Germany in Our Time

Germany in Our Time

A Political History of the Postwar Years

ALFRED GROSSER

Translated by Paul Stephenson

PRAEGER PUBLISHERS
New York · Washington · London

PRAEGER PUBLISHERS
111 Fourth Avenue, New York, N.Y. 10003, U.S.A.
5, Cromwell Place, London S.W.7, England

Published in the United States of America in 1971
by Praeger Publishers, Inc.

Published in West Germany under the title *Deutschlandbilanz*
© 1970 by Carl Hanser Verlag, Munich

Published in France under the title *L'Allemagne de notre temps*
© 1970 by Librairie Artheme Fayard, Paris

English translation © 1971 by Praeger Publishers, Inc.

Library of Congress Catalog Card Number: 77-130529 *10 26 71*

Printed in the United States of America

Contents

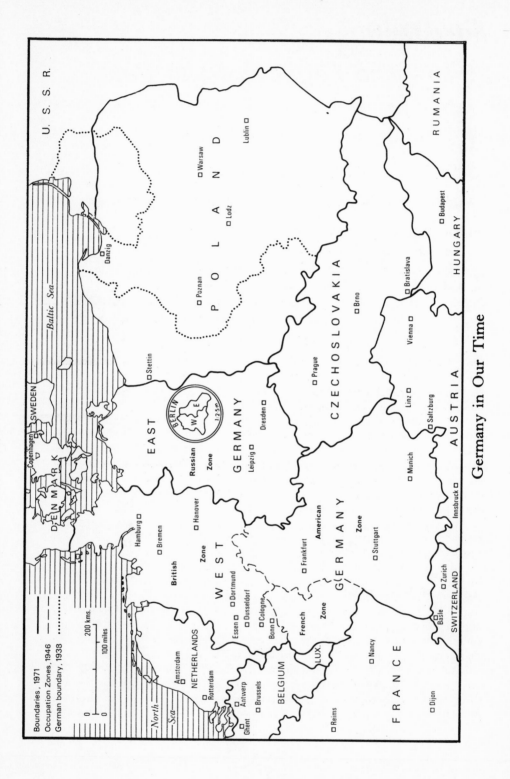

Germany in Our Time

Introduction:
1945—The Legacy of the Past

WHEN we speculate about our own country or its neighbors, we generally do so in terms of the future. But this inevitably involves consideration of the present. What are the existing realities whose development we must attempt to forecast? What hopes and fears guide the decisions of those who influence events, be they rulers of society, consumers of resources, or fighters for political causes? How do suchpeople see the future, and how are they setting about transforming the present? As soon as we ask these questions, we are in turn obliged to consider the past. Current realities cannot be understood without knowing how they came to be as they are. Hopes and fears cannot be dissociated from individual personalities, and these too are a product of past experience.

Whether we are dealing with a human being or a nation, a purely contemporaneous approach gives a misleading, two-dimensional impression. But the historical viewpoint has at least two grave dangers of its own. The first is that when we judge an individual, a group, or a nation in the light of its own past, we forget that each is subject to outside influence at every turn and that countries whose history is very different often go through similar shifts of attitude and policy at a given juncture. Thus, it may be stated here and now that one of the conclusions of this book will be that Germany today is less intelligible as the product of an age-long national development than as an element in a society that transcends national boundaries and also as an entity composed of two parts, each of which belongs to a different and relatively homogeneous section of a divided world.

The second danger of the historical approach is that it lays too much emphasis on continuity. Of course, complete breaks with the past are rare in history—indeed, they are impossible. Great as political upheavals may be, they do not annihilate social and economic conditions or bring about a complete change in the ideas and beliefs of individuals. But there are times when the breach of continuity is so sharp and the changes that take place in social organization, in the structure of power, and in public opinion are so abrupt and far-reaching that it is hazardous to interpret events in terms of a continuous evolution. Russia in 1917 is a case in point, and in the same way we may regard 1945 as marking a clear break in German history.

This is not, however, a self-evident fact. It is, of course, easy to see that 1945 was a more important turning point in Germany than in Britain or even in France. The mutilation of the national territory, the beginnings of political division in what remained of Germany, the loss of external and internal sovereignty, and the collapse of the country's institutions—all these things meant an upheaval on even a larger scale than that which accompanied the establishment of the Empire in 1871 or its collapse in 1918. But, as against this, there was in the three western zones after 1945 a definite continuity of social organization and social values. There was much talk of "restoration" in the 1950's, but it was less a question of reviving forces and institutions that had ceased to exist than a discovering that there had not, after all, been a total break in 1945. Despite their checkered history with its abrupt changes, such organized groups as the churches or the Social Democratic Party were able to point to a continuous evolution that suffices to refute the notion of 1945 as an absolute zero.

Nevertheless, Germany in ruins—Germany as a mere object of international relations—was clearly an altogether different phenomenon from the Germanies of the past. At the same time, that past continued to be singularly real in 1945. It was part of the national scene in a fuller sense than that in which the past is always present—that is to say, as a common system of reference reflecting shared habits of life and thought, or as the expression of a political culture of which individual citizens may be only partially conscious. It was present as part of the mental image of Germany and the Germans, entertained by the foreign masters on whom the fate of every German depended. Germany in 1945 was not the same country as it had been in the immediate past, but the treatment meted out to Germans was dictated by that past. Even twenty-five years later, the idea that other nations and their leaders have of Germany, and their behavior toward her, is not wholly independent of their notion of what Germany was before the break of 1945.

Above all, the past is still present in the question that was asked again and again after the war and has not yet ceased to affect German public life: *Wie konnte es geschehen?* How could it have happened? Those who argue about this question are not always as clear as they should be as to the prior question: *Was ist geschehen?* What did happen? What happened to explain Hitler's sudden rise in 1930-32, or his seizure of absolute power in 1933-34? What happened in the ensuing twelve years to make up the whole ghastly sum of horrors, of sufferings inflicted and endured?

Whatever the precise answer to these questions, the reference to "what happened" is fraught with moral condemnation. While it is right that it should be, the effect is that German politics since the war, both as the German people sees them and as they are analyzed by German and foreign historians, political scientists, sociologists, and economists, are judged with reference to the moral standard that condemns "what happened," but that is often left out of account in studying the present or the past of countries other than Germany.

Thus it is hardly possible to conceive of a dispassionate approach to Germany since World War II or a neutral presentation of its problems. Nonetheless, it is both possible and desirable to judge with a mind unclouded by the past, to examine the facts with scrupulous accuracy and in the light of those coherent principles that may be applied to all political systems. The first step is to react against a tradition of long standing, which is now fortunately on the decline in Britain, the United States, and France as well as in Germany itself.

2

This is the view that led so many analysts to consider Germany as a phenomenon *sui generis*, a country set apart by the inexorable fatality of its history and by the chain of events that led to Adolf Hitler, seen as an extreme but not otherwise unusual instance of the odious type of leader produced by German society or encouraged by German ideology.

What we are concerned with in this study is neither fatality nor necessity, still less any kind of explanation based on racial characteristics, but simply those elements of the past that throw light on the present. If the present were other than it is, we should give prominence to different aspects of the past: the retrospective gaze of an analyst of present-day reality is not exactly the same as the historian's.

Germany as a political unity is just one hundred years old. Up to 1870, the Germans were in search of a legal and political framework that would transform their fragmented nation into a state. In Germany, the very word "nation" has a meaning and associations of its own, being endowed by history with a political and ideological coloring that places it on the side of authority and conservatism. In the United States, the nation was born of a struggle for independence and human rights, and the Bill of Rights is an integral part of the Constitution. In France, two nations have existed side by side since the Revolution: that of right-wing nationalism and that of Jacobin patriotism. In their joint heritage, the idea of national greatness combines with that of imparting universal values. Thus France embarked on conquest with a clear conscience, acting in the name of liberty—whether in Europe after the Revolution of 1789 or in Africa and Asia under the Third Republic. Any war waged by France was, by definition, a disinterested struggle to defend justice and civilization and to extend their sway outside her borders. At the same time, the nation was incarnate in the Republic; the Communist Party's attempt, after 1935 (the birth of the Popular Front) and especially after 1941 (the transformation of the imperialist war into an anti-Fascist one), to reconcile the tricolor with the red flag was the less shocking since, after all, the three colors were those of a revolutionary regime. If the French right wing has, from time to time, invoked the Marseillaise against the internationalist left, it could only do so by forgetting the words of the song.

In Germany, the idea of nationalism was espoused by the left and the right not simultaneously but at different times. Until the failure of the 1848 revolution, nationalism was linked with liberalism if not identified with it. It set out to oppose the legitimacy of the people to that of princes by uniting into one nation the various groups of subjects of powerful or petty sovereigns. The black, red, and gold colors of German democracy were originally those of the Jena *Burschenschaft*, the student corps whose first members fought in the war of liberation, from Leipzig to Waterloo. The Hambach rally at Whitsun of 1832 was held under these colors in the name of national unity and political freedom.

After the 1848 revolution had failed, however, national unity was created by an authoritarian state. Authority—*Obrigkeit*—took in hand the creation and defense of a nation based on the people, it is true, but not, to use Michelet's terms, the people as a force or *volonté commune*: rather the people as a racial entity, a community of subjects obedient to their temporal or spiritual masters. In other circumstances, a different tradition might have won the day. As it was, under the German Empire everyone's tasks were clearly laid down: it was for Authority to command and for the citizen to practice the domestic and professional virtues of his station, political virtue being summed up as obedience to the lawful powers. This view was based on a particular Christian tradition of long standing: Luther himself could be invoked in its support. (Similarly, toward the end of the seventeenth century a theologian of note had written a large volume on the question whether it was lawful to cut wood on Sundays; the conclusion was affirmative, provided that one had been ordered to do so. The person who commits the sin is the one who gives the order. In 1945 and after, more serious matters than tree-felling were at stake in the retrospective discussions that took place on the subject of the *Befehlsnotstand*, the plea of exculpation on the ground of superior orders.)

But the German Empire did not consist wholly of dutiful subjects accepting as one man the decisions of authority. Bismarck wrestled with two forces he considered dangerous to authority and to the power of the nation-state: the Catholics and the Socialists. His struggle was a losing one: at the last prewar elections in 1912, the Social Democratic Party (SPD) and the *Zentrum* (the Catholic Center) emerged as the two largest parties, with 34·8 and 16·4 per cent of the votes respectively. They were very different from each other, but the fact the civil power regarded them both as its enemies produced a situation quite unlike that in France, where the Catholic Church supported authoritarian regimes but found itself at odds with the victorious republicans. In Germany, there was no overriding reason why the Catholic and Social Democratic parties should not, after 1918, act as pillars of the republic which took over from an empire that had been not only military and industrial, but, above all, Protestant and aristocratic.

It did not come easily to the *Zentrum* to consider itself responsible for the State at large. In 1887, the Cardinal Secretary of State wrote to the Nuncio at Munich that "the Holy See recognizes the services rendered by the *Zentrum* and its leaders in defending the Catholic cause" and he observed that the Catholics' task was to protect their religious interests, which were identical with those of the Vatican.[1] On July 7, 1933, two days after the *Zentrum* dissolved itself, one of its most respected leaders noted in his diary: "There is nothing we can do now but follow the bishops' example and continue as best we can, within the National Socialist Party and in cooperation with it, to protect our religious interests."[2]

As for the Socialists, they were not merely the victims of a *Kulturkampf* in Bismarck's day; they were banned for twelve full years, under the law of October 21, 1878, which prohibited all associations of a "Social Democratic, Socialist, or Communist" character that aimed to "subvert the political and social order," or that, more simply, presented a threat to peace "and particularly concord among different classes of citizens" (*Bevölkerungsklassen*). Although Wilhelm II lifted the ban in 1890, he continued to regard the Socialists as the "internal enemy," men without honor or patriotism. The SPD became stronger and stronger numerically, as a result of which it had a privileged

4

position in the Second International; but it had no real influence on politics and the power situation, which in part explains its doctrinal intransigence. If, in 1905, the French Socialist groups merged in the SFIO (*Section Française de l'Internationale Ouvrière*) with a program inspired by Guesde rather Jaurès, it was because, at the Amsterdam congress in the previous year, the Germans had pressed for a united front and cast their weight in favor of orthodoxy.

However, in Germany as in France, August, 1914 showed how completely national solidarity outweighed the solidarity of the proletariat. The outbreak of the war and its duration in fact produced stronger tensions within the SPD than in the SFIO, so that in 1917 the party underwent a schism. Like the *Zentrum*, it had accepted the Kaiser's dictum—"I no longer recognize parties, only Germans"—which in practice meant depriving the parties of what little control they still exercised over the government. Only on October 28, 1918 was the Imperial constitution amended: as the state was about to collapse, the German Government was made responsible to the Reichstag. At the same time, the cabinet was reshuffled to include the party leaders, who were thus saddled with the blame for the country's defeat.

That defeat came after four years of war, the responsibility for which was fixed on Germany by the victorious powers. In 1951, a group of German and French historians drew up a joint statement that ran:

There is no documentary evidence to justify us in attributing a premeditated will to war in 1914 to any European government or people. Lack of confidence was extreme and government circles were obsessed with the idea that war was inevitable; each suspected the other of aggressive designs; the risk of war was accepted by all, and the only safeguard seemed to lie in systems of alliance and the piling up of arms. Certain elements in the German General Staff considered Germany's chances of success to be greater in 1914 than they would be in the years following; but it cannot be inferred that the German Government's policy was based on this consideration. The great majority of both Germans and French were against war; but in Germany, especially in military circles, there was a greater disposition to accept it if it came. This was a consequence of the place held by the army in German society.[3]

The army in question refused to admit that it had been beaten on the battlefield. Testifying in November, 1919 before a parliamentary commission of inquiry, Field Marshal von Hindenburg declared: "The German army was stabbed in the back." This legend took shape and became widely accepted because Germany was not defeated on its own soil: when the armistice was signed on November 11, 1918, German troops were still fighting in France. When the Allies decided twenty-five years later, to demand unconditional surrender and occupy the whole of Germany before ceasing hostilities, they were largely influenced by a determination not to allow the "stab in the back" legend to take root for a second time.

True, there was a revolution in Germany and a republic was proclaimed two days after the armistice was signed in the forest of Compiègne. But revolution was the child of defeat and not vice versa. Was it a genuine revolution? Certainly there was a change of regime and of political philosophy: the legitimacy of an autocrat was replaced by that of majority suffrage. On November 25, the governments of the *Länder*—Germany's component states

5

—decided at a joint conference to hold general elections for a Constituent Assembly. The Social Democrats were the dominant party in the workers' and soldiers' councils, and in their view there could be no liberty without democracy, that is, a system of decisions based on majority vote.

However, the revolution was only to a very limited extent a social one. On November 15, 1918, an agreement was signed between trade unions and managers' organizations that gave the workers such benefits as the eight-hour day, collective bargaining, and recognition of the unions as representatives of labor. In return, the unions tacitly agreed not to subvert the social order or attack the foundations of economic power. They were prepared to work with management to save the country from chaos and to maintain or restore a particular form of order, which involved a relationship between social forces that was certainly not biased in favor of the wage earners.

Trade unionism in Germany has never represented the militant wing of the workers' movement. It did not, as in Britain, give birth to a Socialist party; nor, as in France, did it take up a position to the left of the political parties, regarding with mistrust their participation in the parliamentary game. Before the war, the SPD fought the political battle single-handed; the *Allgemeiner Deutscher Gewerkschaftsbund* (or General Federation of Trade Unions) was more like a fraternal society than a fighting force, despite its Socialist tendency and the fact that, in 1913, it comprised 2·5 million members out of the 3·3 million Germans belonging to unions of all kinds.

By the end of 1918, the SPD itself was more interested in order than in subversion. Its chief representative, Friedrich Ebert, was invested with power from two widely different sources: from Wilhelm II's Chancellor, Prince Max of Baden, and from the workers' and soldiers' councils. This dualism faithfully reflects both the reality and the limits of the breach of continuity that took place in 1918.

There were others who wished for a much more thoroughgoing change. In 1917 a minority group of the SPD had set itself up as an independent body —the USPD—and from this a further group hived off which, through the Spartacist Union (*Spartakusbund*), gave birth on December 30, 1919 to the German Communist Party (KPD). A few days before this, Berlin had been in a state of civil war, the so-called red week, in which the revolutionaries were ranged against the collegium of people's commissars presided over by Ebert, with Noske, another Social Democrat, as Commissar for Defense. The Spartacists were crushed without difficulty. Their two chief leaders, Karl Liebknecht—the son of one of the founders of the SPD—and Rosa Luxemburg, were arrested and murdered on January 15, 1919. The victory and the murders were the work of crack military units whose officers were not only hostile to revolution but profoundly anti-democratic and anti-liberal.

In France, while the guillotine and the Terror are not forgotten, it has long been customary, even in the textbooks of history used in Catholic schools, to assess the outcome of 1789 in a favorable light. The young Frenchman's mental imagery is so conditioned that he thrills to the romanticism of the nineteenth-century barricades, and the days that saw the second overthrow of absolute monarchy in July, 1830 are known as the *trois glorieuses*. In short, the general attitude of mind is friendly to revolutions, and there is a widespread readiness to believe that the capture of the Winter Palace in 1917 was an act of the same kind as the storming of the Bastille, which gave France its national holiday. In Germany, on the other hand, from 1919 onward, "revolution" no longer awoke memories of 1848, but was instead associated with the idea of a savage and barbarous revolt that had been put down by a fortunate conjunction of widely different forces interested in the defense of social order. This hostile view of revolution in Germany was at least as influential as the persistence of the revolutionary myth in France. Its effects are visible in the weakness shown by the Social Democrats in the 1920's, despite their millions of votes, in comparison with extreme right-wing groups that for years had only a small membership; they may equally be discerned in the complete lack of sympathy between the workers' organizations and the rebellious students of 1967–68.

The Versailles peace conference opened on January 18, 1919. On the 19th, elections were held for the Constituent Assembly, which met at Weimar. On June 22, by a majority vote, the Assembly accepted the visitors' ultimatum and agreed that the German delegation should sign the treaty that had been drafted without German participation. On July 31, by a vote of 262 to 75, the Assembly adopted the republican constitution.

The Weimar Republic never wholly recovered from this coincidence in time between national humiliation and the birth of Germany's first democratic regime. It is not unusual in history for a democracy to be born of national defeat—such was the case with the Third Republic in France—but the treaty of Versailles was very different from that of Frankfurt, and not primarily because of the severity of its terms. In 1871, the annexation of Alsace and Lorraine and the war indemnity of 5,000 million gold francs, together with the occupation of French territory until the whole sum was paid, were certainly not acts of generosity on Germany's part. If the Germans had won the war of 1914–18, they would have imposed much harsher terms still, as we know from their wartime plans and the formidable treaty of Brest Litovsk with defeated Russia. But, while all peace treaties are concluded on unequal terms and are largely imposed by the victors on the vanquished, Versailles was a *Diktat* of a much more spectacular kind, representing as it did a sort of double outlawry of Germany. The Germans were not allowed to take part in the negotiation of the treaty (whereas, for example, Talleyrand had been free to exercise his diplomatic wiles at Vienna in 1814-15) and in the document that they were called upon to sign they were treated not only as the losers but also as a guilty party. Moreover, Germany was to become an outcast from international society at the very moment when it had at last adopted the forms of political organization extolled by its conquerors.

The Weimar constitution created a parliamentary regime that, if it functioned amiss, could be upheld thanks to the powers vested in the President, but in such a way as to falsify its nature. The Chancellor, who headed the government, was responsible to the Reichstag, but he was appointed and could be dismissed by the President, who himself was elected by universal suffrage and whose mandate was therefore no less legitimate than that of

7

parliament. In a way very similar to the French constitution of 1958, the Weimar system could be interpreted either as a parliamentary regime in which the presidential power took second place to that of a government with a majority in the assembly, or as a presidential regime in which the Chancellor or Prime Minister was the mere appointee of the head of state. The latter interpretation did not become a reality until 1930, but it did so then to such purpose that it remained a more vivid memory than the ascendency of the government and parliament during the presidency of Friedrich Ebert (who, it is true, did not owe his position to universal suffrage but was elected by the Reichstag, which prolonged his term until 1925) or during the greater part of Hindenburg's first term (1925-32).

There is, however, an important qualification: from the very outset, the President, at the request of successive governments, made use of Article 48 of the constitution, which conferred on him wide powers in what were supposed to be exceptional circumstances.

In the case of a *Land* not fulfilling the duties imposed on it by the Federal constitution or the Federal laws, the President of the Federation may enforce its fulfillment with the help of the armed forces. Where public security and order are seriously disturbed or endangered within the Federation, the President of the Federation may take the measures necessary for their restoration, intervening if necessary with the help of the armed forces. For this purpose he may temporarily abrogate, in whole or in part, the fundamental rights laid down in Articles 114, 115, 117, 118, 123, 124, and 153.

That is to say, virtually all public liberties. True, the section that followed provided that the President, immediately after taking any such measures, had to inform the Reichstag, which was empowered to demand their withdrawal; but there was an inherent danger in allowing the President to annul civil rights, even as a temporary measure. For the most part, Article 48 was used to legalize economic and financial decrees; but a month after Hitler became Chancellor, a law based on it made possible a dictatorship under which liberty was suppressed for good and all. The question of how to provide emergency powers without running the risk of destroying what they are meant to safeguard is not unique to Germany; in 1958 in France, it arose in the debate over Article 16 of the draft constitution for the Fifth Republic. In Germany in the 1960's, the memory of Article 48 gave additional intensity to the long debate on the subject of the emergency laws (*Notstandsgesetze*).

The main feature of the Weimar system, both as it actually was and as people remembered it, was the dominant role of the political parties; these were not specifically mentioned in the constitution but their existence was implied by the provision that elections to the legislature had to be based on the proportional system. The electoral law of 1920 provided for full proportional representation, with one deputy for every 60,000 voters (the size of the Reichstag therefore varied considerably according to how many votes were polled), with a remaining number of seats allotted on a nationwide basis. Proportional representation meant there was less risk of wasting one's vote by giving it to a small party, since such a party had a good chance of being represented in parliament. Consequently, there was a multiplicity of parties, thirty-eight of which, for example, figured on the ballot in July, 1932.

8

Nonetheless, the number of parties playing any real part in politics was fairly small, and the real problem was that more and more powerful parties were opposed to the very basis of the political system. The three "Weimar parties," which had had the courage in 1918 to take responsibility for clearing up the consequences of defeat and for installing the new regime, were not really dominant except in the Constituent Assembly. There, the SPD polled 37·9 per cent of the votes, the *Zentrum*, 19·7 per cent, and the Democratic Liberals (*Deutsche Demokratische Partei*), 18·5 per cent. But, in the election of June, 1920, the SPD suffered from a left-wing breakaway, the *Zentrum* lost members to the Bavarian People's Party, which drew off Catholic voters to the right, and the Liberals began on a downward slope that was to bring them below 5 per cent of the poll in 1928 and 1 per cent or less in 1932. On the extreme left, the Communists made progress after 1924 but never achieved 17 per cent of the poll. As regards the right wing, the extremists' sudden rise after 1930 should not blind us to the fact that at any time after 1920 it was very hard to draw a dividing line between those who accepted the rules of the game and those who hoped to transform the regime into something of a more authoritarian stamp.

Certainly there appeared to be a lack of authority in the first few years of the Republic. More than one of the *Länder* experienced riots and *coups d'état.* The abortive Munich *putsch* of November, 1923 was only one of a long series of upheavals. One form that violence took was political assassination: the most eminent victims were, in 1921, Matthias Erzberger, a signatory to the armistice, and, in 1922, Walther Rathenau, the Minister of Foreign Affairs. The murderers did not risk a great deal: throughout the Weimar period, judges, for social and ideological reasons, were indulgent toward those who resorted to violence as a weapon in the "national" cause and severe toward the men and parties who had come to terms with Germany's conquerors and impaired national unity by demanding social change.

In both internal and external affairs, the atmosphere was poisoned by the problem of reparations, the total of which had not been fixed at Versailles. In 1923, the French and Belgians occupied the Ruhr as a sanction for nonpayment; this provoked passive resistance, which in turn touched off an inflationary crisis. At that time and for a half-century afterward, the word "inflation" had associations in Germany very different from those in France or Britain. To non-Germans it has signified a financial and economic phenomenon that is no doubt deplorable in itself but that one can learn to live with. To the Germans it has meant *die Inflation*—the inflation, that of 1923 when the price of a newspaper rose to 200 marks in April, 2,000 in July, 150,000 on September 1, 500,000 on the 15th, 4 million on October 1, 25 million on the 15th, 2,000 million on November 2, and 8,000 million on November 8. In more technical terms, the fiduciary circulation of the mark, which was 2,300 million in 1913, had risen to 41 milliard in 1919; it stood at 90·4 milliard in 1921, 124 in January, 1922, and 484 in October of that year. In January, 1923 it leapt to 2 billion and in July of that year to 44,000 billion; in October it was over 3 trillion.

The inflation was a social tragedy, ruining millions of humble people while at the same time providing the State and industrialists with a brutal and

9

inhuman means of wiping out their monetary debts. Once the financial catastrophe was over, it could be seen that it had indeed been only financial: German industry had remained intact and was able to expand rapidly as soon as the monetary situation had been restored; the collapse itself was to some extent an aid to progress. On two later occasions, in 1932 and 1946–48, Germany once again seemed to be at the end of its tether and recovered with equal rapidity, with credit for the recovery rebounding to the regime that happened to be in control at the time. In 1933, Hitler benefited from Brüning's stabilization of the economy, and in 1948 the Federal Republic and the Christian Democratic Party (CDU) reaped the reward of the monetary reform imposed by the occupying powers. In 1924, the republican regime gained credit from the stabilization, the more so as the external situation also improved—thanks in part to the victory of the *Cartel des gauches* at the French elections and the triumph of Briand's policy over Poincaré's—though the reparations question remained an irritant in international affairs until 1932. Hindenburg, it is true, was elected President in 1925, but only after having presented himself at the second ballot as a "national" candidate against the *Zentrum* leader Wilhelm Marx (who enjoyed SPD and Democratic Liberal support) and only because the Communists maintained their own candidate, while the Bavarian Catholics preferred the aged marshal (Protestant though he was) to a candidate of their own faith supported by the "reds" of the SPD. Hence, Hindenburg's election did not in any way signify a danger to the regime as such.

On the contrary, despite various troubles, the years from 1924 to 1929 were a period of peace and stability in political and economic affairs. As far as art and science were concerned, there was little to worry about: in these fields, Weimar represented a golden age. Movements that had been born in the years of adversity came to fruition: a prodigious liveliness and fecundity were evident on every hand, from architecture to journalism and from physics to the cinema. But because this intellectual ferment tended to challenge accepted values in both private and public life, Germans of the nationalist tradition associated Weimar with cultural decadence. Another reason for their doing so was that Jews were deeply engaged in most of these activities.

The international financial and economic crisis, which began with "black Friday" on the New York stock exchange in October, 1929, hit Germany with special severity, partly because German industrial development had largely depended for the previous few years on American credits that were now to be called in, and partly because of the intransigence of French foreign policy, which prevented the moratorium on German debts from taking effect in time. A further reason was that Germany was (and is) much more dependent on international trade than France, which meant that it was strong at times of worldwide prosperity and very vulnerable to a sudden slump.

The central importance of the Depression, however, was not its cause but its consequences: it brought about the collapse of the German regime. In what sense? We are not dealing here with an instance of direct causation, of remorseless fatality. The same crisis that "caused" Hitler's rise to power in Germany led, in the United States, to Roosevelt's victory and the New Deal. One may say, however, that had it not been for the economic crisis, the Weimar Republic would probably have succeeded in consolidating its strength, and the

National Socialist Party would not have shot forward from 800,000 votes in the elections of May, 1928 to 6,400,000 in November, 1930. The slump, with its accompanying unemployment, destitution, confusion, and panic, increased by tenfold the general longing for a new order.

This longing was also felt in the United States, but there it was canalized by one of the two great parties within an accepted institutional system: the citizens and their leaders alike were confident in the power of democracy to bring about a new economic and social order. In 1930, Germany presented a very different picture: the country was deeply divided, and the cry for a change from liberal democracy was all the stronger since the regime was of recent date and its leaders had suffered their power gradually to ebb away. Economic conditions are never the direct causes of political events; they operate indirectly through institutions, beliefs, and actions, which may themselves have other than economic causes. Thus, the Depression that began in 1929 was preceded by a hardening of the attitude of the Communist International from 1928 onward. Under Stalin's aegis, the Comintern decided that Communist parties everywhere should play a lone hand, denouncing the Social Democrats as "social traitors" and "social Fascists." Consequently, the German parties of the left and center had to fight on two fronts, while the KPD set out to improve its popularity and influence with the masses by outdoing the nationalists and declaiming against Versailles, reparations, and the League of Nations in no less strident terms than the extreme right.

This latter section of the community is hard to define precisely. Did it, for instance, comprise all the individuals and groups who took part in the joint rally held at Bad Harzburg on October 11, 1931? These included Adolf Hitler, with a nationalist program against the Marxists and a Socialist one against the capitalists; the Stahlhelm (Steel Helmets), an ultranationalist ex-servicemen's organization; General von Seeckt, no longer at the head of the Reichswehr; and Dr. Hjalmar Schacht, the "savior of the mark" in 1923, who had resigned from the presidency of the Reichsbank in 1929 in protest against the Young plan on reparations. There was also Alfred Hugenberg, the leader of the German National Party (DNVP), which was more and more openly combating the regime in the name of nationalist and authoritarian principles. Hugenberg was also a German equivalent of William Randolph Hearst, controlling chains of newspapers, an information agency, and the largest film concern. The "Harzburg front" did not survive beyond 1932, but it symbolizes a decisive factor in Hitler's victory—namely, the support given him by a right-wing organization of a different type, whose power was due to its own economic resources and which had no intention of playing Hitler's game, but hoped to make use of him to preserve the social order while transforming the political scene at home and abroad.

March 27, 1930 saw the fall of the sixteenth government formed in Germany since the elections of 1919. The Chancellor, a Social Democrat, was overthrown because his party could not or would not agree to a compromise on the scale and financing of aid to the unemployed, who already numbered over 3 million. Faithful to its social ideals and insufficiently conscious of the needs of the economic situation, not to speak of the danger to the republican

GERMAN ELECTIONS 1928–33

Election	May 20, 1928		Sept. 14, 1930		July 31, 1932		Nov. 6, 1932		March 5, 1933	
Registered electors (in millions)	41·22		42·96		44·23		44·37		44·69	
Percentage voting	74·60		81·41		83·39		79·93		88·04	
	per cent of votes	seats	per cent of votes	seats	per cent of votes	seats	per cent of votes	seats	per cent of votes	seats
NSDAP (National Socialists)	2·6	12	18·3	107	37·2	230	33·0	196	43·9	288
DNVP (Hugenberg)	14·2	73	7·0	41	5·9	37	7·2	52	8·0	52
DVP (Stresemann)	8·7	45	4·5	30	1·1	7	1·7	11	1·0	2
BVP (Bavaria)	3·9	16	3·0	19	3·2	22	2·9	20	2·7	18
Zentrum	11·9	62	11·7	68	12·4	75	11·9	70	11·2	74
DDP (later, Staatspartei)	4·9	25	3·7	20	1·0	4	0·9	2	0·8	5
SPD (Social Democrats)	28·7	153	24·5	143	21·5	133	20·4	121	18·3	120
KPD (Communists)	10·6	54	13·1	77	14·2	89	16·8	100	12·3	81
Others	14·5	51	14·2	72	3·5	11	5·2	12	1·8	7
Total		491		577		608		584		647

regime with which it was so closely linked, the SPD withdrew from the governmental majority. It had done so many times before, but on this occasion the effect was to exclude it from power for almost four decades.

For the next two years Heinrich Brüning—the *Zentrum* leader, a financial expert, and a Christian trade unionist—governed with the President's support, sometimes with a parliamentary majority and sometimes by decree. Almost at the outset, a mixed majority including extremists and Social Democrats rejected his deflationary measures and obliged him to dissolve the Reichstag. The elections increased tension at home and intensified the external crisis: the more unstable Germany appeared to be, the more she was distrusted by foreign governments and public opinion and the less inclined they were to give the German Government a chance of maintaining its prestige at home by pointing to successes in the foreign field. In retrospect, Stresemann's death on October 3, 1929 appears symbolic.

While deflation opened the way to financial and economic regeneration, its immediate effects were disastrous in the social and political sphere. So rapid was the rise of Hitler that when, as leader of the NSDAP (National Socialist German Workers' Party), he decided to stand for the presidential election in March, 1932—having, shortly beforehand, obtained German nationality by a legal subterfuge—the center and left-wing parties could find no one to back except Hindenburg, by then eighty-four, whose election they had opposed seven years earlier. The Field Marshal did not gain victory until the second ballot (on April 10). He despised Hitler, resisting his claims until convinced by those about him that the people wished to be governed by the *Führer*. This took place a little over nine months later—a short period, but one full of commotion and surprises.[4] On May 30, 1932, Hindenburg dismissed Brüning and appointed as Chancellor Baron Franz von Papen—a Catholic to the right of the *Zentrum*, a brilliant horseman and mediocre politician, popular with the President but lacking parliamentary support. Papen dissolved the Reichstag and lifted the ban on the uniformed Nazi "Storm Troops" (SA—*Sturmabteilungen*) that had been imposed in April by Brüning and his Minister of the Interior and Defense, General Groener. This sharply increased the violence of street fighting: during the weeks that elapsed before the Reichstag elections of July 31, dozens of people were killed and hundreds seriously injured.

In those elections Hitler's party obtained 37·2 per cent of votes cast and 230 seats in the Reichstag, of which Hermann Göring became the President. For the first time, the Nazis had a lead, and a very considerable one, over any other party. Also for the first time, the Reichstag presented a picture that was later to be (unjustly) looked on as a permanent characteristic of the Weimar regime: namely the extreme right and the extreme left—the Nazis and the Communists—between them commanded an absolute majority, so that any government could be overthrown by their combined opposition.

Nevertheless, power eluded Hitler. It was in fact wielded by nobody at this time, certainly not Papen, whose decrees of September 4 were overruled by 515 votes to 42. So a fresh dissolution took place, followed by elections on November 6. These fell out badly for Hitler, who lost 2 million votes, and also for Papen, who was supported by no one and was finally dismissed by Hindenburg (who nonetheless continued to regard Papen with confidence). On December

13

3, 1932, General Kurt von Schleicher, a complex personality who had long been influential and was Papen's Minister of Defense, became Chancellor. His aim was to win over the left wing by an advanced social policy and to "tame" the NSDAP by playing on its internal rivalries. Both these attempts misfired. On the one hand, Hitler was to manage to overcome the conflict within the Nazi Party as well as its financial troubles, which had made things look black for him at the end of 1932. On the other, many capitalists were frightened by Schleicher's "left-wingism" and therefore transferred their support to Hitler, who was as conciliatory toward them in private as he was "anti-plutocratic" in public; in this way, he obtained the funds he needed.

On January 4, 1933, Hitler and Papen came to terms and let it be publicly known that they had done so. On the 15th, the Nazis scored a limited success in a small regional election, which was then inflated into a triumph by Dr. Joseph Goebbels' propaganda. On the 23rd, Hindenburg refused Schleicher's request for another dissolution. On the 26th, Hitler, Papen, and Hugenberg set to work to plan the new government. On the 28th, Schleicher resigned, Papen was charged with investigating the political possibilities, and on January 30, 1933 Hitler became Chancellor.

In 1920, when the civilian Kapp was installed in power by a military coup, the workers and civil servants went on strike; within a few days, the legal government was back in Berlin. In 1933, the change was nonviolent: Hitler was appointed Chancellor in due legal form. The Communists alone called for a strike; on January 31, the SPD organ *Vorwärts* declared that, while the strike was a legitimate weapon with which to defend the people's rights and liberties, the ammunition of the working class should not be wasted without cause.

According to many people, especially the men and institutions that made common cause with Hitler, there was nothing in the nature of a breach or an upheaval: witness the new Chancellor's reassuring statements and the composition of his government. Von Papen was Vice-Chancellor and Hugenberg was Minister of the Economy; Baron von Neurath kept the Foreign Affairs portfolio which he had held under Papen and Schleicher. The Ministries of Finance and Justice likewise remained in the same hands. True, the new Minister of Labor was the chief of the Stahlhelm, but this was a patriotic and not a revolutionary body. Apart from Hitler, only one Nazi, Wilhelm Frick, became responsible for a department (Interior) of government (on January 30); Dr. Goebbels' Propaganda Ministry was created in February, 1933. Those who expected to tame Hitler and make use of his party regarded the Economic Ministry as more important than the Interior; they did not realize that Frick would have control of the State police, while Herman Göring, who became Prussian Minister of the Interior, was thus in charge of the police force of much the biggest of the *Länder*.

No one suspected in those days that control of the police and propaganda, and a modicum of disregard for law, would be sufficient to ensure the conquest of power. From the outset, a purge of the civil service was set in motion, and one newspaper after another was banned. Far from lessening, the brutality of the party's uniformed bands became more flagrant and widespread, under the increasingly benevolent eye of the police.

For the next seven weeks the picture was one of violent contrasts. On the one hand, gestures of reassurance and appeals to the pride of national unity: on March 21 Hitler celebrated the "day of national awakening" at Potsdam in front of Frederick the Great's tomb, with Hindenburg present in full uniform. On the other hand, undisguised terrorism, with the liberal newspapers full of reports of dismissals and arrests. When the new Reichstag assembled on March 23, its members were soon to know that Hitler would not be tamed by the enjoyment of supreme power, that his appeals to force and the excesses of his followers were |not simply the marks of a tawdry opposition movement.

The election was held on March 5, Hitler having earlier obtained the President's agreement to a dissolution on January 31. Despite moral and physical pressure, despite the mass arrests of Communist leaders after the Reichstag fire of February 27, and despite the mobilization of the electorate that produced a poll of 88 per cent, Hitler's triumph was incomplete: 43·9 per cent of the votes went to the Nazis and 8 per cent to Hugenberg. With 288 and 52 seats respectively, they had an absolute majority in a Reichstag composed of 647 members, but not the two-thirds required for amendments to the constitution. Wishing to become a dictator by ostensibly legal means, Hitler therefore submitted to the Reichstag an enabling bill (*Ermächtigungsgesetz*) empowering his government not only to pass laws but to do so in violation of the constitution.

The *Vossische Zeitung*, one of Germany's most respected and courageous newspapers, had, in a long article on March 21, warned the deputies in vain that—coming on top of the suspension of rights on February 28 under Article 48 of the constitution—the new measure signified the end of judicial independence and legal guarantees in every sphere of public and private life, signified, in fact, the end of all the liberties that have been the heritage of modern peoples since the American Declaration of Independence. Thanks to the vote of 153 non-Nazi deputies, Hitler's enabling act was carried by 441 to 94. The "nays" were all Social Democrats: there should have been 120, but the others were either in prison or on the run. The 81 Communist deputies had already been stripped of their parliamentary mandate by decree. The Bavarian Party, the five Democratic Liberals, and, above all, the 74 representatives of the *Zentrum* voted for the law by which they, their parties, and their supporters alike were deprived of power.

From then on, events moved rapidly. The press was muzzled. The trade unions, with their 5 million members, allowed themselves to be intimidated into association with the government that they had attempted to fight: on May 1, they took part in the official ceremonies in honor of "national labor day." On the 2nd, their premises were occupied by the police and SA; the property of the General Federation of Trade Unions was seized and its leaders arrested. Between May and July, political parties of all kinds ceased to exist. The SPD was banned; many of its leaders were already in prison, in hiding, or in exile. Hugenberg resigned at the end of June; his party had by then disappeared. At the same time, the police arrested the leaders of the Bavarian

Party. The *Zentrum* dissolved itself on July 5. Two days earlier, Vice-Chancellor Papen had telegraphed from Rome to the Minister of Foreign Affairs: "From my discussions today with Pacelli [Cardinal Secretary of State], Archbishop Gröber [of Freiburg], and [Monsignor] Kaas [leader of the *Zentrum*], it appears that the dissolution of the *Zentrum* upon the signature of the Concordat is regarded here as decided upon and approved."[5]

The Concordat was in fact signed on July 20. A law of July 10 registered the submission of the Protestant churches. On the 14th, another law forbade the revival of old parties and the creation of new ones. On November 12, in fresh elections to the Reichstag, 661 Nazi deputies were returned. A law promulgated on December 1 declared the unity of the Nazi Party and the state.

At the last elections at which there was any choice—although even these were subject to coercion—the Nazis secured less than 44 per cent of the votes. There was thus no massive endorsement by the German people of Hitler's seizure of power. But, on January 30, 1933, the Nazi Party had 1·5 million members, and on March 5, 17 million electors voted for it—a success unparalleled in German party history, enhanced by the blindness and weakness of most of its enemies. The Communists, to the very last, deluded themselves as to what Nazi repression would mean. The Socialists protested faintly, if at all, when Communists were persecuted. The Democratic Liberals and the *Zentrum* paid little attention to the arrest and ill-treatment of Socialists. The Catholic Church was content to look after its own flock. Each thought he would be spared if he did not join forces with his neighbor: this was true even of those German Jews who thought Nazi anti-Semitism was only aimed at the small fry and that Jews of consequence had nothing to fear if they kept quiet. And while all these stood idly by, millions of other Germans flocked to the support of the new regime in obedience to a psychological urge that has been most pertinently analyzed not by a historian or a sociologist, but by a playright in the admirable last act of Eugène Ionesco's *Rhinoceros*.

Hitler became Chancellor on January 30, 1933. Within a few months, he established a system of absolute rule that tolerated no opposition, exacted obedience throughout public life, and sought to impose itself equally in private. The "night of the long knives" was not only an opportunity to eliminate by murder the SA leaders who might have shown a will of their own within the party and to wreak revenge on individuals; nor was it merely an overture to the rule of Himmler, the SS, and the Gestapo. A law of July 3, 1934 declared: "The measures taken on June 30 and July 1 and 2 to put down treacherous attacks were legitimate acts of State defense." Arbitrary murder became justified; soon there would be no need of law, scarcely even of judges. Did not Carl Schmitt, the best-known professor of public law, state on the day after the massacre that: "The true leader (*Führer*) is always a judge as well. His right to judge is part of the right of leadership. Anyone who seeks to separate or oppose the two is setting up the judge as a rival leader or the instrument of such a rival. . . . Our *Führer's* action was in fact a proper exercise of jurisdiction: not under the law, but itself constituting supreme justice. . . . All law emanates from the *Führer*."[6]

In short, law no longer had any meaning, and neither did the individual as such. Goebbels' dictum "You yourself are nothing, the nation (*Volk*) is everything" sums up the various facets of Nazi totalitarianism. Culture, for example, was to have no meaning except in so far as it served and glorified the people and the *Führer*. At Berlin on May 11, 1933, the bonfire onto which thousands of books were hurled with chants of execration symbolized the breach with the living culture of the immediate past and foreshadowed the fearful impoverishment of Germany's intellectual life by forced emigration, the rapid or slow murder of creative minds, and the regimentation that condemned the rest to sterility. What need was there of free research in the artistic or academic field? An eminent philosopher and university rector said to his students: "It is not doctrines and ideas that should constitute your rule of life. The *Führer* alone is Germany's sole present and future reality and its law."[7]

The national spirit was to be fostered unceasingly by a universal *mystique* and by training the young from childhood up. In 1936, it became compulsory for teenagers to join the party youth organizations. Unity was preserved by the strict control of professional life and the day-to-day supervision that the party and police exercized over every individual. It was strengthened by the elimination of all who endangered it by lack of submission or by belonging to an "alien race."

The regime of terror was soon established and was constantly made more thorough. The concentration camps—as foreigners too often forgot during and after the war—were set up from the beginning, in 1933, as places of confinement and torture for thousands of Germans. And the persecution of the Jews—at first by boycott, ill-treatment of various kinds, and pressure to emigrate, then later by a whole range of punitive and confiscatory measures of increasing severity, and finally by the *Endlösung* of extermination—far surpassed in its scale and barbarity the treatment inflicted on the regime's political antagonists, real or potential. The same may be said of the treatment meted out to despised nations, particularly in Eastern Europe. Over-all, the number of internments and executions and the steady expansion of the police apparatus, both overt and secret, show clearly that Hitler did not rely solely on mystic enthusiasm as a means of imposing his will.

Such measures also testify to the continued existence of an opposition—or, rather, several oppositions, whose motives and activities varied a great deal, as we shall see when examining how judgment was passed on Germany as it lay in ruins after the collapse of the Nazi regime. One of the great retrospective questions at that time was: "What could have been done?" It is a question asked almost more often than "What was in fact done?" It largely thrust into the background a third question, legitimate though this one was: "Why should we have done anything against the regime?" It was, after all, a regime recognized by foreign governments, and the whole world seemed to do homage to it at the Olympic Games in August of 1936. A regime that made Germany strong; that provided work: 14.5 million wage earners in October, 1933 and 20.8 million in 1938, by which year there were only 200,000 unemployed as against 3.7 million five years earlier. A regime, moreover, that doubled production during the same period. (Few people in Germany or outside it realized that the level of industry in 1933 was only 66 per cent of that of 1928, so that doubling it merely meant achieving an index of 132 compared with the last predepression year.) Finally, it was a regime led by a man who spoke of peace and justice for Germany and her people—who, for their part, could not or would not imagine that he planned to conquer vast territories and enslave other nations.

As early as February 3, 1933, Hitler told the army chiefs that, as Germany had insufficient "living space," she must plan for "the conquest of more space in the east and its ruthless Germanization" (*rücksichtslose Germanisierung*). In August, 1936, he ended a long memorandum on the aims of the Four-Year Plan with two terse formulas: "(1) The German army must be fit for action (*einsatzfähig*) in four years. (2) The German economy must be fit for war (*kriegsfähig*) in four years." In May, 1939, he reiterated to the Reichswehr commanders, "Danzig is not the real issue, it is a question of extending our living space in the east."[8]

Thirty years after Hitler came to power, one of the main German daily newspapers published a significant cartoon: It depicted the SA troops parading under the Brandenburger Tor at Berlin, as they had actually done on the evening of January 30, 1933. As the last men passed under the arch, the front ranks of the Red Army followed on their heels.[9] The consequence symbolized by the drawing was logical rather than practical. As in all other countries at all times, the whole of Germany's past weighed on it in 1945. But the mutilation and division of Germany, its people's sufferings, and its position among the nations of the world were the direct result of the preceding twelve years—a period infinitely more decisive and fraught with catastrophe than the years from 1919 to 1933, the "fourteen years" to which Hitler never ceased referring as a symbol of the national humiliation and abasement to which, as he contended, he had fallen heir. How much more disastrous was the inheritance that he left behind him when he took refuge in suicide on April 30, 1945.

Part I
The Conquerors' Germany

1

The Take-over

WHEN a country is conquered, it may happen that the whole of its territory is annexed by the victorious powers and it disappears from the map. More often, the victors dictate terms to the government of the defeated state, irrespective of whether it was that government which conducted the war or whether the defeat brought about a change of political regime.

In 1945, however, Germany did not disappear, nor was a German Government forced to carry out the Allies' terms. Instead, the most powerful members of the victorious coalition took upon themselves the exercise of the country's internal and external sovereignty; no authority could be exercised in or over Germany except insofar as they might delegate or retrocede it. The totalitarian regime had had its total war, and it had ended in total dispossession. The change in the basis of legitimacy was so far-reaching that, twenty-five years later, the question of the responsibility assumed by the Big Four still figures crucially in the debate on the German question, completely though the problem has altered in its nature, context, and scope.

The assumption of authority in 1945 was not altogether in accordance with the lofty principles that had been proclaimed at the birth of the alliance. On August 14, 1941, Churchill and Roosevelt proclaimed the Atlantic Charter, the terms of which were endorsed in the following month by the Soviet representative at an inter-Allied conference in London. Among other things, it said that no territorial changes should follow an Allied victory except by the freely expressed will of the peoples concerned, and that all peoples should have the right to choose the form of government under which they would live. On the other hand, it must be recognized that the Allies, as they later proclaimed at Yalta, were determined to destroy "German militarism and Nazism," and it might be considered that military victory was not in itself sufficient to ensure the fulfillment of this aim.

The Big Three alliance was by no means of long standing. The 1938 Munich agreement between the Western democracies and the Fascist states had excluded, if it was not actually directed against, the Soviet Union; and, on August 23, 1939, the Russians signed a pact with Hitler for the partition of Poland, on whose behalf Britain and France were about to take up arms. Germany and Russia's new friendship was shortly afterward "sealed in blood"; Molotov was to congratulate Hitler on the fall of Warsaw and to declare, at the fifth extraordinary session of the Supreme Soviet.

The warmongers have declared against Germany a sort of ideological war which recalls the old wars of religion. . . . Hitler's ideology, like any other, can be agreed with or not: it is a question of political taste. But anyone can understand that ideologies cannot be destroyed by force or put an end to by war. That is why it is senseless and even criminal to wage a war like this for the "annihilation" of Hitlerism under the pretense of fighting for "democracy".[1]

As Stalin declared on July 3, 1941, it was the German attack in June of that year which "forced" the Soviet Union into war.

Roosevelt and Churchill had little hesitation in giving Russia the maximum help. An Anglo–Russian treaty of alliance was signed on July 12, and on the 27th Harry Hopkins, Roosevelt's special adviser, arrived in Moscow to arrange lend-lease for Russia. Relations between America and the Soviet Union had not previously been cordial: the United States was the last of the great nations to recognize the Soviet regime, doing so in 1933 at the beginning of Roosevelt's first term. But in 1941 the President was anxious to build friendship and confidence not only for the war alliance but also for the peace to come. Lend-lease was granted free of interest or conditions of any kind. Nevertheless, the Russians remained suspicious and exploded into violent accusations on the slightest pretext. A betrayal of the alliance, a separate peace, a return to the interwar *cordon sanitaire* policy—the Russians continued to express their fear of these things. One cannot say they were wholly wrong; we know today that, in a secret memorandum of 1942, Churchill spoke of "erecting barriers after the war against communist barbarism."[2] But Churchill, for his part, was surely right in believing that the Soviet view would always be the one implied in Molotov's complacent speech at the end of the Polish campaign: "The capitalist world has had to withdraw a little recently, while the Soviet Union has increased its territory and population."[3]

The immediate task that lay before the Big Three was to destroy Germany. But what was meant by Germany? From a very early stage, the Soviet Government had refused to condemn the German nation wholesale. On February 23, 1942, Stalin, then People's Commissar for Defense, issued an Order of the Day (No. 55) in which he said: "It would be absurd to identify Hitler's clique with the German people, the German State. History shows that Hitlers come and go, but the German people, the German State remain."[4] After the victory of Stalingrad, he promoted a "Free German Committee" in order to stiffen resistance to Hitler inside Germany. Roosevelt's own attitude was most clearly expressed in a memorandum of August 26, 1944 to Stimson, his Secretary of War: "The German people as a whole must have it driven home to them that the whole nation has been engaged in a lawless conspiracy against the decencies of modern civilization."[5] It is worth noting that, in his youth, Roosevelt had been in Germany, "where he had attended school and had formed an early distaste for German arrogance and provincialism."[6]

It was this attitude that led to the celebrated demand for "unconditional surrender," which was first formulated at the meeting between Roosevelt and Churchill at Casablanca in January, 1943. The demand applied not merely to the army but to the entire German people, and its meaning, as Secretary of State Cordell Hull immediately pointed out to the President, was not altogether clear. But Roosevelt continued to uphold it against all opposition. At the end of 1944, General Eisenhower pleaded with him to define the slogan more clearly, lest it should inspire the German army to an even more desperate resistance, but the President answered that it was not yet time to do so. Stalin had expressed disapproval at the Tehran conference the year before. Although he himself had spoken of "unconditional surrender" in an Order of the Day of May 1, 1943, he did so only with reference to Hitler's army. But Roosevelt stuck to his guns; in 1945, the Yalta declaration read: "We have agreed on common policies and plans for enforcing the unconditional surrender terms which we shall impose together on Nazi Germany after German armed resistance has been finally crushed. These terms will not be made known until the final defeat of Germany has been accomplished."

In addition to planning for victory, it was necessary to decide how a defeated Germany should be dealt with. Many plans, some of them well considered, were evolved on the British and American side. Germany was to be transformed and kept under strict control, but the planners emphasized both the danger of allowing her to starve and the fact that the countries of Europe were economically interdependent. Every plan provided for German disarmament, but how was this to be understood? For Sumner Welles, then Undersecretary of State, the essential was to dismember the country and, above all, to destroy military influence, avoiding a return to the situation prevailing after World War I when "Allied support was given time and again to the old-line military organizations because it was thought that these alone could prevent Germany from going Communist."[7]

The group of younger planners responsible for dealing with Germany's economic power was instructed that disarmament must include "the eradication of these weapons of economic warfare," as Roosevelt wrote to Hull in September, 1944 after reading a report on I.G. Farben. At another time, he wrote, "The history of the use of the I. G. Farben Trust by the Nazis reads like a detective story."[8] There was no overt opposition to this view, but later, when the Allied military governments in Germany were set up, they included a large number of men concerning whom Senator Kilgore wrote, in a report drawn up at the end of 1945, "Nazi industrial organization is not repugnant to them and they have shown every disposition to make their peace with it." And, in fact, the director of the economic section of the British military government, Sir Percy Mills, had been a member of the Federation of British Industries delegation that had signed a gentlemen's agreement with the *Reichsgruppe Industrie* at Düsseldorf in March, 1939. And his U.S. colleague, William H. Draper, Jr., was a former treasurer of the American bank whose credit had fostered the prodigious growth of the *Vereinigte Stahlwerke* the largest steel trust in Germany.

During the war years, however, the influence of such men was still not felt, the American policy went even further in the opposite direction when, in September, 1944, Roosevelt took to his Quebec meeting with Churchill a memorandum of four typed pages from his Secretary of the Treasury, Henry Morgenthau. This brief note, soon to be known as the Morgenthau Plan, had been drawn up in reaction to a series of meetings at which Harry Hopkins and Stimson had opposed Morgenthau's view and gradually won Cordell Hull over to their own. Morgenthau's plan provided for the cession of East Prussia and Upper Silesia to Poland and of the Saar and adjacent territory between the Rhine and the Moselle to France; for the creation of a federation of German states; for forced labor by German personnel outside Germany, by way of reparations; for the internationalization of the Ruhr, together with Bremen, Kiel, and Frankfurt; and, last but not least, for the total dismantling of all industrial and mining equipment so as to transform Germany into a pastoral country.

On September 6, Roosevelt was still hesitating about accepting Morgenthau's views. The Quebec conference opened on the 11th. On the 13th, Roosevelt sent for Morgenthau and, on the 15th, Roosevelt and Churchill initialled the typescript, which thenceforth carried the endorsement: "O.K., F.D.R., W.S.C." What had happened? The President no doubt desired to plan a Carthaginian peace for Germany and failed to see that it could not survive, even in penury, if Morgenthau's ideas were carried out. Churchill was at first strongly opposed, declaring that he did not want to see England after the war "chained to a dead body." But he changed his mind, apparently for two reasons. Morgenthau pointed out to him the advantage to Britain of the disappearance of German economic competition and, more important, in exchange for a stroke of the pen, to which he probably attached no undue weight in the circumstances, Churchill obtained a substantial advantage: Roosevelt agreed to a British occupation of the Ruhr after Germany's defeat, leaving the Americans to take the South German zone previously assigned to the British.

On September 16, Eden arrived at Quebec. Having, ever since 1941, maintained that it would be folly to reduce Germany to starvation after the war, he protested violently and had a sharp altercation with Churchill. Hull emphasized to Roosevelt the disastrous effect the plan would have on world opinion and upon Germany, whose resistance it would only strengthen; he also stressed its impracticability. Through the efforts of Stimson, Hopkins, and Hull, the President was in the end partly convinced.

The Morgenthau Plan was never in fact an official part of Anglo–American policy in Germany, but neither was it officially disavowed until a statement issued by President Truman on July 3, 1945. Its influence can to some extent be detected in two basic documents, the Potsdam agreements and a U.S. Chiefs of Staff directive, JCS 1067; these together formed the textbook of American policy in Germany up to July, 1947.

But disagreements in Washington had little effect on the Big Three meetings, for the good reason that Roosevelt alone spoke for the United States and his will determined the course of the discussions. The first conference, held at Tehran at the end of November, 1943, was chiefly devoted to the conduct of the war, but two decisive factors in Germany's future were considered: dismemberment and the eastern frontiers. The principle of dismemberment was scarcely questioned. At Washington in March, Eden, Roosevelt, and Hopkins had envisaged isolating Prussia by the formation of two or three other German states, and Litvinov, the Soviet ambassador, had agreed in principle to this in a conversation with Hopkins. At Tehran, Stalin "spoke bitterly of the attitude of the German workers in the war against the Soviet Union" and said that "there would always be a strong urge of the Germans to unite and that the whole purpose of any international organization must be to neutralize this tendency by applying economic and other measures, including, if necessary, force."[9] For his part, Churchill proposed the creation of an Austro–Bavarian state. Roosevelt favored a fivefold division of Germany, and this came up again for discussion at Yalta. But at Tehran no decision was taken.

Nor was the question of Germany's eastern frontier decided at Tehran, though it was discussed at length in somewhat imprecise terms. The problem was in fact looked at from the point of view—identical in geography but not in politics—of the western frontier of Poland. Having agreed that Poland's frontier with Russia should be the "Curzon line" proposed by the British Foreign Secretary in 1920 and not the frontier of 1939, which had been fixed in 1921 after the Russo–Polish war, the Allies sought to compensate Poland in the west for what it was to lose in the east. Here again there was no dispute of principle. A transfer of population was envisaged, but the extent to which Poland should advance was not defined.

A tripartite body, the European Advisory Commission, was set up in London—pursuant to an agreement by the three Foreign Ministers—to continue the work of planning for the immediate postwar period. Its principal task was to draw up a protocol delimiting the future zones of occupation in Germany, and this took the best part of a year, from January to November, 1944. The work was speeded up after the Big Three decided, on November 11, 1944, to bring France, by then liberated, into the Commission. The final protocol delimiting the zones was then signed on the 14th, it being thought desirable to get the matter settled before the French representative's arrival, because it was not yet known if France would be one of the occupying powers. There was no dispute concerning the limits of the Soviet zone or the special regime for Berlin; agreement was reached without much trouble on both points. But Anglo–American discord regarding the zones continued even after the Quebec meeting in September. The occupation of the Ruhr having been settled to Britain's advantage, there still remained the question of Bremen, Hesse, and other areas. The U.S. Government, very dissatisfied, was slow to confirm its representative's signature, and as the Soviet ratification waited upon the American, there was a danger that the agreement would still be inoperative when hostilities ceased. At last, Hopkins, passing through London en route to Yalta, saw the need for quick action. American ratification was obtained at Yalta on February 1, 1945, and the Russians followed suit on February 6. The British had already signed in December.

The documents signed at London on September 12 and November 14, 1944 took on an importance that their signatories could hardly have dreamt of. Drawn up while the war was still in progress and final victory lay months ahead, they were to determine the fate of Germany and the Germans for decades to come, surviving the divisions and conflicts of the Big Four and invoked by German leaders from Adenauer to Brandt as an essential element in the solution of the German question.

The protocol of September 12 provided for the division of Germany into three zones, comprising the national territory within the frontiers as these existed on December 31, 1937; that is, including the Saar (returned to Germany after a referendum held in 1935 in accordance with the treaty of

Versailles) but excluding all territory seized by Hitler. The zonal boundaries were defined, with the eastern zone allotted to the Soviet Union; it was not yet determined which powers should occupy the northwest and southwest zones. Within the Soviet zone, the area of Greater Berlin as defined by a German law of April 27, 1920 was to be occupied jointly by the three powers. The city was therefore divided into three sectors, the northeastern portion being assigned to the Russians while the northwestern and southern still remained unallocated. Greater Berlin was to be jointly administered by a *Kommandatura* composed of the three section commanders.

The protocol of November 14 filled in the picture by assigning the northwestern zone of Germany to the British and the southwestern to the Americans; by a supplementary article, the U.S. military were given control of Bremen and its immediate surroundings so as to provide the American forces in Germany with a port of their own. But the main feature of the November 14 eleven-article agreement on the postwar control of Germany was that it defined the nature and structure of the occupation. The three commanders-in-chief were to exercise supreme authority in Germany on behalf of their respective governments, each in his own zone and all three jointly in matters affecting Germany as a whole. Together they constituted the Control Commission, which was to sit in Berlin, operate under a rotating chairmanship, and take decisions by a unanimous vote. Article 7 of the November agreement endorsed the September arrangements concerning Berlin. Article 6, which was never actually applied, suggested that supreme authority in Germany would not be exercised directly but through German central institutions including ministers, "controlled" (or supervised in the proper sense of the word) by the Allies.

Both documents were finally ratified on February 6. Two days earlier, the Big Three conference, which was to last a week, had opened at Yalta. France was not invited, but she occupied a large part of the discussions about Germany. Should she be allotted a zone as one of the occupying powers? Should she be a fourth member of the Control Commission and thus participate in the administration of Germany as a whole? Churchill and Stalin argued the question before Roosevelt, who was at first inclined to Stalin's view but later came round to Churchill's. Stalin argued that France had "opened the gates to the enemy" in 1940 and that her subsequent contribution to victory had been insignificant. Churchill pleaded at length for French participation, emphasizing that Britain could not bear the whole brunt of containing Germany in the west. At last Stalin declared that he would accept Roosevelt's view provided the British and Americans gave France a zone carved out of their own. It was finally agreed, in the words of the communiqué, that "France should be invited by the Three Powers, if she should so desire, to take over a zone of occupation and to participate as a fourth member of the Control Commission."

At Yalta, the question of dismembering Germany was again discussed, and again inconclusively. The (unpublished) final protocol stated:

The United Kingdom, the United States of America, and the U.S.S.R. shall possess supreme authority with respect to Germany. In the exercise of such authority they will take such steps, including the complete disarmament, demilitarization, and the dismemberment of Germany as they deem requisite for future peace and security. . . . The study of the procedure for the dismemberment of Germany was referred to a committee consisting of Mr. Eden (Chairman) Mr. Winant, and Mr. Gousev [the three members of the European Advisory Commission]. This body would consider the desirability of associating with a French representative.

While involving no formal agreement on the dismemberment of Germany, this decision suggests that the three powers were agreed that it should take place, a fact which throws doubt on the exact interpretation of the London agreements.

There was much discussion of Poland, both its future government and its frontiers with Germany. The rivalry between the London government-in-exile and the Communist regime set up at Lublin in 1944 (which moved to Warsaw in January, 1945) was at its height. Stalin reiterated his desire for a Poland "amicably disposed" toward the Soviet Union. There was little difficulty in agreeing upon Poland's new eastern frontier, but it was otherwise wite the western frontier, which had been the subject of discussions between thh London Poles and the American and British during the later months of 1944. These discussions gave rise to two confidential letters. The first, dated November 2, was written by the Permanent Undersecretary at the Foreign Office on behalf of the Prime Minister. It agreed to Poland obtaining the Oder line and the port of Stettin, but did not define the southern end of the new frontier; it also promised British support even if the United States attitude should be unfavorable. The second letter, dated November 17, was signed by Roosevelt, who said that he would acquiesce in any frontier settlement agreed to by Poland, the Soviet Union, and Britain. If a transfer of populations was desired by Poland, he would not oppose it.

On December 15, Churchill spoke in the House of Commons about the advantage to Poland of obtaining richer territories in the west than it was losing in the east, and he added:

The transference of several millions of people [that is, Poles] would have to be effected from the east to the west or north, as well as the expulsion of the Germans— because that is what is proposed: the total expulsion of the Germans—from the area to be acquired by Poland in the west and the north. For expulsion is the method which, so far as we have been able to see, will be the most satisfactory and lasting. There will be no mixture of populations to cause endless trouble, as has been the case in Alsace-Lorraine. . . . Nor do I see why there should not be room in Germany for the German populations of East Prussia and of the other territories I have mentioned. After all, 6 or 7 million Germans have been killed already in this frightful war, into which they did not hesitate, for the second time in a generation, to plunge all Europe.

Agreement had not yet been reached, however, on the extent of the territories to be allotted to Poland in the north and west. The Soviet proposal at Yalta ran: "It has been decided that the town of Stettin shall be Polish and shall mark the western frontier of Poland, which shall be continued along the Oder and then along the Western Neisse." Churchill opposed this, saying that Poland could never absorb so much territory. His proposal, with which the

Americans concurred, was to give Poland the line of the Oder together with Upper Silesia. Later, the Poles at Potsdam contended that, apart from Poland's loss of territory in the east, it was entitled to the Oder–Neisse frontier as compensation against Germany; this would give Poland wider access to the sea and a more defensible frontier for the future.

Much was at stake. The Anglo–American proposal meant fixing the frontier along the Eastern Neisse, which flows through the town of Neisse and approximately bounds the 3,750 square miles of Upper Silesia, with a prewar population of 1·5 million. The line of the Western Neisse, on the other hand, involved the transfer not only of Upper Silesia but also of the 10,250 square miles of Lower Silesia, which included Breslau and Liegnitz and a population of 3·5 million, as well as a fair slice of Brandenburg. It was found impossible to reach a compromise, and the Yalta communiqué read:

The three Heads of Government consider that the eastern frontier of Poland should follow the Curzon line with digressions from it in some regions of five to eight kilometers in favor of Poland. They recognize that Poland must receive substantial accessions of territory in the north and west. They feel that the opinion of the new Polish Provisional Government of National Unity should be sought in due course on the extent of the accessions and that the final delimitation of the western frontier of Poland should thereafter await the Peace Conference.

For its part, the Soviet delegation was more interested in reparations than in any of these questions. Soviet spokesmen continually reverted to this essential war aim, which they justified by pointing to their immense losses of men and material and to their contribution to the common victory. French membership on the Reparations Commission was, in their eyes, "an insult and an attempt to humiliate the Soviet Union."[10] The Soviet delegation at Yalta proposed that, after the war, "the German national economy should, first, be deprived for two years of the use of all its factories, heavy machinery, machine tools, rolling stock, and foreign investments and, secondly, should make annual reparations payments for ten years in manufactures or raw materials."

Eden pointed out that these proposals were self-contradictory: it is impossible to confiscate a defeated nation's current production if you have already confiscated the factories and machines by which it produces. The Americans for their part emphasized that there must not be a repetition of the previous postwar period, when German reparations had been financed by U.S. loans. Roosevelt said there would be no loans to Germany this time; he wanted the country to be self-sufficient and able to keep itself from starvation. Then they talked figures. The Soviets proposed to fix reparations of 20 milliard dollars, of which 10 would go to Russia, 8 to America and Britain, and 2 to the remaining countries. The final protocol envisaged three types of reparations in kind: the removal of assets within two years of Germany's surrender, annual deliveries of goods from current production for a period to be fixed, and the use of German labor. It also established a tripartite Reparation Commission at Moscow, to which a resolution was addressed by the Russians and Americans suggesting that it should "base its discussions upon the Soviet Government's proposal that the total reparations indemnity should be fixed at 20 milliard dollars, of which 50 per cent should go to the U.S.S.R." The British delegation was opposed to the mention of any specific sum.

The Yalta conference marked the high point of cooperation between the Big Three, especially in the matter of Germany. The Potsdam meeting, held five months later, took place in a very different atmosphere. Much had happened in the interval. Germany's collapse had begun; her forces in Italy had been routed; and, in mid-March, telegrams had been exchanged between Stalin and Roosevelt, the former violently accusing the Americans and British of working for a separate German surrender in the west, and the latter refuting the charge.

On April 12, Roosevelt died. On the 25th Russian and American troops made contact near Torgau. On the 30th, Hitler killed himself in Berlin, having appointed Admiral Dönitz his successor. On May 1, Dönitz spoke on the radio to the German people: "Our *Führer*, Adolf Hitler, has fallen. . . . He was swift to recognize the appalling danger of Bolshevism and devoted his life to combating it. . . . In his personal struggle to stem the Bolshevik flood he was fighting also for Europe and the whole of civilization. . . . The British and Americans, therefore, are no longer waging war for their own nations but solely to assist the spread of Bolshevism in Europe."

This interpretation of the war of 1939—a rather free one, to say the least—was the prelude to a German offer to capitulate to the west while continuing the war in the east. Eisenhower refused it out of hand, as his government had refused similar offers from Himmler a few days earlier. The U.S.S.R. was kept scrupulously informed of these German approaches. On May 7 and 8, the surrender was signed at Reims and Berlin, and, on the 9th, Stalin addressed a message to the German people in which he said: "While celebrating this victory, the Soviet Union has no intention of dismembering or destroying Germany." His representative on the Dismemberment Committee (which only met twice) had already stated, on March 26, that "the Soviet Government understood that the Yalta decision regarding the dismemberment of Germany was not an obligatory plan for partition but a possibility for exercising pressure upon Germany for the purpose of rendering it harmless if other means proved insufficient."[11]

On June 5, a declaration was issued at Berlin by Allied commanders Eisenhower, Zhukov, Montgomery, and de Lattre de Tassigny, acting on behalf of their governments. Comprised of fifteen articles, it spelled out in detail the notion of the unconditional surrender not merely of an army but of a nation.

On July 1, in accordance with the London protocol, the American troops withdrew from those parts of Saxony and Thuringia in the Soviet zone to which their advance had carried them, while British and American units took over their respective sectors of Berlin, which had been taken by the Red Army. These two moves were of the utmost importance. In later arguments concerning the right of the Western powers to station troops in Berlin, the Russians ignored the fact that the latter's presence there was not the result of a unilateral gesture of benevolence on the part of their Soviet ally, but represented the fulfillment of a pact previously concluded. The Western Allies paid the "price" for the occupation sectors of Berlin on July 1, 1945: the territory of the German Democratic Republic (G.D.R.) would be a great deal smaller than it is today if Germany had been partitioned along the line of junction of the victorious troops on the day of the German surrender.

The Potsdam conference of the Big Three, which opened on July 6, 1945, included a different cast of personalities: Truman had succeeded Roosevelt and, in the middle of the conference, when the British election results were known, Churchill was replaced by Attlee—though this was not to alter the British line in any way. Stalin alone was unchanged. Besides Germany, there were a number of problems on the agenda: Iran, the Rumanian oil plants, the international zone of Tangier, the Black Sea straits, and the peace treaties with Germany's former satellites. Germany, however, was the chief subject of discussion. It was not difficult to define certain basic principles for "the treatment of Germany during the initial period of control." The Allied aims included:

The complete disarmament and demilitarization of Germany and the elimination or control of all German industry that could be used for military production. . . . To convince the German people that they have suffered a total military defeat and that they cannot escape responsibility for what they have brought upon themselves, since their own ruthless warfare and the fanatical Nazi resistance have destroyed the German economy and made chaos and suffering inevitable. . . . To destroy the National Socialist Party and its affiliated and supervised organizations [and] to dissolve all Nazi institutions; [to arrest and try war criminals and to remove undesirable persons] from public and semi-public office, and from positions of responsibility in important private undertakings.

These principles were drawn—verbally to some extent and, as regards their content, completely—from JCS 1067, which was the U.S. Commander-in-Chief's directive from May onward, though it was not made public until October 17.

But to which Germany or Germanies were the principles to be applied? President Truman arrived at Potsdam with a dismemberment plan that envisaged a southern state comprising Austria, Bavaria, Württemberg, Baden, and Hungary, with its capital at Vienna. He also proposed a permanent international four-power control of the Ruhr–Rhineland–Saar area. Apparently, he had not taken account of Stalin's declaration of May 9 or the *volte-face* which it implied. In any case, the idea of dismembering Germany was dropped. There was to be only one Germany. But what were to be its boundaries? The quadripartite Berlin statement of June 5 on the occupation zones had referred to the frontiers of December 31, 1937, and the British and Americans expected to negotiate on this basis; but they found themselves confronted with a new situation. At Potsdam, they learnt that the Russians had, on April 21, signed an agreement with the Warsaw Poles entrusting to them the administration of the territory east of the Oder and Western Neisse. Eden, and after him Bevin, protested vigorously; and Truman later wrote, with obvious exaggeration in view of the American position at Yalta: "At Potsdam we were faced with an accomplished fact and were by circumstances almost forced to agree to Russian occupation of Eastern Poland and the occupation of that part of Germany east of the Oder river by Poland. It was a high-handed outrage."[12]

Churchill was prepared to accept the Oder line but not the Western Neisse, arguing that the moral responsibility for expelling such a large number of Germans was too great. The Polish leaders were sent for and maintained their claim to the entire territory made over to them by the Soviet Union. The final agreement about Germany's eastern territories read as follows:

The conference has agreed in principle to the proposal of the Soviet Government concerning the ultimate transfer to the Soviet Union of the city of Königsberg and the area adjacent to it as described above. . . . The President of the United States and the British Prime Minister have declared that they will support the proposal of the conference at the forthcoming peace settlement. . . . The following agreement was reached on the western frontier of Poland. In conformity with the agreement on Poland reached at the Crimea conference, the three Heads of Government have sought the opinion of the Polish Provisional Government of National Unity in regard to the accession of territory in the north and west which Poland should receive. . . . The three Heads of Government reaffirm their opinion that the final delimitation of the western frontier of Poland should await the peace settlement. The three Heads of Government agree that, pending the final determination of Poland's western frontier, the former German territories east of a line . . . along the Oder River to the confluence of the western Neisse River and along the western Neisse to the Czechoslovak frontier . . . shall be under the administration of the Polish State and for such purposes shall not be considered as part of the Soviet zone of occupation in Germany.

This text became the subject of conflicting interpretations. By the Russians and Poles, it was held to allot the territory in question finally to Poland, and this interpretation was more and more clearly acted on in the years after Potsdam. In January, 1949, the Polish parliament passed a law bringing the "recovered territories" under the control of the Polish Ministry of the Interior; and, in June, 1950, the governments of Poland and the German Democratic Republic signed an agreement recognizing the Oder–Western Neisse line as the definitive frontier. The Poles and their Soviet allies quoted Truman's speech of August 9, 1945, broadcast on his return from Potsdam: "The territories to be administered by Poland will give her the chance to provide a better life for her people and a better defense of her frontier with Germany." They have continued to argue that the word "delimitation" does not concern the general line of a frontier but only the fixing of its details.

The Western powers argued that the agreement did not give the territory in question to Poland but postponed any final decision until the signing of the peace treaty. Legally this view seems unassailable. But as time went on, there was a tendency to claim—in view of the different terms in which the agreement referred to Königsberg and to the other territories—that the signatories to the agreement made no commitment to Poland at all. This was hardly a sustainable position, and Churchill for his part continued to uphold the line he had taken at Yalta and Potsdam—that, in the peace treaty, Poland should be given the line of the Oder and Eastern Neisse—while protesting against the Russo-Polish *fait accompli*.

The only one of Russia's allies to have already accepted the Oder–Western Neisse frontier was not represented at Potsdam. General de Gaulle, then head

31

of the French Provisional Government, had discussed the matter in some detail during his visit to Moscow in December, 1944; on the 2nd, Stalin had declared that "Poland's former territory in East Prussia, Pomerania, and Silesia should in justice be restored to her." The General made no objection, merely asking in return that Stalin should support the French claim "concerning the Rhine." On December 6, he told Stalin: "We are in no way opposed to what Marshal Stalin said the other day with reference to Poland's western frontiers. A solution on these lines would, it seems to us, serve to prevent Poland reaching an understanding with Germany"[13]—which, in the General's view, would be dangerous both to France and to the Soviet Union.

The Russo–Polish interpretation of Potsdam was reinforced by the confusion that attended the settlement of another important issue, the transfer of population. According to the agreement, "The three Governments, having considered the question in all its aspects, recognize that the transfer to Germany of German populations, or elements thereof, remaining in Poland, Czechoslovakia, and Hungary, will have to be undertaken. They agree that any transfers that take place should be effected in an orderly and humane manner." This last provision was to remain a dead letter, but the decision clearly meant that the three countries referred to were to be rid of their German minorities. But how was the expression "in Poland" to be interpreted? The Russians and Poles claimed that Poland extended beyond her 1939 frontiers as far as the Oder–Neisse line, and that the intention was to expel the millions of German inhabitants of the area newly administered by Poland, many of whom had already fled before the advancing Red Army. Though difficult to justify by the letter of the agreement, this interpretation was not far removed from what Churchill had previously had in mind, and it gained in force from the fact that the expulsions were virtually acquiesced in by the Western powers. A December 6, 1945 decision by the Control Commission at Berlin accepted the entry into the British and Soviet zones of 3·5 million Germans from "Poland," at a time when, according to the Polish authorities, only 2·1 million were left in the former German territories. So Molotov was able to claim, in a speech of September 16, 1946, that the Western powers had implicitly recognized the Oder–Neisse frontier, since the transfer of population could not be regarded as a mere "temporary expedient."

The area of the former German territories east of the Oder–Neisse line is about 44,000 square miles, or 24 per cent of the entire area of Germany in 1938. Their mainly agricultural population of 9·5 million provided food for 13·5 million Germans. In addition, 17 per cent of German coal production in 1938 was from Silesian mines. The influx of some 12 million Germans— "expelled from their homes" (*Heimatvertriebene*) in the Western terminology, or "resettled" (*Umsiedler*) in the Eastern—posed enormous economic and social problems in the reception areas. And, finally, the amputation of a quarter of Germany's territory complicated the reparations problem from Potsdam onward, the Soviet Union maintaining against the West that the wealth of the remaining three-quarters should provide the total sum—for it was unthinkable to make confiscations from the territory which had been assigned to Poland.

The section of the Potsdam agreement dealing with reparations was the outcome of arduous discussion. Two of the three types of reparations proposed at Yalta were not mentioned: confiscation from current production and the use of German labor abroad. Out-and-out confiscation, for which no total figure was fixed, was to be effected by the Soviet Union, both for itself and for Poland, in the Soviet zone, while the British, the Americans, and other countries were to take their share from the western zones. The U.S.S.R. was also to receive, from the western zones, in exchange for coal, foodstuffs, and other specified materials, 15 per cent of all industrial equipment in excess of Germany's peacetime requirements, and a further 10 per cent of it outright. The preceding section of the agreement, however, contained a phrase that looked harmless enough but was, in fact, vital: "Payment of reparations should leave enough resources to enable the German people to subsist without external assistance." This was the principle maintained by Roosevelt at Yalta; but no one at Potsdam seems to have asked whether, if it were respected, the payment of reparations would ever be possible for a ruined and overpopulated Germany, deprived of her richest agricultural lands.

The contradiction was certainly not resolved by the "Economic Principles" in section II of the agreement: "In order to eliminate Germany's war potential . . . productive capacity not needed for permitted production [whose amount the agreement does not fix] shall be removed in accordance with the reparations plan recommended by the Allied Commission on Reparations and approved by the Governments concerned or, if not removed, shall be destroyed." Here there is a serious confusion between two distinct proceedings: the destruction of arms factories and plant for security reasons, and the transfer of industrial equipment abroad by way of reparations. This confusion, which was already apparent in the Yalta debates, became inextricable in subsequent years. In the same way, the indefiniteness of the word "excessive" complicated the task of "eliminating the present excessive concentration of economic power as exemplified in particular by cartels, syndicates, trusts, and other monopolistic arrangements."

The agreement did at least presuppose that the economic principles it set out would be applied in common by all the signatories. According to paragraph 14 of section II: "During the period of occupation Germany shall be treated as a single economic unit. To this end common policies shall be established in regard to . . . (d) import and export program for Germany as a whole; (e) currency and banking, central taxation, and customs; (f) reparation and removal of industrial war potential." Further, it was laid down in the "Political Principles" that "so far as is practicable, there shall be uniformity of treatment of the German population throughout Germany." At the same time, however, "the administration of affairs in Germany should be directed toward the decentralization of the political structure and the development of local responsibility."

Besides the negative purposes of the occupation—demilitarization and denazification—the "Political Principles" also indicated a positive aim: "to prepare for the eventual reconstruction of German political life on a democratic basis and for eventual peaceful cooperation in international life by Germany." Apart from decentralization, other measures were to be taken to this end: "All democratic political parties with rights of assembly and of public discussion shall be allowed and encouraged throughout Germany; . . . Subject to the necessity for maintaining military security, freedom of speech, press, and religion shall be permitted, and religious institutions shall be respected;" and "the formation of free trade unions shall be permitted."

2

Nuremberg and Denazification

IT WAS the first time since 1814 that Germany had known war within its own frontiers—and what a war! The towns were in ruins. Of Frankfurt's 177,000 houses, only 44,000 still stood; in Nuremberg, scarcely one house in ten was undamaged; 53 per cent of the buildings in Hamburg had been turned into 43 million cubic meters of rubble. Not one of the great cities had escaped the pitiless bombings for which the Luftwaffe had set the pattern in its raids on Rotterdam and Coventry. The fighting on land and Hitler's scorched earth policy had increased the devastation; not only viaducts and bridges crossing great rivers but even the footbridges over village streams had been destroyed. Apart from the peasants of central Germany, few Germans still lived in their homes. Millions of townspeople had fled from the bombings into the country; millions more had fled west before the advance of the Red Army, and there had been the beginnings of a movement the other way at the first appearance of Allied troops in the west. The population seemed to consist only of women and children and old men, and even boys of fifteen had been given rifles. 1,650,000 men had been killed in action, 2 million were prisoners, and 1,600,000 were missing. Food supplies and transport had completely broken down; there were no mails or newspapers; administration had collapsed, and chaos was unchallenged.

Into this chaos more millions of Germans were to be thrown, expelled from the countries of Central and Eastern Europe and from the German territory east of the Oder–Neisse line. These expulsions began before the Potsdam conference and reached their height in the winter of 1945–46. The conditions under which they were carried out were appalling. From this point of view, the rights and wrongs of the matter are a secondary issue. No doubt it is important to judge whether or not Czechoslovakia, which had been a multinational state, had the right to expel the Sudeten German minority who had lived there for centuries, but whose existence—and also the behavior of some—had been the cause of Czechoslovakia's enslavement and ruin. But whatever the rights of the case, millions of human beings were forced to leave their homes at twenty-four hours' notice for unknown destinations with no more than fifty or sixty pounds of baggage apiece, were transported in herds, and forced to make long marches in cold and hunger. Their sufferings can certainly be explained, but nothing can justify them.

Nevertheless, these sufferings were the consequence of Hitler's "total war," during which the invaded peoples had suffered atrociously until his regime collapsed in total defeat. France, Belgium, and to a still greater extent Poland, the Ukraine, and Yugoslavia had endured massacre, looting, deportation, and systematic devastation. Of the millions of men, women, and children thrown into concentration camps—Dachau, Auschwitz, Buchenwald, Ravensbrück— only a few emaciated survivors were rescued by the Allied troops. It would not have been surprising for atrocities on this scale to be visited with brutal vengeance; and for the first few days or weeks, especially in many places along the Red Army's line of advance, looting, rape, and other forms of brutality took place on a large scale. As was later observed, "Many East German men and women had personal grounds to hate the Russians."[1] The victors' policy, in principle, was not to take revenge but to judge and mete out punishment as rapidly and as fairly as possible, in such a way that justice should be seen to have been done. What the victors forgot was the weight of suffering by which both sides were oppressed—the majority of countries in the victors' camp and also defeated Germany. From the start, this made fairness and calmness almost impossible; it guaranteed in advance that there should be no common language between accusers and accused.

This lack of comprehension was accentuated by the fact that the victorious powers who sat in judgment on Germany had not thought out their own position and did not explain it clearly. On the face of it, their double objective was simple enough: on the one hand, to punish Germany, on the other, to bring about such changes that the crimes of the past could never be repeated. But who were to be punished—individuals or groups? What crimes were to be punished—that of giving the order for atrocities, that of physically carrying them out, that of active or passive complicity in their manifold degrees? What was the punishment to be? The duration of the penalty in a given case was no less hard to decide on than its nature. What exactly was to be changed in Germany—the political system, the structure of society, the attitude of the people? What were they to be changed into, and what were the models to be imitated?

It was common ground that the chief Nazi leaders should be punished; but, after that, the victors took different views of what constituted the essence of Nazism and, therefore, of how best to eradicate it. The British leaders regarded it as a sort of disease in the body politic, which would be cured if all carriers of the germ were eliminated. In the French view, Hitler was in the direct line of development from Bismarck: Nazism was bound up with "Prussianism, of which Hitler was the most dangerous incarnation."[2] The totalitarian state was a natural outcome of unitary Germany; punishment would be useless if Prussia and German unity were not at the same time destroyed. Among the Americans, some took the French view and some the British; while the Russians ascribed Hitler's domination of Germany to the country's social structure and above all to the distribution of economic power. Punishment, in the Soviet view, was a secondary matter: the prime task was to carry out a social revolution.

The victors did reach agreement on the method of trying and punishing those they unanimously regarded as the chief culprits. During the war—on January 13, 1942—the representatives of nine German-occupied countries had signed a declaration in London denouncing the occupation with its "regime of terror characterized . . . by imprisonments, mass expulsions, the execution of hostages and massacres," and declaring as a "principal war aim" the punishment by judicial process of all who ordered, perpetrated, or took part in these crimes. In 1945, the Allied powers decided to go further. They endorsed the plan for judging war criminals by special tribunals, either in Germany or in the countries where their crimes had been committed; but they also set up an International Military Tribunal to deal with the major criminals, whether individuals or groups, and with crimes that were far out-side the definitions laid down by the Hague Convention of 1907.

The Tribunal sat at Nuremberg from November 20, 1945 until October 1, 1946. Arraigned before it were the principal surviving leaders of Nazi Ger-many, and also the following groups or institutions: the Reich Government, the General Staff, the SA, the SS, the SD (security police), the Gestapo, and the "corps of political leaders" of the Nazi party. The charter of the Tribunal laid down that: "In cases where a group or organization is declared criminal by the Tribunal, the competent national authority of any signatory shall have the right to bring individuals to trial for membership therein before national, military or occupation courts." The crimes for which they could be convicted were of three orders: first, crimes against peace, defined in accordance with the 1928 Kellogg–Briand Pact, which outlawed war, and including the planning of wars of aggression; second, war crimes, including "murder, ill-treatment, or deportation to slave labor or for any other purpose of civilian population of or in occupied territory, murder or ill-treatment of prisoners of war or persons on the seas, killing of hostages, plunder of public or private property, wanton destruction of cities, towns, or villages, or devastation not justified by military necessity"; and finally "crimes against humanity, namely murder, extermi-nation, enslavement, deportation, and other inhumane acts committed against any civilian population, before or during the war, or persecutions on political, racial, or religious grounds in execution of, or in connection with, any crime within the jurisdiction of the Tribunal, whether or not a violation of the domestic law of the country where perpetrated."

At the end of the long, meticulous yet confused proceedings, the accused organizations were found criminal except for the Reich Government and the General Staff. The Soviet judge protested against these exceptions and also, in a dissenting opinion, against the acquittal of three individuals: Hans Fritzsche (an unimportant aide to Goebbels) and, especially, Franz von Papen and Hjalmar Schacht. Both the latter, after some trouble with the German denazification authorities, were to enjoy many years of quiet and contented life. In retirement, Papen published memoirs full of distortions of the truth and was honored by being made a *cameriere segreto* of the Pope in 1959; he died in May 1969. Schacht, who continued to run a bank until 1963, died on June 4, 1970 at the age of ninety-three. Four of the accused were sentenced to terms of imprisonment. Admiral Dönitz (ten years) was released in 1956. Baron von Neurath was released in 1954, two years before his death; he was Hitler's Minister of Foreign Affairs from 1933 to 1938, and, later, "Protector" of Bohemia and Moravia, and he had received a fifteen-year sentence. Baldur von Schirach, the Nazi youth leader, and Albert Speer, the Minister for Armaments, were both sentenced to twenty years and released on September

37

30, 1966: the former, heavy as his guilt had been, was loud in self-pity, while the latter, the case against whom was less clear, showed discretion and more objectivity. Of the three condemned to life imprisonment, Admiral Raeder and Walther Funk (Minister of the Economy from 1936 onward) were released for reasons of poor health in 1955 and 1957 respectively: they both died in 1960. The third, Rudolf Hess, who was the *Führer's* former deputy, therefore became the sole remaining inmate of the inter-Allied prison at Spandau.

Hitler, Goebbels, and Himmler escaped the Allies' hands by committing suicide. Göring took poison after being sentenced to death at Nuremberg. Martin Bormann, Hitler's immediate aide, was condemned to death *in absentia*. Ten other death sentences were carried out by hanging: they included Joachim von Ribbentrop, Generals Keitel and Jodl, and the most fanatical and poisonous of anti-Semites, *Gauleiter* Julius Streicher.

What exactly was meant by the verdict passed upon organizations as such? The Tribunal declared that all persons were criminal who had become or remained members of certain groups which they knew at the time to be responsible for criminal acts as defined by Article 6 of the Charter. But did a young man who was drafted to a unit of the military SS, as hundreds of thousands were, or to the Gestapo, necessarily know that these bodies committed crimes? And, once enrolled, could he get out without saying why and risking death or a concentration camp? The Nuremberg procedure, however, did not declare a man guilty for the sole reason that he belonged to a criminal group: it only declared him liable to trial, and his actual participation in some specific crime had to be proved before he could be condemned. This, at least, was the position in countries other than Germany. The Control Commission at Berlin, by a law (No. 10) of December 20, 1945, declared it a criminal offense to have belonged to any organization judged as criminal by the International Military Tribunal. The Tribunal itself, in its verdict of September 30, 1946, emphasized that the condemnation of the organizations did not mean that persons brought to trial before other courts should not receive the benefit of normal judicial procedure—an injunction that was not always respected.[3]

In one country only, France, was a law passed that overrode the fundamental legal principles of individual responsibility and of placing the burden of proof on the prosecution and not the defense. A French law of September 15, 1948 laid down that "when a crime . . . is imputable to the collective action of a detachment or group forming part of an organization condemned as criminal by the International Military Tribunal, . . . all individuals belonging to this detachment or group may be considered jointly responsible unless they can prove that they were forcibly enrolled and did not participate in the crime." This law, which was applied only once by a French court,[4] was known in Germany—with good reason—as the *lex Oradour*: it owed its existence to the memory of the massacre in the French village of that name, where the men were shot and the women and children herded into the church and burnt to death. Those responsible for the massacre were tried at Bordeaux in 1953, and on June 27, while the proceedings were actually going on, the French parliament revoked the law of 1948, it having come to light that some members of the unit in question were natives of Alsace.[5]

The verdicts passed on individuals for the most part involved problems that concerned them only. But as the main trial took its course, to be followed by many other less spectacular ones, three questions that transcended individual cases arose more and more frequently: To what extent should obedience to orders constitute a defense? What was left of the evidence concerning crimes committed on such a frightful scale, once it was granted that participating in a crime unawares is less culpable than full complicity? And finally, was it only Germans that had committed the crimes in question?

Article 8 of the Charter said: "The fact that the defendant acted pursuant to order of his government or of a superior shall not free him from responsibility, but may be considered in mitigation of punishment if the Tribunal determines that justice so requires." The purpose of this article is clear. If an accused person were permitted to shelter behind superior orders, in a totalitarian system this would mean that in the end the dictator himself would be the only guilty party. But the article implied that the accused, particularly if he was a soldier, ought to have been prepared to risk his life every time he received an order he judged to be immoral. A French witness at Nuremberg related that he, as a doctor, was made to select patients to be transported to a place where he knew they would be put to death, and the defense cross-questioned him as follows:

"Why did you not say: 'I know what your purpose is, and I refuse to obey this order'?"

"Because it would have meant my death."

"Quite so. And what would it have meant for any German who refused to obey a similar order?"

In every country in the world, a soldier under arms has always been liable to the death penalty for refusing to obey an order; and the defense counsel for members of armed forces recalled this fact at every one of the numerous trials that took place after 1945.

While the excuse of obedience to orders might be advanced for the lower ranks, the excuse of ignorance was continually appealed to in defense of the leaders, especially diplomats and military men. One atrocity would be explained as the independent act of a local authority, another as having been committed by police orders that bypassed the normal hierarchical channels. Each accusation and each trial thus presented special problems, and it cannot be claimed that all of them found equitable solutions.

In any case, the problem of ignorance vastly exceeds the scope of the trials. It concerns not merely those who appeared before the military courts but the whole population of Germany. It was asserted among the victors that the German people could not have failed to know what crimes were being perpetrated in the concentration camps and the occupied countries. The majority of Germans replied that they had known nothing at all. These two assertions, debated for years in the press, in books, and in conversation, are both exaggerated. Many Germans really did have no idea of the crimes that were being committed in Germany's name; but others saw the forced laborers from the torture camps being driven to work, or the machine-gunning or burning of some occupied village. Here again, hasty generalization should have been avoided. But the victors generalized in two contradictory ways. On the one

39

hand, they said to the Germans: "You must take responsibility for crimes of which you cannot have been ignorant," and on the other, they launched a full-scale campaign of information, to prove to these same Germans that the crimes in question had really been committed. It should have been unnecessary to turn such a blaze of limelight upon the Nuremberg trial if the German people already knew all about the horrors that were revealed there.

The publicity campaign would have been better received if the proceedings at Nuremberg had not given the impression of being founded on victory rather than justice. The accused and their counsel were German; the prosecutors and judges were American, British, Russian, or French. No doubt they performed their functions conscientiously; and perhaps it would not really have been possible to set up a tribunal composed of the nationals of neutral states. Which of the neutrals, including for instance Sweden and Switzerland, had kept their hands wholly clean during the war? But Germans remembered the accusation of Versailles; and the sense of uneasiness was increased by charges levelled against the victors themselves, especially when, as time went on, they began to accuse one another. At Nuremberg, the Soviet judge had succeeded in stifling inquiry into the murder of thousands of Polish officers whose corpses were discovered in a mass grave at Katyn. Admirals of the U.S. navy were heard to say that if they had been in the same position as their German opposite numbers, they would have carried on submarine warfare in the same way. So what became of the notion of a "war crime"? The bombing attack that destroyed Dresden on February 13, 1945 had not been directed against any military objective. Between July 25 and August 3, 1943, 40,000 inhabitants of Hamburg had been killed in "Operation Gomorrah," which laid to waste 277,000 homes, 24 hospitals, 277 schools, and 58 churches. Shortly before the Nuremberg trial opened, atomic bombs were dropped on Hiroshima and Nagasaki. A month after it ended, French warships bombarded Haiphong, causing thousands of civilian casualties. In Indochina, Algeria, and Vietnam, the execution of hostages and destructive acts of reprisal were to become the order of the day. In 1956, Khrushchev's speech to the Soviet Party Congress revealed or confirmed a tale of Soviet crimes committed on a massive scale. Twenty-one years after Nuremberg, Israel in its turn was to discover that an occupation cannot be conducted with clean hands.

All this does not detract from the horror and barbarity of German behavior in Poland and the Soviet Union, or prevent us from shuddering at the mention of Auschwitz or Treblinka. But it would have been better if Allied justice in 1945–46 had appeared more evenhanded, more visibly founded on absolute standards. This is true politically as well as morally: those who had admired Nazism in the past would have perceived its barbarity more clearly if greater care had been taken to distinguish those features that were specific to the movement from those that were not.

If the Germans could not be trusted to bring their former leaders to book, might the Tribunal not at least have included a German judge? This would probably have helped to educate the German public, and would also have reminded the world that the German people itself, or a large proportion of it, was a victim of Nazism and had its own accounts to settle with the accused. The risk of a German judge or prosecutor being branded as a traitor by his own people would only have existed if the German nation had been disposed to close ranks against its conquerors in defense of its late masters.

However, the idea of including a German judge was firmly rejected by the United States, the most powerful of the victorious allies. Directive JCS 1067, addressed to the Commander-in-Chief of the U.S. occupation forces in Germany—a document to which we have already referred and whose importance cannot be overestimated—clearly laid down that "Germany will not be occupied for the purpose of liberation."[6] The notion of collective guilt was not expressly formulated, nor was it intended in the sense of the personal guilt of every individual German. But at the very least the directive signified an arraignment of the whole people, which was both unjust and a grave political error.

It was unjust because it deliberately ignored the existence of a German opposition to Hitler, the sacrifices its members had made, and the additional obstacles that the future conquerors had placed in their way. We can understand the bitterness of Kurt Schumacher when he exclaimed, in the autumn of 1945: "While others were signing alliances with the German Government, some of us were already rotting in concentration camps."[7] Between 1933 and 1939, over half a million Germans, not to speak of those driven abroad, were arrested, condemned, or interned on political grounds, while the help or even sympathy extended to them by the outside world had been moderate to say the least. When war came, the moral dilemma of the German opposition was still more acute. Defeat would certainly mean the collapse of the regime, but it would be a defeat for Germany as a whole and not merely for the Nazi Party. In the invaded countries, Nazism could be resisted on ideological and patriotic grounds alike, but to oppose it in Germany partook of treason. Every German had been exposed to the right-wing propaganda, taken over by Goebbels, which attributed the defeat of 1918 to a "stab in the back," and every German soldier had been trained to put honor, which for practical purposes meant discipline, above all else. A law of August 20, 1934 prescribed an oath of absolute obedience to the *Führer*, ending with the words: "I pledge this oath with my life." This led to many tragic crises of conscience for officers and soldiers alike, as was shown by the extraordinary success after the war of Carl Zuckmayer's play *The Devil's General*. In that piece, an air force officer sabotages the planes in his charge, thus bringing death to his closest comrades[8] and hastening the defeat of his country—but also hastening the downfall of an odious regime, as harmful to Germany itself as to the rest of the world. Did he do right? There were many who thought that victory should come first and that the Nazis could be tackled later. Certainly it cannot have been easy to decide that Germany's defeat would be to her own advantage; and the Allies' demand for unconditional surrender made the task of the opposition inside Germany almost impossible, for it compelled the Germans to choose between Hitler and national ruin.

This demand, formulated at Casablanca, was not a casual expedient but part of a consistent attitude. When the Allies were warned by the German opposition in 1940 of the imminent invasion of the Netherlands, they were sceptical of this information because it came from a group whose existence they refused to admit. When, at the beginning of 1942, an American journalist, who had had a long talk in Germany with Jakob Kaiser (one of the underground leaders), tried to see Roosevelt to tell him what had passed and to urge that the movement be given help, the President refused to see him on account of the "most embarrassing" nature of his mission; and Churchill, when he already knew the broad significance of the attempt on Hitler's life on July 20, 1944, described it in the House of Commons (on August 2), as a settlement of accounts among Nazis.

The years 1940 and 1941 were the nadir of the German opposition. All the evidence confirms that it was impossible for its leaders to make any headway during that period of unexampled triumphs. But after the defeat at Stalingrad, the atmosphere changed, and from then on the German resistance comprised two very different and yet inextricably mingled elements. The first consisted of those who wanted to destroy Hitler in order to put an end to Nazi barbarism, and it was exemplified in the admirable Hans and Sophie Scholl who were executed at Munich with four of their fellow-students in the spring of 1943—after the pretense of a trial at which the presiding judge observed that the times were happily past when people could go about proclaiming their "so-called political faith." There had in fact been a number of police reports since 1941 referring to small "antisocial" or "opposition" groups, from which we may conclude that the taste for political independence was alive in a considerable number of young people. Of the same type were such men as the moderate-minded Goerdeler, a former mayor of Leipzig, the trade union leaders Wilhelm Leuschner and Jacob Kaiser, and the "Antifa" (anti-Fascist) groups in Bremen, Lübeck, and a number of the Ruhr towns.

The second group consisted of those who also wished to rid Germany of Hitler, but only because he was leading the country to disaster. Their conscience was untroubled by the destruction of Rotterdam or Warsaw; it was the ruin of German cities that shocked them, and it was Hitler's errors of strategy and not the Nazi regime that aroused their revulsion. Recruits to this way of thinking were chiefly found in the higher reaches of the army and in certain government circles.

Those who planned the attempt of July 20, 1944 represented a variety of groups animated by diverse motives. The very scale of the repressions that followed ought to have convinced the Allies that there was more than one Germany and that if they played their cards right a large part of the population would welcome them as liberators. They could have said to the Germans: "You have been deceived, terrorized, and led to disaster by Hitler's fault. It is for you and us now to bring the guilty men to judgment." As it was, the arraignment of the German people *en masse* revived their feelings of solidarity with the defeated regime at the very time when these were starting to disappear. It also had the effect of inhibiting reflection about the nature of the Nazi regime and the extent to which almost everyone in Germany had compromised with it.

Nevertheless it would be wrong to blame the Allies exclusively for the attitude of those Germans who refused to admit that they knew what Nazism was about. Often the latter's reaction was one of fear. If they acknowledged the truth now, they would have had to admit, at least to themselves, that they had suspected it all along but had refused to give it any serious thought, for fear of having either to act dangerously or to keep their mouths shut and so become accomplices in crime. The fear of knowledge was bound up with the individual's awareness of his sins of omission. Nonetheless, a good many Germans admitted to themselves—and were not afraid to declare openly—that they had been guilty of weakness or cowardice and thus shared the moral responsibility for the crimes of others. Germans of this type did their best to persuade their compatriots to make a similar examination of conscience, which involved no small degree of humility as well as forgetfulness of one's own sufferings. A word that recurs constantly in German writings of this time is *Besinnung* or self-recollection. The responsibility to which it referred was not something that could be weighed by judges or assessed by judicial norms—a fact that the occupants failed to realize when they embarked on their denazification program.

This was of such complexity that it is almost impossible to summarize briefly. One set of laws and directives were promulgated by the Allies collectively through the Control Commission at Berlin. Others emanated from the commanders-in-chief of the respective occupation zones, and others again from German authorities, usually after a hard but unequal tussle with the occupying power. Broadly speaking, there was a period during which the task of denazifying was reserved to the occupants, and a subsequent one in which they transferred it to the Germans; but the two overlapped to some extent. From the SHAEF (Supreme Headquarters, Allied Expeditionary Force) *Handbook for Military Government*, issued in September, 1944 by the "German Country Unit" of the U.S. Government, to the Bavarian *Abschlussgesetz* (Final Law) of August, 1954, the subject is a maze of complex and sometimes contradictory texts.[9]

The first step taken by the Allies was to set up internment camps for persons who were liable to "automatic" arrest by reason of the posts they had held. By the end of 1946, about 64,000 such arrests had been effected in the British zone, 95,000 in the American, 19,000 in the French, and 67,000 in the Soviet zone. These figures do not represent the numbers actually detained in camps at that date, for a good many of those arrested were released, especially younger men and those who had not belonged to any of the organizations declared criminal by the Nuremberg verdict. Mass dismissals took place, and a variety of grounds were established on which individuals were debarred from holding any public office. In 1945-46, about 70,000 such prohibitions took place in the French zone and 320,000 in the British. In the Soviet zone, the criteria were to a large extent social as well as political; in the western zones, especially the American, what chiefly counted was former Party membership. By a law (No. 8) of September 26, 1945, the U.S. military government forbade anyone who had belonged to the Nazi Party or to any organization connected with it to exercise any profession or craft, otherwise than in the form of manual labor or in a completely subordinate position.

Legislation of this kind took no account of the realities of the Hitler period —when an industrial magnate who contributed heavily to Nazi funds might safely abstain from becoming a Party member, while every teacher or civil servant who had his career to think of was at least tempted, for the sake of a quiet life, to join either the Party itself or the appropriate professional organization.

How many people had not in fact been coerced into joining? In any case, many Nazi organizations were concerned with organized leisure rather than with combating Germany's internal or external enemies. And how many organizations were there all told? The Control Commission's Law No. 2 of October 10, 1945 spoke of sixty, whereas, in the French zone, Order No. 61, signed by Laffon (the Administrator-General) and defining the categories of persons who were not allowed to vote, put the number at thirty-eight.

In the innumerable *Fragebogen* (questionnaires) that had to be filled in—they were caricatured in an autobiographical novel by Ernst von Solomon—every German was ordered to tell the whole truth about himself, his past, and, above all, his Party affiliations. One of the cynical jokes that went the rounds at this time was: "Three more ships have arrived in Hamburg—one with a cargo of food and the other two with questionnaires." Another was: "Do you know the three meanings of the initials PG?", the answer being: *Parteigenosse* (member of the Nazi Party), *prisonnier de guerre* (prisoner of war in France and still engaged on forced labor there), or simply *Pech gehabt* (no luck). The third interpretation, of course, covered the first two categories also.

The most important enactment in the American zone was the "law concerning liberation from Nazism and militarism," signed on March 5, 1946 by the German prime ministers of Bavaria, Württemberg-Baden, and Hesse. This called for a fresh screening of the whole population, with a new questionnaire to be filled in by everyone over eighteen, that is, a total for the whole zone of 13 million people. Those who fell into certain categories, comprising about 3·5 million people of both sexes, were to be tried by special courts known as *Spruchkammern*. The net was wide enough to include members of such bodies as the *Reichsbund der Kinderreichen*, an organization for encouraging large families, which had existed even before 1933. The bans already imposed on professional activity were in general maintained in force until made enforceable by the law. The persons concerned were divided into five categories: *Hauptschuldige* (major offenders), *Belastete* (offenders), *Minderbelastete* (lesser offenders), *Mitläufer* (followers), and *Entlastete*, the last term signifying "exonerated" or "discharged" rather than "innocent."

German judges had to be found to cope with the work of applying the law, though to sit on a *Spruchkammer* it was not necessary to have legal qualifications. To attract volunteers, a law was passed on November 20, 1946 in the American zone on the "duty of citizens to cooperate in denazification." But where were judges to be found whom the people would recognize as fair? Against the returned anti-Fascist exiles it was objected that they could not know what the situation under Himmler had been like with all its constraints and inevitable compromises; while members of the internal opposition were often unable to prove their active resistance and were held to be as much compromised as many of the accused. Moreover, all the prospective German judges were considered to be merely puppets of the allies.

The division into five categories applied in all three western zones, but the law took a very different course in each. The proportion of charges dismissed was 52 per cent in the French zone, 33 per cent in the American, and 29 per cent in the British. In the British zone, 58 per cent of cases fell into category 5 and only 10·9 per cent into category 4, whereas in the American and French zones, category 4 accounted for 51 per cent and 45 per cent respectively, and category 5 for only 1·9 per cent and 0·5 per cent. Categories 1 to 3 represented altogether 14 per cent of cases in the American zone, 1·3 per cent in the British zone, and 2·6 per cent in the French.[10] The final classification often depended on the verdict of appeal courts, which provided a kind of Party promotion in reverse for the benefit of luckier persons, especially those who could produce certificates to say that they had played an honorable part in the resistance. A shameless traffic went on in the so-called *Persilscheine*, certificates that proclaimed that their holders were "whiter than white."

Sometimes the Allied authorities applied different criteria than did the *Spruchkammern*. Thus the purge of universities in the American zone was at the outset particularly severe, applying even to well-known anti-Nazis who happened to have held office in reserve officers' associations.[11] Many of those ousted on such grounds obtained academic posts in the French zone. It was, however, generally admitted that a distinction should be made on account of age, and amnesties for younger people came into effect in the British and American zones in August, 1946: those born after January 1, 1919 who were not themselves guilty of any grave offense were exempted from further judicial proceedings or from the penalties to which they had been sentenced. As these young men and women had been only fourteen years old when Hitler came to power, it could not be said that the authorities erred on the side of leniency.

The multiplication of dossiers obviously tended to favor the really guilty, whose cases were lost to sight in the profusion of others. If they had a good lawyer, all they needed to do was play for time. In any judicial system, the passage of time engenders weariness if not indifference, and in the present instance it was clear that the number of cases would have to be drastically reduced if denazification was not to become a millstone for the next twenty years. Moreover, it was not long before many people came to realize that, as the East–West confrontation took shape, the allies would find a use for the very Germans whom they had begun by condemning lock, stock, and barrel.

International considerations apart, the occupation authorities whose job was to administer the country soon found themselves much hampered by those whose job was to rid it of Nazis. Already by July, 1945, General Clay wrote, in a report to Eisenhower: "All too often, it seems that the only men with the qualifications . . . are the career civil servants . . . a great proportion of whom were more than nominal participants (by our definition) in the activities of the Nazi Party."[12] When the Americans discovered that the purges had brought university life to a standstill, they made haste to reinstate numerous professors who had been purged, some of whom had had a good deal to answer for in the past.

In the Soviet zone, the ruling principle was that men can learn to perform whatever duties are required of them and that the social revolution required the elimination of all those who had held the top political and economic posts, however competent they might be. Lesser fry, on the other hand, could be forgiven easily enough once they submitted to the new order of things. In the western zones, one felt as early as 1946 that the severity of the purge in particular cases depended on how useful the person concerned was likely to be to the administration or economy of the zone in question.

45

In the early days of Hitler, certain Jews were officially classed as "economically useful" (WWJ—*wirtschaftlich wertvoller Jude*); and under the occupation, there was in effect a category of "economically useful Nazis." A rigorous purge of teachers was certainly essential to the country's spiritual future—but what happened to the "managers" of the German economy, who had played such an important part in Hitler's accession to power, had flattered and been cosseted by the regime, and had done everything to help it in preparing and prolonging the war? Under the pretext that their assistance had been technical and not political, and on the ground (often well justified) that their abilities were required for coping with the economic chaos, all but the most prominent of them were left alone or reinstated at an early date, including many who were certainly much guiltier than the humble town clerk or elementary schoolmaster who was purged and thrown into destitution.

True, the latter were for the most part deprived of their jobs on a temporary basis only, the implication being that a "Nazi" official could be transformed into a "democratic" one by the simple expedient of being given leave without pay for two or three years. It seemed much more likely that he would merely resume his work filled with rancor and bitterness; and this in fact was the most deplorable effect of a method of "denazification" that was at once too severe and too lenient, too broad and too restricted. The result was to create a kind of social class consisting of the "denazified." Embittered and inclined to feel that they had been punished merely for their opinions, they often turned against politics of any kind for fear of being hauled before other tribunals in the future. Of all the after-effects of a mismanaged "denazification," this was to prove the most lasting.

But denazification was, so to speak, only the negative aspect of the occupants' policy. On the positive side, the task that lay before them was to rescue Germany from chaos and to enable it to construct a democratic political life. These aims would have been more clearly visible if the occupation system had not suffered from so many inner weaknesses and contradictions.

3

The Occupying Powers and the German People

"TOTAL victory means total responsibility." The occupying powers were well aware of the truth thus provocatively formulated by Kurt Schumacher. Each commander-in-chief was faced in his own zone with the double task of bringing order out of chaos and taking long-term measures for democratization.

In any criticism of the occupation it should always be remembered that the task before the Allied authorities was immense: the rebuilding of a German administration to carry out their orders, the restoration of communications, reopening of factories, and provisioniong of the population. In addition, it was necessary to arrange, in the American zone alone, for the repatriation of 2 million "displaced persons," as well as nearly 3 million American soldiers from different parts of Europe, while finding room in Germany for 4·6 million refugees and expellees from countries further east. There can be no question that the achievement of the military governments in coping with these tasks was prodigious.

To deal with the multiplicity of problems, the commanders-in-chief required a large administrative personnel in addition to the occupation troops properly so called. The composition and recruitment of this staff played an essential role in the functioning of the occupation. The trend was progressively to replace military by "assimilated" personnel, that is, by civilians in uniform holding temporary rank. But in practice there were considerable differences between the three Western zones. The British administrators were often of very high ability, and as it was their government's policy to supervise administration even at the local level, they were very numerous—approximately 22,000 in 1946. They administered Germany as though it were a Crown Colony, with the same imperturbable energy and disdain for the "natives." Both officials and soldiers behaved with a distant correctness and lived so far as possible apart from the German population, although the nonfraternization order was revoked at the end of 1945. From 1946, however, the quality of the British personnel fell off perceptibly. As the occupation continued, the better elements wanted to return home to permanent work, and they were often replaced by men who had been unable to find well-paid jobs in England. Politically, the British occupation was in general conservative, in spite of there being a Labour Government in power.

The U.S. administrators were only about 5,000 strong at the end of 1946, although their zone was a little larger and nearly as populous as the British (41,500 square miles as against 37,700, and 17·1 million inhabitants as against

22·3 million, according to the 1946 census). In local affairs, they exercised control but did not directly administer. The chief positions were held by technicians from government service, the army, and the academic world, but after 1946 these were gradually replaced by industrialists and businessmen. Most of them alike insisted on enjoying the "American way of life" and failed to understand what an effect the luxury, which seemed to them normal, might have upon famished Germans. Nor did the American troops imitate the restraint of their British comrades. The intoxication of victory and the scramble for repatriation led to an extreme relaxation of discipline. Early in 1946, General McNarney listed in an order of the day the principal misdemeanors in the army he commanded: wholesale blackmarketeering, absence without leave, dangerous driving, drunkenness, venereal disease, slovenly appearance. From 1946, discipline improved, but the black market continued to flourish: ᵗhe temptation to swap cigarettes for Leica cameras was too great.

The Americans, like the British, were supposed to live more or less separately from the Germans. Many public places were "off limits" to troops, and no Germans were allowed to live in any building occupied by Americans. Long after the occupation was over, a whole row of houses in Frankfurt near the I. G. Farben headquarters building, which had been the seat of the military government, were still practically empty because a few Americans happened to live there. When, after the establishment of the Federal Republic, the Americans built a large new embassy at Bad Godesberg, the architect gave a press conference at which he pointed out with pride that the diplomatic staff could live and eat on the premises and have their laundry done without ever setting eyes on a single German.

On the other hand, even before the ban on fraternization was officially removed, many Americans made friends with Germans and especially German girls. Apart from the increase of illegitimate births, this had a definite political importance. Never having lived under an occupation themselves and knowing almost no history, the soldiers rebelled against the harshness of their government's policy. How could the hospitable family of Lisbeth or Hanna have anything in common with the Nazi criminals? Thus the soldiers imitated in their own way the attitude of military chiefs like General Patton, or of the businessmen turned administrators. Patton was removed from his command in Bavaria for having opposed denazification on the ground that there was no more difference between Nazi and anti-Nazi Germans than between Americans of the Republican and Democratic parties; and the "administrators" would not admit that *Bankdirektor* Müller could ever have been anything but a decent and completely nonpolitical businessman. Such reactions, which were for the most part spontaneous, practical, and unspoken, had a profound effect on the day-to-day application of American policy.

The French zone, with 16,500 square miles and 5·9 million inhabitants, was by far the smallest of the three, but it had the largest number of occupation personnel. This was not because the French administrators were proportionately more numerous than the British, but because of the proximity of France. Although the personnel of the other zones were allowed to bring their families, in the French zone the definition of "family" was wide enough to include grandmothers-in-law and great-nephews. Prone to make confiscations on their own account, accessible to the temptations of the black market, arrogant and exacting toward the Germans, and meanly seeking to enjoy the fruits of a victory to which most of them had contributed nothing whatever, these lazy and parasitic hangers-on were the scandal of the French occupation regime. Nor were the working personnel irreproachable. They had been recruited haphazardly and at the same time as the first postwar purges in France, with the result that a good many of the officials were former "collaborators" who were escaping from embarrassments at home. Such men were not very well qualified to undertake denazification in cooperation with colleagues who had been members of the French Resistance.

If discipline among the troops was better in the French than in the American zone, it was very poor in the central, regional, and local administration. The French Commander-in-Chief at Baden-Baden behaved like a proconsul and was not overly attentive to instructions from Paris; and the delegates at Coblenz, Freiburg, and Tübingen were in no hurry to obey orders from Baden-Baden. At the district and *Kreis* level, it was the same. Everyone was revelling in the process of government and the enjoyment of an almost unchallenged authority. In order to represent the French Republic worthily in a country believed to respect only force and to admire munificence, a large part of the occupation budget was spent on luxury. Fleets of cars, armies of servants, lavish entertaining, game preserves, special trains and steamers—such was the example set by the higher grades and imitated so far as possible by the local satraps. This provocative façade prevented the majority of Germans from appreciating an important element of the French occupation—a number of officials who not only took their work seriously but were also probably the only ones in all the three military governments with a thorough grasp of Germany's psychological problems.

All in all, the outward aspect of the three zones hardly gave the impression of virtuous conquerors come to raise the morality of vanquished delinquents. Yet this was the dominant theme of the whole "re-education" program. All Germans, especially the young, had been exposed to an evil influence, were in a certain sense badly educated, and must therefore be re-educated so as to become good democrats. And since it was agreed that true democracy was the system that existed back home in the United States, Britain, or France, all that was needed was to establish in Germany, whether by persuasion or force, the American, British, or French system of general and political education. The effect of this simple creed was that German youth in the western zones were exposed to three very different influences, not to speak of the far more thorough indoctrination that went on in the Soviet zone.

In the American zone, for instance, education was based on the principle that healthy democracy is a matter of the political development of the individual, independent of any framework of political or religious theory. Accordingly, clubs, youth parliaments, and nonpolitical, nondenominational groups were made to flourish at the expense of movements with a clear ideological tendency. On the same principle, the U.S. military government would not allow newspapers of any political trend, but granted licenses only to organs of information whose editorial roster had to include representatives of different political tendencies—a rule that led to grave problems in 1946–47 when it came to ousting Communist editors. As the Americans possessed considerable resources, they were able not only to establish *Amerikahäuser* (America Houses) but also to finance all kinds of centers and institutes for German youth; these benefits reached their peak in 1950 and the years immediately thereafter, when the McCloy Fund financed a large number of student hostels, children's villages, and other welfare institutions.

The British and French, feeling that the American system tended to promote a vague, invertebrate type of idealism, went the other way and encouraged the clear expression of the most diverse points of view. It may be said with confidence, however, that the most fruitful method of approach to the younger generation of Germans was that which took shape in the French zone.

The French cultural effort in Germany took many forms: from the impressive colleges for teachers to the creation of Mainz University, from the drafting of textbooks (some disastrously bad) to the sacrosanct institution of the *baccalauréat*. Being on a much wider scale than the work of the other occupying powers, it had more successes and also more failures. But its really original features were developed in opposition to the general tendency of the administration, in particular to the isolation of the zone that had been exalted into a dogma. A German trade unionist or political leader was not allowed to leave the zone to meet a colleague in the British or American zone; the people of Mainz and Freiburg could, in theory, buy foreign newspapers, but only with foreign currency they were forbidden to own.

A few officials perceived the inconsistency of this policy and had the courage to take the necessary steps. They saw the unreason of blaming young Germans for being nationalistic while at the same time forbidding them any contact with the world outside Germany; and they were wise enough to reject the pharisaism of "re-education," admitting that not everything in Germany was bad and that everything that was happening in France was not perfect. They saw that German youth must be free to learn and to meet the youth of other countries, and realized that many Hitler Youth leaders had been more remarkable for their good qualities than for fanaticism and that it was absurd to treat them as pariahs for the rest of their lives. Already in 1945, though cautiously at first, international meetings were arranged, and a movement was thus started that was to spread steadily as the efforts of the "Youth and Sport Section" (later called the "International Relations Section") of the cultural affairs division of military government were supported and multiplied by private initiative in France.

Ever since the end of the war, there had been French people who believed that the future could not be built upon aversion and fear. Most of them had been in the Resistance movement, and many in German prisons and concentration camps; and they did not accept the theory of collective guilt. They understood that the majority of Germans were weak, undecided, and profoundly shaken by the ruin of their country, and that these people were going to be exposed to the conflicting influence of two minorities. One of these minorities consisted of those Germans who, inspired by nationalism and hatred of the conqueror, looked back with nostalgia to their country's recent greatness. The other consisted of those who sincerely desired to join in building a new world in which nationalism would have no place. To refuse help to the latter group would mean increasing the influence of the former, and in the fullness of time the rest of the world would get "the Germany we deserved."[1] The world should therefore so act as to support the courage of the young generation, of religious believers both Protestant and Catholic, of trade unionists and anti-Nazi intellectuals who wanted to rebuild and transform their country. They were asking for help. To refuse it because they were Germans would be a betrayal of the ideals of the Resistance.

The young people of the two countries who met in Germany in 1945 numbered a few dozen. The figure rose to 1,000 in 1946, 1,200 in 1947, 2,000 in 1948, and 5,000 in 1949—in which year the French frontier was at last opened to young Germans, who had till then been blamed for knowing nothing about France and at the same time prevented from learning anything. The establishment of contacts between people of maturer years was necessarily slower, but there too a beginning was made immediately after the war.

These organized meetings and contacts, supplemented as time went on by independent groups and individuals, were on different lines to the attempts at Franco–German *rapprochement* that had taken place before 1933. Those concerned were not interested in sentimental effusions, and their purpose was not merely to promote superficial friendships between individuals. They wished to build a common future based on a correct reading of the lessons of the past. There were endless discussions on collective responsibility, French policy after World War I, the occupation, the Saar, German nationalism—the purpose throughout being that the youth of each country should learn what the past had meant for the other, and then, while their knowledge was still fresh, be ready to put it at the disposal of the people at home. Talk about the past is sterile if both sides merely dwell upon their own grievances; it becomes fruitful if it leads them to counteract this tendency in their respective countries. Thus, if the French, on returning home, described the German experience under the bombings and if the Germans described French sufferings under the occupation, then the discussions had served their purpose. It was for the Germans to make known to their compatriots the full horror of the massacre at Oradour, and for the French to protest in France against the law of September, 1948.

But discussion of the past was only the first stage of Franco–German contacts, and it was always a surprise to the participants when they went on to discover how similar their current problems were. The French found that they had much more to offer than historic literary and artistic values, as the Germans were also interested in the many and fruitful new experiments taking place in France immediately after the war. The performances of the Théâtre National Populaire were a tremendous success with audiences at Frankfurt and Berlin, to whom they revealed a new form of theatrical art. The whole notion of "culture" was enlarged when it was found that contemporary France had not only literary and theatrical values to offer but also research work like that of "Economie et Humanisme," new kinds of youth activities, studies in electoral geography and the sociology of political parties, or the educational experiment of the *classes nouvelles*.

Special organizations were created in order to further these Franco–German contacts. The *Bureau international de Liaison et de Documentation* was set up in

1945 at Offenburg in Baden by an army chaplain, the Jesuit Father Jean du Rivau, and in that year it began publishing two parallel reviews, *Dokumente* and *Documents*, for the purpose of informing Germans about France and the French about Germany; it also organized numerous contacts and exchanges. The *Comité français d'Echanges avec l'Allemagne nouvelle*, set up in 1948 on the initiative of Emmanuel Mounier, was directed by a committee of journalists, writers, politicians, and persons in academic life, all of whom—though their religious and political convictions were as varied as they could be—derived their inspiration from the spirit of the French Resistance. Until its dissolution in 1967, the Committee issued an information bulletin, *Allemagne*; it organized public Franco–German debates on such subjects as the press, political parties, or youth problems, and it also selected individuals and groups in France for seminars and other contacts in Germany.

Immediately after the war, such activities, insofar as they were taken note of at all, may have seemed of minor importance. Today it can be seen that the system of exchanges to which they led served to create a permanent human infrastructure in the field of Franco–German relations, the solidity of which was an essential factor in making possible the "European" policy of the 1950's and 1960's.[2]

At the same time, the French intellectual presense in Germany helped to satisfy in some degree the appetite for intellectual adventure that, along with so many less-pleasing phenomena, has been a characteristic of the postwar years in Germany. It was not only because money had lost its value in the years after 1945 that Germans flocked to the theatres, joined countless societies, and bought innumerable magazines, the profusion of which was abruptly cut short by the currency reform.

However, German life under the occupation was dominated first and foremost by more elementary forms of hunger. At the end of 1946, there were in Hamburg 100,000 sufferers from edema due to undernourishment, and in Cologne only 12 per cent of the children were of normal weight. According to U.N. experts, the daily requirement of calories for health and normal work is 2,650; but the official ration in Germany was 1,500 and the real ration often much below 1,000. Whole families were crowded in underground bunkers without water or light. Clothes and medicines were unprocurable, and money had lost its value. The result was a profound demoralization, for what point was there in working if a few cigarettes would buy as much food as a bus-driver's monthly wage? And why go hungry when you could get packets of chocolate or coffee beyond price simply for obliging an occupation soldier? Railway stations and subways were filled with boys proposing bargains of every sort; and if, in the first year of the Federal Republic, there were 15,000 prostitutes in Cologne as compared with 1,500 before the war, it was perhaps because the misery and privation of 1945–47 had given rise to habits which were not so easily unlearnt.

The penury and demoralization of those days had two lasting consequences. First, many Germans in the next decade retained a vivid memory of what they had been through and judged economic and social conditions by reference to the immediate postwar periods so that they were relatively contented with their lot. Second, each individual felt a deep longing to forget the humiliation and degradation of attitude and behavior that had been forced upon him and to make sure that others forgot it also. The effect of this was a desire to multiply the external signs of prestige and respectability, in a recrudescence of outdated values that became one of the more unattractive features of the Federal Republic.

Influential people abroad saw the need to do something about Germany's deplorable state. Many private individuals, in rich America and impoverished Britain, had been sending food parcels to Germany ever since the end of hostilities; and religious and other charitable organizations combined in a movement whose proportions are partly explained by the German origin of a large number of Americans. The campaigns of Victor Gollancz in England and Herbert Hoover in America, however, attracted the most attention. Gollancz observed discretion and did not allow his indignation over the miseries of Germany and the mistakes of the Allies to blind him to the past and present sufferings of other countries; but the former President of the United States went much further and almost represented Germany as the innocent martyred victim of ruthless conquerors. Many an American family felt morally obliged to help a German family without realizing, very often, that there were also families in Caen or Belgrade to whom a food parcel would not have come amiss.

German gratitude was on the whole somewhat tepid, and foreign help was accepted as though it were a very inadequate atonement for undeserved suffering. Unbiased observers might feel that there was a concerted playing-up of Germany's unhappy plight, aimed at inducing a relaxation of the harsh rigors of occupation and discouraging any idea of reducing the level of German industry. The figures in the Hoover report, which showed that famine would have been much worse without the official Anglo–American aid, were hardly quoted at all in Germany, and from Gollancz's book[3] the photographs of emaciated German children were much more often reproduced than the descriptions of Nazi concentration camps. Listening to complaints from almost every German they met, foreign visitors were invariably struck by their extraordinary self-centeredness. People in Germany were quite unconcerned at hearing about the meager rations in occupied France or wartime Britain, and were even unaware that the French and British were still rationed. When they were told, the information was received with smiles of incredulity.

To sum up in a word the most tragic aspect of those dismal times, it was incomprehension. Visitors to Germany did not comprehend the misery of the Germans, who in turn could not or would not comprehend the horrible acts of which their misery was the sequel. Many allowed no credit for foreign aid or for the efforts of the occupying powers to set the German economy to rights, but had eyes only for the Morgenthau Plan aspects of the occupation. Accordingly, in later years they saw their country's prodigious economic recovery as taking place in spite of the victorious powers, and their pride in it was mingled with arrogance and defiance.

This, however, was not the attitude of the German statesmen on whom the Allies conferred gradually widening responsibilities. It was the good fortune of these men that the German people vented their bitterness and misery on the victors who displayed all the trappings of power and refrained from blaming their German associates who appeared to be acting under orders, yet who showed a sufficient degree of independence to gain them credit for the successes of the occupation though not its failures.

Even if the Allies had wanted to, they could not have exercised the sovereignty they had assumed over Germany by direct administration alone, without the help of Germans. In any case, it was part of their objective to revive and democratize German political life; they disagreed as to the definition of democracy, but were unanimous in practice in seeking to impose it by authoritarian means. Whether in the creation of new institutions or in the choice of men, their constant and often crude methods of intervention were a poor advertisement for democratic ways. Arbitrary appointments and dismissals were carried out on the most unexpected grounds. The Prime Minister of Bavaria, Dr. Fritz Schäffer (who was to become a finance minister in the Federal Government), received a letter of dismissal on September 28, 1945, having been appointed exactly four months earlier, because he had voted for Hitler's Enabling law in March, 1933 while a member of the Bavarian People's Party in the Reichstag. On October 6, Brigadier Barraclough, the military governor of the North Rhine *Land*, summoned the mayor of Cologne—an elderly gentleman named Konrad Adenauer—and read out a letter dismissing him on the ground of administrative incompetence.[4] As late as 1948, Dr. Ludwig Erhard owed his appointment as Economics Director for Bizonia to the fact that his predecessor, Johannes Semler, had been forced to resign on account of his sharp criticism of occupation policy.

German administrators were not always forced to knuckle under or resign. In the western zones at all events, the occupying powers were generally prepared to listen to criticism and to answer it, either because they did not want to undermine the authority of newly-fledged institutions they themselves had created, or, in some cases, because the institution the malcontents represented was one they were not fully able to control. This applied, for example, to the Protestant Bishop Theophil Wurm of Württemberg, who spoke out as freely under the occupation as he had done in Hitler's day, and to Dr. Kurt Schumacher, the vehement spokesman of the Social Democrats. Similarly, in the French zone, violent protests were heard in the *Land* parliaments against the dismantling and food policies of the occupying power.[5]

In retrospect, however, the aspect of cooperation is seen to have predominated. Close personal ties were formed, such as the friendship between the American Colonel William W. Dawson, a professor of law and an administrator of exceptional quality, and Dr. Reinhold Maier, the Minister-President (Prime Minister) of Württemberg-Baden, whose memoirs contain a moving account of their relations.[6] Above all, it was the occupants' choice of personnel that to a large extent determined the leadership of the future West German state. Many of those they appointed or allowed to exercise a leading role in 1945–46 remained in office in the *Länder* after the occupation ended, or went on to fill leading posts in the Federal Government.

Dr. Reinhold Maier, for instance, who took office on September 24, 1945, had as his Minister of Education Dr. Theodor Heuss, who, like him, had been a Liberal member of the Reichstag up to 1933 (when they had both voted for the Enabling Act). Dr. Maier was to remain head of the government at Stuttgart until 1953. At Tübingen, the French created a "Secretariat of State" for

South Württemberg–Hohenzollern, to which they appointed the bilingual law professor Carlo Schmid. At Munich, Dr. Wilhelm Hoegner, the Social Democrat who succeeded Schäffer on October 3, 1945, had as his Minister for Trade and Industry the nonparty Dr. Erhard. The tiny *Land* of Bremen was governed by Wilhelm Kaisen from 1945 till he retired in 1965. At Hanover, the capital of Lower Saxony, Hinrich Kopf was in charge from 1946 until his death in 1961, except for the years 1955–59 when he was out of office owing to a defeat at the polls. At Düsseldorf (North Rhine–Westphalia), the second Amelunxen cabinet, formed in December, 1946, included as Minister of Food and Agriculture, from January, 1947, the Christian Democrat Heinrich Lübke.

Many other political leaders who were "discovered" by the occupying powers or who came into view at this period as members of new or revived parties continued to forge ahead when Germany again became master of its own affairs. They had done good service at a time of exceptional difficulty. Their good fortune lay in the fact that the return to prosperity and, above all, the reversal of the international situation (which turned Germany's Western conquerors into her allies) prevented their compatriots from regarding them as "collaborators" or traitors, either during or after the occupation. The only sphere of activity in which approval by the Allies came to be regarded as a stigma by the new nationalists of the 1950's and 1960's was that of the press: the term *Lizenz-Presse*, referring to the licenses issued by the occupying authorities, was used with the same pejorative implication as that with which former Vichyites in France speak of the *presse issue* of the Resistance.

The Allies left lasting traces of their rule in a great variety of fields: for instance, workers' codetermination in the coal and steel industries, where the main lines of the military government system of 1947 were confirmed by a German law of 1951; or local government in the former British zone, where the basic features of the reform molded on British practice were adopted in the *Gemeindeordnungen* of North Rhine–Westphalia and Lower Saxony in 1953 and 1955 respectively. "We had one disappointment," observes an official responsible for the British scheme, referring to the fact it was not followed in Schleswig-Holstein.[7]

The *Länder* were constituted gradually by the occupying powers. As early as July, 1945, the Soviet military administration formed *Länder* out of the provinces of Brandenburg and Saxony-Anhalt. On September 19, proclamation No. 2 by the U.S. Commander-in-Chief created the *Länder* of Bavaria, Greater Hesse, and Württemberg-Baden. Bremen ranked as a *Land* in the American zone from January, 1947. In the British zone, the initial situation was complicated by varying historical traditions and the problems of the Ruhr and the Rhineland. In August, 1946, four Prussian provinces were formed into the *Länder* of Schleswig-Holstein, North Rhine–Westphalia, and Hanover; soon afterwards, Hanover was combined with the tiny *Länder* of Brunswick, Oldenburg, and Schaumburg-Lippe to form Lower Saxony, while in January, 1947 Lippe-Detmold was merged into North Rhine-Westphalia. In the French zone, South Württemberg–Hohenzollern and South Baden were formed at an early date; the Saar, as we shall see, was treated as a separate entity, while the *Land* of Rhineland–Palatinate was not created until April, 1946.

The *Länder* of the French zone are those whose boundaries illustrate most clearly the artificial character of most of the units of which the Federal Republic is today composed. Just as the independent African states of the 1960's are not based on racial or historical groupings but on the accidental drawing of colonial frontiers, so the *Land* boundaries were in part predetermined by those of the occupation zones. The effect of this was most marked in the French zone, which, ín accordance with the decision at Yalta, was carved out of those of the British and the American.

The *Länder* were not necessarily endowed at once with constitutions, elected assemblies (*Landtage*), and governments headed by minister-presidents. Here again there was much variation from one zone to another as regards the setting up of institutions and the real or nominal delegation of power to the new German authorities.

The Big Three had agreed at Potsdam that German political life could not be revived except on the basis of political parties. These in fact already existed. The Soviet military administration was set up on June 9, 1945; on the following day, it authorized the formation and activities of four anti-Fascist parties: the Communists (KPD), Social Democrats (SPD), Christian Democrats (CDU), and Liberals (LDPD). In the western zones, the Communist Party was authorized on June 11, the SPD on the 15th, the CDU on the 26th, and the Liberals on July 5. The functioning of these organizations gave rise to a number of problems—in particular, to the question of direct or indirect control by the occupying powers and to the contradiction that appeared on the face of things between the division of the country into zones and *Länder* on the one hand, and, on the other, the fact that the names of the parties, if not their actual organization, transcended these geographical limits.[8] The French authorities showed most concern to maintain the separateness of their zone, while the Russians did most to give the parties under their control an individual character. On July 14, 1945, the four authorized parties in the Soviet zone united to form an anti-Fascist bloc, which was later to serve as a basis for single-list elections; and on April 22, 1946, the KPD and SPD in that zone merged into a single party, the SPD as such being thenceforth prohibited.[9]

Disagreements on how to restore German political life were not the only ones that divided the occupying powers. At the outset, differences of economic policy were at least equally serious. These were not only ideological, bearing on the question of how far rights of ownership and the structure of economic power should be respected, but were also due to divergences between the circumstances of the victorious powers.

The Russians and French had been invaded and looted by Germany, and their main interest as occupying powers was compensation for the damage they had suffered. They proceeded at once to order confiscations and the removal of plant; the French in an unorganized way, the Russians systematically and on a vast scale. Troops and officials lived off the country, the more easily because these two zones were primarily agricultural. The German economy was restored for other purposes than an improvement of the inhabitants' rations. As a French official report put it in 1947: "The German population has been set to work in the principal sectors of production, especially those necessary to the recovery of the French economy."[10] The situation in the other zones was very different. The British and Americans brought their rations with them; their zones being industrial and urban, they were obliged to import food into Germany to prevent the populations of those devastated areas from dying of starvation. The total cost of the occupation to the two powers was $700 million a year. Naturally, they wanted to revive Germany's industrial production so that it could be exchanged for agricultural products, and they wished to lower the economic barriers between the four zones. Had it not been agreed at Potsdam that Germany should be treated as an economic unit? Yet the Russians were failing to inform the Control Commission of the confiscations in their zone and showed no enthusiasm for a common import and export program. In May, 1946, General Clay declared that until such a program existed there would be no further contribution to Russian reparations from the U.S. zone.

Nevertheless, on March 26, 1946, the Control Commission had reached agreement on the very harsh terms limiting Germany's industrial production. After the defeat, German industry was in fact at a standstill, but not destroyed. So little was produced and the devastation of the country was so evident that its potential might seem to have been drastically reduced. But this was not so. Although the towns lay in ruins, the destruction of plant was only 10 per cent for metallurgy, 10–15 per cent for the chemical industry, 15–20 per cent for engineering, and 20 per cent for textiles. There were a number of reasons for this comparative immunity: the efficient camouflaging of factories and the German system of dispersal, the Allies' concentration on the bombing of towns "to sap the population's morale," which left the factories relatively intact, and, finally, the "selective" bombings that spared certain factories in which non-German firms had an interest. The immense I. G. Farben head office, which remained intact at Frankfurt while three-quarters of the town was destroyed, stood as the symbol of a war that was more total for some people than for others.

Such productive capacity as did survive the war was considerably diminished by the victors' policy. The plan of March 26, 1946 fixed the level of production at about 50 per cent of 1938, the best prewar year. Among the products completely banned were petrol, synthetic rubber, and radioactive material; steel was limited to 7·5 million tons a year—less than the 1938 production of *Vereinigte Stahlwerke* alone; the basic chemical industry was reduced to less than 40 per cent of its 1936 production, and the pharmaceutical industry to 80 per cent. Furniture, glass, and bicycles were almost the only articles whose manufacture was uncontrolled; but there was to be the maximum possible production of coal.

This policy was intended to destroy the economic basis of German military power and also to make available "surplus" plant for distribution as reparations to the victors. At the same time, it sought to decentralize Germany's industry and break up the system of trusts and cartels that had made it possible for six banks and seventy combines to control two-thirds of German industry and for six combines to own, in 1938, 98 per cent of the foundries and 95 per

cent of the steel output of the Ruhr. The limitation on production, the confiscations, and the restructuring of industry were in theory three separate
objectives, but in practice they soon appeared as three inextricably combined
methods toward a single end—the permanent weakening of the German
economy.

When in due course this tendency was reversed and it became official policy
to revive the economy, there were some who thought, or pretended to think,
that a return to the former level involved the reintroduction of some features
of the former industrial organization. For two years, from 1945 to 1947, a
struggle went on within the U.S. military government between those who
wished to maintain the distinction between these objectives and those who
preferred to confuse the issue and persuade American and German opinion
that the elimination of the former masters of the German economy was simply
another aspect of the Morgenthau policy. Yet, when the British arrested Hugo
Stinnes and thirty-nine other members of the mining cartel on September 6,
1945 and took over control of the Krupp works on November 16, this did not
appear to damage Germany's productive capacity in any way. By 1949, on the
other hand, Article 18 of the Ruhr International Authority agreement appeared out of date and discriminatory against Germany when it made the
Military Security Board responsible for preventing persons convicted or liable
to be convicted "of having encouraged the aggressive designs of the National
Socialist party" from holding managerial or proprietary interests in the coal,
coke, or steel industries of the Ruhr or in the professional and commercial
organizations of those industries.

Such confusion would never have been possible had the Allies not, at the
outset, completely misunderstood Germany's economic situation. The chairman of the Inter-Allied Reparations Agency declared in March, 1947: "The
over-industrialization of Germany for military purposes has created conditions
in which, despite destruction and the exceptional wear and tear of war, there
remains an industrial potential which in any case . . . is vastly superior to the
requirements of a peace-time economy." After the publication of the first
Anglo–American plan to raise the economic level of Bizonia, the same Agency
reported: "The effect of the new plan will be to retain sufficient capacity in the
Bizonal Area to approximate the level of industry prevailing in Germany in
1936, a year that was not characterized by either boom or depressed con-
tions."[11] In other words, Germany's peacetime production needs in 1947 were
supposed to be no greater than in 1936. This might have been so if there had
been no ruined towns, no loss of territory east of the Oder, no partition of the
country, no refugees, no occupation costs, and no social changes resulting
from the war. Certainly, the Germany of 1938 was overindustrialized; but could
one reasonably say the same of western zones of Germany after the war?

In 1939, the present area of the Federal Republic contained a population of
39·3 million. The 1946 census showed a population of 43·7 million, in spite of
military and civilian war casualties; by the 1950 census, after the return of
prisoners and a new influx of refugees from the eastern regions, there were
47·7 million. The density of population increased in this way from 417 inhabitants per square mile in 1939 to 463 in 1946, and 505 in 1950. Such figures do
not necessarily mean poverty; but a country so densely populated, unless it is

to live off charity, must be able to feed its people, either by itself producing the food it needs or by importing it in exchange for raw materials or manufactured goods.

Prewar Germany, in spite of possessing rich agricultural lands in the east, was obliged to import 20 per cent of its food. The deficit for the three western zones, when cut off from the regions east of the Oder–Neisse line and then, almost immediately afterward, from the Soviet occupation zone, was more than 50 per cent. Efforts were made in all three zones to increase agricultural production, but it was indispensable that industry should produce not only for reconstruction needs but also, and above all, in order to pay for food imports. Since these were required to feed a considerably increased population, it was misleading simply to compare current production needs with those of 1936. The average index for 1950 (based on 1936) was in fact 109·5, but when allowance is made for the increase of population the figure falls to 86. West Germany had no alternative but to die of starvation or continue to live off the charity of the United States, unless it could revive and develop its industry. If the Allies had agreed unequivocally that this was the only solution, the Germans would have been less critical of their economic policy, even when it was in other respects inconsistent and vacillating.

The three restrictive principles, as we have seen, were confiscation, limitation of output, and the transformation of industry. Occupation costs and the various types of reparations deliveries come under the heading of confiscation. From 1946 to 1950, in the three western zones combined, the annual percentage of total taxation reserved to meet occupation costs was, in the successive years, 42, 38, 33, 26, and 28. (For the French zone separately the figures for the four years 1946–49 were 86, 49, 41, and 38). The 1950 figure represents 96 marks per head for the total population, or 210 marks per head—the monthly salary of a clerical worker—for the active working part of it. The money was spent in a variety of ways, and too often it was used to buy luxury goods for occupation personnel and their families.

The nations that had suffered at Germany's hands had an incontestable right to reparations and exercised it in various ways. The German merchant marine had been divided among the Big Three at Potsdam, and they reallocated part of their shares to other countries. The transatlantic liner *Europa* was given to France and renamed the *Liberté*. German industrial patents were annulled, and it was later claimed that the free use of German patented processes was equivalent to a reparations payment of several milliard marks. Prisoners were kept at work abroad long after the war. At the end of 1945, there were 470,000 of them in France in factories, construction works, and agriculture, and when they were released (between April, 1947 and April, 1948), 116,000 of them remained in France on labor contracts. Between 1946 and 1948, 9·5 million cubic meters of timber were sent from the French zone to France as partial compensation for the 30 million cubic meters taken from French forests during the German occupation, and the Saar, with its coal and steel resources, was incorporated into the French economy. But the intention was to obtain the bulk of reparations from the dismantling of industrial plant.

What should have been done was to decide quickly which factories or parts of factories were to be confiscated and to organize their speedy removal to, and

59

reassembly in, the confiscating country. But in fact it was done slowly and by fits and starts, and confusion was allowed to arise between dismantling for removal and outright destruction as such. After 1947, and still more after 1949, the occupying powers changed their policy, first permitting and then encouraging Germany's economic revival. As a result, there were continual hesitations and reversed decisions, while the list of factories for dismantling shrank steadily from 1,800 in March, 1946, to 858 in August, 1947 and 697 in February, 1949—in which year, however, most of the actual dismantling was done, including 93 per cent of all removals of metallurgical equipment after 1945.

The results of dismantling were often a disappointment, for the material lost much of its value when disassembled. Moreover, one part of a factory might go to Belgium and another to France, while a third was left to rust in Germany. And after 1948, a new and unwelcome development began to occur: the no longer new equipment received by the confiscating countries was liable to be replaced in Germany by ultramodern machinery from the United States. In all, about $1 milliard worth of plant was removed, but with delays and hesitations and to a growing chorus of German protest. The removals created unemployment; at Duisburg-Hamborn, the livelihood of more than 100,000 people depended entirely upon the Thyssen steelworks, which remained on the list for dismantling until 1949. Clearly, said the Germans, this policy condemned Germany to remain in misery. It could indeed be replied that the other European countries had the right to priority in reconstruction, and this principle was asserted in many Allied pronouncements from 1945 to 1949; but the dismantling was effected in such a way, and with so many apparently arbitrary decisions, that the argument was deprived of much of its force.

In theory, the purpose of destroying industrial installations was to prevent the future production of war materials; but a number of the factories listed for destruction could have been converted to peaceful uses, and a great many that were not condemned were by no means incapable of switching to war production. The fact is that it is no longer possible today to speak of a factory as producing exclusively for peace or for war, and it was natural that the Germans should get the impression that the real motive for dismantling was fear of German competition. It became clear that the occupation authorities were being subjected to two kinds of pressure: a factory producing watches, for example, would be suppressed because a British firm wanted to eliminate a rival, while another, producing poison gas, would escape because it belonged to a company in which an American group was financially interested.

France in particular seemed to be insisting upon the limitation of German production, especially of steel, much less in order to prevent Germany from getting priority in reconstruction, or to make more coal from the Ruhr available for export, than because she was opposed to the slightest recovery of economic power by her formidable neighbor. The variations of the permitted maximum for steel production make a long story, which lasted until the announcement, on July 25, 1952, of the termination of the Ruhr Authority and the lifting of all restrictions upon the German metallurgical industries.

As regards the reorganization of industry, here too the motives of the occupying powers might well appear ambiguous. Especially on the French side, the objectives of denazification and democratization sometimes served to disguise the wish to weaken German industry and the fear of letting it reform itself too thoroughly. The development of the "deconcentration" policy cannot be described in detail here. The British set up control groups for coal and steel and effected a preliminary decartellization; the Anglo–American law No. 75 entrusted German experts with the task of reorganization; and the tripartite law No. 27 of May 16, 1950 paved the way for the settlement finally accepted by the Federal Government. Anglo–American differences, French vetoes, and open or covert German obstruction acted and reacted upon each other in complicated ways, and the participants changed their ground continually as the European and world political situation evolved.[12]

The majority of Germans disapproved of nearly all the measures adopted by the occupying powers. The currency reform of June, 1948 alone escaped criticism, if not of its details at least of its principle. It was the indispensable preliminary to Germany's economic revival, and the visible signs of its success appeared miraculous. Overnight the shop windows became full, factories reopened or speeded up, and the nationwide poverty seemed suddenly transformed into a relative prosperity. The index figure for industrial production, which was 51 in June, rose to 61 in July and 79 in December.

It became apparent that western Germany's poverty was not so extreme as had been thought and that farms, factories, and stores had been carefully saving stocks of provisions, raw materials, and goods until the day when there should be a sound currency. A chemist who, on June 17, "regretted" to have to tell a housewife that the medicine she needed for her sick child was unprocurable, found himself, on June 20, suddenly able to provide it, although no delivery van had been seen to call at his shop in the interval. Far from paying any penalty, the peasants, industrialists, and merchants who had made illegal secret hoards were greatly favored by the method of application of the reform.

The very complicated process was based in theory on two principles, but only one of them was in fact applied. There was a drastic deflation without any spreading of the losses involved. Owners of real property had a great advantage over people with money savings. The general rate of exchange was 10 new DM (Deutsche Mark) for 100 old RM (Reichsmark); but debts and transferable securities were almost the only items to which this rate was in fact applied. Those with cash reserves and bank deposits were worse off, getting about DM6·5 for RM100; and as for private investors in the public funds, they got nothing at all. Meanwhile, official prices and salaries were unaltered, being simply made payable in DM instead of RM; but since real prices had hitherto been those of the black market, the working class and salaried employees were among those who gained from the deflation. The real victims were people with savings, many of whom fell into utter destitution. In the confused debate that raged for four years around the problem of "equalizing burdens" (*Lastenausgleich*), disasters inflicted by the currency reform (*Währungsschaden*) were treated as comparable to those of the war and the occupation.

But the creation of the Deutsche Mark, besides being the first step on the road to economic recovery, was even more significant as a factor in bringing about the division of Germany.

4

Cold War, Political Division and Limited Sovereignty

EVEN if the four powers had sincerely meant to cooperate for the purpose of governing Germany as a single economic whole, the structure of the occupation would have hampered this objective. As it was, one of the four, namely France, set its face against uniformity of treatment for fear that this might lead to the revival of a unitary German state; while the Soviet Union almost at once set about transforming the large slice of Germany entrusted to it so thoroughly that the resulting differences themselves became a cause of division. Finally, the increasingly strained relations between the former Allies led them to change their minds about defeated Germany and to regard its population not so much as political novices who had to be taught the meaning of democracy, but rather as potential auxiliaries in the East–West conflict.

The Control Commission in Berlin, consisting of the four commanders-in-chief, held its first meeting on July 30, 1945, and by August 10 it had settled its method of functioning. Besides the Commission proper, there was a Coordinating Committee of the deputy military governors and a system of directorates analogous to ministries. The Commission's competence extended over Germany as a whole, but each commander-in-chief exercised supreme authority in his own occupation zone and therefore possessed a sort of dual personality. At Berlin, he had one vote out of four in deciding whether to issue a directive to himself at Baden-Baden, Frankfurt, or the British zonal headquarters in Westphalia. Since it is easier to govern alone than as a quartet, the "zone commander" personality generally prevailed over the Commission personality. The zones soon came to resemble independent countries, with frontiers almost impassable for men and materials alike.

The sealing off of the zones would have been less complete if the Commission had been able to agree on setting up central German administrative bodies. In spite of the growing conflict between the Russians and Americans—the friction over details in Germany, the darkening international horizon, and the discovery by Britain and America of what the U.S.S.R. meant by "friendly" governments in the Balkans and elsewhere—the factor that at this time prevented agreement on a minimum of unity in the day-to-day administration of Germany was the use of the French veto.

France had not been invited to Potsdam and was therefore not bound by the decisions of the three powers. But these decisions had to be implemented by the Control Commission, to which France belonged and which could not act without the unanimous consent of its members. The fact that France became a member of the Council of Foreign Ministers, set up with the task of framing the future peace treaties, did not resolve this fundamental contradiction. On August 7, however, the French Government informed the three powers that it accepted the main lines of the Potsdam agreement, with the reservation that "it could not assent *a priori* to the apparent intention to revive for a certain period a central German government."

French policy at this time aimed at the creation of separate German states forming at most a confederation without a central authority, as well as at the complete detachment from Germany of the Saar–Rhine–Ruhr area. This meant opposing all measures of a centralizing tendency and, in particular, the setting up of central German administrative bodies. But Potsdam had provided for the establishment of such bodies in various spheres, including transport and finance; they were to be headed by German "state secretaries" acting under the direction of the Control Commission. The French veto prevented their coming into existence. This veto, incidentally, was by no means purely "Gaullist." As late as September, 1946, at the French Radical Pary congress, M. René Mayer, a future prime minister of his country and President of the European Coal and Steel Community, protested in his report on foreign affairs at the setting up of a central bank in Germany and at the re-establishment of the Reichsbahn, the national railway system—"the most Prussian institution in Germany!"[1]

The Saar territory, which lay within Germany's 1937 frontiers and which France now sought to detach, was one over which she had exercised economic control in the past. By the treaty of Versailles, it was separated from Germany, placed under League of Nations administration, and joined to France by a customs union. At the referendum held in accordance with the Treaty of January 13, 1935, 90·8 per cent of the population voted for reunion with Germany, 8·8 per cent for the *status quo*, and 0·4 per cent for union with France. In 1945, the Saar became part of the French occupation zone, and from an early stage it was treated as a separate entity. In January, 1946, its area was increased from 741 to 993 square miles by the transfer of two districts from the *Land* of Rhineland-Palatinate, and on the night of December 21–22, 1946 a customs barrier was erected between it and the rest of the French zone. In elections held on October 5, 1947, 97·7 per cent of the population voted for one or the other of the parties that had been allowed to function by the occupation authorities, and which, with the exception of the Communists, had all endorsed the draft constitution published on September 27. The preamble to this document, which the Saar parliament adopted by 48 votes to 2, declared the Saar to be an autonomous territory linked to France by an economic union; the French Republic was responsible for the defense of the territory and for representing its interests abroad, and a French representative was to be appointed to supervise the customs and monetary union and the application of the new statute.

From time to time during the 1950's and even afterward, ideas were put forward for an "Austrian solution" to the German problem, with reunification under four-power supervision. But these never had more than a speculative existence. Austria, it is true, was under four-power occupation like Germany, with separate zones and a quadripartite regime at Vienna; but from

63

the outset an Austrian government also functioned with authority over the whole country, whereas in Germany the French veto prevented any form of nationwide administration by German bodies. More important still, the occupation of Austria was purely military. The powers made no attempt to transform the foundations of political life in their respective zones as they did in Germany, especially in the Soviet zone. The Russians never Sovietized their part of Austria, whereas in Germany they soon brought about economic and social changes that made it unreal to speak of a unification of the country, given the absence of such changes in the western zones.

This is not to say that Russian behavior in Germany was always consistent, or that they treated the population of their zone with leniency, especially in economic matters. Understandably enough, their policy was dominated by an obsession with reparations. Dismantling was carried out in successive waves, the last of which dated from the autumn of 1947 and the spring of 1948, a long time after Marshal Sokolovsky's statement on May 21, 1946 that dismantling and removals had come to an end. Altogether, more than 1,300 factories were dismantled and some 4,500 miles of railway track was removed.[2] Levies on current production took the form of direct orders to German industry and the confiscation of entire concerns, which were turned into "Soviet companies" (*Sowjetische Aktiengesellschaften* [SAG]); by the spring of 1948, these employed about a fifth of the East German industrial labor force and accounted for a third of total production.[3]

From the very beginning, however, the Russians used the services of privileged Germans with whose help they planned to transform the basis of German life not only from what it had been under Hitler, but also from the social and political order that had existed under the Weimar Republic. On April 30, 1945, a group of ten émigré German Communists arrived in the eastern sector of Berlin from Moscow. Their leader was Walter Ulbricht, a former member of the SPD and the Spartacists and a founder of the KPD, who had been the leading spirit of the "Free German National Committee" in the Soviet Union. From 1945 onward, as the Soviet authorities introduced measures for the nationalization of industry and for land reform, the Communist minority gradually worked themselves into positions of power in the administrative and political bodies that were set up. Once the new forms were created and real power was in the hands of the Socialist Unity Party, the Russians could extend a hand of friendship to the greater part of the population, which they had all along taken care not to condemn indiscriminately. The German denazification commissions in the eastern zone dismissed over 400,000 people from administrative or economic jobs, but the "smalltime Nazis" did not forfeit any civil rights except that of being elected to representative bodies. Even this was restored to them by Marshal Sokolovsky in a decree of August 16, 1947, which put a stop to legal proceedings except in the case of former leaders and persons accused of specific crimes. By a further measure of February 27, 1948, the denazification commissions were finally wound up.

This leniency, however, was not prompted solely by the desire to facilitate political development in a part of Germany that was undergoing economic and social transformation. As with the change of attitude at this period in the western zones, its main cause was the alteration of the world political scene.

It had not taken long for the former allies to find themselves at odds. The meeting of the Council of Foreign Ministers in October, 1945 had achieved nothing; the Italian treaty, Austria, the Balkans, Iran, the Far East—all had been nothing but fields for controversy between the Anglo–Americans and the Russians. So both sides began to look at Germany with new eyes, feeling that perhaps the Germans could be made use of in the quarrels between their conquerors. But in that case a milder and more sympathetic attitude was indicated, so that one could saddle the opposing party with responsibility for the harsh measures of Potsdam and the occupation. The race for Germany's favors began at the Paris sessions of the Council of Foreign Ministers between April and July, 1946, with disputes about denazification, reparations, and the self-sufficiencies of the occupation zones. M. Bidault insisted that France could not agree to any centralized German administration until the questions of the Saar and the Rhineland had been settled. Mr. Molotov criticized the policy of decentralization, the excessive scaling down of industry, and the identification of the German people with Nazism. In the end, the conference decided practically nothing about Germany.

On September 6, 1946, U.S. Secretary of State Byrnes made a speech at Stuttgart that completely transformed American policy in Germany, or at least the manner of its enforcement. He did indeed reaffirm to his German audience U.S. support of a revision of the 1939 frontiers in Poland's favor, while leaving to the final peace settlement the decision as to the amount of territory to be ceded. But at the same time he announced the end of the occupation's punitive phase and held out prospects of a less gloomy future. One passage in his speech, however, showed that he well understood the problems involved in a change of policy motivated by other considerations than Germany's own welfare: "It is not in the interest of the German people or in the interest of world peace that Germany should become a pawn or a partner in a military struggle for power between the East and the West."

The debate between the allies became so sharp that the Control Commission's work was at a standstill. The only points of agreement were those relating to a past era, such as law No. 46, which abolished the State of Prussia. The fourth session of the Council of Foreign Ministers opened in Moscow on March 10, 1947 in a tense atmosphere. On the 12th, the American President defined in a message to Congress what became known as the Truman Doctrine: Communism was to be held in check by granting aid, primarily economic and financial, but also military, to any country seemingly threatened by it.

The conference was a fiasco. There were accusations and counter-accusations about the way in which denazification had or had not been effected. Six points concerning German economic unity, put forward by General Marshall, then U.S. Secretary of State, were discussed amid considerable confusion: the utilization of resources in common, an import and export program, reparations, financial reform, freedom of movement, and centralized German administrations. Bidault demanded more coal for France and asked Molotov to support France's economic annexation of the Saar, which, begun in the previous December, had been accepted without enthusiasm by Britain and America. When Molotov failed to respond, Bidault ceased his efforts to mediate between the Russians and the Anglo–Americans. There was further discussion of two drafts of a four-power treaty, proposed in 1946 by Byrnes and Molotov respectively, neither of whom had found the other's acceptable. Although the conference lasted until April 24, no important decisions were reached except as regards the repatriation of German prisoners of war, to be accomplished before December 31, 1948. A further meeting of the Council was arranged for November in London, but no one expected it to yield any results, nor did it. The mutual reproaches were yet more violent and the discord sharper. Bidault was more stubbornly opposed than ever to any centralized administration for Germany unless Molotov would relent on the Saar question.

The failure of the Moscow conference in the spring of 1947 marked the beginning of the cold war and the splitting of the world into two parts. Its consequences were felt especially in France and Germany. In France, it led to the withdrawal of the Communists from the government in May and to a deepening of the gulf between them and the other parties. In Germany, it hastened the division of the country on geographical lines, which was both a cause and an effect of the world schism.

When Molotov came to Paris to discuss with his West European colleagues the offer of aid put forward by Marshall in his speech of June 5, 1947, it was a foregone conclusion that no agreement would be reached. Ever since the end of April, the German press in the eastern zone had attacked with increasing violence the "imperialist" and "Nazi" policies of the U.S. occupation. On October 5, the Cominform came into being and declared in its first manifesto that the sole war aim of America and Britain had been to rid themselves of the economic competition of Germany and Japan—an accusation very similar to the theme of Soviet propaganda before June, 1941. The manifesto went on to say that the world was divided into two fronts, one imperialist, the other socialist and democratic, and that there must be no Munich with the imperialists. On October 25, General Clay gave permission for the press in the U.S. zone of Germany to campaign against Communism.

From the breakdown of the Moscow session dates also the progress of both parts of Germany towards sovereignty—first economic and internal sovereignty and then political and external. The first Economic Council in Germany was set up on May 25, 1947 in the Anglo–American Bizonia (created by an agreement, signed at New York on December 2, 1946, which provided for the economic merging of the British and American zones and for a joint export and import agency [JEIA]).

It was impossible in any case to remain forever in the situation, envisaged at Potsdam as provisional, which gave the victors dictatorial powers; unless, of course, it were held that victory confers absolute power in perpetuity. But the gradual restoration of German sovereignty should have followed the rebirth of democratic sentiment and achievement. Instead, it took place as a function of East–West discord, and the wider the chasm the more the victors on each side of it tried to conciliate "their" part of Germany by promoting it in the scale of sovereignty.

The temptations in the West were two: either to pretend that the democratization intended at Potsdam had already been achieved, or else to reject the Potsdam principles *in toto* and abandon the idea of a special process of democratization for Germany. Both these temptations were such as to strengthen the hand of those members of the military governments who were more concerned with the East–West conflict than with any profound structural reform. On October 10, 1946, General Clay could still say, in a vigorous note to William H. Draper, the director of his economic department: "I am certain that the revival of democracy in Germany is dependent on our ability to develop an economy which is not controlled by a handful of banks."[4] But by July, 1947, Mr. Draper's assistant, whose job was the dissolution of cartels, was handing in his resignation on the ground that he found the task impossible.

As the schism in the world developed, and partly as a result of it, the notion of European unity came to the fore. The first impetus was given by the Marshall Plan, and, as the European idea took shape, its twofold character became clearly marked: it combined a constructive internationalism with timorous anti-Communism, the relative strength of the two attitudes and the mode of their expression varying according to the individual and to the world situation. The directives of JCS 1779 to the U.S. Commander-in-Chief were as categorical about denazification and demilitarization as those of JCS 1067, which they replaced on July 11, 1947; but the preamble stated that "an orderly and prosperous Europe requires the economic contribution of a stable and productive Germany." On July 12, the representatives of the sixteen countries receiving Marshall aid declared in Paris that "the Germany economy should be integrated into the economy of Europe in such a way as to contribute to a a raising of the general standard of life."

Nothing could be more obviously true; but why had it taken the breakdown of the Moscow conference to make people aware of it? In the following year, western Germany duly became a beneficiary under the Foreign Aid Act of April 3, 1948 and a member of the Organization for European Economic Cooperation (OEEC), which was set up on April 16. True, Germany was only represented in that body by the three commanders-in-chief. Nonetheless, Germany received a substantial amount of aid—about $1,400 million, in addition to gifts and credits previously granted under GARIOA (Government Aid and Relief in Occupied Areas) to the extent of $2,000 million.

Germany at this time was not a mere passive recipient of orders from the occupying powers; the people made their views known with increasing clarity through political parties and the *Land* governments and assemblies (*Landtage*). By and large, their minds were moving in the same direction as those of the occupying powers, with a similar ideological split developing between the genuine majority in the western zones and the *de facto* rulers with their sham majority in the eastern. In the Soviet zone, at the elections held on October 20, 1946 for the five *Landtage* of Saxony, Saxony-Anhalt, Thuringia, Brandenburg, and Mecklenburg, the Socialist Unity Party (SED) had received an average of 47·5 per cent of the votes compared with the Christian Democrats' 24·5 per cent and the Liberals' 24·6 per cent. In the three western zones, different though the character and policy of the occupation was between one and another, the principal contending parties scored comparable results in each zone in elections at all levels. (The Bavarians went to the polls on January 27, 1946 for municipal elections in small communities, on April 28 and May 26 for rural and urban district elections, on June 30 for the *Land* constituent assembly, and on December 1 for the *Landtag*.) The two dominant parties in the western zones were the Christian Democrats and the Social Democrats, with the Liberals a long way behind. The Communists scored patchy results, the best being in North Rhine–Westphalia, but were far behind the three main parties.

Just as the failure of the Moscow conference in April, 1947 marked the breach between the victors and their division into two camps, so the breakdown of an all-German meeting at Munich in June signaled a split between two opposing groups and foreshadowed the creation of two Germanies. The Bavarian Minister-President, Hans Ehard, had invited the heads of government from the *Länder* in all four zones, if only by way of demonstrating that Bavaria was not seeking to make itself autonomous. Lengthy preparations for the meeting took place in the western zones, without the participation of the five minister-presidents from the Soviet zone. The three western occupying powers had stipulated that there should be no discussion of German unity. This was something of a relief to the major German parties, which were not agreed among themselves as to the exact status of the heads of government, the Socialists in particular fearing that they might claim to represent completely sovereign *Länder* and thus set the seal on the fragmentation of Germany. On the evening of June 5, the day before the conference was due to open, the five representatives of the Soviet zone arrived at Munich and, in a preliminary discussion, at once demanded that the question of German unity be placed on the agenda. They also repeated demands they had put forward on May 28 that the venue of the meeting should be transferred to Berlin and that it should include representatives of political parties and trade unions. When Ehard refused to accept what he regarded as an ultimatum, the five Soviet zone ministers left for home after issuing a sharply worded joint declaration.

The meeting thus opened on June 6 as a purely western gathering. The Saar was unrepresented, as the result of a ban by the French authorities, which came in for lively criticism. On the 7th, the heads of government adopted a series of declarations, two in particular dealing with the economic distress of the German people and "political aspects of the situation." They proclaimed "the great objective of the economic and political unity of Germany" and their will to cooperate peaceably with all nations, and declared that "our existence as a state can only be rebuilt by means of genuine democracy in which all the fundamental rights of human freedom are guaranteed."[5]

This last phrase was an allusion to the state of affairs in the Soviet zone, where the SED was asserting its influence by less and less democratic methods, in particular using the "mass organizations" under its control to clip the wings of rival parties. Meanwhile, on the institutional level, the Russians on June 14 responded to the creation of the Economic Council in Bizonia by setting up a "German Economic Commission" to direct and coordinate the *Land* administrations. In November, the SED invited all anti-Fascist parties, as well as trade unions, management committees, groups and associations of peasants, academicians, and so forth to take part in a "German People's Congress for

Unity and a Just Peace." This duly assembled at Berlin on December 6 with 2,215 participants; the Christian Democrats refused to attend, with the result that their leaders, Jacob Kaiser and Ernst Lemmer, were dismissed by the Soviet governor. A second People's Congress, held on March 18, 1948—the centenary of the German revolution, as the organizers expressly recalled—elected a "German People's Council" (*Deutscher Volksrat*).

By now, the situation in the western sector was evolving rapidly. On February 9, 1948, the "Frankfurt Charter" was issued: it created a sort of German economic government for Bizonia, appointed by the occupying powers and comprising an executive body and a legislature. The Economic Council was under the presidency of Erich Köhler, who later became the first President of the Bundestag. The Administrative Council, under the chairmanship of Hermann Pünder (who had been Brüning's *Staatssekretär* in 1931–32), had six directors and six assistant directors with functions corresponding to those ministers. Four of them were to serve in Adenauer's first cabinet in September, 1949.[6]

On February 24, the Communists seized power in Prague—an event that did more than the creation of the Cominform to bring home to the West that danger in Europe might threaten from a quarter other than Germany. The talks that were in progress between Britain, France, and the Benelux countries took on a different tone, and the Western Union that resulted was military in character rather than economic, social, or cultural. The Brussels treaty of March 17 mentioned the possibility of German aggression, but only in one of the eight general statements of intent contained in the preamble. Article 4, which provided for automatic military aid if any of the parties should be the object of an armed attack in Europe, did not specify the potential aggressor. At the same time, the five signatories, and especially France, sought to persuade the United States to join in establishing a mutual defense system. In order to obtain an American guarantee, France found herself obliged to subordinate her German policy to wider national issues and waive her opposition to the course of events in Germany. This meant ceasing to treat the French zone as a separate entity and accepting the gradual formation of a federal German state that would include in its territory the Rhineland if not the Saar. France's decision was announced by M. Bidault, then Foreign Minister, at a London conference of the three occupying powers and the Benelux countries. The communiqué issued on June 7 indicated the wide range of recommendations that had been made to all governments. These included the establishment of an international Ruhr Authority "which did not involve the political separation of the Ruhr area from Germany." The delegates stated that they recognized, "taking into account the present situation, that it is necessary to give the German people the opportunity to achieve on the basis of a free and democratic form of government the eventual re-establishment of German unity at present disrupted." Moreover, "the delegates have agreed to recommend to their governments that the military governors should hold a joint meeting with the minister-presidents of the western zone in Germany. At that meeting the minister-presidents will be authorized to convene a Constituent Assembly in order to prepare a constitution for the approval of the participating states." The constitution was to embody "a federal form of government which adequately protects the rights of the respective states, and which at the same time provides for adequate central authority"—a vague formula calculated to lead to tension and conflict. Finally, France agreed to the joint conduct of the external trade of the trizonal area pending the establishment of German institutions that would make possible a full economic merger.

Before the minister-presidents met at Coblenz on July 8 to discuss the documents the three commanders-in-chief had drawn up on July 1 on the basis of the London agreement, the Berlin crisis broke. This episode, bringing the world to the brink of war, had a decisive effect on all aspects of the German problem.

The breach between the former allies in Germany had been virtually complete from the time Marshal Sokolovsky walked out of the Control Commission meeting on March 19 in protest against Western policy; the Commission was never to meet again, though it was not formally dissolved. Considering that a healthy German economy depended on currency reform, and having failed to obtain Soviet agreement to a common plan, the Western authorities issued a decree on June 18 for a reform in the trizonal area. On June 23, the Soviet military government replied with a reform in the eastern zone which was also intended to apply to the whole of Greater Berlin, and they suspended coal and electricity supplies to the western sectors of the city. On the 24th, the Western commanders decreed that a slightly modified western mark should have currency in their sectors. On the same day, the representatives of the "people's democracies" at Warsaw protested against the "Western military alliance," "Western encouragement of German revisionism," and "unilateral currency reform," and demanded four-power control of the Ruhr and the creation of a central government. On the 28th, the Americans announced the plan for an "air lift" to break the blockade of the western sectors; and on July 1, the four-power *Kommandatura* ceased to function.

The problem of access to Berlin was a complicated one.[7] What was in fact happening, however, was not a juridical dispute but a test of strength. The Russians persistently denied that a blockade was in force at any time, though they took restrictive measures from the end of March onward. Ever since the municipal elections of October 20, 1946, when the SED obtained only 19·8 per cent of the total vote as against the Socialists' 48·7 per cent, the Christian Democrats' 22·1 per cent, and the Liberals' 9·4 per cent, Berlin had provided a sort of index of the relative strength of East and West. It was not until November 30, 1948 that a separate municipality was created in the Soviet sector and the city was administratively divided. The Russians apparently believed that the air lift would not last through the winter and that the Western powers would abandon the city. But the United States made it a question of prestige. The air lift did succeed, more or less, in keeping the three western sectors provisioned, and a counterblockade of the Soviet zone of Germany was put into force. In February, 1949, negotiations to end the crisis were begun, and an agreement, announced on May 5, provided for the lifting of all restrictions on movement affecting Berlin and the eastern zone.

The air lift saved Berlin, and it also left a lasting mark on West German policy, especially in the external field. German–American solidarity was cemented by the winter of 1948–49. The other Western nations had of course helped to fly in coal and food to the beleaguered city, but it was the U.S. Government and General Clay that organized the air lift and mobilized resources, the bulk of which were American. From then on, no foreign policy was acceptable to the West Germans except on the basis of meriting the Americans' confidence so that they would continue to extend their protection over Berlin and West Germany. This was a point that, ten years later, General de Gaulle was to find some difficulty in realizing.

Another effect of the crisis was to bring about, overnight as it were, a kind of moral transformation of Berlin into a symbol of liberty instead of Prussianism and Nazidom. The East–West conflict was no joke for the Berliners, who suffered real privation, but it was gratifying to them to find themselves in the same camp as the greatest power in the world and to enjoy their protectors' recognition as defenders of moral values.

While Berlin was being kept alive by the air lift, preparations went steadily forward for the creation of the West German state on the basis of the London agreement. On July 26, 1948, the eleven Minister-Presidents (or mayors in the case of Hamburg and Bremen) jointly adopted a law for the establishment of a constituent assembly to be known as the Parliamentary Council. According to this law, which the *Landtage* ratified in August virtually without alteration, the Parliamentary Council was to consist of delegates of the *Länder* elected not by universal suffrage but by the *Landtage* themselves, on the basis of one delegate for every 750,000 of the population. Preparatory work for the Council was carried out by a commission of experts, the *Verfassungskonvent*, which met at Herrenchiemsee from August 10 to 23 and drew up a long document as a basis for the Council's debates.[8]

The Council sat at Bonn from September 1, 1948 to May, 1949. It was made up of 65 members (including 27 Christian Democrats, 27 Social Democrats, 5 Liberals, and 2 Communists) plus 5 delegates from Berlin including Jacob Kaiser and Ernst Reuter, the Socialist mayor of the western part of the city. The Council elected as its chairman the leader of the CDU in the British zone, Konrad Adenauer. The bulk of the work was done in the "main committee" (*Hauptausschuss*), of which Carlo Schmid was chairman and in which Theodor Heuss played an important part. The debates were complicated by the frequent, not to say constant, intervention of the occupying powers, either by means of written memoranda or through the "liaison officers" of the respective military governors.

The Council's dialogue with the Allies was not conducted without assistance: outside its walls, Kurt Schumacher carried on a fairly successful blackmail operation on the theme of: "It is as much in your interest as in ours that we should get things settled." The chief bone of contention, regarding which the members of the Parliamentary Council were also divided among themselves, was the nature of the proposed federation and the amount of power to be granted to the central authority.

On May 8, the Council finally approved the Basic Law of the future state on a third reading by 53 votes to 12, the minority including the two Communists

71

and six of the eight members of the Bavarian CSU (Christian Democrats). On the 12th, Generals Clay, Robertson, and Koenig addressed to Adenauer a "letter of approval" setting out a number of reservations concerning the residual powers of the Allies, the police powers of the German authorities, and the status of Berlin. The text was then submitted to the *Landtage* for ratification, on the understanding that it would be accepted by all the *Länder* if ratified by at least two-thirds of them. It was in fact ratified by all except Bavaria, and thus came into force on May 23.

The military governors, who were henceforth replaced by an Allied High Commission, pointed out in their letter that the Basic Law in no way infringed the rights of the occupying powers as they themselves had defined them shortly before in a draft Occupation Statute. The new state would not be free to use its economic power as it wished: the International Authority for the Ruhr, set up on December 28, 1948, would see to that. It was also to remain completely disarmed, and, on January 17, 1949, the military governors signed a directive setting up a Military Security Board at Coblenz "to ensure the maintenance of disarmament and demilitarization in the interests of security" and to "recommend to the military governors measures necessary to prevent the revival of military or para-military organizations." (The Board was not legally abolished until 1955, so that the situation that arose after 1950 was paradoxical to say the least.) Again, before the new state came into existtence it was made to suffer a slight loss of territory on its western frontier. On March 26, 1949, a six-power communiqué announced that thirty-one rectifications would be made along the frontier with the Netherlands, Belgium, Luxemburg, and France. The total area affected was only 52 square miles, with a population of some 13,500.

The main reservation, however, was that the sovereignty of the new state was doubly limited: the powers it enjoyed were only delegated, and they were very incomplete in themselves. An agreement signed in Washington on April 8, 1949 declared that the three Western governments retained the supreme authority which they had assumed by the Berlin declaration of June 5, 1945. On April 10, the three military governors had proclaimed the Occupation Statute, which began "In the exercise of the supreme authority which is retained by the Governments of France, the United States, and the United Kingdom." It was to enter into force simultaneously with the Basic Law, and included the following provisions:

1. The Federal State and the participating *Länder* shall have, subject only to the limitations in this Instrument, full legislative, executive and judicial powers in accordance with the Basic Law and with their respective constitutions.

2. . . . Powers in the following fields are specifically reserved:

(a) disarmament and demilitarization, including related fields of scientific research, prohibitions and restrictions on industry, and civil aviation;

(b) controls in regard to the Ruhr, restitution, reparations, decartellization, deconcentration, nondiscrimination in trade matters, foreign interests in Germany and claims against Germany;

(c) foreign affairs, including international agreements made by or on behalf of Germany;

(f) respect for the Basic Law and the *Land* constitutions;

(g) control over foreign trade and exchange;

3. It is the hope and expectation of the Governments of France, the United States and the United Kingdom that the occupation authorities will not have occasion to take action in fields other than those specifically reserved above. . . .

4. The German Federal Government and the governments of the *Länder* shall have the power, after due notification to the occupation authorities, to legislate and act in the fields reserved to these authorities, except as the occupation authorities otherwise specifically direct. . . .

5. Any amendment of the Basic Law will require the express approval of the occupation authorities before becoming effective. . . .

The Basic Law itself contains no reference whatever to this subordination to the Allies, but reads as if it had been elaborated by a sovereign independent state, though one of a transitional nature and deprived of part of its territory. One would have to read the preamble very carefully to discover in it any hint of dependence on the Western powers; the problem of the partition of Germany, on the other hand, is clearly present and is expressly referred to in the final article, 146:

Preamble
Conscious of its responsibility before God and mankind, filled with the resolve to preserve its national and political unity and to serve world peace as an equal partner in a united Europe, the German people

in the *Länder* Baden, Bavaria, Bremen, Hamburg, Hesse, Lower Saxony, North Rhine–Westphalia, Rhineland–Palatinate, Schleswig–Holstein, Württemberg-Baden and Württemberg–Hohenzollern

has, by virtue of its constituent power, enacted this Basic Law of the Federal Republic of Germany to give a new order to political life for a transitional period.

It acted also on behalf of those Germans to whom participation was denied.

The entire German people is called upon to accomplish, by free self-determination, the unity and freedom of Germany.

Article 146
This Basic Law shall become invalid on the day when a constitution adopted in a free decision by the German people comes into force.

The above text, and especially the words "by virtue of its constituent power," are in fundamental contradiction with the formula used by the Allies. It is in fact impossible to define clearly the nature of the new state, since its powers derive from two quite different sources: the delegation of authority by three of the Big Four, and the ratification by the German people, acting freely though indirectly through the *Landtage*, of a document drawn up by a German Constituent Assembly. A further difficulty arises from the "transitional" character of the Federal Republic: how far would any international commitments undertaken by it be binding on a state that might come into existence in accordance with Article 146?

On May 10, before its dissolution, the Parliamentary Council designated Bonn as the capital of the new Republic, by a not especially flattering vote of 33 against 29 for its rival Frankfurt. The U.S. High Commissioner, John J. McCloy, was appointed on the 18th and his French and British colleagues,

André François-Poncet and Sir Brian Robertson, on May 19 and June 1 respectively. Between September 7 and 20, the Bundestag and Bundesrat were constituted; Theodor Heuss was elected President of the Republic, Konrad Adenauer became Chancellor, and the government assumed its duties.

At the same time, another German state was coming to birth in the east. On May 15, elections were held in the Soviet zone for a third People's Congress, which, on May 30, adopted a constitution for the German Democratic Republic (G.D.R.), excluding East Berlin. In October, Wilhelm Pieck became President of the Republic and Otto Grotewohl its head of government, while the Soviet military administration was replaced by a Control Commission "charged with exercising control over the fulfillment of the Potsdam and other joint decisions of the four powers in respect of Germany." The G.D.R. constitution, like that of West Germany, says nothing about the delegation of powers, but it is also silent as to the division of Germany. The preamble declares that "the German people . . . have adopted this constitution." According to Article 1, "Germany is an indivisible democratic Republic" and "there is only one German nationality" (*Staatsangehörigkeit*), a view also taken by lawyers and other authorities in the West. By Article 2, the G.D.R. adopted as its colors, as the Federal Republic (F.R.G.) already had done, the black, red, and gold of 1848 and the Weimar Republic; also according to Article 2, "the capital of the Republic is Berlin."

As was to be expected, each of the opposing camps regarded the other's German state as illegal, but on what grounds? The Allies did not challenge one another's right to delegate their power, in whole or in part, to German authorities, for if they did they would first have to answer the question: "Can the indivisible power of the four be transferred by any of them separately?" According as the answer is yes or no, either German state has as much or as little right to exist as the other: there are two states or none. So, the argument from the delegation of power being of no avail, each side fell back on the principle of free popular consent, as proclaimed in the two constitutions, and each denied the right of the opposing regime to call itself democratic. Soviet General Chuikov denounced the F.R.G. for being dominated by *revanchist* and militaristic forces. The Western powers retorted on October 10 and 12, in statements by the three High Commissioners and Dean Acheson, then U.S. Secretary of State, that the population of the Soviet zone had not had a chance to express its wishes through free elections. Was there one German state or two? It would be a long time before the question was answered. For the time being, however, neither of the newborn Republics was a true state, since neither enjoyed full sovereignty.

Part II
The West German Democracy

5

The Foundations of the State

WHEN the institutions of the Federal German Republic were set up, they were able to function more or less harmoniously because the brunt of the work had already been accomplished: the important decisions were taken before the decision-taking machinery existed. When the new state was born, the period of dramatic changes was already over—indeed, its birth was a sign of that very fact.

This does not mean that nothing significant happened after 1949, that there was no further change or that it was a matter of no consequence that Adenauer and Erhard won at the polls on August 14, 1949, that the National Democrats (NPD) were defeated on September 28, 1969. The important fact, however, is that restrictions dating from the time when Germany was a mere object of policy were maintained in force at a time when it was once more becoming an independent agent. The effect was to reduce initiative and limit the stakes of political life, while at the same time softening the clashes of ideological and social rivalry. To the frequently put question "Was there any alternative?" the answer seems quite clear: "Perhaps in 1947, but certainly not in 1949."

In previous chapters we have followed stage by stage the development of events during the four years from Germany's surrender in 1945. It seems unnecessary to do the same for the next twenty-one years, since continuity was their principal feature once the initial situation had been put under control. The history of the Federal Republic can of course be written chronologically, but it seems more useful to consider its various aspects individually, bearing in mind however that each institution, each political and social force is both a cause and an effect of the country's evolution as a whole. No doubt various "turning points" can be discerned, but none are so decisive that events and institutions can be understood only by reference to them. For instance, in October, 1963, the Federal Republic ceased to be Adenauer's Germany; but the power and prestige of that extraordinary man had already been dwindling for at least four years, and his departure was not attended by any profound upheaval. A sharper break was that of October, 1969, when the Christian Democratic Party (CDU) went out of office for the first time, an event which caused many individuals and groups that had looked to it for ideas and guidance to rethink their position. The Social Democrats (SPD), on the other hand, had become part of the governing coalition as early as December, 1966, but without imposing such changes as would have amounted to a breach of continuity in politics or public life. This is true even as regards policy toward Eastern Europe, where there was a change of emphasis rather than direction.

Certain dates, too, are of major importance as regards the Republic's position in international affairs: 1955, when the Paris agreements came into force, the Bundeswehr was created, and normal relations were established with the Soviet Union; August 13, 1961, when the symbolic division of Berlin became a physical reality; March, 1970, when Brandt as Chancellor conferred at Erfurt with Stoph, the East German Premier. It will of course be part of our task to study how these events came about and what they signified.[1] The list of them in itself suggests one of our basic themes—namely, the sensitivity of West German political life to developments outside the Republic. It is, of course, a general truth that a state's domestic and foreign policy can hardly be dissociated and that the latter is bound up with the condition of international relations as a whole. In many countries, indeed, internal politics are directly influenced by the international scene: the alliances and antagonisms of French left parties during the past fifty years cannot be fully understood without reference to those of the Soviet Union. But the Federal Republic has always been more directly dependent on the international situation than most other states, by reason of the circumstances of its birth and the specific limits placed on its liberty of action.

As with all other members of the international community, Federal Germany is increasingly influenced by events beyond its own frontiers, and has in consequence experienced changes of attitude and opinion that it is hard to date or trace to the origin with any certainty. The attainment of more complete sovereignty in 1955, or Adenauer's resignation, had less effect on the evolution of German Catholicism than that evolution had on Brandt's accession to power and the revision of German policy toward the Communist bloc. This being so, a chronological as opposed to an analytical approach would have the disadvantage of obscuring the presence or absence of continuity that can be discerned in each of several aspects of political life, especially if we understand this term as including in some degree social and ideological realities.

The Roots of Legitimacy

During the twenty years and more since it was founded, the Federal Republic has scarcely ever been faced with an internal challenge to its legitimacy; the overwhelming majority of its citizens accept it as a state fully entitled to require that they should cooperate in its functioning and obey its decisions. This, if we reflect on it, is a remarkable fact. Whereas the Weimar constitution was adopted by an assembly elected by universal suffrage and free to deliberate without interference from the victorious powers, in 1948–49, the German people had no direct part either in appointing the Parliamentary Council or in ratifying the Basic Law, and the occupying powers intervened time and again in the drafting process. Yet the legitimacy of the Weimar regime was incessantly challenged from one quarter or another, even before it was engulfed by National Socialism. Germany in the 1920's, though shorn of territory by the treaty of Versailles, was at least the only state laying claim to represent the German people; it was more or less fully sovereign and was accepted as a permanent feature of the international scene. The Federal Republic, on the other hand is, a country of imperfect sovereignty and uncertain frontiers, which officially describes itself as transitory. Is the line between it and the other Germany a frontier? And is the line between that Germany and Poland the frontier of "Germany" pure and simple? Again, West Berlin belongs to the Federal Republic but is not part of it; and the very term "West Berlin" is only one of practical convenience, without prejudice to the legal and to some extent political conception of Berlin as a whole. Although the Federal Republic has become an economic power of the first rank, it is still in theory less independent than, say, Algeria—a country with no history, no structure, and no resources—under the Evian agreement of 1962, which brought it into being: "The Algerian State shall freely give itself its own institutions and choose the political and social regime that it considers best suited to its interests. In the international field it will determine the policy of its choice and pursue it in full sovereignty."

The Occupation Statute, it is true, was not maintained for long in the full rigor of 1949. In March, 1951, the Federal Government was authorized to establish a Ministry of Foreign Affairs, and in May, 1955 the Statute was superseded by the ratification of the Paris agreements of October 23, 1954. But it was not until May 27, 1968 that the three powers informed the German Minister of Foreign Affairs that, in view of the constitutional amendments concerning the state of emergency (*Notstandsverfassung*), the rights held or exercised by them under Article 5 of the convention on the termination of the occupation regime were considered to have lapsed. The rights in question were those that entitled the powers, in case of emergency, to resume a large measure of the sovereignty they had restored to Germany in and after 1949.[2] Nor has there yet been any modification of Article 2 of the convention, which lays down that the "full authority of a sovereign state over its internal and external affairs," guaranteed to the Federal Republic by Article 1, does not apply to the most basic national problems: "In view of the international situation, which has so far prevented the reunification of Germany and the conclusion of a peace settlement, the Three Powers retain the rights and the responsibilities, heretofore exercised or held by them, relating to Berlin and to Germany as a whole, including the reunification of Germany and a peace settlement."

In practice, all these elements of uncertainty and weakness have had less effect than might have been expected, owing to decisions and events that took the sting out of the major difficulties and also to changes in the political or ideological sphere that played an overriding part in legitimizing the Bonn regime. The humiliation of foreign domination was felt less once West Germany was not merely the protégé of the occupying powers but their ally against a common danger. Within a very short time, the High Commissioners ceased to have any power over the German Government and the Occupation Statute became in practice a dead letter. This was due mainly to the energy and astuteness of Dr. Adenauer, who from 1951 was his own Minister of Foreign Affairs and, as such, was able to hint to his U.S., British, and French opposite numbers that they should instruct the High Commissioners not to interfere with the German Chancellor, who was theoretically their subordinate.

The Oder–Neisse line remained a source of tension, but even before 1949 the German leaders had resolved to do their utmost to bring about the economic and social integration of the refugees.[3] The Federal Government from time to time made concessions to refugee organizations, but in the long run the policy of integration was bound to have an assuaging effect: despite pressure, the German authorities did not adopt a policy similar to that of the Arab governments who saw to it that the Palestine refugees remained refugees for good and thus kept alive the claim of their homeland. As to the division between the two Germanies, it had and continues to have its effect on Federal policy but it did not prevent the new state, with its smoothly functioning institutions, from basing its claim to legitimacy on popular consent—in contrast to the other Germany, which could not rest its title on the free expression of public opinion. This situation had, as it were, a cumulative effect. In order to stand up to Ulbricht's Germany, it was important to make the Federal institutions work smoothly, overlooking as far as possible their provisional character; in this way, the legitimacy of the West German state was strengthened, but at the same time the division between the two Germanies also came to seem, and to be, less provisional. The strengthening of legitimacy in the West was in part due to the regime's taking less and less account of the preamble and Article 146 of the Basic Law and regarding itself more and more as a permanent entry. But this led in no small measure to the stabilization of another phenomenon—namely, the existence of two German states. It was natural enough for the West German leaders to wish to rescue the new state from the uncertainties attendant on its provisional character, with all the risk of internal conflict and disorder that this involved. But they might have realized or admitted before twenty years had elapsed that the very success of their efforts, whether in power or in opposition, had created an insuperable obstacle to German reunification, to which there were so many obstacles already.

Be that as it may, the Federal Republic of Germany, from 1949 onward enjoyed one major advantage, which also redounded to the benefit of its first Chancellor and the party that triumphed at the first elections. Whereas the Weimar Republic and its leaders had borne the blame for the hapless situation of a defeated Germany, the Germans spent the worst years of their history since the Thirty Years' War, that is to say from 1944 to 1948, under the rule of Hitler and then of the occupying powers. The state born in 1949 took shape and developed when the effects of economic revival were already making themselves felt and Germany's international prestige was undergoing a fairly rapid recovery. In the 1920's, the words "republic" and "democracy" meant surrender, humiliation, and misery; in the 1950's they coincided, in time at all events, with the ideas of bringing order out of chaos and of restoring Germany's economic and diplomatic position. This, too, was a source of strength and legitimacy to the Federal regime.

Besides benefiting from prosperity, the Federal Republic was able to buttress its position by a twofold hostility, directed at the Nazism of the past and Communism in the present. In respect of both, there were compromises from time to time, but the regime's firmness was sufficient to ensure that public life was not "de-ideologized"—as has been too often claimed—but, on the contrary, was based on uncontroversial foundations as far as ideology is concerned. It was to the Republic's benefit that it found itself constrained to take up a strongly negative position in these two directions, the effect of which was again to strengthen its claim to legitimacy despite the incompleteness of its sovereignty and its territory.

The rejection of Nazism was based on conviction in the case of the leaders and a large proportion of the people, and also on concern for Germany's good name. Apart from the adoption of a philosophy and a system different from Nazism, it involved deciding, for example, what attitude should be taken toward the Nazi past of this or that individual and how Nazism was to be referred to in public life.[4] From the outset, the new regime shouldered the heavy burden of the past: while repudiating the idea of collective guilt or penal responsibility, it accepted liability for the crimes committed in Germany's name. As for the West Germans' rejection of Communism and, in particular, the dictatorship that was being set up in the Soviet occupation zone (called, since 1949, the German Democratic Republic), it was fortified both by an almost unanimous conviction and by the desire for inclusion in one of the two international camps that had taken shape in 1947. In and after 1949, however, the term "anti-Communism" covered many ambiguities by reason both of the varying motives that lay behind it and of West Germany's international position.[5] It signified the defense of those liberties that had been suppressed in the Soviet zone, but in Hitler's time it had itself been used as a pretext for suppressing liberties. From 1946 onward, anti-Communism was a natural standpoint for those who, faced with the creation of a political and ideological monolith in East Germany, wished to found their own state on a free and pluralistic basis. But an anti-Communism based on the love of liberty had to be instilled into a people that had, for years, been indoctrinated with intensive anti-Communism based on Nazism. In addition, defense against the Communist menace was to enable the infant Republic to become the ally of three of the victorious powers and, at the same time, to live down Germany's Nazi past. Anti-Communist solidarity was the road that led to *Gleichberechtigung*—the "equality of rights" with other states that had been the slogan of the late 1920's and early 1930's.

Since the Communist threat presented itself in a military light, it was natural that this solidarity soon took on military forms; this meant risking that the ideological emphasis in the new state would shift from one kind of anti-Communism to another. However, West German rearmament did not become a reality until 1955, by which time the cold war was beginning to give way to a *détente*. But it was not until the 1960's, when the *détente* became more marked, that anti-Communism lost its place as an ideological foundation of the regime, no less essential because it was ambiguous. This was facilitated by the fact that the equality of rights was more or less achieved in 1955, and also by the continued inner strengthening of the F.R.G.: the more stable the regime became and the more smoothly its institutions worked, the less need was there to define its purposes in negative terms.

It remains true, however, that the Federal Republic had made its decision once and for all against Communism, which explains why its claim to legitimacy never really suffered as a result of the division of Germany. In 1948, the great majority of West Germans made a choice that is very rare in the twentieth century, preferring the maintenance of a certain political and economic system to the achievement of national unity. Faced with a situation where reunification might mean a danger, however slight, of Germany as a whole being Communized and where, if there were no reunification, it was certain that West Germany would preserve its liberties, they opted firmly for the second alternative. The option was a theoretical one, since the choice hardly existed as a practical issue, but it was nonetheless decisive as regards the ideological foundation of political life.

The Rule of Law, Citizens' Rights and the Constitutional Court

In opposition both to Nazi despotism and to the predominance of political ideology in the other Germany, the founders of the F.R.G. were resolved to enshrine the rule of law as the supreme value of the new state, protecting the citizen against all abuses of power, not excluding those committed by the majority. When, in the debate on the *Spiegel* affair, the Christian Democratic deputy Max Guede, a former Advocate-General at the Federal High Court at Karlsruhe, said in effect that "We are all agreed here that while democracy is of course a good thing, the rule of law is as vital to us as the air we breathe,"[6] he was expressing the idea that even the will of the majority must submit to a common law and that only so can minority rights be protected. As for the Social Democrats, they had only to remember the brave and optimistic words that their leader Otto Wels addressed to Hitler on March 23, 1933 in explanation of the SPD refusal to vote for the Enabling Act: "We see the facts which give you power now. But the people's sense of law and justice (*Rechtsbewusstsein*) is a political force too, and we shall not cease to appeal to it."

The notion of a *Rechtsstaat*, a state based on the rule of law, has dangers of its own: that of legalism, for instance—a fondness for texts that petrify reality, the temptation to hide behind the written word and so avoid change or action of any kind; these are vices not confined, as some might think, to French justice or French administration. Greatest of all is the danger of excessive respect for laws whose purpose is not to maintain liberty but to suppress it. During the demonstrations by German students in the 1960's, a curious paradox came to light: whereas the Basic Law was emphatic in affirming the unconditional right of citizens to express their opinions publicly and collectively, the old Penal Code that was still in force was concerned primarily with the maintenance of public order, even the very undemocratic type of order that had prevailed in Imperial Germany. In France, it is easier than it should be for the authorities, in defiance of fundamental rights, to prohibit rallies and demonstrations. But those who infringe the ban are not generally brought to trial; when they are, the judges are lenient, while if the acts of disobedience are numerous, their judicial consequences are soon wiped out by an amnesty. In West Germany, on the other hand, the right to demonstrate was taken much more seriously, but at the same time the authorities applied the traditional Penal Code (which was not altered until 1970), bringing large numbers of people to trial and imposing a good many severe sentences.

By and large, however, fundamental rights (*Grundrechte*) are taken very seriously, as the drafters of the constitution had intended. Whereas these rights only figured in Part II of the Weimar constitution, where they were mentioned in the same breath with "fundamental duties," they are set out in the first section of the Basic Law of the F.R.G. Nor is this merely a preamble enunciating general principles, as in the French constitutions of 1946 and 1958. Article 1 says: "The following basic rights shall be binding as directly valid law on legislation, administration, and judiciary." Although this and the eighteen articles that follow are much less detailed than the corresponding articles (109–65) of the Weimar constitution, they repeat several important provisions from that document. Some statements of principle are clearly designed to mark the break with Nazism: "The dignity of man shall be inviolable. . . . The German people acknowledges inviolable and inalienable human rights as the basis of every human community, of peace, and of justice in the world." Practical conclusions are also drawn. Thus, as Hitler deprived émigrés and other anti-Nazis of their German nationality, Article 16 lays down that no one may be deprived of German citizenship against his will if the effect would be to render him stateless. The same article says that "No German may be extradited to a foreign country." This gave rise to some awkward problems in the case of war criminals and even persons guilty of common law crimes, especially those that involved the death penalty in the country concerned. This penalty was abolished in West Germany by the Basic Law and has never been reintroduced, despite numerous campaigns inspired not (as might be thought) by the trial of former Auschwitz warders, but by cases of the murder of taxidrivers.

The equality of all citizens before the law is declared in Article 3 and spelled out in two further provisions. The first, which says that "men and women shall have equal rights," has caused difficulties for legislators who have sought to translate it into precise formulas and for governments that have wished to make it a reality. Twenty-one years after the Basic Law came into force, there are still many obscurities, and the level of women's pay remains obstinately below that of men. The tragicomic argument over homosexuality, which German law forbade in the case of men but not of women, was not resolved until 1969, when the Penal Code was amended to confer equal immunity on both sexes.

The third paragraph of Article 3 merits attention: "No one may be prejudiced or privileged because of his sex, descent, race, language, homeland and origin (*Heimat und Herkunft*), faith or his religious and political opinions." The enumeration here is inspired by anti-Nazism and the policy of facilitating the integration of refugees, but the article is also, in theory, applied in such a way as to prohibit favoritism based on denominational or party affiliations in the allocation of important posts at Bonn or in the *Länder*.

Article 4 guarantees freedom of faith and conscience, and adds: "No one may be compelled against his conscience to perform war service as a combatant. Details shall be regulated by a Federal law." The first rules for the application of this principle were embodied in the Basic Law itself by an amendment of 1956, without prejudice to the specific provisions of military legislation. By this amendment, Article 12—which guarantees freedom from compulsion in work matters—was altered to provide that conscientious objectors might be obliged to perform civilian labor in lieu of military service, but such labor could not be of longer duration than the military service it would replace and must have nothing to do with the armed forces.[7]

As education falls within the competence of the *Länder* and the SPD and CDU were particularly at odds in this domain, Articles 6 and 7 merely emphasize the value of marriage and the family and lay down that, while the care and upbringing of children is the natural right and duty of parents, the entire educational system is under the supervision of the state. Parents or guardians have the right to decide whether a child shall receive religious instruction, which "shall form part of the curriculum in the state schools with the exception of nonconfessional schools. . . . No teacher may be obliged against his will to give religious instruction." This last provision has often been a dead letter in parts of the country where any teacher seeking to take advantage of it would have difficulty getting a job. The article on religious instruction is supplemented by two of the "Concluding Provisions": Article 141, which states that the rule concerning the curriculum in state schools does not apply to a *Land* whose law provided differently on January 1, 1949, and Article 140, which declares that the provisions of Articles 136–39 and 141 of the Weimar constitution, concerning the rights of the churches and the practice of religion, are an integral part of the Basic Law. Thanks to Adenauer's "anticlericalism," these secularist provisions were adopted without difficulty by the Parliamentary Council.[8] But the constitution-makers forgot to decide as to the validity or otherwise of the 1933 Concordat, an omission that was to give rise to a serious problem. It was also more or less overlooked that Article 141 of the Weimar constitution dealt with the rights of religious bodies in the army as well as in prisons and hospitals. When Germany came to rearm after 1954, this article served as the basis of agreements with the churches, the terms of which aroused lively controversy within the Evangelical Church.

The Basic Law does not say much about social and economic rights, though Section II is introduced by the statement in Article 20 that "the Federal Republic of Germany is a democratic and social federal state." The list of fundamental rights does not include the right to strike. However, the freedom to form trade unions is clearly implied in Article 9, paragraph 3 of which is particularly interesting: "The right to form associations to safeguard and improve working and economic conditions shall be guaranteed to everyone and to all professions. Agreements which seek to restrict or hinder this right shall be null and void; measures directed to this end shall be illegal."

Article 15, drawn up at a time when the CDU was still adhering to the leftish program adopted at Ahlen in 1947, permits nationalization: "Land and landed property, natural resources and means of production may, for the purpose of socialization (*Vergesellschaftung*), be transferred to public ownership or other forms of publicly controlled economy by way of a law which shall regulate the nature and extent of compensation." During the 1965 election campaign, the Liberals made a symbolic but unsuccessful appeal for the abolition of this article.

The drafters of the Basic Law had a more urgent preoccupation than the proclamation of rights, however important: namely, how to prevent abuses by and deny liberty to, the foes of liberty. Mindful of the rise of Nazism and the present threat of Communism, the Council laid down, in Articles 5 and 9, that: "Art and science, research and teaching shall be free. Freedom of teaching shall not absolve from loyalty to the constitution. . . . Associations, the objects or activities of which conflict with the criminal laws or which are directed against the constitutional order or the concept of international understanding, shall be prohibited." Further, Article 18 provides that:

Whoever abuses the freedom of expression of opinion, in particular the freedom of the press (Article 5, paragraph 1), the freedom of teaching (Article 5, paragraph 3), the freedom of assembly (Article 8), the freedom of association (Article 9), the secrecy of mail, post, and telecommunications (Article 10), property (Article 14), or the right of asylum (Article 16, paragraph 2), in order to attack the free, democratic basic order, shall forfeit these basic rights. The forfeiture and its extent shall be pronounced by the Federal Constitutional Court.

As we shall see in chapter 7, the same idea was expressed in Article 21 concerning political parties.

Article 24, in the section on the respective rights of the Federation and the *Länder*, states a principle also to be found, though in a different form, in the preamble to the French constitution of 1958: "The Federation may, by legislation, transfer sovereign powers to international institutions. In order to preserve peace, the Federation may join a system of mutual collective security; in doing so it will consent to those limitations of its sovereign powers which will bring about and secure a peaceful and lasting order in Europe and among the nations of the world." It will be seen that the Basic Law as drafted in 1949 refers only twice, and in a more or less negative way, to the possibility of Germany possessing armed forces; once in the context of conscientious objection and then in that of the limitation of sovereignty. In due course, the Chancellor and the CDU argued from these provisions that rearmament in itself was allowed by the constitution.

It would of course be idle to pretend that basic rights have always been guaranteed as fully in practice as they are on paper. But they play a real part in German political life, if only because the Basic Law created an institution designed to act as their champion, namely the Constitutional Court, which loses no opportunity to insist on their validity. This was seen, for example, in the Court's decision of January 29, 1969 on the subject of natural children. The last paragraph of Article 6, as drafted in 1949, contained an injunction to the legislature: "Illegitimate children shall, through legislation, be given the same conditions for their physical and spiritual development and their position in society as legitimate children." No such legislation having been passed in the intervening twenty years, the Court, in a judgment arising out of a suit brought by an under age girl, issued what amounted to an ultimatum to the legislature: if a law was not passed within the few remaining months of the session, the courts were directed to ignore the legislation in force insofar as it conflicted with the spirit of the constitution on this point. Thus admonished, the legislature did its duty and, on August 19, 1969, passed a law, which entered into force on January 1, 1970.

There could be no clearer affirmation of the power of the constitution to override the ordinary laws, expressing as these do the will of the parliamentary majority in a form that can be amended without much difficulty. The French tradition in this respect is very different. The Third Republic scarcely possessed a coherent constitution; in 1946, Article 91 of the constitution of the Fourth Republic declared: "The Constitutional Committee shall examine whether laws passed by the National Assembly imply a revision of the Constitution." On November 6, 1962, the Constitutional Council of the Fifth Republic declared itself incompetent to pronounce on laws that "having been adopted by the people in consequence of a referendum, constitute the direct expression of national sovereignty." Both these formulas clearly imply the power of the majority to override the terms of the constitution. In the Federal Republic, on the other hand, the Basic Law is designed to establish the *Rechtsstaat* "not only on the will of the legislature at a given time, but on values that are equally binding on the legislature and the state." This formulation by the President of the Constitutional Court[9] shows clearly that the latter's task, like that of the U.S. Supreme Court, is not merely to give a legal interpretation of the constitution but to define and expound the system of political ethics by which the nation is governed. Hence the importance of the Court's role in the political life of the Federal Republic.

As compared with France, the judiciary as a whole plays a more important part in the organization of powers. The French people exercises sovereignty "through its representatives and by means of referenda," but the German people do so "by means of separate legislative, executive, and judicial organs" (Article 20 of the Basic Law). There are Federal supreme courts for various purposes: the Finance Court at Munich, the Administrative Court at Berlin, the Labor and Social Courts at Kassel, and, at Karlsruhe, the Federal High Court (*Bundesgerichtshof*), which broadly corresponds to the French Cour de Cassation (and also to the Cour de Sûreté de l'Etat, as it has direct jurisdiction in cases involving treason). The existence of all these as well as of lower Federal courts leads, as might be expected, to conflicts of jurisprudence. In 1949, the Basic Law (Article 95) envisaged the creation of a supreme Federal court to crown the edifice, but this idea had to be abandoned: an amendment of June, 1968 provides for the establishment of a panel (*Senat*) or conciliation commission to ensure unity of jurisprudence.

The Federal Constitutional Court (*Bundesverfassungsgericht*), which also sits at Karlsruhe, is much more directly associated with the political process and is the only judicial body that, properly speaking, is designed to act as a counterpoise to the executive and the legislature. Its powers, composition, and procedure were outlined in the Basic Law and defined by a law of March 12, 1951, amended by three other laws of July 21, 1956, June 26, 1959, and August 3, 1963.[10] As with the Basic Law itself, which, respected though it is, has been amended twenty-six times in twenty years by a two-thirds vote of the legislature, proposals have been made repeatedly for a complete revision—the most important aspect of which would be to give the Court more freedom to determine its procedure, which at present is largely imposed on it by parliament through the 107 articles of the Court's statute.

The powers of the Constitutional Court are manifold and extensive. It rules on the forfeiture of basic rights by individuals and on the constitutionality of political parties, which are automatically banned if its decision is adverse. It acts as an appeal court for disputed elections to the Bundestag, and as a High

Court to try the President of the Republic if he should be impeached by the Bundestag or the Bundesrat. It may also try any member of another Federal court who is, by a two-thirds majority of the Bundestag, accused of improper conduct. Further, the Court is the sovereign interpreter of the Basic Law in jurisdictional disputes between constitutional organs or between the Federation and the *Länder*. It pronounces with immediate effect on the constitutionality of laws, so that any law condemned by it is *ipso facto* revoked. It also decides, in case of doubt, whether a rule of international law is part of Federal law. Any citizen may appeal to the Court on the ground that he has suffered wrong through a violation of the constitution, especially the deprival of one of the basic rights. However, if any other legal remedy is open to him, the Constitutional Court will only try the case in the last instance, unless it considers the matter of sufficient general importance for it to take immediate cognizance.

In other cases, the right of access to the Court is not enjoyed by everybody. Only the Bundestag, the Federal Government, or a *Land* government may apply to it for a declaration that an individual has forfeited his basic rights. Only the Bundestag, the Bundesrat, or the Federal Government may plead that a political party be outlawed, except that, in the case of a regional party, the *Land* government in question may do so. For a judgment on the constitutionality of a Federal law, application must be made by the Federal Government, by a *Land* government, or else by one-third of the members of the Bundestag.

Until 1956 (when the provision was revoked), the Court might also give an advisory opinion (*Rechtsgutachten*) on a specific question of constitutional law at the request of the President of the Republic or at the joint request of the Bundestag, Bundesrat, and Federal Government. Although in theory such an opinion had no binding force, it naturally prejudged the way in which the Court would decide if a concrete issue were before it. For this reason, Adenauer as Chancellor put pressure on President Heuss in December, 1952 to withdraw his request for an opinion on the constitutionality of the treaty for the establishment of the European Defense Community (EDC). The abolition of the power to obtain advisory opinions was a further limitation on presidential authority, but the reasons for it were understandable; such opinions were all the more binding as they were given by the full Court, whereas ordinary appeals were tried by one or other of its two divisions or panels (*Senate*). The respective functions of these are strictly delimited, and joint sessions are only held in the event of a disagreement between them in regard to competence or jurisprudence.

In 1956, some functions were transferred from one *Senat* to the other, ostensibly because one of them was overworked but in fact because the parliamentary majority wished to limit the sphere of action of a "red" *Senat* and increase those of a "clerical" one. Such doubts as to the judges' impartiality were understandable in view of the procedure by which they are appointed and replaced. The Basic Law (Article 94) says that "the members of the Federal Constitutional Court shall be elected half by the Bundestag and half by the Bundesrat." The detailed procedure was laid down in a 1951 law. Two lists are drawn up by the Federal Minister of Justice, the first comprising the names of all judges of other Federal courts who agree to be nominated and are at least forty years of age (the law requires that several members of each *Senat* shall be chosen from among members of the Federal judiciary and hold office for the remainder of their careers as judges, that is, until they reach retiring age). The second list contains the names of all persons proposed by a party group in the Bundestag, or by the Federal Government or a *Land* government, who are over forty, have qualified for the profession of a judge or medium-rank civil servant, and have "particular knowledge of public law and public affairs." These persons must signify in writing that they agree to be nominated; if elected, they must give up all other duties, the only exception being for university professors. Those elected from the second list serve for a term of eight years and may be re-elected. Since the intention was to renew half the Court at a time, a distinction was made at the 1951 election between those appointed for only four years and those for the full eight.

The Bundesrat votes for the judges by direct suffrage and a two-thirds majority is required. The Bundestag adopts an indirect procedure, the judges being elected by a commission consisting of twelve deputies and reflecting in its composition the strength of the respective parties in the Bundestag itself. The President of the Court is chosen alternately by the Bundestag and the Bundesrat. Further points for decision were, what majority should be required for the decisions of the Bundestag and what should be the total number of judges? The 1951 law stated that each *Senat* should consist of twelve members and that the Bundestag commission should vote by a three-fourths majority, corresponding roughly to a two-thirds majority of both houses of the legislature. Under Adenauer, the CDU government and party fought hard to get these clauses modified so as to reduce the size of the court from twenty-four to twelve, doing away with the two-division system altogether, and to provide that the judges would be elected by a simple majority. While there was some truth in their argument that a majority of one-third possessed a kind of veto, there is no doubt that Adenauer's object was not to facilitate the working of the Court but to strike at the root of its independence. He was, however, unsuccessful. After endless argument and incidents, the law passed in 1956 made little change in the former one. Since 1958, each *Senat* has consisted of only eight judges, three from the Federal (first) list and the other five from the second, to serve for terms of eight years with the possibility of re-election. The electoral commission of the Bundestag, whose members are bound to secrecy, votes by a two-thirds majority, as does the Bundesrat.

Was Adenauer justified in complaining that the Socialists had given a "red" complexion to the first *Senat*? Had the second more of a CDU tinge? In our view, the answer is "no" in both cases. Naturally the opinions of a particular judge in matters of public or constitutional law were and are known, if only from his teaching and writings. For instance, some passages in the Court's judgments concerning political parties could safely be attributed to Professor Leibholz, whose ideas they faithfully reflected, and in 1966 he was challenged on grounds of presumed partiality; eventually he admitted the validity of the challenge and a decision of the Court declared his admission to be justified, thus opening the door to future attacks on individual judges.[11]

However, one cannot speak seriously of political prejudice. Once a judge is elected, he identifies himself with his office and becomes a member of a corporate body. Who, in 1956 or thereabouts, still remembered that Dr. Erwin Stein had been the CDU Minister of Education in Hesse from 1947 to 1950, or that Professor Martin Drath had acted as a legal adviser to Socialist trade unions before 1933? The Court's first President, Dr. Höpker-Aschoff, had represented the Liberal Party on the Parliamentary Council at Bonn, but his former political allegiance had nothing to do with his celebrity: if he was regarded as a great President until his death on January 15, 1954, it was because he showed the same courage and nobility of views in that office as he had before and after 1933.

His successor Josef Wintrich, a senior member of the Bavarian judiciary, had a less remarkable personality and a less distinguished past. When he died in office on October 19, 1958, the Bundestag and Bundesrat reached agreement that one of them would elect a political personality to the Court and that the other would appoint him its President. The person chosen was Gebhard Müller, the CDU Minister-President of Baden-Württemberg, whose government was a coalition including the Socialist and Liberals. His term was renewed in 1963, the year in which Wintrich's would have come to an end.

Since the Court was established, it has had to take numerous decisions in the most varied fields. As an example of the application of the basic constitutional rights to a legal provision of an apparently technical nature, we may take the Court's ruling of January 17, 1957, when the first *Senat* annulled Article 26 of the income tax law of 1951, amended in 1952, under which husbands and wives were obliged to declare their incomes jointly, and the method of assessment heavily penalized marriage as against concubinage. This, the Court ruled, was a violation of Article 6 of the Basic Law, which lays down that "marriage and family shall be under the special protection of the state." While making clear that it was not opposed to tax reductions for married couples, the Court insisted that Article 6 forbade interference of any kind with the private life of families. It suspected that the intention of the offending clause was not purely financial but social as well, namely to encourage women to stick to housework by making it less profitable for them to take jobs—a method of combating unemployment that the Nazis had used in their time. The Court expressly declared that the legislature had no right to seek to impose its view as to the way in which married couples should conduct their lives.

The most awkward issue which came before the Court was that of the European Defense Community. Its uneasiness throughout this affair was due, we may say, to the feeling that law was being treated as a continuation of politics by other means. Although the Court never had the opportunity to say so clearly, it took the view that the problem of rearmament was essentially political and that the objections the Socialists raised against the treaty of Paris on January 31, and July 7, 1952 were intended to foist onto the Court responsibilities that it was not meant to assume. The judges first found a legal reason for not giving a decision: they were incompetent to rule as to the constitutional character of a measure that had not yet gone through all the legislative stages. They then procrastinated in replying to President Heuss's request of June 12, for an advisory opinion, until they were obliged by a false step of the Chancellor's to adopt a more definite attitude and fix a date for their reply. At

Adenauer's instigation, the government parties appealed to the Court to pronounce against the opposition's insistence that the ratification of the treaty required a two-thirds majority. This was justifiable in theory but had an air of sharp practice that exasperated the Court, as the article under which the complaint was brought was one designed to protect a minority group against the abuse of power by a majority. When President Heuss at the last moment withdrew his request for an advisory opinion, his decision seems to have come as a relief to the Court, which continued to abstain from pronouncing on the EDC, though it rejected the government's plea on March 7, 1953. The action of the French Assembly in killing the treaty on August 30, 1954 relieved the Court of considerable embarrassment.

The Court's attitude over the "Article 131" cases, although it attracted less attention, was in fact more significant. This article of the Basic Law provides that "the legal status of persons, including the refugees and expellees who were employed in the public service on May 8, 1945 and who have left service for reasons other than those based on civil service regulations, and who hitherto have not been employed or been in a position corresponding to their former one, shall be regulated by Federal legislation." Several provisions of the so-called 131 law of 1951 led to complaints from officials who considered that their basic rights had been infringed. These complaints were rejected by the Court in a judgment of December 17, 1953. Without going into the details of this award, which aroused much controversy, we should notice that it dealt at considerable length with two basic questions that have been touched on in the introduction to this work and in the previous chapter: the question of the continuity of the German State in 1933 and, again, in 1945. As regards 1945, the Court drew a subtle distinction between three ways in which the life of a state may suffer interruption: a change of regime (*Systemwechsel*), the disappearance or destruction of the state (*Staatsuntergang*), and its collapse (*Staatszusammenbruch*). This last conception makes it possible on the one hand to assert the continuity of the state and on the other to hold that all juridical links between the German Reich and the members of its civil service came to an end on May 8, 1945. But the Court went further than this: it gave a severe and fully documented description of the public service under the Nazi regime and concluded that the nature of the bond between the state and its officials had undergone a complete change in 1933 and that, from that year onward, the notion of established rights took on a completely different sense. The text of the Court's ruling of December 17, 1953 is a lesson on the nature of Nazism and a sort of definition in reverse of the function of the civil service in a democracy.

In other cases, the Court showed less firmness and more legalistic subtlety, as for instance over the Concordat. When the educational law of Lower Saxony was promulgated on September 14, 1954, the Federal Government took exception to eleven of its articles and requested the Court to pronounce that "the *Land* . . . by disregarding the Concordat of July 20, 1933 between the Holy See and the German Reich, had infringed the right of the Federal Government to require that the *Länder* conform to the terms of international treaties to which the government is a party." The matter was debated on June 4–8, 1956 and again on March 26, 1957; the second *Senat* rejected the

Federal Government's complaint, but in such a way as to give victory to neither side. On the one hand, it ruled—against the opinion of many jurists of a Socialist turn of mind—that the Concordat had never ceased to be valid; but, on the other hand, it declared, after a long and subtle argumentation, that the Basic Law imposed no obligations on the *Länder* in educational matters. The Federal Government and the Vatican were left to find a way out of this paradoxical situation, the upshot of which was that, in February, 1965, a separate Concordat was concluded between Lower Saxony and the Holy See.

One of the Court's more spectacular decisions was that of February 28, 1961, in which it overruled the government's proposal to create a second television network. In chapter 9, we shall consider the theoretical and practical importance of the wide interpretation thus given by the Court to Article 5 of the Basic Law regarding freedom of opinion and information.

The Court has frequently intervened in electoral or quasi-electoral matters. In August, 1958, it condemned the Social Democratic opposition, which then controlled the *Land* governments of Hesse, Bremen, and Hamburg, for organizing referendums on the question of atomic armaments: a party must not misuse regional institutions to achieve its objectives on the national level. In January, 1957, it pronounced in favor of the Federal legislature and against two small parties that had appealed to it against the restrictive clauses of the law governing elections to the legislature. On several occasions, on the other hand, it annulled clauses of municipal electoral laws that discriminated in favor of national parties and against candidates representing purely local interests.

Last but not least, the Court has intervened directly in politics by using its right under Article 21 of the Basic Law, which we shall study in more detail later, to pass judgment on political parties. In October, 1952, it declared the extreme right-wing *Sozialistische Reichspartei* (SRP) to be illegal, and on August 17, 1956 it outlawed the Communist Party in a reasoned judgment that covers over 300 pages of the volume recording the Court's decisions. In June, 1958, it ruled that private donations to parties were not deductible for income tax purposes, and in June, 1966 it declared that state subsidies to parties, which as we shall see had been granted in large quantity, were illegal. However, it permitted the state to assist electoral campaigns on a large scale, with the funds allotted to a given party to be proportional to the votes obtained by it. In December, 1968, the percentage of votes a party had to secure to qualify for this form of bounty was reduced by legislative action, at the Court's behest, from 2·5 to 0·5. This ruling caused a good deal of uneasiness: the government and parliament, and not they alone, felt that the Court had taken a further step in a dangerous direction by going into details that were hardly in its province, and that it should have confined itself to laying down principles and seeing that they were respected. As has happened so often in the United States, the press raised the warning of "government by judges," and the Court's prestige was seriously affected.

Its reputation has also been harmed by the frequent revision of its statute. On December 11, 1969, the Federal Government produced the draft of a "fourth amendment to the law on the Federal Constitutional Court," which embodied the practice of the U.S. Supreme Court whereby judges in the minority on a particular issue furnish dissenting opinion explaining the reasons for their vote. The draft—adopted by the Bundestag in first reading on March 13, 1970—also provided that all the judges would be elected for a period of twelve years, without the possibility of re-election; and it modified the rule as to the retroactive legal consequences of the annulment of laws or decisions by the Court. In addition, there were reported to be a whole series of proposals for minor changes in the Court's procedure.

Despite this, it remains true that the Court is the most noteworthy of the Federal Republic's institutions, especially as compared, for example, with Great Britain, where no need is felt to codify or interpret the rules on which public life is based, or France, where the Constitutional Council has a minor role and the task of "ensuring respect for the constitution" is entrusted to the President of the Republic, himself elected by a political majority.

6

Political Institutions

PRINCIPLES, rights, and prohibitions are not enough: a state must have institutions to enable it to function and develop as a political entity. The system provided by the Basic Law has undergone amendments and modifications since 1949 and has had its share of criticism, but on the whole it has evolved smoothly and without crises. One point, however, gave rise to a problem at the outset—namely, the choice of the Federal capital; and after twenty-one years, it is still not clear whether Berlin is a part of the West German Republic.

Bonn was finally chosen as the provisional capital after two very close votes in the Bundestag on September 30 and November 3, 1949, the outcome being partly due to pressure of a somewhat unedifying kind. As a result, the Federal parliament and administrative bodies were located in a small town, pleasant enough but far from central, and lacking most of the necessary facilities for setting up offices, installing a large telephone system, and housing members of parliament and administrative officials. Bonn was chosen by a very narrow margin in preference to Frankfurt, a large city in the middle of West Germany and an important rail and road center, which had been the capital of Bizonia since 1947. Historically, Bonn stood for the old romantic Germany composed of small states, while Frankfurt was a symbol both of industrial and commercial progress and of the liberal and democratic movement for Germany's unification that began in 1848. No doubt the vote might have fallen out differently but for the fact that a Socialist government was in power in Hesse, of which Frankfurt is the chief town, and that Dr. Adenauer, the CDU candidate for the chancellorship, was a citizen of the village of Rhöndorf, situated a few miles from Bonn. But the strongest argument in favor of the university town on the Rhine lay in its very inadequacy, which served to underline the provisional character of the Federal Republic: Frankfurt, by contrast, might have given the impression of being a real capital, whereas this right belonged to Berlin alone.

As regards the status of Berlin, the Federal Republic of Germany* was faced from the outset with an Allied veto it has never accepted. Article 1 of the West Berlin constitution of September 1, 1950 states that:

1. Berlin is a city and also a German *Land.*
2. Berlin is a *Land* of the Federal Republic of Germany.
3. The Basic Law and other legislation of the FRG applies to Berlin.

* *Bundesrepublik Deutschland:* English abbreviation, FRG.

93

However, the drafters of this constitution (which ignores the partition of Berlin, considering it null and void) were obliged by the veto of the Allied powers to suspend the application of paragraphs 2 and 3, and Article 87 states as a temporary provision that the Berlin Assembly may "pass a law recognizing that a law of the Federal Republic applies to Berlin without modification." Under Allied pressure, the Parliamentary Council was forced to agree that Berlin should not take part in Federal elections, that its Assembly should only send delegates to Bonn, and that although the delegates would sit in the Bundestag they would have no voting rights. But from 1949 to 1957, the notion of Berlin as the true capital of Germany was constantly reaffirmed, and West Berlin was in practice more and more assimilated to the status of a *Land* of the Federal Republic, though without prejudice to the rights of the occupying powers and the quadripartite control that still existed on paper.[1]

Since 1954, Berlin has been the venue for the election of the President of the Republic, and a certain number of Federal bodies are permanently located there, including, as we have seen, the supreme Administrative Court. The Bundestag occasionally meets in Berlin, as it did for the inauguration of its third session on October 15, 1957. Dr. Adenauer and his party had to show firmness in rejecting, in the previous February, proposals of the Socialist opposition for the permanent transfer of the Federal authorities to Berlin. On the other hand, in 1953 Adenauer himself took into his government a Berlin representative, Robert Tillmanns. In the Bundesrat, the chamber that represents the *Länder*, the Mayor of Berlin became President for the first time in 1957 (under the annual rotating system), though he does not, properly speaking, possess a vote. The Berlin delegates to the Bundestag do not vote on laws, but they take part in all debates and vote at committee sessions. In Berlin itself, the application of Federal laws is enacted with less and less formality. Originally, the Assembly adopted without change each measure as it was passed by the Bonn legislature; the next phase was to adopt by a single vote all Federal measures on the day's agenda; finally, Federal laws were simply promulgated by the Mayor of Berlin without any intervention by the city legislature.

The distinction may at times give the impression of hairsplitting: Berlin delegates take part in electing the President of the Republic, not always without conflict, as in 1959 when Gerhard Schröder, then Federal Minister of the Interior, opposed their right to do so. They likewise have a say in electing the President of the Bundestag, but can cast only a symbolic vote when it comes to electing the Federal Chancellor. In November, 1966, a move was made to abolish this limitation, but the U.S. Ambassador at once interposed the 1949 veto on behalf of the three occupying powers. In consequence, the result of the election was announced as follows by the President of the Bundestag, whose own election had involved only a single ballot:

"Number of votes cast: 473, plus 22 by Berlin deputies, total 495; one invalid vote.

"Number of affirmative votes: 340, plus 16 by Berlin deputies, total 356 members of the Assembly.

"Number of negative votes: 109, plus 3 by Berlin deputies, total 112 members of the Assembly.

"Number of blank votes: 23, plus 3 by Berlin deputies, total 26 members of the Assembly.

"Thus the number of votes in favor of Dr. Kiesinger, counting those from Berlin, is 356. Even if the Berlin votes are not counted, the result is the same, since the total of 340 votes is well in excess of the figure of 249, which represents an absolute majority of deputies other than those from Berlin."

In October, 1969, the Social Democrats again sought to ensure Willy Brandt's victory by having the Berlin votes, with their Socialist majority, included in the count, but they soon desisted from the attempt. Only six months before, Klaus Schütz, the SPD Mayor of West Berlin, had once again had occasion to recognize the sovereignty of the occupying powers by requesting them to ban the local branch of the National Democratic Party (NPD).

A Federal State

Difficulties of another kind arose over the integration of the Saar, which politically became a *Land* like the others on January 1, 1957 and was assimilated into the economy between that date and July, 1959. But at the very beginning, in 1949, the Federal Republic was confronted with what seemed a basic structural problem: the lack of ethnic and cultural unity of most of its constituent *Länder* and their irrationality from the economic and administrative standpoint.

Article 118 of the Basic Law as approved by the occupying powers envisaged the formation of a southwestern *Land*. After many setbacks and lengthy negotiations in which the occupation authorities took a major part, the *Land* of Baden-Württemberg was created in 1952: it comprised the former territories of Baden, Württemberg-Baden, and Württemberg-Hohenzollern, and thus reduced the number of *Länder* in the Federation from eleven to nine. The decision was based on a referendum in the territories concerned. The legitimacy of this method was contested by the *Land* government of Baden, whose opposition to the proposal for a *Südweststaat* was based primarily on religious grounds: the population of Baden was 70 per cent Catholic, and the regime, which was under fairly strong clerical influence, feared the influence of Protestant Württemberg in the new state. It might have been possible to avoid combining two regions with such different traditions by forming two new *Länder*—Württemberg and Greater Baden—instead of only one, out of the three set up in 1945. But the partisans of the *Südweststaat* urged the necessity of creating in the southern part of the Federal Republic, alongside Bavaria, a second counterweight to North Rhine-Westphalia, which, with its 14 million inhabitants and its industrial potential, had become—as the politicians of other *Länder* put it—"the Prussia of the new Germany." The constitution of the new *Land*, the name of which was only settled after long debate, entered into force in November, 1953.

The long and detailed Article 29 of the Basic Law went much further, since it envisaged a complete reorganization of the Federal territory "with due regard to regional unity, historical and cultural connections, economic expediency, and social structure," especially in regard to areas transferred from one *Land* to another after the German surrender. The military governors, in their letter of approval of the Basic Law, stipulated that no effect should be given to

95

this article until a peace treaty was signed. In point of fact, it became legally applicable when the High Commission was abolished in May, 1955. By that time, however, ten years had elapsed since the reorganization of German territory by the occupying powers, people had grown accustomed to the new boundaries, and it seemed unlikely that they would or could be altered. In November, 1955, after a commission presided over by Dr. Hans Luther (a former Reich Chancellor) had sat for three years and produced a voluminous report, the Federal Minister of the Interior declared it was not essential for any reorganization to take place. However, recourse was had to the procedure whereby a territorial change might be made if 10 per cent of the electorate in a given area expressed a wish to that effect by signing a special register, and if Federal legislation in accordance with their wishes was subsequently ratified by a referendum, in which an absolute majority was required.

The time limit prescribed by the constitution expired at the beginning of 1956, by which time fourteen applications had been made. In September, 1956, 15 per cent of Baden voters expressed a wish for the dissolution of Baden-Württemberg. In April, 13·4 per cent of the half-million electors of the Oldenburg district (*Verwaltungsbezirk*) of Lower Saxony voted, chiefly on confessional grounds ,for their territory to be made into a separate *Land*. The greatest number of applications related to the *Land* of Rhineland-Palatinate, the abolition of which had been recommended by the Luther commission. In the districts where over 10 per cent voted for a change, votes of 20·3 and 25·4 per cent were cast for union with Hesse and 14·2 per cent for Rhineland-Westphalia, while, in the southern part of the *Land*, 7·6 per cent desired a merger with Bavaria and 9·3 per cent with Baden-Württemberg.

In the end, the procedure laid down in Article 29 proved so intricate that none of the changes were carried out. But the problem of *Land* boundaries recurred from time to time, and on July 2, 1969, despite government misgivings, the Bundestag adopted a revised version of Article 29 in seven long paragraphs, prescribing stricter time limits for the various procedural stages. It was laid down, for instance, that wherever a popular initiative received a sufficient number of votes, a referendum should be held before March 31, 1975, or June 30, 1970 for the Baden area of Baden-Württemberg. However, on June 7, 1970, 1·3 million voters in Baden opted for the continued existence of the present *Land*, as against only an 18 per cent vote for separation.

The uncertainty as to their boundaries did not prevent the *Länder* from having a genuine political existence: the Federation (in German, *Bund*) is truly federal—less so than the United States, where the central power is much weaker in relation to the individual states, but much more so than France or Britain. The *Länder* existed before the *Bund*, and each of them already had a government and a *Landtag* when the Federal institutions were set up. Accordingly, the Basic Law declares in Article 30 that "the exercise of the powers of the state (*staatliche Befugnisse*) and the performance of state functions shall be the concern of the *Länder*," though this is at once qualified by the words "insofar as this Basic Law does not otherwise prescribe or permit." The scope of this reservation limits the importance of regional politics, but they are not negligible and may sometimes appear to offer a better field than Bonn for the achievement of personal ambitions. Of course, it is less impressive to be a

Landtag deputy than a member of the Bundestag, and there is no doubt that it is a political promotion to move up from one assembly to the other. But some functions are less easy to evaluate in terms of relative prestige and influence. A *Land* minister may think it worth while to surrender his portfolio in order to become a member of the Bonn parliament: a case in point is Helmut Schmidt, who was Senator (i.e. Minister) of the Interior at Hamburg when elected to the Bundestag in 1965. On the other hand, a Federal minister may leave Bonn to become a Minister-President (Prime Minister) in his own *Land*, as did Heinrich Hellwege of Lower Saxony in 1955. In the first case, the ambition to carve out a political career on the national plane provided a motive for accepting a temporary loss of power; the exchange proved well justified, as Schmidt became chairman of the parliamentary SPD in December, 1966 and Federal Defense Minister in October, 1969. As regards Hellwege, the portfolio of Bundesrat affairs was an unimportant one and it was more tempting for the leader of a small party (the *Deutsche Partei*), to exercise power in and from Hanover. The calculation, however, proved wrong: the Socialists returned to power in Lower Saxony in 1959 and Hellwege's political career came to an end.

There have also been cases of a switch from *Land* to Federal politics and back again, or vice versa. Thus Klaus Schütz, who in 1954 became a member of the Berlin Assembly at the age of twenty-eight, went to Bonn in 1957 as a deputy to the Bundestag; in 1961, he was a Berlin Senator; in December, 1966, *Staatssekretär* (State Secretary, similar to a deputy minister) for Foreign Affairs at Bonn; and, finally, governing Mayor of Berlin from October, 1967. The most striking case is that of Kurt Georg Kiesinger, who in 1958 became Minister-President of Baden-Württemberg in disappointment at being kept out of the Federal Government by Adenauer although he was chairman of the foreign affairs committee and a party spokesman of long standing. Thanks to his success in *Land* politics and the fact that, being at Stuttgart, he was not involved in the intrigues of Bonn, he became in 1966 the CDU candidate for the office of Federal Chancellor, to which he was in fact elected. Again, in 1970 it became known that Gerhard Stoltenberg, a Federal minister till October, 1969, was returning to Schleswig-Holstein as *Land* Prime Minister, with the hope of a comeback at the highest level to Bonn.

Political forces vary from one *Land* to another, and so in consequence do majorities and governments. The situation in a *Land* may be influenced by that at Bonn: Adenauer, though a defender of "state rights" in Rhineland politics, tried more than once to secure the election of *Land* governments patterned on the coalition he himself directed. In the Federal elections of September, 1953, the CDU received an absolute majority of votes in Baden-Württemberg, which was governed at the time by a Socialist-Liberal coalition. The Minister-President, Reinhold Maier, thereupon resigned on the ground that his team had clearly lost the confidence of the electorate. This led to an all-party coalition and to the disappearance of a regular opposition. Maier's action, while creditable in itself, created a very dubious precedent. A similar situation arose in Bavaria after the Federal elections of September 15, 1957 as the CDU, which was not represented in the *Land* government, scored 57·2 per cent of the votes. At first it was vigorously contended that Federal and *Land* politics were two different things; but, a month later, the CSU (corresponding in Bavaria to the CDU) was sharing power at Munich with part of the former coalition, while the Socialists were relegated to the opposition. The formation of the Grand Coalition on the Federal level in December, 1966 favored the creation or survival of similar *Land* governments, and its breakup led to the dissolution of the coalition government of Lower Saxony in February, 1970.

Similarly, *Landtag* elections are often treated, by electorate and politicians alike, as though they were Federal elections held within the confines of a single *Land*, with no purpose other than to reflect or influence Federal politics. Nevertheless, the political differences between one *Land* and another are very pronounced, as will be seen from a glance at the variety of parliamentary majorities.

From the outset, the three principal parties in the F.R.G. were at one and the same time associates and adversaries, a fact that had two important consequences. To begin with, the antagonism between the SPD and the CDU, lively though it was at Bonn, did not degenerate into an irreconcilable conflict. Second, although the SPD was out of office at the Federal level till 1966, this did not mean that it was wholly deprived of important political responsibilities. Its leaders had a chance to show and exercise their abilities in the *Land* capitals, and the party militants were not tempted to regard themselves as a foreign body within the political system.

At the beginning of 1970, the composition of the *Landtage* was as follows:

Länder	Majority	Opposition
Baden-Württemberg	60 CDU; 37 SPD	18 FDP; 12 NPD
Bavaria	110 CSU	79 SPD; 14 NPD
Bremen	50 SPD; 10 FDP	32 CDU; 8 NPD
Hamburg	74 SPD	38 CDU; 8 FDP
Hesse	52 SPD	26 CDU; 10 FDP; 10 NPD
Lower Saxony	66 SPD; 63 CDU	10 FDP; 10 NPD
North Rhine–Westphalia	99 SPD; 15 FDP	86 CDU
Rhineland–Palatinate	49 CDU; 8 FDP	39 SPD; 4 NPD
Saar	25 CDU; 4 FDP	21 SPD
Schleswig–Holstein	35 CDU; 3 FDP	30 SPD; 4 NPD
Berlin	81 SPD; 9 FDP	47 CDU

Proceedings in the *Landtage* are generally uneventful, and governments are, with few exceptions, stable. Often the governing team remains the same for years on end—at least, this frequently happened in the past, and there is still the case of Helmut Lemke, who has been Minister-President of Schleswig-Holstein since 1955. However, the great generation of postwar *Landesväter*, or patriarchal rulers of the *Länder*, has now left the political scene, its successors belonging for the most part not to the next generation but to the next but one (a state of affairs we shall later consider in a wider context). For instance, in 1965, Wilhelm Kaisen, then aged seventy-eight, relinquished power in Bremen, and, after a two year interim, the city elected as its mayor Hans

Koschnick, aged thirty-eight. Georg August Zinn was Minister-President of Hesse from 1950 till April, 1969, when he had a heart attack at the age of sixty-eight; he was succeeded that October by Albert Osswald, aged fifty and thus appreciably senior to Helmut Kohl at Mainz (Rhineland-Palatinate), who, in May, 1969, became Minister-President at thirty-nine, succeeding Peter Altmeier, the incumbent since 1947.

As a rule, the *Land* governments order their affairs conscientiously and efficiently, despite the frequent problems created by their relations with Bonn in the fields of administration, legislation, and finance, not to mention coordination with one another. The need for consultation with the Federal authorities has involved the creation of innumerable agencies. The North Rhine–Westphalia Ministry of the Interior, to name only one, is represented on about sixty *Bund-Länder* commissions dealing with matters within its competence.[2] The obscurities of Section VIII of the Basic Law incessantly give rise to tension between Federal and *Land* agencies, and this produces a curious result at the local level: the municipalities, the range of whose powers would make a French *maire* green with envy, often enjoy better relations with the distant Federal ministry than they do with the nearby *Land* authorities. The Federal Government thus tends to appear in the role of protector of the municipal liberties guaranteed, by Article 28 of the Basic Law, against encroachment on the part of the *Länder*, who for their part accuse Bonn of trespassing on their responsibilities.

Under Section VII of the Basic Law, three types of legislation are distinguished: the *Länder* are competent in all fields other than those of "exclusive" and "concurrent" legislation as defined in the Basic Law. The Federation has the exclusive right to legislate on eleven main subjects, including foreign affairs, nationality, currency, customs, Federal railways and air traffic, post and telecommunications, trademarks, copyrights, and publishing rights, Federal-*Land* cooperation in criminal police matters and the protection of the constitution, the establishment of a Federal office of criminal police, and measures against international crime. "In the field of exclusive legislation of the Federation, the *Länder* shall have powers of legislation only if, and so far as, they are expressly so empowered in the Federal law" (Article 71). Article 72 states that:

1. In the field of concurrent legislation, the *Länder* shall have powers of legislation so long and so far as the Federation makes no use of its legislative right.
2. The Federation shall have legislative rights in this field in so far as a necessity for regulation by Federal law exists because:
  1. a matter cannot be effectively regulated by the legislation of individual *Länder*, or
  2. the regulation of a matter by a *Land* law could prejudice the interests of the other *Länder* or of the *Länder* as a whole, or
  3. the preservation of legal or economic unity demands it, in particular the preservation of uniformity of living conditions extending beyond the territory of an individual *Land*.

Among the twenty-three subjects of varying importance to which concurrent legislation applies are: civil and criminal law and the organization of the

99

courts and the legal profession; matters of civil status; the right of association and assembly; matters relating to refugees and expellees; war damage and compensation; economic and labor legislation; the promotion of scientific research; transfer of land and resources to public ownership; and "prevention of the abuse of economic power" (anticartel legislation). From a French or British point of view, one is struck by the extent of authority vested in the *Länder*—for instance, as regards criminal law; while, by American standards, the powers enjoyed by the Federation are extremely wide.

In point of fact, the trend toward centralization from 1949 onward was necessary and was kept within proper bounds: the Federal legislators brought order into a system that had grown intricate and obscure, especially in all matters relating to the consequences of the war, such as compensation and the integration of refugees. Using the power, conferred by Article 75 in certain very limited fields, to issue "general provisions" (*Rahmenvorschriften*), they passed a number of "outline laws" laying down general principles for the *Länder* to translate into detailed provisions—a device that considerably reduced the freedom of action of the *Landtage*.

The privileged domain of the *Länder*, however, in which they enjoy full sovereignty in principle, is that of cultural and educational matters, including teaching on all levels, and relations with the churches (though in respect to culture, the municipalities also have wide powers). The provision in Article 32 (3) of the Basic Law that "insofar as the *Länder* are competent to legislate, they may, with the approval of the Federal Government, conclude treaties with foreign states" is applicable in this field, an example being the Concordat concluded by Lower Saxony;[3] while the controversy over the teaching of French illustrates the emptiness of cultural agreements concluded by the Federation without the concurrence of the *Länder*: in a 1955 convention, France and the Federal Republic undertook to promote the teaching of each other's language; but, in most parts of Germany, English was in fact taught as the first foreign language in secondary schools, and the convention brought about no change in this state of affairs. In reply to French protests, the Federal Government has always pointed out that it has no power over the *Land* governments in this matter. Such is the penalty incurred by France for its opposition, after 1945, to the creation of a central power in Germany. The procedure finally adopted for Franco-German cultural negotiations is noteworthy: apart from liaison between the directors of cultural affairs in the respective foreign ministries, a treaty of January 22, 1963 provides for regular contacts between the French Minister of National Education and a German Minister-President specially empowered to represent the *Länder*. Until 1966, the minister in question was Kurt Georg Kiesinger of Baden-Württemberg, which in part explains Paris's favorable reaction when he became Federal Chancellor in that year; subsequently, the role was taken over by Heinz Kühn of North Rhine–Westphalia.

Coordination of the eleven educational systems within the Federal Republic is more or less achieved by the "permanent conference of ministers of education" (*Kultusminister*). Its secretariat—the only part of the institution that is in fact permanent—has no power to take decisions, for which full dress agreements are needed. Thus, on April 10, 1968, the ministers met in extraordinary session—it was in fact their 122nd plenary meeting—to adopt a long series of "directives [*Leitlinien*] for an up-to-date code of law concerning universities and the structural reform of higher education."[4] These directives did not succeed in obviating profound differences between the laws drafted or enacted in the various *Länder* as an answer to the crisis in university life. It should in fairness be added that the universities themselves enjoy considerable independence of the *Land* governments, so that coordination between them is effected not by ministers but through a "conference of rectors."

There is, however, a movement to limit the absolute sovereignty of the *Länder* in cultural matters, and this finds expression both in public opinion and in actual practice. Despite valuable experiments in teaching methods and school reform, particularly in Hesse and Hamburg, there have been many complaints of the indifference of the *Länder* to the needs of intellectual, scientific, and artistic development, not to mention their difficulty in finding the necessary resources. Even if they do find them, there is a clear risk of wasted investment due to excess of competition and lack of coordination. Sufficient warning of what can happen in this respect is afforded by the Swiss *cantons* and the new African states.

From the outset, the Federal Government attempted to whittle down some of the powers of the *Länder*, particularly in the Ministry of the Interior and, after 1953, of the newly created Ministry of Family Affairs, whose functions were later extended to cover youth problems in general. More important was the creation in 1962, at the time of the reshuffle due to the *Spiegel* affair, of the Ministry for Scientific Research, which became increasingly active after 1965 under Gerhard Stoltenberg, a young CDU minister with a large following in his party and an industrial background that made him responsive to the demands for technological development. In October, 1969, he was succeeded by Professor Hans Leussink, who has tended to emphasize the role of his ministry vis-à-vis the *Länder* by exerting pressure on the latter's governments rather than directly on the ministers of education.

By a "state agreement" (*Staatsabkommen*) concluded at Königstein on February 19, 1959, the Federation and the *Länder* undertook to share equally the cost of subsidizing the German Research Community (*Deutsche Forschungsgemeinschaft*) and the research institutes controlled by the Max Planck Association. An "administrative agreement" (*Verwaltungsabkommen*) of June 4, 1964 was renewed and extended by a further agreement of February 8, 1968, which markedly increased the Federation's share in university and scientific development. Two years later, on February 13, 1970, Chancellor Willy Brandt and the Minister-Presidents agreed to set up a working group to frame a uniform policy on education and training (*einheitliche Bildungspolitik*).

The 1968 agreement refers expressly to the proposed reform of the entire financial system of the Federal Republic: this was finally promulgated on May 12, 1969 and entered into force on January 1, 1970 as the twenty-first amendment to the constitution. An end was thus put to a dispute that had gone on for twenty years, the decision for a basic reform having been taken by the *Bund* and the *Länder* almost six years earlier. It had in fact been clear ever since the first year of the Republic's life that Section X of the Basic Law did not regulate in a satisfactory manner the distribution of revenues between the *Bund* and the *Länder* or among the *Länder* themselves, some of which were much wealthier than others. The occupying powers had done their best, in particular by their memorandum of March 2, 1949, to prevent the creation of a Federal financial administration. Under Section X, the collection of income and corporation taxes was a matter for the *Länder*, which were to turn over an unspecified proportion of this revenue to the *Bund*: by subsequent laws and agreements, the proportion was fixed at amounts varying between 27 and 39 per cent. Among the *Länder*, an equalization system was fairly soon in operation whereby each *Land* received at least 94 per cent of the average total of tax receipts per head of population. (There were, however, frequent conflicts on specific points, for example, as regards the location of the registered offices of large companies.) This meant, for instance, that for the year 1967 the "rich" *Länder* had to provide DM1,600 million for distribution among the "poor." The former included North Rhine–Westphalia, Hesse, Baden-Württemberg, and, above all, Hamburg, where in 1967 the receipts per head from income and corporation taxes stood at an index of 193 and 234 respectively, counting the national average as 100 (whereas in Schleswig the figures were 79 and 35).[5] The "rich" *Länder* came, in the course of time, to see an advantage in making concessions to the "poor" so as to form a common front against the *Bund* and also to ward off a redrawing of *Land* boundaries, which would have been the most logical solution to the problem of inequality.

After much upheaval and many procedural delays, a constitutional amendment was enacted in 1969; it modified six articles of Section X and added a new section, VIIIa. This consisted of two articles defining the "joint responsibilities" (*Gemeinschaftsaufgaben*) of the *Bund* and the *Länder*, especially in the field of higher education and research. The rules for the allocation of revenue are still extremely complicated. The *Länder* receive the revenue from income taxes, death duties, motor vehicles, and casinos, and also the beer tax, expressly mentioned in the new law (as it also was in 1949). The *Bund* receives *inter alia* the revenue from customs and taxes on consumption, except beer. Income and corporation tax receipts are divided equally between the *Bund* and the respective *Länder*. A Federal law is to determine, in accordance with principles laid down in the Basic Law, the allocation of receipts from the turnover tax, account being taken of the rights of municipalities.

The revised law does not completely resolve what has been seen to be a basic difficulty since 1967: how can the Federal Government oblige the *Länder* to conform to its economic policy in administering their own resources, particularly at a time of "stabilization"? But, in general, the reform reflects the same tendency as the development of the Ministry of Research: the trend in Germany is toward centralization, whereas in France, regionalism has become the order of the day. However, the two countries are so far apart in this that the respective tendencies would have to go on for a long time before their systems came to resemble each other at all closely.

The Presidents of the Republic

The *Länder* also play a direct part in the workings of Federal Government— chiefly through the Bundesrat, which represents the *Land* governments, but also in the election of the President of the Republic. This is carried out by secret ballot and without debate in the Federal Assembly (*Bundesversammlung*), a body that meets for this purpose only. At the first and second ballot, an absolute majority is required; at the third, a relative one is sufficient. One half of the Assembly consists of the members of the Bundestag—the lower house of the Federal parliament—and the other delegates from the *Landtage* (known as *Wahlmänner*). These are chosen by proportional representation, each *Landtag* electing a number corresponding to the population of the *Land*. This system was decided on because it was felt that the French method, whereby the President was elected by both legislative chambers, would give the Bundestag excessive weight as compared with the Bundesrat, which has only one-twelfth as many members. In actual fact, however, the system makes only a slight difference to the relative strength of the parties as reflected in the Bundestag, since the *Landtag* delegates do not attend the election (held at Berlin) as representatives of their *Länder* but as Christian Democrats, Socialists or Liberals. Nevertheless, if ever the voting were close, the difference could be sufficient to affect the election, as is seen from these figures for March, 1969 (which include the Berlin representatives):

Party	Deputies	Delegates	Total
CDU/CSU	252	230	482
SPD	217	232	449
FDP	49	34	83
NPD	0	22	22
Total	518	518	1036

The President's powers are extremely limited, as the drafters of the constitution were anxious to avoid what they regarded as one of the main defects of the Weimar system. He is elected for five years—two years less than in France or the Weimar Republic, but one year longer than the life of a parliament—and cannot be elected for more than two successive terms of office. His functions are more restricted than those of the presidents of the Third and Fourth French Republics: he does not preside over cabinet meetings and thus has no direct influence on government decisions. He does appoint the Chancellor, but his right to do so is limited, both in law and in practice, as compared with the situation in Italy or in the Fourth French Republic. In the first place, if the Bundestag does not accept the President's candidate, it may elect another Chancellor without reference to him, and, as we shall see, the President has no opportunity of making a second nomination. Second, as parliament is composed of large, well-disciplined groups, the President does not have the task of selecting a candidate among several who might, as far as voting strength goes, be equally capable of forming a coalition cabinet.

The role assigned to him by the constitution is that of a head of state who, like the British monarch, personifies the nation by performing duties of a largely symbolic character. The Basic Law lays down that the President shall represent the Federation for purposes of international law, conclude treaties with foreign states on its behalf, and receive and accredit envoys; he appoints and dismisses Federal judges and Federal officials and also (by an amendment of 1956) officers and noncommissioned officers. He exercises the right of pardon. But the main feature of his office, again as in Britain, is that it enables him to exercise personal influence, over and above any specific constitutional function. At the same time, legal provisions relating to the presidency have played a significant part, if only as subjects of controversy, in German political life during the tenure of the three men who have held office since 1949.

On September 12, 1949, as the result of an agreement between the CDU and the FDP, the Federal Assembly, which then consisted of 804 members, elected Theodor Heuss on the second ballot by 416 votes to 312, the rival candidate being Kurt Schumacher of the SPD. Five years later, on July 17, 1954, the three principal parties re-elected Heuss, for a second term. This time the full membership of the Assembly was 1,018, and of 986 votes cast, 871 went to him on the first ballot: his prestige was by then such that no one felt obliged, for the sake of principle, to put up a rival candidate. During his ten years at the Villa Hammerschmidt, he exerted a real influence on the tone of political life in the Republic. Some of his moves were unsuccessful, such as the proposal for a new national anthem. But his horror of pomp and rhetoric, his studied modesty and simplicity, and his sincere attachment to democracy soon caused the presidency to be accepted as an essentially civilian institution.

A native of Swabia, aged sixty-five at his election in 1949, Heuss spoke with the accent of his homeland and displayed all its geniality and sense of humor. He had studied art, history, and economics in his youth and in 1905 became the editor of a review owned by the philosopher, sociologist, and essayist Friedrich Naumann; his future wife, Elly Knapp, was also a disciple of Naumann, who was Heuss's friend as well as his preceptor.[6] A woman of great intelligence and humanity with a gift for organization, Frau Heuss was particularly active in the field of social welfare from 1949 until her death in 1952. From 1909 onward, Heuss belonged to liberal parties under the Empire and to the Liberal Democrats during the Weimar period. From 1912 to 1918, he edited the *Neckarzeitung* at Heilbronn, which he revived at Heidelberg in 1945 under the name of *Rhein-Neckar Zeitung*. He was a reader at the School of Political Sciences at Berlin from 1920 to 1933, and became a member of the Reichstag in 1924. He opposed Hitler, more especially in a book that was less outspoken than it might have been,[7] but voted for the Enabling Act on March 23, 1933. For a time, he wrote for the *Frankfurter Zeitung*, the last paper to display a spirit of cautious independence under the Nazis; later, he was forbidden to write and led a hand-to-mouth existence. In 1945–46 he was for some months Minister of Education in Württemberg-Baden. In 1947, he became professor of modern history and political science at the Stuttgart Technical Institute, the professorial title remaining with him for the rest of his life. From 1946 onward, he worked for the revival of the Liberal Party (FDP) and became its chairman, first in the U.S. zone and, in 1949, throughout Trizonia. He served on the Parliamentary Council as a representative of the *Landtag* at Stuttgart.

An intellectual even more than a statesman, the first President of the Republic was a profoundly cultivated man in the humanistic spirit of the eighteenth century; as his friend Albert Schweitzer once wrote to him, they both represented a culture that lay in ruins and of which few survivors were alive in the modern era.[8] As President, he won hearts as a plain man, careless of protocol, joking in gruff tones, and never seen without a cigar; he took trouble with his speeches, not for the sake of elegance but in order to get his message across clearly. As a political teacher, his constant aim was to call into being a new Germany that should turn its back on the Nazi past in an impulse of collective shame though not of collective guilt, while at the same time preserving the best elements of the culture of former days. His principal speeches, for instance at Bergen-Belsen where he spoke of the concentration camps, or on July 20, 1954, the tenth anniversary of the attempt on Hitler's life, are outstanding for their thought and style alike. Perhaps the most characteristic of all was a speech delivered at Hamburg on March 12, 1959 to 800 lieutenants and cadets of the new military academy: there, he not only displayed his usual humor and aversion to demagogy, but courageously told his audience that "the independent military history of Prussia and Germany is at an end" and that they should in future pay heed to the doctrine of Jean Jaurès, the French Socialist, regarding the "nation in arms." He added that it made him "freeze up" when anyone spoke of tradition in political or sentimental terms and, finally, he told his hearers to bear in mind that "a merry laugh is not a disciplinary offense."[9]

Fonder of ideas than of fighting, and preferring shades of meaning to downright statements, Heuss was the antithesis of Chancellor Adenauer, and neither of them would have been well qualified for the other's post. Their mutual relations were not always easy, particularly over the EDC crisis in December, 1952; they were frankly bad during the last few months of Heuss's second term, owing to the manner in which the Chancellor played with the dignity of the President's office.

To find a successor to Heuss was no easy matter, and he was even sounded out as to whether he would agree to serve for a third term, for which it would have been necessary to amend the constitution. The only statesman with comparable gifts of mind, culture, and tolerance without cynicism was no doubt Carlo Schmid, and many looked in his direction; he was a Social Democrat, but not a "party boss," and had shown impartiality in the role of Vice-President of the Bundestag. But the CDU was determined to vindicate its claim to the topmost office in the state, especially after the electoral triumph of 1957, which had given it an absolute majority. The party's first choice fell on Heinrich Krone, a former *Zentrum* leader and chairman of the parliamentary CDU, but he refused. The Chancellor, for his part, wanted to make use of the presidency to remove from the ranks of his own potential successors a man he judged incapable of shouldering the responsibility of power—namely, the Vice-Chancellor and Minister of the Economy, Ludwig Erhard, the "father of the economic miracle." To appoint Erhard to the presidency would be the most honorific way of placing him on the shelf. On February 24, 1959, the CDU decided to put him forward as their candidate, but on March 3 he refused the nomination after a stormy interview with the Chancellor. On

April 5, the party set up a nomination committee to make recommendations to the Chancellor, but it then suddenly became known that Dr. Adenauer was entering the lists himself. His decision, taken in solitude and communicated to President Heuss by telephone, was ratified by the party on the following day.

The frequent uncomplimentary, not to say insulting remarks that the Chancellor let fall concerning Erhard left little room for doubt as to his motives, which were summed up in a cartoon in the Paris *Express* on April 16. This showed Adenauer smiling at his friend de Gaulle, who held by the hand a little Prime Minister in short trousers, and saying: "Soon I'll have a Debré of my very own." In a radio speech, Adenauer informed the nation that the President's job was a much bigger one than was generally supposed—an observation that Heuss, not surprisingly, considered lacking in tact. The Chancellor then departed on a vacation. To the journalists who came to see him off, he displayed a copy of the Basic Law, which, he said, was to be his holiday reading. Having (presumably) studied it, he discovered the unwelcome fact that if he became President he would not be in a position to appoint whomever he liked as Chancellor. Say, for example, that he were to nominate the Finance Minister, Franz Etzel: it would only need the abstention of a few CDU deputies to deprive Etzel of an absolute majority, and the parliamentary CDU would then be free to elect Erhard to the chancellorship regardless of the presidential wishes. Such were the terms of the constitution. On June 6— with the meeting of the Federal Assembly three weeks ahead—Adenauer withdrew his candidature for the presidency.[10]

At the last moment, the CDU produced a candidate who, while he aroused no special enthusiasm, had no enemies and many friends—the Minister of Agriculture, Heinrich Lübke. He was elected on July 1, at the second ballot, by 526 votes against 386 for Professor Carlo Schmid (SPD), 99 for Dr. Becker (FDP), and 22 abstentions. In a broadcast just before the election, Heuss explained why he had not been willing to stand for re-election on the basis of an amendment to the constitution: "It is not just an old man's need for a rest. Nor is it a desire on my part to shirk responsibilities that I have always accepted within the limits that the law permits. No, I want you to see the handing over of the presidency as an educative process for the benefit of the ordinary citizens. . . . Many years ago I expressed the idea by saying that democracy is leadership with a time limit [*Heerschaft auf Frist*]." The allusion to the Chancellor was subtle, but clear enough.

Lübke's presidency opened in difficult circumstances. The Chancellor had dealt a blow to the prestige of the office, and Heuss's personal aura had departed with him. For many months afterward, almost till his death on December 12, 1963, the ex-President (*Altbundespräsident*) was, with his own consent, received everywhere—at assemblies and rallies of German organizations of all kinds, in Paris, Israel, and India—as if he were still the representative of the Federal Republic, a second President as it were. Gradually, however, the modest dignity of his successor won the respect of his fellow citizens. An active member of farmers' organizations in his youth, Lübke had represented the *Zentrum* in the Prussian *Landtag* from 1931 to 1933; he was arrested on April 1, 1933 when Hitler dissolved the *Deutsche Bauernschaft*, a peasants' organization of which he was secretary-general, and was again imprisoned for twenty months in 1934–35. As President, he was given due credit for his soberly-worded speeches, and it was not held against him that he did not write them himself or deliver them as effectively as his predecessor. The most striking of them, imbued with a high moral standard and thoroughgoing condemnation of the past, was delivered at Bergen-Belsen on April 25, 1965, the twentieth anniversary of the Allies' discovery of the concentration camp and the liberation of its few survivors.

A year or so earlier, on July 1, 1964, Lübke had been re-elected at the first ballot by 710 votes out of 1,024. The FDP candidate received 123; the SPD voted for Lübke in the belief that he was in favor of a "grand coalition" that would enable them to achieve power.[11] The coalition was in fact formed two years later, after the President—more outspokenly than befited his office— had expressed the hope that the CDU and SPD might join forces. In so doing, he gave a handle to criticism, but in other ways he made more legitimate attempts to exercise his limited powers to the full. According to the constitution, senior officials are appointed by the President, and so are Federal ministers (on the Chancellor's advice). Is the President entitled to reject the Chancellor's nominees? In the Fourth French Republic, this question was not dealt with in legal terms: the President could exercise behind-the-scenes influence on nominations to important posts, which were then endorsed by the Council of Ministers under his chairmanship, and he had no hesitation in advising the Prime Minister as to the choice of his cabinet. In Britain, the sovereign has no specific right of decision, but in 1945 Attlee's choice of Ernest Bevin as Foreign Secretary instead of Hugh Dalton was apparently due to the fact that George VI had discreetly suggested the change. However, when Lübke refused to sign the appointment of a certain Federal judge and when he tried to prevent Gerhard Schröder from keeping the foreign affairs portfolio in 1965, he was accused by the great majority of legal experts and journalists of attempting to violate the constitution. Their attitude owed something to memories of Weimar and also to suspicions of Gaullism, the French President being just then highly unpopular in West Germany. The main reason, however, was that at the time when Lübke thus sought to influence the political game he was becoming gravely discredited for other reasons, both personal and political.

In the first place, his "style" had completely altered. His modesty had turned into conceit: he insisted on deciding everything and talking about everything, and was less and less disposed to allow others to write his speeches. Unfortunately, his technique as an orator went from bad to worse, with *gaffes* and solecisms at every turn. His slips, truisms, and general lack of education made him a laughingstock; and his compatriots were indignant when they heard that during the many foreign trips he was fond of undertaking, the diplomats had to exert all their skill to prevent his behavior at official functions from creating serious incidents. It was less an occasion for anger than for ridicule when he refused a formal request from the French Government to agree to the modest purple ribbon of the *palmes académiques* being conferred on Klara Fassbinder, an author and the translator of Claudel who was also a bellicose old lady of leftish views and a fanatical champion of pacifist causes of all kinds.

The second main reason for Lübke's unpopularity was connected with his past life. As usual in such cases, the first accusations, with supporting documents, emanated from the German Democratic Republic.[12] Lübke, it was alleged, had been imprisoned not on political grounds but for swindling. What was more, in the architect's office where he worked during the war, he had designed barracks for concentration camps. The charges swelled in volume during 1967; the President denied them all, but did not sue anyone for libel. In a televised address on March 1, 1968, he defended himself in highly infelicitous terms. His chief accuser, Henri Nannen, the editor-in-chief of the illustrated weekly *Stern*, attacked with redoubled virulence: "He may deserve our pity, but certainly no longer our respect."[13] Most of the President's fellow politicians kept silent; the few who took up arms in his defense recalled that in 1925 his predecessor Friedrich Ebert had been slandered and had died fighting his slanderers.

The affair was undignified on both sides. If Lübke had been a man of moral stature he would have said on television: "Yes, I did sometimes compromise with the Nazis. So did everyone else who wanted to stay alive during those twelve years. That is why you see me here as the representative of the German people, who, like all other peoples, were less than 100 per cent heroic, but are trying to make up for their past weakness by leading as democratic a life as possible." As for Nannen, he increased the discredit of the presidency by refusing to treat it, if not the President himself, with the deference which in other countries, and particularly France, the law enforces (to what may seem an excessive degree).

The upshot was that, on October 14, 1968 the President announced not that he was retiring, but that the election of his successor would be advanced so as to take place the following spring. The official reason for this was not devoid of substance: the President's term was due to expire at the same time as that of parliament, and the coincidence of the two elections would have the unhealthy effect of tending to "politicize" the contest for the presidency. In the event, however, this was not avoided. The new President did not take up his duties until July 1, 1969, instead of September as he normally would have done; but the presidential election became, in effect, a stage of the parliamentary campaign, and for the first time there was a head-on contest along party lines. The two main groups designated their candidates in October, 1968. The CDU nominated Gerhard Schröder, who had been Minister of Foreign Affairs from 1961 to 1966 and was Minister of Defense in the Grand Coalition under Kiesinger; the SPD put forward Gustav Heinemann, Kiesinger's Minister of Justice. The FDP decided at an early stage to take a decision unanimously but not until the last moment. Just before the Federal Assembly met in Berlin on March 5, 1969, they made it known that they would vote for Heinemann. The only other group represented in the Assembly, the NPD, opted for Schröder. At the first ballot, Heinemann secured 514 votes, which was 5 less than an absolute majority, while Schroder received 501; there were five abstentions and three blank votes.[14] At the second ballot, the figures were 511 to 507, with five abstentions. At the third, in which a relative majority is sufficient, Dr. Heinemann was successful by 512 votes to 506, there again being five abstentions.

The vote was important for several reasons. The SPD-FDP coalition that brought Heinemann to the presidency was a precursor of that which made Willy Brandt Chancellor seven months later; that is to say, it made the latter event easier to envisage, though by no means inevitable. The Liberals, by their decision to vote as a block, saved the Republic from a moral disaster of the first order. If any member of the FDP had taken advantage of the secret ballot to vote for Schröder, the latter would have owed his election in part to the twenty-two delegates of the extreme right, whose preference was not in doubt: the virulent *Deutsche National-Zeitung* on March 14 carried the headline "Heinemann—a disaster for Germany." Finally, the new President's record and personality were such that his election redounded to the prestige both of the Republic and of his office.

Gustav Heinemann was born on July 23, 1899. He studied law, economics, and history, and became a doctor of laws and of political science before embarking on a barrister's career. As a student, he was an active member of the society affiliated to the then liberal party, the DDP. In 1930, he joined a small Protestant group, the *Christlich-Sozialer Volksdienst*, and after Hitler seized power he was active in the Protestant opposition. He took part in the Synod, held at Barmen in 1934, which refused to obey the Nazis and led to the foundation of the Confessing Church, a center of courageous opposition to Nazi tyranny.[15] After the war, he played an important part in the life of German Protestantism and was President of the Evangelical Synod from 1949 to 1955. A member of the CDU since its formation, he was mayor of Essen till 1949, a member of the *Landtag* of North Rhine–Westphalia, and Minister of Justice for that *Land* in 1947–48. In 1949, he became Minister of the Interior in Adenauer's first government, but resigned in October, 1950 in protest against the Chancellor's rearmament policy.[16] In 1952, he left the CDU and founded the All-German People's Party (*Gesamtdeutsche Volkspartei*) on a platform of neutralism.[17] In 1957, seeing that his party was not making progress, he dissolved it and entered the Bundestag as an SPD member. As Federal Minister of Justice after 1966, he instituted a liberal reform of the penal code and stood for a sympathetic policy toward rebellious youth.

Before and after the presidential election, his adversaries laid stress on his changes of party allegiance and his "leftism," particularly in foreign affairs; they also contended that his ideas had evolved to such an extent as to show a lack of stability. His friends and admirers, on the other hand, had long respected his high and consistent moral standards, political courage, lack of self-interest, dignity, and profound sense of democratic behavior.

Apart from one false step immediately after the election—an interview, ill-judged to say the least, that appeared in the *Stuttgarter Zeitung* of March 8[18]—President Heinemann has acted with both circumspection and firmness. While he was undoubtedly delighted to be able to appoint Willy Brandt as Chancellor, he regards the presidency as conferring on him the right and duty to represent all citizens of the Republic. In so doing, he is at least as much concerned to form their views as to reflect them. On such occasions as the twenty-fifth anniversary of the attack on Hitler's life, the thirtieth anniversary of the outbreak of war, or the first postwar visit of a German President to the Netherlands (in January, 1970), he has referred to the past in forthright terms.

	Adenauer I CDU/ CSU–DP–FDP 9/20/49	Adenauer II CDU/ CSU–DP–FDP 10/20/53	Adenauer III CDU/ CSU 10/18/57
Chancellor	Adenauer (CDU)	Adenauer (CDU)	Adenauer (CDU)
Vice-Chancellor	Blücher (FDP)	Blücher (FDP)	Erhard (CDU)
Foreign Affairs	Adenauer (CDU)[1]	Adenauer (CDU)[4]	von Brentano (CDU)
Interior	Heinemann (CDU)[2]	Schröder (CDU)	Schröder (CDU)
Justice	Dehler (FDP)	Neumayer (FDP)[5]	Schäffer (CSU)
Economy	Erhard (CDU)	Erhard (CDU)	Erhard (CDU)
Finance	Schäffer (CSU)	Schäffer (CSU)	Etzel (CDU)
Defense	—	Blank (CDU)[6]	Strauss (CDU)
Agriculture	Niklas (CSU)	Lübke (CDU)	Lübke (CDU)[11]
Labor	Storch (CDU)	Storch (CDU)	Blank (CDU)
Transport	Seebohm (DP)	Seebohm (DP)	Seebohm (DP)[12]
Posts	Schuberth (CDU)	Balke[7]	Stücklen (CSU)
Reconstruction	Wildermuth (FDP)[3]	Preusker (FDP)	Lücke (CDU)
Refugees	Lukaschek (CDU)	Oberländer (BHE)[8]	Oberländer (CDU)[13]
All-German Affairs	Kaiser (CDU)	Kaiser (CDU)	Lemmer (CDU)
Bundesrat Affairs	Hellwege (DP)	Hellwege (DP)	von Merkatz (DP)[14]
Economic Cooperation*	Blücher (FDP)	Blücher (FDP)	—
Family Affairs	—	Würmeling (CDU)	Würmeling (CDU)
Atomic Energy	—	Strauss (CSU)[9]	Balke (CSU)
Federal Treasury	—	—	Lindrath (CDU)[15]
Health	—	—	—
Scientific Research	—	—	—
Ministers of State	—	Tillmanns (CDU) Schäfer (FDP) Kraft (BHE)[10]	—

*Overseas development aid.

Notes to the Table of Federal Cabinets
[1] From 3/15/51 onward.
[2] From 10/11/50: Lehr (CDU).
[3] Till 3/10/52. From 7/16/52: Neumayer (FDP).
[4] From 6/6/55: von Brentano (CDU).
[5] From 11/8/56: von Merkatz (DP).
[6] From 6/6/55. From 11/8/56: Strauss (CSU).
[7] From 12/9/53 to 10/16/56: Balke (CSU). Previously Schuberth, in charge of current affairs; from 11/14/56 to 10/22/57, Lemmer (CDU).
[8] From 6/6/55: von Merkatz (DP).
[9] From 11/8/56: Balke (nonparty: CSU from 1/16/64).
[10] CDU from 7/11/55.
[11] Till 7/1/59. From 9/9/59: Schwarz (CDU).
[12] CDU from 7/1/60.
[13] Till 5/3/60. From 10/28/60: von Merkatz (CDU from 7/1/60).
[14] CDU from 7/1/60.
[15] Till 2/27/60. From 4/8/60 to 11/7/61: Wilhelmi (CDU).
[16] From 12/14/62: Bucher (FDP).
[17] From 12/14/62: Dahlgrün (FDP).
[18] From 12/14/62: (Spiegel affair): von Hassel (CDU).

Adenauer IV CDU/ CSU–FDP 11/14/61	Erhard I CDU/ CSU–FDP 10/18/63	Erhard II CDU CSU/FDP 10/26/65	Kiesinger CDU/ CSU–FDP 12/1/66	Brandt SPD– FDP 10/21/69
Adenauer (CDU)	Erhard (CDU)	Erhard (CDU)	Kiesinger (CDU)	Brandt (SPD)
Erhard (CDU)	Mende (FDP)	Mende (FDP)[28]	Brandt (SPD)	Scheel (FDP)
Schröder (CDU)	Schröder (CDU)	Schröder (CDU)	Brandt (SPD)	Scheel (FDP)
Höcherl (CSU)	Höcherl (CSU)	Lücke (CDU)	Lücke (CDU)[30]	Genscher (FDP)
Stammberger (FDP)[16]	Bucher (FDP)[25]	Jaeger (CSU)	Heinemann (SPD)[31]	Jahn (SPD)
Erhard (CDU)	Schmücker (CDU)	Schmücker (CDU)	Schiller (SPD)	Schiller (SPD)
Starke (FDP)[17]	Dahlgrün (FDP)	Dahlgrün (FDP)[28]	Strauss (CSU)	Möller (SPD)
Strauss (CSU)[18]	von Hassel (CDU)	von Hassel (CDU)	Schröder (CDU)	Schmidt (SPD)
Schwarz (CDU)	Schwarz (CDU)	Höcherl (CSU)	Höcherl (CSU)	Ertl (FDP)
Blank (CDU)	Blank (CDU)	Katzer (CDU)	Katzer (CDU)	Arendt (SPD)
Seebohm (CDU)	Seebohm (CDU)	Seebohm (CDU)	Leber (SPD)	Leber (SPD)[35]
Stücklen (CSU)	Stücklen (CSU)	Stücklen (CSU)	Dollinger (CSU)	
Lücke (CDU)	Lücke (CDU)	Bücher (FDP)[28]	Lauritzen (SPD)	Lauritzen (SPD)
Mischnick (FDP)	Krüger (CDU)[26]	Gradl (CDU)	von Hassel (CDU)[32]	
Lemmer (CDU)[19]	Mende (FDP)	Mende (FDP)[28]	Wehner (SPD)	Francke (SPD)[36]
von Merkatz (CDU)[20]	Niederalt (CSU)	Niederalt (CDU)	Schmidt (SPD)	
Scheel (FDP)	Scheel (FDP)	Scheel (FDP)[28]	Wischnewski (SPD)[33]	Eppler (SPD)
Würmeling (CDU)[21]	Heck (CDU)	Heck (CDU)	Heck (CDU)[34]	Strobel (SPD)[37]
Balke (CSU)[22]	—	—	—	—
Lenz (FDP)[23]	Dollinger (CSU)	Dollinger (CSU)	Schmücker (CDU)	—
Schwarzhaupt (CDU)[24]	Schwarzhaupt (CDU)	Schwarzhaupt (CDU)	Strobel (SPD)	—
—	Lenz (FDP)	Stoltenberg (CDU)	Stoltenberg (CDU)	Leussink[38]
Krone (CDU)	Krone (CDU)[27]	Krone (CDU)[27] Westrick (CDU)[29]	—	Ehmke (SPD)[39]

---

[19]From 12/14/62: Barzel (CDU).
[20]From 12/14/62: Niederalt (CSU).
[21]From 12/14/62: Heck (CDU).
[22]Till 12/14/62.
[23]From 12/14/62: Dollinger (CSU).
[24]From 12/14/62: Lenz.
[25]Till 3/27/65. From 4/1/65: Weber (CDU).
[26]Till 2/7/64. From 2/17/64: Lemmer (CDU).
[27]Permanent chairman of the Federal Defense Council.
[28]Till 10/27/66.
[29]Head of the *Bundeskanzleramt* (Chancellor's Office) till 9/16/66.

[30]Till 3/28/68; then Ernst Benda.
[31]Till 3/26/69; then Ehmke (SPD).
[32]Till 2/5/69; then Windelen (CDU).
[33]Till 10/2/69; then Eppler (SPD).
[34]Till 10/2/69; then Frau Brauksiepe (CDU).
[35]Posts and Transport.
[36]Renamed "Ministry for Inter-German Relations."
[37]Youth, Family and Health Affairs.
[38]Nonparty.
[39]Minister of State in charge of the Chancellor's Office.

At the same time, he breaks through existing customs and protocols so that economic power or social prestige is no longer a *sine qua non* for Germans who desire access to the President. However, it is too early to assess his political influence on the basis of the past year or so, especially as the chancellorship is held by a man who in many respects stands very close to him.

Four Dissimilar Chancellors

Under the constitution, in practice as in the intention of its drafters, the President is not the source of power: the government does not derive its authority from him, nor does he have much influence over its acts. His chief right is to be informed as laid down in the standing orders of the Federal Government, formulated in 1951: "The Chancellor will keep the President continuously informed of his policy and the acts of the various ministries by sending him the necessary documents, by written reports on matters of particular importance, and by oral explanations as the need arises." The President is not, even symbolically, the head of the armed forces. In ordinary times, the post of commander-in-chief is held by the Minister of Defense under Article 65a of the Basic Law, adopted in 1956. In the case of military emergency (*Verteidigungsfall*), it is vested in the Chancellor under Article 115b of the new section, Xa, which became law in 1968.

The drafters and amenders of the Basic Law were concerned to ensure the stability of governments and due freedom of action for the Chancellor and his ministers, while respecting the essential principle of a parliamentary regime— namely, that the head of the executive should derive his authority from an assembly elected by universal suffrage. "The Federal Chancellor shall be elected, without discussion, by the Bundestag on the proposal of the Federal President." If the President's nominee secures an absolute majority in the Bundestag, there is no problem: he is elected, and the President duly appoints him. This is what has in fact taken place on each occasion, the procedure giving rise to no particular excitement except in 1949 and 1969, when Adenauer in 1949 and Brandt in 1969 received 202 and 251 votes respectively: the total number of deputies in those years, respectively, was 402 and 496, so that the absolute majority in each was 202 and 249. If Dr. Adenauer had forgotten to vote for himself in 1949, it would have been necessary to apply the following paragraphs of Article 63—those whose existence he overlooked in 1959:

If the person nominated is not elected, the Bundestag may, within fourteen days after the ballot, elect a Federal Chancellor by more than one half of its members.

If the Federal Chancellor is not elected within this time limit, a new ballot shall take place immediately, in which the person who receives most votes shall be elected. If the person elected receives the votes of the majority of the members of the Bundestag, the Federal President must, within seven days after the election, appoint him. If the person elected does not obtain this majority, the Federal President must, within seven days, either appoint him or dissolve the Bundestag.

The experience of Weimar in Germany and the Third and Fourth Republics in France had shown that it was not so hard to find a Chancellor or Prime Minister; the real problem was to keep him in power, avoiding government crises and, in particular, the situation in which the cabinet might be over-thrown by a combination of mutually hostile opposition parties. To obviate this, the Parliamentary Council hit upon the idea of a "constructive vote of no confidence," expressed as follows in Article 67:

The Bundestag may express its lack of confidence in the Federal Chancellor only by electing a successor with the majority of its members and submitting a request to the Federal President for the dismissal of the Federal Chancellor. The Federal President much comply with the request and appoint the person elected.

There must be an interval of forty-eight hours between the motion and the election.

The working of this procedure has twice been exemplified in the biggest *Land*, North Rhine–Westphalia, whose constitution of 1950 contains a similar provision. On February 26, 1956, the CDU Prime Minister, Karl Arnold, was overthrown following the election of his successor Fritz Steinhoff of the SPD, as a result of the Liberal and Center parties switching their support; the two men embraced in friendly fashion when the result of the vote was made known. On December 8, 1966, as the result of another shift by the Liberals, Franz Meyers of the CDU, who had been Prime Minister since the previous July, was replaced by Heinz Kühn of the SPD. However, Article 67 has never been applied on the Federal level. On the only two occasions when the Chancellor has resigned during a legislative term—Adenauer in 1963 and Erhard in 1966—it was due to the attitude of their own party rather than to opposition by its smaller ally, and the question of a constructive no-confidence vote did not arise. Nor has any Chancellor ever invoked the suicidal provisions of Article 68, which entitles him to solicit a vote of confidence: if he does not then obtain the support of an absolute majority, he may request the President to dissolve the Bundestag within three weeks, but "the right of dissolution shall lapse as soon as the Bundestag, with the majority of its members, elects another Federal Chancellor." In November, 1966, the SPD, then in opposition, tried unsuccessfully and with doubtful propriety to secure a vote compelling Dr. Erhard, then Chancellor, to put the question of confidence in this risky fashion.

Thus there has never been a state of "legislative emergency" (*Gesetzqe-bungsnotstand*) or deadlock such as may in theory arise from the application of Article 68—a case where the government is not overthrown and the Bundestag not dissolved, but the measure in respect of which the government sought its vote of confidence is not adopted. In the Fifth French Republic, the problem is solved by making it possible to pass a law without an affirmative vote by the Assembly: if the censure motion does not obtain an absolute majority, the bill is considered to have been passed. At Bonn, the complicated procedure of Article 81 is intended to meet the case: the President, with the approval of the Bundesrat, may declare the bill adopted on grounds of urgency and despite the lack of approval by the Bundestag.

Article 65 lays down that the Chancellor "shall determine and assume responsibility for general policy"—a phrase that has left room for endless debate on the exact limits of his authority vis-à-vis Federal ministers. This seems to be restricted by the provision in the same article that "the Federal

Government shall decide on differences of opinion between the Federal ministers," and by the government's standing orders, which rule that such differences are resolved by a majority of the cabinet, the Chancellor having no more than a casting vote if opinions are equally divided. In practice, however, the Chancellor's authority over "his" ministers (the possessive is justified inasmuch as the President appoints and dismisses them on his advice) depends on a number of factors. First among these is the Chancellor's personality: thus Adenauer had his own method of organizing the cabinet's deliberations. Second is the composition of the government's majority: for example, it was natural enough that a vote should be taken within Kiesinger's cabinet, representing as it did a coalition of the two main parties, on the question of re-valuing the Deutsche Mark. Third is the position of individual ministers, which may be strengthened either by party support—as when Dr. Erhard, backed by the parliamentary CDU, stood out against Adenauer on economic matters—or by formal provisions—for example, the strong position that standing orders confer on the Minister of Finance, which was made full use of by such strong characters as Fritz Schäffer from 1949 to 1957, Franz Josef Strauss in the Kiesinger cabinet, and now Alex Möller in Brandt's.

The office of Vice-Chancellor carries few, if any, formal privileges beyond that of taking the chair at cabinet meetings in the Chancellor's absence. If the Vice-Chancellor is a man of little personality or if his party does not play an important part in the coalition, his practical role will be negligible. It is another matter if, like Brandt vis-à-vis Kiesinger, he is a man of stature at the head of a large party and an important ministry. But, even when he is deputizing for the Chancellor, he does not have at his command the resources of the *Bundes-kanzleramt*, or Chancellor's secretariat, which in the latter's hands is a powerful instrument of coordination and drive.

For many years the Federal democracy was ironically described as a *Kanzler-demokratie*, while at the same time it was praised for combining a parliamentary system with governmental authority. New methods of mass communication made it necessary for authority to be personified in some degree, and, this being so, it was not unnatural for it to be personalized as well. Even, in 1969, the CDU adopted as its election cry *Auf den Kanzler kommt es an* ("It's the Chancellor that matters"). But in fact the political influence of the head of government has varied a good deal from person to person and in different circumstances. The Parliamentary Council's action in conferring wide powers on him, at least in theory, was encouraged by the two chief political personalities of that time, Konrad Adenauer and Kurt Schumacher, each of whom expected to win the first election and intended to govern without the other. Whatever the circumstances had been, their mutual antagonism and hatred would have sufficed to exclude the possibility of a "grand coalition" between their parties. Both were fond of power and determined to exercise it undivided. They knew, moreover, that whichever of them lost the battle might well not be in a position to seek his revenge at the next election: Adenauer was seventy-three and Schumacher, though almost twenty years his junior, knew that only willpower could keep his body alive, crippled as it was by injuries received in World War I and in Hitler's camps. He died, in fact, three years after Adenauer's victory. The latter, however, remained Chancellor for fourteen years and continued to indulge his bent for politics until he died in his ninety-second year, on April 19, 1967.

Adenauer at seventy-three was four years older than Disraeli at the outset of his long premiership, from 1874 to 1880. It is an age at which men usually prepare to withdraw from public life, but at which they are revered and given chairmanships—a source of power for those who know how to use it. In January, 1946, it was not Adenauer but Friedrich Holzapfel who called the first important meeting, at Herford, of the CDU executive board in the British zone. But Adenauer, as the oldest man present, took the chair and was in due course formally elected chairman, with Holzapfel as his deputy. It is true that, besides the prestige of age, he had a background of experience that went beyond the sphere of local and regional politics.

Konrad Adenauer was born on January 5, 1876 at Cologne, where his father was a secretary to the provincial court of appeal. He was the third of four children; the family were not well off, and after leaving school he worked for a short time in a bank before he was able to become a law student. After taking his degree, he spent two years in the state prosecutor's office at Cologne and afterward entered the office of an eminent civil lawyer, *Justizrat* Kausen, who was also the chairman of the *Zentrum* group in the municipal council. Thanks to Kausen's patronage, he was appointed in 1906, at the age of thirty, to a counsellor's post in the office of the mayor of Cologne. In 1917, he was elected mayor, a post he held until 1933, having been re-elected with some difficulty in 1929. The mayors of the great Rhineland towns were persons of consequence, elected for twelve years at a time and enjoying considerable scope in the exercise of wide municipal liberties. Adenauer remained a Rhinelander throughout his life, preserving the local accent and a lively dislike of Prussianism; Berlin, in particular, long represented to him, as a devout Catholic, not only the capital of Prussia but also a city of sin, a modern Babylon. Apart from this, his long tenure in the mayor's office implanted in him a fondness for thorough organization that was tinged with authoritarianism, for a stable executive ensuring the firm conduct of affairs and rising above the pettiness of everyday politics.

In the aftermath of Germany's first defeat, day-to-day events in the Rhineland were not lacking in drama. As mayor, Adenauer took part in discussions and activities concerning the province's future, which he envisaged in terms of a German confederation. In a memorandum of December, 1923 addressed to the French authorities, he wrote: "A lasting peace between France and Germany can only be built in the manner that I suggest, by strengthening the influence of western Germany within the Reich and by creating common economic interests between western Germany and France."[19]

He became a member of the executive committee of the *Zentrum* and was at one time in the running for the Reich chancellorship, but held out for measures that would have caused serious trouble with wage earners. Heinrich Brüning, his junior by nearly ten years, became Chancellor in 1930. There was no love lost between the two, either then or after 1945, when Adenauer saw to it that Brüning, who had been teaching at Harvard since 1933, should not occupy a position of any influence in the second German Republic, though he was allowed to become a professor of political science at Cologne from 1951 to

1954: he afterward returned to the United States and died there on March 30, 1970. However, in Weimar days both Adenauer and Brüning were opposed to the rise of Nazism. As President of the Staatsrat, the upper house of the Prussian legislature—for the Rhineland was, willy-nilly, still part of Prussia—Adenauer supported the legal government headed by the Socialist Otto Braun after Papen's *coup d'état* of July 20, 1932. In March, 1933, he was removed from the Staatsrat and also from the office of mayor: the Nazis were in full cry against him, their official grounds being the costliness of his administration and his alleged support of separatism in the Rhineland after 1918. Between 1933–45, he lived in seclusion: the Nazis molested him from time to time and he was twice interned—for a few days after June 30, 1934 and for a longer period after July 20, 1944, though he had not taken an active part in the conspiracy against Hitler. He escaped, was recaptured, and finally released in November. In March, 1945, the U.S. military invited him to become mayor of Cologne once again; but on October 6, as we have seen, the British brigadier in charge of military and civil affairs in the North Rhine province dismissed him from his post and from the city and forbade him to carry on any political activity. This measure, the ostensible grounds for which were lack of energy and administrative inefficiency, did Adenauer more good than harm. The rebuff he had received from the occupying power proved that he was in no sense a "collaborator," and he was able to put it about that this action by an officer in the service of the Labour Government had been inspired in a highly unpatriotic fashion by the Social Democrats. In November, the ban on his activity was lifted, and from then on his career coincides with the development of the CDU, the chairmanship of the Parliamentary Council,[20] and finally the government of the Federal Republic and the leadership of its largest party.

The man who reached, late in life, such political heights was, in his personality, a model of balance and serenity. His family life had always been above reproach. His first wife, Emma Weyer, died in 1916 after bearing him three children, one of whom, Max, became *Oberstadtdirektor*, or head of the Cologne municipal organization, in 1953. By his second wife, Auguste Zinsser, who died in March, 1947, he had four children, one of whom took holy orders. A cousin of Auguste's was married to John J. McCloy, who became U.S. High Commissioner at Bonn in 1949. Konrad Adenauer was a typical *père de famille* of the old school, affectionate and authoritarian, genial in a somewhat aloof manner, accustomed to being respected and obeyed. In his village home at Rhöndorf, he spent his leisure gardening, listening to music, and browsing through books. Not that he was, properly speaking, an intellectual: his solid piety, his rather hidebound moral standards, and his fondness for simplifying issues were not qualities that encouraged speculation, critical analysis, or the discernment of fine shades. Perhaps his lack of self-criticism was a source of added vitality; if so, he was in this respect not unrepresentative of the nation under his rule.

His capacity for work, or rather his staying power, was extraordinary. During negotiations he would often insist on continuing without a break, even after several hours, in the knowledge that he could remain fresh and alert for longer than the rest of those present, despite being much older than they. He did not follow business in all its details, but left it to his aides to keep the files up to date and to pass a brief note to him at the right time. He possessed the art of choosing efficient aides who were chiefs of staff rather than advisers (let alone friends). Without knowing it, he answered to the description of the "man of character" given by Charles de Gaulle in 1932 in *Le Fil de l'épée*: "The passion for self-reliance is obviously accompanied by some roughness in method. The man of character incorporates in his own person the severity inherent in his effort. This is felt by his subordinates, and at times they groan under it. In any event, a leader of this quality is inevitably aloof, for there can be no authority without prestige, nor prestige unless he keeps his distance." Only the banker Robert Pferdmenges, four years his junior, could really be called Adenauer's friend as well as his adviser.

Not that the Chancellor's manner was a harsh or brutal one. On the contrary, he was adept at the kind of repartee that amuses while it strikes home. He had a lively sense of humor and was fond of a joke, though he did not like being the butt of irony. He could make an audience of ordinary citizens laugh and could put the Bundestag at its ease, though he had none of the qualities of a rabble-rouser or a practiced rhetorician. His high-pitched voice with its Rhineland accent and somewhat monotonous delivery, together with his horror of pompous and emotive language, often made his speeches sound as if they were reports of a highly competent managing director rather than examples of the eloquence that carries conviction by its warmth of feeling or intellectual mastery. Schumacher once remarked that Goethe had a vocabulary of 29,000 words and that Adenauer's was more like 500, on which a woman deputy commented: "Even if Adenauer knew 200 more, he wouldn't use them. That is precisely his strength."[21] When he addressed large audiences, he would descend to their level rather than raise them to his. He did not shrink on such occasions from exaggerated arguments and empty phrases, nor from hitting below the belt—as he did in the election campaign of 1961, when he spoke disdainfully of "Herr Brandt, alias Frahm" and refused to defend his adversary against the slanders that his own friends were heaping on him.

Adenauer was variously accused at different times of being a demagogue or a dictator who took decisions without regard for public opinion. It would be truer to say that he had an idea of democracy in which there was no room for extremes. He did not impose his views on others, nor did he let the nation at large, or even its representatives, share in working out his policy. He came to his own conclusions as to what was needed and then submitted his actions to the judgment of the electorate, having first decided, with the flair of a true statesman, what artifices were most likely to make these palatable to public opinion. As time went on, the need to disguise his purposes became less: his successes enhanced his prestige and vice versa. His popularity became an essential feature of German policy. It was of a frank, straightforward kind, and while one may speak of a "personality cult" in this context, the phrase implies nothing of the morbid idolatry that we associate with Hitler or Stalin. It does, however, recall the somewhat childlike state of mind that has led other countries to turn, after a defeat, to aged leaders—Mannerheim, Pétain, Hindenburg, or, in France after 1870, Theirs. We may also be reminded of Eisenhower's presidency. In all such cases, the phenomenon is that of a troubled nation relieving its anxieties by the choice of a trusted father figure.

Such, at least, was the position during the period of Adenauer's increasing success, from 1949 to the electoral triumph of 1957. Soon afterward, his stock began to decline, the stages being marked by the affair of the presidential succession in 1959, the *Spiegel* incident in 1962, and, finally, his reluctant surrender of power in 1963. By this time, both his own party and its FDP allies had grown tired of the perpetual argument that ran: "The people would not understand it if I did not stay on for at least two years after winning the election. . . . It wouldn't do to have a change within less than two years of the next election." Not by accident, his retirement from the chancellorship took place exactly halfway through a legislative term. The event may be seen partly as an ungrateful revolt by the rank and file, and, to a much less extent, as due to the feeling that Adenauer's powers were failing (like Churchill's at a similar juncture) and that it was time he went. The basic reason was probably the same as that which caused the departure of his friend de Gaulle in 1968–69: namely, the revenge of the injured female who figured alternately as a Cinderella or a wallflower in the work of a well-known German cartoonist, and whose name was domestic affairs. Her dazzling rival, foreign policy, was always the one pictured as stepping into an elegant carriage or partnering the eligible hero, except when he briefly took the floor with her homely sister for an electoral waltz.[22] When the charmer reached the end of her successful career, the neglect from which the other had suffered became all the more apparent.

The decline in Adenauer's prestige toward the end of his chancellorship was fortunate from his successors' point of view. Here too there is a comparison with France: it is easier to take over the reins of power from a great man when he has suffered setbacks that make him appear vulnerable and no longer unique. Not only is this lucky for his successors, but for democracy as well, since it facilitates the changeover from an exceptional leader to his less brilliant subordinates or adversaries, without which the regime cannot be normal or lasting.

Unlike M. Pompidou in France, Dr. Ludwig Erhard did not have the skill to use this good fortune properly. His election by the Bundestag on October 16, 1963 was in itself a triumph over the former leader, who had done his best during the previous four years to prevent Erhard coming to power and who continued to work against him afterward. But did not the outcome prove that Adenauer had been right in denouncing him as a man of small political stature? Erhard had been the wonder-working Minister of the Economy ever since 1949 and also Vice-Chancellor, a post of no influence in itself, since 1957. Many of the CDU members who advanced him to power had misgivings, seeing him more as an electoral war horse than as a gifted leader. But, after all, what was the general opinion of Truman at the time of Roosevelt's death, or Cardinal Roncalli when he became the successor to Pius XII? Yet President Truman showed himself a statesman of decision, and John XXIII a great hope. Ludwig Erhard, unfortunately, was not transformed by his new responsibilities.

This was perhaps because, after having been in 1948 the champion and embodiment of a certain economic policy, he became Chancellor without ever having engaged in politics as such. He was born at Fürth in Bavaria on

February 4, 1897, joined the army in 1916, was badly wounded at Ypres and, demobilized in 1919, was a sergeant in the Bavarian artillery. After graduating from the Higher School of Commerce at Nuremberg and studying management economy and sociology at Frankfurt University, he took a doctor's degree and abandoned commerce for research. From 1928 to 1942, he was a research assistant, then deputy director, and finally director of the Economic Research Institute attached to the School at Nuremberg. When dismissed on account of not having joined the Nazi Party, he set himself up as a private economic adviser. The U.S. occupation authorities called him in to reorganize industry in the Fürth-Nuremberg area, and, from October 3, 1945, he became, as a nonparty technician, Minister for Trade and Industry in the second *Land* government to be formed in Bavaria, which, as already mentioned, was a coalition under Socialist leadership. He did not retain this job in the next government, which was predominantly CSU, but in 1947—when he became professor of political economy at Munich University—he moved from the Bavarian governmental sphere to that of Bizonia, initially as chairman of the advisory commission on currency and credit.

From February, 1948 onward, his name was associated with the economic "new order," which we shall study later on in its philosophical and practical aspects and of which he was a doughty champion, first, as an independent and, later, on behalf of the CDU. When he became Chancellor, the mistake he made was perhaps to play down his own fighting spirit in order to act the part of a "people's Chancellor" (*Volkskanzler*), as though his policy should and would in the last resort be accepted by everyone, whatever their party or way of thinking, except for a few fractious critics. Instead of this, he soon found that he had plenty of opponents and that the majority of these belonged to his own party and to the government coalition. Adenauer's personality and prestige had obscured the fact that the Chancellor's power was limited in two ways. Except from 1957 to 1961, the governments he had led were coalitions, and he sometimes had to make wide concessions in return for the support of a small group. This happened, for instance, in 1953, when he took on as ministers two members of the BHE (refugees' party) whose past was by no means unblemished. Again, on October 20, 1961, he made a deal with the FDP which was intended to be secret but soon leaked out,[23] and which involved bypassing constitutional procedures, not only by laying down future government policy in every detail but by providing that every step taken by the government or the parliamentary party should be subject to the prior approval of a "coalition committee." In addition, the chairmen of the two parliamentary groups were to attend cabinet meetings as of right. However, within a few weeks, the agreement, which was never applied, had fallen into oblivion, and the Chancellor went on governing as before.

Adenauer, who was not only Chancellor but also chairman of the CDU, knew how to resist pressure from his own party or any other, whether inside or outside parliament. Unlike him, Erhard had trouble in standing up to both the Liberals' mounting hostility and the frequent attacks from an ever growing number of CDU members. His party colleagues allowed him to win the 1965 elections, in which he gained a larger majority than Adenauer had in 1961; but within a short time, economic difficulties began to dim his reputation and make his placid aversion to change look foolishly optimistic. *Land* elections, particularly that of the North Rhine–Westphalia on July 10, 1966, confirmed the verdict of public opinion polls that Erhard was not good for the party's image, and from thenceforth his days were numbered, irrespective of the attitude of the SPD opposition. On October 27, following a dispute over the 1967 budget, the FDP withdrew its four ministers from the cabinet. From then on, affairs were conducted as if Erhard had ceased to exist—so much so that on November 28 the *Süddeutsche Zeitung* reminded its readers, almost without irony, that the Republic still possessed a Chancellor who had neither been outvoted nor resigned. The CDU, with ingratitude rare even by political standards, had completely jettisoned its former champion. As a German weekly put it in a brilliant parody, people were hastening to clear their names from the slur of having worked with him, in the same way they had rushed to clear them from a different slur after 1945.[24]

The quest for a successor began not in parliament but within the ruling party. On November 10, the CDU/CSU parliamentary group chose Kurt Georg Kiesinger on a third ballot as their prospective Chancellor. He began his soundings, but on the 25th met with a refusal from the Liberals, who hoped to exploit the situation in which they held a balance between the two main parties. Next day, the latter two reached agreement through their negotiating committees on the formation of a government. Erhard resigned on the 30th, and on December 1 Kiesinger was elected Chancellor, his team comprising of ten Christian Democrats and nine Socialists.

The third Chancellor was a man of more charm and subtlety than his predecessor, with at least equal self-confidence and probably a greater measure of touchiness, so that his courtesy, though exemplary as a rule, sometimes deserted him in front of a hostile audience. The hostility in question drew its arguments from his remoter past; it had not shown itself during the postwar years, when he had been an influential member of the Bundestag, chairman of its foreign affairs committee in 1954–58, vice-president of the consultative assembly of the Council of Europe in 1955, and, from 1958, Minister-President of Baden-Württemberg. As to his earlier history, he was born at Ebingen (Württemberg) on April 6, 1904, his father being a commercial employee. He studied law at Tübingen and Berlin, where he practiced after joining the Nazi Party in 1933. During the war, he did not serve in the army but in the foreign ministry, where he was in charge of liaison with the Ministry of Propaganda. In consequence, he was automatically arrested by the Allies in 1945.

The questions of principle raised by Kiesinger's background and his position in German public life in 1966 are of such importance that they will be considered at greater length in chapter 9. For the present, we may note two political consequences. On the one hand, the controversy that arose concerning the Chancellor weakened his own position and that of his party; but, as against this, the association of Brandt with Kiesinger in the new government meant that each conferred respectability on the other. Brandt's impeccable record of opposition to Nazism afforded a guarantee of the Chancellor's democratic sentiments, while the latter's action in entrusting the foreign affairs portfolio to a man who had emigrated in 1933, become a Norwegian subject, and recovered German nationality only in 1947 represented, in the eyes of many electors, a certificate of Brandt's honor as a German patriot.

The Grand Coalition inevitably transformed the Chancellor's role, obliging him to conciliate rather than to impose his will, and thus providing a constant temptation to delay decisions so as not to exacerbate differences between the two parties that had been so long at odds, or between one ministry and another. Conciliation in the realm of policy seldom took place at cabinet meetings but rather at informal gatherings held periodically on a shady lawn at Kressbronn on Lake Constance—the so-called Kressbronn circle comprising the Chancellor and his chief ministers, the chairmen of the two parliamentary parties, and various high officials. On the administrative level coordination was the business of the Chancellor's Office, but this body proved inadequate to the task and Werner Knieper, the state secretary in charge of it, was able neither to keep order among ministerial departments nor to collaborate effectively with the Chancellor. He was replaced by Karl Carstens, a professor of public law and state secretary in the Ministry of Foreign Affairs, who saw his job in terms of coordination rather than authority. In any case, the approach of the 1969 elections meant that the two parties tended to become rivals rather than associates, at least as early as 1968. It proved impossible to honor an undertaking to reform the electoral law, with the result that the Minister of the Interior, Paul Lücke of the CDU, resigned on April 2, 1968.

Nevertheless, the Grand Coalition achieved results of great importance in many different spheres. Its economic policy was a spectacular success, and it unquestionably imparted a new direction to the country's foreign relations. The law on the status of parties, for which the Basic Law had called since 1949, was at last enacted in 1967. The controversy over the constitutional amendments concerning the state of emergency was resolved by the measures voted in 1968, while the following year saw a reform of penal law and a new "financial constitution." Thus, notwithstanding many fears and predictions, there was no paralysis of the decision-making machinery: the conjunction of the two great parties did not result in a political or legislative deadlock. There might thus have been a possibility of its continuing into the period of the sixth legislature, but just before the elections a violent controversy arose within the government on the subject of the revaluation of the mark, for which Karl Schiller pressed in vain against the opposition of the Chancellor and Franz Josef Strauss. Despite the heat aroused by this argument, the respective party experts on finance and economics would not have been averse to a second spell of cooperation; but personal relations between the two leaders deteriorated to such a point that it was clear the coalition would not be renewed unless there proved to be no alternative in view of the composition of the new Bundestag.

As the election returns came in during the evening of September 28 it looked at first as if there might be a revival of the "little coalition" between the CDU/CSU and the Liberals. But the latter party had changed its character, and in any case it became clear toward midnight that a Socialist-Liberal coalition was arithmetically possible. After surprisingly rapid negotiations, facilitated by the CDU leaders' tactical blunders vis-à-vis the Liberals, Willy Brandt became Chancellor on October 21, 1969.

The new coalition presented two distinctive features. In the first place, although the lesser partner was extremely small, with only thirty seats in the Bundestag, it was allotted three important ministries—namely, Home, and Foreign Affairs, and Agriculture. This was not only because the FDP held in its hands—or rather in the hands of a few of its parliamentary members—the ministerial fate of the SPD, but also because it was very much in the latter's interest to keep their Liberal allies afloat. If they should ever disappear from the Bundestag for want of the magic 5 per cent of votes, the distribution of the spoils would in all probability be such that the CDU would continue to gain in strength and would be able to govern without sharing power with anyone.

Second, the Brandt government naturally bears the imprint of its leader, whose career and personality we shall study when describing the party of which he is the head and which has brought him to power. His character has evolved with the years, but he has long been noted for his rejection of the "charismatic" view of leadership. In his first official statement of policy, he significantly used the phrase: "We are the elected of the people [*Gewählte*], not the elect [*Erwählte*]." His aim is to use power in a sensible and efficient manner. Efficiency, likewise, is a major object of the younger generation of Socialist leaders, who plan to improve the apparatus of government by applying methods that have stood the test in the nationalized industries: exact data on which to base decisions and machinery for determining policy with the minimum waste of energy in the light of previously formulated middle- and long-term objectives. Horst Ehmke, formerly dean of the Freiburg law faculty, a state secretary, and later Minister of Justice in the Grand Coalition, became under Brandt a minister of state in the Bundeskanzleramt and set about modernizing its structure and working methods. The administrative changes so far made or announced do not, of course, guarantee that correct policies will be adopted, or even that decisions will be taken clearly and promptly: witness the hesitation over economic and financial alternatives in the first half of 1970. But they do bring into the open a number of questions that have so far been dealt with in an empirical rather than a systematic fashion.

How should the preparation of forecasts be organized? In a country whose dominant philosophy was formerly that of allowing free play to more or less unpredictable forces, the evolution of social ideals and technology has led to a general fondness, not to say mania, for studying methods of organizing information and acting upon it. This phenomenon, of course, existed before Brandt came to power; but until then, the government's idea of advance planning chiefly took the form of setting up a small group of high officials in the Chancellor's office or the Foreign Ministry; their task was to look ahead but they had no special means of informing themselves and no direct influence on current decisions. The present intention is to rationalize the process of decision-making, in particular by simultaneous computer processing of alternatives in the most varied fields of government, the optimum choices thus obtained being then translated into specific decisions. This method of approach gives rise to serious conflicts of opinion between ministers and the Chancellor's Office, since the former wish to be masters of their own departmental policy and to share in the framing of major decisions by the cabinet on a collective basis.

How is the public to be kept informed of government policy and the reasons for it, given that the absence of such information is a grave cause of inefficiency? Adenauer himself recognized the importance of the part played by the government spokesman, who is also head of the Federal Press and Information Office, and who, under standing orders, is entitled to be present at cabinet meetings. Felix von Eckardt, who occupied the post with hardly a break from 1952 to 1962, became a well-known figure in public life, but was primarily an executor of policy. Under the Grand Coalition, Günter Diehl, a Foreign Ministry official, played a much more important part in the Chancellor's scheme of things, so that he appeared at times to be formulating policy rather than merely expounding it. When Brandt became Chancellor, Diehl's place was taken by his assistant, the journalist Conrad Ahlers, whose arrest in 1962 had been a key development in the *Spiegel* affair. In the name of public relations, he set about reorganizing and enlarging the office, though it was already of great size by comparison with other democratic countries.[25]

After the government apparatus has submitted facts and proposals to the Chancellor and his ministers, and the latter have taken decisions upon them, what is the best method of ensuring that these decisions are properly handed down and acted on? This involves the role of the *Staatssekretäre* (state secretaries), who form a link between the political and the administrative system, and particularly the state secretary in the Chancellor's Office, at the very center of the governmental machine. Up to 1967, these officials were in effect deputy ministers, similar to the French *secrétaires d'état*: they superintended the heads of departments (*Ministerialdirektoren*) in their ministries, and often played a more important part than the ministers themselves. This was particularly true of Peter Paul Nahm in the Ministry for Refugee Affairs, to whom the main credit is due for the success of integration; it is also true of Alfred Hartmann in the Ministry of Finance and Ludger Westrick in the Economics Ministry. Westrick was so highly valued by Ludwig Erhard that he made him state secretary in the Chancellor's Office and, when he reached the retirement age for officials, promoted him to ministerial rank in the same office, there being no age limit for politicians. Westrick's role was even more important than that of Sherman Adams in President Eisenhower's entourage; he might almost have been taken for the Chancellor himself, and when he resigned on September 15, 1966, it was a portent of Erhard's fall from power.

When Adams was involved in charges of corruption, Eisenhower's reply was: "I need him." Adenauer might have said the same for different reasons about Hans Globke, whom he kept in office first as a departmental head and, from 1953, as a state secretary and close adviser, despite his record as a senior official of the Ministry of the Interior in the Nazi period and author of the official commentary on the Nuremberg racial laws of 1935. Globke was not a policy-maker but an ideal civil servant, skilled at operating the governmental machine and at briefing the Chancellor on matters requiring decision. Horst Ehmke did not aspire to be either a Westrick or a Globke; but his situation was ambiguous in so far as he was a politician of exceptional ability performing a job which had hitherto been that of a high official and thus giving it a new dimension, so that he tended to become a sort of Vice-Chancellor responsible for the infrastructure of power.

Under Article 36 of the Federal law on the civil service, the state secretaries, who form the topmost grade of that service, are government appointees; so are other important officials, such as the head of the Federal press bureau and the public prosecutor in the Supreme Court of Appeal. The holders of these posts can be placed *en disponibilité* (or, in "temporary retirement," as it is called in Germany), and the Brandt regime has made full use of this provision to install nominees of its own: the CDU has complained that the rules are being abused in imitation of the American "spoils system."

Finally, what is the best way of organizing liaison between government and parliament? From time to time, German observers had advocated the institution of parliamentary undersecretaries, more or less on the British model, who would perform this function while at the same time learning to exercise ministerial responsibility. The Grand Coalition passed a law on March 15, 1967 providing for the appointment of junior ministers of this type, known as *parlamentarische Staatssekretäre*.[26] At the time of writing, three years later, it is proposed to widen their powers so as to enable them to participate more fully in the handling of state affairs, as the ministers have more work than they can handle without delegating responsibility to the civil service, which is supposed to be politically neutral. The function of ensuring liaison between government and parliament has come to appear of secondary importance, as in practice it has for a long time been carried out through the chairmen of the parliamentary groups of the parties in power.

The Bundesrat and the Bundestag

In theory, the Federal Republic enjoys a parliamentary constitution. In fact—as in Britain, France, and most other countries except the United States with its "presidential" regime—parliament's real powers are very limited, even in its own field of legislature. When a government is formed, lengthy negotiations take place between the parties not only in order to distribute portfolios but also in order to reach agreement on a policy and thus on the legislation that will be needed to carry it out. Bills are drafted by the civil service and are, as a rule, steered through parliament by ministers much more efficiently than if the initiative were left to the Bundestag. This tendency is observable in all modern states, but especially in the Federal Republic. Out of the 2,395 laws passed during the five legislative terms from 1949 to 1969, 34 were proposed by the Bundesrat, 535 by the Bundestag, and no fewer than 1,826 by the government.[27] There are several causes of this phenomenon, such as the enlarging of the state's competence, the scope of legislation, the complexity of drafting on technical subjects, and so forth. But the result is to make the executive increasingly dominant over parliament and to create a sense of frustration in the latter, as its theoretical powers are encroached on by ministers on the one hand and party committees on the other.

The Bundesrat is the linear descendant of the eighteenth-century Imperial Diet (Reichstag), the Frankfurt Bundestag (1815–66), the Bundesrat under Bismarck, the Reichsrat of the Weimar Republic, and the Conference of Minister-Presidents that met from 1947 to 1949. Article 50 of the Basic Law says that "the *Länder* shall participate through the medium of the Bundesrat

in the legislation and the administration of the Federation." Though a legislative assembly, it has retained the essential characteristic of its predecessors,
that of being composed of "members of the governments of the *Länder*"—
that is to say, of the executive power. Although the *Länder* are not represented
on a basis of strict equality irrespective of population, as in the U.S. Senate,
the smaller ones are still greatly favored over the larger. "Each *Land* shall have
at least three votes; *Länder* with more than 2 million inhabitants shall have
four, *Länder* with more than 6 million inhabitants shall have five votes." The
distribution is thus as follows:

Land	*Number of delegates*	*Population in millions* (end of 1968)*
North Rhine–Westphalia	5	16·9
Bavaria	5	10·4
Baden–Württemberg	5	8·7
Lower Saxony	5	7·0
Hesse	4	5·3
Rhineland–Palatinate	4	3·6
Schleswig–Holstein	4	2·5
Hamburg	3	1·8
Saar	3	1·1
Bremen	3	0·8
	41	58·1
West Berlin	4	2·1

*The figures in this column are rounded to the nearest tenth.

The Bundesrat's powers are sufficiently wide to bring about a situation in
which, as has been observed, the politics of the *Länder* are often influenced by
Federal considerations. Thus, for example, a small party may claim its reward
at Bonn for concessions made in a *Land* capital, or the ruling party at the
Federal level may seek to make the Bundesrat more amenable by increasing its
own majority in that body or by decreasing that of its opponents. At the
beginning of 1970, the SPD deliberately exacerbated the political crisis in
Lower Saxony so as to secure an SPD majority at Hanover, while the CDU
did its best to block government policy in the Bundesrat, where the CDU
Land governments had, in theory, a one-vote majority.

We should not, however, overrate the importance of these tussles or be
taken in by their sometimes spectacular character. The Bundesrat has in fact
become very largely what the makers of the constitution wished—namely a
chamber representing the *Länder* and an assembly of "wise men" counter-
balancing the centralizing pull of the government and the more demagogic
tendency of the Bundestag. When, for example, on June 11, 1957, the Bundesrat unanimously threw out a government bill under which the Federation

would have taken 40 per cent of the proceeds of income and corporation taxes, it was acting as the mouthpiece of the dissatisfied *Länder* and not of CDU or SPD politicians.

To make clear the technical significance of this revolt, we should explain the somewhat complex legislative procedure of the Federal Republic. Bills may be proposed by the government or by either house of parliament. Under Article 76, "Federal Goverment bills shall first be submitted to the Bundesrat, which shall have the right to give its opinion on these bills within three weeks. Bundesrat bills shall be submitted to the Bundestag by the Federal Government, which must add a statement of its own views." The Bundestag, being the main legislative body, does not have to consult anyone before deliberating on bills proposed by its members. Wherever a bill originates, it is for the Bundestag to vote on it as the first step in the legislative process. If the vote is favorable, the bill is referred, or referred back, to the Bundesrat. If the latter is in agreement, there is no problem; if not, its powers depend on the nature of the bill. If it belongs to the category of "Federal" measures for which the Bundesrat's consent is necessary (*Zustimmungsgesetz*), the latter has an absolute veto. In the case of other bills, the Bundestag may override the Bundesrat's opposition by a qualified majority. Article 77 provides that if the Bundesrat adopts the veto by more than half of its votes (as is in fact necessary for all its decisions), then an absolute majority is required in the Bundestag. If the Bundesrat decision is taken by a two-thirds majority, the Bundestag vote must comprise an absolute majority of its members and at least two-thirds of those voting.

On paper, these rules would seem likely to give rise to endless conflict; but the constitution-makers provided an auxiliary body known as the Mediation Commission (*Vermittlungsausschuss*), which for the past twenty years has shown itself to be extremely effective. It consists of eleven members of the Bundesrat, one for each *Land*, and an equal number of Bundestag deputies. The commissioners hold office on a personal basis and are not responsible to a parliamentary group or *Land* government. They meet in closed session, away from the spotlight of publicity, and determine by majority vote the changes that they think will make a bill acceptable to both houses. The Mediation Commission itself has no powers of decision: the two houses must vote on the modifications proposed. It is usually the Bundesrat that appeals to the Commission, as it is permitted to do within two weeks of receiving a bill from the Bundestag. Sometimes, the Bundestag or the government have recourse to the Commission in the first instance in order to avoid a clash with the Bundesrat over a bill that requires its approval. The Commission's record is remarkable: during four parliaments, 256 bills were submitted to it and its proposals were rejected only twenty-one times. For the most part, bills are referred to the Commission before the final stage of the legislative process. As regards bills requiring the approval of the Bundesrat (1,489 out of a total of 2,395 in twenty years), there have only been forty-three cases in which this has been refused, and in twenty-four of these the Bundesrat has subsequently agreed to a compromise suggested by the Mediation Commission.

Most of the Bundesrat's work is done in committee, plenary sessions being fairly infrequent (56 in 1965–69, as compared with 535 committee sessions). One representative of each *Land*, who may be a senior official, sits on each committee. Every bill referred to the Bundesrat by the government or the Bundestag goes to the competent committee, whose report—often unanimous —is then submitted to the *Land* governments. The committee system constitutes one of the main features enabling the Bundesrat to share effectively in Federal administration as provided by the constitution. Whereas the Bundestag deputies are often unable to conduct technical arguments on equal terms with Federal ministers who are backed by the resources of their departments, the Bundesrat can draw on the expertise of civil servants in the *Länder* as a counterpoise to the arguments put forward by the Federal bureaucracy.

In 1949, the city of Bonn had no single palace or public building of any sort that could conceivably have served the needs of a parliament. It was necessary to build, and to build fast. Very soon there arose on the banks of the Rhine a white structure, modern but not aggressively so, to which new and taller wings had constantly to be added. Though built outside the center of town, the parliament was increasingly hemmed about by other buildings, some of which continued to have a makeshift appearance. Inside the main building, only those with long experience could find their way about the maze of corridors and staircases leading to the various deputies' and party offices, conference rooms, and secretarial bureaus that were shuffled round again and again to cope with developing needs and expanding manpower. Finally it became necessary to erect a new building, if only so that the deputies might at last have reasonable office space. The new thirty-story edifice was prepared for occupation in successive stages, and at the same time some alterations were made to the conference chamber. This is neither semicircular in shape like the French National Assembly nor longitudinal like the House of Commons. The deputies enter from a main corridor through one or other of three doors reserved for them, under the central public gallery that is often filled with an audience of likable young people who have been brought to see how democracy works. On either side of the chamber, under huge windows that fill it with light, two other galleries—diplomats on the left, reporters on the right— look down on the people's representatives. As in Paris, the political left and right occupy their appropriate places as seen from the viewpoint of the President of the assembly, so that the ambassadors have the best view of the CDU deputies and the journalists of the SPD. The party leaders sit in front as at Westminster; the President, as at the Palais Bourbon, sits behind and above the rostrum, beneath which stenographers busy themselves.

For the first twenty years, a long desk extended on either side of the President's seat, facing and looking down on the deputies. The side on his left, opposite the Social Democrats, was reserved for members of the Bundesrat, while the side on his right was occupied by the government, the Chancellor sitting next to the speaker's tribune. This arrangement had a symbolic importance: whereas in the French parliament ministers sat in the front row of the speaker's audience—their position among the deputies corresponding to the political facts of republican life—at Bonn they appeared as lordly spectators presiding over the parliamentary contest. However, in 1969, the government bench was brought down to the same level as the deputies.

Bundestag sessions are generally quiet and rather dull: they became more so in 1953 with the disappearance of the Communists and the extreme right.

SIX LEGISLATIVE ELECTIONS

					August 14, 1949			September 6, 195:		
Size of electorate	..	..	..	..	31·2[1]			33·2		
Votes cast	..	..	..	..	24·5 (78·5%)[2]			28·5 (85·8%)		
Invalid votes		..	..	..	0·8 (3·1%)[3]			0·9 (3·3%)		
Party					Votes[1]	Per cents[3]	Seats	Votes	Per cents	Seat
CDU/CSU	..	..	..	..	7·4	31·0	139	12·4	45·2	243
SPD	..	..	..	..	6·9	29·2	131	7·9	28·8	151
FDP	..	..	..	..	2·8	11·9	52	2·6	9·5	48
German Party[4]	..	..	..	..	0·9	4·0	17	0·9	3·3	15
Refugees[4]	..	..	..	..				1·6	5·9	27
Bavarian Party	..	..	..	..	1·0	4·2	17	0·5	1·7	
Extreme right[5]	..	..	..	..	0·4	1·8	5	0·3	1·1	
Communists	..	..	..	..	1·4	5·7	15	0·6	2·2	
"Neutralists"[6]	..	..	..	..				0·3	1·1	
Others	..	..	..	..	2·9	12·2	26	0·4	1·2	3
Total	..	..	..	..	23·7	100	402	27·5	100	487

Notes
[1]In millions.
[2]Per cent of electorate.
[3]Per cent of votes cast.

There are sometimes expressions of indignation from the floor, but these are more often feigned than real; there are stormy moments, but they seem somewhat artificial and devoid of passion. One of the reasons for this indifference is the rarity of debates in which the issue has been in doubt—at least until Brandt became Chancellor. As a rule party discipline is such that the voting can be predicted with almost complete accuracy. Yet this is also true of the House of Commons, where the debates can nevertheless be of great interest. There are many reasons for the difference, which is partly a matter of personalities and partly of the rules of procedure and the accepted method of debate. There is a dearth of good parliamentary speakers; picturesque independent characters are kept out by the electoral law, and it is usually the same official spokesmen who take the floor time and again on behalf of the main parties. They are forbidden to read their speeches, but this rule has not sufficed to produce an atmosphere of debate: the effect is rather that of a sequence of monologues, each speaker paying little attention to his predecessor. In general, there is almost as much absenteeism as in the French Assembly, a fact which no standing orders have been able to cure and which is often the subject of complaints in the press and in parliament itself. The reasons are various. In the first place, as government in Germany is less centralized than in France, the deputies do not have to spend so much time contacting administrative authorities in the capital. For similar reasons, they do not have to be at their constituents' disposal for three days of every week. In fact, the German

128

September 15, 1957			September 17, 1961			September 19, 1965			September 28, 1969		
35·4			37·4			38·5			38·7		
31·1 (87·8%)			32·8 (87·7%)			33·4 (86·8%)			33·5 (86·%7)		
1·2 (3·8%)			1·3 (4·0%)			0·8 (2·4%)			0·6 (1·7%)		
Votes	*Per cents*	*Seats*	*Votes*	*Per cents*	*Seats*	*Votes*	*Per cents*	*Seats*	*Votes*	*Per cents*	*Seats*
15·0	50·0	270	14·3	45·3	242	15·5	47·6	245	15·2	46·1	242
9·5	31·8	169	11·4	36·2	190	12·8	32·3	202	14·1	42·7	224
2·3	7·7	41	4·0	12·8	67	3·1	9·5	49	1·9	5·8	30
1·0	3·4	17 }	0·9	2·8					0·05	0·1	
1·4	4·6										
0·2	0·5								0·05	0·2	
0·3	1·0		0·3	0·8		0·7	2·0		1·4	4·3	
								}	0·2	0·6	
			0·6	1·9		0·4	1·3				
0·2	0·8		0·1	0·2		0·1	0·3		0·9	0·2	
29·9	99·8	497	31·6	100	499	32·6	93·0	496	33·8	100	496

[4]In 1961 and 1969, *Gesamtdeutsche Partei.*
[5]DRP (*Deutche Reichspartei*) till 1961; NPD (*Nationaldemokratische Partei Deutschlands*) in 1965 and 1969.
[6]GVP (*GesamtdeutscheVolkspartei*) in 1953; DFU (*Deutsche Friedens-Union*) in 1961 and 1965.

electoral law is such that many deputies have no constituency at all, though this does not prevent their having to lead a double life, partly at Bonn and partly in the *Land* for which they were elected. Unlike French deputies, German ones are partly paid on a "time" basis: in addition to a basic salary, they receive travel expenses and a further allowance proportionate to their attendance at plenary sessions and committees. Nevertheless, their total re-numeration is a good deal less than that of their French colleagues, who are in the enviable position of enjoying a salary equated by law to that of the highest grade of the civil service. The chief reason why deputies fail to attend plenary sessions is the same as elsewhere: the most important work is done in committee. Moreover, it is impossible for a deputy to be expert in all subjects and he therefore prefers to let his colleagues attend debates on matters of which he is ignorant.

The committees, which have varied in number and size, are composed according to the relative strength of parties in the Bundestag. In the sixth session, there were seventeen of them, with between seventeen and thirty-three members each, plus two *ad hoc* committees on sport (including the Olympic games) and penal-law reform. By and large, the committees' spheres of activity correspond to those of government departments. The chairmen are, properly speaking, not elected but are nominated by the standing committee known as the Council of Elders (*Ältestenrat*), consisting of the President and Vice-President of the Bundestag and a varying number of deputies representing the parliamentary groups. There is usually little objection to the nominations, which maintain a just balance between the parties. Even after its electoral triumph in September, 1957, the CDU took only fifteen chairmanships for itself, leaving nine to the SPD and two to the FDP; and the committee for All-German Affairs ratified, though by a narrow margin, the Council's proposal for the reappointment as chairman of Herbert Wehner, whom the CDU had practically accused of treason during the electoral campaign. The deputies, in fact, wish the committees to work seriously in a nonpolemical atmosphere. In the sixth Bundestag, the CDU, though in opposition, chaired the committees on foreign affairs (Gerhard Schröder), defense, the budget, financial and legal affairs: altogether it had nine chairmanships, the same as the SPD, while the FDP had one (economic affairs).

Committee meetings are neither public nor secret: deputies who are not members, ministers, members of the Bundesrat, and high officials have the right to attend, and those who take part in the meetings may inform the public of what takes place. Only the committees concerned with foreign affairs, the reunification issue, Berlin, defense, and the protection of the constitution meet behind closed doors and in secret. Like hearings of U.S. congressional committees, regular meetings are sometimes preceded by sessions open to the press and public. Standing Order 73 lays down that experts and representatives of particular interests (*Interessenvertreter*) shall be invited to attend these, a procedure that has the advantage of ensuring that open expression is given to arguments and facts which are more usually adduced behind the scenes. Public hearings (*Öffentliche Anhörungen*) of this kind were infrequent in the early days (only two in twelve years), then a little less so (six in 1961–65), while fifty-eight were held during the fifth session of the Bundestag, notably those dealing with the "state of emergency" legislation and university affairs.

Committee debates on government and private bills generally take place between the first and second reading. Under the Bundestag standing orders, which are fairly complicated, on the first reading of a bill only its main principles are discussed; amendments are not permitted and the decision, which can be and usually is taken without voting, is solely on the question of referring the bill to committee. The second reading takes place at the latest two days after the distribution of the committee's report: this time, there is as a rule no general debate, but the bill is discussed article by article and amendments are introduced; a further reference to committee is possible at this stage. The third reading may commence immediately after the vote on the second reading if the latter has not led to any amendments being adopted; otherwise it begins not later than two days after the second-reading amendments have been circulated. At the third reading, there is another debate on the general principle and on any fresh proposals for amendment, which on this occasion must be put forward by a parliamentary group or at least fifteen deputies (whereas on second reading any deputy is free to propose an amendment). The vote for adoption or rejection of the measure is held only after the third reading. Bearing in mind that the Bundesrat also has to be consulted, one may think the system extremely complicated; but in practice the first and third readings are often purely formal, and debate on the second is much shortened by the work done in committee. Nevertheless, all critics of the system, as well as the deputies themselves, complain of its inefficiency and especially the piling-up of bills for consideration in the last few weeks of each session. In June–July, 1969, there were about ninety of these, and on some days there was scarcely a moment when the bell summoning deputies to vote (by show of hands, roll-call, or a division as at Westminster) was not echoing through the precincts of the parliament building.

It certainly happens that the deputies pass many laws they have not studied and do not fully understand. This is due partly to methods of work and partly to the way in which the laws are drafted. An attempt was made to improve matters in the "little parliamentary reform" adopted in July, 1969, which entered into force in October. The Bundestag elected in that year was slightly younger than its predecessor (78 deputies aged under forty) as against 73 in 1965, and 63 over sixty as against 109), equally lopsided as regards the sex of deputies (only 7 per cent are women as compared with 55 per cent of the electorate), and much the same as regards social and professional origins (163 officials as against 149, 59 managers and industrialists as against 53, and 51 farmers as against 59).[28] Each deputy is to have an "assistant" of his own, and groups of deputies may commission small working parties for purposes of research and documentation, over and above the 100 new Bundestag officials who are at the committees' disposal. Under the new scheme, the work of the Bundestag is to be planned three months in advance, each week being ear-marked for a single broad subject such as social or defense policy. Debates are to be "organized," though much less strictly than in the French Assembly, the chief spokesman of each party being allowed forty-five minutes while others are limited to a quarter of an hour. The functions of the principal organs of the Bundestag have been slightly modified, though without altering their balance. The *Ältestenrat* has had its powers widened and is no longer sub-jected to the rule of unanimity, but the "bureau" (*Vorstand*), consisting of the President, Vice-Presidents, and secretaries, still retains its privileges. The President and Vice-Presidents are elected separately, by secret vote, for the whole period of the legislature. At the first and second ballots, an absolute majority is required; at the third, a simple majority decides between the two candidates who received most votes in the previous ballot. The President has fairly wide authority, especially as regards drawing up and amending the agenda and determining the list of speakers; but his prestige depends at least as much on his personality as on his formal powers.

The first holder of the office, Dr. Erich Köhler, was a former chairman of the Economic Council at Frankfurt. He was not a success as President of the Bundestag and withdrew in 1950. His place was taken by Dr. Hermann Ehlers, a fellow member of the CDU with a more superficially Protestant background, being a trained theologian and a consistorial councillor. His remarkable abilities lent luster to the presidential office. He was re-elected in 1953 but unfortunately died on October 29, 1954. His successor was Dr. Eugen Gerstenmaier, also a Protestant theologian, whose candidature pre-sented difficulties at the outset, as the Chancellor appeared to be foisting him on a reluctant assembly. However, his personal qualities soon won recognition and he was re-elected at the opening of the third Bundestag by 437 votes to 54 abstentions. Thereafter, he appeared destined to hold the office for life, frustrated as far as his own ambition was concerned—he would have liked to become President of the Republic, Chancellor, or Minister of Foreign Affairs —but wielding undisputed authority in the Bundestag and much respected outside it by his own party and by public opinion. His quick temper caused him to be involved in one or two disputes and it was also said that he was not indifferent to money, but the scandal that broke at the end of 1968 and obliged him to resign on January 31, 1969 was of an unexpected kind: he was accused of having exerted undue influence on the terms and application of a law for the compensation of victims of Nazism, and to have accepted large sums by way of consolation for not having been made a professor by the government of the Third Reich. He was no doubt to blame, in particular for maintaining that his career continued to suffer at a time when he held the office of Bundestag President; but the hue and cry against him would have been less fierce but for the opportunity it afforded certain critics of discrediting a genuine opponent of Nazism.

The rules required his successor to be a member of the CDU, and the party leaders put forward Kai-Uwe von Hassel, a former Minister-President of Schleswig-Holstein, who had been an unsuccessful Minister of Defense in 1961–65 and was relegated to the post of Minister for Refugees in the Grand Coalition government. An unexpected revolt on the part of some younger deputies almost led to the nomination of one of their number, Heinrich Köppler, the parliamentary secretary of state for home affairs, whose meteoric rise received a further boost in this way. However, on February 4, 1969, von Hassel finally won the day within the parliamentary group and the Bundestag itself. He turned out to be an effective president, and, in October, the SPD and FDP agreed not to deprive the CDU of the post but to allow von Hassel to retain it in the new Bundestag. His duties were the more arduous since he no longer had the assistance of the veteran secretary-general (*Bundestagsdirektor*) Hans Trossman, who retired at this time after twenty years of onerous administrative duties.

In theory, the Bundestag possesses several means of calling the government to order. It has less power over the budget than the U.S. Congress, but more than the British Parliament and, in practice, a good deal more than the French. The cumbersome procedure of "interpellation" (*Grosse Anfrage*), which requires thirty signatures and does not necessarily lead to a debate, has not been used on a large scale since the first legislature: 160 instances in 1949–53, as against 97, 49, 34, and 45 in the four succeeding parliaments. "Written questions" (*Kleine Anfrage*) are more frequent, about 400 being put down during each parliament: they require the signature of fifteen deputies and are submitted to the President with a brief explanatory statement. The government's reply, which may be oral or written, is supposed to follow within a fortnight. But the commonest procedure is that of "questions for oral answer" (*Mündliche Anfrage*), the number of which in five successive parliaments has grown from 392 to 1,069, 1,373, 4,786, and 10,480. These are questions put down in writing and answered by the minister concerned in the course of an hour's "question time." They may concern the most varied subjects, and since an evasive reply may be countered by supplementaries (*Zusatzfragen*) from other deputies, the minister may be subjected to a real interrogation. This occurred on November 7–9, 1962, the SPD parliamentary group having put down eighteen questions on the 5th with a request for urgent answer; aided by numerous supplementaries from the floor, and also by the minister's compliance in allowing himself to be cross-questioned, they succeeded in making Franz Joseph Strauss contradict himself and finally admit that he had had a hand in the arrest of Conrad Ahlers in Spain—this being the crucial point of the *Spiegel* affair. Since then, questions of this type have been used more and more widely, not only because they are a means of calling the government to account but also because they help to inform the public and enliven parliamentary life.[29]

The Bundestag has another, more direct means of control over an important aspect of the executive power. The rearmament legislation of 1956 provided for the appointment of an Ombudsman in the shape of the Parliamentary Defense Commissioner (*Wehrbeauftragter des Bundestags*), who enjoys unrestricted powers of investigation and may receive complaints directly from officers and private soldiers. The institution was some time getting under way, as it was not easy to find a suitable man: he had to be politically acceptable to the main parties, knowledgeable in military matters, and free from the suspicion of being opposed to soldiering on principle. On February 19, 1959, General Helmuth von Grolman, formerly commander of a cavalry division and state secretary for refugee affairs in the government of Lower Saxony, was elected by 363 votes to 49. By October of that year, he had received 2,200 complaints. In July, 1961, however, he was obliged to resign as a result of having shown overmuch fondness for young soldiers. Five months later, the Bundestag elected as his successor one of its own number, Admiral Hellmuth Heye, who in turn had to resign in November, 1964 after some articles of his criticizing the structure and behavior of the armed forces had appeared in a sensational magazine.[30] The third holder of the post, and the first not to have been a high-ranking officer, was Matthias Hoogen, who, at the time of his election on December 1, 1964, was the CDU chairman of the legal affairs committee. Despite numerous conflicts with his assistants, he remained in office till 1970.

The commissioner's duties include submitting an annual report to the President of the Bundestag, which is then debated and approved by that body and which gives full information on the attitude and morale of the armed forces. The main part of the commissioner's task, however, consists in investigating the complaints he receives against the military authorities. In 1969, his last full year of office, Hoogen received over 7,000 complaints, which led in about twenty cases to penal or disciplinary sanctions and in 400 others to various measures such as admonitions, the cancelling of orders or regulations, and so on. On March 11, 1970, he was succeeded by the fourth holder of the office, Fritz-Rudolf Schultz. A major in the reserve, holder of the Military Cross with oak-leaves, an owner of vineyards in private life, he was a member of the Bundestag from 1957 onward and vice-chairman of the parliamentary FDP from 1963. His election was somewhat difficult—he received only 8 votes more than the necessary absolute majority of 260 (the Berlin delegates being entitled to vote) one reason being that, although a specialist in military affairs, he had taken no part in debates on the social role and psychology in the armed forces.

To sum up, parliament in the Federal Republic is a vigorous institution, more so in any case than in the Fifth French Republic, even though it is undergoing the same decline in West Germany as in other European countries.[31] But there are at least two distinctive features of the German situation. In the first place, a whole range of groups opposed to government policy describe themselves as the "nonparliamentary opposition" (*ausserparlamentarische Opposition*), and their action in thus denying the right of the people's representatives to speak in their name must in some degree detract from the authority of parliament. Second, the stability of past governments and the existence of a few large, tightly organized parliamentary groups have combined to reduce considerably the traditional role of parliament as an institution. In the course of time, two different situations have developed. For some years, the real struggle for influence was not between the government and parliament but between a government with a solid majority and the dominant parliamentary group on which the majority rested, that is, the CDU/CSU. Later, in 1966–69, when the two main parties were in alliance and relations between the executive and legislature were even less interesting in their public aspect, parliament recovered a measure of influence—though in a novel and unspectacular way—by reason of the fact that the two parliamentary groups had to compromise with each other in order to work together. The respective chairmen—Rainer Barzel for the CDU and Helmut Schmidt for the SPD—thus became key men of the Grand Coalition, but their activity was, so to speak, marginal to the official role of the Bundestag. This fact was the reflection of a basic reality—namely, the decisive part played by the big parties in the political system as a whole.

7

Elections and Party Politics

FROM 1949 to 1961, parliamentary life in the Federal Republic became progressively simpler: the electors concentrated their votes more and more on the three big parties, and, by the end of the period, all members of the Bundestag belonged to one or another of the main groups. Contrary to many predictions as regards the effect of the Grand Coalition, the voters actually seem to be more and more in favor of a bipartisan setup.

Year	*CDU/CSU + SPD + FDP* (*in per cents*)	*CDU/CSU + SPD* (*in per cents*)
1949	72·1	60·2
1953	83·5	74·0
1957	89·7	82·0
1961	94·3	81·5
1965	96·4	86·9
1969	94·6	88·8

One reason for this trend is that the electoral law is so drafted as to encourage the citizen not to "waste" his vote. Another reason lies in the privileged position the constitution accords parties as dominant forces in the political game: the voter's task is not merely to bear witness to his own state of mind or abstract preference, but to use the election as a means of influencing the power situation.

The Law and the Elector's Choice

Nevertheless, Article 38 of the Basic Law, following Article 21 of the Weimar constitution, reflects the traditional liberal conception of individual deputies representing an undifferentiated citizenry. "The deputies of the German Bundestag . . . shall be representatives of the whole people, not bound by mandates or instructions and subject only to their conscience." But this seems, at most, to be intended as a reminder that members of parliament should be independent of economic and social groups: for Article 21 of the Basic Law, which significantly occurs at the beginning of the section on institutions— between the statement of general principles and the article on the colors of the national flag—provides that

1. The parties shall participate in forming the political will of the people. They can be freely formed. Their internal organization must conform to democratic principles. They must publicly account for the sources of their funds.

2. Parties that, according to their aims and the behaviour of their adherents [*Anhänger*—not simply members], seek to impair or abolish the free and democratic basic order or to jeopardize the existence of the Federal Republic of Germany, shall be unconstitutional. The Federal Constitutional Court shall decide on the question of unconstitutionality.

3. Details shall be regulated by Federal legislation.

Paragraph 1 clearly influenced Article 4 of the constitution of the Fifth French Republic, which runs: "Parties and political groups play a part in the exercise of the right to vote. The right to form parties and their freedom of action are unrestricted. They must respect the principles of national sovereignty and of democracy." But, while this article was intended to reassure the parties that they had a right to exist, it is less far-reaching than its German counterpart. To "play a part in the exercise of the right to vote" is simply to act as a channel for the expression of the voters' wishes at election time; whereas to "participate in forming the political will of the people" involves acting as a permanent sounding board and also performing an educative function. When the Federal law on parties, foreshadowed in paragraph 3 of Article 21, was finally promulgated on July 24, 1967, the first two of its forty-one articles described their role in forthright terms:[1]

1. Parties are, in constitutional law, a necessary component of the free and democratic basic order. . . .
2. Parties shall participate in forming the political will of the people in all fields of public life, and especially by:
influencing the formation of public opinion; promoting and intensifying political education; encouraging the active participation of citizens in political life; training citizens capable of assuming public responsibilities; nominating candidates in Federal, *Land*, and municipal elections; influencing political developments in parliament and government; formulating political aims and applying them to the process of forming the political will of the people; and endeavoring to bring about a constant and active relationship [*lebendige Verbindung*] between the people and the organs of the state.

Paragraph 2 of Article 21 has been brought into operation on two occasions. On November 19, 1951, the Federal Government applied to the Constitutional Court for a declaration that the Socialist Reich Party (SRP) was unconstitutional. The Court's procedure was set in motion, and on January 24, 1952 a search was carried out in the national and regional headquarters of the SRP and the homes of its leaders. On July 15, an interim order was issued forbidding the party to carry on propaganda. On October 23, the first division of the Court gave its verdict ordering that the SRP be dissolved. The party had been formed on October 2, 1949, after the first Bundestag elections on August 14, at a time when the Allies' permission to do so was no longer requisite. Most of its leaders and members came from the *Deutsche Rechtspartei* (German Party of the Right), which had received 1·8 per cent of the votes cast in the election and five seats, all in Lower Saxony. Two deputies, Fritz Dorls and Franz Richter, were among the leaders, together with Count Westarp and ex-General Remer: the latter, at Berlin, had been responsible for defeating the *coup d'état* of July 20, 1944. The SRP later scored a few electoral successes, most notably in Lower Saxony in May, 1951, when it gained 11 per cent of the votes and 16 seats in the *Landtag* of 158 members.

The Court's judgment banning the SRP began by giving a detailed interpretation of Article 21. In the first place, it observed, the "basic order" of which the constitution speaks is an order dependent on values, namely those of liberty, equality, and the dignity of the human person. The foundations of such an order must include "respect for the human rights enumerated in the Basic Law, especially the right of every person to live and develop freely, the sovereignty of the people, the separation of powers, the responsibility of the executive, administration according to law, independent courts, a multiparty system with equality of opportunity for all parties, and the constitutional right of an opposition to form itself and carry on its activities." It will be seen that the Court is here developing a specific and, as it were, classical conception of democracy, and proclaiming that any party which flouts that conception is unconstitutional. The nature of a party's internal organization is among the factors that may be examined in order to determine its aims; it may very probably "seek to impose on the state the structural principles that it had adopted for itself," but "this inference must be verified in each particular case." In so doing, less attention should be paid to the letter of the party's statutes than to the way they operate in practice and, as Article 21 says, to the behavior of its adherents. This term, in the Court's view, included "at least all persons who are active (*sich einsetzen*) in favor of the SRP, even if they are not actually members of it."

The Court had little trouble in proving that the SRP was genuinely neo-Nazi, that is, that it regarded itself as the successor to the NSDAP, addressing its appeal to veterans of the latter, using its vocabulary, and invoking its ideology: totalitarian, racist, and hostile to the parliamentary system. When the defendants protested, through their lawyers, that their party program and statements embodied declarations of loyalty to the Basic Law, the Court replied that these "did not constitute evidence as to the party's real aims," and it recalled that Hitler in his time had sworn to obey the Weimar constitution. The SRP then advanced a fresh argument: was it not unjust to condemn a party on the strength of words or actions for which parallels could be found in the case of other bodies that were accepted as democratic? Had not other parties done their best to recruit ex-Nazis? To this plea the Court replied with two arguments of unequal value. The first was clear enough: "The SRP is not condemned for having sought support among former Nazis, but for constituting a group of incorrigible adherents to Nazism who had not changed their views"—their purpose being not to strengthen democracy but to uphold and propagate the ideas of National Socialism. The Court's second argument was more involved. An act considered in itself may or may not be unconstitutional: "only the general consideration of a number of separate acts makes it evident that their purpose is to undermine and eventually abolish the existing order." The Court's difficulty is clear enough: it was well aware that no party at the time was wholly democratic in its behavior, but it nevertheless had to be

137

possible to apply Article 21 to prevent the rise of a totalitarian party. The Court's attitude, however, implied the assumption by the judiciary of wide powers of political interpretation.

What are the legal consequences of banning a party? In the first place, the law lays down that its property shall be confiscated. As regards the SRP'S seats in parliament, the Court ruled—refusing to see in this any infringement of Article 38 of the Basic Law—that "the mandate of deputies to the Bundestag or *Landtage* who were elected as candidates of the SRP, or who belonged to the SRP at the time when this judgment was delivered, is hereby annulled. The deputies in question shall not be replaced by others; instead, the membership of the assemblies in question shall be reduced by a number of seats equal to those annulled. This shall not affect the validity of parliamentary decisions already adopted." As regards local and municipal councils—except of course those of Hamburg and Bremen, which have the status of *Länder*—the Court took no action to annul representatives' mandates, since these bodies were essentially administrative and "did not, properly speaking, take political decisions." This is an ingenious distinction, but it is by no means wholly in accordance with reality as far as municipal powers are concerned.

The lesson administered by the Court had its effect. The parties of the extreme right that succeeded the SRP—the *Deutsche Reichspartei* and subsequently the NPD (*Nationaldemokratische Partei Deutschlands*)—were much more circumspect in stating their aims, though it is by no means certain whether an application to the Court against them would have been successful. In any case, for reasons we shall see later on, the Federal Government refrained from action even during the period of NPD gains in 1967, a fact that cast a curious light on the banning of the Communist Party. This measure, which has remained in force, was the result of a plea by the government made on November 22, 1951, three days after it moved against the SRP—the idea being to strike a balance in castigating extremists of the right and left. The Court commenced action against the Communists on January 24, 1952, the same day as in the case of the SRP. But this time the proceedings took longer, both because the defendants used every possible device to gain time and because the Court itself was plainly anxious to postpone judgment, if not to avoid the issue altogether. The arguing of the case did not begin until November 23, 1954 and it continued until July 5, 1955. There was then a long interval, which would no doubt have been longer still if the government had not exerted pressure. Finally, on August 17, 1956, the first division of the Court handed down a judgment, which comprises over three hundred pages of its official record. The judges were at pains to avoid basing their arguments on historical events outside Germany, but they expatiated on Marxism-Leninism and on Stalin's writings. Referring to twenty-six works or particular statements of Stalin, Lenin, and Marx, they demonstrated with scrupulous care the incompatibility between Communism, founded on the dictatorship of the proletariat, and the "free and democratic basic order." To the objection that the German Communist Party (KPD) had been authorized as a democratic party by the four powers in 1945, the Court replied that, while this was certainly so, the powers' view was based on a negative conception of democracy, which they treated as identical with anti-Nazism; the Basic Law, however, had defined democracy in a positive sense, and the KPD must be judged in the light of this.

"The banning of the KPD is not legally incompatible with the re-authorization of a Communist Party in the event of elections being held throughout Germany." By so declaring, the Court gave its answer in advance —though not a very convincing one—to those who saw the ban as an additional obstacle to German reunification.

The reasons for the ban were not wholly founded either on the KPD's principles or on its acts. "A party is not unconstitutional merely because it does not recognize the basic order founded on democracy and liberty: there must also be evidence of a combative and aggressive attitude toward the existing order." But, under Article 21, "there need not be a definite attempt [at subversion]: it is sufficient that the party's political acts should be governed by an intention of principle and a permanent attitude of hostility toward the basic democratic and liberal order." Why this complicated distinction? In the first place, freedom of opinion must be respected, and, moreover, there was another party in Germany (the SPD itself) that had once invoked Marxist and revolutionary principles. Second, there were not many concrete misdeeds that could be laid to the KPD's charge in the Federal Republic, and it was not felt desirable to allude to "infiltration" from the G.D.R.

As the proceedings developed, the KPD passed to the counter-attack, invoking the right of resistance and maintaining that attacks on democratic liberties in the Republic frequently took place with impunity. In reply, the Court took its stand on dangerous ground by stating that "the right of resistance must only be used in a conservative sense, that is to say, to protect or maintain the legal order of things (*Rechtsordnung*) in time of emergency" should it appear that recourse to law would be of no avail. This was a considerably narrower version of the duty of resistance than that laid down in Article 19 of the Bremen constitution or Article 147 of that of Hesse. For instance, it implicitly limited the right to strike in the form in which it was upheld by the most powerful trade union, that of the iron and steel workers. Moreover, it entailed a very specific interpretation of Article 20 of the Basic Law, which declares that "the Federal Republic of Germany is a democratic and social [*sozialer*] federal state." In the Court's view, society is composed of groups that, provided the legislator acts in accordance with justice, must not and need not conflict except in a free interplay of forces that must exclude any domination of one group by another. No attention is paid to the idea that the preservation of the "free democratic" order might signify the perpetration of a state of injustice and, in a truer sense, of disorder.

The Court's judgment had a mixed reception. One of the arguments most frequently used against it was that it gave a handle to East German propaganda concerning reunification and even as regards standards of liberalism: the G.D.R. could boast that a CDU and a Liberal Party continued to exist on its territory (even though both were in fact subservient to Communist leadership). The liveliest criticism was directed not against the Court but against the government. Despite reservations on this or that aspect of the verdict, most observers took the view that the Court had no choice but to pronounce a ban, if it were not to give the impression of absolving Communism from any suspicion of being totalitarian. But why had the government put such pressure on the Court when the latter was obviously not desirous of being involved? And what had the government succeeded in doing, other than extinguishing a political group that was in any case dying a natural death?

As early as 1946, the Communist Party had appeared very much weakened in comparison to its prewar status. At Duisburg, for instance, where it had gained twice as many votes as the Socialists in 1932, it now had only 87,000 votes to their 214,000. At Essen and Düsseldorf, the picture was the same. From 1946 onward, the party had continued to decline throughout West Germany. At the general election of 1949, it gained 1·4 million votes (5·7 per cent) and 15 seats, while in 1953 the figures fell to 610,000 (2·2 per cent) and it disappeared from the Bundestag. Even in its best constituency, Remscheid-Solingen, it gained only 12 per cent of the votes as opposed to 21 per cent in 1949. In the *Land* elections it was the same story. In Bremen, it scored 11·4 per cent, 8·8 per cent, 6·4 per cent, and 5 per cent in 1946, 1947, 1951, and 1955; in Hesse, 10·7 per cent, 4·7 per cent, and 3·4 per cent in 1946, 1950, and 1954; in North Rhine–Westphalia, 14·0 per cent, 5·5 per cent, and 3·8 per cent in 1947, 1950, and 1954. In these circumstances, the ban appeared positively unsporting, and it did the KPD at least as much good as harm: from East Germany, the Communists were able to proclaim that if they were allowed to take part in the elections, everyone would see how matters really stood. Nor was the ban calculated to have much effect on anti-Communist feeling in the Federal Republic, which was already very strong. Later, when a whole ideological evolution had taken place and the Federal Republic had acquired full confidence in its own existence and that of its institutions, the old arguments were discarded and a Communist Party was once more authorized. Not the same Communist Party, for it would have been a difficult matter juridically to lift the ban on the KPD. But in October, 1967, the *Länder* ministers of the interior decided that there need not be any objection to the creation of a new Communist Party. So, on September 26, 1968, Kurt Bachmann, who had been a member of the KPD since 1932 and its leader at the time of the ban, held a press conference at Frankfurt in which he announced that a new party had come into existence. The DKP (*Deutsche Kommunistische Partei*) held its inaugural congress on April 12–13 and elected Bachmann as its president. Its basic documents, the party statutes and "fundamental declaration," invoked Marxist principles but avoided those that the Constitutional Court had pronounced illegal: the dictatorship of the proletariat, for example, was replaced by the "struggle to ensure the leading role of the working people in the state and society." The DKP, it was made clear, did not supersede the KPD, which in theory continued to exist underground with the aged Max Reimann as its secretary-general—which did not prevent him from being one of the founders of the new party.

If the Federal Republic had maintained the Weimar system of voting, the KPD would still have had eleven deputies in the second Bundestag (1953). But the drafters of the constitution in 1948–49 believed that full proportional representation had been to blame for the proliferation of parties, the parliamentary disorder, and the paralysis of government in Weimar days. They therefore cast about for a different method, which should, however, be other than the majoritarian system as practiced in Britain and the United States. Although soundings had taken place since 1945 at the *Land* and municipal level and more was known about the electorate's views than in France during the same period, the German authorities felt, as their French opposite numbers had done, that some form of proportional representation was necessary to obtain a political conspectus of the country. Hence the law of June 15, 1949, which was amended at various times right down to May, 1968 but which has not been altered in its main lines. It provides for a sort of "personalized proportional representation," in the following way: Each voter marks his ballot twice, choosing a candidate in one column and a party in the other. In each constituency, one deputy is elected by a plurality of votes (as in Britain), but the "direct" seats thus filled represent only half of those in the Bundestag The remainder are filled from lists drawn up by the parties in each *Land*, in such a way that when each party's "direct" seats and "list" seats are added together, the party will have as many representatives in the Bundestag as it would have if the "second column" votes were allotted proportionally, on the d'Hondt or "highest average" system.

To take an imaginary example: in a *Land* where there are twenty seats to be filled and ten constituencies, the CDU candidate is successful in eight constituencies, the SPD candidate in two, and the FDP in none, while the three parties respectively obtain 50 per cent, 40 per cent, and 10 per cent of the "second votes." On the proportional system, these percentages entitle them to ten, eight, and two seats respectively. Consequently the CDU is allotted two "list" seats in addition to its eight "direct" ones; the SPD similarly gets another six, and the FDP gets two.

It will be noticed that a party may gain a higher number of direct seats than its quota under the proportional system. There is the more chance of this since the direct seats represent half the total on a national basis but not always at *Land* level: for example, in Bavaria 47 seats out of 86 are "direct," but in North Rhine–Westphalia it is only 66 out of 155. In Schleswig-Holstein in 1961, there were 14 constituencies, and, in principle, 6 "list" seats to be filled. The CDU candidates headed the poll in 13 constituencies, but in the *Land* as a whole the CDU, SPD, and FDP scored respectively 42 per cent, 36 per cent, and 14 per cent of the "second column" votes. Out of the total of 20 seats, this would give the CDU 9, the SPD 8, and the FDP 3. The solution in such cases is to create additional "list" seats (known as *Überhangsmandate*) for the benefit of the smaller parties: thus, in the example given, Schleswig-Holstein sent 24 deputies (13 + 8 + 3) to the Bundestag instead of 20. In the same way a single *Überhangsmandat* was created for the Saar, so that the Bundestag in 1961 consisted altogether of 247 + 247 + 4 + 1, or a total of 499 deputies. In 1949, there were two *Überhangsmandate*, in 1953 and 1957 there were three, but none in 1965 and 1969.

What is the advantage of enabling the elector to vote for a candidate as well as for a party? As a rule, he simply marks his ballot twice in the same row, voting for the candidate put forward by the party to which his second choice is given. Nevertheless, it may happen that the candidate who tops the poll is not a representative of the party that gets the most votes. For example, at Mannheim in 1957, the CDU scored 74,900 votes and the SPD only 70,200, but Carlo Schmid with 76,200 "first" votes beat the CDU candidate with 73,300. Even if the majorities do not differ in this way, a comparison of the first and second votes will often provide an index of a candidate's personal appeal to voters who favor parties other than his.

The system thus enables the elector to differentiate his choice. If he favors neither of the two main parties but finds that they are rivals for the "direct" seat, he will cast his votes for the party he prefers and for whichever of the "big party" candidates is more acceptable to him. In 1969, the SPD obtained 400,000 more personal votes than list votes; the FDP, on the other hand, scored 1,900,000 list votes, but only 1,500,000 votes were cast for its candidates.[2] Finally, the system makes it in the parties' interest to put forward candidates who can put up a good fight at constituency level.

When the rules were drawn up in 1949, it might have been feared that they would encourage the idea that there were two categories of Bundestag members, the first being genuine "representatives of the people" while the second being, so to speak, second-class deputies, having either been defeated in their constituencies and rescued by the *Land* list or else "elected" by the proportional system without ever having had to face the electorate. In fact, however, no distinction has ever been made between the two categories, either in the Bundestag itself or by the public. A more serious problem is the degree of power enjoyed by the party authorities who drew up the supplementary list, on which the order of precedence is laid down in advance. After directly elected candidates have been ticked off the list, further seats are allocated in accordance with this order, which also operates in the event of a member's death: there is no by-election, his place being simply taken by the next candidate on the party list.

The party leaders are placed at the head of the list so as to confirm their authority and ensure that they get a seat—and sometimes also to confer distinction on a party at *Land* level. Thus in 1969 there was a contest over who should head the CDU list in North Rhine-Westphalia, the final order being Gerhard Schröder, Rainer Barzel, and Hans Katzer: this had a political significance, whereas there was no dispute within the SPD over the party list being headed by "Willy Brandt, journalist, residing at Bonn-Venusberg."

The lists are drawn up at *Land* level, and the party federations are jealous of their independence though naturally they pay attention to national headquarters. The constituency committees, for their part, do not like "carpetbaggers." Under Article 17 of the 1967 law, candidates must be chosen by secret ballot: in not a few cases, the effect of this has been to prevent genuine competition. However, the method of choosing candidates in a constituency is, by and large, more democratic than in most other countries.[3] The party may, on the other hand, fail to "reinsure" a candidate, either by leaving him off the list or by giving him a low place on it. In 1953, Carlo Schmid almost missed re-election because his party, the SPD, struck him off the list on account of some rash words he spoke in criticism of its leaders. In 1969, Reinhold Rehs, the chairman of the refugees' association, who had just deserted the SPD for the CDU, was beaten at Verden in Lower Saxony and missed election to the Bundestag, the party not having judged that he rated a place on its list: an interesting token of the decline of a pressure group.

The dual-vote system does not in itself mitigate the effect of proportional representation in multiplying parliamentary groups. To remedy this, the electoral law lays down conditions that must be met before a party can be represented in parliament under the proportional system. In 1949, it was stipulated that a party must either receive at least 5 per cent of the votes in a *Land* or gain one direct seat. In 1953, this was altered to one direct seat or 5 per cent of votes on a nationwide basis; since 1957, the requirement is 5 per cent of votes on a national basis or three direct seats. Thus the conditions have become progressively more severe from the point of view of small parties. However, the rule concerning one or more direct seats is of dubious effect, since it enables a large party to make a "client" of a small one by the following simple process. The large party puts up no "direct" candidate in a given constituency and says to the voters: "Give your first vote to candidate X representing party Y, but mind that you give your second vote not to party Y, but to us." Except in the case of an unnatural alliance, as between the SPD and the Bavarian Party in 1957, the principle is, as a rule, faithfully observed, the electors showing considerable understanding of how to use their two votes. For instance, at Celle (Lower Saxony) in 1957 the result was:

Party	First votes	Second votes
CDU	no candidate	38,600
SPD	31,200	28,700
DP	40,100 (elected)	14,500

In 1953, this stratagem enabled the small *Zentrum* Party to survive for a time, and it enabled the DP in 1957 to secure seventeen seats although only 3·4 per cent of votes were cast for it. But as, in such cases, the small party's survival depends entirely on the good will of the larger, it is soon obliged to choose between merging with it or taking an independent line and disappearing from parliament in consequence.

In 1953, the requirement of 5 per cent on a national basis eliminated the regional Bavarian Party. The same rule had a drastic effect in 1957 on the BHE (Union of Expellees and Dispossessed), which lost 243,000 of its 1,600,000 votes, thus falling below the crucial level and forfeiting every one of its twenty-seven seats. The blow to its supporters and party militants was one from which they did not recover. In general, the effect of the 5 per cent rule is to hasten the fall of a party that is on the downgrade, as was seen once again on September 28, 1969 when the NPD came just short of the qualifying number of votes. Yet the same rule had previously helped the NPD to gain ground. When a party is too small, the electors do not waste their votes on it, but if it appears capable of reaching the 5 per cent mark they may be more disposed to give it a leg up. Apart from thus affecting the voters' behavior, the rule has a decisive effect on the working of state institutions. If, in September,

1969, 226,000 more electors had voted for the NPD instead of some other party, it would have had twenty-five seats in the Bundestag instead of none at all, and the Brandt-Scheel coalition would have been arithmetically impossible. In the same way, the whole strategy of the FDP for 1969–73 is dominated by a well-founded apprehension aroused by its score of only 5·8 per cent at the last election.

Under the Grand Coalition, on the other hand, the FDP had even more reason to fear what might happen if the two major parties agreed to base elections on the "relative majority" system. The SPD, however, finally came to the conclusion that the CDU, which seemed to be permanently in the lead in the largest number of constituencies, would remain in power indefinitely if the change were made. To everyone's surprise, the election of September 28, 1969 showed a change in the position as regards "direct" seats in most constituencies. In 1965, the CDU/CSU had won 154 of these to the SPD's 94; in 1969, the respective figures were 121 and 127. This meant that the FDP could not afford to be as greedy as they had been in 1966, lest the other two parties should feel tempted to renew the Grand Coalition and elbow them out of the Bundestag by introducing a voting system based on plurality. For the time being, however, the proportional method has guaranteed the survival of a three-party system and prevented it turning into a virtual two-party one on the British model.

The 5 per cent rule does not operate to limit the financial aid granted to parties by the state. The position in regard to this is both clear and complex. Its complexity is due to successive judgments of the Constitutional Court, which have introduced new factors and new formulas; but basically the German parties are highly privileged as compared with the situation in most foreign countries. Their heyday as regards state aid was between 1955 and 1966. After the Court's ruling of June 24, 1958, which laid down that donations to parties were not deductible for income tax purposes, the Bundestag created a budgetary item of "grants in furtherance of political education by parties." The sums involved rose from DM5 million in 1959 to 38 million for each of the years 1964, 1965, and 1966; they were shared in their entirety between the parties represented in the Bundestag—namely, the SPD, FDP, CDU, and CSU (the last two being counted separately). In addition, large sums for the same purpose were granted by the *Länder*.[4] In 1965, the SPD received a total of DM19·7 million from public funds, the CDU 18·1 million, the CSU 5·8 million, and the FDP 7·4 million.

On June 19, 1966, the Constitutional Court forbade the financing of parties by the state, while nonetheless sanctioning grants for parliamentary activity and especially for campaigning purposes. As a result, the parties cut their budgets considerably, reducing salaried staff, closing down a number of periodicals, and restricting their information and propaganda activities. But the 1967 law on parties defined the notion of electoral campaigning in wide terms. It provided for the creation of a fund of DM2·50 per registered voter, to be divided among all parties that had secured at least 2·5 per cent of second votes. The law further empowered the *Länder* to provide campaign funds at their level, the figure decided on by them being DM1·50 per voter. At the Federal level alone, the four parties represented in the Bundestag would have received on this basis over DM96 million for the period of 1965–69. To this must be added the grants made since 1967 to the parties' large institutes of democratic education—DM3·5 million each to the CDU's Konrad-Adenauer-Stiftung and the SPD's Friedrich-Ebert-Stiftung, plus extra grants to both of these for aid to students, and DM1 million each to the CSU's Hanns-Seidel-Stiftung and the FDP's Friedrich-Naumann-Stiftung. However, the Court's judgment of December 3, 1968 obliged the Bundestag to amend the law, and since July, 1969, any party that secures 0·5 per cent of the votes qualifies for an electoral grant. At *Land* level, the position was still uncertain in the spring of 1970, as the Court had not been asked to rule as to the qualification in non-Federal elections; but it would probably pronounce in favor of a party that appealed to it after gaining between 0·5 and 1·5 per cent of votes. In any case, on the Federal level alone, Adolf von Thadden's NPD was entitled, on the strength of the September, 1969 elections, to receive about DM3·5 million from the Federal treasury. He had in fact already drawn a large part of this sum before the election on the basis of the 1965 results, and was in 1969 in a position to claim the remainder, whereas the FDP had to surrender part of the advance it had received.

Federal and *Land* money are not, of course, the parties' only source of revenue. The 1967 law finally gave effect to the provision in the constitution that the origin of party funds should be made known publicly. Thus the parties' accounts for 1968 were published in the official gazette (*Bundesgesetz-blatt*) on October 20, 1969, in the form laid down in 1967, which was later revised in accordance with a judgment handed down by the Court in 1969. The law originally stated that it was not necessary to declare the names of physical persons who had given less than DM20,000 or corporate bodies that had given less than DM200,000. Starting with the accounts for 1969, the lower limit of DM20,000 applies to physical and juridical persons alike. The 1968 figures show how much more important membership dues are to the SPD (DM18·9 million, compared with 8·1 million for the CDU/CSU, 1·2 million for the FDP, and 630,000 for the NPD), while the official figures for donations are: CDU, 5 million; CSU, 2 million; SDP, 2·5 million; FDP, 2·1 million; and NPD, 1 million. As the figures are given for the *Land* federations as well as for party headquarters in each case, the reports are enlightening as regards the structure of the respective parties and the support they enjoy in different areas. Even though the accounts cannot, of course, be taken wholly at face value, their publication is a remarkable step forward in the process of democratic information.

The Social Democratic Party (SPD)

The 5 per cent hurdle and the grant of public aid in proportion to electoral support are of course calculated to favor the big parties and make it very hard for the smaller ones to gain ground. This is a good thing insofar as it contributes to the stability and efficiency of the nation's institutions, but it is also attended by some risk. Since it is almost impossible to progress by slow degrees, a new party can hardly make its way except by appealing to emotion or exploiting a state of crisis. Moreover, the absence from public life, and especially from parliament, of any parties that can give continuous and organized expression to minority views tends to favor sporadic, irregular movements and to encourage malcontents to blame the system as such rather than the government of the day. In this way, the very smoothness with which the country's institutions function is taken as a sign of the neglect of real problems, of a divorce between the parties that operate within the institutional framework and the national life that goes on outside it.

During the first two decades of the Republic's life, these dangers seemed of little account compared with the advantages of having two strong, self-assertive parties as rival poles of attraction for the great bulk of the electorate. The parties in question were at one and the same time very close to each other and very different: inevitably close insofar as they stood for a similar type of regime and aimed to capture the support of the same intermediate mass of voters, yet profoundly different in their political beliefs, their general spirit, and their methods of recruitment. As with the British Conservative and Labour parties or the American Republicans and Democrats, it would be absurd to overlook the points of resemblance, but equally unrealistic not to appreciate the depth of the political, sociological, and ideological differences.

In 1945, the SPD had to its credit a history, going back several decades, of organization and militancy. Like the other social democratic parties of Europe it also had the advantage that its ideas were generally popular: faced with the task of clearing up the debris of war, everyone was more or less socialistically inclined. On the other hand, the SPD was deeply marked by its years of exile: there seemed good reason to fear that the German people might distrust men who had not been in Germany at the time of her collapse and who in many cases had spent the war years in enemy territory. This fear led initially to the adoption by the SPD of a tough nationalist line, intensified by the personality and ideas of its postwar chief and by its leaders' anxiety to wipe out the old, damaging reproach that the Socialists were men and women without patriotism. Their fears as to the political consequences of exile appeared for a long time to be unfounded. The public in various polls expressed hostility toward ex-émigrés in general, but this did not affect the personal following of Erich Ollenhauer, the party's vice-chairman and, later, chairman, or Max Brauer, who became mayor of Hamburg immediately after his return from America in 1946, or, again, Erich Lindstaedt, who became the unchallenged leader of Socialist youth on his return from Sweden. The theme did not take on any dramatic importance until 1961, when the Mayor of Berlin became a candidate for the chancellorship; and since then it has never played an important part in any electoral contest, although the SPD and its opponents did their best respectively to diminish or play up its importance in the minds of marginal voters.[5]

On October 6, 1945, those of the SPD leaders who had survived the war and the Nazi period met at the monastery of Wenningsen near Hanover to plan the reconstruction of the party. The debate was dominated by three personalities: Kurt Schumacher, who had formed a revived Socialist Party in the British zone; Erich Ollenhauer, newly arrived from London and representing the party's executive in exile; and Otto Grotewohl from Berlin, where he was head of the Socialist Party in the Soviet zone. Grotewohl proposed the immediate formation of a new executive to prepare a merger with the Communists. Schumacher, supported by Ollenhauer, held out for independence and persuaded the delegates to postpone the election of an executive until the party congress, to be held in 1946. On April 22, the creation of the Socialist Unity Party (SED) was forced through in the Soviet zone, and on May 10, the SPD congress at Hanover elected Schumacher and Ollenhauer chairman and vice-chairman of the party, which now existed only in West Germany. In the case of the CDU, as we have seen, the break between East and West did not finally take place until December, 1947, and even then the party did not cease to exist in the Soviet zone.

The SPD was not only the first political group to be affected in this way by the division of Germany, but it was also the party that suffered most from having to limit its recruitment and activity to the western zones. Before 1933, Prussia had been the stronghold of German Socialism; in 1946, 48·6 per cent of Berliners voted for the SPD, and West Berlin is still one of its strongest constituencies. In the whole region east of the Elbe and outside Greater Berlin, 34 per cent of the electorate was Socialist before Hitler came to power. Moreover, a sizeable number of the "western" leaders of the SPD were natives of eastern Germany. Schumacher was born at Culm (Chelmno) south of Danzig, and Ollenhauer at Magdeburg; of the 131 SPD deputies elected to the Bundestag in 1949, 50 were born outside Federal territory, whereas the CDU figure was 15 out of 139. Thus the SPD, like the Protestant Church (as we shall see later), was wounded to the depths of its being by the division of Germany. Its truncation, moreover, was only gradually made up for by the reforging of links with international Socialism.[6] As late as June, 1947, at the Zurich meeting of COMISCO (Committee of International Socialist Conferences), a proposal for the admission of the SPD was rejected despite the plea of Dr. Schumacher, who had suffered grievously at the Nazis' hands: the British, French, Dutch, and Scandinavians were in favor, but the Belgians, Greeks, Italians, and Swiss abstained, while the Palestinian Jewish and East European unions opposed the motion, so that it failed to get the necessary majority. Thanks to a Belgian change of mind and the reaction to the foundation of the Cominform, the SPD became a member of COMISCO at the Antwerp congress at the beginning of December, 1947. When, at the Frankfurt congress in July, 1951, the Information Bureau was replaced by a Socialist International properly so called, it might have seemed that the SPD was at last truly assimilated, but in fact it remained for some time longer in a state of partial isolation. The favorable attitude taken up by the SFIO (French Socialist Party) in 1947 was the work of a single man, Salomon Grumbach. Within the British Labour Party, Crossman's knowledge of Germany was more than outweighed by Dalton's Germanophobia. Nevertheless, the SPD looked on its British and Scandinavian opposite numbers as truly fraternal parties, both because of the personal ties formed by the German leaders in exile and because of the others' political strength and the nature of their social backing. Dr. Schumacher's hostility toward the EEC powers was in large measure due to his scorn of the SFIO and of the Italian Social Democrats under Saragat. The Europeans, for their part, showed no great love for the SPD: for several years, Guy Mollet and Paul-Henri Spaak presented a curious spectacle as they endeavored to spare the Federal Republic the supreme disaster of being governed by their Socialist brethren.

Although support for the Christian Democrats was more widely based, the SPD was the largest and best organized political group in the Federal Republic—in fact, its only mass party. However, once prosperity returned, the German people were less interested in joining organized groups, including political parties, with the result that the number of SPD adherents and local committees declined from 1947–48 onward: it steadied around 1955–56 and rose again in the 1960's. At the end of 1947, the party's membership stood at 875,000; it fell gradually to 580,000, but reached 800,000 in 1968.

The SPD has always been a thoroughly organized party, so much so as to provoke periodic complaints of "bureaucratization" and the neglect of internal democracy: a number of proposals to remedy this were put forward at the party's Nuremberg congress in 1968. According to SPD statutes, the congress (*Parteitag*) is the supreme source of authority, but real power clearly belongs to the executive (*Parteivorstand*), if only because a great many officials at the local, regional, and national level depend financially on the party, as do many delegates to the congress. Nevertheless, local and especially district (*Bezirk*) committees have a life and independence of their own, which is manifested on both the political and the personal plane. Thus, in March, 1969, at the congress of the Hesse-Süd district, the second largest, with 71,000 members, a motion calling for the establishment of normal relations between the F.R.G. and the G.D.R. as "sovereign states of the German nation, possessing equal rights" was passed by an overwhelming majority despite a message from party headquarters and despite the pleading of the latter's representative, the minister and trade union leader Georg Leber. Similarly, Willy Brandt and Helmut Schmidt have at times had the utmost difficulty in handling their respective districts of Berlin and Hamburg. In both cases, these were due in the first instance to the revolt of local party officials against the brilliant personalities who were neglecting day-to-day party life. At the Nuremberg congress a reaction of the same sort led to the failure of Klaus Schutz, the Mayor of Berlin, and Horst Ehmke, state secretary in the Federal Ministry of Justice, to secure election to the executive: their rise to fame had been too rapid, too neglectful of the prescribed degrees of advancement within the party. Nevertheless, the fact that brilliant careers are not prevented by the hostility of the party bureaucracy proves that a change has taken place. The leaders have grasped that men of talent must be found and given suitable jobs when they are available; especially now that the party has come into power at Bonn, it will no longer do for such jobs to be reserved for party stalwarts of low capacity. A case in point is the career of Katharina Focke, a woman of brains and elegance who has played an active part in support of the European movement. She joined the party in 1964 and became a member of the *Landtag* at Düsseldorf two years later. She was not elected to the steering committee of the parliamentary group, but in the election of September, 1969, after a brilliant campaign, she was victorious in the solidly CDU constituency of Cologne-South: her adversary was a man of importance, Fritz Hellwig, a member of the

Commission of the European Economic Community and a former chairman of the economic affairs committee of the Bundestag. Three thousand more votes were cast for her at this election than for her party. Within a month she was appointed parliamentary secretary of state in the Chancellor's Office, with responsibility for European questions, cultural affairs, and Federal-*Land* relations.

At the top level, the exercise of authority within the party has altered in line with changes of organization and personalities. The salaried members of the executive committee, who are always at the ready, are naturally more powerful than the unsalaried members who live in all parts of the Republic. The party's central bureau, the *Parteipräsidium*, enjoys a degree of authority that depends on the individual qualities of the chairman and his deputy or deputies. Kurt Schumacher was authoritarian by temperament and strove to impose his political views, while leaving administration to the conciliatory vice-chairman, Erich Ollenhauer. In due course, the latter succeeded Schumacher and had as his vice-chairman Wilhelm Mellies, a colorless personality whose death in May, 1958 caused little stir. During this period, the party was run on more easygoing lines; but when Herbert Wehner succeeded Mellies, the result was to confer unprecedented power on the vice-chairman in charge of organization. In May, 1968, a new office was created—that of secretary-general (*Bundesgeschäftsführer*): its importance was underlined from the outset by the fact that a minister, Hans Jürgen Wischnewski, gave up his portfolio in order to take it on.

In the early days of the Federal Republic, the SPD headquarters remained at Hanover. This fact, together with the traditional primacy of the party machine over the parliamentary SPD, tended to restrict the latter's role within the party. But after the move of headquarters to the "shanty" at Bad Godesberg—less like a refugee hut in 1970 than formerly, but still poky and uncomfortable—the Bundestag group has progressively increased in importance, especially as it now includes the chief party leaders. The interplay between the party management, the parliamentary group, and, since 1966, the Federal Government is subtle and complicated, the balance of forces varying according to the topics and personalities involved.[7] The steering committee of the parliamentary group has the double task of keeping the deputies in line with government and party views and interpreting their wishes to the party in the hope of influencing government policy. In the first year of the sixth Bundestag, the chairman of the committee was Herbert Wehner; there were five vice-chairmen, of whom the eldest was born in 1907 and the youngest in 1932, and four "secretaries" (*Parlamentarische Geschäftsführer*) whose role, especially when the Brandt government's majority fell so low, was not unlike that of the whips at Westminster.

One of the four was a woman, Annemarie Renger, who entered parliament in 1953 after being Schumacher's secretary from 1945 to 1952. During his lifetime, it was on her shoulder that the veteran leader leant with his single arm as he moved forward on his single leg toward the rostrum in the Bundestag or at a political meeting. A tragic figure, yet the unchallenged head of the SPD, Schumacher's energy and strength of purpose were all the greater for his physical disablement. In like fashion, he held that the Federal Republic should be all the more intransigent in its dealings with the Allies by reason of its weakness—an attitude very similar to that of General de Gaulle during and after the war. Under his leadership, the party took a tough line in opposition, not only in foreign policy but also in economic affairs, as predictions of disaster came thick and fast from the party's economic expert, Professor Erich Nölting. Schumacher did not, however, take decisions in isolation but instead consulted especially his closest party colleagues such as Ollenhauer and Fritz Heine, the member of the executive in charge of information matters, who never did become a member of the Bundestag.[8]

When Schumacher died on August 20, 1953, it was natural for the SPD to choose Ollenhauer as its leader. His policy, though conducted with less vehemence and more discretion, was at first the same as that of his former chief. But the electoral defeat of 1953, the spectacular success of Erhard's economic policy, the international *détente*, and the temporary resolution of the European problem (with the signature of the Paris agreements in October, 1954)—all these events combined to impel the SPD to modify its course and to cease presenting itself to the electorate as a party of *Nein-Sager*, of opposition for opposition's sake. In this as in many other cases of political evolution, it is impossible to disentangle the part played by conviction from that of electioneering. To take first the party's attitude toward religion: while it was never secularist after the fashion of the SFIO, its opposition in the postwar period to denominational schools and to any form of church influence in politics was strong enough for Catholic bishops and parish priests usually to dissuade the faithful from voting for the SPD and still more from joining it. Nonetheless, quite a number of left-wing Catholics did vote for it against the CDU. The SPD had to tread warily in order to combine two very different objectives: to win over from the CDU the bulk of the Catholic working population, especially in the Ruhr, and to undermine FDP influence among the liberal and anticlerical *bourgeoisie*, especially in Württemberg. But the formula adopted at the 1954 congress was further removed from orthodox Marxism and closer to, say, the Labour Party's attitude in Britain than mere tactical considerations would have required. It ran: "The ideas of Socialism are not a rival form of religion [*Ersatzreligion*]. The Socialist movement has different tasks from a religious community. In Europe, the intellectual and moral roots of Socialist ideology [*Gedankengut*] are Christianity, humanism, and classical philosophy."

This formula was reaffirmed in the new "basic program" adopted at a special congress held at Bad Godesberg on November 15, 1959: the party had suffered its worst setback in the 1957 election, when the CDU increased its lead even though the SPD obtained more votes than in 1953. The latter once again saw the need to change its program and methods: as far as political doctrine was concerned, it had virtually done so at its Munich congress in 1956, where the burning question was that of the character to be given to the "second industrial revolution," that of automation (pending the atomic revolution)—that is, it was concerned with such problems as the training of technicians, the organization of leisure time, and the harmonizing of technical and specialized education with culture and citizenship. Compared with these, the old Socialist theme of the nationalization of key sectors of the economy was scarcely in evidence. Heinrich Deist, who had been the party's economic theorist since Nölting's death, was careful not to invoke the latter's ideas: he even declared that free competition was a key element in Social Democratic economic policy.

The Bad Godesberg program, which crystallized the party's evolution, was couched in terms that the authors of the previous program, adopted at Heidelberg in 1925, would have found hard to recognize. The preamble declares *inter alia*:

Democratic Socialism, which in Europe is rooted in Christian ethics, humanism, and classic philosophy, does not set out to proclaim eternal verities, not because it lacks interest or understanding of philosophy or religious truths, but because it respects the right of human beings to decide for themselves in matters of faith, independently of the state or of political parties. . . . The SPD stands for freedom of the mind. It is a community of men and women who represent different beliefs and schools of thought, but who share common moral values and political aims. The party's object is to establish a way of life in accordance with those values.

The program endorses the principle of national defense, but calls for a general ban on nuclear weapons, and is opposed to their being manufactured by the Federal Republic. The section on foreign policy is fairly short;[9] the passages dealing with economic and social affairs are lengthy but lacking in precision. They advocate full employment, as in the past, but stipulate that it must be based on a stable currency: for a long time the SPD was accused of being the "inflationary party." Pointing out that the modern state exerts more and more influence in economic matters, the program calls for a "planning policy related to the economic cycle," but goes on to say that "free competition and free enterprise are important elements of Social Democratic economic policy" and concludes with the motto: "As much competition as possible, as much planning as necessary." The party is opposed to the concentration of economic power in the hands of private enterprise or the state: accordingly, the program speaks, without undue emphasis, of nationalization, but also of decentralization. But the key sentence, which explains better than any other the evolution of the party's ideology, is to be found in the last section entitled "Our Course": it declares that "The SPD, which was a party of the working class, is now a party of the whole people." In other words, the SPD, like the British Labour Party or brother parties in Austria and Sweden, is setting its sights on appealing to the majority of an electorate in which the working class is more and more of a minority.

To do this, however, a new program is not enough. The defeat of 1957 was also due to electoral techniques that neglected elementary psychology. While the CDU had called in experts to help it choose its slogans and even the color of its posters—a shade of blue "recommended by market specialists"—the SPD relied on its "poor but honest" image to win the voters' hearts, and displayed somber posters with yellow lettering on a black background. The party, in fact, appeared to have no better idea of how to attract the masses than to allow its regular publisher to put out a collection of cartoons of its leader, in the last of which a fat, naked Ollenhauer was seen on his knees praying to

Marx: "Lord, grant me a political idea, for the elections are at hand and I am sore afraid."[10]

It was after this that the party made a radical change in its outward image, beginning with the removal of Fritz Heine in 1958 and continuing to the Nuremberg congress of 1968 with its elegant female stewards. The main decision reached at Godesberg was that, in a period when a leader's popularity depends on his television personality, the party needed a more glamorous candidate for chancellorship. With praiseworthy loyalty and self-effacement, Ollenhauer accepted the view that he himself was deficient in personal magnetism and that the party's nominee for the post of Chancellor in 1961 should be the Mayor of Berlin, Willy Brandt.

Born at Lübeck out of wedlock, on December 18, 1913, Herbert Frahm—as he then was called—became a Socialist at a tender age and was later an SPD militant and a reporter for the *Lübecker Volksbote*. He left Germany immediately after Hitler came to power, and took the name of Willy Brandt during his long and often difficult years of émigré life in Norway and later Sweden. He returned to Germany in 1945 and worked in Berlin as a correspondent for Scandinavian newspapers. In 1948, he became the Berlin representative of the SPD executive committee, and also married his second wife, the Norwegian Rut Hansen. He was elected Mayor of Berlin in 1957. The decision to put him forward as a candidate in 1961 was to some extent inspired by the success of John F. Kennedy: Brandt, like him, was a smiling, likable young man with a pretty and intelligent wife. Perhaps, however, it was a mistake to go to the extreme of presenting as an adversary to the aged Chancellor a young leader who had not yet won his spurs in politics—even though at Berlin he was so much in the public eye that one was often not quite sure, looking at the photographs that showed him playing host to foreign leaders, whether this was a mere aspirant to power or the representative of all Berliners without distinction of party.

The election of 1961 was a partial setback; but Brandt nevertheless became vice-chairman of the party at the congress of May, 1962 and, after Ollenhauer's death on December 14, 1963, he was elected chairman at an extraordinary congress on February 16, 1964. A few days later, on March 16, another change became necessary owing to the death of Heinrich Deist, the party's economic expert and author of the most important sections of the Godesberg program. His post was filled by Karl Schiller, once a member of the NSDAP, who had taken his doctorate in political economy in 1935 at the age of twenty-four. Ten years later, he was a professor of the subject at Hamburg and, in 1947, he was Senator (that is, minister) for the Economy in the *Land* government.

The SPD election campaign of 1965 laid more stress than ever on the ideological *rapprochement* with its adversary the CDU, as though the slogan were: "The same thing, but better." The outcome was again disappointing: the SPD gained some seats but still scored less than 40 per cent of the poll, while the CDU remained at its peak. Brandt's discouragement led him to announce that he would give up the struggle for power. But at the Dortmund congress in June, 1966, the party confirmed him in the chairmanship and also re-elected the two vice-chairmen. The first of these, Fritz Erler, born in 1913, had been a valiant opponent of Nazism and had spent many years in prison: of all Socialist leaders, he was probably the best known and most respected in foreign capitals for his character, intelligence, and ability. He fell seriously ill in 1965 (his death occurred on February 22, 1967) and relinquished the leadership of the parliamentary group to Helmut Schmidt, at first on a temporary basis and then permanently at the end of 1966.

The other vice-chairman, Herbert Wehner, was an unusual personality.[11] Born at Dresden on July 11, 1906, the son of a cobbler, he joined the Communist Party in 1927 and lived in Moscow and in Sweden from 1935 to 1946. He returned to Germany as a Social Democrat, convinced that the party's task was to reconcile the working class with the state and to pursue a patient, sensible, reliable policy. From 1962 onward, he set about preparing the way for the Grand Coalition with the CDU, which he saw as the only way to vindicate the "reds" once and for all in the eyes of the *petite bourgeoisie*, and also to achieve an effective policy toward the Communist bloc. His reckoning proved to be sound, although his policy of patience and the appeal to reason achieved its triumph at a moment when the younger generation was once again becoming susceptible to Utopian dreams and the lure of impatient, irrational action. In October, 1969, when he left the government to become chairman of the parliamentary group, he could reflect with satisfaction that the transformation of the SPD was in large measure accomplished. Above all, this was true of its leader. Willy Brandt, now Chancellor, was a different personality from the young hero of 1960: he had been matured by the setback of 1965, and, at Dortmund in the following year, the party had re-elected him by 324 votes out of 326—not merely as a candidate for the chancellorship but as its true leader. As a member of the coalition government, he showed himself adroit, tenacious, and circumspect, with the ability to listen to his colleagues and subordinates as well as to foreign representatives.

In addition, the new Chancellor constituted a link between two very different generations. On the one hand were the tried and true militants of the party, faithful to its traditional style and tone, as well as the leaders who had had no chance to give fully of their services and had worn themselves out in opposition. Fritz Erler died before he could give the SPD and Germany the benefit of his exceptional qualities; Carlo Schmid, in October, 1969, had to forgo the post of Minister of Research that would have suited him a few years earlier, because he was no longer physically equal to it and because what was needed was not a man of culture but a technician. On the other side of the gap were the unsentimental representatives of efficiency and a rationalized world: Helmut Schmidt, the party vice-chairman, and Horst Ehmke, despite their age difference (they were born respectively on December 27, 1918 and February 4, 1927), belonged to the generation of those who aim to give the old party a new image. An image, be it noted, that does not please everybody or even all members of the young generation, such as the Socialist youth organization. At all times and in all Social Democratic parties, youth leaders have tended to kick over the traces and denounce the softness and conservatism of their elders, though this has seldom prevented them from becoming sober party dignitaries in due course. From Erich Ollenhauer to Helmut Schmidt and Hans Jürgen Wischnewski, the *Jungsozialisten* and Socialist student groups have served as training grounds for party cadres, as also have the *Falken* ("falcons"), a youth movement attached to the party but not directly controlled by it (one of its postwar leaders, Heinz Westphal, was appointed state secretary for youth matters in 1969). But the conflict of generations is more serious at a time when, as we shall see, it affects the whole outlook of society. The Social Democratic University Union (SHS) was founded as a riposte to the Socialist Students' Union (SDS), which broke away from the SPD; but, in 1968 the SHB in turn took issue with the party line, and in March, 1969, there was a partial breach accompanied by financial sanctions. The challenge of the *Jungsozialisten* was more outspoken still: at their congress in December, 1969 they showed more affinity with dissidents outside the party than with its leaders.

Even within the party, the new course has not yet been adopted without opposition. When the Grand Coalition was formed, it was on the cards that a left-wing group would break away. The Brandt-Wehner policy was approved by only a narrow margin at the Nuremberg congress in March, 1968. But unity was restored by the approaching elections and the formation of the Brandt government thereafter, more especially as the result of the poll confirmed the leaders' calculations. At Saarbrücken on May 13, 1970, the party congress confirmed Willy Brandt as chairman by 318 out of the 331 valid votes cast. Herbert Wehner received 331 votes "for" and only 16 "against," as compared with 270 and 57 at the Nuremberg congress, while Helmut Schmidt scored an easy victory over Gansel, the vice-president of the Young Socialists, by 256 votes to 65.

The party's "new look" did not deter its left-wing critics from voting for it in the name of efficiency, while it also gained votes from new sections of the public who were attracted or reassured by its image—or at all events discontented with their previous allegiances, to the extent that they would support the SPD if it proved, as in 1967–68, to be associated with a revival of prosperity. This sociological evolution among such classes as employees and technicians, or women and Catholic voters, is certainly the aspect that most disquiets the CDU, although the latter, despite a slight falling off in strength, is still decidedly the larger of the two main parties.

The CDU and the Exercise of Power

Thanks to the three years' transition afforded by the Grand Coalition, the SPD had time to prepare itself for the role of the chief government party. The Christian Democrats, on the other hand, had no interval in which to learn the part of an opposition. The night of September 28–29, 1969 was dramatic: several hours after the polls had closed, Rainer Barzel, the chairman of the CDU parliamentary group, was seen on television explaining to the other two parties why they had lost, and a smiling Kiesinger was applauded by his supporters. Then, after the shock of the final result and Willy Brandt's sudden bid for the chancellorship, the CDU was left wondering how it should conduct itself in opposition.

Not only had the CDU always been in power at Bonn, but the Christian Democrats were in charge even before they existed as an organized party, since their first federal congress (*Bundesparteitag*), at Goslar, did not take place until October, 1950, when Adenauer had been Chancellor for more than a year. Even then it was not, strictly speaking, "Federal," for the party as constituted at Goslar did not include the Bavarian Christian Democrats, who formed the separate Christian Social Union (CSU). For the purpose of ascertaining the winner of the Federal elections, it is certainly correct to add together the CDU and CSU results; but, when it comes to the distribution of ministerial posts and, in general, the question of power relationships in German political life, it must never be forgotten that they are two distinct parties that together form a "working association" (*Arbeitsgemeinschaft*) and a joint but not homogeneous parliamentary group, with a CSU *Landesgruppe* as one of its components. Each party has its own organization and congress, to which the other's chairman is invited. At the Bundestag elections of 1957, the Bavarian group of Christian Democrats were actually opposed to the CDU in one of the *Länder*. In the Saar, the Christian People's Party, which was for a long time led by Dr. Hoffmann, the head of the "pro-French" government, became, in June, 1957, a *Land* association (*Landesverband*) of the CSU, after the Chancellor had failed to unify the two Christian parties. Thus the Saar was represented in the third Bundestag by one member from the FDP, two each from the SPD and CSU, and three from the CDU. Twelve years later, the chairman of the CSU hinted to the CDU that if the latter were to adopt an unduly leftward position he would not shrink from carrying out a similar maneuver in all the *Länder* or from encouraging the formation, outside Bavaria, of groups of "friends of the CSU."

For a long time, the dominant personality of the CSU was neither the party chairman Josef Müller nor the Bavarian Minister-Presidents Ehard and Seidel, but Dr. Alois Hundhammer. This cultivated man, an ardent Catholic and a brilliant talker, was a former leader of the Bavarian People's Party and had been interned by the Nazis. As Minister of Education from 1946 to the end of 1950, he wielded a moral dictatorship over Bavarian cultural and academic life, restoring corporal punishment in the schools and exercising behind-the-scenes censorship over radio programs, while his large black beard became a vivid symbol of clericalism and intolerance. After 1953, the CSU began to escape from his control, becoming gradually more liberal and a good deal more interdenominational. At the 1957 congress, he was defeated by Franz Josef Strauss, who was to become chairman of the CSU in March, 1961. From 1957 onward, Dr. Hundhammer was merely Bavarian Minister of Agriculture, a post he retained until February, 1969, when he decided to retire at the age of sixty-nine. It may well be that the single-minded and disinterested austerity of this unbending "clerical" was closer to the genuine spirit of democracy than the energy and ambition of his successful rival.

Franz Josef Strauss was born in Munich on September 6, 1915; he entered public life after being demobilized in 1945. A founding member of the CSU, he became its secretary-general in 1949. He was a member of the Bundestag from its first session and of the Federal Government from 1955 onward, being Minister of Defense from 1956 to 1962. He fell from office over the *Spiegel* affair, but remained in firm control of the CSU and increased the party's homogeneity, especially in parliament. In fact Erhard, as Chancellor, had a three-party coalition to contend with, and, in 1965–66, the forty-nine CSU deputies gave him as much trouble as the forty-nine Liberals. The formation of Erhard's second government was made more difficult by Strauss's objections to Schröder and to FDP chairman Erich Mende, though in the end these were overridden. In November, 1966, the public announcement that the CSU would support Kiesinger in the second ballot played a large part in ensuring the latter's victory over Schröder.

The formation of the Grand Coalition enabled Strauss to rejoin the government, the Liberals' hostility toward him having no doubt been greater than that of the SPD. He was glad to accept the Finance Ministry, thereby presenting himself as a serious and responsible statesman who had made peace with many of his former enemies.[12] But his temperament more than once got the better of his political judgment, especially during the 1969 election campaign, when he insulted and denigrated his opponents with almost equal zeal and in a similar style to that of the *Bayern-Kurier*, the CSU newspaper he controlled. The party's election program was decidedly tougher than that of the CDU, whether in regard to the German problem or to the protection of public safety against the "terror of extremist groups." The results, announced on September 28, were encouraging: the CSU was still well ahead of an absolute majority (54·4 per cent, as against 55·6 in 1965), and the NPD hardly exceeded the 5 per cent mark in Bavaria, showing that it had paid the CSU to stress the right-wing elements in its program. But the failure of the CDU/CSU to secure the chancellorship threw them into profound disarray for lack of a clear-cut strategy. Should they try to defeat the Brandt government by means of a liberal policy aimed at winning left-of-center votes, or take a hard line and go all out for right-wing support? Strauss, at the outset, clearly tended to favor the latter course, but the CDU, after a short delay, adopted the former, at all events in domestic affairs; by the middle of 1970, it had also come round officially to Strauss's views on policy toward the Communist bloc.

The CDU (*Christlich-Demokratische Union*) was born, in a sense, as a left wing party. It had, in fact, a multiple origin—at Berlin, Cologne, Düsseldorf, and Hamburg. The initiative at Berlin came from anti-Nazi resisters who had been interned in the Moabit prison. The first nucleus consisted of Christian trade unionists, Protestants of various political backgrounds, and Catholics from the old *Zentrum*. They wished to build a new Germany with a completely transformed social and economic structure, purged of all the Nazi poisons. At the same time, they wished the new party to be fully interdenominational. The same ideas were prevalent in the Rhineland. The "guiding principles" laid down at Cologne in July, 1945 were to a large extent endorsed and developed in the Ahlen program of February 3, 1947, the motto of which was "CDU supersedes [*überwindet*] capitalism and Marxism."[13] This document, inspired by Karl Arnold, the Minister-President of North Rhine–Westphalia, and his trade union and left-wing Catholic friends, drew a sharp distinction between political freedom and economic liberalism. It asserted the failure of capitalism in measured terms, condemning both monopolies and state capitalism while calling for economic planning and control through a system of corporative organs under parliamentary supervision, on a principle similar to that advocated by the trade unions. But the Düsseldorf program of July 15,

1949—that of the party's first Federal election campaign—rejected all planning, whether of production, labor supply, or internal and external markets: the only government economic action it envisaged was through taxation and import policy. What it proposed, in fact, was Dr. Erhard's "social market economy": when the latter belatedly joined the CDU, it was not he who accepted the party's doctrine but the party that had decided to adhere to the doctrine of its future Economic Minister. Or, to be more precise, the choice of Ludwig Erhard as the standard-bearer of the election campaign meant the victory of the liberals within the party over its "socializing" wing. This victory was due to several causes, the chief of which was not specifically German. As in Belgium, Italy, and France, the Christian Democratic movement had chosen, in 1945, to adopt a leftist position, and had won exceptional success because the bulk of the conservative voters had little choice open to them—the traditional right-wing parties being in eclipse or permanently destroyed. Such a situation cannot last long: either the party leaders will modify their program to keep their supporters or they will stand firm and watch their majorities dwindle as other parties are formed that, in large measure, correspond to the voters' real wishes. The Christian Social Party in Belgium, the *Democrazia Cristiana*, and the CDU opted for the first course: it was left for the MRP in France to water down its program and yet to lose most of its support at the polls.

In addition, the CDU had specific reasons for abandoning its initial platform. It would have been absurd not to cash in on the triumphant success of the policy advocated and put into effect by the Economics Director of Bizonia immediately after the currency reform, in opposition to Professor Nölting with his call for a planned economy. Moreover, this state of affairs provided the dominant personality of the CDU with a justification of his own likes and dislikes: Dr. Adenauer had never been on very cordial terms with Karl Arnold, whereas among the Chancellor's few friends in public life to whose advice he was likely to listen were the liberal banker Robert Pferdmenges and High Commissioner John J. McCloy. This personal factor should not, however, be overstressed, especially as Adenauer was also on excellent terms with Hans Böckler, the first chairman of the trade union federation (DGB) (as late as 1951, the CDU introduced a law on codetermination in industry in concert with the SPD opposition). The evolution of the CDU was in fact parallel with that of the Federal Republic as a whole: in economic matters, the SPD's Godesberg program of 1959 was far to the right of the Ahlen program.

On the other hand, Konrad Adenauer's personality had a lasting effect on the structure and behavior of the CDU. For many years, the typical problem of a dominant party within a parliamentary regime, namely the balance of strength between the government, the party organization, and the parliamentary group, scarcely arose at all, though there were some disagreements, particularly in the economic field.[14] The Chancellor was himself chairman of the party, and the chairmen of the parliamentary group (Heinrich von Brentano until 1955 and, from 1961 onward, when Brentano was Minister of Foreign Affairs, Heinrich Krone, the secretary-general of the *Zentrum* before 1933) were absolutely devoted to their leader. Moreover, the government scored one electoral success after another without finding it necessary to bring the party machine into action to mobilize support at the polls. Why indeed should it trouble to strengthen the party organization and improve its structure, weak though these were? The more the party remained decentralized, the more solid was the Chancellor's authority.

The constituent units of the CDU were originally set up as "*Land* parties," later renamed "*Land* associations" (*Landesverbände*). There are sixteen "federations" on a territorial basis, including the Saar and West Berlin: one each for North Rhine and Westphalia, three for Lower Saxony (Hanover, Brunswick, and Oldenburg), and four for Baden-Württemberg (North and South Baden, North and South Württemberg). To these should be added two federations of a more or less symbolic character, one for the G.D.R. (*Exil-CDU*) and one for the Oder-Neisse territories (*Oder-Neisse-CDU*). The latter was dissolved in November, 1968; the refugees who belong to the former are, for the most part, also members of the party associations for their places of residence in the Federal Republic. The associations vary considerably from one area to another. In some, for instance at Essen and Cologne, they are large and well organized; in others, they exist mainly on paper. Like the SPD, the CDU grew at the outset with extreme rapidity. About the middle of 1947, the federations claimed a total membership of about 650,000, the British zone being the one in which the highest proportion of the electorate (about 8 per cent of CDU voters) were federation members, while the proportion in the French zone was the lowest. The figures began to drop at the time of the currency reform. In April, 1954, the party claimed 215,000 members, or about 40 per cent less than in 1948. Since then, there has again been an increase, the figure settling around 300,000 in the 1960's.

In theory, the supreme party authority is the congress (*Parteitag*), the structure of which was altered in May, 1956. Up till then, the federations were represented in proportion to the number of votes gained in each *Land* at the previous Bundestag elections. At the Stuttgart congress, it was decided that in future the federations would send one delegate for every 100,000 votes (subsequently amended to 75,000), plus one delegate for every 1,000 party members. In this way, the federations were encouraged to step up recruitment and improve their organization. The first effect of the reform was to make the federations of North Rhine and Westphalia still more dominant: under the old system, they accounted for 28·9 per cent of the delegates; under the new, for 33·6 per cent.

Under its statutes, the party is governed by the executive committee (*Vorstand*), which has steadily grown in size from twenty-seven members to over sixty. Apart from the party managers at the national level, its *ex officio* membership consists of the following (the theoretical total is of course reduced by duplication of functions): the eighteen chairmen of federations, the Chancellor, Federal ministers and *Land* Prime Ministers who are party members, the chairman of the parliamentary group and his deputy; the chairmen of CDU organizations (two for women, one for young people, one for the local government union, one for the social commissions, and one for the "middle class" of traders and craftsmen); fifteen "especially deserving" party members, and three co-opted members. Clearly, this is much too unwieldy a body to be

effective, especially as the federations have always been jealous of their independence, with the result that the Chancellor and chairman have had their
hands free when it came to major political decisions.

Date	Chancellor	Party Chairman	Chairman of Parliamentary Party
9/1949	Adenauer	Adenauer	Brentano
10/1950	Adenauer	Adenauer	Krone
10/1963	Erhard	Adenauer	Brentano
11/1964	Erhard	Adenauer	Barzel
3/1966	Erhard	Erhard	Barzel
12/1966	Kiesinger	Erhard	Barzel
5/1967	Kiesinger	Kiesinger	Barzel

A change was first made at the 1962 congress, when, to assist the Chancellor
—who was, after all, getting on in years, a new post was created, that of
"managing chairman" (*Geschäftsführender Vorsitzender*). However, Josef
Hermann Dufhues did not play the same sort of role vis-à-vis Konrad
Adenauer as Léon Martinaud-Déplat did in the French Radical Party in
Edouard Herriot's declining years. A more significant change took place in
1963, when the new Chancellor was up against the fact that Adenauer was
still party chairman and was determined to prove that his successor was not a
statesman. The parliamentary group, however, was more favorable to Erhard
than to the aged leader whose prestige was on the decline: the more so as
Brentano, who was gravely ill, was replaced as chairman of the group by the
hardheaded Rainer Barzel, who was resolved to make the most, while it lasted,
of Erhard's appeal to the electorate as the father of the "economic miracle."
When Brentano died on November 14, 1964, Barzel became, as of right, what
he had so far been provisionally: the very active chairman of a parliamentary
party, exasperated by the behavior of its former idol and also by the Chancellor's weakness. Barzel first showed his power during the German-Egyptian
crisis of the first weeks of 1965, when he seems to have put pressure on Dr.
Erhard to make statements that were on the whole pro-Israeli, while Dr.
Schröder was anxious to preserve diplomatic relations with the Arab states.
In November, 1965, it was as painful to listen to the Chancellor reading the
government's program as it was impressive to hear the clear, forthright, cool,
and intelligent speech of the chairman of the parliamentary group.

Rainer Barzel, who was born in 1924, had made his way rapidly in politics.
Thanks to Karl Arnold's patronage, he became secretary-general of the joint
presidium of the Rhineland and Westphalian federations. In 1957, he entered
the Bundestag and, departing from his former ideological position, ranged
himself with the party "hard-liners," especially on the reunification question.
In February, 1959, he founded the "Save Liberty" organization, which was
particularly intransigent vis-à-vis the Communist bloc. He became Minister
for All-German Affairs in 1962 but did not join Erhard's cabinet, preferring to

work through the parliamentary group. He might have remained in this key position in the expectation that time would do its work and that his own ambition to rise still higher would gain acceptance in and out of the party. When Adenauer declared, on his ninetieth birthday (on January 5, 1966), that he would not be a candidate for the party chairmanship at the next congress, it seemed almost certain that Dufhues would be elected; but he, at the age of fifty-four, had just had a serious illness and, after much hesitation, he decided not to stand. The first week of February was filled with intricate maneuver and uncertainty. Unless a third man could be found whom everyone would accept, the issue was between Erhard and Barzel. The chief point in the former's favor was an electoral one: if he were standing for the presidency, it would not do for him, while still Chancellor, to meet with a rebuff within the party, which would also be bad for the party's prestige. Against Dr. Erhard was Adenauer's persistent hostility and a general feeling that, being unsuccessful at his present job, he would be ill-advised to take on another as well. Barzel was strongly supported by the two great federations of North Rhine–Westphalia, but his ambition was too obvious and the risk of appearing to split the party was against him. He allowed his name to be put forward on February 7, while the Chancellor was in Paris. The latter was furious, and on return announced himself as a candidate. On February 17, the executive unanimously decided to recommend to the congress at Bonn, to be held in March, that Erhard should be elected chairman and Barzel first vice-chairman while Dr. Adenauer would become honorary chairman for life, with the right to speak in all the party's chief assemblies.

The conflict was not truly resolved, but there was not a deadlock either: Rainer Barzel was still moving up. However, he encountered a setback on November 10, 1966, when the parliamentary party met to elect a candidate for the chancellorship, for which a majority of the 251 votes was required. Eugen Gerstenmaier having withdrawn, three candidates remained, a few votes being cast for Dr. Hallstein, who was then president of the Commission of the EEC. The voting in three successive ballots was as follows:

Candidate	Ballot		
	(1)	(2)	(3)
Rainer Barzel	56	42	26
Walter Hallstein	14	3	–
Kurt Georg Kiesinger	97	118	137
Gerhard Schröder	76	80	81

For some months, Erhard remained party chairman but exercised no influence; then, at the Brunswick congress in May, 1967, Kiesinger—who was now Chancellor—succeeded, despite some hostile maneuvers, in being elected chairman by a huge majority. He was aided in his new function by another Swabian for whom, at the 1966 congress, the post of secretary-general had been created over and above that of Federal administrative secretary (*Bundesgeschäftsführer*). The amiable and energetic Bruno Heck combined this post with that of Minister for Family and Youth Affairs until he left the government in October, 1968 to devote himself to the electoral campaign and, in principle, to reforming the party organization, the inadequacy of which he had denounced in strong terms.[15] However, to succeed in this he would have had to persuade the Chancellor to take his own position as party chairman seriously; and why should Kiesinger be expected to act differently from his predecessors in this respect? All three CDU Chancellors neglected the problem of party management. Adenauer did on exactly one occasion visit the Headquarters in Nasse Street, but neither Erhard nor Kiesinger ever set foot within the premises of the organization over which they presided.

The situation altered when the party went into opposition. Kiesinger, it is true, was re-elected for two years by the Mainz congress in November, 1969, while the secretary-general's term of office had still two years to run. But this was a purely formal act: the party could not throw over the central personality of its election campaign, even though his speech at the congress, which was clumsy both in content and in form, showed that he was not the right leader for the defeated party. Kiesinger's chairmanship became similar to Erhard's toward the end: soon people were making jokes about the disappearance of the ex-Chancellor and talking of the likelihood of his resigning.[16]

The age level of the party presidium was considerably reduced at the Mainz congress. While Dufhues' candidacy was defeated by a large margin and Gerhard Schröder, who gained 267 votes, was—at fifty-nine the oldest and least successful of those elected, Gerhard Stoltenberg (aged forty-one) received 451 votes and Helmut Kohl (aged thirty-nine) who, as Minister-President of Rhineland-Palatinate was host to the congress, received 392; this was ten votes more than Hans Katzer (aged fifty), a former Minister of Labor who represented the party's working-class wing. Any of these four might have hoped to replace Kiesinger, but they had little chance compared with Rainer Barzel, who had established himself at the outset of the new session as the CDU's chief political spokesman.

There was a similar rejuvenation at party headquarters, where Kraske, the administrative secretary-general, was replaced in February, 1970 by a man of forty-one, Rüdiger Göb, while the chief information officer, Arthur Ratke, became a state secretary in the Schleswig-Holstein government. His place was taken by Willi Weiskirch, a noted journalist and a former Catholic youth leader. Heinrich Köppler, a friend of Weiskirch who was himself a former chairman of the Catholic youth organization, was on his way to occupy posts of the first importance after having served as party leader for Rhineland-Westphalia: a former parliamentary secretary of state, he surprisingly obtained this key party appointment in November, 1969, and increased the party's vote in the election of June, 1970.

Meanwhile, the youth organizations directly attached to the party had been getting restive. In October, 1969, the RCDS (*Ring Christlich-Demokratischer Studenten*) called for Kiesinger's resignation and his replacement by Helmut Kohl. The *Junge Union*, the CDU equivalent of the *Jungsozialisten*, held a countrywide rally (*Deutschlandtag*) on November 9, 1969, at which they amended their statutes so as to narrow the age limit for membership from forty to thirty-five (still a good way beyond adolescence!) and showed an increasingly critical spirit vis-à-vis the party leadership, to the point of drawing up a complete political program.[17] However, the *Junge Union* of 1969–70 did not adopt a leftward position within the party: contrary to its attitude in the 1950's, it had taken a tough line against the SPD during the Grand Coalition, and its monthly journal *Die Entscheidung* began publishing articles severely criticizing President Heinemann.

The CDU held an extraordinary congress at Hamburg in November, 1970 for the purpose of adopting a more attractive and striking version of the "Berlin program of action" drawn up in November, 1968 at the instance of Bruno Heck. The party's aim is to regain control of voters who are tending to fall away, especially in the big Rhineland towns. To do so, it must rely on specifically political methods: the falling off since 1965 in Catholic areas is due to the fact that the faithful are less organized than they used to be, partly for sociological reasons connected with increased urbanization and partly because of changing tendencies in the Church itself. In 1965, the drop in Catholic support was offset by a distinct gain in Protestant areas.[18] The CDU is, in fact, a genuinely interconfessional party, unlike the *Zentrum* of Weimar days; but, in this respect, it has varied a good deal in different regions and at different social levels. From the outset, the proportion of Protestant votes was greater in areas where the population was less Catholic: in mainly Protestant areas the CDU could be regarded as a Christian party, while in Catholic areas, it wore the appearance of a Catholic one. The Catholic element predominated among party workers and members of parliament, but leading posts were fairly evenly divided between Catholics and Protestants, if only to preserve the interconfessional image. Nevertheless, the fact that Konrad Adenauer was a Catholic—as were the three successive chairmen of the parliamentary group and, naturally, the chairmen of the CSU—gave the impression that Protestants took second place within the party. The headway the party made in Protestant areas in 1965 is largely to be explained by the substitution of Protestants for Catholics in the key posts of Chancellor (Erhard for Adenauer), Minister of Foreign Affairs (Schröder for Brentano), and Minister of Defense (Hassel for Strauss). The apparent weakness of the Protestant element, as well as the desire to strengthen ties between the party and the Protestant church, led in 1951 to the creation of the "Evangelical CDU/CSU Working Group" under the chairmanship first of Hermann Ehlers and, from 1955, of Gerhard Schröder, who owes much of the weight he carries in party circles to his connection with this body.

The Decline of Small Parties

Going into opposition has had at least one advantage for the CDU: it may expect to attract to itself all discontented elements to the right of the SPD. However, the benefit of this is limited by the fact there are few organized bodies left from which it might hope to gain voters, whereas in 1953 and 1957 its conquests were made at the expense of other parties.

Among those represented in the first Bundestag, two were purely Bavarian (assuming that the CSU is not counted as a separate party). The Union for Economic Reconstruction (*Wirtschaftliche ·Aufbauvereinigung*—WAV) was already moribund at the 1949 elections: it was founded in 1945 by a Munich lawyer, Alfred Loritz, a virulent and demagogic speaker who attracted attention for a time in Germany and abroad, even being spoken of as a "new Hitler." The fact is, he never had any precise ideas, solid organization, or genuine following. Most of those who voted for him were not native Bavarians, as his extreme advocacy of federalist views might have suggested, but refugees in search of a political mouthpiece. He reached the peak of his success on August 14, 1949, when he gained 14·4 per cent of the votes in Bavaria, but by then his party was already falling to pieces, over half its local branches having been dissolved in 1948. At the 1950 *Landtag* election, WAV gained only 2·8 per cent of the votes and therefore obtained no seats; at the municipal elections of 1952, its score fell to 0·3 per cent. It put forward no candidates for the legislative elections in 1953, by which time it had virtually disappeared from the Bundestag. In October, 1950, four of its twelve deputies, all representing refugee organizations, split off and established links with the *Zentrum*: in December, 1951, six others joined the German Party (DP) after an eleventh member of the group had gone over to the *Deutsche Rechtspartei* (DRP). Loritz was thus left alone to be the butt of the assembly. In April, 1953, he was joined by a handful of isolated right-wing extremists, but the fact caused no stir in political circles.

The Bavarian Party (*Bayernpartei*—BP) had more solid electoral foundations. Its program called for the creation of an "autonomous Bavarian State within a German and European community." It advocated a corporative system in the social field and wished to establish "a culture rooted in the life of the Bavarian people." This particularist and traditionalist party fell into the habit of allying itself with groups that have seemed completely alien to it. Within the Bundestag, it formed an association at the end of 1951 with the revived *Zentrum*, with which it formed a working group called the "Federalist Union." Its success of 1949 was not repeated: from 20·9 per cent of the votes it fell to 17·9 per cent at the *Land* elections of November, 1950, and 9·2 at the Bundestag election of 1953, which, as we have seen, did not entitle it to a seat. However, it rose again to 13·2 per cent at the *Landtag* elections of November, 1954, and took part in maneuvers that led to a highly unexpected coalition: leaving the biggest party, the CSU, alone in opposition, the Socialists, Liberals, refugees, and "Bavarians" formed a government in which Josef Baumgartner, the chairman of the *Bayernpartei*, was Vice-Premier and Minister of Agriculture, while another member of the party was Minister of Internal Affairs. This raised the BP's hopes for the Bundestag elections of 1957, and, after elaborate maneuvers, the party succeeded in concluding a double alliance. On the one hand, it linked itself with the *Zentrum*, hoping that their combined votes in North Rhine-Westphalia and Bavaria would enable the Federalist Union to clear the 5 per cent hurdle. On the other, it made a pact with the SPD whereby the latter agreed not to put forward candidates in four constituencies where the total number of votes gained by the two parties in 1953 and 1954 was such that they might in theory expect to obtain three direct seats under the electoral law. It remained to be seen what the voters would think of this unnatural alliance. On September 13, they gave their answer in no uncertain terms: the CSU swept ahead, gaining all four seats and between 54 and 64 per cent of "second votes" in the constituencies in question.

The Bavarian Party's only consolation was that its ally in North Rhine–Westphalia was crushed in an even more spectacular fashion, gaining only 0·8 per cent of *Land* votes. The *Zentrum* had been revived in October, 1945 by a Catholic group of somewhat leftward tendencies who desired to reconstitute what had been one of Germany's oldest and most influential political parties. They were, however, unable to compete against the growth of the CDU. There were several attempts to unite the two parties, but they broke down because the *Zentrum* finally decided that conservative influence was too strong in the CDU. Although the *Zentrum* was a Christian—and more especially a Catholic—party, it feared that a two-party political system of SPD versus CDU would lead to a disastrous alternation of clerical and anticlerical governments. It thus became a party of the left, strongly opposed to capitalism and fairly close to the SPD except in religious matters. But the electoral law obliged it to seek the patronage of one of the big parties, and it was with CDU help that the *Zentrum* chairman, Johannes Brockmann, was elected for Oberhausen. Before long, he was the only representative of his party in the Bundestag: the second candidate elected was in reality a Christian Democrat, and the third died in January, 1954. In accordance with the electoral law, his place was taken by the next candidate on the *Zentrum* list, but in May, 1955 he was deprived of his party membership and joined the CDU.

The *Zentrum* lost its strongest personality in 1951 when its chairman, Frau Helene Wessel, resigned from the party to devote herself wholly to the campaign against rearmament in which she was allied with Dr. Gustav Heinemann, the former Federal Minister of the Interior who had resigned in 1950. In November, 1952, together they founded the All-German People's Party (*Gesamtdeutsche Volkspartei*—GVP), which attracted a good many students and working-class militants by its vigorous attacks on rearmament and its pleas for German reunification, as well as by its leaders' sacrifice of personal ambition and its hostility to bourgeois tendencies in the Federal Republic. However, this popularity brought no comparable success at the polls. The fortunes of the GVP were followed with attention by the New Left in France, which in large measure shared its views and, though it was less aware of this, found itself in a similar situation—namely, that of exercising intellectual influence out of proportion to its electoral chances. The least bad result achieved by the GVP in any regional election was in Hesse, where it obtained 1·7 per cent of votes in the legislative election of 1953. Its best constituency result was scored by Dr. Heinemann himself at Siegen in Westphalia, but with 8·9 per cent he was still far behind the CDU, the SPD and, even, the FDP candidates. Analysis of the figures showed that he had gained his votes from the Communists and, especially, the Socialists, which was not what the party had hoped for. This being so, would the party not be better advised to turn itself into a left-wing of the SPD, at all events in matters concerning the army and reunification, rather than continue to maintain a political existence without prospects? For over three years the debate went on in the GVP; finally, the advocates of fusion won the day, and, at an extraordinary congress on May 19, 1957, it was decided to dissolve the party. In return for advising their followers to vote for the SPD, Dr. Heinemann and Frau Wessel were included in the latter's lists, the former in third place for Lower Saxony and the latter ninth on the North Rhine–Westphalia list. Helene Wessel remained a member of the Bundestag until she died, at the age of seventy-one, in October, 1969, having lived long enough to receive a decoration from her former co-chairman, by then President of the Republic.

In the 1949 elections, there was not as yet any party concerned specifically with refugee interests; yet, when 1953 came round, the BHE's opportunity had already passed. The "Union of those expelled from their homelands and of the dispossessed" (*Bund der Heimatvertriebenen und Entrechteten*) was founded in Schleswig-Holstein in January, 1950, and on the 9th of that month it had already scored a striking success, gaining 23·4 per cent of votes at the *Landtag* election. Even so, it was a long way from commanding the support of all those whom it claimed to represent, since 36 per cent of the *Land* population then consisted of refugees. The BHE was set up on a national level in January, 1951, but its first congress, at Goslar, was not held till September, 1952. Its chairman was Waldemar Kraft, a former captain in the SS who was born in Pomerania in 1898. The BHE regarded itself as a "special interest" group acting through the medium of a political party. Besides refugees, it sought to appeal to all the "dispossessed," that is, to victims of the war and also of denazification. Its recipe for helping its clientèle was to advertise its presence as widely as possible, especially by being represented in *Land* governments. From September, 1950, it had a share of power in Schleswig-Holstein with the CDU, the FDP, and the German Party (DP); in Lower Saxony, it joined with the SPD from 1951 to 1955 and with the other parties against the SPD from 1955 to 1957; while in Hesse it shared power with the SPD from January 1955 onward.

However, the BHE leaders soon discovered that the refugees were being integrated into national life so fast that it was not a paying proposition to exploit their economic distress. Their propaganda accordingly laid more and more stress on political grievances in regard to reunification and the lost territories. The party's name was modified by prefacing to it the initials GB (*Gesamtdeutscher Block*—All-German Bloc). On the eve of the 1953 elections, however, its policy was still indecisive, with Kraft making vague and contradictory attacks on the Chancellor's foreign policy. Alongside the chairman, who was at this time deputy Prime Minister at Kiel, a strong personality was coming to the fore as a representative of the refugees in Bavaria. This was Professor Theodor Oberländer, seven years younger than Kraft and a specialist in East European affairs. He had taught at Königsberg and Prague and had been discharged from the army in 1943 on the ground, or so he claimed, that he had refused to ill-treat the Russian population; on the other hand, he had unquestionably demanded the expulsion of Poles from the territory annexed by Germany after 1939. In the elections, twenty-seven members of the BHE, including Kraft and Oberländer, were returned to the Bundestag, and the party decided to take a hand in Federal Government, the two leaders becoming respectively Minister Without Portfolio and Minister for Refugee Affairs. For a time, Oberländer looked like a strong man and possibly a dangerous one: he replaced Kraft as chairman of his party and, within the government, persuaded the Chancellor to widen considerably the powers of his own ministry. But, in Germany as elsewhere, ministerial rank and the parliamentary game have a softening effect on political attitudes. Within a few months of accepting office, Kraft and Oberländer were accused by their associates of spinelessly adhering to Adenauer's policy, ceasing to think for themselves and, in short, betraying their party. Those who thus attacked them had feared, with some reason, that the result of joining Adenauer's government would be that the party leaders would have to endorse a foreign policy that did nothing to bring reunification closer, and that they would get no credit for the economic integration of refugees; instead, public opinion would give credit to Erhard's policy. For these reasons, the BHE parliamentary group, in July, 1955, repudiated the two ministers and seven of their friends and went into opposition. On September 15, 1957, Oberländer, now a CDU candidate, scored a resounding electoral success in Lower Saxony with 56,081 first votes as against 51,700 second votes, this being five times more than the BHE candidate. In the same election, Kraft became a CDU member of the Bundestag for North Rhine–Westphalia.

The remnant of the BHE elected as their chairman the minister of agriculture in Lower Saxony, Friedrich von Kessel, a Silesian *Junker* of no great brilliance who, before 1933, had been a member of Hugenberg's party, the DNVP (German Nationalists). At the Fulda congress of June, 1956, the party seemed full of hope: it claimed 162,000 members and announced that it was going to conduct a vigorous election campaign. Its basic theme was the recovery of the Oder–Neisse territories, Memel, and the Sudeten area: Sudeten refugees played a decisive role in the party, which asserted the continued validity of the Munich agreement. The Sudeten spokesman and Bundestag deputy, Frank Seiboth, was in fact its strongest personality: at the Düsseldorf congress in April, 1957, he received more votes as vice-chairman than von Kessel as chairman. The task of organizing election propaganda was entrusted to him: economic questions and the equalization of financial burdens were no longer important issues; the great question was foreign policy. But the electoral law was still an obstacle: could the party afford to cut loose from its protectors? Speakers declared themselves confident of achieving the necessary 5 per cent, but not everyone was so sure. In the event, the party lost on all fronts. The congress did not dare to adopt resolutions too outspoken either on the Sudeten question, on which it expressed itself in moderate terms, or on the European treaties, which were excluded from its deliberations. At the same time, negotiations with other parties fell through, and the BHE had to play a lone hand in the election. The result, while less than catastrophic, was such as to deprive the party of representation in the legislature. The most spectacular individual defeat was that of Dr. Linus Kather, a picturesque character who had been a CDU deputy and chairman of the German Expellees' League (*Bund vertriebener Deutscher*). His influence in refugee circles was rated so highly that, in the early summer of 1952, the Chancellor had asked his Minister for Refugee Affairs, the unexcitable Hans Lukaschek, to stand down in Kather's favor. Lukaschek refused. After the 1953 elections, Kather thought his hour had come. Infuriated by what he regarded as Adenauer's treachery in giving the post to Oberländer, he joined the latter's party and became a mortal enemy of the Chancellor, even to the point of standing for election against him at Bonn in 1957; he received 4,116 votes to his adversary's 129,549. Thereafter, the fortunes of the BHE declined rapidly, despite an attempt to save them by merging, paradoxically enough, with the German Party, which had also fallen on evil days. The merger took place in April, 1961, and the joint party was named the *Gesamtdeutsche Partei*.

In 1949, the German Party had seventeen representatives in the Bundestag. They came from the northeast of the Federal Republic: Schleswig, Lower Saxony, Hamburg, and Bremen. The party was founded in June, 1945, as the *"Land* Party of Lower Saxony" (*Niedersächsische Landespartei*), and regarded itself as the heir to the Guelph particularists who had, in former days, relied for support on the Hanoverian aristocracy, Protestant clergy, and peasants; but its extension beyond Hanover was inspired by a much less regionalist ideology. It was indeed the explicit aim of the DP to become a right-wing conservative party. It showed from the first a predilection for the Imperial black, white, and red flag and for organizing public rallies with parades and military music. One of its leaders, Hans Christoph Seebohm, remained Federal Minister of Transport until 1966, thus sharing with Erhard a record for governmental longevity; he soon attracted attention by intemperate language, which continued to be his speciality, especially in regard to the Czechoslovak frontier.

However, in 1953 the survival of the DP was an open question. In that year, the party succeeded, by allying itself with the CDU, in capturing fifteen seats with 3·3 per cent of the votes, but, in exchange, it moderated its tone to such an extent that it virtually disappeared behind the CDU. Throughout the second Bundestag, it loyally supported the government. Two of its leaders attracted notice: Hans Joachim von Merkatz, an excellent parliamentarian and respected member of the Council of Europe who later became a minister, and Heinrich Hellwege, the party chairman (from October, 1952) who, as we have seen, was first a Federal minister and then Minister-President of Lower Saxony. It was he who, in November, 1957, expelled the FDP and BHE from his government because of their links with the DRP (extreme right) and replaced them by members of the SPD while keeping the support of the CDU —despite the fact the election was fought on the slogan "Keep to the right, vote to the right," and that the DP's unwritten motto at this period was still *Kanzlertreue mit Rechtsblick* (loyalty to the Chancellor, but with a rightist outlook).

As the election drew near, the DP sought to regain some independence, contrary to the advice of von Merkatz who himself became a member of the CDU. The tie-up with the former BHE proved disastrous, especially in Lower Saxony, which had till then been the DP's most faithful area. The electors seemed to disapprove of the alliance and, for the most part, to choose between two ways of punishing the DP—either by adhering to the former party line and voting CDU, or by giving their votes to the only small party that had any chance of achieving the 5 per cent minimum, namely, the FDP, whose growth in 1961 was largely due to the accession of these right-wing votes. This is shown by the fact that the FDP vote slumped in Lower Saxony after its delegates had supported Dr. Heinemann in the presidential election of 1969.

The FDP (*Freie Demokratische Partei*), or Liberal Party, was established in the three western zones as late as November, 1948, and its first congress was held in June, 1949. A Liberal Democratic Party (LDPD) had been formed in the Soviet zone in 1945; and Württemberg-Baden, in January, 1946, saw the birth of a Democratic People's Party (DVP), which later became, without changing its name, a regional constituent of the FDP. In August, 1952, the DVP chairman, Reinhold Maier, was called to account before an extraordinary congress of the FDP, which deliberated on whether to expel him for having formed the government of the new *Land* of Baden-Württemberg with the aid of the SPD, contrary to the views of the party leadership and the parliamentary group at Bonn. The congress decided to take no action. Apart from reflecting a difference of view as to the powers of the regional federations of the FDP, the incident was symptomatic of the party's duality of origin. The FDP was at once the party of republican liberals, whose roots went back to the political tradition of 1848, and that of the right-wing *bourgeoisie* who pressed for undiluted liberalism (or *laissez-faire*) in the economic field. Thanks to the ambiguity of the term "liberal," it was usually possible to blur the distinction. The former attitude was strongest in southwest Germany, where it was exemplified in such men as Reinhold Maier and President Heuss himself; while the stronghold of the second tendency was in the Ruhr, where one of its chief representatives was Adenauer's Vice-Chancellor Blücher, who became party chairman after Heuss was elected to the presidency.

In the field of religion and education, the FDP was much more united. It "combated the false modern doctrines of Marxist and biological materialism" and was opposed to secularist education "because it exposes the youth of wide social strata in the big towns to the danger of growing up with insufficient knowledge of the religious and cultural values of Christianity, and, consequently, without a proper understanding of the Western tradition as a whole." At the same time, the party denounced clericalism and voted against the confessional school system, advocating instead the *Simultanschule* or "community school" with a curriculum "designed to impart a knowledge of the religious and cultural heritage of the Christian West in all subjects of instruction that lend themselves to this purpose." The views of the FDP in these matters, therefore, were somewhere between those of the SPD and the CDU, whereas, in the economic and social sphere, the CDU was intermediate between it and the SPD.

From 1952 onward, however, the FDP began to change and its variations are almost as hard to follow as those of the French Radical Party. In the Bundestag, it sat further to the right than the CDU and it strongly opposed the bill providing for workers' co-management (or co-determination: *Mitbestimmung*) in the coal and steel industry. Dr. Dehler, Adenauer's first Minister of Justice, spoke more and more violently against the trade unions, while the FDP as a whole warned insistently of the dangers of CDU clericalism and the Chancellor's excessively "European" policy, despite the fact that Franz Blücher, as Vice-Chancellor, was responsible for international economic cooperation. The electoral results of this medley of views were not encouraging. The Chancellor left Dr. Dehler out of his 1953 cabinet, which was a mistake: the Bavarian lawyer, with his frankness and warmth and his irreproachably anti-Nazi past, was—whatever his intemperance of language—a man of great charm and energy. At the Wiesbaden congress in May, 1954, he was elected party chairman in place of Blücher, who was considered too soft vis-à-vis the Chancellor. The FDP thus entered on a period of semi-opposition or "critical participation." The first serious crisis broke out over the Franco-German agreement concerning the Saar: on the occasion of his visit to Paris in October, 1954, the Chancellor refused to take account of the FDP's proposals, though they were quite close to the solution that was eventually adopted. When the Saar statute came up for ratification in February, 1955, the entire parliamentary FDP, with the exception of the Vice-Chancellor, voted against it.

In February, 1956 came the "Düsseldorf revolt": the *Land* association of the FDP in North Rhine–Westphalia came out in favor of a change in the composition of the government, and on February 20, Karl Arnold, the CDU Minister-President, was overthrown. When the FDP congress met at Würzburg in April, profound changes had taken place. The party was torn in pieces: sixteen deputies had left its ranks, including the Federal ministers and the Vice-Presidents of the Bundestag. The remaining thirty-six FDP deputies had gone into opposition, and no one at Würzburg raised a voice in favor of returning to the government fold. Dehler was re-elected chairman, but his prestige suffered gravely from the party's defeat at the municipal elections in the autumn. On January 6, 1957, he announced that he would not again stand for the chairmanship, and the party committee thereupon unanimously invited Reinhold Maier to accept nomination.

The real victors in the crisis were apparently the "Young Turks" of Düsseldorf. Their leader, Wolfgang Döring, was born in 1919, and his closest associates—Willi Weyer, the *Land* minister of reconstruction, and the Bundestag deputies Walter Scheel and ex-officer Erich Mende—were of the same generation. Their links with the Socialists went back to 1953. They had as yet no precise economic and social program, but wanted a more active foreign policy especially in the matter of reunification (as expressed later in the electoral slogan "Germany first, Europe afterwards.") In October, 1956, Döring, Scheel, and Mende went to Weimar to confer with the leaders of the Liberal Party in the G.D.R., a step that was less than popular in the Federal Republic as it brought no concrete result. However, the Düsseldorf group had at least shown that they intended to neglect no chance of bringing reunification closer. Did this denote a return to the policy of right-wing liberalism dominated by the nationalist *Reichsidee*? But, as against this view, Dr. Pfeiderer, a left-wing liberal and former diplomat, had in 1952 put forward a reunification plan that the Chancellor had judged too neutralistic, though he subsequently appointed its author ambassador to Yugoslavia.

At the Berlin congress of January 24–26, 1957, the party seemed to be moving toward the left: a majority of the twenty-seven members of the new committee were known to favor the idea of a coalition with the SPD. Döring was given the task of organizing the election campaign under the supervision of the party chairman. The program was a straightforward one: there was no difficulty in agreeing on slogans, such as "Strengthen the Third Force," or in appealing more or less openly to nationalism. A poster inviting Germans to take a stand between clerical black and socialist red afforded a pretext for reproducing the Imperial tricolor. But there were disagreements on economic and social matters, which were interesting as they showed that the liberalism of the Rhineland and that of the southwest had to some extent changed places. While Döring insisted that "It will never be our object to preserve an outworn social order," Reinhold Maier denounced "an excess of social legislation at the Federal level, to meet equally excessive claims from below." When Germany was reunified, he declared, the party's role would be to resist the determination of the SPD and the inclination of the CDU to preserve so-called social achievements in the G.D.R. It was difficult to tell which of these attitudes represented the dominant party view.

The setback of 1957 was felt the more severely since the CDU/CSU commanded an absolute majority and the FDP was thus excluded from government. The hardest hit were the "Young Turks," who put up a very poor showing in North Rhine–Westphalia. But the party was in any case due for rejuvenation, and, at the 1960 congress, Reinhold Maier agreed not to stand again for the chairmanship. His successor was Erich Mende, a Catholic from Silesia, aged forty-three: a little overconscious of his physical appearance and not quite energetic enough in his role as a party leader, he was, from 1963 onward, a Vice-Chancellor and minister. Under his leadership, the FDP's voice remained uncertain,[19] but it is hard to see how this could have been avoided: there were as many schools of thought within the party as among the voters who supported it and those whom it hoped to win over. The role of an opposition within the government is never easy to play, but the attitude of "Yes, but . . ." is less difficult to sustain on the basis of coherent objections, whereas the FDP found itself criticizing its powerful ally first from a rightist standpoint and then from a leftist one. At times it risked an appeal to liberal opinion, as when it mobilized against Franz Josef Strauss over the *Spiegel* affair and brought about his downfall. One of the few moments of real human dignity in that tragicomic episode was Wolfgang Döring's speech to the Bundestag on November 7, 1962, when the ablest of the FDP leaders—who unhappily died a few weeks later, on January 17—struck a personal note in defense of his friend Rudolf Augstein, while appealing to the Chancellor to respect the rule of law. At other times, the party sought a more facile success, as in the controversy over the time limit for the prosecution of Nazi offenders: the resignation of the FDP Minister of Justice, Ewald Bucher, on the eve of the 1965 election was designed to gain credit with voters who took the view that it was time to let bygones be bygones.

The FDP's hesitations over ideology and tactics, both in the *Länder* and at Federal level, went a long way to explain both the exasperation of the two major parties with its "pendulum tactics" and the formation of the Grand Coalition in 1966. As the sole parliamentary opposition group, the party continued to snipe at the government from all directions at once, but by degrees it came to adopt a more consistent line, especially after the election of a new chairman at the Freiburg congress in January, 1968. Erich Mende had been obliged to stand down because the party did not share his view that it was proper to combine the office of chairman with a seat on the board of the American firm Investors' Overseas Services, which he had accepted in the previous September. As the only "old-timer" of importance—Thomas Dehler—had died in July, the chairmanship went to Walter Scheel. His election presented no difficulty at a time when his friends were again in power in North Rhine–Westphalia, and the party was beginning to enjoy fresh prestige in the important field of training and education. This was due to the spectacular activity of a new recruit, Ralf Dahrendorf, who, in 1960, was appointed to a chair of sociology at the age of thirty-one: he was the author of penetrating studies of German society and vigorous pleas for the reform of the school and university system. Within the FDP, he joined forces with a woman of great charm and energy, Hildegard Hamm-Brücher, who had written books boldly advocating democratic and other reforms in this field and had become state secretary for education in Hesse.

Apart from the educational theme, the FDP, not without confusion and much internal conflict, attempted to outflank the government in the matter of a more fluid Eastern policy. The chief result, in February, 1968, was the production of a draft "general treaty" with the G.D.R. In general, the party's leftward trend was to a large extent due to the increasingly strong influence of a man of exceptional ability and will power, Hans Dietrich Genscher. In 1956, at the age of twenty-nine, he had been engaged as a "research assistant" by the parliamentary FDP; three years later, though not himself a deputy, he was its secretary. When he entered the Bundestag in 1965, he was already the key man of the party, which he steered toward an alliance with the SPD; the election of Dr. Heinemann to the presidency was a personal success for him. However, the Bundestag election campaign, based wholly on the theme of rejuvenation and modernization, (*Schneidet die alten Zöpfe ab!*—"Down with the old fogeys!"), was disastrous in arithmetical terms, though by the same token a political triumph: although the party barely scraped over the 5 per cent hurdle, it was represented in force in the new government, with Walter Scheel and Genscher as Ministers of Foreign and Home Affairs respectively, while Dahrendorf and Frau Hamm-Brücher became state secretaries, the one for foreign affairs and the other for scientific research. The party's left wing had risen to power on the ruins of the election; to give the right wing some satisfaction, the strongly conservative Josef Ertl was made Minister of Agriculture. At the beginning of 1970, Erich Mende launched a counter-offensive to induce the party to pay more attention to the conservative vote, but this was repulsed with little difficulty.

The course adopted by the party's younger leaders is a risky one: many of its supporters have deserted to the CDU, and those that remain will be tempted by the SPD. The party must find some way to attract voters before the decline becomes irremediable. There can be no question of outflanking the SPD to the left, and the party no longer aims to conquer right-wing votes from the CDU except in matters of social organization, where the FDP stoutly maintains its hostility to codetermination. The party is thus reduced to attempting to find a niche between its two rivals by presenting not so much an alternative program as an alternative style. The rejuvenated FDP has little chance of increasing its vote in the direction of conservative nationalism and its economic liberalism is not calculated to appeal to those who blame the SPD for departing too far from Socialist principles. Sure enough, the election results of June 14, 1970 in North Rhine–Westphalia, Lower Saxony, and the Saar were unfavorable to the FDP, its percentage of the vote falling—as compared with the *Landtag* elections of 1966—from 7·4 to 5·5, 6·9 to 4·4, and 8·3 to 4·4 respectively. At the party congress that followed, Walter Scheel was re-elected by a large majority, but the FDP's future remained somber.

In any case, no political force has ever succeeded in establishing itself to the left of the SPD, the latter's situation in this respect being similar to that of the British Labour Party or the Democrats in America, and very unlike that of the French or Italian Socialists. A party thus placed can lay itself out to appeal to the central mass of moderately inclined voters without the risk of losing support to a hard-line rival. The SPD is not free from internal dissension, especially in Berlin, but it may take comfort, after three years of alliance with the CDU, from the results of the 1969 election, in which extreme left-wing competition was negligible. The German Peace Union (*Deutsche Friedens-Union*— DFU), founded in 1960, was scarcely able—in that year or in 1965—to capture the adherents of Dr. Heinemann's former party. In 1969, the international atmosphere was more relaxed than in the early 1950's, and the DFU leaders had less appeal to left-wing intellectuals than their predecessors, in some cases because their good will seemed unduly naive and in others becouse they did not show enough independence vis-à-vis the Communist bloc. As a result, the DFU was far from being in the ascendant when it decided to join forces with the new Communist Party (DKP) to form a "League for Democratic Progress" (*Aktion für demokratischen Fortscritt*—ADF). The alliance was the more ill-fated as the DKP had welcomed the Soviet invasion of Czechoslovakia, which repelled from the ADF a good many leftist critics of the SPD. In these circumstances, the left-wing intellectuals adopted different attitudes at the election: some were for abstention, others for supporting the SPD (but not seeking, like Günter Grass, to transform it from within), and a few others for the ADF.[20] Among these were Protestant clergymen and university professors such as Wolfgang Abendroth, who launched an appeal embodying the group's election program and calling on the faithful to combat the threat of Fascism and put pressure on the SPD to adopt a more leftist course. The result was a total failure. At Waldshut in Württemberg, the ADF put up against Kiesinger a young woman named Beate Klarsfeld, who had made a name for herself by attacking him at every turn on account of his past: she scored 644 votes to Kiesinger's 60,373. The best performance of the ADF in any constituency scarcely exceeded 1 per cent of the votes, and, in the country as a whole, it scored only one-seventh as many votes as its rival of the extreme right, the NPD (*Nationaldemokratische Partei Deutschlands*).

The NPD had already picked up some DFU votes in *Land* elections, a phenomenon reminiscent of the shift of French Communist votes toward Poujadism in 1955–56: a vote of sheer discontent may drift from one extreme to its opposite. There is, however, one fundamental difference between the German and the French electorate—namely, that, in times of economic crisis or profound social unrest, the tendency is for extremism to manifest itself on the left in France, but on the right in Germany. This was once again illustrated by the way in which the NPD gained ground during the recession of 1965–67.

The NPD was founded at Hanover on November 28, 1964. Several of its leaders and much of its following had belonged to the *Deutsche Reichspartei* (which was not officially dissolved till 1965), or, especially in Schleswig and Lower Saxony, to the *Gesamtdeutsche Partei*. The NPD has not at any time been the sole mouthpiece of German right-wing extremism, which exists in multiple forms.[21] Its leaders—particularly Adolf von Thadden, who emerged victorious from a series of tussles within the party—are fairly moderate in their utterances; this cannot be said of local meetings, where unbridled language is the order of the day. The party's long and carefully drafted official program contains relatively few references to the past. It demands a general amnesty and recalls that Germany is still in subjection to her conquerors. The older generation of Germans should no longer be kept in the dock. The NPD abominates massacres and war crimes, by whomever committed and at whatever period. It rejects the charge that Germany was wholly or mainly responsible for either of the world wars: those who accept this charge and submit to foreign domination have, it claims, paralyzed German policy for decades. In foreign affairs, a European policy is upheld as the best means of fighting American and Soviet imperialism, especially the former. The Yalta spirit must be overcome. The party vigorously opposes the abandonment of any part of German territory in the east. "Our claim to the Sudetenland must be given up by no one, no government and no party. Our claim to eastern Germany [that is, the Oder-Neisse territories] must be given up by no one, no government and no party." In internal affairs, the program includes familiar social themes—public and private morality, elimination of class conflict, rejection of cultural cosmopolitanism, and negative economic aims that need cause no surprise (the party is against big stores, foreign workers in Germany, industrial combines, and aid to undeveloped countries).[22]

Many of the party's leaders, though not von Thadden himself, held propaganda and other jobs in the NSDAP; but the rank and file members, and, still more, those who vote for the party, are of varying backgrounds. Analysis has shown that there were a considerable number of potential NPD supporters in each of the other parties and in all sections of the public.[23] The party's successes in and after 1966 gave rise to fears that it would expand rapidly: it gained 7·9 per cent of votes in Hesse on November 6, 1966; 7·4 per cent in Bavaria on November 20; 6·9 per cent in Rhineland-Palatinate on April 23, 1967; 7·1 per cent in Lower Saxony on June 4; 8·8 per cent at Bremen on October 1; and 9·8 per cent in Baden-Württemberg on April 28, 1968. The student riots seemed to give it a useful chance to appeal to respecters of law and order. The coalition government was in two minds as regards applying to the Constitutional Court to declare it illegal. Was not the NPD, if nothing else, a successor to the SRP, which was banned in 1952, and was it tolerable that it should carry on propaganda with the help of public funds? On the other hand, was it certain that a ban would be forthcoming, given the prudence of the NPD leaders and the fact that the party's general behavior was more peaceable than that of student organizations, which no one spoke of banning? Was not the NPD too large to ban? Contrariwise, would it not be better to trust the electorate and the 5 per cent rule? In the end, it was decided to take no action, and this decision was repeated by the Brandt government, which defended it in a reply by Genscher to a written question by F. J. Strauss.[24] The policy of "playing it cool" had in fact paid off—though only just. In the 1969 election, the NPD failed to clear the 5 per cent hurdle except in the Saar and Bavaria (5·7 per cent each), Rhineland-Palatinate (5·2 per cent), and

Hesse (5·1 per cent), which meant that its nationwide total was below 5 per cent. The party held a post-election congress at Wertheim (Baden-Württemberg) in February, 1970, having been banned from Berlin by the Allies and from Saarbrücken by the municipality for fear of demonstrations; the atmosphere was one of dejection.

The party's defeat may be ascribed to several causes: the economic revival in 1968, the failure of NPD deputies to dramatize their party's activity in the *Landtage*, the dying-down of student disturbances (the election itself took place during the vacation period), and the success of attacks on an NPD that, surprisingly enough, was made to figure not as a victim of student or trade union intolerance but as an instigator of unrest. But the 1969 result does not mean that the NPD is done for or that some other party of the extreme right may not come to the fore at a future date. However, the prime condition of its rise—the existence of the Grand Coalition—is no longer present: the CDU and CSU are available as a refuge for right-wing malcontents.

In any case, the future of small parties, whatever their place in the political spectrum, is not rosy. The big parties have every opportunity to grow bigger still, especially at election time when they can call in public relations agencies and take full advantage of modern advertising techniques. A striking description of such methods was given as long ago as September, 1958, by Franz Meyers, the Minister-President of North Rhine–Westphalia, to the CDU congress at Kiel. In a report on "scientific" electioneering, he raised the question of whether the methods used were wholly in accordance with the traditional idea of democracy: the answer he gave was, in effect, "Yes, provided they are used by us."

Since 1965, "us" has meant the two great parties that have the ability and the desire to penetrate every milieu, attracting the most varied elements of an electorate that is less and less fixed in its choice: the most striking conclusion to emerge from detailed analysis of the 1969 election[25] is not that the SPD or the CDU has been more or less successful in this or that area, with this or that socio-economic class or age group, but rather that there is a general slackening of party ties, a decline of permanent loyalties, and a frequency with which voters change their allegiance. One may infer from this that German society is becoming more homogeneous, if only by the softening of traditional dividing lines of ideology and social or cultured habits. On the other hand, this state of affairs is quite compatible with a different psychological tendency. Citizens of the Federal Republic have grown accustomed to voting for one of the two main parties because there is no reasonable alternative to doing so; but their choice does not necessarily reflect in full measure the aspirations and discontents of individuals and groups, who may be inclined to seek the satisfaction of their wants and feelings through institutions other than those of representative democracy.

8

Economic and Social Forces

The Doctrine of Prosperity

West German democracy cannot be understood without some idea of the economic development that underlies and supports political life. The German public has had time to grow accustomed to prosperity: continued expansion ceased to be a matter of wonder after the first ten years, and by degrees people started to compare what they had with what they still lacked, rather than with what they had had to go without during the dark years. When the new state began to function in 1949, it was still uncertain whether, and if so how, the start given to the economy could be followed up by a period of steady progress, and there was a haunting fear of crises similar to those that had afflicted Germany between the wars. In 1968–69, relief was felt that the country had overcome the "recession" of 1966, in which year the gross national product (GNP) grew by "only" 2·3 per cent, and 1967, when it remained static and the unemployment figure rose above 300,000.

The currency reform of June, 1948 marked the spectacular beginning of an economic rebirth. In June, 1952, the President of the *Landtag* of North Rhine–Westphalia had occasion to announce that larger chairs were to be installed in the chamber of that assembly: those provided six years earlier had grown too small to accommodate deputies who had enjoyed the benefits of the "social market economy" for the preceding four years!

Production had already begun to revive during the occupation. In 1946, it had stood at an index of 33 compared with 1936: this rose to 90 by the summer of 1949, when the institutions of the new state were being created, but prosperity was still a good way off. Unemployment was on the increase, and there was a heavy adverse balance of payments. In the course of the next ten years, production rose by 126 per cent. Whereas in September, 1950 there were 1,580,000 unemployed as against 13,827,000 at work, by September, 1961 it was reckoned that virtual full employment had been achieved, the figures being 95,000 and 20,933,000—and this despite the fact that 3 million East Germans had taken refuge in the Federal Republic since its creation. The demand for labor was such that, after August 13, 1961, when the Berlin wall stopped further migration from the G.D.R., recourse was had to importing foreign workers. In 1969, over 1·5 million Italians, Greeks, and Turks were employed in the Republic, where the working population was over 26 million,[1] with less than 200,000 unemployed and over 700,000 jobs vacant.

In 1946, the occupying powers in the four zones had imposed a limit on Germany's total steel production of 7·5 million tons per annum. In 1969, the figure for the Federal Republic alone was 44 million. A favorable trade balance was achieved in 1952, and in 1961 the excess of exports over imports—though the latter had quadrupled—stood at DM6,600 million.* The favorable balance had grown to such proportions that the mark was up-valued by 5 per cent on March 6, 1969 and postwar debts were repaid ahead of time. In the mid-1960's, the pace had slackened: in 1965, foreign trade showed only a small profit and the balance of payments was in deficit. But expansion was soon resumed, and, in October, 1969, the over mighty Deutsche Mark was again revalued, this time by 8·5 per cent.

The population of the Republic (including West Berlin) had swelled to over 60 million by 1968—a density of 629 per square mile, as compared with 429 for the same area in 1933. Not only did the GNP, expressed in real terms, treble itself in twenty years, but per capita production was constantly on the increase. From 1950 to 1966, real wages rose by 139 per cent, while the average working week was shortened by 10 per cent.[2] During the Federal Republic's first twenty years of existence, no fewer than 10·5 million new dwellings were built on its territory.

Naturally the picture has its lights and shades, and some sectors are better off than others. The coal and textile industries are far from equaling the prosperity of such key branches of the economy as chemicals and electronics. The unemployment peak of January, 1967 was 2·6 per cent of the working population in the country as a whole, but at Gelsenkirchen it was 4·2 per cent and at Passau, 18·4 per cent,[3] the figure varying not only between sectors but between geographical areas. Nevertheless, all the important figures go to show that economic prosperity is a continuing phenomenon and that, twenty-five years after Germany's collapse, conditions of life in the Federal Republic are such that its more critical citizens accuse their compatriots of surrendering to material comfort and treating it as the sole measure of well-being.

Is this an "economic miracle"? At all events, it is a remarkable achievement, and its causes deserve close examination. How far was it due to a specific economic policy? Was the "social market economy" genuinely liberal and inspired by considerations of social welfare? Granted that the government's policy was dictated by an economic philosophy, may we not also say that the return to prosperity has led to the domination of a particular ideology in the Federal Republic?

Among the factors that made recovery possible from 1948 onward, one that the Germans are inclined to forget is that the occupation did not weigh too heavily on the country. As we saw, the Allies made it known that they intended to levy reparations and restrict the development of German industry. The levies were certainly onerous, and factories were being dismantled as late as 1950, but it cannot be said that reparations were a crushing burden on the Republic. Up to about 1950, the country's poverty served as an excuse to dodge the issue, and afterward, it became too late in the day to rake up old scores. This process of double reasoning was particularly evident in relation

*From March, 1961 to September, 1967, the DM–£ rate was between 11·09 and 11·22. In October, 1967, it was 9·63; in 1968, 9·5 (average); in January, 1969, 9·58; in October, 1969, 8·83. The DM–$ rate was close to 4 from 1961 to October, 1969, when it became 3·66.

to the Saar; on the other hand, an exception must be made for the treaty of 1952 with Israel. As for shackling German production, this idea vanished with the introduction of the Schuman Plan. On balance, the Allies' intervention must be put on the credit side of the economic ledger, since West German recovery was greatly helped by American aid. The billions of dollars in loans and especially gifts, provided at first in the form of Aid to Occupied Areas (GARIOA) and later under the Marshall Plan, played a decisive role, the more so as West Germany—unlike Britain and France, which received even larger amounts of aid—had neither an army to maintain nor present and former colonies to aid; nor was Germany engaged in colonial warfare. To be sure, the Republic was obliged to bear occupation costs till 1955. But even if the annual charge of DM7,200 million had been paid in full and had represented wholly unproductive expenditure, which was not the case, and even if we leave out of account the influx of dollars due to the presence of American troops, the proportion of the budget devoted in this way to defense was less than the corresponding figure for the Western Allies, despite the fact that the Republic contributed in various ways to the cost of stationing American and British troops on German soil.

The U.S. occupying authorities also helped to influence events by upholding an economic system that was to figure prominently in West German theory and still more in the official explanation of developments as they took place.[4] This did not, however, prevent conflicts arising: in fact, at the outset Allied pressure was exercised more strongly in the field of economic policy than in any other. Apart from General Clay himself, no one among the occupying authorities approved of Ludwig Erhard's 1948 decision to do away with controls and trust to private enterprise. Pressure was put on him and on Dr. Schäffer, the Finance Minister, until the aftermath of the Korean boom, when it was finally admitted that their policy had paid off. Up to then, they had been blamed chiefly for not taking measures to stimulate expansion, while appearing outrageously indulgent to high rates of profit and large incomes. On April 4, 1950, the German ministers sought to introduce a "minor fiscal reform" that considerably reduced the tax burden on the groups in question: it was vetoed by the High Commissioners on April 20, the Americans especially being indignant that taxes should be lowered at a time when the Federal Government was asking them for extra aid. However, under the combined effect of the ministers' arguments and violent press criticisms of the High Commissioners' interference in German internal affairs (though their action was perfectly justified under the Occupation Statute), the Allies gave way on the 29th and the reform entered into operation almost intact.

Whatever the appearances, this reduction of taxes was in fact a logical part of Erhard's "social market economy"—or, as it might be translated, free-enterprise economy with a social conscience. This burly, sanguine, self-confident man, little given to theorizing but full of will-power, seemed to embody the robust energy of a whole section of the population that only asked to be given a free hand and was not impressed by the forecasts of skeptical experts. Erhard's economic doctrine derived from what has been called the "Freiburg school," the head of which, Walter Eucken, died in 1950. Thereafter, its chief representative was a German professor named Wilhelm Röpke, who had emigrated in 1933 and was teaching at Geneva. He was fifty years old when the Federal Republic came into being and afforded him the rare opportunity of seeing a government put his ideas into practice, so faithfully indeed as to produce an amusing incident in 1950: the Federal ministers, desirous of answering their critics on the basis of an authoritative foreign opinion, sought the advice of Professor Röpke and were gratified to find that their neoliberalism met with his entire approval.[5]

The object of the social market economy was to create a truly competitive market, free from domination either by the state or by private monopolies. Economic laws should be allowed to operate freely, subject to such conditions as would ensure all round and "social" development of the economy instead of one based solely on private profit. "An undigested Keynesianism is no less discredited than the *laissez-faire* idea that the state should play no part in economic life. If the state does intervene, the important thing is how and why it does so—intervention in itself is neither good nor bad."[6] In Erhard's view, economic and political freedom were intimately and organically linked, as we may see from his speech on the 1948 currency reform:

Various liberalizing measures have recently been announced in the field of capital and consumer goods. The welcome given to these measures shows that our people are tired of administrative tutelage and set much store by their right of free choice as consumers. If we had taken a single step further in the wrong direction it would have meant a death blow to democracy, the negation of our people's democratic rights. Only when every German can freely choose what work he will do and where, and can freely decide what goods he will consume, will our people be able to play an active part in the political life of their country.[7]

Many would find it hard to accept this equation of political with economic liberalism and would feel that the law of a completely free market has more in common with that of the jungle than with right and justice. But the school of thought that opposed Erhard in Germany in 1948–49 had little chance of winning the day. The opposing doctrine, professed by the Social Democrats, sought to encourage production by means of credit, to equalize incomes through fiscal and social security measures, and to combat unemployment by all means including lavish government expenditure. This policy, which was also that of the British Labour Government, involved a system of rationing, price control, and strict regulation of foreign trade. But the Germans had just lived through fifteen years of planned economy, the first twelve of which had ended in the greatest cataclysm of their history, while the following three had seen the disappearance of rationed products and the astronomic prices of the black market. Moreover, the advocates of full employment were vulnerable on the ground that their system seemed to mean the encouragement of inflation— a poor offering in a country where, ever since 1922, that word has had the same overtones as "plague" or "cholera."

In French politics, it may be said that the left traditionally thinks in terms of consumption and redistribution in accordance with social justice, and the right in terms of a balanced budget. At Bonn, Dr. Schäffer, with the help of the *Bank deutscher Länder* at Frankfurt (renamed the *Bundesbank* in 1957), steadfastly pursued a policy of classic financial austerity, while Ludwig Erhard gave absolute priority to economic development, not directly in order to satisfy consumer demand but to step up production and exports in the belief that this would automatically lead to increased consumption. This policy was radically different from that adopted in France in 1945, but is akin to the Soviet preference for an economy based on production as opposed to consumption. At the same time, the *laissez-faire* aspect of German policy operated in favor of strong and forceful elements, of private "enterprise"— which fully justified its name as the socio-economic class it designates was brought to the forefront of society. The policy meant, among other things, that war victims and the unemployed received a meager dole while the new rich began to flaunt themselves in luxury. But were the poor deprived thereby of any goods they would have been able to enjoy under a different system? Erhard believed that they were not: he considered that the appetite for gain was the best possible stimulus to the economy, on the sole condition that the businessman spent only a small part of his income on expensive cars paid for out of profits, or on tax-deductible expense account meals at restaurants. For the system to work properly, it was necessary that the bulk of the profits should be ploughed back into fresh production, the ambition to grow richer or to acquire greater economic power being stronger than the desire for present enjoyment.

On the whole, Erhard's calculation proved to be justified. As he had hoped, industrial development financed itself on a large scale and thus required a minimum of borrowing. Out of DM2,000 million invested in the iron and steel industry in 1953 and 1954, about 1,300 million came out of the industry's own profits, as against 200 from Federal and *Land* credits and 200 from the "investment aid" that was part of the government's contribution to heavy industry. Under the relevant law, the rest of German industry was obliged to turn over 3·5 per cent of its own profits for two years to a special bank created for the purpose, the *Industrie-Kreditbank*. In addition, a whole range of measures was taken to stimulate exports.

The success of foreign trade was perhaps the most spectacular and decisive achievement of the social market economy. At the outset, conditions had appeared catastrophic. Germany had forfeited practically all her markets, at first owing to the Nazi policy of autarky and then by the effects of her collapse. But the impoverishment of the population forced industrialists to look for customers abroad; they were helped in doing so by the fact that Dr. Schäffer's policy of financial stability made their prices competitive, as did the foreign competition they met with on the home market owing to Erhard's liberalization of trade. The Korean boom also played a large part, though at first it set off a serious crisis: the rise in raw material prices, speculation, and fear of war led to a foreign-trade deficit and a financial crisis from which Germany was rescued with the aid of her fellow members of the European Payments Union. But Erhard's unconquerable optimism proved justified against the fears entertained by Schäffer and John J. McCloy—which they had induced the Chancellor to share. The Federal Republic, debarred from producing arms and thus possessing unused capacity for the production of machinery and capital goods, was in a position to profit by the surplus income of arms producers and those who supplied them with raw materials. From 1951 onward, West German foreign trade grew at a triumphant rate.

For the next ten years or so, Erhard's success appeared to be complete. Even the SPD opposition seemed to be converted, as witness the Godesberg program of 1959. But as time went on, he carried the rationalization of his philosophy to unwarrantable lengths, and those in political circles began to doubt the wisdom of confining government action to stimulating economic activity while otherwise leaving the market to look after itself. At the beginning of the 1960's, the situation was in fact somewhat paradoxical. From Erhard's utterances, one would have supposed that his policy as Economic Minister consisted of intervening and directing as little as possible, allowing the maximum free play to existing methods and institutions: in short, having no economic policy at all and, in the last resort, rendering his own ministry superfluous. But anyone who looked at the ministry's organization chart would discover that, in addition to departments concerned with European economic cooperation, with trade and smaller-sized enterprises, with mines, metallurgy, and power supply, with processing industries, foreign trade, development aid, and currency and credit, it also included an Economic Policy Bureau with a subsection on "economic policy and international cooperation," which was further divided into offices dealing with "basic problems," regional economic structures, production and raw materials, state budgeting and investments, foreign trade, transport, statistics, and trade cycle policy, plus another subsection on "specific tasks of economic policy," with subdivisions for price policy, military and civil defense, farm and building policy, the regulation of competition, taxation, state-controlled markets, and price supervision. Clearly, all this apparatus could not exist simply for the purpose of doing nothing; nor, evidently, was this the view of Erhard's closest collaborators. Alfred Müller-Almack, four years younger than he, a professor and director of the Institute of Political Economy at Cologne University, had been an official of the ministry since 1952, first as a head of department and, from 1958, as state secretary: Erhard had always made it clear that he owed a great deal to him. In January, 1963, after the breakdown of the Brussels conference on Britain's entry into the Common Market, he tendered his resignation. Erhard was loathe to accept it, which led to a violent scene between him and the Chancellor, but Müller-Almack finally went off to an important job in the European Coal and Steel Community at Luxembourg. The other state secretary, Ludger Westrick, was three years older than Erhard; a lawyer by training and an industrialist of long standing (iron and steel, then aluminium, and finally coal), he was, as we have seen, a key figure in the ministry from 1951 onward.

Even more than his immediate staff, Erhard was known for his hostility to planning and his aversion even to economic forecasts. But from 1960 onward, an increasing number of leading industrialists and others began to show an interest in "flexible planning" on the French model. It would seem that, at Brussels, Professor Hallstein, the president of the Commission of the EEC and a former state secretary for foreign affairs, was persuaded of the merits of the French doctrine by Robert Marjolin, his vice-president and a fellow jurist. At all events, a dispute on the subject broke out between Erhard and Hallstein in the European parliament at Strasbourg, while the former was even more outspoken in a debate on economic policy in the Bundestag in April, 1963. On this occasion, he drew a sharp distinction between "forecasting" (*Vorausschau*), which he accepted, and "prediction" (*Voraussagen*), which he did not, although the examples he gave of the second might rather seem to belong to the first. Thus, after speaking with studied irony on the subject of attempts to estimate future demand for automobiles, he went on:[8]

I shall resist this with all the strength of which I am capable, for it is like giving the devil your little finger to hold. One day you are free, the next you are a slave. I will not surrender the German market economy in this fashion, whatever anyone may say or think. Have other countries done so well with all this planning [*Planungen*]? I don't like to say this, because it may sound like criticizing them, which is not my intention. I need not give any names, but there are countries that are in the middle of their fourth four-year plan today, and we all know well enough how far the first three have got them.

Dr. Deist: "Things are quite different in Western countries."

Erhard: "But I'm talking about Western countries!" (Laughter.)

Dr. Deist: "May I ask which country you have in mind? Come out into the open! Which country?" (Renewed laughter.)

Erhard: "Since I must, I hope I shan't be misunderstood. I was referring to France."

Dr. Deist: "That is absolutely wrong." (Cries of "Oh, oh!" from the CDU/CSU benches.)

Erhard: "Just one moment. France is in the middle of her fourth four-year plan. Before that she had three others. No one can say that those three plans put the French economy on a healthy footing. It is only since France, under a strong government, has introduced and imposed the methods and principles of a market economy, according to clear-cut ideas of economic order—only since then has she found a cure for her troubles." (Applause from the CDU and FDP.)

This point of view is exactly similar to that of de Gaulle's economic adviser Jacques Rueff, himself a friend and disciple of Wilhelm Röpke: the French currency reform of December, 1958 was in fact conceived and carried out in a thoroughly Erhardian spirit. But whereas in France, despite statements on the "burning necessity" of planning, it was gradually superseded, in the field of long-term measures, by a policy of stimulating business activity, in Germany the evolution was in the opposite direction. In 1963, Erhard himself accepted what had been one of the SPD demands in the election campaign of 1961—namely, the institution of a *Volkswirtschaftliche Gesamtrechnung* or general survey of the economy, the equivalent of the *comptes de la nation* in France. The Grand Coalition launched the idea of medium-term financial planning (*Mittelfristige Finanzplanung*, known for short as "Mifrifi"), while the law of June 8, 1967, introduced by Karl Schiller, on "economic stabilization and growth" was supposed to modify the structure of the economy as well as stimulate it. The Brandt government emphasized the planning aspect still further: in March, 1970, a professor of economics named Reimut Jochimsen, aged thirty-seven, who was due to become rector of Kiel University on April 1 —a man as rotund and optimistic as Ludwig Erhard had been in 1950, but more of an intellectual and, above all, more conversant with modern economic methods—was appointed director of planning at Bonn under the direct supervision of the Chancellor (whom he had aided during the election) and of Horst Ehmke, a personal friend who, like him, had first studied and later taught at Freiburg University where Eucken originally evolved his theories.

If Erhard's successor believed in the necessity of increased public credits and planned state activity, it was because they recognized the shortcomings of the social market economy. Quite apart from any criticism that might be made on the "social" side, it had serious deficiencies from the purely economic point of view: research, and training had been much neglected, and investment in infrastructure of value to the economy as a whole was so inadequate that the Federal Republic had begun to lag behind other states whose industrial progress had been less conspicuous. However, as in other countries, public investment was in any case limited by nondoctrinal factors. Concern for a balanced budget is a motive for cutting down on any expenditure that is not likely to show an early profit in either economic or electoral terms. In the Federal Republic, the Minister of the Economy has only a limited influence on the Federal Bank, which plays a fundamental part in determining financial policy and, consequently, economic policy as a whole. In 1964–65, Karl Blessing, who had been the chairman of the Bank since 1957, was the real author of the trade-cycle policy that brought about the recession.[9] In 1969, the open alliance between the Bank and the Minister of the Economy in favor of revaluation despite the Chancellor's objections was a matter of coincident opinions rather than joint action. On January 1, Blessing was succeeded by Karl Klasen; as he was said to have been against revaluation, his appointment was taken as a sign that the government thought it valuable to have a man of independent judgment as chairman of the Bank.

The government's concern with electoral aspects is a function of the strength of pressure groups, which act upon it as well as on the parties and the Bundestag. To be sensitive to this pressure is not necessarily to sacrifice the public interest, since pressure groups are part of the public. Their strength is not always in proportion to their numbers: for example, road haulers are a much smaller group than farmers, but it was a long while before Georg Leber, the Minister of Transport in the coalition government, was able to put into effect any significant part of his plan to rationalize the road and rail freightage system.[10] The haulers maintained a propaganda barrage that aroused response even within the government, although the minister's plan was clearly in the interest of the economy as a whole, aiming as it did to turn the railways into a commercial public service for purposes of long-distance transport and to speed up the circulation of goods by improving road-rail coordination.

When it comes to agriculture and, especially, to the prices of farm produce, all "market economy" countries are in the habit of putting a damper on their free trade policies. The U.S. Government does not dream of treating the powerful American farming community in the spirit of economic liberalism it invokes when the prices of South American or African raw materials are in question. The Federal Republic's remarkably efficient system of agricultural protection made it possible to keep the prices of home produce at a level that was the envy of French farmers until the progress of the Common Market enabled them to share in its benefits to a considerable extent. Largely owing to the vigorous activity of the German Farmers' Union (*Deutscher Bauernverband*) under its boisterous and effective chairman Edmund Rehwinkel, whose strength between 1954 and 1969 depended chiefly on the union's two powerful branches for Bavaria and Lower Saxony, German agriculturists were able increasingly to influence government policy in their favor. The important law of September 5, 1955, introduced by Heinrich Lübke, was based on the "parity" principle that French farmers in due course placed in the forefront of their demands. Article 1 states that "the social situation of persons engaged in agriculture shall be raised to the same level as that of comparable occupational groups." The government was obliged under the law to submit to parliament annually a "green report" on the position of agriculture during the preceding year and a "green plan" stating what measures, including credits, were contemplated in order to remedy the shortcomings described in the report. From 1968 onward, the two documents were combined.[11] Under pressure from the *Bauernverband*—including threats from Herr Rehwinkel that his followers would vote for the NPD instead of the CDU if their demands were not met— the German negotiators at Brussels succeeded in making the Federal Government's agrarian problems a matter of European concern, thus helping to create an insoluble problem of surpluses and the financing of excess production.[12] At present, the Brandt government and the new chairman of the *Bauernverband*, Freiherr Constantin Heereman von Zuydtwyck—who, at thirty-eight, entered upon his duties on January 1, 1970, after the union had been under interim collective leadership for nearly a year—are in almost as difficult a situation as their French opposite numbers. The price-oriented policy of subsidies has not made it possible to solve any structural problems, while the gap between the farmer's average earnings and that of the rest of the nation is getting wider. Out of 2,350,000 farmers and agricultural workers, it is expected that over 1 million will leave the land in the course of the next decade. This is likely to mean a good deal of social and economic tension, the effects of which will not be confined to Germany, especially if attempts are made to shift responsibility for the situation to foreign countries: Heereman, for instance, has stated that many young farmers of his generation believe that West German agriculture is handicapped because, as they put it, the farmers are still virtually paying reparations to France.[13]

While agricultural difficulties seem to be common to all countries whether their creed be Socialism or economic liberalism, and while no liberal country is true to its principles where agriculture is concerned, the social market economy experienced a more notable setback in the coal sector, which was for a long time the foundation of German economic power. The Ruhr is in a state of crisis owing to the competition of American coal, which has been aided by the sharp fall in freight costs, and owing still more to the drop in oil prices. Protectionist measures such as a tax on imported coal and fuel oil did not make up for the lack of an over-all policy in regard to power supply. Under the Grand Coalition, a law passed on May 15, 1968 did at last provide for a complete reorganization of the coal industry. As is always the case when there has been overproduction and industry is running at a loss, private interests welcomed state intervention, which led in this case to the setting up of a single holding company, the Ruhrkohle AG. This does not in itself ensure that the necessary partial reconversion of the Ruhr basin will be carried out, but it may well be that a fuel policy cannot be framed for Germany in isolation: as with agriculture, the problem is of European dimensions, and divergent national solutions can only be temporary expedients. Meanwhile, the troubles of the mining industry have immediate repercussions on society at large.

The resort to a policy of concentration in the Ruhr was not criticized even in France, although it was not so long ago that French circles were up in arms against the creation of a central selling office for German coal, notwithstanding the fact that the *Charbonnages de France* themselves enjoyed a monopoly situation. French opposition to German economic concentration diminished during the 1950's and died out during the 1960's, since it no longer appeared a rational aim to weaken the German economy. But as long as such opposition was a part of Allied policy, it singularly complicated the discussion of cartel problems within Germany. According to the neoliberal school of thought, it was the state's duty to intervene to ensure free competition. Ludwig Erhard fought a long and hard struggle to secure firm anticartel legislation. Between his statement of intention to the Bundestag on October 13, 1950 and the final vote on July 4, 1957 lies the history of a "seven years' war" of discussion and intrigue, amendments and maneuvers which it would take a whole volume to trace even in outline. The law to prevent restrictive practices (*Wettbewerbsbeschränkungen*) was, in its final form, a leaky tub compared to the seaworthy vessel Erhard had hoped to launch. One reason was that he was unable wholly to win over public opinion to his antitrust views because of the fact that such legislation, like the breaking up of the chemical and iron and steel industries, had been associated with the occupying powers. Erhard was opposed to deconcentration as a matter of economic efficiency, but was in favor of breaking up cartels in order to liberate prices; public opinion, however, found it hard to appreciate the distinction between the two attitudes. The Federal Office for the Supervision of Cartels (*Bundeskartellamt*)[14] has become an important institution for the prevention of harmful agreements in accordance with EEC doctrine, but it is of negligible effect in preventing the most typical development of modern industry—namely, the exercise of steadily increasing power by fewer and fewer enterprises. In the steel and chemical industries, this tendency gained still greater momentum in the late 1960's. In Germany as in France, the need to rationalize production and marketing and to compete with big American or Japanese concerns is invoked to justify a trend that, even more than in the past, raises in an acute form the question of the relationship between economic and political power.

The solution to this question in Germany is only simple if we fail to see things as they really are. It is in fact no easy matter to say who exactly possesses economic power. The age of great captains of industry seems in any case to be over, even though the state is relinquishing control over some major enterprises. The Volkswagen works were "denationalized" on the basis that the Federation and Lower Saxony each retained 20 per cent of the capital stock, 60 per cent being sold to 1·5 million small shareholders and the greater part of the proceeds being assigned in 1961 to a public foundation, the *Volkswagenstiftung*, subsidizing higher education and research; but so far there has been no successor of the caliber of Heinrich Nordhoff, who ran the nationalized enterprise from 1948 until his death in 1968. In the same way, the death of Alfried Krupp on July 30, 1967 has come to seem an event of symbolic importance. By the early 1950's Krupp was once more a power in the land. He had regained possession of his family home, the Villa Hügel at Essen, which had been occupied after the war by the Allied antitrust commission. On March 4, 1953, he signed an undertaking to divest himself of his coal and steel interests as required by the Allies, but no buyer was ever found for them. Times had indeed changed since, at the Nuremberg trial in 1947, he had been sentenced, by a loose interpretation of justice, to twelve years' imprisonment in his father Gustav's stead. The name of Krupp became increasingly important in ship-building and in the industrialization of developing countries. Little by little, however, it appeared that the financial basis of the new empire was insecure; in January, 1967, the government intervened, and the banks carried out a rescue operation at a price that amounted to expropriation. Alfried's heir, Arndt von Bohlen und Halbach, exchanged his interest in the Krupp enter-prises for a comfortable pension of DM2 million per annum, while his father's fortune was used to endow a foundation named after him and devoted to encouraging science, education, and the arts in Germany and abroad.[15] The enterprises themselves passed into the hands of the true beneficiaries of the new policy, with the blessing of the Allies who rescinded their anticartel measures in August, 1968.

These beneficiaries were the banks, who constitute a major power in the German economy. It may be mentioned at once, however, that one of the chief banks that assumed control of the Krupp group was the trade union (DGB) bank, which will be described later on. Moreover, the chairman of the Iron and Steel Workers' Federation, Otto Brenner, was appointed to the board of directors together with Walter Hesselbach, the chairman of the DGB bank, while the iron and steel works remained subject to the principle of comanage-ment for which the trade unions had fought successfully in 1951. The chair-man of the board of directors of the group, however, was also the chairman of the board of directors of the *Deutsche Bank*, Hermann J. Abs. This financier, head of one of the "big three" banks that dominate the complex private bank-ing system of the Federal Republic (the other two being the *Dresdner Bank* and the *Commerzbank*), has for many years been a key figure in German economic and public life. Whether or not one accepts—as his less friendly biographers do not[16]—that his role in the Third Reich was simply that of a banker out to increase his business, he certainly acted as an adviser to Adenauer, negotiated international agreements, and had a hand in many aspects of economic policy. About 1961, when he was sixty years old, he could boast of an even greater range of chairmanships and holdings than the other banker and counsellor to Adenauer, Robert Pferdmenges.[17] Since then, his influence has grown still further, thanks in part to the simple way in which German joint stock companies operate: the banks do not need to become big share-holders in industrial enterprises in order to control them, since they utilize the shares of which they are custodians, voting on behalf of the mass of small and medium shareholders. Nevertheless, great banking personages are disappear-ing as fast as captains of industry: Robert Pferdmenges has had no successor, and Abs will not either. The bankers' power is becoming largely depersonal-ized, and in any case its political effects are hard to trace. This, in fact, is true as regards the whole interplay of economic and political forces. Who makes whom do what?

In our view, there are three basic trends. In the first place, the "big guns" of the economy have confirmed the statesmen in their hostility to adventures abroad: economic expansion must be protected from political shocks in the foreign field even more than at home. Second, the economic tycoons have not so much tried to impose this or that policy as to inculcate a philosophy, which was also that of Ludwig Erhard—namely, the view that economics are the true yardstick of national progress and that politics have the subordinate and accessory function of allowing the economy to develop. Economics have an intrinsic value and politics an ancillary one, at all events in internal affairs; the only kind of politics in which Adenauer cared seriously to engage were international ones. Finally—a simple but basic consequence of the previous point— the primacy of the economic factor means that any large-scale welfare program is out of the question. This does not mean that the social market economy is a complete misnomer; it means, however, that relationships between social forces are allowed to take shape with little government interference.

The Favored and the Handicapped

Today's social élite is obviously of quite a different character from that of the Kaiser's Germany. The types who were once savagely caricatured in the pages of *Simplicissimus* have all but disappeared, if only because the bases of their influence have ceased to exist—namely, the great German estates in the east and the army, conceived and organized as a dominant element in society. It is true that, thanks to family tradition and to methods of recruitment in which social connections played a large part, the upper class were able to benefit by the trend toward restoration in the 1950's, so that in 1956 they accounted for 17 per cent of diplomatic service.[18] Titles, especially princely ones, and double-barreled names still have considerable power to impress the ordinary citizen. Nor has the class of *Junkers* who run big estates and take part in politics entirely died out: a good example is Freiherr Karl Theodor von und zu Guttenberg (the husband of Princess Rosa Sophie of Arenberg), who specializes in foreign affairs and was parliamentary state secretary in the Chancellor's Office from 1966 to 1969. But while titles of nobility are of some use, they do not mean anything in themselves except to make it more likely that their owners will figure in gossip columns.[19]

The *Machtelite*, or power-wielding élite, is in fact difficult to identify, since the Federal Republic has, properly speaking, no "establishment" as in Britain—or in France, with its great administrative schools and the concentration of leadership in the capital. Wealth and power by no means necessarily go hand in hand. Social mobility, while still limited in many ways, is greater than in Britain or France: it is easier in Germany for newcomers, not from the poorest circles but from the middle ranks of society, to become members of the governing class.[20] Wealth does not always confer influence, but it is a source of strength, and the differences between incomes are enormous. As in other similar countries, they are of course regional as well as hierarchical: the average monthly wage may be four times as high in one *Kreis* as in another.[21] But the 16,000 or so inhabitants of the Federal Republic who admit to an annual income of over DM1 million (about £112,000 or over $260,000) are to be found in all parts of the country, while the 500,000 dwellers in shanty-towns inhabit the outskirts of most of the bigger cities: there are about 19,000 of them at Cologne, 16,000 at Hamburg, and 15,000 at Mannheim. These shanty-towns are quite as squalid as those of France or the United States, and the affluent society puts up only a feeble fight against their existence, condemning their swarms of children to poverty and delinquency: 75 per cent of the young people in reformatories came out of the "slum milieu."[22]

Between the two extremes there are wide differences of various kinds, particularly as between branches of industry in which salaries and wages differ greatly from one sector to another.[23] According to one's preferred method of calculation it is possible to show that the differences are either increasing or tending to diminish, leaving out of account the small minorities of the very poor and the very rich. But, whether real poverty is on the increase or not, two things seem certain. In the first place, in Germany as in other countries, not only is there no actual pauperization, but there are a growing number of families attaining a real standard of prosperity. Second, and here the situation differs from that in France, wealth in the Federal Republic is not ashamed to show its face but is widely displayed and held up for the admiration of the populace. Articles on "how I became a multimillionaire" or "my life with a rich husband" appear regularly in the mass-circulation illustrated papers, especially the tawdriest of them, *Jasmin*, which is also the most vulgar and hypocritical.

At the same time, wealth helps to provide wealth. The income tax, which is a good deal higher and rises at a sharper rate than in France, has been used since the early days of the Federal Republic as a means of evening out inequalities. In 1951, an American inquiry commission published a report on the integration of refugees that caused a considerable stir.[24] The Sonne report (named after its chairman) observed that: "Some circumstances have made it easy for a few to obtain large incomes. . . . There is a tendency on the part of some elements of the business and financial community to be too self-seeking and too little interested in the general welfare. . . . It has been said that, through the lack of courage to stop the dictator in time, the first German Republic was lost. Care must be taken to avoid losing the new Federal Republic through greed." What the commission failed to see, however, was that this "greed" was the motive force of an economic recovery that was to make it possible, by legislation and by the ordinary effects of a developing economy, to achieve the integration of refugees in a much shorter time. It should be added that the influx of millions of dispossessed people, prepared to work hard to rebuild their lives, was in itself an economic asset. The refugees were a plentiful supply of cheap labor, no less useful in speeding the work of reconstruction, once it got under way, than in keeping wage claims down. Having appeared at first to be an insurmountable barrier to recovery, they were later seen as a first-class stimulus to the economy. But for this to be so, it was necessary for the authorities to extend fiscal, legislative, and administrative aid to those who settled in West Germany in 1945 and in the years following.

"Refugee" is an inexact term, used to cover several categories of inhabitants of the Federal Republic. First, the *Heimatvertriebene*—those "driven from their homelands," that is, from areas that were part of eastern Germany in 1937 and also from other countries of Central and Eastern Europe. In the census of September 13, 1950, they numbered 7,978,000, including 4·5 million from former German territory (East Prussia 1,375,000, Silesia 2,090,000, and others from eastern Pomerania and Brandenburg), and 3,436,000 from various countries, including 1,918,000 Sudeten Germans from Czechoslovakia. Second, the *Zugewanderte*—"immigrants" or resettlers—who had come to live in West Germany from the Soviet zone, having previously been expelled from territories further east; and, finally, the *Flüchtlinge*—refugees properly so called, that is, former inhabitants of the Soviet zone, which became the G.D.R. These latter two categories were in the course of time lumped together: their number had grown to about 3,600,000 by the end of 1960, before the few months of intensified flight westward that was stopped by the erection of the Berlin wall on August 13, 1961.[25]

All the figures concerning refugees should be treated with great caution. The system adopted and maintained by the Federal statistical bureau is, to say the least, open to challenge: the children of expellees and refugees, even those born in West Germany in the 1960's, are themselves still rated as belonging to these categories.[26] On this basis, it was reckoned that the population of the Federal Republic in April, 1968 included 9,108,000 refugees (using this general term for convenience), or 15·3 per cent of the total, with a ratio of 17·1 per cent—the highest of any age group—for youths between fifteen and twenty; no fewer than 3 million "refugees" were under fifteen, which meant that they were born after 1952. This would be a less misleading picture if the refugees had remained in watertight groups, with Pomeranians or Silesians forming separate, self-contained communities like the Italian or Polish inhabitants of New York or Chicago. But, fortunately, no such thing took place, thanks to aid from the community as a whole and because, after all, a Brandenburger is no more and no less a foreigner in Württemberg than a man from Hamburg. Admittedly, those who arrived in Bavaria from Pomerania in the early days were often nicknamed *Polacken*—a bitter irony for those who had just been driven from their homes by Poles.

When the flood of refugees started pouring into Germany and, later, when the agreed transfers of population began, the occupation authorities and their advisers adopted a very simple method of placing the new arrivals. They were directed to the most under-populated areas—except those in the French zone, for the French Commander-in-Chief refused to accept refugees on the ground that France was not a signatory of the Potsdam agreement that authorized the transfers. The local residents had to do the best they could to make room for them as lodgers; but the overcrowding was such that many had to be accommodated in camps of hastily improvised huts. Once they were installed, it soon became clear that the idea of settling them in underpopulated districts, though superficially plausible, was in fact mistaken. In a purely physical sense, there was of course more room for new arrivals in sparsely populated areas; but such areas were sparsely populated precisely because they were not capable of supporting a larger population. The whole movement in the nineteenth and twentieth centuries had been away from the poor districts and the countryside and toward the rich districts and the towns, where the growth of industry and commerce offered more chances of work. But now an impoverished region like Schleswig-Holstein suddenly received a 60 per cent increase of population, and Bavaria, which had little need of more agricultural laborers, an increase of 30 per cent. The result, as could easily be foreseen, was that those who sought work were settled far away from places where they could find it. There were few unemployed in the Ruhr, where many branches of industry and commerce were short of labor, but the refugees seeking work were mostly in Schleswig or Lower Saxony. From 1950 onwards, the German Authorities tried to remedy the situation by new transfers of population, shifting 300,000 "surplus" refugees per year into the *Länder* that still required more labor.

The fact that only 0·6 per cent of the refugees were originally settled in towns of any size, while 8 million were directed to rural areas, added greatly to the problem of assimilating them. In a large city, there is very little communal life: the inhabitants have no deep roots, and new arrivals are accepted without comment. But small towns and villages have their own customs and a more pronounced local speech and way of life. In them, the refugees were generally received not merely as intruders who deprived you of half your house and shared your kitchen, but as foreigners into the bargain This was hardly surprising, if one thinks for instance of the stolid unprogressive dwellers in some remote Hessian valley, with its precapitalist agriculture, facing the impact of refugees from a large Sudeten industrial town. The refugees would then be skilled workers, tradesmen, or industrialists, having nothing in common with the locals, and relations between the two groups would be made up of suspicion and misunderstanding. The conflicts were so serious that in several areas a regular atmosphere of class war developed: this term was all the more apt because in many cases the refugees were in fact proletarianized. There having been no agrarian reform, former peasant proprietors were compelled to work as farm laborers along with other refugees— intellectuals, tradesmen, artisans—who had no country experience at all. In the Federal Republic as a whole, 25 per cent of the working peasants were refugees in 1950, while, in May, 1949, 96 per cent of holdings of over half a hectare (about 1·4 acres) were still in the hands of the original inhabitants. But it was not only in the country that the refugees became proletarianized. Of those who were active in 1950, 16 per cent had been independent in 1939 and another 21 per cent had been working in family businesses. By 1949, this was true of only 5 and 3 per cent respectively, while the remaining 92 per cent were working for wages.

The government's legislative measures took effect by degrees, and were to serve as a model in France, in 1962–63, for the resettlement of colonists from Algeria. Geographical mobility was aided by the housing program, increasing prosperity helped to ease living conditions, and the refugees became integrated more and more rapidly. The young people made their way without too much of a psychological upheaval, and their elders showed a surprising degree of adaptability in settling into their new environment. It might have been expected that in areas with a high proportion of refugees they would have had a visible if not a transforming effect on society, but nothing of this kind seems to have occurred.[27]

Integration and assimilation are different things. The Federal Government's constant dilemma has been that to assimilate the expellees altogether would be tantamount to recognizing the Oder-Neisse frontier, since it would mean giving up all idea of their returning to their homeland. Consequently, encouragement was given to associations and organizations that upheld the right of return, whether the homeland in question was part of prewar Germany or not. Professor Oberländer, when Minister for Refugees, often uttered far from conciliatory words on this subject, and even a man like Dr. Gerstenmaier has not always spoken with good sense and moral courage. On August 4, 1957, in a speech to the *Karpathendeutsche Landsmannschaft* (the association of Germans from the Carpathians), he urged them not to lose their racial identity and traditions or be absorbed into the West German population, and spoke in involved terms, but with a clear enough intention, of their returning home to Slovakia one day when the German Reich was restored.[28] Twelve years later—also in an election speech—Heinrich Windelen, the Minister for Expellees, Refugees, and War Victims, spoke more discreetly to a rally of the *Landsmannschaft Ostpreussen*, but still went so far as to say: "Germany, in the history of European peoples, does not consist solely of the Federal Republic and the Soviet occupation zone. The frontiers of that Germany are beyond the Oder."[29]

A *Landsmannschaft* (literally, an association of compatriots, or natives of the same region) has been defined in Germany as a group whose objectives are not specifically material or political but which constitutes an "expression and representation of the lost *Heimat* and its people." Altogether, there are a dozen or so of these associations, composed of former inhabitants of Pomerania, Silesia, Brandenburg, and places further afield such as Hungary and the Bukovina. Their activity takes the form chiefly of cultural propaganda, reminding their own members and Germans in general of the material and, above all, the artistic and intellectual riches of the lands they have been compelled to abandon. They issue magnificent brochures describing the past splendors of Breslau or Königsberg, and recall incessantly the men of learning, poets, and philosophers given to Germany by the lost regions. The great rallies that regularly take place at Easter or Whitsun are dominated by the sense of belonging to a community and by nostalgia for the land of one's birth. The *Sudetentag* is attended by up to 300,000 men, women, and children. All these manifestations and publications might be harmless enough if they were not often accompanied by explicit claims. The *Landsmannschaften* profess loyalty to the "Charter of German Expellees" adopted on August 5, 1950, in which they unconditionally renounced vengeance and the use of force. But oratorical excesses remained frequent even in the 1960's, and the various bodies have not always dissociated themselves firmly enough from groups like AKON (Aktion Oder-Neisse), founded in 1962, which has put out violently anti-Polish propaganda accompanied by maps showing the German frontiers as they were in 1914.[30]

The Federation of *Landsmannschaften* (VDL) was created in 1952 under the chairmanship of Dr. Lodgmann von Aue, a Sudeten German spokesman: it presented itself as a semipolitical rival to the "League of German Expellees" (ZVD, later BVD) led by Dr. Linus Kather, then a CDU deputy, who confined himself to defending the refugees' material interests. Five years later, in July, 1957, the two organizations decided to merge after the forthcoming election. Kather, who had become a member of the BHE in 1954, was still chairman of the BVD, while the VDL was presided over by Baron Manteuffel-Szoege, a CSU deputy. Despite the electoral debacle of the BHE, the new organization under their joint presidency was set up in October, its title being the *Bund der Vertriebenen: Vereinigte Landsmannschaften und Landesverbände* (BdV); a definitive statute was adopted in September, 1958.

The BdV has undergone various changes of front. Its early leaders belonged mostly to the CDU; then, at a congress in February, 1964, it elected as its chairman a remarkable figure, Wenzel Jaksch. Aged sixty-seven, he had an animated career behind him: as chairman of the Sudeten Social Democratic Party and a member of the Czechoslovak parliament, he had fought Henlein and the Nazis until 1938, when he took refuge in Britain. He stayed there till 1949, the Czechoslovak Government having asked the British not to let him out of the country. He then went to Germany where he became a member of the Bundestag and of the SPD executive. Both before and after becoming chairman of the BdV, he was a virulent spokesman for the expellees (although not one himself in the usual sense of the term), so that one might wonder whether the SPD was influencing the BdV through him or whether the BdV was preventing the SPD from taking a clear stand on the question of frontiers and the assimilation of refugees. He was re-elected in May, 1966, but died in an accident on November 27. His successor, Reinhold Rehs, was also an SPD deputy, though, as we have seen, he joined the CDU before the 1969 election. By March, 1970, when the CDU deputy Herbert Czaja became chairman, the BdV had lost much of its importance owing to the government's new eastern policy, which itself might not have been feasible without some moderation of attitude of the refugee bodies. In May, 1969, for instance, one of the most intransigent among them, the *Sudetendeutsche Landsmannschaft*, condemned NPD propaganda out of hand and refused to link itself with the extreme right.

The interplay between the government and parties on the one hand and the refugee associations on the other has always been complicated. The *Landsmannschaften* were kept in a good humor by subsidies and fair words, and gained in official standing from the fact that their press and rallies were supported from government funds. Having thus become more representative, they were in a position to claim further aid—and so the process went on, the true extent of their following being a matter of conjecture rather than of verifiable numbers. In any case, a distinction must be drawn between organizations of a mainly cultural type and others, such as the *Deutsche Jugend des Ostens*, which have inspired young men with thoughts of "returning" in triumph to the east at some future date.

All in all, it seems beyond dispute that the Federal Republic has done an admirable job of social integration: the absorption of the refugees was by no means a foregone conclusion, and while the passage of time and demographic changes have had their effect, they would have operated differently if it had not been for the policy of successive governments. One has only to think of the story of the Palestine refugees to realize that time may exacerbate hatred instead of softening it. When, in October, 1969, Willy Brandt decided to abolish the Ministry for Refugees, this was not only a decisive step and an important political event, but the logical consequence of a more or less steady evolution toward what may be called the normalization of German society in relation to neighboring countries.

Most of the public money spent on the integration of refugees came from a source that was and is used to furnish aid to many classes of people who suffered hardship as a result of Germany's tragic years: namely the fund for the "equalization of burdens" (*Lastenausgleich*) established under a law of August 14, 1952. Its provisions are extremely complicated and cover widely different categories of victims: the expellees of 1945, ex-émigrés of 1933, and Germans who suffered war damage or whose savings were swept away by the currency reform. Benefits under the law are also extremely varied, comprising loans, pensions, and grants for housing or the purchase of furniture; but the main element consists of rehabilitation grants calculated at a moderately progressive rate: DM50,000 for a loss of 1 million, and a minimum grant of DM800 for a loss of 500–1,500. Funds were provided by what appears at first sight a drastic measure: apart from certain public bodies, the central banks, and religious or charitable institutions, all persons and organizations were required to contribute one half of their assets to the compensation fund. The "solidarity tax" levied in France after the Liberation appears tiny by comparison. But the contributions payable under the German law were based on the tax figures for 1948–49, and those assessed in this way on their capital and income at the time of the currency reform were permitted to pay in quarterly installments spread over thirty years. By 1969, twenty-one *Novellen* or supplementary laws had been passed defining and extending the scope of the law, but no very substantial pensions had been granted under it. The Brandt government's first social measure was to vote, with the almost unanimous support of parliament, increases of between 16 and 25 per cent in pensions payable over the next three years to 2,600,000 war victims, especially widows: the sums paid to them would otherwise have continued to fall behind social security grants, including civilian pensions.

This is not the place for a detailed description of the German social security system,[31] but a few characteristic features should be noted. Notwithstanding the Basic Law, families are not especially favored, and the allowances instituted for the first time in 1954 are low compared with those in France: originally, DM25 for the third and each subsequent child, they were raised to DM25 for the second child, 50 for the third, 60 for the fourth, and 70 for each one after that. On the other hand, unemployment insurance is more comprehensive and insured persons do not have to contribute part of the cost of sickness benefits. Most notably, a substantial sum is paid out directly by firms to their employees in the form of "voluntary social grants," the amount of which is sometimes decided by the firm itself and sometimes agreed by a process of collective bargaining. Supplementary pensions are granted in this way to most executives, many clerks, and a fair number of workers.[32] The system is based on seniority, a fact that considerably increases the wage earner's dependence on the firm, as do other forms of assistance including, frequently, housing.

Such is the chief "market economy" aspect of a system of allowances that is one of the most highly organized imaginable and is far removed from *laissez-*

faire principles. Redistributing wealth on a large scale and involving every paid worker in an elaborate scheme of codified benefits, the German "welfare state" is more reminiscent of the British Socialist model than of traditional liberalism. This is true, *inter alia*, in the field of housing; or, more correctly, it used to be, as the part played by the government in building and investment has been diminishing since the late 1950's, though it still accounts for 200,000 of the 500,000 dwellings built annually. Immediately after the war, when in France there was no more than a light tax on under-used living space, the West German Government requisitioned large dwellings and obliged the owners to take in additional occupants. The housing program that followed was extraordinarily successful, owing in part to various methods of encouraging prospective owners (tax relief, low-interest mortgages, and so forth) and also to a rationalization of building techniques that stands out sharply by comparison with French conditions.[33]

The welfare-state image also holds good to some extent for the new subproletariat of foreign workers, who are better looked after than in France, inasmuch as their reception and conditions of employment are organized in detail by the authorities and various religious and other bodies, often in concert with the governments of their countries of origin. At the end of January, 1970, there were in the Federal Republic 330,000 Italian workers, 297,000 Yugoslavs, 272,400 Turks, 206,800 Greeks, 149,200 Spaniards, and 32,800 Portuguese. The conditions in which they live are far from ideal, however: apart from hostels, of which there are too few, they are frequently cheated over rent, especially those who have been smuggled into Germany by modern methods of slave-trafficking. The problem of the temporary integration of these men and women—who do not count as permanent immigrants—is by no means yet solved, and this can be clearly seen from their own attitudes and reactions.[34]

But is the German population itself becoming integrated or more homogeneous? Certainly, as in all industrial societies, ways of life tend to differ less and less. Social groups have their specific problems, but every individual belongs to a large number of groups. One's occupation is of course an essential factor, insofar as it determines one's income level and mode of life. But sex and age are also relevant as a key to social status and attitudes.[35]

For a long time, German women were supposed to confine themselves to the three K's—*Kinder, Küche, Kirche* (children, kitchen, and church). Those who imagine that this is still the case overlook the fact that women in Germany outnumber men and that an increasing proportion of them are paid workers. At the beginning of 1970, there were in the Federal Republic 32 million women as against 29 million men. About a quarter of the manual laborers and half the clerical workers were women. Nevertheless, they are still at a double disadvantage in spite of their electoral and social importance and the equality prescribed by the Basic Law. As in most other countries, they seldom achieve posts of responsibility and, owing in part to the lack of promotion, they receive unequal pay for equal work, to a greater extent perhaps than in France. The German husband and father still tends to see himself as the head of the family and his wife in terms of two of the K's—as a mother and housekeeper who has no need of rest or sparetime amusements. As in other countries, one hears a good deal about increasing sexual freedom, but there are other aspects of female emancipation that are still far from being a reality, and this is not without its bearing on the nature of the political regime. One might ask whether a Muslim country can call itself Socialist and yet still maintain the inferior status of women.

Age creates problems of its own at the top and bottom of the scale. We shall consider the state of youth and education in the next chapter. But it should be pointed out at once that youth in Germany is not a single category, since the social milieu that a boy or girl belongs to generally determines the kind of career they can expect to enjoy. At ten, they are all in primary school, but, at sixteen, most of them are in a technical school of some kind, while a small minority is at a grammar school (*Gymnasium*)—and, of these, a small fraction will go on to university.[36] As for old people, they tend to be neglected by society, which is not a phenomenon peculiar to Germany. As elsewhere, women and old people, both being underprivileged, tend to vote for the party that offers them reassurance and are afraid more of change than of remaining in their present "inferior" position. At the 1965 election, 56 per cent of women over sixty voted for the CDU, while the SPD achieved its greatest success (48 per cent) among men between thirty and forty-five.[37] But, as we have suggested, political and social changes are gradually diminishing the importance of sex and age as indices of political behavior. In the opinion of all observers, especially institutes for mass observation and the politicians who consult them, the dominant factor is, to an ever greater extent, the socio-economic group to which a person belongs, that is to say, his job. This is borne out by the fact that organizations which represent social groups, or claim to do so, are usually based on particular trades or professions. Women's associations are weak, and old people's do not exist. The German farmers' association is a powerful one, but less so than the trade unions and the employers' federations.

Employers and Trade Unions

The employers' power is manifested at enterprise level, within a particular branch of industry, and ultimately at the national level, where it competes with the workers' representatives for political influence and economic advantage, either by direct pressure on the government or by subtler methods. Despite differences of size and structure from one enterprise to another, and despite the fact that different branches of industry often have divergent interests and are able to take direct action on their own account, there are in the Federal Republic two nationwide organizations representing employers. The duality does not mean that they are in competition with each other but that, unlike the situation in France, the owners of businesses draw a distinction between their function as producers and entrepreneurs and their function as employers. The Federation of German Industry (*Bundesverband der deutschen Industrie*—BDI) is not a rival to the Federation of German Employers' Associations (*Bundesvereinigung der deutschen Arbeitgeberverbände*—BDA) but exists for different purposes, although in practice the fields of action overlap when it comes to contacts or disputes with the government or the workers' unions.

The BDI possesses powers that the *Conseil National du Patronat Français* might well envy. Whereas the latter represents an amalgamation of the most varied interests, the BDI is dominated by heavy industry, particularly iron and steel.[38] This is partly due to a difference of ideology: whereas in France the "little man" is traditionally an object of respect, and power is obliged to conceal itself, in Germany people are readier to believe that what is good for the big industrialists is also good for society. Terms like *"die Wirtschaft"* (the economy) and *"die Industrie"* are almost personifications: they have overtones of respectful admiration which are lost if one translates them into French or English.

The BDI represents thirty-nine industrial unions[39] whose subscriptions, while not especially large, suffice among other things to support the Industrie-Institut at Cologne, an important center of economic and political research, which turns out high-class theoretical studies and propaganda of both a heavy and a persuasive kind. Its typical themes have altered in two ways over the years. During the immediate postwar period, the owners were suffering from denazification and were glad of the trade unions as defenders of German industrial interests; this, however, did not last long, and since then the industrialists have generally maintained an aggressive attitude toward the trade union federation and its attempts to share economic power. At the same time, they have become less rigid in their adherence to *laissez-faire* doctrines. Even before the Grand Coalition came into being, the BDI had watered down its dogmatic attitude almost as much as the SPD. A pamphlet like the one distributed before the 1957 election would never have seen the light of day in the 1960's, its theme being that all European countries where the Socialists were in power were in a mess from the economic and social point of view: the reader was invited to pity the miserable fate of Sweden and to shudder at the harm done to France by the foolish and harmful institution known as social security.[40]

In 1959, on the tenth anniversary of the founding of the BDI, Adenauer described its relations with the authorities in idyllic terms that were not without justification:[41]

The *Bundesverband der deutschen Industrie*, under its president Herr Fritz Berg, has given loyal help in the fulfillment of all these great and difficult tasks. I should like to say a word of hearty thanks to the federation as a whole, and to testify that it has always clearly understood the links between that part of the economy it represents and the remainder of the German economy, as well as the links between the economy and social problems. I wish also publicly to confirm that in the many negotiations we have conducted over the past ten years, Herr Berg has always emphasized these major aspects and given them priority over more limited aims. . . . He never acted as a representative of selfish or onesided interests, least of all the onesided interests of heavy industry.

In actual fact, the BDI's relations with the government and the CDU amounted to a state of symbiosis in which the BDI was often able to obtain the action it wanted or prevent measures it disliked; sometimes, however, it failed, as in the case of the revaluation of the mark in 1961, when Erhard and Karl Blessing were able to convince the Chancellor that Berg was in the wrong. The latter, who was born in 1901, had been chairman of the BDI since its foundation. Like his French opposite number, Georges Villiers, he was not himself a big industrialist (he was the head of a metal-products firm employing about a thousand workers): none of the big bosses wanted the exacting job or was prepared to see it given to a competitor from some other branch of industry. Unlike M. Villiers, on the other hand, Fritz Berg always exercised personal influence both behind the scenes and in public, sometimes by making dramatic statements. In the end, he damaged his own credit with one of these: during the wildcat strikes of September, 1969, when it was reported (falsely) that the strikers had threatened a general manager's wife, he remarked that she ought to have fired on them, and that if one had been killed it would have restored order.

The atmosphere of the employers' federation (BDA), in which about 800 associations of great diversity are represented, has never been so bellicose, though its relations with the workers' unions have grown tougher with the passage of time. In June, 1951, Dr. Walter Raymond, the BDA president, was able to say: "Never in our history have relations between employers and wage earners been so good, I may even say so cordial, as today."[42] This was at the time when the comanagement law was coming into force with the support of both the main parties: the all-out reconstruction effort inspired a sense of partnership in the common cause, and the bosses did not as yet seem all powerful on the political plane. Moreover, the BDA, being more concerned with social relations than the BDI, was accustomed to speak a more moderate language. Within a few years, however, things had changed. In October, 1956, it was learned that the Ruhr collieries had been invited by their employers' association to create a "solidarity fund" of DM6 million by contributions of 5 pfennige per ton of coal produced during the year. The president of the association let it be known that he was acting on instructions from the BDA, which planned to introduce similar funds in all branches of industry. Dr. H. C. Paulssen, who had succeeded Dr. Raymond as BDA president in December, 1953, was a Thuringian, the manager of an aluminium factory at Constance: a man of affability and understanding and by no means a fire-eater, he believed in social justice of a paternalistic kind but was opposed to comanagement and what he regarded as the excessive powers of the workers' unions. He was succeeded in 1964 by Professor Siegfried Balke, who had been a Federal minister from 1953 to 1962; in December, 1969, Balke was in turn replaced by Otto A. Friedrich, a manager who had written interesting studies on social relations, and a brother of the eminent American political scientist Carl J. Friedrich. Under these two presidents, the BDA's relations with the workers' unions were strained at times but seldom violent, the tension usually taking the form of tough negotiation. It must be admitted that the philosophy and practice of the trade union federation went far to explain the moderate attitude displayed by the employers; while the latter, by their shrewdness, contributed to the observance of moderation by the unions.

At the end of the war, as we have seen, the Allies encouraged the revival of the trade union movement, which they regarded as the best available instrument for the democratization of Germany. The first instructions issued to the U.S. military government before the surrender, on April 28, 1944, already envisaged the formation of trade unions while banning political activity. Many of the Germans who began organizing unions after the end of hostilities had been among the leaders before 1933. Whatever their original labels, the fact they had survived the war and the Nazi persecution and were not obliged to join forces, vis-à-vis the Allies, inclined them to work together to create a unified movement. There was one serious obstacle: in the Soviet zone, a new central organization had been formed at the outset, but the Western powers insisted that local groups be formed in the first instance, in line with their general policy for the reconstruction of the political and administrative system. The British Commander-in-Chief was the first to allow a central organization for his zone as a whole, while his American and French colleagues would only allow it on a *Land* basis. After 1948, American policy changed fairly rapidly, but in February, 1949, the French were still vetoing a central organization for the whole of western Germany, and the veto was not lifted until two months later, after the signing of the Atlantic Treaty and the merger of the French zone with the other two. At last it was possible to hold the constituent conference that brought into being the Federation of German Trade Unions (*Deutscher Gewerkschaftsbund*—DGB). This assembly was held at Munich on October 12–14, 1949, and Düsseldorf was chosen as the headquarters of the federation. Its first president was Hans Böckler, the most respected of the surviving prewar union leaders.

The DGB is not the only German trade union federation. There are two other large bodies, the *Deutscher Beamtenbund* (DBB) for the civil service and the *Deutsche Angestelltengewerkschaft* (DAG) for white-collar workers: these claim over 700,000 and nearly 500,000 members respectively. Although the DGB includes nearly as many public servants (616,000) as the DBB and many more clerical workers (nearly 900,000) than the DAG,[43] these latter have a life and importance of their own. The DBB for a long time set its face against the idea of a strike in the public service. The DAG draws its membership chiefly from the banks, commerce, and noncareer civil servants: it sets out to represent a distinct social category consisting of executive and clerical workers (like the *Confédération Générale des Cadres* in France), whereas in the DGB these are classed together with manual workers in each separate occupation.

At first sight, the structure of the DGB resembles that of the big labor organizations in France, with the sixteen *Gewerkschaften* corresponding to the *fédérations* and the eight *Landesbezirke* (district unions) corresponding to the *unions départementales*. In fact, however, there are major differences, as the terminology itself suggests. In France, the basic unit is the local professional or craft group—the *syndicat* in the original sense of the term. In Germany, the local unit is only a section or subsection of the union, which embraces all the workers in a particular occupation. It is therefore misleading to translate *Industriegewerkschaft* as "federation," though we may sometimes do so for convenience: the German unions have a centralized and hierarchical structure that is one of their sources of strength. The *Landesbezirke*, on the other hand, also possess an importance of their own except in areas where the role of heavy industry is overwhelming. Thus in North Rhine–Westphalia, although the *Landesbezirk* includes a third of the members of the DGB in all occupations, it has not much power compared with the metallurgical and mining unions,

I. G. Metall and *I. G. Bergbau*; but in Bavaria, the chairman of the *Landes-bezirk* for a long time enjoyed considerable freedom of speech and action, especially when the post was held by such a strong character as Max Wönner.

The system as a whole is dominated by three organs, of which the congress takes first place. The manner in which delegates are appointed makes it, in effect, an assembly of permanent officials: at first they met every two years, but, at Hamburg in 1956, it was decided to increase the interval to three. Between congresses, the governing body is the federal commission (*Bundes-ausschuss*), composed of members of the executive committee (*Bundesvorstand*), the chairmen of the *Landesbezirke*, and representatives of each federation: two for those with under 300,000 members, three for those between 300,000 and 1 million, and four for those over 1 million, which at present means *I. G. Metall* only. The executive consists of permanent members elected by the congress, including its president, plus one representative of each federation. Its function is to see that the statutes are observed, to coordinate action by the federations, and to carry out tasks entrusted to it by directive or resolutions of the congress or the federal commission. Its headquarters are at Düsseldorf, where in 1967 a huge ultramodern building was erected by the organization at a cost of about DM20 million.

The powers of the president and the executive are limited insofar as the most powerful of the sixteen federations have no wish to see their freedom of action curtailed. This was seen during the early months of 1969, when *I. G. Metall* succeeded in preventing the election as president of Kurt Gscheidle, an SPD deputy and vice-president of the Post Office Workers' Federation (although he was at first proposed unanimously by all sixteen federations), because he wanted to reform the statutes in such a way as to strengthen author-ity at the center. Certainly, the unions differ enormously in importance. At one extreme comes *I. G. Metall*, with 1,965,000 members at the end of 1968; then Public Services and Transport (ÖTV) with 964,000; Chemical (534,000); Building (503,000); and Mining and Power (409,000, with a traditional empha-sis on coal as against other sources of power); at the other extreme are the trade unions of leatherworkers (63,000), farmers (53,000), and artists (34,000). Even within the central organs, the strongest federations enjoy a privileged position. They are represented in the congress in proportion to their size, so that, for in-stance, *I. G. Metall* alone had 131 delegates out of 430 at Munich in May, 1969. The giants are also exceptionally strong financially: it is the federations that collect members' annual dues, of which 15 per cent went to the central organi-zation from 1949 to 1952 (when the figure was lowered to 12 per cent), plus their quarterly contributions to a central Solidarity Fund. A union member's dues are set at the value of one hour's work per week. He is unlikely to fall into arrears, as the sum is often subtracted from his pay-packet, a system that is highly convenient to the DGB treasury and arouses the indignation and envy of French trade union officials when they learn of it. As wages are especially high in the metal industry, *I. G. Metall* provides about one-third of the total budget of the DGB.

When the DGB was first set up, its membership stood at 4·9 million. In 1952, it passed the 6 million mark, but it has hardly grown at all in absolute terms since then, which means a relative decline in view of the steady increase in the labor force. In recent years, there has even been an absolute decline also: the figure was 6,537,000 at the end of 1966, 6,408,000 at the end of 1967, and 6,376,000 a year later, though it rose to 6,482,000 at the end of 1969. The proportion of union members varies greatly from one sector to another: it is especially high among miners, metalworkers and railway workers, and low in trade and agriculture. The causes of the relative decline are twofold. The wage earners are, to some extent, alienated by the cumbrous bureaucracy of the unions, and many of them do not see why they should have to join in order to secure benefits that they receive in any case without having to fight for them. In reality, of course, nonmembers enjoy the fruits that come out of the struggle and negotiations carried on by the unions, and the Miners' Federation has put forward the idea of compulsory contributions by all workers, whether members or not. Even without resorting to such measures, the wealth of the German unions is tremendous by comparison with those in France, for instance. Apart from the accumulation of dues and unused strike funds, they are able, in accordance with true economic liberalism, to own and manage enterprises of all kinds. In 1958, six trade union banks merged to form the *Bank für Gemeinwirtschaft* (Bank for Social Economy), the volume of whose transactions makes it the fourth largest private bank in the Federal Republic. The building society *Neue Heimat* and its thirty-odd affiliates owned about 230,000 dwellings at the end of 1968, making it probably the biggest owner of real estate in the country. The DGB controls a fishing fleet that is the second largest in the country by tonnage, a chain of cooperatives with 6,200 shops, two popular insurance companies, and so forth.

Part of the money is devoted to training party workers and officials and keeping them supplied with information. The Trade Union Institute of Economic Studies (*Wirtschaftswissenschaftliches Institut der Gewerkschaften—* WWI), formerly at Cologne and now in a modern building alongside the Hans-Böckler-Haus at Düsseldorf, employs a staff of about fifty, half of whom are researchers; since 1960, it has operated a computer system for the central archives of wage rates and prices that were instituted in 1954. In discussions related to collective bargaining, employers and trade unionists are thus each in a position to rely on data prepared by an institution that belongs to them. In addition, "social academies" and "higher schools for workers" enable the younger workers especially to study economic, political, and social problems at evening classes and through meetings and training programs. These institutions do not always depend directly on the DGB, but the latter runs special Federal-level schools to train future union executives, who are taught labor legislation and political economy, the legal aspect of social security, and also the arts of debate and public speaking. On a more broadly cultural plane, the DGB organizes the annual Ruhr Festival (*Ruhrfestspiele*) at Recklinghausen. This festival, which includes lectures and round-table discussions on political themes, amateur and professional stage shows, films, art exhibitions, and talks, has from its inception been sharply criticized by the left wing of the DGB.

The benefits of this educative work are evident, but it has disadvantages too. Most of the training courses do not impart general education so much as the technical instruction needed by a future trade union official. Some veterans of the movement remember how they used to study at home after a day's work at the factory: their ideas may not have been too systematic as a result, but self-education helped them to become disinterested and more broadminded, whereas the big schools at the *Land* and Federal level may, they fear, only turn out experts in the art of negotiating wage agreements. As a reaction against this "technocratic" tendency, *I. G. Metall*, in June, 1968, started to build a new type of education center (*Bildungszentrum*) at Sprockhövel near Bochum, with the object of developing critical minds by nonauthoritarian methods, following the example set by *I. G. Chemie*, which completely overhauled its training system in the late 1950's.

Financial power is vital to labor, since the threat of a strike carries much more weight when the employers know that the unions are rich enough to make it a long one. One of the chief reasons, though not the only one, why strikes are rare in Germany is that the unions have no need to organize work stoppages to prove that they are entitled to speak for the workers, a fact everybody recognizes, and that they can generally get what they want without going to extremes. Thus, in 1967 alone, important agreements were arrived at in the chemical industry in January, in the Hessian metal works in November, and in the public services in December, while the calling of a strike for October 30, in the Württemberg metalworking industry, led the Federal Minister of the Economy, Karl Schiller, to offer mediation, with the result that agreement was reached on the 28th. The decision of the union leaders to call the strike had been approved by 87 per cent of those voting.

The DGB's "instructions concerning direct action in industrial disputes" (the term for such action is *Arbeitskampf*) are very strict, and are binding on member unions under Article 19 of its statutes. No strike may be declared until every effort at negotiation has been exhausted. A local union may not start a strike without the authority of its national federation. Once the strike has been authorized, there must be a referendum of all union members of more than three months' standing, and a majority of 75 per cent must be obtained before the strike can commence. Nor will work automatically stop even when this majority has been obtained, for "in deciding whether to authorize direct action, federations must take into account not only the result of the referendum but also such general considerations as the state of business and the repercussions of a strike on other works and other sectors of the economy." But, in practice, authorization to hold a referendum implies authorization to put its verdict into effect. This is the negotiators' decisive weapon, as the employer knows that the call to strike will be obeyed. The procedure for the return to work is similar, the federations supervising the union negotiators. The DGB executive has, in theory, only the right to be informed by the federations before any far-reaching action is undertaken. But according to Article 11 of the instructions, headquarters will give financial support only in return for the right to supervise the development and conclusion of the strike. This makes arbitration between unions possible, while the federations, thanks to their own funds, are able to arbitrate between categories.

The classic illustration, and indeed the only one, is that of the metalworkers' strike in Schleswig, which began on October 24, 1956 after a vote that mustered 88 per cent of union members. The issue appeared a minor one—it concerned payment for the first few days of sick-leave—but a point of honor was at stake:

the workers wanted equality of treatment with the white-collar staff and felt disparaged by the employers' practice, which implied that absence from work on health grounds was due to genuine illness in the case of office workers but probably to malingering where factory hands were concerned. The conflict lasted four weeks and was conducted with lavish expenditure on both sides. The employers were subsidized by their "solidarity fund" and launched a massive campaign against *I. G. Metall* as a wrecker of industrial peace. The strike committee ran a four-page daily newspaper for the strikers and their families and a huge entertainment program, ranging from Christmas trees to films and variety shows with popular singers. Press conferences, posters, and loudspeaker vans were brought to bear on public opinion. During the strike, those of the strikers who were union members received about half their ordinary wage. The first attempt at mediation was a failure: 97·4 per cent of the strikers rejected the proposals, which had already been turned down by *I. G. Metall*. On January 30, 1957, there was a more unexpected turn of events: although *I. G. Metall* had put its signature to a compromise, 76·2 per cent of the strikers voted to reject it and to fight on. On February 9, against the union's advice, they turned down a third proposal, but this time only by 57·7 per cent, which, as we have seen, is an insufficient majority under federation rules. Accordingly, the men went back to work on February 15. Subsequently, *I. G. Metall* was ordered by the Federal Labor Court to pay a large indemnity to the employers for breach of contracts entered into before the strike. German law is strict in labor matters and, like the DGB, it forbids wildcat strikes. Article 10 of the DGB's statutes declares firmly that: "The representatives of any union within whose sphere a strike occurs without having been properly decided upon and authorized must take action to ensure a prompt return to work, while safeguarding the workers' interests so far as possible."

In the first years of the Federal Republic, the DGB seemed the very incarnation of the political ideals of the new Germany. It was in tune with the parliamentary system inherited from nineteenth-century Europe, and it regarded universal suffrage and freedom of thought and assembly as bulwarks of political democracy. It therefore fought tooth and nail against both the Communists and the neo-Nazis, who were jointly dubbed "enemies of democracy" by a periodical of the North Rhine–Westphalia *Landesbezirk*. But, in the DGB's view, democracy as thus defined is far from complete, since it only takes account of the citizens' political, or rather electoral, functions and not of economic factors—whereas, it is argued, the downfall of the Weimar Republic was due to the fact that Germany's economic power rested in the hands of a small group of men who used it to enable Hitler to destroy political democracy. By degrees, the German workers have obtained political equality, but in the economic sphere they are as badly off in the twentieth century as they were a hundred years ago from the political point of view. Certainly working conditions have come a long way since the first "social law" of April 6, 1839, which forbade the employment of children under nine years old. But the issue today is not how to improve material conditions but how to obtain a share in power. A share, not the whole: it is not the DGB's ambition to destroy capitalism. It does stand for the socialization of basic industries, but its demand

201

is for equality between capital and labor, not their abolition as separate categories. It is empirical rather than doctrinaire, concentrating on the achievement of codetermination at every level of economic power: in individual plants, in whole branches of industry, in the framing and application of economic policy in each *Land*, and in the Republic as a whole. In a bill introduced on May 22, 1950, the DGB proposed an equal sharing of power and responsibility throughout the economy, from the factory board with its equal representation of managers and workers to the Economic Council: this, it claimed, would automatically safeguard political democracy and transform the condition of the working class. To the objection that the workers were not qualified for such responsibilities, the DGB replied that in the nineteenth century the same had been said about their unfitness to exercise the vote—in Prussia, for instance, the population had been divided for voting purposes into categories according to wealth—yet nobody in our day would challenge the principle of political equality on the ground that the workers were insufficiently educated.

As we saw, the occupation authorities introduced comanagement in 1947, and, when the Federal Republic came into being, a German law was needed to replace the Allied legislation. Every aspect of the problem was debated at length by the unions, the employers' associations, the political parties, and the churches. At the beginning of 1951, the question was about to be discussed and settled by parliament, when the DGB took direct action. It organized a referendum throughout the coal, iron, and steel industries and announced, after obtaining 95 per cent support, that there would be a general strike on February 1 unless the government undertook to sponsor a bill that satisfied the unions' claims. On January 25, there was a decisive interview between the Chancellor and Hans Böckler, which produced agreement. The strike was called off and the law in question was steered through parliament by the CDU with the help of the SPD, overriding the views of the right-wing opposition and a part of the government majority.

This law, of May 21, 1951, provided for comanagement on a parity basis in all coal mines and iron and steel works with more than 1,000 employees. The management of each concern was entrusted to two bodies, a board of directors (*Aufsichtsrat*) of eleven members, whose function is policy-making, and a management committee (*Vorstand*), which is a sort of executive. The members of the board are chosen as follows: there are four representatives of the owner (or owners) and four of the employees, and to each of these groups is added a fifth member who must not belong to the firm or have any financial interest in it. The eleventh member is then nominated jointly by the employers' and workers' representatives. As to the *Vorstand*, its three members, who are equal among themselves, are the business manager, the production manager, and the *Arbeitsdirektor* or manager responsible for welfare. The last-named cannot be appointed or dismissed by the board of directors without the majority consent of the five workers' representatives.

Of the original four "worker" members of the board, only two—one manual and one clerical—need be members of the firm: the other two may, for instance, be full-time union officials. But even the first two must be approved by the trade union federation concerned. The law does provide that the workers in the firm shall elect them, but candidature is not open to all. Candidates "are proposed by the factory committees after consultation with the unions involved and with their central organizations. . . . The electors may only vote for candidates proposed by the factory committee and the central organizations."

It was not only the law itself, but the prerogatives it granted to the DGB that incensed the employers and the conservatives in parliament. They considered it intolerable that trade unionists from outside the firm should sit on the board, and that the federation should have to approve the candidature of the workers' representatives. The DGB replied that the retired generals and diplomats and the magnates from other industries who traditionally sat on boards were also outsiders to the businesses they were called upon to direct; as for the trade union control of nominations, it eliminated "official candidates" who might be elected under pressure from the management. This latter was not a particularly strong argument, and the procedure laid down in the law tends greatly to favor centralism and bureaucracy in the DGB, lessening the power of the rank and file and increasing that of the higher levels. The rule that some of the workers' representatives might come from outside the business was more justifiable: the trade union colleges had not yet turned out a sufficient number of militants to ensure the presence in every firm of enough manual and clerical workers capable of functioning effectively as board members when it came to examining a balance sheet or deciding on a price and investment policy. It should be added that the members nominated by the DGB have shown themselves fully alive to the interests of the enterprises in question, from which they receive large salaries, while the *Arbeitsdirektor* has as a rule succumbed to the influence of the managerial outlook.

An even stronger attack, however, was directed against the way in which the law had come to be adopted by what was described as an intimidation of parliament (*Parlamentsnotigung*). To this the DGB replied that the employers had their own ways of influencing deputies and political parties without resorting to strike action. Their adversaries retorted that trade unionists constituted the largest single group in the Bundestag: there were in fact 197 trade union deputies in 1965 and 218 in 1969.

Attacks of this sort were no more than a small cloud on the DGB's triumph in 1951, but in 1952 the wind changed. Hans Böckler had died on February 16, 1951, a few days after his great success. He had won the confidence and respect of the Chancellor as well as of his own forces; but it is unlikely that if he had lived, he could have altered the course of events. His death was symbolic, but it also created a vacuum just when the DGB was in need of firm leadership. At an extraordinary congress held at Essen in June, it elected as its new president Christian Fette, are presentative of the Federation of Printers and Stationers. The choice of this colorless personality represented a compromise: he was a Socialist, like his predecessor, but was thought of as a moderate compared with Walter Freitag, the president of *I. G. Metall* and a member of the SPD group in the Bundestag. Although the DGB is not officially linked with any political party, in practice it has always had close ties with the SPD, and, from 1949 onwards, many of its leaders belonged to special committees of the party. Up to 1951, this was of no particular importance: although the two great parties were already at odds over economic policy, their views on social

203

matters were much alike and appeared to be shared by the churches. Even after the formation of the first Federal Government and the breach between the parties headed by Adenauer and Schumacher, the DGB could follow its own course without much interference: it was too powerful in itself to be taken under the wing of any party. The parties, in fact, needed the unions and not vice versa. The dispute over the Schuman Plan brought about a curious situation: the Social Democratic members of the DGB organization, in their capacity as members of the SPD, were opposed to the treaty, but the DGB as such, with the support of these same members, was cautiously in favor of it.

Things changed under the impact of rearmament and of the law on the constitution of enterprises. The proposal to rearm West Germany caused grave unrest in trade union circles, as it did in other fields of public opinion. The unions were particularly divided in 1952, but opposition to remilitarization in any form seemed still to be in the ascendant. However, Christian Fette agreed to take part in the discussion of ways and means before the unions had made up their minds on the principle. At the same time, he showed hesitancy and maladroitness in the campaign for the extension of the comanagement system to all types of enterprises. On May 15–16, demonstrations took place involving about 350,000 union members, and the DGB announced that they would be repeated. On May 29, the printers' federation launched a newspaper strike for which it was later sentenced by the labor courts to pay heavy damages as a penalty for seeking to influence the legislature by means of "unconstitutional pressure, contrary to law and good order." Then the agitation died down, the demonstrations were called off, and, in July, the Bundestag passed a law that, while it granted considerable powers to the unions and works councils, was a long way from introducing full comanagement. However, under the law of October 11, 1952, the workers' representatives were given some share in the social and economic management of industrial firms in general. On October 17, at the DGB's ordinary congress at Berlin, Walter Freitag was elected president by 184 votes, against 154 for Christian Fette, and 18 abstentions.

The fight for comanagement being lost, the congress resolved to do battle for the forty-hour week. The new president, who had joined the SPD and the trade union movement in 1908 at the age of nineteen and had spent years iu concentration camps, took a much more cautious and temporizing line than had been expected: he was anxious to preserve harmony in the trade union movement and was circumspect in his attitude toward the CDU. The DGB's slogan in the election campaign was "Vote for a better Bundestag." Apparently the previous one was officially deemed incapable of improvement, for the unions were at once accused of infringing political neutrality. The CDU victory in the elections on September 6, 1953 was considered a defeat for the DGB, and its weekly organ, *Welt der Arbeit*, hastened to say that "the unions naturally accept and respect the clear verdict of the electorate." However, on the 16th, the DGB received a joint letter from the social committee of the CSU—headed by such men as Karl Arnold and Jakob Kaiser, who were themselves trade unionists—and the Catholic and Protestant workers' associations, demanding that "Christians" be co-opted onto all the central organs of the DGB and that they should in addition be enabled to form trade union groups of their own. On the 30th, the DGB executive unanimously refused these demands. For some days it looked as if there might be a split, but Arnold and Kaiser did not want to push matters to a breaking point, and the advocates of a separate Christian organization were not certain as to how they would succeed when it came to recruitment.

After a brief lull, the DGB once again swung toward a more aggressive position under the influence of Dr. Viktor Agartz, a codirector of the Economic Institute who had violently opposed the Schuman Plan and whose closest associates, particularly the young sociologist Theo Pirker, had been in the forefront of the antirearmament campaign in Bavaria. Agartz was the hero of the third ordinary congress of the DGB, held in Frankfurt in October, 1954, where his speech denouncing government policy and rejecting rearmament in violent terms was acclaimed as the basis of a "new action program." Three months later, the "hard line" was even more in evidence when, on January 14, 1955, the 30,000 workers of the metallurgical works controlled by the industrial magnate Herman Reusch went on strike in protest against the latter's statement that the adoption of the 1951 law was due to gross blackmail at a time when the power of the state was not yet firmly established. On the 20th, the Federation of Employers' Associations spoke out against comanagement, and, on the 24th, the miners and metalworkers downed tools for twenty-four hours. The Chancellor attempted to restore calm in a broadcast in which he declared that there was no threat to comanagement. In 1956, it was in fact extended to holding companies, contrary to the employers' wishes.

However, the DGB hard-liners had overrated their strength, and Agartz's star paled rapidly: a harsh, dictatorial man, he was scarcely popular even with his own adherents. An intrigue that he conducted within the WWI against his colleague Professor Gleitze furnished a reason, which would have been found in any case, for ousting him from that body in December, 1955, but his fall from grace had begun earlier than that. Walter Freitag and such leaders as Ludwig Rosenberg—the executive's expert on economic affairs and, prior to Freitag's election to the presidency, on international affairs—were opposed to anything that could be labeled fellow-traveling or to a doctrinal position that would drive even the best-disposed Christians into schism. The break with the "left wing" took place in October, 1955, but the DGB's standing was not impaired thereby. On October 30, a "Christian Trade Union movement" was founded by three CDU deputies who were members of the DGB—two Catholics and a Protestant, all of whom had been active members of Christian workers' associations since their youth. The attempt was a fiasco, rallying only some 20,000 members: it was in fact opposed by a variety of different quarters. Karl Arnold and Jakob Kaiser disapproved of the breakaway while at the same time sharply criticizing the DGB. The latter's vice-president, Matthias Föcher, though himself a representative of the "Christian" viewpoint, stayed firmly where he was. The Catholic bishops made extremely prudent statements, and many Protestants spoke out in favor of unity.

All in all, the DGB was not weakened by the crisis, and when the Chancellor attended its congress at Hamburg in October, 1956 the effect was to give the impression that he was conducting a reconnaissance to assure himself of its monopoly of representation. The executive for its part reverted to a cautious attitude and made little further use of its potential strength. In the period before the 1957 election, the DGB took care to avoid a crisis on the lines of 1953 and to demonstrate its political independence, not to be confused with neutrality, which was impossible in the nature of things. In 1961, its pre-election appeal also avoided party politics, merely urging workers of all kinds not to "waste their votes on splinter groups."

Had the effort to avoid partisanship left the DGB with any doctrine at all? Following the example of the SPD four years earlier, the DGB on November 22, 1963 adopted a "Basic Program" at an extraordinary congress at Düsseldorf. This was a long document that laid stress on the defense of public and private liberties and on the demand for comanagement on a parity basis at all levels; it also set forth detailed objectives in the field of social policy. In the economic field, it expressed itself in favor both of planning and of liberalism; but the key sentence was contained in the preamble: "Paid workers, who constitute the overwhelming bulk of the population, are still deprived of command (*Verfügungsgewalt*) over the means of production." Thus the point at issue is use, not ownership. Later in the document, detailed attention is given to the various techniques of control of economic power.

In the previous year, Ludwig Rosenberg had succeeded Willi Richter, an SPD deputy, in the presidency of the DGB, which the latter had held since 1956. Born in 1903, Rosenberg had lived in London as an émigré from 1933 to 1946 and had been a member of the DGB executive since 1949. He enjoyed considerable prestige in ICFTU (the International Confederation of Free Trade Unions). During the seven years of his presidency, the DGB was involved in two major political issues: the question of nuclear armaments for Germany and the "state of emergency" legislation. The first was straightforward: the DGB unanimously condemned the acquisition of any nuclear armaments by the Federal Republic, a viewpoint clearly stated in the Basic Program. As to the emergency powers legislation, the influence exerted by the DGB in common with other extraparliamentary forces gave rise to problems inasmuch as the SPD was now a member of the government coalition and was engaged in discussing a compromise with the CDU; on the other hand, an alliance with forces further left carried with it dangerous risks of ideological contagion. In May, 1966, the DGB congress at Berlin emphatically condemned the proposed constitutional and legislative changes as harmful to democracy, and, in November, 1967, Rosenberg made a strong speech on the subject in the Beethovenhalle at Bonn. But after the measures were finally adopted in 1968, the unions at once withdrew from the organization known as *Notstand der Demokratie* ("An Emergency for Democracy"), with the result that it ceased to exist.

It was in fact Otto Brenner, the president of *I. G. Metall* and doubtless the strongest personality in the German trade union movement during the past twenty years, who, more than anyone else, put a stop to the operation he had launched in spite of the reservations of DGB headquarters. His youth, spent in difficult circumstances as a riveter, endowed him with a sense of working-class realities that made him popular with union members, while his later career, first as a researcher and then as a union "boss," gave him the appearance and manner of a caustic and aggressive intellectual, respected by businessmen and more than capable of keeping up his end with them. From 1951, he was an SPD member of the *Landtag* of Lower Saxony; in December, 1952, he succeeded Walter Freitag as joint president of *I. G. Metall*, and became its sole president at the congress of September, 1956. This congress also conferred additional powers on the executive in regard to strike action. The statutes continued to require the holding of a referendum before a strike was called on an industrial issue, but the union leaders were thenceforth authorized to call for a stoppage in the event of attack on the rights and existence of the unions or the endangering of basic democratic rights in the Federal Republic. This, to say the least, opened up the possibility of a "political strike," which had been the object of reprobation in the past.

In October, 1956, Brenner, in his report to the DGB congress at Hamburg, spoke of the necessity of transforming the working of the economy by a genuine system of comanagement that would be a distinct form of nationalization. The ideas he advanced were not very different from those of Viktor Agartz, and to this extent also resembled the DGB's original program. In Brenner's view, while it was not necessary to think in terms of a class struggle, the idea of the Federal Republic as a classless society was mythical and absurd. During the next twelve years, he remained associated with the critical intelligentsia and joined with some other independent spirits of the SPD and DGB to publish the review *Neue Gesellschaft* (*New Society*), a franker and more interesting journal at all events than the DGB's official monthly the *Gewerkschaftliche Monatshefte*. However, his audacity was kept within judicious bounds and, once the SPD was associated with the government, he showed much sobriety in order to spare embarrassment to his colleagues who had become ministers.

Naturally the relationship between the SPD and the DGB has undergone a change of tone since December, 1966, and especially since October, 1969. The DGB's attitude must be one of critical and cooperative independence vis-à-vis a government three of whose members are former presidents of trade union federations. The most sharply felt difficulty is over comanagement: it was revived during the election campaign of 1969 and by the publication, in January, 1970, of a report on the subject by the Biedenkopf commission. This academic body, foreshadowed in the government declaration of December 13, 1966, was set up a year later under the chairmanship of Professor Kurt Biedenkopf: it performed its task with great thoroughness, receiving testimony from dozens of general managers, works managers, and members of directors' boards, and collating about a thousand detailed questionnaires. The massive final report was moderate in its terms but recommended an extension of comanagement in all enterprises. While frank in its expressions of opinion, it took occasion to rebut many criticisms. Once again, a lively debate on ways and means was unleashed, and a flood of publications followed.[44]

At the same time, the DGB began to take initiatives in regard to Federal Germany's relations with the Communist bloc. For a long time, it had been violently anti-Communist, refusing all contact, even at a low level, with the French CGT and restraining attempts by any of its member unions to establish links with those of the G.D.R., whose independence was of course highly questionable. In 1956, *I. G. Metall*, at the instance of Otto Brenner, censured a surprise resolution to this effect that had been issued by the printers' union. The idea of contacts was revived from 1965 onward by Heinz Kluncker, the president of the Public Services Federation. The DGB, however, was by no means in advance of the government on this issue. Ludwig Rosenberg's attitude was itself involved in contradictions, partly because, while he accepted in 1967 an invitation to the DGB to meet Soviet trade unionists in Moscow, he also criticized America's Vietnam policy: the *Gewerkschaftliche Monatshefte* went so far as to publish an article on this subject criticizing George Meany, the president of the great American combination of unions, the AFL-CIO. On October 8, 1967, *Welt am Sonntag*, which like the rest of the Springer press had denounced the DGB president for his "anti-Americanism" and "naiveté" where the Communists were concerned, published an interview with Rosenberg in which he categorically rejected the idea of contacts with the G.D.R. trade unions, "which are not worthy of the name."[45] Two years later, in March, 1970, it was learned that a meeting was to take place in Berlin between Herbert Wahrnke, the president of the East German DGB, and his Federal opposite number, Heinz Oskar Vetter, who succeeded Rosenberg on May 21, 1969.

Vetter's election had not gone altogether smoothly; the leaders of the main federations had agreed on his candidature shortly before the congress, after the withdrawal of Kurt Gscheidle. He was fifty-one years of age, vice-president of the Miners' Federation, and quite unknown to his fellow delegates. He made an unimpressive showing at the congress, and was elected by only 267 votes to 20 against and 133 abstentions. Not surprisingly, he was congratulated on the result by the president of his federation, Walter Arendt. As time went on, however, his authority increased, especially after Arendt became Minister of Labor in the Brandt cabinet, which improved Vetter's negotiating position.

In general, the DGB has little cause for apprehension as far as the government is concerned. The same cannot, however, be said as regards its prospects in themselves. This is less because of attacks from the right—although such an important daily as the *Frankfurter Allgemeine Zeitung* has never relaxed its firm opposition to the unions—than because of a twofold discontent on its left wing, among the rank and file, and on the part of the young generation. The warning was sounded by the wild cat strikes of September, 1969 in the Ruhr and the Saar, at Bremen and Kiel. They did not mean that the DGB was necessarily losing control over the working masses. A warning of this sort had already come at the end of 1955 and the beginning of 1956, when the Communists scored some successes in the elections of works committees, but these had had no sequel. The strikes of 1969, however, showed that besides the danger of apathy on the workers' part there was another, which had already been seen in Britain and Sweden: namely, that manual workers who were in a state of revolt against the social order and its economic consequences for the individual might reject the authority of an organization that, while no doubt skilled in negotiating benefits, was too much a part of the existing social structure and too bureaucratic to be sensitive to workers' needs, except perhaps in the case of certain unions such as those in the chemical industry.

In addition, the DGB had failed to understand the impatience and aspirations of many young people, most of all those within its own ranks. Certainly little is heard of these young people at congresses: in 1969, only four of the delegates were under thirty, while 364 were over forty. There is an organization of young trade unionists, the *Gewerkschaftsjugend*, with 600,000 members, but it is closely controlled by the executive committee of the DGB: it is not an autonomous body, and the "Federal Secretary for Youth" (*Bundesjugendsekretär*) is not so much a spokesman for the young people as an agent for executing the committee's decisions in regard to them. On the other hand, a steadily growing trend toward critical independence has been in evidence since the late 1960's. At the federal conference of May, 1969, the 146 delegates adopted—by large majorities—resolutions calling for the recognition of the G.D.R. and the Oder-Neisse frontier, contacts with the East German trade unions and with "progressive students," and the setting up of a committee of the DGB to prepare for a general strike in the event of a government abusing the emergency powers legislation.

Thus the DGB is affected, though by no means threatened as yet, by forces of protest that are also making themselves felt in other parts of German society, although for many years that society has been regarded as peculiarly submissive to the rules by which it is organized.

9

Moral and Intellectual Trends

THE forces that underlie political life and contribute to its demands and stresses do not consist solely of economic facts and exigencies due to material circumstances and human wills and needs—the clashes or unspoken antagonisms between more or less tightly organized groups based on wealth or status, the ambition to acquire tangible goods and measurable advantages. Besides these, we must take account of all the factors that go to form, sustain, or undermine beliefs of every kind, from the principles on which communities are based to those regarded as giving meaning to the life of the individual and inspiring his public and private actions.

In the Federal Republic as elsewhere, there are specific forces that reflect these beliefs and at the same time act upon them, and which have a direct or indirect bearing on politics. Chief among these are the churches, the press, and education. In all these fields, there is a stronger tendency in Germany than elsewhere for opinions and attitudes to be framed with reference to a past that is still in the present, and whose influence is slow to disappear.

The Burden of the Past

The past in question is not, like that of France, a centuries-long sequence of events presented to schoolchildren as bearing the imprint of a continuous national history from Vercingetorix to General de Gaulle—a pageant whose chief figures and episodes are commemorated at every turn as a stimulus to national pride. It is in fact astonishing how little one hears, in German public life, of the nation's history from the Hohenstaufen to Bismarck, and we shall have more to say about this in our last chapter. In the present context, the past we are concerned with consists almost wholly of the dark days of the Nazi era. From the earliest days of the new German democracy, foreigners and Germans alike evaluated that democracy according to the manner in which it interpreted the Nazi past and came to terms with it.

From the outset, therefore, the question of civic consciousness in the new Germany presented itself in two distinct but interconnected forms. The German people, and especially the young generation, had to be convinced of the need for active participation in public life, which meant that they had to be made aware of political, social, and juridical facts; and, at the same time, they had to be informed of, and taught to understand, the worst aspects of the recent past. The occupying powers had done a good deal in the way of "democratization," but unfortunately, as we saw, they made many mistakes through adopting the paternalistic notion of "re-education," the implications of which are Pharisaical and far from democratic in themselves. The Allies' best achievements were those that enabled Germans, especially young people and also leaders and militants of all kinds, to become acquainted with facts and currents of opinion outside Germany. This work of international education, continued and developed by German institutions, was of great value because it affected the most diverse circles and because the young people who benefited from it immediately after the war later came to occupy an ever growing number of leading posts in public life.

The Federal Government in its turn wished to contribute to the work of training citizens, but its situation was a difficult one: if it did too little, it would be accused of failing to encourage democracy; and if it did too much, there would soon be a cry of "propaganda." The government certainly did not avoid all the dangers of intervention: in 1956, for example, through its control of financial aid to the film industry, it saw to it that a film on Stresemann was toned down in such a way as to turn that statesman into a forerunner of Adenauer's policy. Again, in 1956, Dr. Schröder had difficulty in defending himself against an SPD interpellation after he had held up the government grant to the Socialist students' association because its president had written an article sharply criticizing parliament. Some ten years later, a Social Democratic official, Conrad Ahlers, stopped the grant to an FDP youth publication that had not shown proper respect for the Grand Coalition. But, on the whole, the various organizations that receive public funds to help them carry on political education have not had much reason to complain that their freedom of research and speech was curtailed as a result. It is true, however, that until the National Students' Union passed into the hands of dissenting groups and the assumptions of liberal society were called in question, relative unanimity prevailed as to the main principles of the "basic liberal and democratic order" the nation had set itself to preserve and develop.

The government itself set up a remarkable institution, originally under the curious name of *Bundeszentrale für Heimatdienst* (or "Federal Center for Home Front Activity"). This title, borrowed from a Weimar organization, was changed in 1963 to *Bundeszentrale für politische Bildung* (Federal Center for Political Education). This institution, whose object is to foster democracy by means of knowledge, publishes the weekly *Das Parlament*, which gives a lively and impartial account of parliamentary debates, with supplements on history and current affairs. The Center also publishes numerous pamphlets, subsidizes larger works, and organizes lectures, acting in this way as a supplier of material to teachers, universities, and educational associations. Apart from articles expounding the nature of Federal institutions and the citizens' rights and duties, the tenor of its publications is anti-Nazi on the one hand and anti-Communist on the other. Thanks to its activity, Germans are better informed than they would otherwise have been about the Nazi massacres and the German opposition to Hitler. In the late 1950's anti-Communism became its dominant theme; ten years later, this had somewhat receded, while the tone and reasoning of the publications was still at times calculated to favor a somewhat narrow spirit of conformity.

Since education in the strict sense does not fall within the province of the Federal government, we must look to the *Länder* for enlightenment as to the civic aspects of the school system. The syllabuses and directives in this field vary from one *Land* to another. "Political" or "civic" (*staatsbürgerlich*) instruction was introduced at an early stage in Hesse and was systematized in Baden-Württemberg from 1957 onward by the training of special teachers: it is now fairly general throughout the Republic, chiefly in *Gymnasien* but also in technical schools. The curriculum basically includes instruction on the workings of parliamentary democracy and also on past history. To enliven the subject, much use is made of methods such as games and competitions. University extension courses do much to instruct adults, as do the trade unions and churches. Nevertheless, the system of political education has been criticized as inadequate and even as permanently in danger of collapse, especially by those who attack its content because of disagreement as to what would be put in the place of Nazism—the answer to this question having hitherto been, a form of democracy characterized by political pluralism and social evolution at a moderate pace.[1]

At the school level, syllabuses are of course no use without adequate textbooks and good will on the part of teachers: this proved as true in the field of history as in that of instruction in civics. Some teachers indeed took their task seriously: a form master might spare his class an hour's arithmetic at the end of term in order to make them listen to the broadcast of a Bundestag debate, which they would then discuss. But most, for fear of giving themselves away, would avoid the more awkward aspects of the past by teaching history only as far as the nineteenth century. The older teachers had taken warning by successive purges and the changing face of historical Truth, and their young pupils were uncertain what they were supposed to think. The average university graduate had been taught nothing about current events: the academic world, in Germany as in France or Britain, prefers its history to be well matured. As regards school textbooks, a good deal was done: in particular, an international institute at Brunswick under Professor Georg Eckert organized bilateral conferences for the production of texts, which were adopted as the basis for some German manuals. Some of the better books in use still contain some passages on the Nazi period that are, to say the least, questionable; but the image of the past is changing, in part as a result of the efforts that have been made. For instance, a certain opinion poll regularly puts a question on responsibility for World War II. Between 1952 and 1957, the percentage of those who put the blame on Germany increased steadily from 32 to 62, while those answering "other countries" or "both sides" diminished respectively from 24 to 8 and from 18 to 8 per cent.[2]

The reluctance of many history teachers, and many parents too, to recall the years from 1933 to 1945 is natural enough. What is the point, and what is the effect, of retracing the history of past crimes or bringing them to the knowledge of those who were not even alive when they were committed? The answer to this question is not as simple as it may seem to the non-German reader. Certainly the mention of Nazi atrocities in schoolbooks and elsewhere was a necessary sign of the democratization and moral rehabilitation of postwar Germany; and it was right that men and women who had been adults in

1933 or even in 1945 should be reminded again and again of what the Nazi regime, which they had cheered so loudly, had meant to other nations, and to those Germans who opposed Hitler or to whom he denied the name of Germans. It is right, too, that the great majority of people in Germany today who were children or still unborn in 1945 should know what their country meant to other countries at a recent period of its history. But we must also understand the implications of this state of affairs, both in Germany and outside it.

In Germany, it has meant a permanent humiliation of national pride, to such a degree as to call in question even the most traditional ceremony of respect for the dead. In November, 1966, on the *Volkstrauertag*, or national day of mourning and remembrance, the writer Rudolf Krämer-Badoni was invited to address the Saarland associations of ex-servicemen and war victims. Instead of making the speech his audience expected, he addressed them thus: "How—I ask you and I ask myself—are we to commemorate those who fell in the last two wars? Can we speak of them as of the defenders of Thermopylae, who fought to the last man against the barbarian hordes? No, we cannot. It is we ourselves who were the barbarians in the last war."[3] And he went on to recall the Nazi crimes and atrocities, praising those who had resisted Hitler as the true defenders of civilization against barbarism. We may understand the feelings of the president of an association of ex-prisoners of war who expostulated: "We have come here to remember our dead sons and not to be told about the Nazis." It is not easy to confess to the young generation that one's own generation was guilty of cowardice. In this respect, people in other countries should be prepared to judge themselves by the same standards as the Germans—even though some German psychologists have held that Germans especially are, as a people, incapable of doing penance for crimes committed in their name.[4]

Having made this point, we may certainly agree that it is better for Germans to be told about Hans and Sophie Scholl than called on to admire their country's wartime victories. In 1968, on the twenty-fifth anniversary of the martyrdom of the two students, it was clear that there was still plenty to be done in this direction—their story was unknown to the majority of people even in Munich, their native city, although the Institute of Political Studies there is named after them.

It is also to be desired that the Nazi period should not be "tarted up" and presented in a more or less humorous, anecdotal fashion, as has been done by certain picture papers of wide circulation, which at other times pride themselves on their democratic and anti-Nazi attitude. Thus, in 1966, *Quick* published the memoirs of Emmy Göring, the "first lady" of Hitler's Reich, with an introductory leader that was a masterpiece of hypocrisy. While recognizing that millions had lost their lives thanks to Nazism and that Germany's leaders for the past twenty years had been striving valiantly to reconstruct their shattered country, the editor offered his readers the chance of reading a "first-hand account" of the "true character" of the men who cast a spell over the Germans of their day.[5] About the same time, when Speer and Baldur von Schirach were released from Spandau, the manifestations were positively indecent; the highly democratic weekly *Der Stern* lost no time in purchasing at a high price, and publishing the following year, the memoirs of the Youth Leader of the Third Reich, imbued with sincerity and entitled "I believed in Hitler."

The victims of Nazism received no such monetary rewards, although the compensation paid to them has not been negligible: government and parliament showed much good will, though the legislation has frequently had to be clarified and supplemented. Thus the law of May 11, 1951 on compensation for members of the public service was amended by seven further measures ending with that of September 9, 1965—which led to the "Gerstenmaier affair." The important law of September 18, 1953, known as the "second Basic Law," was also widened in successive stages over the next twelve years. By the end of 1968, a total of some DM30,000 million had been paid out under the various measures of compensation and restitution. All the same, many of those entitled to compensation died before they could receive it. In December, 1955, the Bundestag unanimously adopted a third amendment to the law of 1953, the preamble to which recalled that "resistance to National Socialist tyranny [was] a meritorious action for the good of the German people and state;" but, in the course of the debate, some painful facts came to light as regards the amounts so far paid out (only DM1,000 million in 1948–54) and, above all, the lack of good will shown by the administration and courts. The departments involved had worked slowly and made impossible demands for the production of papers: a former prisoner was asked to give the names of his warders, and a young woman who had seen her whole family perish at Auschwitz and bore her camp number tattooed on her wrist was told to produce two certificates attesting that she had been a concentration camp inmate. Out of 1,125,000 applications submitted by September 20, 1955, only 320,000 had been dealt with: the number in which compensation had been granted was 143,000.

Although this slowness and procrastination was less marked toward the end of the 1950's, it contrasted sharply with the treatment extended to "victims" of a different class. The "131 law" was generous to former Nazi dignitaries. The widow of Count Berthold Stauffenberg, who was executed with his brother after the attempt on Hitler's life on July 20, 1944, received a pension of DM200 a month, her husband's rank having been that of a legal adviser in the Ministry of Marine. The head of Hitler's navy, Grand Admiral Raeder, was condemned to death by the Nuremberg tribunal, and his widow's pension was fixed at DM2,246 a month. The Federal High Court ruled that the former Chief of Police at Lübeck was entitled to DM18,000 compensation for the requisitioning of his apartment in 1945. The Constitutional Court, however, took a different view of cases like these: in a series of decisions on February 19 and 20, 1957, it approved the action of the legislature in excluding former members of the Gestapo from the benefits of the "131 law," and recalled the considerations on which its judgment of December, 1953 had been based. Nevertheless, courts and administrative authorities continued to set precedents in the opposite sense.

A large proportion of the victims who received compensation in and out of Germany consisted of Jews who had escaped the horrors of the Nazi massacre. For ten years or so, the public was slow to realize the enormity of this crime, its reluctance being partly due to the effects of the Nuremberg trial, which we have already discussed. But in 1956–57, the subject was brought home by two events of unequal moment: Alain Resnais' short film *Nuit et Brouillard*, a restrained but deeply moving production, and the *Diary of Anne Frank*. The former gave rise to an incident at the Cannes festival, when the German representatives withdrew in protest against its being shown. This provoked a sharp reaction in Germany: with the help of the CDU deputy Paul Bausch, chairman of the Bundestag committee on the press, radio, and cinema, the film was shown in Bonn to an audience of 700 consisting mainly of students together with journalists, deputies, and officials. In reply to a questionnaire that 412 members of the audience filled in, 347 of them expressed the view that the film should be publicly shown in Germany. A version was then made with government approval, Jean Cayrol's commentary being replaced by a German adaptation. The horrifying scenes from it, which appeared on Bavarian television, aroused conflicting reactions, but Anne Frank's diary had a more lasting and widespread effect. In March, 1955, an edition of 40,000 copies was published in the cheap Fischer-Bücherei series; by July, 1956, sales were over 100,000, and in January, 1957, they exceeded 200,000. Then came an avalanche: by May, 1957, 400,000 copies had been sold. A play based on the book had meanwhile been performed in several German cities, the merits of the production varying from one to another: at Düsseldorf, Munich, and Hamburg it struck the right note, while at Aachen the effect was one of caricature. Public reactions varied also: as in Paris and New York, some found in the play merely an outlet for easy sentimentality, while others were indignant at what they considered an arraignment of Germany. In many cases, however, the audience reacted to the play as its theme demanded, by leaving the theater without applauding and in dead silence.

The little Jewish martyr became a symbol. On June 12, 1957, when she would have been twenty-eight years old, a plaque was unveiled at the house in Frankfurt where she was born, and commemorative meetings were held at the university and the Paulskirche. The initiative came chiefly from youth movements, and in general it was the young who felt most strongly. At the end of February, 1957, a three-line notice appeared in the Hamburg press advertising a "remembrance visit" by young people to the graves at Bergen-Belsen: those who attended were asked to pay DM5.20 toward expenses. Erich Lüth, the organizer of the pilgrimage—we shall hear more of him presently—had expected 80 or 100 people to respond: the actual number was 2,000. Some school classes got up collections so that the less well off could take part; others had to overcome objections by their teacher. At the site of the murder camp where Anne Frank had perished, a young man of twenty-eight made a speech. As Hans Nüssen, he had been a fanatical member of the Hitler Youth; his name was now Hans-Hanoch Nissan and he had come from a *kibbutz* in Israel, having emigrated to that country and embraced Judaism as a result of learning about the Nazi atrocities.

President Heuss referred to Anne Frank's diary in October, 1957 in a message to the congress—held at Munich—of twenty German Associations for Cooperation between Christians and Jews (*Gesellschaften für christlich-jüdische Zusammenarbeit*): in his view, the reactions aroused by the book were an

215

encouraging sign at a time when people had been more and more inclined to forget the past. Efforts have never been lacking, however, both to combat the tendency to oblivion and to instill opposition to racism, for example, by the meetings, film shows, and lectures organized in the course of "brotherhood weeks." At times, the fight against anti-Semitism has taken on a sharper form, as in the Harlan affair. In Hitler's time, Viet Harlan, the film producer, had made a film of *Jew Süss*—which amounted to an incitement to massacre. When brought before a denazification tribunal, he was acquitted on the ground that he had acted under duress, whereupon he immediately resumed filmmaking. He soon had plenty of capital, for he knew his business and could turn out sentimental and edifying productions that appealed to a wide public; but a vigorous campaign was launched against him by Erich Lüth, the official responsible for press matters in Hamburg, and was supported in a large number of towns by trade unionists, students, and youth movements of every color. Lüth, having urged a boycott of Harlan's films, was prosecuted for interfering with freedom of opinion and condemned to pay a heavy fine— which was defrayed for him by a collection. When the president of the court urged him to "make his peace" with Harlan, he replied that it was not a question of himself but of 6 million murdered Jews. The matter was taken to the Constitutional Court, which ruled that Lüth was in no way to blame in calling for a boycott and had acted in accordance with his rights as a citizen.

The movement he set on foot bore the name of "Peace with Israel," which was intended to apply both to conditions within Germany and to foreign relations. A reparations treaty between Germany and Israel was signed in September, 1952 after long negotiations linked with the name of Professor Franz Böhm, a CDU deputy who was as zealous in combating the evil influences of the past as in defending the market economy. Before this, on September 27, 1951, Chancellor Adenauer had made a statement to the Bundestag that was received with approval by every parliamentary group; in it, he recalled that "in the German people's name unspeakable crimes have been committed, which demand moral and material reparation." In chapter 11, we consider the significance of these sentiments and their reception by the Bundestag in relation to Germany's foreign policy and the reactions of public opinion to the Near East crises of 1967 and after.

A good deal has been done in the Federal Republic to ensure reasonable living conditions for the remnants of the Jewish community, who with their children number only some 20,000 according to religious statistics. Perhaps, indeed, these efforts have gone too far: anti-Semitism can be aroused by too much striving to eliminate it. The press is faced with a perennial dilemma: if it says nothing about untoward incidents, it is accused, especially by foreigners, of hushing them up; if it gives them prominence, the effect is to call attention to the peculiar status of Judaism and to foster the conviction that Jews are radically "different," from which it is only a short step to hostility. For this reason, the Central Council of German Jews and their weekly *Allgemeine Wochenzeitung der Juden in Deutschland* opposed the introduction of special "pro-Jewish" laws after the anti-Semitic incidents of the winter of 1959–60 when, not for the first time since 1945, Jewish cemeteries were desecrated and swastikas painted on synagogues. Such incidents were no more than a striking reminder of what was already known, but public reactions to them were of considerable interest.[6] Both before and after 1959–60, there were disquieting occurrences, such as mass reactions in favor of persons convicted of anti-Semitism—for example, for a highschool teacher named Ludwig Zind, who in 1958–59 was sentenced for having publicly expressed the view that the surviving Jews would be better dead; he escaped from Germany and went to live in Egypt. Similarly, a group of scouts who formed teams to restore an abandoned Jewish cemetery were subjected to criticism and persecution.[7] Nor should we overlook the tendentious practice of the best-known German encyclopedia, which suppressed the Jewish origin of such respectable Jews as Kafka and Rathenau while stressing that of the wicked revolutionaries, Rosa Luxemburg and Karl Marx (whose father's "real" name was given as Marx Levi).[8]

On the whole, however, it may be said that while the latent anti-Semitism in the Federal Republic finds frequent expression in private attitudes, it is hardly noticeable in public life. Moreover, the effect of the Arab-Israeli crises in reviving its traditional manifestations has been much less marked in Germany than in France, where we have seen since 1968 how strong a prejudice lingers against Jews, whether in the political field or nurtured by some fanciful scare of the "white slave" variety.[9]

During the Allied occupation, the crimes committed by the Nazis between 1933 and 1945 were punished only to a limited extent: many of their perpetrators, in any case, remained unknown, as the documents that would have identified them were out of reach. In 1958, a central office representing the *Länder* ministries of justice was set up at Ludwigsburg for the purpose of tracking down the criminals, its efforts being aided in large measure by the return of German archives from the United States. The Ludwigsburg office also attempted, sometimes with success and sometimes not, to obtain additional documents from the Soviet Union, Poland, and the G.D.R.

Before long, however, the question of prescription was raised. Should there be any restriction on the bringing of prosecutions against people who, in many cases, had for years past been living a normal professional and social life in which nothing distinguished them from their neighbors? Foreign observers thought it entirely proper that there should be none. In France, particularly, although the doctrine of amnesty is well established and is used to forbid even the mention of crimes allegedly committed in France's name, the idea that the punishment of Nazi crimes might be subject to a time limit aroused great indignation. This was not so much because the crimes were on a different scale as because of the fundamental divergence between the moral standard applied to Germany and that applied to France, where the principle is that oblivion is necessary for social peace. When it was learned in 1969 that Mgr. Defregger, the coadjutor bishop of Munich, had as an officer in Italy shared responsibility for the mass murder of civilians, few Frenchmen reflected that, after all, the same kind of blame might justly have been leveled at French officers who had fought in Indochina or Algeria.[10]

In the Federal Republic, no question of an amnesty was raised, but the maximum period of prescription allowed by the law—namely, in murder cases—was twenty years. What was to be done in 1965? After much lively argument and a full-dress parliamentary debate in which the young CDU deputy Ernst Benda came to the fore and which led, as we have seen, to the resignation of Ewald Bucher, the Minister of Justice, a legal subterfuge was hit upon that enabled the issue of principle to be evaded. Since the Federal Republic had only come into existence in 1949, the period of prescription could not run from 1945: the problem was thus postponed until 1969.

Both Gustav Heinemann, who was Minister of Justice in 1968, and Horst Ehmke, who succeeded him in March, 1969, held strongly that there should not be prescription pure and simple. After further controversy, a law was passed on May 9, 1969 along the lines of a proposal put forward in Hamburg in February, 1965. This provided that there should be no time limit on prosecutions for genocide, and that for ordinary murder the period should be extended from twenty to thirty years. Thus no prosecution for a murder committed before 1945 could be initiated after 1979, by which time most actions would probably have lapsed owing to the death of the accused. Even in 1965–67, out of 194 persons brought to trial, 62 per cent were aged between fifty and sixty and 26 per cent between sixty and seventy; by 1975, the average age of this group will be over seventy.

In fact, however, prescription for second-degree murder (*Totschlag*) has already existed since 1960, and many criminals have benefited by this thanks to the unexpected application of Article 5 of the Penal Code, which, as revised in 1958, provides that an accomplice to a murder committed from a heinous motive may be tried on a different basis from the principal author if his own motive was not a heinous one. The Federal High Court, when consulted, ruled that this provision could be invoked in favor of men accused of thousands of murders in concentration camps or in the lands east of Germany.

The promulgation of the 1969 law in the midst of an election campaign was an act of political courage: the public was by no means in favor of the extension of the time limit, and the government took care not to publish the results of a poll it had carried out on the subject. Another poll, hardly more encouraging, was carried out by the second television network, which asked viewers: "If someone murdered Jews during the Nazi period, do you think he should be prosecuted today or not?" The vote in favor was 44 per cent (but 47 per cent for those aged between sixteen and twenty-four; against, 46 per cent.[11] Yet the nature and extent of the atrocities committed had been once again brought into public view as a result of spectacular trials, particularly that at Frankfurt, which lasted twenty months, involved 350 witnesses from all over the world, and terminated, on August 18, 1965, with the conviction of a majority of the twenty-two defendants, all of whom were concerned in the operation of the Auschwitz death camp. The investigation went back to 1958, when it was begun almost casually as the result of a denunciation. The quality press gave the trial much publicity,[12] with the result that many young Germans came to understand more fully what Auschwitz stood for; the publicity, too, was not without effect on the outcome of the debate on the prescription issue.

There had of course been previous trials of the same kind, all of which gave ground for uneasiness by reason of the lenient attitude shown by the judges. Naturally there could in any case be no common measure between crime and punishment; but when, to take only one instance among dozens, a Flensburg jury sentenced one Fellenz, against whom the attorney-general had demanded the maximum penalty of life imprisonment for the murder of 40,000 human beings, to a term of four years' hard labor—less the three years and eleven months he had spent in custody awaiting trial—it is hard not to feel indignant, especially on reading that the sentence expressly provided that the accused remained in possession of his civil rights (*bürgerliche Ehrenrechte*, or "rights of honor" as they are called). Moreover, the sentences, light as they were, were in many cases further reduced owing to premature release "on health grounds"; thus Robert Mulka, the chief defendant at the Frankfurt trial, was released a year after being sentenced to fourteen years' hard labor.

Nor is it only popular juries that have behaved in this way: their lenience has often been outdone by professional judges. A whole collection of Gilbertian judgments could be compiled. In one case, systematic murder and torture are excusable because their perpetrator was inspired by passionate anti-Semitism, the fault thus lying with those who taught him to hate the Jews; in another, the fact that the criminal acted in cold blood is held to diminish his responsibility, since it shows that he acted without passion and therefore from motives of pure obedience to his superiors. A fact should be recalled here which we mentioned in discussing the failure of denazification: it was necessary to pass a law offering all judges who had been members of special courts during the Nazi period the chance of retiring before reaching the age limit. A certain number of them eventually did so; they need not have troubled, however, as on December 6, 1968 a Berlin court acquitted Hans Joachim Rehse, formerly a member of the worst of Hitler's courts, the *Volksgerichtshof* under Roland Freisler, whose hundreds of death sentences included those passed on the conspirators of July 20, 1944. In conformity with a decision of the Federal High Court quashing Rehse's conviction, the Berlin court in its oral judgment and in a written exposé published some weeks later held that the *Volksgerichtshof* had been a normal judicial body and that the accused, being a member of it, had exercised his profession as a judge in a normal manner and in accordance with law and conscience. The Constitutional Court's ruling of December, 1953, which clearly exposed the falsity of such reasoning, might as well never have been uttered. The effect of the judgment at Berlin was to provoke a noisy manifestation by some thousands of young people belonging to the "nonparliamentary opposition." How indeed could they be expected to show respect for judges who on the one hand claimed to protect the liberal order against violence on the part of dissident students, and on the other exonerated their fellow magistrate who had shed blood as the faithful servant of a totalitarian regime bent on the extermination of its enemies?

In the academic world, a similarly unhealthy situation prevails. If we compare the movement of student protest during the 1960's in the Federal Republic with that in other countries, the first point to note is that many German professors did not, to say the least, have an impeccable record of civic virtue, and were thus not best qualified to set themselves up as defenders of liberal democracy. The students, who were moderate in their demands— but not moderate in their zeal for democracy—were not concerned to bring

about wholesale resignations, especially on the part of seniors who had themselves been young at the time of their transgression; but they did expect a
degree of frankness and modesty. The year 1964 was studded with incidents
involving the past careers of university rectors and deans. Did this involve the
conclusion that "no former servant of Hitler and Rosenberg should occupy
any position of prominence in Germany whatsoever?"[13] The question is not
easy to answer, and it is difficult to lay down hard-and-fast criteria. It was
certainly disgraceful that Otto Ambros, who had been in charge of the manufacture of poison by I. G. Farben*at Auschwitz-Monowitz and had hired out
moribund prisoners from the camp to provide labor for the SS, should have
again become a member of several boards within a few years after the "purge"
of the giant chemical trust. If we read the works published by Theodor
Maunz during the Nazi era, particularly that on police law which defended the
prerogatives of the Gestapo, we may be astonished that this professor of
public law, who was Bavarian Minister of Education from 1957 onward,
should not have been forced by public protest to resign his position until 1964.
On the Federal Government level, the clearest and most scandalous case was
that of Friedrich Karl Vialon, who was secretary-general of the Ministry of
Economic Cooperation (overseas aid) from 1962 to 1966: at Riga, where he
was head of the financial department of the office of the Reich Commissar for
the Eastern Territories from 1942 to 1944, he had signed appalling instructions for the "hire" of Jews to prospective employers and the seizure of their
property, including substantial quantities of shoes and underwear.

The case that aroused most publicity of all was that of Hans Globke, the
most trusted member of Adenauer's staff, who in 1936 published a commentary on the Nazi racial laws that, by his own admission, is "horrible and repugnant" to read. As to its effect at the time, the most divergent evidence has been
adduced: some say that it aggravated the force of the law, others that it created
loopholes that may have saved lives. Adenauer himself always stood up for
Globke, whom he took with him everywhere and finally promoted to State
Secretary. Globke was thus received in audience by the Pope, and on September 10, 1955 Khrushchev drank a birthday toast to him at the Kremlin. He
retired in 1963, aged sixty-five, after Adenauer withdrew from the chancellorship. He maintained till the last that he had never known anything about the
camps and had remained in his key post in Hitler's Ministry of the Interior
because the Church had asked him to do so. But, whatever the facts may have
been and whatever his motives, was it really necessary to let a man with such
a past share in the exercise of power? Assuming that we answer "No" to this
question, must we then hold that Günter Grass was right when he inveighed
in 1966 against Kiesinger becoming Chancellor? Should we defend the action
of Beate Klarsfeld, the excitable young woman who slapped Kiesinger's face
in public, or that of the writer Heinrich Böll, who sent her a bouquet of roses
after she had received a sentence of imprisonment (converted, on appeal, to a
suspended sentence) for her misdemeanor?

In our opinion, the conclusion in regard to Kiesinger does not follow. The
documentation assembled by Beate Klarsfeld[14] does not really amount to

*I. G. of course stands here for *Interessengemeinschaft* or trust, and not *Industriegewerkschaft* (trade union) as in chapter 8.

much, and we remain of the opinion expressed in our answer to Günter Grass on this subject.[15] As for Kiesinger's joining the Nazi Party in 1933, this was something the Catholic bishops had certainly not forbidden, nor was it an act of such heavy political consequences as voting for the Enabling Act, as Heuss did on March 23. During the war, Kiesinger was in charge of liaison between the Foreign and Propaganda Ministries and was a member of the council for broadcasting in occupied countries; this indeed gives more ground for disquiet, but his case is in no way comparable with that of F. K. Vialon, and we are bound to respect the testimony in his favor of such a courageous opponent of the regime as the clergyman Grüber. But above all, when Grass in his open letter asks how young people could object to the NPD as long as a man with Kiesinger's past was Chancellor, this argument plays directly into the NPD's hands, implying as it does that anyone with Kiesinger's past is politically a marked man for the rest of his life, whatever services he may have rendered to democracy since the war. What better way could there be of encouraging all the former hangers-on of Nazism to keep clear of the big parties, especially the CDU, and vote for the NPD instead?

Granted, we prefer Willy Brandt's record to his predecessor's; but it was hardly to be hoped for that the Federal Republic should be governed exclusively by heroes of the anti-Nazi resistance. In any case, if men are to be barred because of their past misdeeds, where is the line to be drawn? A writer who belongs to the extreme right has taken a malicious pleasure in collecting numerous statements by journalists, politicians, and academic figures of excellent repute and proving that they too were once members of the pro-Hitler chorus.[16] In some cases, it is true, past themes have been revived, as they were by Hans Zehrer, who once worked on the monthly *Die Tat* and was chief editor of *Die Welt* from 1953 to his death in 1966: in 1929–33, he inveighed against anti-Nazi intellectuals, and many of his editorials from Hamburg struck a similar note. But such cases are not numerous, while on the other hand there are publicists of the extreme right who gave no hostages to Nazism. One such was Leonhard Schlüter, the owner of a publishing firm that specialized in memories of the past: he was appointed Minister of Education for Lower Saxony in May, 1955, but was forced to resign by a rebellion of students at Göttingen University.

The whole problem is extremely complicated and beset with hypocrisy. A notable case was that of Erwin Schüle, the advocate-general who was in charge of the Ludwigsburg office for tracking down former Nazi criminals. In May, 1966, it appeared that he too did not have clean hands: the Russians had forwarded documents showing that he was implicated in cases of execution and ill-treatment. He resigned, but two years later it came to light that the charges were unfounded: the Russians announced that they had made a mistake. No one gave any publicity to this fact, partly because it was a good joke to call in question the past of a man holding such a position. There was more hypocrisy on the occasion of Ilse Koch's suicide: the spine-chilling stories in the popular press about her sadistic treatment of prisoners at Buchenwald were read with avidity because, among other things, they proved that the real, the only criminals were beings of a different stamp from you or me.[17] Altogether, no doubt, there is a strong dose of hypocrisy in the whole conception of

Vergangenheitsbewältigung, that is to say of "overcoming" the past without forgetting it.[18]

How do things stand in this respect in 1970, twenty-five years after Hitler's death? Two things may be stated at once. First, the extreme right, which barely conceals its admiration for the past, is of negligible importance: there are tiny groups and publications without number, but they have no real influence. Second, time is doing its work: in the nature of things, there are fewer and fewer men alive who held posts of responsibility in 1933–45. But what are the feelings, deep down, of the millions of former "little Nazis" who followed Hitler not because they wanted foreign conquest and concentration camps, but because he satisfied their love of order and dislike of "unruly elements"? These people vote and behave like reasonable beings; as the social environment changes, their *raison d'être* as a group tends inevitably to disappear. But every now and then, the challenge of left-wing intellectuals or turbulent students, not to speak of more truly violent elements, provokes outbursts of rage and hatred that are more dangerous to Germany's political health than a dozen journalistic rags extolling Hitler's victories.

There is, however, one element in society that has special difficulty in throwing off the weight of the past—namely, the army. In this case, the gradual disappearance of those who played an important part in serving Hitler will doubtless not of itself set minds at rest, either within the institution or among those who contemplate it from outside.

We shall see in chapter 11 how the decisions were taken that led to rearming Federal Germany. To understand the shock they produced we must remember the fierce antimilitarism of the victorious Allies, the bans they imposed and the promises they extracted from the Germans. The wholesale condemnation of professional soldiers went much too far: as in the case of denazification, it created a bond of interest among those who had done nothing wrong, those who had carried out orders contrary to the laws of war, and those who were themselves responsible for criminal acts. By the time judgments had cooled and distinctions came to be made, rearmament was already under consideration and the impression given was not that of belated justice but of seeking to cajole those whose services were required. Meanwhile the task of "re-educating" Germans had been a complete success as far as antimilitarism was concerned: youth movements, trade unions, and churches were all convinced that there must be a long period of training in civic duties and liberal democracy before there could be any question of again putting Germans into uniform.

At the time when plans for a German contribution to the defense of Europe were first discussed, gliding and fencing were still officially banned as "militaristic" pursuits. This would have been absurd if the very principle of rearmament had not involved a transformation of the idea of democracy. In 1949, a young German who expressed a horror of wearing uniform was praised to the skies for his attitude; now, instead of being a model pupil of Germany's accusers, he was himself accused. No doubt there was a greater measure of consistency among the anti-Nazis who continued to oppose every form of totalitarianism than among the former Nazi stalwarts who found their services required once more. Yet a German NCO who was ordered to prepare to fight on the same terrain as before against the same enemy might be forgiven for thinking that the war that threatened was simply a continuation of the previous one.

The battle over the rearmament issue was long, confused, and vehement. In Germany itself, as in France, people of divergent ways of thinking found themselves on the same side. Among those who said "yes" to the Chancellor's policy were democrats convinced of the danger of Soviet aggression and sincere "Europeans," but also skeptics who viewed the plan with resignation, former victims of "slander" who saw the chance of a come-back, and political realists who grasped that here was West Germany's opportunity. Among the "noes" were some who feared for German democracy or the effect on reunification, the *"ohne mich"* or "count me out" group with its anarchical tendency, conscientious objectors with high moral standards, victims of denazification who held that the authorities should first apologize to them, and nationalists who could not stomach any limitation of Germany's rights in the military field.

Necessarily, the conditions in which rearmament was prepared were out of the common. Although the principle of a German contingent had been accepted in the autumn of 1950, no practical progress could officially be made until the entry into force of the Paris agreements in May, 1955. In November, 1950, Theodor Blank, a CDU deputy and member of the executive of the Miners' Federation of the DGB, assumed the title and duties of "Representative of the Chancellor for Matters Connected with the Strengthening of Allied Forces" (*Beauftragter des Bundeskanzlers für die mit der Vermehrung der alliierten Truppen zusammenhängenden Fragen*)—a euphemism that must be admired for its ingenuity. From January, 1951, onward, Herr Blank took part in the negotiations for a European army, with the technical assistance of former Generals Hans Speidel and Adolf Heusinger. No one objected to these two names at the time; it was only in 1957, when Speidel was appointed to a NATO post, that a campaign was launched against him. For the moment, even the Socialists considered that if two former generals had to be chosen, these men were preferable to others. For close on to five years, they were, technically, civilians: only in November, 1955 was President Heuss able to sign their commissions as four-star generals, the highest rank in the Bundeswehr. Whatever their merits as human beings and soldiers, as lukewarm servants and cautious opponents of Nazism, it was inevitable that jokes of the following kind should start going the rounds:

Among the last lot of Germans repatriated from Russia was a general who had commanded a division at Stalingrad and was given twenty-five years in prison by a Soviet court. In the transit camp he ran across a former officer of his unit and they got talking. "By the way," says the general, "what became of Grand Admiral Dönitz, the submarine commander?" "Dönitz?" says the officer in surprise. "Why, he's at Spandau." "At Spandau? Whats an admiral doing there?" "Why, he's in prison, of course." "Ah, yes, of course. And what's Rommel's old chief of staff doing, General Speidel?" "Oh, he's in Paris," "In prison, I suppose?" "No, he's at NATO." "Oh, yes, of course. And Meyer, the tank general?" "Well, he's in Canada." "Yes, I see, with NATO." "No, no, he's in prison, of course." "Yes, of course. And how about our old chief of staff, General Heusinger?" "He's at Bonn."

"I see. Is he in prison?" "Good heavens, no, he's at the Ministry of Defense." Whereupon the repatriated general applies for admission to a lunatic asylum.[19]

This tale reflects what was passing through many minds, but it overlooks an important fact in connection with the new German army, namely the creation of a "Personnel Advisory Committee" (*Personalgutachterausschuss*—PGA) by a law of July 23, 1955 in which all parties concurred except the *Deutsche Partei*; the Bundestag at the same time elected the thirty-eight members of the commission from a list, drawn up by the government, comprising "persons respected in public life" and former regular officers known for their humane qualities and not themselves candidates for any high military or civil position. The chairman of the PGA was Dr. Otto Rombach, a former state secretary and Mayor of Aachen who had been dismissed by the Nazis in 1933. Among its other members were Frau Annedore Leber, the widow of a Socialist deputy who had been in a concentration camp and was executed after the coup of July, 1944—she herself had also been interned and had written an account of the German resistance; Fabian von Schlabrendorff, author of *The Secret War Against Hitler*; and General von Senger und Etterlin, the defender of Monte Cassino, who had always kept the Gestapo from interfering in his command and had been running a first-class educational establishment since 1949. The only restriction the law imposed on the commission's work was that it must be kept secret: apart from this, it was free to adopt its own rules. Despite the diversity of its members' origins and their political and religious convictions, it was almost always unanimous in its decisions. It finished its labors in 1957, having examined 600 cases in 400 sessions, plenary or otherwise. About 100 proposed appointments were eliminated either by an adverse vote of the commission or because they were withdrawn before it announced its decision. As early as December, 1955, it showed its independence by rejecting four colonels who had performed important duties under Herr Blank.

On a more permanent basis, the constitutional amendments and laws of 1955–56 embodied a whole system of guarantees for the political control and "liberalization" of the new army. The institution of the Parliamentary Commissioner was created, as we saw in chapter 6, and firm guarantees were given to conscientious objectors, both by amending the constitution in the sense of greater precision and by the details of the conscription law of July 6, 1956, the debate on which showed a remarkably high level of seriousness. Under this law, a request for exemption from military service must be submitted two weeks before the individual concerned appears before the draft board. If the board finds him unfit for service, the application lapses. If not, he is interviewed by a four-member commission consisting of a chairman with advisory functions, appointed by the minister, and three assessors "qualified by experience:" one of these is appointed by the *Land* government and the other two are chosen annually by lot from a list representing various districts of the *Land*. The definition of an objector is "any person who is opposed on conscientious grounds to all use of force as between states," that is to say, it recognizes only a general and systematic objection based on conscience and not, for example, the attitude of someone who might object to serving lest, as a result, he may one day be obliged to fire on fellow Germans.

In practice, there have been few difficulties in applying the law, except on occasion as regards the civilian duties to be performed in lieu of military service. The commissions have shown much good will and understanding in carrying out their task. For a long time, the number of applications for exemption was in fact low: it averaged 3,400 a year from 1956 to 1967, four-fifths of these being recognized as genuine. Seventy per cent of the applicants were students or had at least passed their *Abitur*. The figure then rose sharply as a corollary of the protest movement at schools and universities: in 1967, it was twice as high as in 1966, and in 1968 it again quadrupled. In 1969, the *rate* of increase fell off, the figure being 14,374 as against 11,798 the previous year, out of a contingent of 177,000. In 1969, there was actually a falling-off as regards one category of applications included in the figures, namely those from soldiers already in service, who asked for a discharge on conscientious grounds; in that year, these numbered 2,508.

This increase in the number of objectors took place at a time when the new army was once again questioning itself on its own organization, its mission, and its place in society. Its self-interrogation took the form of numerous and often clumsy statements by generals and of a manifesto by some young officers. The questions they raised have never ceased to be ventilated, for the good reason that it is hard to find satisfactory answers to them.

When the Bundeswehr uniforms were seen for the first time, the prestige of a military career stood at its lowest level, and since then it has not appreciably risen. Opinion polls show again and again that a general is far less looked up to than a bishop or an industrialist, a professor or a minister of state, and that few are attracted by military life: so few indeed that in 1969 the army was short of at least 2,580 officers and 31,000 NCO's. Recourse was had to press publicity to remedy the situation, and it is significant that the advertisements were aimed (as they are in other countries) at young men interested in acquiring technical skills they could afterward turn to good use in other walks of life.

Certainly successive governments and Ministers of Defense—not excluding Helmut Schmidt, the present incumbent and a Socialist—have always indicated their respect for the army and shown indulgence toward those of its leaders who were guilty of ill-chosen language. But it must be realized that many officers, not necessarily of the highest rank, feel that the army is, so to speak, under a permanent cloud, and that most citizens put up with it as an institution but would get rid of it if they could. This goes far to explain the political behavior of individual officers in recent years. For the first decade or so, they almost all voted for the CDU as a matter of course. Then it became clear that some were gravitating toward the SPD, out of discontent and in order to find a new political and social orientation, while others moved toward the NPD. In the 1965 elections, the polling stations in places where the military were most in evidence registered in some cases a third more and in others twice as many votes for the extreme right as compared with the regional average.[20]

Despite appearances, the relationship between the army and political society is not the same as in France, for instance. France, of course, knows the meaning of antimilitarism, and the French army too has doubts concerning its place in society and its significance from the military point of view. But there are also considerable differences. In the Federal Republic, the absence of a truly national theme prevents many citizens, and especially young people, from regarding the army as a symbol of the nation and as performing a useful function for that reason alone, whatever its importance in the practical sphere. Second, the French army has a tradition of past military glory to which it can appeal, whether the battles in question were always victorious or not, whereas the soldiers of the Bundeswehr must speak of their fathers' triumphs in a whisper, disavowing the past as completely as they can—even though books about Rommel are bestsellers both in Germany and abroad. When the German navy launched a ship named after an admiral who was sentenced at Nuremberg, the outcry that resulted was no doubt fully justified, but we should nevertheless understand its psychological effects.

Finally, the German army is bound to have doubts about its own military role because it is debarred from access to what are officially called in France "modern armaments," that is to say, nuclear weapons. It is never particularly pleasant to think of oneself as the "poor bloody infantry" of an alliance. The most serious crisis that has broken out between the Federal Government and the army leaders had much more to do with purely military aspects of organization and weaponry than with any question of the army interfering in politics. This was the dispute in the summer of 1966 between, on the one hand, Kai-Uwe von Hassel and his state secretary Gumbel and, on the other, General Heinz Trettner, the inspector-general of the Bundeswehr, and General Werner Panitzki, the inspector of the air force. The affair, which ended with the resignation of both generals, arose, it is true, over what seemed to be quite a different question—namely, the right of military men to join a trade union. The ÖTV (Federation of Public Servants and Transport Workers Union) had begun to recruit army members with the government's approval: the latter stuck to its position and received spectacular support from General Count Wolf von Baudissin, at that time NATO chief of staff, who himself publicly joined the ÖTV, an event one could scarcely imagine happening in any other country. This officer, together with General Ulrich de Maizière—who took General Trettner's place in 1966—had, from 1951 onward, been the chief advocate of two ambitious and controversial ideas: that of the soldier as a "citizen in uniform" and that of "*Innere Führung*," an ambiguous term by which is meant both the system of command within the army and the self-discipline of the individual officer. In 1969, after both officers had retired, these principles were called into question by their successors, who were more inclined to revert to orthodox ideas of discipline and less prone to break with military tradition in general.

Nevertheless the reformers seem to have gained their point inasmuch as there is a strong conflict of generations within the army, and the young officers who make themselves heard put forward extremely modern-sounding views—so much so that they fall at times into sociological jargon, as in the case of the "nine theses" advanced by a group of twenty lieutenants.[21] According to them, an officer is a man engaged in doing a job like any other; he discusses the orders he receives and is prepared to discuss his own, and he regards military discipline as a good thing provided it is the result of self-discipline based on the maturity of the individual. He is in the service of peace: his duty is to restore it in case of conflict, to maintain it, and, as a citizen, to help to organize it (*Friedenswiederherstellung, Friedenserhaltung, Friedensgestaltung*). For young officers of this way of thinking, the problem of "overcoming the past" is certainly no longer an issue.

The Churches

Among the organized forces that help to shape German democracy by their influence on public life, the churches continue to hold a privileged position, notwithstanding the changes that are taking place in them and in society at large. This is due first and foremost to their legal status. In France, ever since the separation of Church and State, religion has been a purely personal affair and does not figure in official records. But in Germany, where there has been no such separation, a person has to state his religion in almost every form he fills out. In February, 1957, the Bundestag passed a law on marital status, the government draft of which provided that the marriage lines should indicate the religious denomination of the husband and wife. The relevant committee replaced this by the provision that, "if they agree" (*im Falle ihres Einverständnisses*), there should be an indication of their legal membership or nonmembership in a church or a religious or ideological body (*Weltanschauungsgemeinschaft*). The Socialists attempted in vain to have the whole passage deleted, or at least amended by altering "if they agree" to read "if they so desire" (*auf Wunsch*). Thus it was necessary, under the law as adopted, to raise a specific objection in order that one's religion might remain a private affair.

In the same way, one has to take a positive step in order to cease belonging officially to one's church, and until doing so one remains liable for the church tax (*Kirchensteuer*), which is levied by the state on behalf of the respective churches. Not many people do divest themselves of church membership in this way, and if they do so it is usually a case of Catholics becoming Protestant or vice versa. In 1966, for example, 22,000 people left the Catholic Church while 13,000 entered it; the corresponding figures for the Protestant denominations as a whole were 38,000 and 32,000.[22] At the 1961 census, 51·1 per cent of the population were Protestants, including 0·5 per cent belonging to "*Freikirchen*" or churches not affiliated to the main organization, while 44·1 per cent were Roman Catholics, and only 2·8 per cent were *gemeinschaftslos*, that is, not members of any religious denomination.

The *Kirchensteuer* provides the churches with considerable revenues. In 1968 alone it represented over DM1,700 million for the Protestant churches and over DM1,300 million for the Catholics. Its amount is fixed as a percentage of income tax, varying from 8 to 10 per cent in different areas. The proceeds of the tax, together with gifts and income from properties, are used to finance all kinds of activities, including some 10,000 kindergartens, thousands of homes and orphanages, and about 1,000 hospitals. There is also a particularly active religious press, and much is done for foreign workers in Germany and for the provision of aid to developing countries. At the same time, the fiscal situation of the churches has led to increasing discontent. From the financial point of view, while the citizen grudgingly accepts the burden of highly progressive taxation by the state, he is less pleased that the church should profit every time he moves into a higher tax bracket. As an independent agent, he wonders

227

if this sort of duress is really appropriate to the present day; and from the point of view of Christian ethics, he may ask whether such well-endowed churches are really servants of the poor or merely "charitable organizations" of a social type.

However, the most important aspect of the religious "establishment" is its role in education. Each *Land* is empowered to determine as it thinks fit the part played respectively by confessional schools (*Bekenntnisschulen*) and non-denominational or "community" schools (*Gemeinschaftsschulen*), which may either take pupils of different denominations or be secular in the French sense, with religious instruction excluded from the normal curriculum. The Catholic Church has long held out for confessional schools. In 1967, for instance, the Vatican intervened directly in the debates on school legislation in Baden-Württemberg and North Rhine–Westphalia, by means of a letter from the nuncio, Mgr. Corrado Bafile, to the foreign minister: this led to a fresh dispute over the 1933 Concordat, an issue that might be thought to have been closed since the judgment of the Constitutional Court and the Lower Saxony Concordat of 1965. In this matter, the Catholic Church is fighting a rearguard action against the general trend of opinion which is strongly opposed to separate confessional schools, though these remain the norm in a *Land* such as Bavaria. This trend is based on material necessity and the need to reorganize education, and also on changes within the Church itself. Meanwhile, the most absurd situations have existed at times, and some of them still do. In a new quarter on the outskirts of Bonn, a particular school building was used, from the moment it was put up, by Catholics and Protestants according to the time of day: at certain hours, Catholic pupils were taught by Catholic teachers using Catholic books, while at others the Protestants took over. And there are many complaints about the "segregation" of school bus services, with separate vehicles picking up Catholic and Protestant children.

The sharing of buildings as just described has little to do with the fact that in the postwar devastation many churches, both Catholic and Protestant, were used by either denomination. At that time there was, it is true, a certain effacement of the barrier between the two Christian communities, while some years later they were again sharply divided and sometimes even antagonistic. Shortly before his death in 1954, Herman Ehlers, the President of the Bundestag, said of his fellow members of the CDU: "In 1945 we worked together because our faith helped to bring us together. Today we work together although our faiths divide us."[23] During the 1950's, it was not only within the CDU that a strict balance had to be kept between the two confessions: throughout the state apparatus, it was of such importance to hold the scales even that candidates whose religious views were unknown often came off worst in the competition for posts which they desired but which had to be awarded to one side or the other.

By degrees, however, the religious criterion has lost much of its importance thanks to the progress of the ecumenical spirit and the decline of sectarianism even in parochial circles—although the story is still told of the Catholic parents who were appalled to hear that their son intended to marry a Protestant, but learnt with relief that she was only a prostitute. This anecdote would not be so very improbable in many a small town, and, as far as statistics go, we learn that 70 per cent of the marriages contracted in 1968 were between persons of the same denomination. Nevertheless, a profound change is taking place, as may be shown by a small example. As late as 1960, a visitor to Cologne Cathedral might buy for 50 pfennige a pamphlet on mixed marriages that described their consequences in frightening terms and summed up by saying that even the best mixed marriage was an unfortunate marriage (*Unglücksehe*), since, if the Catholic partner were the first to die, the children's faith would be in great danger, and, moreover, he or she would have no one to pray for them. In 1969, at the same stall and for the same price, one could buy a pamphlet showing how much common ground there was not only between Catholics and Protestants but between Christians and atheists, and declaring that atheism in the West was "an atheism of human solidarity."[24]

In the chaos of 1945 the churches appeared to be the only institutions still unshaken, the only refuge to which people could turn for material and moral succor, the only voice that could speak for a shattered Germany. But how far were they morally entitled to share in building a new society based on rejection of the principles of the Third Reich?

On August 23, 1945, the Catholic bishops assembled at Fulda and issued a declaration giving an account of the behavior of German Catholics under the Nazi regime. The bishops recalled how they themselves had "intervened on behalf of human rights" and "resisted the state's encroachments upon the life of the Church," and they acknowledged the bravery of parents who had made a stand for Catholic schools. At the same time, they regretfully acknowledged that:

Many Germans, including some in our own ranks, allowed themselves to be deceived by the false doctrines of National Socialism and looked on with indifference while crimes were committed against freedom and human dignity; many lent support to the criminals by their attitude, and many became criminals themselves. A heavy responsibility lies upon those who might, by their influence, have prevented these crimes and who not only did not do so but actually helped to make them possible and thus became the criminals' accomplices.

The bishops' statement was not quite so clear as it looked at first sight. In the first place, were some of the bishops themselves included among those who "might, by their influence, have prevented these crimes"? What about the Pope himself? Few historical problems have given rise to such passionate controversy as this one: some of the best informed books appeared in the 1960's and were provoked by Rolf Hochhuth's play *The Deputy*, a work of uneven merit.[25] The debate, which still goes on, touches fundamental problems of faith and morals. What is the Catholic Church's reply to the question "Who is my neighbor"? How does the Church define the evil aspects of political society that it feels called on to combat, and has it the right and the duty to attempt to influence that society on moral grounds?

Between 1933 and 1945, the Catholic Church, in Germany as elsewhere, tended to distinguish sharply between the rights of Catholics and those of others. All the evidence shows that the Church in general cooperated with the Nazi regime and only made a stand when it seemed to be attacking Catholics or Catholicism. Under the Concordat of July, 1933, Catholic bishops were obliged to swear an oath of allegiance to the Nazi Government at a time when it had already set up concentration camps and was persecuting Communists, Socialists, and Jews. No doubt the Church's behavior was no different from that of the great majority of Germans and organized forces in Germany; but the example of everyone else is not a defense against actions of doubtful morality. In all the documents one reads, one is struck by the persistence of the theme: "We must look after the Catholics first." When the bishop of Münster, Count von Galen, spoke out against euthanasia—successfully, since one of Hitler's massacres was halted thereby—would he have done so with such emphasis if Catholics had not been involved? We may well ask this question when we observe that a distinction was invariably drawn, for reasons unconnected with mere tactics, between Jews by faith and those who were baptized. And while the Church in Germany bent most of its efforts to defending its own members, the Pope himself seems to have been concerned above all with the fate of his German flock, and to have been paralyzed in defending the rest of humanity by fears of what might happen to German Catholics.

There was, moreover, a high degree of interdependence between the attitudes of the German faithful and those of their pastors at all levels including the Vatican. If it was true that reminding German Catholics of their duty as Christians would have had the effect of estranging them from Rome, does this not mean that their "fidelity" was more of a sociological than a religious character? Is it in fact the case that, rather than make a stand against Hitler's war policy or the subsequent wholesale atrocities, the Vatican thought it more important to retain the allegiance of Catholics who were such by baptism but not by conduct or Christian morality? This is a point, perhaps, in which the Catholic Church as a whole has changed most fundamentally since 1945—as witness, for instance, the stand taken by some bishops in the southern states of the United States against segregationist members of their flock, or, above all, the attitude of the French episcopate to the Algerian war. When Mgr. Duval, the bishop of Algiers, spoke out against the great majority of local Catholics in protest against the treatment of Muslims, he was bearing witness to a different conception of duty toward one's neighbor than were the German bishops or the Holy See during the Nazi period.

It should be added that German Catholics, clergy and laity alike, were for the most part Germans first and Catholics afterward: that is to say, they tended to regard as "neighbors" their compatriots rather than their fellow Catholics or mankind in general. This, of course, is not an attitude confined to Germans; but the bishops in Germany were more infected with the nationalist doctrine of mystic brotherhood than their opposite numbers in other countries. Another point we must bear in mind is that until very recent times the Catholic Church's quarrel with totalitarianism has been mainly a function of the degree to which it interfered with private life and with specifically religious matters. When, in 1937, the Vatican condemned Nazism in the encyclical *Mit brennender Sorge* and Communism in *Divini Redemptoris*, it did so mainly on the ground of the former's paganism and the latter's atheism, both of which were actively and aggressively opposed to religious freedom and the rights of individual believers, especially those who were fathers of families. In comparison, the suppression of public liberties, the insistence on political conformity, and the persecution of opponents seemed to be matters of secondary concern. This is not altogether surprising, since the eighteenth-century values enshrined in the American Constitution or the French Declaration of Human Rights, while they can certainly be found in the Gospel, are not, as a whole, very much in line with Catholic tradition. Freedom of conscience and the toleration of enemies are not precisely part of the Roman heritage. Pius XI signed the Concordat in 1933 because he took Hitler for a faithful disciple of Mussolini and thought he would be tamed by the exercise of power. Apart from the profound misunderstanding of Nazism, what is important here is that Italian Fascism was acceptable to the Papacy.

For that matter, why should it not have been? The Church is supposed to be neutral as between one political regime and another. If "render unto Caesar" means anything at all, surely it applies to the organization of the state? Here, Papal teaching and the Church's opponents are at one: it is not the business of Rome to interfere in the workings of political society, and the more it does so, the more it is liable to criticism. Even some of its own members deny that it has any right to attempt to influence governments or those who obey their orders. When the German bishops, on March 28, 1933, lifted the ban on National Socialism and enjoined the faithful to respect lawful authority and abstain from illegal or subversive action, were they not simply conforming to the electorate's decision of March 5 and the Reichstag vote of the 23rd? If they had spoken otherwise, would they not have been encroaching on Caesar's domain? One might, however, feel, as they apparently did not, that even in 1933 the Nazi regime was setting itself against Catholic values, since persecution had begun and the prisons were full. Similarly, the Church may well take the view, which many of its adversaries dispute, that laws affecting education or marriage involve important principles of religion. Obviously, conflict is bound to arise over the justification of a decision by the Church to remain silent or to intervene—against who or what? A particular act of government, or a regime as such? Faced with Nazi rule in Germany, ought the Church to have protested in single instances or condemned the system root and branch? If it had done the latter, what would this have meant for German Catholics? Should the Church have called on them to disobey the civil power and attempt its overthrow? A wholesale condemnation would have made the Church an instigator if not an organizer of rebellion—a role hardly consistent with the respect for constituted authority that is part of its tradition. In his famous sermons in the summer of 1941, Bishop von Galen denounced the power of the Gestapo and the system of arbitrary arrests, but he also said: "We Christians are not revolutionaries. We shall go on doing our duty.... We shall go on fighting against the enemy outside our gates; as to the enemy within, the one who is torturing and beating us, we cannot take up arms against him."

The German clergy paid a heavy tribute to Nazi barbarism. At Dachau alone, the Americans found 326 German priests, not counting the many who had perished. But those members of the German resistance who were inspired by Catholic faith received no encouragement from the Church as an institution: the most that was sanctioned was to refuse to carry out some specific act, and in no circumstances must the faithful seek to overthrow the regime by violence. But how else is one to overthrow a totalitarian regime? In any case, one can imagine other ways in which the Church might have intervened. A Lenten pastoral issued in 1960 by the bishops and Church commissioners in East Germany contained a passage headed "You must not take part directly and expressly in acts that offend the Christian conscience," and included the words: "If the exercise of a certain profession obliges you to turn away from the Church or to lead a life contrary to Christian precepts, we must counsel you with a heavy heart to give up that profession." The Church never uttered such words in 1933–45, even in unspoken reference to Catholics serving in the SS.

By 1960, however, the Catholic Church had evolved in many respects, and in Germany, at least, that evolution cannot be thought of apart from the lasting memory of what took place under Nazism. In 1962, three weeks before the opening of the second Vatican Council, the bishops at Fulda issued a further declaration:

In this historic hour we exhort all those under our pastoral care to do penance from the bottom of their hearts for all the appalling crimes committed by godless rulers in the name of the German people and in violation of fundamental human rights.

In thus appealing for penance we recall once again with special emphasis the inhuman acts aimed at the destruction of that Jewish people which transmitted to humanity the revelation of the one true God and to which Jesus Christ, the Savior of the world, belonged according to the flesh.

German Catholicism, in fact, had entered upon a mood of self-examination. Since 1945, its attitudes in general have been marked by a double tendency, which has had its effect on interconfessional relations. To begin with, in the mid-1950's, a sort of regression took place in many fields, while in others there seemed to be an impasse. Despite geography, Catholicism in Germany seemed to be somewhere between the French and Spanish positions in such matters as Church-State relations, the idea and practice of tolerance, education, social problems, attitudes to Communism and intervention in politics. But whereas German Catholicism was, at that time and in most respects, somewhat on the conservative side by international standards, there has since been a change, and at the beginning of the 1970's one may feel that Germany has, as it were, returned to its rightful place between France and the Netherlands.

In the field of industrial relations, the *Katholikentag* (assembly or congress of German Catholics, first held in 1848), in a meeting at Bochum in 1949, solemnly pronounced in favor of comanagement in a statement that declared that "the right of codetermination, enjoyed by all who are concerned together in social, personal, and economic matters, is a natural right, part of the Divine ordinance and corresponding to their joint responsibility." The Bochum resolutions were strongly influenced by the editors and friends of the review *Frankfurter Hefte*. Immediately afterward, however, there were signs of a reaction. Cardinal Frings, the archbishop of Cologne and president of the episcopal council, was not wholly in agreement with the resolutions: in the same year, he published a book that was much more cautious in tone and did not clearly favor the participation of wage earners, on an equal basis, in the management of industrial and commercial enterprises. He appealed to the employers' generosity and goodness of heart, and urged that "working-class children who are especially gifted intellectually or morally" be given a chance to rise in the social scale. While touching on the problem of the workers' sense of alienation, the book did not call in question the structure of society as such.

In subsequent *Katholikentage*, problems of social justice came much less to the fore. The hierarchy showed less and less sympathy for "left-wing" Catholics, and there was no occasion on which German prelates took a hand in social conflicts and supported strikers in the name of justice, as often happened during the same years in France. Whereas many of the French clergy looked on Catholic activities in working-class circles as a way of proving that the Church was no longer solely the ally of the *bourgeoisie*, whatever it may have been in the past, in Germany the stress in such activities was chiefly on reclaiming the workers for Christianity. The most energetic intervention by the hierarchy took place in 1956, in connection with collective bargaining in the Ruhr iron and steel works, when the owners were prepared to agree to a 42-hour week provided Sunday were made a normal working day. Chancellor Adenauer, the Catholic Church, and to some extent the Protestants raised strong objections to this, but were unable to prevent the *Land* government from endorsing the agreement reached between the owners and the Metal Workers' Union.

As regards relations with the Soviet bloc, the Church was faced with two problems: that of Communism and Soviet power, and that of the position of Catholics in East Germany. The anti-Communism of German Catholics was not identical with that of the Church in France, or rather it generally coincided with that of a particular section of French Catholicism, being based not only on religious and moral grounds but also on a belief in the superior merits of "Western civilization" which, for the most part, ruled out any consideration of objections to that civilization from behind the Iron Curtain. As regards the East German Catholics, relations were marked by a kind of uneasiness, which came to the surface at the *Katholikentag* held at Cologne from August 29 to September 2, 1956, when Bishop Spülbeck of Meissen in East Germany summed up the situation in a remarkable address:

You must talk to one another, and by so doing preserve the unity of our German language, which will otherwise be split asunder by our separation. You, my brothers and sisters from the GDR, must not turn this congress into a Wailing Wall for your discontents. And you, my dear friends in the West, must not regard us simply as poor relations on a visit. . . . You have heard the distress of soul of our brothers in the GDR—can you go on living as carefree as before? Your standard of living may fill us with envy, but is there not also much distress among you, and throughout the world? Should you not think of accepting restrictions of your own accord?[26]

The congress did not go very far into these questions: it did its best to avoid awkward topics, and many East Germans went away disappointed. But how far was it possible to tackle themes with political implications, when the Church appeared more than ever identified with a particular party? Here again there was a significant difference as compared with France. At an international meeting of Catholic journalists at the Abbey of Maria Laach, the French team were divided on all points save one: they rejoiced in their own divisions in so

233

far as these reflected a political pluralism, the exact contrary of the idea of a single Christian party. In the Federal Republic, on the other hand, the dominant view was that prevailing, for instance, in Belgian political life—namely, that Catholics should compromise among themselves, even if they could not reconcile all their differences, so as to form a single party that could make itself felt in matters directly affecting the Church, especially school questions.

In this spirit, on June 2, 1957, Bishop Keller of Münster made a speech to the Catholic Workers' Union (KAB) that attracted much attention. Having laid down that education, while exclusively a question for the *Länder*, was a fundamental issue for Catholics, he declared that the question "Can a believing Catholic vote in good conscience for the SPD?" must be answered with a "categorical negative." Similar though less emphatic statements were made in the ensuing weeks, and on Sunday, September 8, a pastoral letter read in all churches gave the faithful a clear intimation that they should vote CDU. The Chancellor, realizing no doubt that statements like that of Bishop Keller were apt to antagonize Protestant voters, sought to broaden the debate by declaring that Germans had the choice between Christianity and Communism, an alternative the designers of CDU posters expressed in the form: "Ollenhauer instead of Adenauer? Marxism instead of Christianity?"

There was, indeed, a more open-minded Catholic minority that continued to exist and to make itself heard: such men as Father von Nell-Breuning or Walter Dirks had a deeper insight into social and political realities. But they were at this time much less representative of German Catholicism than the vehement *Rheinische Merkur*, which judged and condemned without a shadow of self-doubt, while the weekly *Michael*, which had been the mouthpiece of some of the more unruly young Catholics, had turned into the very sedate *Allgemeine Sonntagszeitung*.

The change of direction in the 1960's was symbolized by the attitude of Cardinal Frings at the Vatican Council, where, to the surprise of many, he ranged himself with the more liberal prelates. This is not to say that German Catholicism had, before then, been stationary or retrograde in every sphere: throughout the postwar period, its theologians had been remarkable for the wealth and vitality of their ideas. Nor, on the other hand, did political attitudes change overnight: in 1965 the bishops' pre-election manifesto was a scarcely disguised call to vote for the CDU, though this did not prevent the SPD from increasing its support by 15 per cent and the CDU from dropping by 0·5 per cent in areas whose population was over 75 per cent Catholic. Nevertheless, it was clear in the early 1960's that an evolution had begun, and after 1965 it gathered momentum rapidly. In May, 1969, the bishops' conference, with the election in view, came out strongly for political pluralism. Prior to this, the central committee of German Catholics had issued a declaration of neutrality as between political parties. This committee had taken the noteworthy step of including the Social Democratic minister Georg Leber among its leaders, and had incidentally also changed its name. It had evolved in 1952 from the central committee of the *Katholikentage*, as a body responsible for coordinating the work of Catholic organizations in general. Described as an "association (*Zusammenschluss*)—authorized and supported by the episcopate—of forces active in the lay apostolate of the Catholic Church in Germany," it was in fact

looked on by the hierarchy as a means of gaining control of Catholic movements and groups. In June, 1967, its plenary assembly adopted a new statute
defining it as an association, "recognized by the conference of German
bishops, of institutions, groups, and persons active in the lay apostolate"
et cetera. This change was responsible for some confusion in the committee's
ranks, its members being less and less certain of their role vis-à-vis the hierarchy, the Catholic community, and society at large.

The Catholic youth organizations, on the other hand, which are combined
in the *Bund der Deutschen Katholischen Jugend* (BDKJ), have, if one may so
put it, become rejuvenated. After the war, this association, under the leadership of Josef Rommerskirchen and Heinrich Köppler, showed much firmness
in maintaining its freedom of decision in secular matters and in cooperating to
a marked extent with other youth movements. In spite of its large membership,
it gave the impression of being an avant-garde movement, particularly in the
international field. Then, after a period during which it simmered down and
lost its drive, it began once again to show independence and initiative, as well
as a sense of responsibility in balancing between the Catholic "establishment"
and organized movements of youthful protest.[27] These latter made a spectacular appearance at the *Katholikentag* at Essen in September, 1968, which
was doubtless a livelier gathering than any of the eighty-one that preceded
it.[28] Several of the sessions were disturbed, and many were dominated, by the
group of revolutionary youths who styled themselves the KAPO, adding a
K (for *katholisch*) to the initials of the "nonparliamentary opposition." But
the main feature of the congress was perhaps the unprecedented phenomenon
of dissent between a majority of German Catholics and the Pope on the
subject of birth control and the encyclical *Humanae Vitae*.

In these ways, the *Katholikentag* demonstrated that, in Germany as in
other countries, the problem of relations between the Church and political
society has in some degree changed its nature. Relations with parties are of
less importance, and pluralism is more and more accepted and practiced. But
this is largely because the whole basis of political society is under challenge, a
fact that tends to blur the distinction between parties operating within the
same institutional framework, and also because the definition of politics has
considerably widened, so that activities the Church formerly claimed to
regulate in terms of individual morality are now recognized as matters of
concern to the community.

There remains, however, at least one specifically German problem—namely, the "German problem" itself. After the more rigid positions of the 1950's
had been relaxed, two major questions still remained unsolved: that of the
Catholics in East Germany and that of relations with the Churches further
east, especially in Poland. Here West German Catholicism has shown itself
rather timid, because Catholics in the G.D.R. are a small minority and because it is divided from Catholicism in Poland by two formidable obstacles.
How can the Church in Germany admit the possibility of a Catholic community in close liaison with a Socialist society? And how could it accept the
idea of the territories east of the Oder-Neisse line being organized into Polish
dioceses? That is a step that even Rome had not yet taken by the middle of
1970.

On November 18, 1965, on the occasion of the second Vatican Council, the Polish episcopate addressed to their fellow bishops in Germany a long letter signed by Cardinal Stefan Wyszyński and thirty-five archbishops, bishops, and auxiliary bishops. Despite the harsh wording of some passages and the incompleteness, to say the least, of its survey of history, the letter definitely constituted a peace overture. The reply, dated in Rome on December 5, was signed by Cardinals Joseph Frings, Julius Döpfner, and Lorenz Jaeger, together with thirty-nine other dignitaries of the Catholic Church in West and East Germany. It was shorter than the Polish bishops' letter and was clumsily phrased: by appearing to suggest to the Polish bishops some kind of negotiation concerning the frontier and the "right to one's native soil" (*Heimatrecht*), the German bishops placed their Polish colleagues in a situation of great embarrassment vis-à-vis the Warsaw Government, which was only too delighted to have an opportunity to impugn the Church's patriotism.[29] The exchange of letters thus failed in its purpose. More than two years later, on March 2, 1968, a group of Catholic intellectuals known as the Bensberg Circle published a memorandum calling for a dialogue with the Poles, to be conducted without prior conditions and in an unprejudiced spirit, with full awareness of what Poland had suffered at Germany's hands. This courageous document, which did not however commit the Catholic Church, came three years after another memorandum that did fully commit the Protestant Church in Germany.

The German Protestants' examination of conscience was more thoroughgoing, but less fully representative than that of the Catholics. The leaders who met in 1945 to lay the foundations of a new union of evangelical churches in Germany went further than the Catholic bishops along the path of introspection and humility; but they themselves represented only one section of Protestantism as it had existed in Hitler's Reich.

The confession of errors was made in accordance with the Biblical precept "Let each remember his own sins." At Stuttgart, on October 18, 1945, the leaders of the new Evangelical Church in Germany (*Evangelische Kirche in Deutschland*—EKD), founded at Treysa on August 31, received the delegates of what later became the World Council of Churches with the words: "We accuse ourselves for not having confessed our faith with more courage, prayed with more devotion, believed with more joy, and loved with more fervor." At Treysa, the Protestant leaders had already laid bare their fundamental error: "A mistaken view of Lutheranism led us to think that our whole duty toward the state was to render obedience ourselves, to preach obedience to Christians, and show them how to obey, except only if the state should command what was manifestly sinful."[30] The men who spoke thus were among the founders and leaders of the small group of German Protestants who did fight against Nazism.

The "German Christian" movement, which came into being in 1932, had espoused the Nazi ideas of blood and race and believed in a "hero-Savior, suitable for German piety." When Hitler came to power, he encouraged these

Deutsche Christen to found a unified *Reichskirche* embracing the twenty-nine German Protestant churches, under a "Reich bishop" who enjoyed the *Führer*'s confidence. The movement grew more and more pagan, and in the end it was nothing but an instrument of Nazi dictatorship. But it had to contend, in and after 1933, with the opposition of Protestant dignitaries and a group of young theologians headed by men like Martin Niemöller and Hans Lilje. In May, 1934, at the Synod of Barmen (Wuppertal), the Confessing Church (*Bekennende Kirche*) was brought into being by these leaders and proclaimed itself the only authentic German Protestant Church. Internal dissensions led to a schism in 1936, but each group continued to fight against the "German Christians" and the Nazis. It was the leaders of these groups of the Confessing Church who assembled at Treysa in Hesse in 1945, and the name they chose for the new unified body was profoundly significant. From 1933 to 1945, the "German Evangelical Church" (*Deutsche Evangelische Kirche*) had implied by its name a specifically German type of Protestantism, whereas the new title denoted the Evangelical Church *in* Germany—in other words, a German branch of world Protestantism. The presense of foreign churchmen at Stuttgart, and their fraternal attitude—refusing to act as accusers and prompt to examine their own consciences—enabled the EKD to begin its life inspired by the ecumenical spirit, which it has not since lost.

As finally organized at Eisenach in 1948, the EKD consisted of a federation of twenty-seven autonomous *Landkirchen*, each under a bishop (*Landesbischof*) or president (*Kirchenpräsident*). It was not itself, properly speaking a church, but an organization empowered to represent the member churches vis-à-vis the civil power, to coordinate their activities, and, when necessary, to act as the mouthpiece of German Protestantism. Its controlling bodies were the general Synod of 120 members, 100 of whom represented the *Landeskirchen* in numbers corresponding to their respective size; the churches' conference, with one representative for each member church; and the church council, a sort of executive composed of twelve elected members. One of the council's three permanent bureaus, the *Kirchliches Aussenamt*, dealt with foreign relations. The EKD comprised two large groups of churches. First, ten of the thirteen Lutheran *Land* churches had combined in 1948 to form a United Evangelical Lutheran Church affiliated to the Lutheran World Federation at Geneva: its dominant figure, until his retirement in 1969, was Hans Lilje, the bishop of Hanover. Second, there was a "United Church" going back to old Prussian days, having been set up by administrative decree in 1818: the churches included in it were of a less dogmatic complexion.

The Protestant leaders sought to eradicate the tradition of blind obedience to authority, and for this purpose to develop a civic sense in both clergy and laity and to educate them in political, social, and international realities. In 1945, they set up "Evangelical Academies," which were a pronounced success, although not all of them maintained an equal level of vigorous thought, independence, and courage in their approach to burning questions of the day. Among the laity, the *Kirchentag* (church congress) movement developed under the leadership of Reinold von Thadden-Trieglaff, who became its president. The *Kirchentage*, like the *Katholikentage*, were huge gatherings of the faithful, held after preparation at the parish level. Apart from the plenary meetings, each *Kirchentag* split up into study groups that concentrated on various aspects of the chosen theme for the year. In the social field, the EKD's activity was facilitated by the existence of "social secretariats" in the member churches.

For more than twenty years, however—up to the time of the meeting of the EKD Council in West Berlin on September 26, 1969 at which it was obliged to recognize the formation of the Federation of Protestant Churches in the G.D.R.—no social problem was of such concern to the German Protestant movement as that of its own unity, which is indissolubly linked to the question of the unity of Germany itself. The *Kirchentag* held at Berlin in 1951 took as its motto: "We are brothers nevertheless." Almost as many Germans from the G.D.R. attended it as from the West. The EKD made no distinction between them: the Lutheran *Land* churches of Hanover or Bavaria were in theory closer to those of Saxony or Thuringia than they were to the churches of Baden or the Palatinate. Although the population of the F.R.G. was three times that of the G.D.R., the latter was four-fifths Protestant and contained 43 per cent of the Protestant population of Germany as a whole. The political schism, therefore, was most keenly felt by the Evangelical Church, which strove at all costs to prevent it from becoming more complete.

In a similar way, world Protestantism was concerned at this time to slow up, as far as might be possible, the division of the world into two camps. At the ecumenical conference held at Lund in Sweden in August, 1952, delegates from the Communist countries were impressed by the "fraternal spirit" they encountered. The most prominent of them, the Czech theologian Hromadka, declared after the meeting that "several of the German delegates had manifested a remarkable spirit of solidarity among themselves"; yet in the political context the delegates from behind the Iron Curtain, and Hromadka in particular, had proclaimed their confidence in the governments of the "people's democracies." The leaders of the ecumenical movement were anxious at all costs to maintain their spiritual unity in spite of political differences, taking the line that the same evangelical premises can lead to varying political conclusions. The same principle is upheld, in theory at all events, by the EKD, whose leaders make it clear that when they express political opinions they are speaking only for themselves as individuals. But can the distinction between the man and his function always be maintained? From 1950 to 1957, this question was a perennial bone of contention within the EKD, owing to the profound difference of opinion between its chief leaders on the issues of rearmament and reunification. From the autumn of 1950 onward, a campaign against rearmament was conducted almost without a break by Pastor Niemöller, head of the Protestant Church in Hesse and director of the *Kirchliches Aussenamt*, and Dr. Heinemann, the statesman and future President of the Republic, who was head of the General Synod. The former's impetuousness and a certain lack of realism on the latter's part often betrayed them into inopportune statements, which the press blew up into inflammatory slogans. This did not deter them, since their paramount aim was to avoid a repetition of 1933, when silence and abstention had led to catastrophe. Others, who had been no less anti-Nazi than they, objected that the political course for which they had opted was not necessarily the only right one. It must be added, however, that the sharpest attacks on them within the Evangelical Church came from elements that had, in former days, been closer to the *Deutsche Christen* than to the Confessing Church.

In March, 1955, Dr. Heinemann ceased to be president of the Synod, while Niemöller was replaced as director of the *Aussenamt* on June 8, 1956. This, however, did not put an end to the controversy. At the meeting of the Synod at Berlin on June 27–29, 1956, 62 of its 120 members signed a resolution expressing grave misgivings over rearmament. On July 23, Eberhard Müller, the director of the Evangelical Academy at Bad Boll, organized a meeting in the Holy Cross Church at Bonn which was unofficially supported by government circles and in which he violently attacked the movers of the resolution, especially Dr. Heinemann and Pastor Helmut Gollwitzer, a professor at Bonn University. A reconciliation was effected at the Frankfurt *Kirchentag* in August, 1956, but trouble flared again when on February 22, 1957, the EKD signed an agreement with the Federal Government about Protestant chaplains for the Bundeswehr. After a lively debate, this was ratified by the Synod in March: much had indeed happened since, in 1950, the same body, assembled at Berlin-Weissensee, had issued a statement condemning German remilitarization. The evolution of the EKD in this respect was similar to that of the president of its council, Bishop Otto Dibelius of Berlin and Brandenburg, who had had to fight an increasingly sharp battle with G.D.R. leaders over their attempts to paganize young people, to stifle church action, and to prevent contacts between the two Germanies. Nevertheless, it had seemed at Frankfurt in 1956 that these contacts might once more be encouraged. Among the delegates from the G.D.R. were Johannes Dieckmann, the president of the *Volkskammer*, who stayed only a short time, and Otto Nuschke, the chairman of the CDU in the G.D.R., who was Minister for Church Affairs in the G.D.R. Government. Clergy and laity from the G.D.R. took Nuschke to task at the congress, with the result that he returned home in a furious temper.

This episode had grave consequences. The *Kirchentage* were supposed to be held alternately in East and West Germany—that at Leipzig in 1954 was a striking manifestation of German Protestant unity—but in April, 1957 Dr. von Thadden had to announce that there would be no congress that summer. The G.D.R. had laid down unacceptable conditions: (1) the EKD must guarantee to prevent anything in the nature of support for the "warlike NATO policy"; (2) no supporter of NATO would be allowed to appear at the congress, and there would be no relaxation of the decrees that forbade entry into the G.D.R. of any persons opposing its peace policy; (3) the leaders must officially condemn the incidents that had taken place at Frankfurt; (4) representatives of the G.D.R. Government must be given an opportunity to expound their peace policy at the congress.

We shall return in the next chapter to the question of G.D.R. policy toward the Protestant churches. Between 1957 and 1969, the links between Protestantism in East and West Germany were gradually severed, circumstances leading perforce to the formation of two separate churches. The immediate effect of the chaplaincy agreement was that Otto Dibelius, who had been bishop of Berlin and Brandenburg since 1945 and became president of the council of the EKD in 1949, was denied access to G.D.R. territory and thus cut off from the main part of his diocese in the heart of Prussia, to which he was linked by many traits of personality. In February, 1961, when Dibelius was almost eighty-one years old—he already had a whole ecclesiastical career behind him when deprived of office by the Nazis in 1933—the EKD Synod replaced him with Kurt Scharf, another dignitary of the church in Branden-burg, who was twenty-two years younger and had been persecuted in Nazi times as a leader of the Confessing Church. After the erection of the Berlin wall, both prelates were denied access to East Berlin; but, in February, 1966, in defiance of the G.D.R. Government under Willi Stoph, the Brandenburg clergy chose Scharf as their bishop in succession to Dibelius, who had remained symbolically in office meanwhile. This action, however, had no practical effect. When, in April, 1967, the Synod elected Bishop Hermann Dietzfelbinger of Bavaria to be president of the EKD council, he too was immediately declared *persona non grata* in the G.D.R.

Nevertheless, it was the Protestants who had taken the boldest initiatives for a more realistic "eastern policy" in the Federal Republic. In the autumn of 1961, eight Protestant leaders drew up a memorandum that, though in-tended as a confidential message to a few deputies of different parties, became public knowledge in February, 1962. The authors of the memorandum, which severely criticized the Federal Government, parties, and public opinion, included Klaus von Bismarck, the director-general of Cologne Radio, and the physicists Werner Heisenberg and Carl Friedrich von Weizsäcker: among other things, they argued in a balanced but forceful manner for the recognition of the Oder-Neisse frontier.[31]

On October 1, 1965, Dr. Scharf, on behalf of the EKD council, issued a statement covering a memorandum of considerably wider scope prepared by the "Public Affairs Office" (*Kammer für öffentliche Verantwortung*) under Professor Ludwig Raiser, and entitled "The position of expellees and relations between the German people and its eastern neighbors."[32] This long document created a considerable stir: its close analysis and firm conclusions contrasted with the government's policy, which we shall study later on. It aroused lively opposition both within and outside the EKD, and by so doing proved that the German Protestant churches were capable of political courage, a fact they again demonstrated by electing Raiser to the presidency of the Synod on May 12, 1970.

In other fields of public life, Protestantism as such was perhaps less in the forefront of progress, except as regards aid to developing countries. The *Kirchentage* continued to be lively and impressive gatherings under the respected leadership of Reinold von Thadden, who had given an exceptional proof of moral integrity: as governor of Louvain from 1942 to 1944, he had done so much to protect the population against his own superiors that he was a welcome guest in the city after the war. In 1964, at the age of seventy-three, he relinquished the chairmanship of the *Kirchentage* and was succeeded the next year by Richard von Weizsäcker, the brother of the Hamburg scientist, who found himself confronted by new problems arising out of the changing state of opinion in German society and in the EKD itself.[33] The *Kirchentag* of 1967 belied the slogan "Peace among us" that its organizers had chosen, and the gathering at Stuttgart in July, 1969 was more turbulent still. However, although the "rebels against society" were fully in evidence, their effect on the proceedings was less violent than at the *Katholikentag* in 1968, partly because the debates of the working groups were concerned frankly and directly with such basic questions as that of democracy within the Church. The result was to give a remarkable picture of the vitality of German Protestantism and its increasing awareness of the present day, though this in turn poses difficult questions in the purely religious field.

It is a further question what is meant by Protestantism or Catholicism, not from the point of view of doctrine or church organization but from that of the faithful considered as "children of God." The vast majority of Germans are officially Christians: does this mean that they are believers, and, if so, in what do they believe?[34] What effects, if any, does their faith have on their social and political behavior? Only a few points stand out clearly. The Catholic Church and the Protestant churches have less and less direct influence on political decisions at the level at which power is exercised, and this is still truer at the level of the ordinary individual. However, Catholics in West Germany are more attached to their Church than Protestants, if only from the point of view of the simplest expression of religious practice, that of attending public worship. In 1966, 64 per cent of Catholics and only 20 per cent of Protestants declared that they went regularly to church on Sundays.[35] When all is said and done, we may ask ourselves whether a *Katholikentag* or a *Kirchentag* has as much effect on the future of the Federal Republic as do a few numbers of *Der Spiegel* or a few television programs.

The Press and Television

When analyzing different types of political society, we generally pay attention to institutions and the relations between them, parties, and the activity of organized groups. We should, however, also take account of the manner in which information circulates.[36] In what way does society exercise the double right of imparting and receiving news? The press, radio, and television clearly constitute a privileged channel of information between social groups, between the governors and the governed. But these media are not a mere automatic system, a machine for collecting and distributing information. They are influenced by those in authority, by the providers of finance, and by the public. They affect the political climate and the attitudes of their readers. There is probably no country in the world where the press is entirely free, if by this we mean complete independence of the two forces that are its Scylla and Charybdis, namely money and political power. However, there are some newspapers of undoubted independence, and these are to be found in "capitalist" states: it is easier, in the last resort, to avoid being enslaved by money than by a totalitarian party or dictator.

Compared with authoritarian states, the Federal Republic and France show more points of similarity than of dissimilarity with each other in press matters. But the differences are real, especially in the field of information, even though radio and television in the two countries are subject to a similar regime. In contrast to the United States, where audio-visual methods of communication are governed by the same laws of private competition as newspapers, in Federal Germany and France, as in Britain before them, these media are now controlled by public bodies on behalf of the community and are financed, in

241

the main, by license fees levied by the administration. Nevertheless the practical results are very different in the two countries. West German radio and television displays much greater vitality, initiative, and independence than its French equivalent, even since the latter's partial "liberalization." Consequently, the criticisms of German practice that are made in this book should be discounted to a large extent by the French reader, while some other features that appear praiseworthy from the French point of view will probably seem to the German reader matters of course.

The principles governing radio and television matters in Germany are clear: as we saw, they were formulated by the Federal Constitutional Court when it ruled, on February 28, 1961, that for the government to control a television network would be a violation of the basic right of freedom of opinion. The Court said in particular:

Radio is more than a simple "medium" in the formation of public opinion: it plays an important creative part in the process. This role is by no means confined to news broadcasts, political comment, and programs dealing with political problems of the past, present, and future. Opinion is also formed by means of radio plays, musical and variety programs. . . . Every radio program is bound to reflect a particular tendency, especially insofar as it involves deciding what not to broadcast, what is thought not to be of interest to listeners. . . . From this point of view, it is clear that freedom, institutionally safeguarded, is no less important for radio. . . than for the press.

This principle is applied in the legal field with considerable strictness. Immediately after the war, it was decided to set up independent corporations in accordance with charters embodied in statutes or agreements between the *Länder*. There are now nine corporations, each with its own radio program and, in the case of six of them, a "third program" on television. They cooperate, through an association known as the ARD (*Arbeitsgemeinschaft der Öffentlich-rechtlichen Rundfunkanstalten der Bundesrepublik Deutschland*), to produce the "first program," their respective shares in which vary from 25 per cent for the Westdeutscher Rundfunk (WDR) at Cologne, and 20 per cent for the Norddeutscher Rundfunk (NDR) at Hamburg, to 3 per cent each for the Saar and Bremen.[37] The "second German television" (ZDF) works on a centralized basis, all its programs being transmitted from Mainz: the agreement establishing it was signed on June 6, 1961 and it began transmission in April, 1963. It is financed by advertising and by the members of ARD, which turn over 30 per cent of their revenue to it.

Each of the corporations has its own charter, but they resemble each other along broad lines. We may take as an example the WDR, which is the largest. Its authority derives from the *Landtag*, which elects by proportional representation a broadcasting council of twenty-one members for five years: no more than four of them may be members of either the *Landtag* or the Bonn parliament. The council in turn elects each year for a seven-year term one of the seven members of the supervisory board. The board, subject to the council's approval, appoints the director-general (*Intendant*) for a term of five years (three at Bremen, nine in Hesse), which may be renewed. While in office, he can only be dismissed for serious reasons and by a vote of five out of seven members of the board, whereas his opposite number in France is appointed by the government and can be dismissed at pleasure.

From the point of view of ensuring the independence of news and comment, a system of this type has two weaknesses. The first derives from the composition of the broadcasting councils, which are supposed to represent social and cultural institutions: the trade unions, churches, and other concerned bodies naturally combine to resist unduly searching analysis of the way in which they conceive and pursue their several interests. They will, in short, do their best to see that radio and television programs skate over awkward issues and do not go far beyond the "least common multiple" of the interests represented. However, the direct influence of the councils is, as a rule, not very great.

The second weakness is due to the distribution of authority within the corporations. The leading posts in each are allocated on a "proportional" basis: the councils have only a limited degree of influence on the decisions of the *Intendant*, but as he generally needs their approval for nominations to the most important posts, a more or less open struggle for power takes place. In some cases, such as the NDR at Hamburg, it is recognized that if the *Intendant* is a Social Democrat, his deputy must belong to the CDU. It is becoming more and more difficult for a man to be appointed *Intendant* simply because he is an able journalist and a genuinely independent personality.[38] However, the danger of undue political influence is much limited by the Federal system: if the CDU abused its majority position in one *Land*, the SPD would certainly retaliate in another. This being so, the most disquieting situation is one in which the Federal Government consists of a coalition of the two big parties: from 1966 to 1969, the tendency was for each to oblige the other by seeing to it that no overcritical programs were broadcast. But the *Intendanten* have almost always shown remarkable independence of the government's wishes, even when these were expressed directly by a Minister of Defense or Foreign Affairs.

Apart from the question of political interference, the German radio and television system is faced with a basic problem that also confronts the BBC in Britain, and the French ORTF insofar as that succeeds in escaping government influence. There are two objections to allowing the journalist absolute freedom vis-à-vis the license-paying public. The first is often heard from politicians who dislike the slant or content of news programs: it may be expressed by the French barons' challenge to Hugh Capet: "Who made you king?" "I, as a minister of state or member of parliament, have received a clear mandate from my fellow citizens. You, the journalist, with your huge audience and powers of influence—you who can address millions instead of the few hundred who come to my meetings—what authority entitles you to give the news according to your own private judgment?" To which it may be answered —after premising that the journalist, while he cannot help being subjective, must seek to be as objective as possible—that his mandate is of a different kind from the politician's. Unlike the statesman or deputy whose business is to act and for whom information is purely and simply a means of action—by conveying ideas, convincing or influencing people—the journalist's appointed task is merely to show people the facts, to communicate knowledge and understanding.

The second objection involves the question of the basic values of a given society. An independent organ of opinion such as a newspaper or private broadcasting system may devote its energies to challenging these values and attempting to substitute others, but can an organ of the establishment do the same? We may well take the view that "a public corporation is not entitled systematically to challenge the existing order. In carrying out its mandate, its duty is to hold a balance between critical detachment and upholding continuity."[39] There will always be tension between the rival claims to a hearing of nonconformist views and those of the prevailing system. From this point of view, journalistic freedom is not so much that of an individual as that of a team conscious of the responsibilities that go with the huge power of mass media in the information field.

In Federal Germany, there is on the whole no lack of courageous and high-quality broadcasting, at any rate in the sphere of information: the cultural level of radio and television programs is not quite so high. Long before the political parties braced themselves to speak plainly on the question of refugees and the Oder-Neisse territories, the issues were presented firmly and dispassionately in television programs by Jürgen Neven du Mont. Other television series, notably those of Helmut Greulich in the "second program," boldly criticized social conditions despite strong objections from "representative bodies," thanks to the firmness with which the *Intendanten* resisted the latter's pressure. Every Sunday, from noon to one o'clock, viewers may see Werner Höfer's "live" program *Internationaler Frühschoppen* (the noun means "morning pint"), in which a German and four foreign journalists discuss in perfect freedom every subject under the sun, government policy included. In Germany, the chairman is sometimes accused of too much caution in skating over delicate points, but any Frenchman who takes part is chiefly impressed by a degree of spontaneity far exceeding what he is used to at home.

Höfer's program weathered a serious incident in 1968. On the first Sunday of March, at the height of the controversy over President Lübke, the subject chosen for discussion was the way in which heads of states should be treated by the press. One of the participants was Henri Nannen, the editor of *Der Stern*, who, as we have seen, was particularly virulent in his attacks on Lübke. Although Nannen had apparently promised beforehand to be moderate in his remarks, he indulged in the most offensive personal comments despite the chairman's attempts to call him to order. The Grand Coalition Government and especially the CDU leaders, had done their best to prevent the program being shown. They afterward called for the blood of the editor responsible, but Klaus von Bismarck, the *Intendant*, firmly defended his subordinate's action.

One should not infer from this that criticism is always given its head, or that out-of-the-way television programs are assured of a long lease on life on the 15 million "little screens" of the Federal Republic. Least of all is this true of satire: when the intelligent, hard-hitting series *"Hallo Nachbarn!"* (Hallo, Neighbors!) was stopped at the end of 1965, there were numerous protests but to no avail.[40] As for "Panorama," the first program's chief "news magazine," three successive organizers—Eugen Kogon, Gerd von Paczensky, and Rüdiger Proske, all journalists of high repute—have either resigned or been dismissed, having given offense by too much critical spirit, and their successor, Peter Merseburger, is obliged, like them, to struggle unceasingly to protect his team's independence.

Nonetheless, it is radio and television rather than the press that continue to offer the readiest opportunities to young men who want to make a career in independent political journalism. In these media, they find themselves in the company of acknowledged intellectuals who occupy posts in the various corporations that are quite well paid and give them plenty of opportunity to express themselves and influence people. Generally speaking, these intellectuals tend to be unorthodox, and some of them are so systematically hostile to the "establishment" that their analysis loses in objectivity. There is some justification for complaints that the radio and television system has been turned into a citadel of nonconformity. The Catholic conservative weekly *Rheinische Merkur* runs a regular column criticizing the content of political information programs, and its strictures are sometimes very much to the point.[41]

At the time of Germany's surrender in 1945, every newspaper in the country had ceased publication. The Allies began forthwith to authorize new publications, whose editorial boards had to be licensed in each zone by the occupying power. In principle, the new journals were supposed to confine themselves to impartial reporting with no specific political or ideological bias, but in practice, as we have seen, the American military government was the only one to insist on representatives of different tendencies being appointed to the board of every newspaper. The journalistic profession was purged on a grand scale, with the result that some completely inexperienced men were given editorial jobs. The printing plants on the other hand, remained in the hands of their former owners, who, when taxed with what they had printed in the past, replied that they had been acting under duress. They were ordered by the occupying powers to sign contracts with the new licensed newspapers; in time, these contracts were replaced by new ones much more favorable to the printers.

Until the currency reform of June, 1948, the papers could not keep pace with a demand that was greatly increased by the public's thirst for news and information of all kinds—and also by the fact that waste paper could be used as a medium of exchange. The number of licenses rose rapidly, and the 140th was about to be granted when control was withdrawn in 1949. At this time, when it became possible to start a new paper freely, the economic basis of the postwar press was not yet solidly established. Capital was still lacking, and it was often impossible to acquire office buildings and printing presses. The printers, however, were now free to publish rival newspapers, financing them in part by the high rates they charged to the licensed press. Not infrequently, a solution was found by admitting the printer-publisher to the editorial board, sometimes with a controlling voice—a practice that seemed to open the way for a revival of old influences, especially when editors who had been "denazified" started to come back into circulation. But, contrary to the fears of those who expected to see a wholesale revival of the Nazi press and the collapse of the papers sanctioned by the occupation, the latter did not suffer unduly by the return to free conditions. As a rule, they survived while changing their character, in the same way as many French newspapers that came into being in 1945. As in France, too, the main lines of change have been in two directions: less emphasis on politics, and more concentration in the press as a whole. The former means that the newspapers are largely nonparty and that they give more prominence to general news than to purely political facts and commentaries; the latter means that the number of papers has diminished and that many of the small ones that survive are less independent than they were, since, unknown to their readers, they print syndicated material emanating from some distant office.

Nevertheless, the Federal Republic possesses a regional press of high quality though small circulation, offering its readers sober analyses, which may be on the dull side but are, if only for that reason, untainted by demagogy. Thanks to the profusion of small advertisements and to the fact that most readers are also subscribers, which is a far better system economically than that of casual sales, some newspapers that sell between 100–200,000 copies, such as the *Kölnische Rundschau*, the *Stuttgarter Zeitung*, or the *Mannheimer Morgen*, are quite able to get on without sensational or frivolous material. Both in the quantity and quality of their news service, they are distinctly superior to the chief French regional dailies. Papers of this kind are not, however, read beyond the limits of a fairly small geographical area, even when their circulation is as high as that of the *Westdeutsche Allgemeine Zeitung* (Essen: nearly 500,000 copies) or the *Hamburger Morgenpost* (over 300,000). In this, as in other respects, Germany has never had a capital city that dominated the nation as Paris does France. The Federal Republic, of course, has no genuine capital at all, and no newspaper published in Berlin or Bonn has a countrywide circulation. Since the decline of the *Frankfurter Rundschau*, long a doughty opponent of anything that suggested a return to the bad old ways, there are only three daily newspapers of a general type that can still be called *überregional* and that exercise political influence despite their limited circulation (250–300,000 in each case). None of these can boast of the same news coverage or international prestige as *Le Monde*, the London *Times* in its best days, or the *New York Times*.

The *Frankfurter Allgemeine Zeitung* has not attained the intellectual level or the political status of the pre-1933 *Frankfurter Zeitung*. It has gone through internal crises that have enhanced its attitude of caution, respect for law and order, and distrust of trade union influence. But like the Paris *Figaro*, which it resembles in many ways, it has a good deal to offer to its readers and is a vigorous champion of pluralistic democracy and liberal institutions.[42] This author, however, confesses to a preference for the Munich *Süddeutsche Zeitung*, the tone and political views of which are similar to those of the London *Guardian*, and which is outstanding in its objectivity, balance, and critical sense and the reliability of its news. To become a paper of international status it should, however, give less space to regional affairs, and a good deal more to developments outside the Federal Republic. The Hamburg *Die Welt*, which treats such subjects more fully, has other weaknesses: since the late 1950's, and especially since the death of its editor Heinrich Schulte in 1963, it has tended to slant both news and views in accordance with the ideas of its owner, the press tycoon Axel Springer, though there have been signs of greater independence since 1968.

Die Welt is in fact only one star in the galaxy of papers controlled by Springer. He relinquished some publications in 1968 but—in addition to some unpolitical weeklies such as *Hör zu*, the radio and television journal—he is still the king of the Berlin press, with the *BZ* (*Berliner Zeitung*), *Berliner Morgenpost*, and the Berlin edition of the *Bild-Zeitung*, all of which have been politically influential at times of East-West crises and during the student disturbances. The *Bild-Zeitung*, which sells over 4 million copies a day in the Federal Republic, has fortunately no French equivalent: to compare it with *France-Soir* would be an insult to the latter. Its screaming headlines with their appeal to individual and mass emotions, its incoherent reporting, its ill-argued editorials, its "splashing" of scandals under the pretext of denouncing them, and its crude, aggressive style with its hectoring statements—in all these ways *Bild* acts as both a narcotic and a harmful stimulant to its readers, which may sound like a contradiction but unfortunately is not.[43]

The controversy in Germany over excessive concentration in the press field has centered around Axel Springer, both because of the latter's strong personality and readiness to take up a challenge, and because his group is the only one of importance as far as the daily press is concerned. It did not come as a surprise when he withdrew from the commission of inquiry set up by the Bundestag in 1967 under the chairmanship of Eberhard Günter, the president of the Federal Cartel Office. After making a close study of the abuses in question, the commission drew up, in July, 1968, important recommendations that have not yet been given legal force by parliament.

The other press groups are less "personalized," have a less definite slant, and are chiefly interested in making a profit out of mass-circulation weeklies and monthlies of very varying quality, most of them illustrated. At the end of 1969, the important publishing house of Bertelsmann, which boasts a "readers' club" (*Buchgemeinschaft*) of 2·5 million members, acquired a large interest in the Springer group, whereas previously it was rather the latter that extended its empire by incursions into the publishing field.

Among the four great illustrated weeklies with a total circulation of well over 6 million, *Der Stern* is the only one of any political significance, and even that devotes the main part of its voluminous space to popular trivia, sentimental fiction, and "reports" on moral questions, that is, sex or crime stories. Weeklies of general interest that give much space to politics are few in number but they are mostly good—except for the *Deutsche National-Zeitung*, which is the nostalgic and aggressive organ of the extreme right: its sales are well below 100,000.

The Protestant press includes *Christ und Welt*, a somewhat right-wing journal that shows an increasing tendency to become secular. On the Catholic side, there is the *Rheinische Merkur*, a small-circulation paper corresponding roughly to *La France Catholique*: it viewed with some jealousy the emergence in 1968 of *Publik*, which, although financed by the episcopate, displays much freedom of style and subject matter. However, *Publik* is far from having achieved the circulation (not that it is very high—under 300,000) or, above all, the influence and quality of *Die Zeit*, which is doubtless the best European weekly combining news and views in the traditional pattern. Its coverage is increasingly broad, comprising political, economic, and cultural topics, and it exercises political influence both by its news columns and by its editorial opinions. It is a paper of the moderate left and is sometimes criticized, much as *Le Monde* is in France, for a certain smugness, a tendency to flirt with the intellectual avant-garde and to judge men and institutions with undue arrogance. When student protest became an issue, *Die Zeit* at first took a very sympathetic line, but, as the disturbances continued, it changed its tune and was denounced for its pains as an organ of the establishment.

Much the same happened with *Der Spiegel*, the other great Hamburg weekly, which the extreme left regards, like *Die Zeit*, as a champion of the detested "system," its very criticisms being an insidious way of setting consciences at rest. The history of *Der Spiegel* is a success story of the first order: in January, 1947, it covered twenty-eight pages and sold 15,000 copies; twenty years later, its circulation was about 1 million and each number ran to about 170 pages, some two-thirds of which were advertising. Its growth was a steady one: sales stood at 121,000 in 1955 and 574,000 in 1963.[44] It may also be regarded as a political event: in many ways, *Der Spiegel* almost ranks as an adjunct to the constitution. Since September, 1950, when it published a long article on suspected corruption over the choice of Bonn as the Federal capital, and a commission of inquiry was set up as a result, there have been a long series of *Spiegel* campaigns leading directly to government action. No less real, though less tangible, is its day-to-day influence—in political circles, where it inspires salutary fear, and on its devoted readers, who keep up a lively correspondence with it. Such influence, of course, is hard to evaluate exactly and is of a somewhat ambivalent kind. Certainly the paper has revealed many scandals and anomalies that would otherwise not have come to light. It is as a rule extremely well informed and is not afraid of filling its columns with full-length political, cultural, and sociological studies. Its "interviews" are exemplary in their thoroughness and aggressive efficiency. In some respects, indeed, *Spiegel* is the very incarnation of press freedom. On the other side of the account, it must be said that its smooth, carefully casual and often malicious style, the frequency of its aspersions, and the relative scarcity of its constructive comments, tend to encourage its readers to abstain from political action and to despise the world of politics lock, stock, and barrel.

The ambiguity of *Spiegel*'s position well reflects the personality of its chief editor, Rudolf Augstein, a man of courage and intellectual brilliance who is ruthless to others and not free from self-satisfaction. When he started the paper in 1946, he was twenty-three years old. A quarter of a century later, he is still actively in charge. When he was arrested in October, 1962 for violating state security by publishing Conrad Ahlers' articles on the Bundeswehr, his colleagues and members of the most diverse groups campaigned in his favor and were right to do so. But one can also understand the resentment of those on whom he passes judgment with ever increasing assurance though not always with perfect consistency. In his fondness for startling effects and trenchant attitudes he has much in common with his rival Springer, who is eleven years older. Both men, it may be said, have exhausted the satisfaction that can be derived from the indirect exercise of power through the press; and, very naturally but for widely different reasons, they both show signs of desiring to wield influence in as direct a fashion as may be possible.

Intellectuals and Students

For a long time, although *Der Spiegel*'s nonconformity showed signs of turning into an orthodoxy of its own, it provided a refreshing dose of the critical spirit in a country where prosperity was fast engendering complacency. The intellectuals, who had been much in evidence during the period of self-questioning immediately after the war, had become, so to speak, irrelevant members of a society that was materially sated and ideologically unified.

In general, except for a brief period in the 1920's, the role of an intellectual in Germany has always been very different from what it is in France. In Germany, the life of the mind has always been one thing, politics and economics another. Whether in disdain or from lack of understanding, men of learning tended to remain outside public life, while writers in their search for eternal verities ignored more transient aspects of reality, which nevertheless have their own importance. The aloofness of the universities in their ivory tower of pure knowledge was not the least of the factors that eased Hitler's rise to power. Whatever view one takes of the duty of "commitment" or the capacity, or incapacity, displayed by intellectuals in political affairs, the fact is that they have usually taken less of a hand in them than their French opposite numbers. Moreover, while postwar Germany was dominated by the notion of building a better moral order, the tendency in the 1950's and early 1960's was to think in terms of maintaining that order and defending it, not only against assault but even against criticism. Thus Erhard, when Chancellor, spoke irritably of his intellectual critics as "tykes" (*Pinscher*). By the mid-1960's, however, there was already a recrudescence of doubt and uncertainty, which increased the strength and prestige of those whose profession it is to think and to ask questions. Not that they had in fact had much to complain of at any time: even when the Federal Republic was at its most conservative, the existence of weekly papers, magazines, paperbacks, and, above all, radio and television meant that plenty of those who criticized the prevailing way of life were able to obtain a good share of the comforts whose excess they deplored. The writers of the *"Gruppe 47,"* led by Hans Werner Richter, showed a bold and generous spirit, while at the same time helping one another to boost their reputation as individuals and as a group, so that one was inclined to think of them as the omnipresent leaders of latter-day German culture; they themselves, however, might well feel that the public tolerated them as entertainers of no serious importance.

Toward the end of the 1960's, and especially under the Brandt government, a twofold development took place, each aspect of which tended to encourage the other. On the one hand, the gulf widened between liberal intellectuals and systematic "rebels," and on the other, intellectuals came to take a more direct part in the working of political institutions. At the end of 1966, Conrad Ahlers left *Der Spiegel* for the Government Press Office, and at the beginning of 1970 Theo Sommer left *Die Zeit* for six months or so to become head of the planning section at the Ministry of Defense under Helmut Schmidt. By this time,

Der Spiegel was a firm supporter of a government that included such out-spoken critics of German society as Ralf Dahrendorf and Klaus von Dohnanyi. Two journalists, a sociologist, and a lawyer: are these "intellectuals" within the meaning of the present discussion? One's answer to this depends on the realities of cultural life and the society of which that culture is a part. In France, for centuries, the "intellectual" was usually a writer dedicated either to his work or to some cause outside it. Today, if we apply the term to all those who claim it by virtue of the fact that they put their names to political mani-festos, generally of a protesting character, its meaning must be enlarged to include artists of every kind, from painters to the theater and film world. Meanwhile, the function of criticizing French society has passed by degrees from novelists and writers to sociologists. This last change is also to be ob-served in West Germany, where the writers of *Ruinenliteratur*—descriptions of the devastation and aftermath of war—are passing from the scene and have no real successors (although Günter Grass's works continue and surpass those of Heinrich Böll), while literature in general is surrendering its position to the "social sciences."

But the strong and weak points of German culture at the present time are not the same as in France, which means that the pattern of prestige and in-fluence is also different. It so happens that the sphere in which postwar Germany has shown the greatest creativity is that of music, which lends itself least to the direct expression of social ideas. Films, on the other hand, have remained for the most part at a low level: the great days of Weimar are only a memory, and for the past twenty-five years the best films seen on German screens have usually been American, French, or Italian. As for the stage, while German theaters are excellently designed and audiences are ready to applaud pioneering works, plays by German-language authors are still rare, the chief being those of the East German, Bertolt Brecht, and the Swiss, Friedrich Dürrenmatt.

The one theatrical genre, however, in which the Germans have excelled since 1945, if not earlier, is precisely that which has most bearing on politics. The satirical *Kabarette* of Berlin, Munich, Düsseldorf, and Hamburg are intelligent, aggressive, well staged, well sung, and well acted: they have only a distant relationship with the art of the Paris *chansonnier*, enslaved as that is to the taste of a well-to-do audience. In Germany, one may often meet in this sphere with a critique of society no less penetrating that those of novelists, sociologists, and the writers of editorials, with the additional grace of humor that is so sadly lacking in intellectual life as a whole, whether in Germany or in France. One must of course remember that intellectuals aspire to exercise serious influence—it would never do for them to try to do so by making people laugh, as if they were no better than Voltaire!

What are they seeking to influence? Politics, of course, and youth, which, as we all know, has the future in its grasp and to which we appeal as if it were always one and the same, unchanging and homogeneous—and as if, moreover, it were identical with the small fraction of itself that goes by the designation "student."

If people remain young until their elders judge them to have grown up, then traditionally the period of youth in Germany is longer than in France or

Britain. It was not until the 1960's that men under thirty-five began to be appointed to responsible posts; the senior civil servant of the future is probably still a *Referendar* or trainee at an age when graduates of the *Ecole Nationale d'Administration* are already in charge of important departments or acting as ministers' private secretaries. If, on the other hand, what causes people to grow up is the experience of suffering, the members of the postwar *Frontgeneration* were mature while still in their teens. It was they who, having beheld the collapse of Nazism with open eyes, provided the youth movements of the 1950's with reliable leaders who understood the need to democratize public life.

The Federal Youth Council (*Bundesjugendring*), set up in 1949, comprises bodies organized on a nationwide basis as well as *Landesjugendringe*, while organizations directly linked with one or another of the political parties are grouped in the *Ring der politischen Jugend*. The Federal Council is dominated by the two large federations of Catholic and Protestant youth and by the "Socialist Falcons," who are regarded as a separate body; they owe their importance to association with the SPD rather than to their numbers, which are much less than those of the *Sportjugend*. At the thirty-sixth congress of the *Bundesjugendring* in November, 1969, the head of the Catholic Youth once again succeeded the leader of the Falcons as president of the main organization.

Article 3 of the Federal Council's statute laid down that the member associations would "resist to the utmost any revival of totalitarian, militaristic, and nationalistic tendencies." Accordingly, the Council fought against a recrudescence of the Nazi past and at the same time denounced the indoctrination of East German youth. In the early 1950's, however, the rearmament crisis brought grave difficulties for the Council, which was divided within itself and attacked from outside for upholding the view of democracy that, till then, had been officially inculcated into young people.[45] The Council's opponents also denied its right to speak for German youth on the grounds that only about a quarter of those in the appropriate age groups belonged to organizations, and that there was little discussion within the latter of problems on which the youth leaders were wont to express their views. These leaders, however, were better qualified to speak for their juniors than many statesmen who studied youth problems from the outside, and they were effectively associated from the outset with a wide range of social and educational activity financed from year to year by the "Federal Youth Plan." Like the trade union leaders, however, the heads of youth organizations tended to evolve into "managers" or bureaucrats, until the appearance on the scene of unorganized "rebel" groups obliged them to rethink their own position and that of the movements they controlled.

At the Ludwigshafen congress in November, 1968, a program was adopted that repeated some themes from the past ("youth" does not exist as a separate class, there are only specific aspects of problems that affect the whole of society; the associations must shoulder their political responsibilities, et cetera), and in general took a middle line between opposition and conformity to adult standards.[46] An appeal was made for young people to be allowed a fuller share in decision-making in all spheres and at all levels, in matters affecting the family, schools, the churches, the state, industrial management, the universities, and so on. This renewed concern with social problems on the part of teenagers and young adults was accompanied by a revival of interest in politics in general, as may be seen by comparing the replies to polls carried out in 1961, 1964, and 1968.[47] Such interest is not necessarily a sign of discontent, and, as in France, care is needed in assessing the significance of "rebellion." The few serious studies that exist on the adaptation of teenagers to society show that few of those who are engaged in earning their living—a category that excludes students—regard their occupation as "alienating."[48] At the same time, it is true that the critical examination of society became much more widespread in the late 1960's as education became "democratized," that is, as more young people were still at school at an age when they would formerly have had to be at work. The *Gymnasien* in particular have been the scene of unrest that was sometimes creative, at other times aimless or destructive.[49] On occasion, it spilled over into the streets, as at Bremen in January, 1968, when pupils protested against a rise in public transport fares. At that time, if not later, the small minority of young people who took part in demonstrations enjoyed the support of the peaceful majority.[50]

The minority in question was chiefly composed of students. These are still a much smaller class than in France, though budgets for higher education have been increasing rapidly, as has the number of enrollments. In 1954, the total student population on the higher level was 137,000, whereof 38,000 were in their first year; in 1961, the figures were 244,000 and 63,000; in 1968, 316,000 and 80,000. During this period, expenditure on higher learning rose from DM600 million to 1,700 and 4,200 million,[51] though this was still not enough to remedy the "disastrous state of education" that has been examined and denounced in a celebrated study.[52]

German universities have long enjoyed a large measure of autonomy, and the social standing of professors was still at its height in the mid-1960's. The academic hierarchy was medieval in its structure, and the revolt of the 1960's was almost as much one of junior teachers as of students. It was directed against the university authorities, since they still possessed effective powers, whereas in France there was initially a degree of solidarity between teachers and students in their hostility to the state, which appeared all-powerful and was therefore saddled with the blame for every grievance. The German students, for their part, had real powers of action and influence. They possessed local representation in the University Students' Councils (*Allgemeiner Studentenausschuss*—AStA), organized at the national level in the Union of Student Associations (*Verband Deutscher Studentenschaften*—VDS). Subscriptions were collected from students at their matriculation, so that the VDS was fully representative as far as numbers went, but its leaders felt at a loss when confronted with a type of problem for which they had received no mandate. Nevertheless, during the 1950's, the VDS, like the Youth Council, came out strongly for the defense and extension of liberal democracy. At that time, during the formative years of the Federal Republic, the chief problem it had to cope with was the revival of the traditional student *Korps*. The generation of students a few years earlier had seen too much blood and too many uniforms to be attracted by the *Mensur*—the ritual saber-duel for the purpose of inflicting manly scars—and the old-fashioned uniform with its cap and ribbons; but in the 1950's, thanks to the *"alte Herren"* or former *Korps* members, these organizations once more became well-to-do and were recognized as offering very real chances of advancement in life through the "old boy" network provided by their elders. Many of the new *Korps* firmly rejected the *Mensur*, but others, including those united under the name of the *Deutsche Burschenschaft*—an incongruous echo of the nineteenth-century groups of liberal students—revived it in secret until such time as *Korps* activities in general became respectable again. These have never had much to do with politics: the *Korps* are inclined to accept the existing social order and to identify with it as far as possible so as to share its advantages. Many students, however, join for the sake of fellowship rather than in the expectation of benefits. In 1968, there were estimated to be over 50,000 student members of about a thousand *Korps*, most of which were Catholic and moderate in tendency. By this time, they were the object of little public attention, as the political climate in the universities had veered sharply leftward.

The "students' revolt" in Federal Germany has given rise to almost as much comment as the events of May and June, 1968 in France,[53] of which it was a contributing cause. It reached its paroxysm between the demonstrations at Berlin against the Shah of Iran on June 2, 1967, in the course of which the student Benno Ohnesorg was shot dead, and the aftermath of the shooting of Rudi Dutschke on April 11, 1968. Later outbreaks, at Frankfurt in April, 1969 and Berlin in July, 1969, took place against a background of relative quiet, the rebels having meanwhile to all appearances won the day as regards influence over their fellow students. The VDS passed wholly into the hands of the extreme left in March, 1969. Just a year earlier, it had held a stormy congress[54] at which the intelligent and capable Hans Joachim Haubold was replaced as president by Christoph Ehmann, an ideologist rather than a politician; at that time, it was divided over the question of orientation but the rebels were in the ascendant. A year later, the Socialist Students' Union (SDS) came to the fore, and the VDS was rechristened the Socialist Fighters' Union (*Sozialistischer Kampfverband*). Within a few months, the latter had almost completely disintegrated, and, in November, 1969, it was abandoned by its new leaders. There was not even a struggle for influence among various left-wing groups such as took place at this time within the *Union Nationale des Etudiants de France*, which in many ways underwent the same sort of evolution as the VDS.

The group that led the VDS to ruin was itself a lost cause: on March 22, 1970, the SDS announced its own dissolution. It had had its difficulties for twenty years: at a stormy congress in August, 1947, under the chairmanship of Helmut Schmidt, the future Socialist leader, the SDS, which was then affiliated to the SDP, took the critical decision to break off relations with East Germany. During the 1950's, it pursued an "anti-Stalinist" course while adhering to a form of Socialism more and more different from that of the SDP. In May, 1960, some members of the SDS broke away to form the Social Democratic Students' Association (SHB), and in July, as we have seen, the SDP officially withdrew its support from the SDS. In those days, however, student protest was confined to specific issues such as nuclear weapons, and to pacifist demonstrations. It was not until later that the students resorted to violence and raised the demand for a general reform of society, beginning with the universities. It is difficult to assess exactly the part played by the SDS in the incidents that became increasingly frequent, especially in Berlin, from 1965 onward. The students' violence, in any case, was largely a response to that of the police: as in France, the methods used by the forces of "law and order" made tens of thousands of young people identify themselves with the cause of an extremist minority. In June, 1967, but for the action of the plain-clothes police officer Kurras in shooting down Benno Ohnesorg, who was not threatening him, the demonstration against the alleged tyranny of the Shah would have had no more serious consequences than the anti-Tshombe rally in December, 1964. The murder of Ohnesorg provoked riots in many other university towns and enhanced the popularity of the bearded, scruffy but keen-witted anarchist Fritz Teufel and, above all, of Rudi Dutschke, a young sociologist who was also an excellent speaker and organizer. At Easter, 1968, when "Red Rudi" was shot and seriously wounded by a youth named Josef Bachmann, street fighting broke out in Berlin, Hamburg, Frankfurt, Munich, and Essen. On these occasions, the rebellious students were clearly the origi-nators of violence, and while the attack on Dutschke had increased sympathy for them in many quarters, the effect of these outbreaks was to reduce their popularity drastically, among fellow students as well as with the general public.

However, although the rebels were to some extent isolated from the summer of 1968 onward, their activity did much to bring about profound changes in the organization and spirit of the university system. The *Länder* worked out elaborate new laws on higher education, usually with a strong emphasis on comanagement: this took the form in some cases of *Drittelparität*, whereby the governing body of the university is composed of one-third each of students, professors and lecturers, and junior teachers and researchers (*Assistenten*). The last category thus find themselves in a key position: at the end of 1969, the president of the Free University of Berlin was a sociology assistant, Rolf Kreibich, elected in opposition to Professor Hans Joachim Lieber by sixty-one votes to forty-nine, while the new president (formerly *Rector Magnificus*) of Hamburg University was a research assistant, Peter Fischer-Appelt.

The street riots that followed the attack on Dutschke were aimed at a mor-ally vulnerable adversary, namely the Springer press, which the demonstrators held to be responsible for Bachmann's action and thus guilty of incitement to murder. But the student rioters' attacks on buildings distracted attention from the main issue. As for Bachmann, who was sentenced to seven years' hard labor in March, 1969 and who committed suicide in prison a year later, he was no doubt an unstable character with hazy ideas that did not necessarily have much to do with those of the *Bild-Zeitung*. Nevertheless, the latter had done its share to create an atmosphere of hatred toward the student rebels, denouncing them as barbarians and malefactors against whom the use of brutal methods was legitimate and desirable.

"We must ask ourselves, every one of us, how far our own actions in the past may have helped to bring about a state of affairs in which anti-Communism culminates in attempted murder." Gustav Heinemann, then Minister of Justice, broadcast on April 14, 1968 this noble appeal for calm and self-discipline.[55] His words were directed not only at the members of *Stammtische*, café habitués and armchair sociologists, among some of whom resentment seems to flow as freely as beer from the cask, but also at the whole trend of opinion encouraged by the Springer press and by the attitude of judges, who are even more inclined in Germany than elsewhere to measure the acts of students and policemen by different standards. Thus, in November, 1967, Detective Sergeant Kurras was acquitted by the Berlin court on the ground that he was not in a position to think calmly at the time of the incident. The amendments to articles of the Penal Code and the law of 1953 on public order, assemblies, and demonstrations,[56] which were adopted in May, 1970 and include an amnesty, would have been a simpler matter if the courts had shown a greater sense of balance and equity. Many judges, it is true, were exasperated by the provocative actions of left-wing student extremists, and so were many moderate critics of the regime who now gradually withdrew their sympathy and support from the rebels. As regards the press, even the hard-hitting satirical *Pardon* abandoned the student cause, leaving as their only faithful ally the monthly *Konkret*, which however continued to devote more pages to sex than to political and academic discontents.

In any case, the German rebels have always been more cut off from the non-academic world than the French *contestataires*. It would have been un-thinkable for the French trade unions to have organized a counter-manifestation in opposition to the students, whereas, in February, 1968, the DGB mounted a huge procession to express its support for the authorities and its protest against the protestors. One reason for this is of course that ideas and attitudes in general are more conservative in the Federal Republic than in France, where "leftism" as such has an emotional appeal that is absent elsewhere. But there is another reason—namely, the genuine attachment of the German public to all that the rebels call in question: liberal institutions, the rejection of fanaticism, respect for due process of law, majority voting, and the secret ballot. This is not to say that the French are less attached to republican liberties than the West Germans: perhaps they are more so. But they are so much more used to seeing them in everyday life that they are less inclined to condemn individuals who from time to time seek the suspension of liberties in the name of liberty. In the Federal Republic, and still more in West Berlin, the basic principles of liberal society are the more appreciated because people remember the Nazi past and because they have only to look at the other Germany to see what comes of abolishing the rules. It is not by chance that the movement of revolt among West German students began to decline more rapidly after the invasion of Czechoslovakia by her Socialist allies.

Part III

The "Other Germany" and the German Problem

10

The "Socialist State of the German Nation"

THE Federal Republic is not the only Germany. It has itself always been conscious of this fact, and has always spoken of German reunification as its aim. But the other Germany, whether or nor an "unknown land,"[1] has from the start been a "distant" one.[2] We shall come back to this question of estrangement, the responsibility for which is not all on one side. The Communists' determination to widen the breach and prevent contacts was matched on the Western side by inflexible condemnation and a refusal to re-examine the problem. During the later 1960's, however, it became increasingly evident that the German Democratic Republic (G.D.R.; in German, D.D.R.) was more than a mere "zone,"[3] although the government and two-thirds of the population of West Germany continued to refer to it as the "eastern zone," "the zone," the "Soviet occupation zone" or the "Soviet zone"[4]—or else, as "Central Germany" (*Mitteldeutschland*), to distinguish it from the territories beyond the Oder-Neisse line. Whatever they called it, ignorance of conditions there was so widespread that only a quarter of those questioned knew, to within 1 million more or less, that 17 million of their compatriots were living on the other side of the barbed-wire curtain.[5]

It is true that the West Germans had not much opportunity of informing themselves adequately. Even the higher quality press was consistently niggardly with its news and comment on the G.D.R., and books attempting to analyze conditions there were few until after 1960;[6] for their part, the G.D.R. rulers, who complained that nothing was known about their state, took care that their own citizens should not learn anything about the West. Both sides, in short, applied the dictum of the satirical poet Morgenstern: "It oughtn't to be real, therefore it can't be." ("*Weil, so schliesst er messerscharf, Nicht sein kann, was nicht sein darf.*")[7] The result is that a writer familiar only with the Federal Republic may feel some diffidence in embarking on an account of the G.D.R., but we nevertheless think it legitimate to do so. Although lacking direct experience of the "other Germany," it seems possible and useful to give a general description of a country that, in many ways, it would no doubt be more appropriate to compare with the other Communist states of Eastern Europe.[8] We do not share the view that intellectual honesty requires us "to study the G.D.R. purely from the standpoint of its own achievements," or that "an outsider's opinion cannot be more than a polemical one."[9] One may try to understand conditions in the G.D.R. without giving up one's own scale of values, especially as no criteria are wholly free from subjectivity. In any

259

case, why should we confine ourselves to "factual judgments" on Ulbricht's Germany when we have thought it natural and proper to apply standards of value in discussing the various aspects of West Germany under Adenauer, Erhard, Kiesinger, and Brandt?

The State and the Party

As we saw in chapter 4, the G.D.R. regarded itself from the outset as a definitive creation: more so than did the Federal Republic, whose Basic Law made it clear that the new state was a provisional entity. The preamble to the G.D.R. constitution of October 7, 1949 declares that that document has been adopted by "the German people"—without saying whether this denotes the whole German people or only part of it—and Article 1 states that "Germany is an indivisible democratic Republic," though it is not specified whether the "German Democratic Republic" referred to in Article 2 is identical with the whole of Germany.

In practice, however, the G.D.R. took much longer than the F.R.G. to place its existence on a solid basis, and to do so it was obliged to turn most of its borders into fortified barriers, at all events along the western frontier. Although Wilhelm Pieck (President of the G.D.R. from 1949 to 1960) spoke as late as 1946 and 1947 of the possibility of a correction of the German-Polish frontier, this problem was settled for all practical purposes before the G.D.R. came into existence; and its leaders had accepted the fact by March, 1948, when Otto Grotewohl, who was soon to become Prime Minister, made a statement to the second People's Congress endorsing the Oder-Neisse line. In November, 1949, the two East German leaders declared it to be a "frontier of peace" (*Friedensgrenze*), and it became officially a "frontier of peace and friendship" by the G.D.R.-Polish declaration and treaty of June 6, and July 6, 1950.

In the West, however, and in Berlin itself, frontier problems existed and were tackled head on. The G.D.R. leaders insistently repeated that West Berlin was situated on their territory, though they did not claim that its 2 million inhabitants and its area of 185 square miles were part of the East German state. As for East Berlin, it was in a special situation: with its 156 square miles and 1·1 million inhabitants,[10] it was officially designated the "capital city of Berlin" (*Hauptstadt Berlin*), thus conforming to the constitution that declared that the capital of the G.D.R. was "Berlin," but ignoring the division of the city between East and West.[11] In this way, the Soviet sector of Berlin was still more firmly incorporated in the G.D.R. than the three western sectors were in the Federal Republic. But the Soviet Union, like the Western Allies, did not allow its German partners to go the whole way: the quadripartite system was safeguarded to some extent, and in 1970 the *Volkskammer* (G.D.R. parliament) still comprised 66 "Berlin representatives" (*Berliner Vertreter*) in addition to its 434 deputies. Like the Berliners who sit in the Bundestag, those of East Germany are not directly elected but are delegates of the Municipal Assembly. Their status is even less precise than in the West, but this is of little importance, as the *Volkskammer* generally votes unanimously and by acclamation.

The severance between the two halves of Berlin was completed on August 13, 1961 when, as the Communists put it, "the G.D.R. established state control of the boundary between the democratic and western sectors of Berlin."[12] Until then, it had not been too difficult to pass from the G.D.R. proper via East Berlin to West Berlin, where one could board a plane for the Federal Republic. All other routes between the two Germanies had long been subject to strict supervision: on May 27, 1952, an elaborate "police ordinance for the special control of the demarcation line" had, among other things, provided for a three-mile-wide "forbidden zone" (*Sperrzone*).[13] Consequently, as G.D.R. citizens were still migrating westward in large numbers through Berlin, it was necessary either to prevent air communication between West Berlin and the Federal Republic or to cut the city in two. The G.D.R. rulers, as we shall see presently, chose the course that appeared least threatening to world peace, but it involved sealing up windows with concrete and erecting fortifications in the very heart of the former Reich capital.

From the establishment of the G.D.R. until 1961, over 2·5 million of its inhabitants had passed through the West German refugee reception centers. The graph of monthly admissions reached a record height in February and June, 1953 (59,000 and 40,000 respectively), the total for that year being over 331,000. After slackening off in 1954 (184,000), the numbers rose in the next three years to 253,000, 280,000, and 262,000; they then declined somewhat, the figures for 1958, 1959, and 1960 being 204,000, 144,000, and 200,000. In the summer of 1961, the rate shot up, partly as a result of measures against people who crossed the border to their daily work (*Grenzgänger*). A press campaign in West Berlin also encouraged the flow of refugees, of whom there were over 30,000 in July alone as compared with under 20,000 in the preceding months. In August, 1961, 47,000 had already crossed when the wall was erected on the 13th. Since then, a small number of *Sperrbrecher* have "crashed the barrier" illegally: (5,701 in 1962, 1,203 in 1967), whereas the number officially allowed to cross has increased: since 1963, pensioners have little difficulty in doing so and, in 1968, they represented 70 per cent of a total of 11,200 migrants.[14]

The Berlin wall, as we shall see, made it possible for the G.D.R. to develop its economy to a remarkable extent. It also stabilized, by the argument of force, a state whose nature had already changed in two ways since it was set up—at all events from the legal point of view, the texts and symbols being for the most part reflections of what had already occurred in practice. The 1949 constitution had stated that "there is only one German nationality" (*Staatsangehörigkeit*); but on February 20, 1967, a "citizenship law" was adopted putting an end to a legal situation that no longer bore any relation to the facts. The preamble to the law states that:

Citizenship (*Staatsbürgerschaft*) of the German Democratic Republic came into existence, in accordance with international law, with the foundation of the German Democratic Republic. It is an expression of the sovereignty of the German Democratic Republic and contributes to the general further strengthening of the Socialist state.

Citizenship of the German Democratic Republic consists in the fact that its citizens belong to the first peace-loving, democratic, and Socialist German state, in which the working class exercises political power in alliance with the cooperative farmers, the Socialist intelligentsia, and other productive classes.

By this last formula the essential change that had taken place was embodied in a basic legal instrument. In 1949, the official slogan had been democracy and anti-Fascism: this was more prudent as far as the outside world was concerned, and the transformation of society lay too far in the future to justify the language of Marxist Socialism. The "national" anthem, written in 1949 by the poet Johannes R. Becher (a Spartacist in 1918 and a leading militant of the KPD from 1923; Minister of Education from January, 1954 till his death in October, 1958), spoke only of reconstruction, peace, and liberty. The G.D.R. adopted the same flag as the Federal Republic: the black-red-gold of Weimar, taken over from the 1848 revolution of which the East German regime proclaimed itself the rightful heir.

Ten years later, on October 1, 1959, the *Volkskammer* decreed that the center of the flag should be adorned with a hammer and a pair of compasses, encircled by a wreath of ears of corn. The change meant the abandonment of a flag common to the two Germanies, with all that this implied, and also symbolized the character of a state based on more specific foundations than those of anti-Fascist democracy. In April, 1967, Ulbricht, the First Secretary of the SED (Socialist Unity Party), said in a speech to its seventh congress that "it has been clear for some time that the present constitution of the G.D.R. does not correspond to the conditions of the Socialist order and the present state of historical development. It was in fact adopted at the time of the democratic anti-Fascist order, and, as is well known, we have now gone far beyond that."[15] On January 31, 1968, after elaborate preparatory work, the *Volkskammer* adopted the final draft of the new constitution. During the next two months, 750,000 meetings, in which 11 million citizens participated, were held in order to discuss 12,000 draft amendments, 173 of which were adopted. They were mostly of a formal character, apart from one relating to religious freedom and another prohibiting the extradition of G.D.R. citizens. On March 26, the Chamber ordered a referendum, which was held on April 6 and resulted in a vote of 94·5 per cent in favor of the draft. The new constitution, which conforms in many respects to the Soviet pattern, came into force on April 9. From the preamble onward, it strikes a very different note from its predecessor:

Imbued with the responsibility of showing the entire German nation the road to a future of peace and socialism,

Mindful of the historical fact that imperialism, under the leadership of the United States of America in alliance with circles of West German monopoly capitalism, has divided Germany in order to build up West Germany as a base of imperialism and the struggle against Socialism, which is contrary to the vital interests of the nation,

The people of the German Democratic Republic,

Standing firmly upon the achievements of the anti-Fascist, democratic, and Socialist transformation of the social system,

Unitedly furthering, in their working classes and strata, the work and spirit of the Constitution of October 7, 1949,

And animated by the will to advance unswervingly and in free decision on the road of peace, social justice, democracy, Socialism, and friendship among peoples,

Have given themselves this Socialist Constitution.

The first paragraph of Article 1 contains a double definition: "The German Democratic Republic is a Socialist state of the German nation. It is the political organization of the working people in town and countryside, who are jointly implementing Socialism under the leadership of the working class and its Marxist-Leninist party."

The first of these statements, whose importance for the foreign policy of both Germanies and their respective allies will be seen as we go on, is supplemented by Article 8 (2):

The establishment and cultivation of normal relations between the two German states, and peaceful cooperation between them on the basis of equal rights (*Gleichberechtigung*), are national concerns of the German Democratic Republic. The German Democratic Republic and its citizens strive, in addition, to overcome the division of Germany forced on the German nation by imperialism and to achieve, step by step, the *rapprochement* of the two German states until their reunification on the basis of democracy and Socialism.

The second sentence of Article 1 (1) gives a clear hint that the institutions described in the constitution are not to be the sole repositories of power. No single one of the thirty-eight articles of Section III—"Structure and System of State Management"—has anything to say about the Party, yet the latter's statutes of 1963 describe it as "the guiding force of all organizations of the working class and workers in general, and of state and social organizations."

Many provisions of the 1968 constitution merely codify changes that had already been introduced. Article 1 of the 1949 instrument described the new Republic as based on the *Länder*, and declared that: "The Republic decides on all issues which are essential to the existence and development of the German people as a whole, all other issues being decided upon by independent action of the *Länder*." But on July 23, 1952, the *Länder* were replaced by districts (*Bezirke*), subdivided into *Kreise*, and the *Land* parliaments and governments ceased to exist. Paradoxically, the *Länderkammer* (second chamber of the G.D.R. parliament) continued to function in a symbolic manner, its members being elected by the districts in 1954 and 1958, until it was dissolved with its own consent by a law of December 8, 1958.

The 1949 constitution provided for a President of the Republic with limited powers, and a Council of Ministers wielding executive power under its Chairman. When Wilhelm Pieck became President on October 11, 1949 he was seventy-three years old. He had joined the SPD in 1895 and, as a Spartacist, had been arrested during "red week" in Berlin in January, 1919. After his release, he became a member of the Central Committee of the KPD. He entered the Prussian *Landtag* in 1921 and the Reichstag in 1928, and played an important part in the Executive Committee of the Comintern. In 1933, he emigrated to France and the next year to the Soviet Union, from whence he returned in 1945. When the KPD and SPD joined to form the SED in 1946, he was co-chairman of the new party; in 1948 he was President of the *Volkskammer* at its session described in chapter 4. When he became President of the Republic, he was already more of a historic figure than a leader, and as long as he was alive there could be no question of changing the character of the office. He died on September 7, 1960; five days later, by an amendment to the

263

constitution, the presidency was abolished and replaced by a Council of State (*Staatsrat*), the organization and powers of which were maintained in the 1968 constitution.

In theory, the latter emphasizes still more than its predecessor the supremacy of the People's Chamber, elected by universal suffrage. It is described as a unique and sovereign body from which all other state organs derive their power:

Article 48
1. The People's Chamber is the supreme organ of state power in the German Democratic Republic. It decides in its plenary sessions on the basic questions of state policy.
2. The People's Chamber is the sole constituent and legislative organ in the German Democratic Republic. No one can limit its rights.
By its activities, the People's Chamber implements the principle of the unity of decision and execution.

Article 49
1. By its laws and decisions, the People's Chamber determines, in a final way binding on all, the aims of the development of the German Democratic Republic.
2. The People's Chamber determines the main rules for the cooperation of citizens, organizations, and state organs, as well as their tasks in implementing state plans for social development.
3. The People's Chamber ensures the enforcement of its laws and decisions and lays down basic principles for the activity of the Council of State, the Council of Ministers, the National Defense Council, the Supreme Court, and the Prosecutor-General.

Article 50
The People's Chamber elects the Chairman and members of the Council of State, the Chairman and members of the Council of Ministers, the Chairman of the National Defense Council, the President and judges of the Supreme Court, and the Prosecutor-General. They may be removed from office at any time by the People's Chamber.

Article 66 (1) seems actually to subordinate the Council of State to the Chamber: "As an organ of the People's Chamber, the Council of State fulfills, between sessions of the People's Chamber, all fundamental tasks resulting from the laws and decisions of the latter. It is responsible to the People's Chamber for its activities."

But the following articles show that the Council is really the key body. This is not only because it exercises the traditional functions of a Head of State [Article 66 (2): "The Chairman of the Council of State represents the German Democratic Republic in accordance with international law;" Article 77: "The Council of State exercises the right of amnesty and pardon"], but because the Council, directed by its Chairman (Article 69), performs multiple functions of an executive, legislative, and judicial character.

Article 71
1. The Council of State deals with all basic tasks arising from the laws and decisions of the People's Chamber, by means of decrees that are submitted to the People's Chamber for confirmation.

2. Decrees and decisions of the Council of State are legally binding.

3. The Council of State's interpretation of the constitution and laws is legally binding, insofar as this task is not performed by the People's Chamber itself.

Article 73

1. The Council of State takes fundamental decisions on matters relating to the defense and security of the country and organizes national defense with the help of the National Defense Council.

2. The members of the National Defense Council are appointed by the Council of State. The National Defense Council is responsible to the People's Chamber and the Council of State for its activities.

Article 74

The Council of State, on behalf of the People's Chamber, exercises continuous supervision over the constitutionality and legality of the activities of the Supreme Court and the Prosecutor-General.

Article 67 declares that "the Council of State is composed of the Chairman, the Vice-Chairmen, the members, and the Secretary," who are all elected for four years. But, though the constitution does not say so, the Chairman and the Secretary are the only ones who perform their functions on a full-time basis. The ordinary members are mayors of cities, party officials, heads of research institutes, managers of industrial plants or farms, and so on. This enhances the Chairman's real power, especially if—as has been the case ever since the post was created—he also happens to be the First Secretary of the Central Committee of the SED, while the Vice-Chairmen are themselves Chairmen of other state organs and the leaders of the other parties. In September, 1960, some observers suggested that Ulbricht had been "kicked upstairs" by virtue of his transfer from Vice-Chairman of the Council of Ministers to Chairman of the Council of State; but those who argued thus showed that they had not studied the new constitution properly. It was significant that at the same time Otto Grotewohl, the Chairman of the Council of Ministers, became Vice-Chairman of the Council of State, thus clearly indicating the subordination of the old body to the new.

The field of activity of the Council of Ministers, which consists of some forty members, is described in Articles 78 and 79 of the 1968 constitution. (The reader may feel that these give a more accurate account of relations between the Council of State and the Council of Ministers than the French constitution of 1958 does of relations between the President of the Republic and the government.)

Article 78

1. On behalf of the People's Chamber, the Council of Ministers organizes the execution of the political, economic, cultural, and social tasks, as well as the defense tasks entrusted to it, of the Socialist state. It functions on a collective basis.

2. The Council of Ministers works out scientifically based forecasts, organizes the economic system of Socialism, and directs the planned development of the national economy.

Article 79

1. The Council of Ministers functions on the basis of the laws and decisions of the People's Chamber as well as the decrees and decisions of the Council of State. It issues orders and takes decisions within the framework of the laws and decrees.

2. The Council of Ministers directs, coordinates, and supervises the activities of the ministries, the other central state organs, and the district councils in accordance with scientific standards of organization.

Grotewohl's death on September 21, 1964 and his replacement by Willi Stoph brought about some change in practice, owing to the two men's difference in age and political background. The former, who was only nine months younger than Ulbricht, originally belonged to the SPD. The latter was twenty years younger and a Communist of long standing; the chairmanship of the Council of Ministers could be for him, as it could not for Grotewohl, a steppingstone to the chairmanship of the Council of State and the office of party First Secretary.

In September, 1960, the President of the People's Chamber also became a Vice-Chairman of the Council of State. Johannes Dieckmann, a still closer contemporary of Ulbricht—only six months younger—had held the former office, which is not of high importance, from October, 1949 until his death in February, 1969, while remaining vice-chairman of the Liberal Democratic Party (LDPD). He was succeeded as President of the Chamber by Gerald Götting, who has been head of the G.D.R. branch of the CDU since 1966. He belongs to the postwar political generation, having been born in 1923, and in 1946 helped to form the Free German Youth (*Freie Deutsche Jugend*—FDJ) a mass organization built on an anti-Fascist basis, which later came under SED control. The replacement of Dieckmann by Götting illustrates both the continued existence of parties other than the SED and their firm integration in the political system, under leaders who played no part in public life before the war.

As we saw in chapter 3, the "united front" (*Einheitsfront*) of democratic anti-Fascist parties was created on July 14, 1945. Among the leaders who took part in its first rally were Wilhelm Pieck, Walter Ulbricht, Anton Ackermann, Franz Dahlem, and Otto Winzer for the KPD; Erich W. Gniffke[16] (who "played along" till October, 1948, when he migrated to West Germany), Otto Grotewohl, and Gustav Dahrendorf for the SPD; Andreas Hermes, Jakob Kaiser, and Ernst Lemmer for the CDU; and leaders of the LDPD. The first and last elections that were relatively free (in the western sense of the term) were held on October 20, 1946: they showed the voters to be equally divided between the SED on the one hand and the CDU and LDPD on the other. In Brandenburg and Saxony-Anhalt, the two latter parties were even in a majority. The next elections were not held until October 15, 1950; by this time two new "bourgeois" parties had been formed and, more important, the "single list" principle had been adopted or imposed. The seats were allocated in the proportion of 45 per cent for the bourgeois parties (15 per cent each for the CDU, the LDPD, and the two others combined), 25 per cent for the SPD, and 30 per cent for the mass organizations, including 10 per cent for the trade unions. Of the 12,235,168 registered voters, 98·53 per cent cast their ballots, of which 13,432 (0·11 per cent) were invalid. In this way, the single list of the National Front scored 99·72 per cent of the poll.

The composition of the fifth People's Chamber is not far different.[17] There are 127 SED representatives, including the Berliners, or 25·4 per cent of the assembly. The Farmers' Union (DBB), the National Democrats (NPDP), the CDU, and the LDPD have 52 seats (or 10·4 per cent each); the trade unions have 68 seats (13·6 per cent), the youth organization, 40 (8 per cent), the Women's Union (DFD), 35 (7 per cent), and the *Deutscher Kulturbund* 22, (4·4 per cent). The mass organizations are directly controlled by the SED, but the "bourgeois" parties are no less under its thumb: they publish newspapers and hold congresses, but have no real political substance. After the showdown with the CDU in 1947, the departure of Kaiser in that year, and of Lemmer to the West in 1949, the party's leadership was taken over by Otto Nuschke, who, like Lemmer, had been a Liberal before 1933 and who, as secretary-general of the *Deutsche Staatspartei*, had had to explain to his fellow members the policy of voting for Hitler's Enabling Act. Until his death on December 27, 1957, Nuschke was Vice-Chairman of the Council of Ministers and head of the Office for Church Affairs: he was not without influence in these posts, and the accusations of selling-out, which were leveled against him in the Federal Republic, would have been more just if they had been less blunt. He was succeeded by August Bach, under whose direction (from 1958 to 1966) the CDU became increasingly attuned to the dominant ideology, the process being apparently complete under Gerald Götting.

The LDPD underwent a similar evolution from acceptance to support of the new social order, which it finally adopted as a party aim. The National Democratic Party (NDPD) was not a spontaneous creation but was founded in 1948, with the object of attracting former professional soldiers and Nazi underlings: its leaders were Lothar Bolz, a KPD member of 1929 vintage who emigrated to the Soviet Union in 1939, and General Vincenz Müller, a former prisoner of war in Russia who joined Bolz on the National Free Germany Committee. The NDPD program came by degrees to be increasingly close to that of the SED.[18]

The merger between the SPD and the Communists in the Soviet zone was both a voluntary act and the result of coercion. Pressure from the occupying power was heavy and multiform; nor was the SPD rank and file consulted about the merger. Some of its Berlin members called for a referendum, which was held in the three western sectors on March 30, 1946, the Soviet commander having forbidden it in East Berlin. The results of the vote were clear-cut. Out of 33,247 registered members, 23,755 or 71·3 per cent took part: 19,529, or 82 per cent of these, were against the merger and 2,937 (12·4 per cent) in favor. However, in reply to a second question: "Are you in favor of an alliance between the two parties that would enable them to work together and avoid fratricidal strife?" 14,663 voted "Yes" and only 5,568 were opposed.

The merger was voluntary, on the other hand, in that it was accepted by most of the leaders of the revived SPD in the Soviet zone, despite Schumacher's vigorous opposition, which he expressed for the last time at a meeting with Grotewohl in Berlin on February 20. Following a decision taken on February 26 at a conference between their governing bodies, the SPD and KPD held separate congresses on April 19 and 20; then, at a joint constituent congress on April 21–22, Wilhelm Pieck and Otto Grotewohl were unanimously proclaimed, amid applause, co-chairmen of the German Socialist Unity Party (*Sozialistische Einheitspartei Deutschlands*—SED).

One may of course explain the behavior of a man like Grotewohl on grounds of naivety or personal ambition. During the Weimar period, he had a fairly unimpressive career in the SPD and in *Land* politics, chiefly in Brunswick, where he was a minister from 1920 to 1924 and, between 1925 and 1933, chairman of the central insurance office. But after 1945, when all over Europe parties and groups were entering into new alliances while retaining their independence, and when practical results seemed to justify this policy, it was not unreasonable that the German Socialists should hope to work out new forms of economic and social organization in conjunction with the Communists, to whom they had been linked by persecution under Hitler. In February, 1946, Anton Ackermann, a member of the Central Committee of the KPD, had published in the first number of the party monthly *Einheit* an article entitled "Is There a German Road to Socialism?" in which he argued that the rapidity of progress and the direction it took would depend on how soon the two parties could be unified. Maurice Thorez, the secretary-general of the French Communist Party and Deputy Prime Minister of France, said in a statement published in the London *Times* on November 18 that "the progress of democracy throughout the world . . . permits the choice of other paths to Socialism than the one taken by the Russian Communists. In any case, the path is necessarily different for each country."

Even in those days, however, it was clear as far as the Soviet zone of Germany was concerned that the first step would consist of a take-over of the unified party by what had originally been its smaller component. At the second SED congress, in September, 1947, the principle of parity was still officially respected. Communists and Socialists were appointed in pairs to the Central Secretariat (the future Politburo)—Pieck and Grotewohl, Ulbricht and Paul Fechner, Franz Dahlem and Erich Gniffke, Ackermann and Otto Meier—the members of each party having, in theory, specific responsibilities within a common sphere of activity. But in the eighty-member Executive (*Vorstand*), some SPD leaders were already missing in 1947 as compared with the previous year. In 1948, thanks to spontaneous defections and the work of "control commissions," the party began to shed those of its members who lacked enthusiasm for the "only possible road to Socialism"—to quote the title of an article in the party daily *Neues Deutschland* on September 24, in which Ackermann performed his "self-criticism" for having advocated a "German way" different from that of the Soviet Union.

The parity rule was officially declared obsolete in January, 1949, by which time the SED had already to a large extent achieved its objective, announced in July, 1948, of becoming a "new type of party," designed not to absorb the masses but to provide them with cadres. At the same time, its top institutions were reorganized. In the Politburo and its Secretariat, the Social Democrats became steadily fewer and less influential. As for the Executive, now called the Central Committee, by the third party congress in July, 1950, it contained only 11 former SPD members out of a total of 51 full members and 30 "candidates." From January, 1951, a drastic purge took place, with 6,000 "inspection committees," composed of 50,000 of the most reliable party members, subjecting their 1·3 million fellow members to the strictest interrogation. About 300,000 were expelled from the party or left it of their own accord, while some half a million others were adjudged fit to exercise responsibilities of every kind, including service in the new *Volkspolizei* or "people's police."[19]

The purge did not completely eliminate the remains of social democracy, but the SED had no longer any real affinity with its non-Communist element. As the years passed, the effect of age was added to those of expulsion or cold shouldering. When, in 1966, the SPD under Williy Brandt embarked on a short-lived dialogue with the SED, the latter's cadres had been almost wholly renewed and few had any SPD experience to look back on.[20] However, despite the passage of time, the SPD is today still dominated by the same elderly man—or rather this man, whose power was not immune from threats during the 1950's, has become the party's undisputed master. Walter Ulbricht's stature and prestige today perhaps denote a certain withdrawal into Olympian grandeur, encouraged by younger leaders who are more directly involved in the conduct of affairs. However this may be, the G.D.R. chief, known as *Spitzbart* on account of his goatee—a man whom nature did not create to inspire warm affection, and who was formerly well hated even within his own party—has come to enjoy general respect in the twenty-five years since he returned from Soviet exile.

In 1945, Ulbricht was only one, though the most important, of the small group epigrammatically described as "aides of the occupying power, aided to power by the occupation."[21] He was also one of the few Communist leaders of Weimar days who were not done to death either by Hitler or by Stalin. However, his party record was not more outstanding than that of Wilhelm Pieck or Franz Dahlem. The latter, in 1928, was a member of the Central Committee of the KPD responsible for trade union relations and, in 1937, was a political commissar with the International Brigade in Spain; he was handed over to Hitler by the Vichy government and imprisoned in the camp at Mauthausen, where he continued to work for the party.

Ulbricht was born at Leipzig on June 30, 1893; his father was a tailor, and he himself was apprenticed to a cabinetmaker. He joined the Socialist youth movement at fifteen and the SPD at nineteen.[22] He was called up in 1915, deserted twice in 1918, and joined the Spartacists in Leipzig, where he helped to establish a section of the KPD at the beginning of 1919. He became a full-time party official, held jobs in Saxony and Thuringia, and in 1923, at the age of thirty, was a member of the Central Committee. Later, a warrant was issued for his arrest for conspiracy, and he went underground. The party at this time was rent by internal strife, and the Secretary-General of the Comintern intervened to place Ernst Thälmann at its head: at the same time he noticed Ulbricht and sent him to the Lenin School at Moscow, where he also worked for a time at Comintern headquarters. Back in Germany in 1926, Ulbricht became a member of the Saxony *Landtag* and, in 1928, of the Reichstag; he was also the KPD representative on the Executive Committee of the Comintern and party secretary for the Berlin-Brandenburg district. He went to France in October, 1933 and returned to Germany in 1939, having served in the KPD in exile at Moscow and Prague and taken part in the Spanish civil war. He spent the years from 1940 to 1945 in Moscow: there he not only survived the murderous effects of Stalin's mistrust, which claimed as its victims four

members of the KPD's Politburo and ten of its Central Committee, but succeeded, by his adaptability and capacity for hard work, in being entrusted
with the preparation and execution of the KPD's plans for defeated Germany
under the Soviet occupation.

Ulbricht no doubt accepted without demur all the twists and turns of
Stalin's policy, including the transformation of Nazi Germany, from 1939 to
1941, into a friendly power engaged in defending itself against Anglo-French
imperialism. No doubt, too, he resembles Stalin in being a man of the party
apparatus, a methodical, tireless worker who likes to keep out of the public
eye. But he is neither cruel nor megalomaniacal. When the time came for him
to carry out his own purges in the SED, they were not bloody and spectacular
affairs like those enacted in the other East European countries during Stalin's
last years, and it was possible in later times to rehabilitate live people instead of
corpses. Paul Merker, for example, an old party militant and member of the
Politburo, was expelled from the SED in August, 1950 as an "instrument of
the class enemy" in connection with the purge in Hungary, and was arrested
in December, 1952 when the SED Central Committee applauded the condemnation of Rudolf Slánský at Prague. Like most of the Czechoslovak
victims—the phrase occurred in eleven out of the thirteen indictments—
Merker was "of Jewish origin," as were the majority of his friends who
suffered disgrace at this time. But whereas the former Secretary-General of
the Czechoslovak Communist Party was condemned to death and executed
along with ten of the other accused, Merker was tried in secret in 1954 and
sentenced to eight years' hard labor. Two years later, he was released, and, in
1964, at the age of seventy, he was honored for "special services to the
workers' movement."

Merker, it is true, had not been a direct rival of Ulbricht's, whereas, in
May, 1953, when Franz Dahlem was removed from the SED Secretariat, the
Politburo, and the Central Committee for "political blindness to the activity
of imperialist agents," the event marked the settling of a quarrel that dated
back to 1934. This took place two months after Stalin's death, when Soviet
triumvirate leaders were endeavoring to persuade Ulbricht to relax in some
degree the severity of his economic policy; the security regime in East Germany had also been tightened up since the announcement in July, 1952 of the
"creation, according to plan, of the foundations of Socialism in the German
Democratic Republic." For the first time, Ulbricht held out against Moscow,
despite two appeals from the Kremlin: the "new course" was not adopted
until June 9, 1953, following a direct order issued on the 5th by the Soviet
High Commissioner and not endorsed by the G.D.R. leader. A week later, an
explosion took place that threatened the regime with collapse but, paradoxically, had the effect of consolidating Ulbricht's position, the Soviet leaders
identifying him henceforth with the system which they had had to send in
tanks to preserve.

The events of June 17, 1953 were described in later Communist writings as
"an attempted *coup d'état*, supported by Western agents, with the object of
overthrowing the regime of the German Democratic Republic."[23] Many
accounts have been published of how the grievances of construction workers
over the raising of output norms despite the "new course" led to a strike on

June 16, followed by demonstrations and, on the 17th, a regular people's revolt. The Soviet military commander proclaimed a state of siege. At Magdeburg, Leipzig, and Dresden, and in most other industrial towns, disturbances broke out ranging from strikes to assaults on prisons. The authorities were at first taken by surprise, but they lost no time in putting down the first working-class rebellion against a Communist regime.

While the police and courts dealt with the strikers and demonstrators, political scapegoats also had to be found. The Central Committee, in a long resolution of July 26, affirmed that "the party's general line was and remains the right one," but admitted that mistakes had been made. Paul Fechner, the Minister of Justice and a former SPD member, was accused of having protected Fascist agents and inflicted heavy and illegal sentences on the workers. He, for his part, emphasized after the events of June 17 that the right to strike was safeguarded in the constitution and that strikers should not be penalized. Together with Fechner, Ulbricht got rid of some party leaders who had tried to use Moscow's new line as a pretext for unseating him. The chief of these were Wilhelm Zaisser, the Minister of State Security and a member of the Politburo, who as "General Gómez" had been chief of staff of the International Brigade in Spain, and Rudolf Herrnstadt, the editor of *Neues Deutschland* and a KPD member since 1924. Both were dismissed but not imprisoned, nor was Franz Dahlem, who was rehabilitated in 1956 and readmitted to the Central Committee in 1957.

Sterner treatment was meted out to the intellectuals who took too seriously the promises of de-Stalinization made by Khrushchev at the Twentieth Soviet Party Congress in February, 1956. During that year, Ulbricht was faced for the last time with opposition within the party leadership, aimed for different reasons at a change of policy in economic matters and over German reunification. The Hungarian rising and its suppression in October-November, 1956 gave the Soviet leaders additional grounds for valuing Ulbricht's steadfast attitude, and this helped him gradually to eliminate the chief figures in the opposition, a process completed in February, 1958 with the removal of Ernst Wollweber and Karl Schirdewan. The latter, a party militant from East Prussia who joined the Young Communists in 1923 at the age of sixteen, had spent the years from 1934 to 1945 in prison and concentration camps. He entered the SED Secretariat in 1952 and appeared to be a possible runner-up to Ulbricht when, in January, 1958, he was stripped of all his party functions and appointed director of the national archives at Potsdam.

Wollweber, who was Minister of State Security in 1958, had taken part as a lad in the naval mutiny at Kiel in November, 1918. His dismissal caused a sensation but was of minor importance against the general pattern of evolution within the party and state, where a younger generation was coming to the fore. Erich Honecker and Willi Stoph, born in 1912 and 1914 respectively, had made their way up in regular fashion under Ulbricht's leadership, having both joined the Communist youth movement in very early years. Honecker was sentenced to ten years' hard labor in 1935 and was still in prison in 1945, while Stoph spent the war years in the army. Thereafter their careers diverged. Honecker was in charge of the G.D.R. youth movement until 1955, when he went to Moscow for two years at the institute of higher political studies. He was a member of the SED Central Committee from 1946 onward, and of the Politburo and Secretariat from 1958, after which he gradually emerged as Ulbricht's second-in-command. It was he who, in January, 1963, presented the new SED statutes to the sixth party congress.

Stoph's first postwar employment was in the Department of Economic Administration. In 1948, he became head of the economic policy department of the SED Executive, and in 1951–52 he held a similar post under the Chairman of the Council of Ministers. He was Minister of the Interior in 1952–55 and became a general and Minister of Defense in January, 1956. In July, 1960, he was promoted to Deputy Premier in charge of the coordination and execution of party and government decisions. He was a member of the party Secretariat from 1950 to 1953, when he entered the Politburo, and, in July, 1962, became First Deputy Prime Minister. When he succeeded Grotewohl as Premier in 1964, he was in fact already performing the latter's functions.

As between the head of the party and the head of the government, there would have been no doubt in 1950 that the former was, by his office, a more important man than the latter. But during the 1960's, the party's role in society began to change. For a long time technical posts in the economy and administration had been filled by party members, but this policy was reversed during the period of expansion after the erection of the Berlin wall, when the SED leaders began appealing to competent technicians at all levels to join the party. This, however, does not alter the fact that the party still dominated the state apparatus and the whole economic and social system. What is changing is the way in which its domination is exercised. Confident of the support of the next generation as a result of the education it has implanted, the party sees itself as embodying the élite of the working population rather than directing the workers from outside. It may be precisely because the party has achieved its basic aims that Stoph appears more likely than Honecker to take over the leadership of the G.D.R. when Ulbricht disappears.

The New Economic and Social Order

Since the SED was founded, its membership has grown slowly from 1·3 to 1·8 million. The changes that have taken place in its methods of recruitment and in its relationship to society are due to the fact that the economic and social revolution in the G.D.R. is already part of history and has been accepted by virtually the whole population since 1961, with enthusiasm, resignation, or calculation as the case may be.

In 1950, private enterprise accounted for 43·2 per cent of total economic production in terms of value. By 1968, this figure had fallen to 6·3, the building industry being the only one in which the private sector represented as much as 10 per cent. There is also a "joint sector" in which enterprises have accepted, willingly or otherwise, a degree of participation by the state, working for it on a contract basis: these enterprises account for slightly under 8 per cent of total production, but employ only 418,000 white-collar workers as against 477,000 in the private sector (including 141,000 craftsmen) and 5,416,000 in the socialized sector. In agriculture, there has been a complete reversal: in 1950,

94·3 per cent of the cultivated area was in private hands, whereas in 1968, 94·1 per cent belonged to "Socialist enterprises."

Until August 13, 1961, anyone who disliked the process of social transformation was able to flee to West Germany, and the number of refugees in March, 1953, for instance, was largely due to measures at the beginning of that month affecting craftsmen and small-scale industry. Over 4,000 doctors left the G.D.R. between 1952 and 1961; however, more than half of the 88,000 or so who were still practicing there at the end of the 1960's were carrying on their profession on a private basis (*in freier Praxis*), although the social security regulations, especially from the financial point of view, were a good deal stricter than in the Federal Republic. Clearly "desertion of the Republic" (*Republikflucht*) was a permanent cause of weakness to the economy, depriving it of technicians and skilled labor. In 1961 alone, 17,400 of the refugees were employed in the metalworking industries. Many took their children with them, thus still further exacerbating the labor shortage.

Despite the initial influx of over 3 million expellees from further east, the demographic situation in the G.D.R. had all along given ground for anxiety; this was not solely because of the refugees who "voted with their feet," even though they were the main cause of the population falling from 19 million in 1948 to 17 million in 1961. A glance at the age pyramid helps to show why there has been virtually no improvement since then: 17,087,000 inhabitants at the end of 1968 as against 17,079,000 at the end of 1961. The surplus of women is even greater than in the Federal Republic, and the years immediately after the war were even more full of hardship and less favorable to the birth rate: of the 17 million inhabitants at the end of 1968, 130,000 were born in 1946 and 181,000 in 1947, whereas the figures for births in 1943 and 1949 were 221,000 and 220,000 respectively. But the pyramid does not suffice to explain the demographic stagnation and the drop in the fertility rate from an already low level of 17 births per 1,000 inhabitants in 1960 to under 15 in 1968. The high proportion of women at work is doubtless a contributing factor. Whatever the reasons, the economic growth of the G.D.R. since its inception and particularly in the 1960's has at least one semimiraculous aspect: how has it been possible for production to increase to such an extent without an expanding labor force? The working population in 1968 was almost exactly the same size as in 1955 (8,172,000 as against 8,188,000). Although urbanization is in progress, the G.D.R. is still a country of middle-sized towns, with only Leipzig and Dresden exceeding the half-million mark; Chemnitz (renamed Karl-Marx-Stadt in May, 1953), Magdeburg, and Halle have between 200,000 and 300,000 inhabitants, and only five other towns have over 100,000.

Demographic problems, however, are not the chief ones with which the G.D.R. economy has had to contend. The Soviet occupation zone represented something under a quarter of Germany as it had been in 1937—23 per cent of its territory and 22 per cent of its population. The area was poor in raw materials, except lignite and potassium: it supplied only 5 per cent of Germany's iron ore production and 2·5 per cent of her coal. Although it possessed important specialized industries, basic industry was lacking: in particular, it supplied less than 10 per cent of the nation's output of steel, a fact that weighed even more heavily than the Soviet example in determining the priority given to heavy industry.

The most crushing handicap was that imposed by the occupying power. Not only was there nothing corresponding to the Marshall Plan, but the Russians from start to finish extracted from their part of Germany an amount not far short of what they had tried to get from Germany as a whole in the inter-Allied negotiations.[24] The initial looting (*Trophäenaktion*), the waves of dismantling from 1945 to 1948, the transformation of enterprises into "Soviet companies" (*Sowjetische Aktiengesellschaften*—SAG)—all these activities, described in chapter 3, were accompanied and followed by levies on current production and indirect forms of tribute such as the lowering of prices and transport charges for reparation deliveries. Only in August, after the revolt of June 17, 1953 did the Soviet Government announce that they would waive further reparations as from January 1, 1954. The SAG's were restored to German ownership, in some cases genuinely while in others the change was more fictitious. Thus the very important Wismut-AG, which was responsible for prospecting and exploiting the G.D.R.'s uranium resources and which employed up to 200,000 people, was turned into a "joint company" with a strong Soviet preponderance.

Even before the new state was born, the SED launched a two-year plan to bring production up to the 1936 level. After its expiration a very ambitious five-year plan came into effect on January 1, 1951, having been adopted by the third party congress in July, 1950: it was to meet the demands of this plan that output norms were raised in 1953. In spite of delay caused partly by the adoption of the "new course," the main lines of the second five-year plan were approved in March, 1956, in a climate of optimism: this was the period of Khrushchev's economic challenge to the West, which was to be "caught up with and surpassed" in the near future. In order to gear the country's economy more closely to that of the U.S.S.R., where the new plan was due to run from January, 1959, it was decided in 1958 to make the last two years of the second G.D.R. plan part of the third. A crucial point was reached halfway through the resulting seven-year plan (1959–65). The growth of industrial output in 1960 fell far below the planned rate, and the collectivization of agriculture, which was forced through in the same year, led to a food shortage. After the erection of the wall in August, 1961, recovery was not achieved all at once. Karl Mewis, the head of the Planning Commission and a member of the Politburo, was dismissed in January, 1963. However, the sixth congress was able to note the presense of encouraging factors, of which advantage was taken in the planning and execution of the plan for 1964–70. The emphasis has since been less on precise objectives than on general forecasts and annual achievements; much is also heard of management techniques and the role of prices in shaping the economy, without prejudice to its Socialist character.

This is particularly the case in agriculture, where the existence of large cooperatives makes it possible to plan on a specialized basis. Originally, the declared objective was merely to dispossess the rich and divide up their estates among the poor, as was done in the land reform of September, 1945–April, 1946. The cooperatives (*Landwirtschaftliche Produktionsgenossenschaften*—LPG) were not set up until July, 1952, chiefly for the benefit of "new farmers"

(*Neubauern*) who had been allotted holdings in 1946. By the end of 1952, there were nearly 2,000 LPG's, and three years later there were three times as many, despite the slowdown after June 17, 1953. The farmers' discontents in 1952–53 were considerably more serious than the workers': the harvest was bad, tens of thousands of farmers could not meet their planned deliveries and were threatened with punishment, and thousands of these fled to the West.

By 1959, over 10,000 cooperatives were in existence, farming 40 per cent of the country's cultivable area. Then, on June 3, a law on "voluntary" collectivization was passed by the *Volkskammer*. It was put into effect from December, 1959 to April, 1960 to the accompaniment of all sorts of pressure, including the public denouncing of recalcitrants, loudspeakers or organized shouting (*Sprechchöre*) outside their farms, and interminable "discussions" with party activists. The new farms were of three types. In the first, the farmer only made over his ploughland to the cooperative; in the second, he also provided meadows and pastureland and some of his livestock. In the third type, everything was collectivized except half a hectare of land, two cows, two sows, and the flocks of sheep. Members of cooperatives are paid in proportion to what they have contributed and, more especially, to their labor (20 and 80 per cent respectively in the third type), this being reckoned in "labor units": the scale of pay is a fairly steep one, substantially favoring the chairman, the chief accountant, and the team leader (*Brigadeleiter*). Official policy is more and more to encourage type 3, for two interconnected reasons: it is more socialistic, and it makes it easier to consolidate holdings and thus rationalize and step up production. At the end of 1960, the number of LPG's was 19,276; eight years later there were 11,834 of them, covering a total area of about 6·5 million hectares (about 16 million acres or 25,000 square miles). There are even "associations of cooperatives" (*Kooperationsgemeinschaften*), comprising several LPG's and covering in some cases an area of some 12,000 hectares (about 30,000 acres).

As a result of rationalization, technical improvements, and industrialization, it is hoped that in time agriculture will cease to be a separate economic sector and the differences between the rural and urban environment will disappear. The position of an agricultural worker is already not so very different from that of a factory hand. The private farmer has become an official or employee of the cooperative, with the loss of independence that that entails but also with the advantages of social security, paid holidays, and a pension. All land workers are supposed, by improving their skills, to increase over-all productivity. In 1965, 74·4 per cent of agricultural workers had no special training; by 1985, it is planned to reduce this figure to 8·5 and to increase the percentage of skilled workers (*Facharbeiter*) from 19·9 to 61·8 per cent; "foremen" (*Meister*) from 3·1 to 23 per cent; instructors (*Fachschulkader*) from 2·1 to 4·2 per cent; and instructors with a university education from 0·5 to 2·5 per cent.[25]

Collectivization did not, to say the least, pay off immediately in terms of productivity. Yields per hectare fell steadily until 1962 and only began to improve in 1963; the 1960 output of cereals, potatoes, and sugar-beet was not overtaken until 1967. In industry likewise, it was not until the later 1960's that a genuine rally took place, a fact that accounts for the widely different estimates of economists writing at approximately the same period. A well-informed study completed in the spring of 1959 showed that the national per capita income was still increasing faster in the Federal Republic than in the G.D.R., and attributed this not only to the drain of refugees but to the G.D.R.'s inefficient investment policy.[26] Four years later, the most thorough study to be published in France, based on 1962 figures, still spoke of a "fairly spectacular" failure, and took the view that "the erection of the Berlin wall was probably the only way to prevent the distintegration of the G.D.R.'s economy and its political system." It had not, however, sufficed to close the gap between the two German economies: "The divergence in standards of living, which tended to grow less between 1950 and 1958–59, has increased in the last few years."[27] Three years after these observations, the word "miracle" began to appear in the headlines and Ulbricht's hopeful forecasts were considered highly reasonable.[28] It would seem, however, that a wholly optimistic view of the future is no less out of place than the former pessimism, for new difficulties made themselves felt at the end of 1969, partly owing to a bad harvest. Older troubles persisted also: errors of management, lack of coordination in exchanges between industries, shortage of power (gas and electricity), and transport problems. But the gross national product again increased by about 5 per cent in 1969, growth being most marked in the electrotechnical and electronic fields and in machine tool construction. Future planning should be aided, moreover, by the decision taken in July, 1969, which entered into force on January 1, 1970, to introduce a unified system of accounting and statistics in private enterprises and those partially state-run.

At all events, the G.D.R.'s economic record gives ground for congratulation in two quite different spheres which are nevertheless doubly related to each other. The development of foreign trade has been steady and considerable, so much so that the G.D.R. has emerged as an economic power on the world scale. This success has been achieved in part at the expense of internal consumption, but the resulting prestige has led, as many reports testify, to a new feeling of self-satisfaction expressed in the phrase "*Wir sind wieder wer*" ("We're somebody again"). The feeling is encouraged to a great extent by the improvement in living standards, though housing is still a black spot. In this field official sources are careful to give only percentages of improvement, and it was left to *Neues Deutschland* to report, in August, 1965, that only 800,000 homes had been built in the fifteen years from 1950 to 1964. In other respects there is real progress, though comparisons between West and East are harder to make than is admitted by either side. Rationing was abolished in May, 1958, but many types of everyday goods are still in short supply; symbols of the affluent society, on the other hand, are more and more plentiful. In 1963, 42 per cent of G.D.R. workers and employees had a television set in their homes, while in 1967 this had risen to 74·5 per cent. The corresponding figures for refrigerators are 15·7 and 43·7, and for washing machines 18·1 and 44·3. However, by 1967, the proportion of car-owners was still only 9·6 per cent.

At this point, however, the difficulty of comparison becomes apparent. The East uses statistical tricks, for example by not giving the over-all proportion of refrigerators to homes. But comparisons in the Federal Republic regularly leave out of account an essential element, namely the provision in the East of equipment and services on a collective basis. Private cars are an index of prosperity, but only of a certain form of prosperity. Crèches, stadiums, libraries, and social benefits must also be taken into account. Admittedly, when all is said and done, the standard of living in the Federal Republic is decidedly higher, and the best proof of this is the continued existence of the wall. But G.D.R. citizens can make three types of comparison with gratifying results: by considering their own situation in the past, the other countries of Eastern Europe, and the position in the Federal Republic as regards *relative* levels of income, that is to say the glaring social inequalities that are apparent to them from West German television programs.

The degree of satisfaction the East Germans feel is increased by the adroit official presentation of what appear to be strictly objective figures. For example, the G.D.R. *Statistical Yearbook* devotes page after page to expenditures on social welfare and culture but says nothing about military and administrative items; yet, while the state budget stands at about 60,000 million marks, the expenditure in question adds up to only some 25,000 million, although everything is done to give the impression that it represents the principal charge on state resources.

Despite all this, it is not an easy matter to assess the degree of contentment among inhabitants of the G.D.R. This is partly because sociological studies, though developing, are still limited and subject to many restrictions,[29] and partly because there is no permitted outlet for discontent, certainly not through representative bodies of any kind. This is true, above all, of the trade unions. The Confederation of Free German Trade Unions (*Freier Deutscher Gewerkschaftsbund*—FDGB), which was set up on June 13, 1945, has a section to itself in the 1968 constitution, where we read:

Article 44
1. The free trade unions, united in the Confederation of Free German Trade Unions, are the all-embracing class organization of the workers. They safeguard the interests of workers, employees, and members of the intelligentsia by means of comprehensive codetermination in political, economic, and social matters.
2. The trade unions are independent bodies. No one may limit or obstruct their activities.
3. Through their organization and organs, their representatives in the elected organs of state power, and their proposals to state and economic bodies, the trade unions play a determining role in shaping Socialist society, in the planning and management of the national economy, in the accomplishment of the scientific-technical revolution, and in the development of working and living conditions, health protection, and labor safety, cultural working environment (*Arbeitskultur*), and the mental and physical recreation (*kulturellen und sportlichen Lebens*) of the working people.
The trade unions cooperate in the drawing up of plans in enterprises and institutions, and are represented in the Social Councils of the associations of nationally owned enterprises (*Volkseigene Betriebe*—VEB) and in the production committees of enterprises and combines. They organize the Permanent Production Councils.

Article 45
1. The trade unions have the right to conclude agreements with government authorities, enterprise managements, and other leading economic bodies on all questions concerning the working and living conditions of the working people.

2. The trade unions take an active part in shaping the Socialist legal system (*Rechtsordnung*). They have the right to initiate legislation and to supervise from the social point of view the maintenance of the working people's legally guaranteed rights.

3. The trade unions direct the social insurance system of workers and office employees on the basis of the self-administration of the insured. They play a part in the comprehensive material and financial care and protection of citizens in case of illness, accident at work, infirmity, and old age.

4. All state organs and directors of the economy are obligated to ensure close cooperation with the trade unions on a basis of full confidence.

In practice, while the FDGB has been entrusted since 1951 with the administration of the social security system, and while its fifteen component unions, whose membership stood at 6·8 million at the end of 1968, exercise at the plant, industry, or national level some of the functions ascribed to them by the constitution, their independence is wholly fictional and they do not represent the workers in anything like the same sense as trade unions in the West. The only parallel that might be drawn is with the French CGT between 1944 and 1947, when the Communists were members of the successive governments, the watchword was national reconstruction, and the powerful trade union organization saw its role as one of enforcing discipline rather than wage claims: it reverted to type only after the wildcat strike at the Renault works in 1947 and the dropping of Communists from the government. In the G.D.R., there was no such regression: on the contrary, the right to strike, safeguarded in 1949, no longer appears in the 1968 constitution, and the FDGB has always played its full part in campaigns to increase output. When, on October 13, 1948 a miner named Adolf Hennecke, at the Karl Liebknecht pit at Gottes Segen ("God's Blessing") near Zwickau, achieved the glorious exploit of fulfilling his norm by 380 per cent, the union threw its weight behind the "Hennecke movement" with the object not only of encouraging labor heroes but of boosting norms generally. When, in May, 1953, the time-and-motion experts came to check the implementation of the 10 per cent rise, we may be confident that they met with no opposition from trade unionists.

The FDGB is only one example, though the most important one, of the general policy of supervising and directing the various social groups through organizations that are themselves directed by the party. Both before and since the introduction of this system of control, the police and courts have been responsible for punishing deviations and seeing that the new society runs no risk of straying from the path that the party has mapped out for it.

"State security" was taken care of well before there was a state. At the end of 1945, special bureaus dealing with political offenses were set up at *Land* and *Bezirk* (district) levels, and a year later they came under the main zonal administration. In February, 1950, the political police, known as the *Staatssicherheitsdienst* (SSD), split off from the Ministry of the Interior to form a separate ministry. The SSD has from the outset been accused in West Germany of infiltration and subversion outside the borders of the G.D.R. Inside the borders, it has had less to do since the political opposition declined and the ordinary police, as well as the courts, began to take over the defense of the workers' and peasants' state. The frontiers of the state are well guarded in both directions: there is a standing order to open fire on any citizen who tries to cross them without leave, which has accounted for about 130 deaths during the eight years since the Berlin wall was erected.

The repression of public enemies was for a long time associated with the name of Hilde Benjamin (née Lange). A lawyer by profession, born in 1902, she joined the KPD in 1927 and married a doctor who perished at Mauthausen. In 1945, the occupying power appointed her chief public prosecutor (*Oberstaatsanwältin*) at Berlin-Lichterfelde. From 1947, she was in charge of personnel at the Department (later Ministry) of Justice, where she supervised the training of "people's judges." She was Vice-President of the Supreme Court from 1949 to 1953, when she became Minister of Justice. Under her auspices, a law was promulgated in December, 1957 that "supplemented" the Penal Code in respect of "crimes against the state and the activity of its organs," with formidable penalties for espionage and "information-gathering," anti-state propaganda (*staatsgefährdende Propaganda und Hetze*), sabotage, and incitement to quit the territory of the Republic. Severe cases may be visited with the death penalty or hard labor for life, for example when the offense "is committed by several persons who have banded together to commit such crimes," or at a time when the G.D.R. is especially menaced.

In 1967, Hilde Benjamin was succeeded by Karl Wünsche, an LDPD leader aged thirty-eight, who himself had been in prison for a short time in 1953. The change, it was declared, was a normal one involving no alteration of policy. This is true in one sense, less so in another. The new minister represents a different generation and quite possibly a different view of the question of a permanent political purge; in any case, over the years, repression has evolved into a system of authoritarian control, with sanctions becoming less harsh as political and social stability has increased. On the other hand, there is continuity in the notion of the judiciary, which was defined many times before its inclusion in the 1968 constitution, Article 94 of which states that: "Only persons who are loyally devoted to the people and their Socialist state . . . may be judges."

The G.D.R. professed from the beginning to be a totally different creation from Nazi Germany, while accusing the Federal Republic of showing scandalous indulgence toward men and women with a Nazi past. Even in East Germany, it comes to light from time to time that some honored citizen has a criminal record, but, when it does, the sentence is a great deal more severe than in the West. Horst Fischer, a doctor who had been guilty of concentration camp atrocities, was executed in 1966. In May, 1969, Josef Blösche was condemned to death for his share in deportations and massacres as a member of an SS "special squad" (*Einsatzkommando*). The penalty for concealing former crimes from the party and state authorities is also more severe than in the Federal Republic.[30] In 1959, Ernst Grossmann was expelled from the SED Central Committee when it came to light that he had been an SS warder at Sachsenhausen. In 1963, the new Minister of Agriculture, Karlheinz Bartsch, lost his post as the result of revelations made in the West and was dismissed from the Central Committee and the Politburo.

However, men who would be branded as "ex-Nazis" if they were citizens of the Federal Republic may occupy important posts in the G.D.R. provided they repented at the appropriate time, especially during captivity in the Soviet Union. This is true in particular of academics and scientists, though the number thus rehabilitated is smaller than in the West. Among the more noteworthy cases is that of Arno von Lenski, born in 1893, an assessor in the Nazi "people's court" presided over by Roland Freisler, of whom we heard in the last chapter: Lenski became a deputy to the *Volkskammer* and a general in the People's Army until he retired in 1958. Another case is that of Herbert Kröger, born in 1913, who joined the NSDAP in 1933 and rose to be an *Oberscharführer* in the SS. He was taken prisoner at Stalingrad and sent to an *Antifa* (anti-Fascist) school in the Soviet Union, where he also assisted Zaisser on the Free Germany Committee. He later specialized in public and administrative law, defended the KPD before the Constitutional Court at Karlsruhe, and was then put in charge of the training of future diplomats. of the G.D.R.

Another aspect of the G.D.R.'s breach with the past is the refusal of its leaders to accept civil liability for the crimes of the Hitler regime. The G.D.R. pays no indemnities, but victims of Nazism are entitled to an "honorary pension" of 600 marks a month, with an extra 200 for the more active members of the resistance—a more equitable system, after all, than that of paying compensation in proportion to the individual's former wealth and position rather than the hardships suffered.

Unfortunately the principle of equal treatment is, to say the least, infringed by anti-Semitism, which exists in the G.D.R. in a more or less open form according to circumstances. Not that there are many Jews left: their communities amount to only 2,000 or 3,000 persons all told, though there have been and are Jews occupying important positions in the country's political and intellectual life. The wave of anti-Semitism in 1952–53, at the close of Stalin's life, led many to flee the country, while others were victimized on the grounds of a "Zionist plot." Some nevertheless remained in important jobs and were able to rise still higher in later years: for instance Albert Norden, the SED propaganda chief, who became a member of the Politburo in 1958 and of the Secretariat in 1963, or Hanna Wolf, directress of the party's Karl Marx University in 1950, who joined the Central Committee in 1958, or again Alexander Abusch, who shared Paul Merker's disgrace in 1950 but became Vice-Minister of Culture in 1954 and Minister in 1958. Since 1967, however, there has been a fresh wave of "anti-Zionism" in the G.D.R., as in the rest of Eastern Europe. In 1968, before the invasion of Czechoslovakia, the party daily *Neues Deutschland* proclaimed that "Zionism is in control in Prague," thus echoing the *Völkischer Beobachter*, which had declared in 1938 that "the Jews are in control in Prague." One should perhaps not be surprised, as Günter Kertzscher, the SED paper's assistant editor and an assiduous denouncer of neo-Nazism in the Federal Republic, himself joined the Nazi party in 1937.[31]

However, at no time and in no way could it be said that the presense in the G.D.R. of individuals with a guilty past has amounted to a restoration of Nazism or a kind of group absolution. This is true above all of the People's Army. Certainly one of the founders of this body in its original form as part of the People's Police—General Vincenz Müller, who died in mysterious circumstances in 1961—had served in the political department of Hitler's General staff and was thus more involved in the political side of the Wehrmacht than Generals Speidel and Heusinger, the first Bundeswehr chiefs. But, whereas all the higher posts in the Bundeswehr were filled by former field officers of Hitler's army, the G.D.R. armed forces were from the start entrusted to men who were politically reliable, even if their technical ability for the time being left something to be desired. We have mentioned the case of Willi Stoph. General Karl Heinz Hoffmann, who succeeded him as Minister of Defense in 1960, was the first chief, in 1956, of the National People's Army (*Nationale Volksarmee*—NVA), although his only experience in the field had been the command of a battalion in Spain in 1936; he had, however, previously studied at a Moscow military academy.

The men have changed, but the uniforms remain the same. Or rather, the NVA has revived a whole range of military traditions, including the goosestep and the cult of 1812-15, Prussia's part in the "war of liberation" against Napoleon. The names of Scharnhorst and Gneisenau are heard much more often in the G.D.R. than in the West: the East Germans see themselves as heirs to a national history that is older than Marx, and in which Prussia's role was not a small one. This is partly because the G.D.R. leaders have resuscitated the military ideal while altering its ideological content. The talk is no longer of Germany's greatness but of defending Socialism; but everything is done, over and above compulsory military service, to interest young people in the army and especially in paramilitary training. The year 1969 saw a massive campaign to popularize the army from the point of view of politics and "military sport" (*Wehrsport*), a term familiar from Hitler's day. Children are taught to love the People's Army and its soldiers at a tender age, as is shown by the following lines from a book of school ceremonies (*Schulfeierbuch*):[32]

> *So wie du wolln wir einst sein,*
> *wenn wir älter sinde—*
> *denn du schützt den Sonnenschein*
> *und den Frühlingswind*
> *und die Ente auf dem Teich*
> *und im Wald das Reh*
> *und des Gartens Blütenreich*
> *und den stillen See.**

Another kindergarten primer explains why the soldiers must keep on the watch: the rich idlers who have fled to West Germany are brewing wicked schemes, "ready to pounce on our Republic like cruel wolves." West Germany is where "the police lock up anybody who wants to prevent war."[33] Phrases of this sort are part and parcel of educational policy and are echoed by the FDJ (Free German Youth), which is pledged by its statutes to "awaken in the hearts of young people passionate hatred and disgust at West German militarism and revanchism and all the hostile forces that threaten their lives and future happiness."[34]

*"When we are older we want to be like you, for you protect the sunshine and the spring breeze, ducks on the pond, deer in the forest, gardens with lovely flowers, and the peaceful lake."

When the FDJ was set up in February, 1946, it was supposed to be open to all young people, with leaders drawn from all parties. It soon, however, took shape as the SED youth organization and, in 1957, officially became "the Socialist Youth Organization of the G.D.R." Its 1963 statutes describe it as "the mass organization of G.D.R. youth," based on the voluntary membership of young people of all classes and backgrounds. It "embodies and constantly reinforces the political and organizational unity of the young generation" and is guided in all its activity by the advice and directives of the SED, whose policy, based on the teachings of Marx, Engels, and Lenin, corresponds to the vital interests of the nation and its young people, and whose over-all task is to guide the whole German people toward a Socialist future.

The statutes have much to say about the FDJ's duties in the field of moral education. It is to "mobilize young people to take part in carrying out the decisions of the SED . . . the People's Chamber, the Council of State, and the government of the G.D.R. in every area of social life," to see that their lives are governed by Socialist ethical and moral principles, that they work, learn, and study in exemplary fashion and "fight against capitalist immorality, selfishness, boorishness (*Flegelei*), drunkenness, and uncomradely behavior especially toward women and girls"; they are also to "show respect for old people and restrain their comrades from bad behavior."

The age of entrance into the FDJ was fixed at fourteen. Later, the "Young Pioneers" were created for the age group ten to fourteen, and, since 1952, there have been two groups aged six to ten and ten to fourteen, the latter being called *Thälmann-Pioniere* after the KPD chairman who died in 1944. The policy of indoctrination is clear enough, especially as children who do not join the Pioneers are thereby cut off from their fellows. The keynote is struck by the "Ten Principles" of Socialist youth policy adopted by the Council of State on March 31, 1967.[35] Like the SED statutes, these define the capacity to think for oneself (*selbständiges Denken*) as the ultimate aim of education, it being postulated that the use of this capacity will lead young people to love their Socialist fatherland and to embrace "with all their heart and mind" the cause of friendship with the Soviet Union.

Indoctrination of this type seems to be carried on more thoroughly than in any of the other people's democracies. At the same time—and the two phenomena cannot be dissociated from each other—the priority given to education and training has led to the provision of an excellent school and university system. Remarkable progress was made even before the law of December, 1958 on the "Socialist development of the school system," which introduced comprehensive schooling and a ten-year curriculum, and the law of 1965 on the "unified Socialist system of education" (*einheitlich sozialistisches Bildungssystem*).[36] The latter naturally requires pupils, apprentices, and students to be given a thorough schooling in Marxism-Leninism. But the whole system represents a genuine endeavor to provide equality of opportunity and long-term education, enabling those who wish it to improve their professional skill and general culture well beyond the years of ordinary schooling.

The G.D.R. is in fact well ahead of the F.R.G. in many respects, such as the number of kindergartens, the ratio of teachers to pupils, the quality of comprehensive technical schools as compared with old-style primary ones, and the creation of new technical institutes. This does not mean, however, that the objective of equality has been attained in all respects. For one thing, the percentage of each age group engaged in higher studies is still small compared for example with France: in 1968, the total number of students was 110,000, including 28,000 studying by correspondence and 3,500 in evening classes. Second, while the sons and daughters of former privileged persons were systematically prevented from going to university, new privileged classes have come into existence: the children of economic and political executives nowadays run little risk of being lumped in with the mass of skilled workers who receive no more than an extra year or two of technical training.

The G.D.R. schools and colleges and the FDJ have a much stronger practical bias than the majority of corresponding institutions in the West. The policy of acquainting young people with the production process at first hand has many advantages, particularly in uprooting ideas of social superiority. Naturally, there is a more down-to-earth motive: the development of the individual's skills is not only intended to draw him out and give him a fuller personality, but, first and foremost, to improve his ability to contribute to raising economic production. Education and the requirements of the economy are of necessity interrelated. Again, young people are given an important place in all spheres of life insofar as they seem better integrated into the political or doctrinal system than their elders. The state's assumption of responsibility for meeting all the needs of young people, whether by means of sport facilities or numerous and well-stocked libraries, is designed to protect them from any influence that might retard the process of integration, especially that of the churches.

A decisive step from this point of view was the introduction of the *Jugendweihe* or ceremony of "youth consecration." Despite sharp objection in 1954 by Protestant and Catholic authorities, the first major celebrations of this secular rite were held in 1955. It consists of a sort of solemn initiation into adult society, preceded by a "catechism" known as the *Jugendstunden*. The law of 1964 on youth matters describes the *Jugendweihe* as a "solid element in preparing young people for life and work in a Socialist society." The ceremony includes an oath of allegiance to the state and Socialism, to the cause of friendship among peoples and particularly with the Soviet Union. In theory it is quite compatible with the religious rite of confirmation, which it is designed to resemble, but the reason for the Protestant and Catholic churches' protests is evident.

Quite apart from the *Jugendweihe*, the number of confirmations and First Communions seems to be declining along with religious practice in general. At Leipzig, in 1949, 6,000 children were baptized; twenty years later, although the birth rate was appreciably higher, the number was only about 1,000. This does not mean that the ceremonies of "Socialistbaptism" (*sozialistische Namensgebung*) or "Socialist marriage" have caught on to any extent.[37] In 1968, less than 5 per cent of marriages were celebrated with Socialist rites, as compared with 15 per cent with religious ones, the other four-fifths being registry office ceremonies. In the 1964 census, about two-thirds of the population, but only 45 per cent of men, described themselves as belonging to a religious denomination. As compared with 1952, the Protestant Church had lost nearly 5 million adherents, while the Catholics, whose number had dropped from 2 to 1·4 million, represented only 8·1 per cent of the population.

This change has been accompanied by an alteration in the government and party line toward religion: in place of aggressive and hostile declarations there are frequent references to the common ground of humanism. The whole educational and cultural environment is nonreligious and the churches are treated as largely irrelevant to society, but the regime is certainly not interested in making martyrs: people are free to practice their religion, a good many churches are built, and numerous theological works are published. But when, for example, the Catholic bishops take up a position in regard to legislation on family matters, their views are treated as those of private citizens and not of the acknowledged spokesmen of a community.[38]

The Catholic Church has adapted itself without much friction, partly because unlike the Protestants it was not organized on an all-German basis. Instead of the Conference of West German Catholic bishops at Fulda, the G.D.R. episcopate meets in a Berlin Conference, attended also by auxiliary bishops and vicars-general, representing the dioceses situated wholly or partly in G.D.R. territory. The problem of the reorganization by Rome of the diocesan system in accordance with the G.D.R.'s present frontiers with Poland and West Germany will sooner or later present itself acutely, especially as the Protestant Church has already adapted its organization to political conditions.

In the previous chapter we traced the principal stages of the division of German Protestantism between East and West. For a time, Provost Heinrich Grüber of Berlin, a former prisoner at Dachau, represented the EKD vis-à-vis the East German authorities, not without effect. This arrangement came to an end in 1958 after the crisis of which the agreement with Bonn over military chaplaincies was either the cause or the pretext. In 1963, the EKD Synod met for the first time without representatives of East German Protestantism. In 1967, however, there appeared briefly to be a fresh hope of avoiding final division. At an April Synodal meeting at Fürstenwald, near Frankfurt on the Oder, held there by the Protestant churches as the G.D.R. Government had barred the EKD Synod from assembling in East Berlin, the delegates adopted a resolution denouncing the pressure to which they had been subjected, affirming that they had no reason to break up the community of the EKD, and rejecting the idea that church unity must be given up because of differences of social system. It was at this time that the EKD elected as its president Bishop Dietzfelbinger of Munich, on the proposal of the East German Synod itself.

The next year, however, the division was made inevitable by Article 39 of the new G.D.R. constitution, which says:

1. Every citizen of the German Democratic Republic has the right to profess a religious faith and carry on religious activities.
2. The churches and other religious communities shall order their affairs and exercise their activities in conformity with the constitution and legal regulations of the German Democratic Republic. Details may form the subject of special agreements.

284

Clearly, any such agreements are bound to entail the church's acceptances of the state on the latter's own terms. Moreover, there was increasing pressure to dissolve ties with the EKD on the ground that it is an instrument of NATO: Gerald Götting and the CDU were even more insistent on this than Hans Seigewasser, the State Secretary for Church Affairs. Accordingly, September, 1969 saw the creation of the Association (*Bund*) of Evangelical Churches in the German Democratic Republic, but this did not entirely resolve the conflict. The new body, in which the various Protestant churches have to a large extent sunk their differences, has declared its willingness to accept the Socialist state without reserve, but in other respects it does not appear satisfactory to the G.D.R. leaders. It is fairly centralized, which may give its authorities too much power, and moreover its first Synod maintained, despite criticism and pressure, a provision in Article 4 of its statutes describing itself as a "separate community of the whole body of Evangelical Christians in Germany."

The Synod elected as "general superintendent" Albrecht Schönherr, who, since January, 1967, had been exercising Bishop Kurt Scharf's functions in East Berlin: he had gained the confidence of the EKD while establishing new ties with the leaders of a state whose basis he was fully prepared to accept. He will need plenty of courage and skill to avoid conflict with the G.D.R. Government and party while endeavoring to prevent a widening of the gulf between the Protestant churches in the two Germanies.

The G.D.R. Government has from the outset done its best to protect its citizens from the influence of the Federal Republic. In one field, however, it has not felt able to take preventive measures. Little as the G.D.R. leaders may like it, West German television and radio play an important part in the information system of the Socialist state, with the result that the people of the G.D.R. know much more about West Germany than the latter's inhabitants know about the East. The impression they thus receive of West German society and culture is far from being wholly alluring. In all other ways, however, everything is done to prevent their having access to any information except that provided by the state. The G.D.R. press is subject to strict control and even stricter self-censorship. Its style is monotonous and drab: as compared with *Neues Deutschland*, the Paris *Humanité* or the London *Morning Star* is an organ of shrewd criticism and entertainment. Out of 297 papers, including regional editions, published in 1968 and selling about 6 million copies in all, 214 were SED organs pure and simple, while 70 belonged to the other four parties.

Intellectual and cultural life has always been livelier than a reading of the press would lead one to imagine. However, it did not take the authorities many years to bring order into the cultural scene and impose a meddlesome system of controls. Among other things, this led to a rapid deterioration of the film industry, which had been far ahead of West Germany's in the immediate postwar years. Toward intellectuals and creative artists, the attitude has varied, according to circumstances, between repression and a more permissive regime. In the early 1950's, the slogan was "Socialist realism," and writers and artists were exhorted to celebrate the development of industry under the five-year plan. During the "new course," it was permissible to take notice of bourgeois humanistic culture: the plays of Giraudoux and Zuckmayer were performed, works by Gerhart Hauptmann and Heinrich Böll were broadcast. However, de-Stalinization was kept within narrow limits, especially when it became too pronounced for Ulbricht's taste, between the Twentieth Soviet Party Congress in February, 1956 and the Hungarian rising in October of that same year.

The crushing of the Hungarians gave Ulbricht his cue to strike at the intellectuals who had taken the example of the "Polish October" too seriously. In March, 1957, Wolfgang Harich, a thirty-five-year-old professor of Marxist philosophy, editor of the *Deutsche Zeitschrift für Philosophie*, and a member of the SED since 1946, was sentenced to ten years' hard labor for demanding intellectual liberty and a more flexible form of Socialism. While the case against him was being prepared, numerous teachers and journalists lost their jobs. During the next few years, Marxist intellectuals of world reputation, such as Alfred Kantorowicz in 1957 and Ernst Bloch in 1961, left the G.D.R. to take up their abode in West Germany, which, however, they continued to criticize. An easier period for writers set in after the erection of the wall, when even the outspoken songs of Wolf Biermann, a young poet who had come to live in East Berlin in 1950 at seventeen years of age, were tolerated. In 1963, Christa Wolf, a thirty-four-year-old "candidate" member of the party's Central Committee, wrote a novel, *Der geteilte Himmel* (*The Divided Sky*), describing with much frankness the attitude of young people to the regime: it received a prize and, what is more important, sold widely.

However, the permissive period ended in 1965, and conformity has since been the rule. Even in 1964, Robert Havemann, a chemistry professor at the Humboldt University of Berlin, was suspended for attempting to interpret Marxism in a liberal sense. After being appointed head of a research center, he was dismissed in December, 1965 for advocating the lifting of the ban on the Communist party in the Federal Republic together with the creation of a regular opposition in the G.D.R. At its session in December, 1965, the Central Committee resolved to launch the second stage of the "new economic system" and also to tighten up on the ideological front. In January, 1966, the Minister of Culture, Hans Bentzien, was removed from his post for "grave mistakes," showing that the official line had taken a sharp turn. When, in 1969, Christa Wolf published a new and very fine novel, partly autobiographical and entitled *Nachdenken über Christa T.*, its circulation in the East was limited to 800 copies.

The new tough line was intensified by fear lest intellectuals and students should be contaminated by the thaw that was taking place in Prague. The G.D.R. leaders' alarm was not without cause: after the invasion in August, 1968, there were numerous manifestations of sympathy with Czechoslovakia, especially by students. Clearly, arrests and sentences had not sufficed to obliterate human feelings, and years of heavily slanted education had not destroyed basic aspirations. Not that the population has ceased to accept the economic and social system of the G.D.R., or that the two Germanies have ceased to be distinct, as witness even the divergences in the language.[39] But the unvaried style of indoctrination in East Germany does not signify that the regimentation of minds is complete or that its citizens have renounced the right of free thought and criticism for good and all.

A Socialist State Among Others?

The invasion and *Gleichschaltung* of Czechoslovakia threw a clearer light on Article 6 (2) of the 1968 constitution, which says that the G.D.R. "practices and develops all-round cooperation and friendship with the Soviet Union and other Socialist states according to the principles of Socialist internationalism." This formula, of course, raises the question of how far the U.S.S.R. regards the countries in question as truly Socialist. "Strictly speaking, the Russians regard this description as true of only the Soviet model. The G.D.R. leaders followed Moscow in criticizing harshly the 'human-face' type of Socialism introduced after Novotný's fall; they condemn Chinese and Albanian Socialism outright; they disapprove of the Yugoslav variety and of Rumania's 'national Communism,' and they show reserve toward the Cuban regime. These criticisms and condemnations vary as and when the U.S.S.R. changes its own attitude toward the respective countries, in tune with its international strategy."[40]

The G.D.R. surpasses all other East European countries in the extent to which the Soviet Union is cited, as a kind of universal standard, in the most varied contexts imaginable. The German-Soviet Friendship Society, with 3·5 million members, 28,700 branches, and 280,000 meetings in 1968, takes its place as a mass organization between the trade unions and the Democratic Women's League. This has been so from the beginning, when Georg Dertinger was Minister of Foreign Affairs of the new Republic. Secretary-general of the CDU in the Soviet zone from 1946 to 1949, he had in Weimar times belonged not to the *Zentrum* but to the Nationalist Party. He was arrested in January, 1953 on charges of espionage and treason, including contacts with Otto Lenz, the state secretary in the Chancellor's office at Bonn, and was sentenced in June, 1954 to fifteen years' hard labor; released in 1964, he was allowed to earn his living as a lecturer until his death in January, 1968. His successor as Foreign Minister was Lothar Bolz, whom we have met as a former KPD member and chairman of the National Democratic Party. However, long before Bolz resigned for health reasons in January, 1965, the real Foreign Minister was Otto Winzer, who had been his deputy since 1956. Winzer, who was born in 1902, joined the Socialist youth movement at the age of seventeen and the KPD at twenty-three. During Hitler's war, he was in charge of propaganda among German prisoners in the Soviet union, and he was with Ulbricht's group which returned to Germany on April 29, 1945. From 1949 to 1956, he was state secretary in the President's Office. Among his deputies and subordinates, the generation trained in political warfare is gradually giving place to those who have gained their experience within the SED.[41]

The G.D.R.'s loyalty to the Soviet Union has not been disturbed by the changes in the Kremlin leadership since 1953. Ulbricht's attachment to Stalin, it is true, was so strong that it was not until November, 1961 that the main thoroughfare of East Berlin ceased to be named Stalin-Allee and became Karl-Marx-Allee for part of its length and for the rest, as in former days, the Frankfurter Allee. It is true, too, that Ulbricht had his moments of tension with Beria and Malenkov, and did not always see eye to eye with Khrushchev. But there was never any question where the G.D.R.'s allegiance really lay. None the less, the nature of that allegiance has undergone changes of some consequence, both on paper and in actual fact. Soviet "supervision of the activity of state organs of the G.D.R." officially came to an end on March 27, 1954, when the G.D.R. was declared a sovereign state and the Soviet High Commission was withdrawn. By the treaty of September 20, 1955, concluded after the ratification of the Paris agreements, which we shall consider in the next chapter, the G.D.R. became "free to decide questions of its internal and external policy, including relations with the German Federal Republic;" the signatories confirmed that their mutual relations were based on "full equality of rights, respect for each other's sovereignty and noninterference in internal, affairs." At this very time, the Soviet Union was engaged in establishing diplomatic relations with the Federal Republic.

From 1955 onward, the Russians did their best to bring about recognition of the G.D.R. by the largest possible number of states throughout the world. They seem, however, to have been faced with insistent appeals by Ulbricht urging them to help stabilize the G.D.R. by repudiating the quadripartite system of 1945. This was particularly the case in Berlin: in February, 1962, clearly as the result of a Soviet concession, compulsory military service was extended to East Berliners two weeks after it was instituted in the G.D.R. proper. The concession was a limited one, for Khrushchev, having long threatened the West that he would sign a separate peace treaty with his German ally, finally stipulated in Article 9 of the U.S.S.R.-G.D.R. friendship treaty of June 12, 1964 that "this treaty does not affect the rights and duties of both parties under existing bilateral and other international agreements, including that of Potsdam."

The most important change that has taken place is in the political weight of the G.D.R. In 1952 or even 1953, Ulbricht had reason to fear that he and his state might be sacrificed to meet the exigencies of a new Soviet policy, as we shall see when considering the Soviet note of March 10, 1952 on the neutralization of Germany. But by 1956, Ulbricht was already a useful ally to Khrushchev as he grappled with the problems of the "Polish October;" and in 1968 the Soviet leaders seem to have taken serious account of his views when deciding to march into Czechoslovakia, a course some other allies looked on with less enthusiasm—including Kádár, though he himself owed his power to Soviet repression at Budapest in 1956.

The G.D.R. units that took part in the collective military action, and thus effected the second German invasion of Czechoslovakia in thirty years, were small in number and largely symbolic, especially as compared with the part played by G.D.R. forces in the Warsaw Pact Organization itself. When the Pact was signed, on May 14, 1955, there was as yet no official East German army, though the People's Police in Barracks (*Kasernierte Volkspolizei*) came into existence in 1948. In May, 1952, when the Paris agreement for a European Defense Community was signed, these units, which had for some time past been equipped with tanks and artillery, became part of the "National Forces" (*Nationale Streitkräfte*). A constitutional amendment of September, 1955 made possible the official creation of the National People's Army (*Nationale Volksarmee*) and the introduction of conscription, which was not, however, enforced until January, 1962, after the wall had removed the danger of recruits escaping to the West. The G.D.R. forces are still more firmly integrated in the Warsaw Pact Organization under Soviet command than the Bundeswehr is in NATO.

The situation as regards economic integration is less clear-cut. In September, 1950, the G.D.R. became a member of the Comecon (Council for Mutual Economic Assistance, also known as CMEA), which had been set up in January, 1949 as an answer to the Marshall Plan and the Organization for European Economic Cooperation. An answer, but not an imitation: the Soviet Union accepted neither multilateralism nor the development of bilateral relations among its satellites. The Polish and Hungarian disturbances of 1956 induced the Russians to stop treating their allies purely and simply as adjuncts to Soviet development in the economic field. But in December, 1965, the suicide of Erich Apel, the chairman of the State Planning Commission of the G.D.R., after his failure to secure any modification of the terms of an economic treaty with the Soviet Union, was a vivid symbol of the unequal relationship from which the G.D.R. as such has never attempted to break free, as for example has Rumania.

At the same time, the G.D.R. has become an economic power in its own right, and its influence both in Comecon and in bilateral relations with the Soviet Union grew considerably during the 1960's. G.D.R. exports in 1950 were valued at 1,700 million marks; in 1953, the figure was 4,000 million, in 1958, 8,000 million, in 1962, 10,000 million, and in 1968, 15,900 million. Out of its total foreign trade turnover (exports plus imports) of 30,200 million marks, 1,200 million represents exchanges with developing countries and 6,000 million with "industrial capitalist countries," while 23,000 million is accounted for by trade with Socialist countries, including 13,000 million with the Soviet Union alone. Considering that in 1946, barely 18 per cent by volume of the external trade of what is now the G.D.R. was carried on with what are now the "Socialist countries," we may see how complete the changeover has been.

Economic integration has never become a reality within Comecon, and the G.D.R. economy has never formed part of an organized whole even to the same extent as the EEC countries, little as that body deserves to be called supranational.[42] Cooperation with the Soviet Union, however, has become increasingly close. Not only has the G.D.R. become the latter's chief trading partner, with 17 per cent of Soviet foreign trade in 1966, but long-term plans exist for mutual supplies and joint production programs.[43]

In foreign policy, the G.D.R., which was recognized from the outset by its fellow members of the Socialist camp, has concentrated on the struggle to achieve diplomatic recognition by other states and membership in international organizations, while, as we shall see in the next chapter, the F.R.G. has been struggling with equal energy to thwart its efforts. These have not met with a great deal of success: although the G.D.R. was recognized in the spring of 1969 by Iraq, Cambodia, Syria, and the Sudan, and in May, 1970 by Algeria, it is obliged in most cases to content itself with trade or consular representation instead of full diplomatic relations.[44] In many countries it also maintains contacts through friendship associations with, in some cases, a counterpart in the country concerned: for example, in France, where an active body known as *Echanges franco-allemands*, founded in 1958, has organized large-scale meetings and visits to the G.D.R. through its secretariat and local committees and carries on propaganda for the recognition of the G.D.R.[45] Its activity was hampered for a time by the measures adopted by the Allied Travel Board in Berlin to prevent G.D.R. citizens traveling to Western countries, as a reprisal against the erection of the wall. These measures were relaxed in 1964 and suspended in 1970, but while they were in force they also seriously interfered with the G.D.R. effort in a privileged domain of international relations, namely sport.

The stress laid in the G.D.R. on sporting activities of all kinds is not, in its leaders' eyes, merely a matter of character building or physical training. The exceptional successes of its champions, especially in swimming, rowing, and athletics, are supposed to afford the world in general, and G.D.R. citizens in particular, a proof of the superiority of Socialism. It is not without political significance that the *Statistical Yearbook* contains long lists of the medals won and places obtained in European and world championships by G.D.R. sportsmen and sportswomen, in every conceivable contest from angling, through ninepin bowling, to table tennis.[46] In addition, sport serves as a microcosm of diplomacy. One by one, the world sporting federations have admitted the respective G.D.R. bodies to membership. In 1955, an all-German Olympics Committee was set up, and the International Committee at Melbourne in 1956 agreed to the participation of a single German team using the same flag and, in the event of victory, parading to the strains of the "Ode to Joy" from Beethoven's Ninth Symphony. At the 1960 games, a compromise was devised owing to the G.D.R.'s introduction of the hammer-and-compass emblem: instead of the flag of either Republic, a banner was used consisting of the German colors and the five Olympic rings. In 1968, there were two separate teams named respectively "Germany" and "East Germany." As we shall see, the Federal Republic made a major concession by agreeing that the games should be held at Munich in 1972.

However, by the time that date arrives the concession will no doubt appear to have been a minor one, as the problem of recognition has evolved a great deal since 1966 and especially since the end of 1969. The G.D.R. leaders' attitude toward German unity had evolved some time earlier: while the treaty of 1955 with the Soviet Union called for reunification, and the demand for a confederation of the G.D.R. and F.R.G. was put forward from 1957 onward, the notion of unity has gradually disappeared from the official East German vocabulary, being replaced by that of relations between two equal German states. The different interpretations that can be read into the terms "equal" and "German" are the crux of the German problem as it appears in 1970.

11

Foreign Affairs and World Policy

"FRANCE, being in the center of the world, must pursue a worldwide policy. She must do so because it is in her power, because everything urges her to, and because she is France."

Many Frenchmen may have smiled—some with admiration, others with sardonic amusement—on hearing their President utter, not for the first time, a grandiloquent statement of this kind.[1] But not all of them would have reflected that such boasts cannot be uttered by anyone who chooses. In particular, no President of Federal Germany, even if he were a second de Gaulle, could have used such words of his own country without being laughed at or accused of deliberate provocation. He would have had to say something more on the lines of: "Federal Germany must not and cannot pursue a world policy, because it is not in her power to do so, because no one wants her to and she certainly does not want to herself, and because she is not the whole of Germany but only part of it. All she can and must do is to try and see that the policy of other countries is not such as to prevent her from having a policy of her own, and that it *is* such as will help to bring all Germans closer together."

Of course, France too is dependent on international developments, if only because the role played by the French Communist Party varies according to the relationship of the moment between the Soviet Union and the West. Moreover, France's liberty of action is in any case very much limited vis-à-vis the really great powers. Nonetheless, she is in a privileged position compared with her German neighbor and ally, whose very existence is a product of the international system and whose fate continues to be closely linked with it.

Compulsion and Choice

In 1949, the main objective of German foreign policy was, of necessity, to secure the right to have such a policy, and to bring about conditions in which it could be exercised.[2] Given the whole situation of the German people at that time, their overriding aim must be to become an active instead of a passive element in international affairs. Such, at least, was the way things appeared, and undoubtedly the recovery of German sovereignty was a matter of imperative concern. Nevertheless, throughout the period from the creation of the F.R.G. and the G.D.R. in 1949 to the conversations between their heads of government in 1970, it has been an objective that could not be conceived or formulated without ambiguity.

One major factor that cut across the desire for complete freedom of action was the policy of European unity. Was not the right course to achieve equality with other states by each pooling a measure of its sovereignty, rather than by Germany striving to achieve independence equal to her neighbors'? This viewpoint was itself the expression of a deliberate choice; but there were other factors over which the West Germans had no control, and which involved them in continual hesitation and permanent contradictions.

The objectives of German unity and a sovereign German state were not identical and probably not even compatible. Ought the West Germans to forego this or that symbol, or even the reality, of independence so as to preserve the chance of reunification, however slender? Having achieved some real or symbolic concession, should they be prepared to give it up again if it appeared that to do so might mean progress toward national unity? Should they accept a possible *diminutio capitis* in the form of special undertakings, or a ban, or the contingent re-establishment of Allied control? Was such a course conceivable after 1955, when sovereignty had been regained in all essentials, or even in 1952, when an agreement was about to be signed with the Western powers that largely did away with Germany's previous servitude? On the other hand, if the West German leaders rejected the idea of any restraint whatever, did this not in fact mean that the independent status of the Federal Republic meant more to them than Germany's existence as a unified nation?

Sovereignty is a good in itself—but if the three occupying powers gave up all their rights in West Germany, would they not be forfeiting all possibility of influencing the fate of Germany as a whole? The continued reference, at all events from a legal point of view, to the quadripartite system of 1945 is incompatible with the full sovereignty of the Federal Republic, though it is no longer invoked to justify a refusal to enter into direct contact with the rulers of the other Germany.

Sovereignty is to be desired—but freedom of action, whether in a real or a purely legal form, must not be allowed to diminish the protection that the Western powers, and specially the mightiest of them, confer on their part of Germany against the fourth occupying power and its Germany. Sometimes legal ingenuity is able to devise a formula, for instance in regard to the stationing of foreign troops on German soil. Their right to be there is acknowledged in accordance with the quadripartite system; the Western Allies waive this right in recognition of German sovereignty; but, as security demands it, they keep their troops in Germany, not as of right but in response to the Federal Government's request.

In some spheres there is contradiction pure and simple. Is West Berlin a *Land* of the Federal Republic, exactly like any other? This is Bonn's basic view, which it loses no opportunity of affirming. But what about the defense of West Berlin by the three powers under the quadripartite agreements of 1944 and 1945, which make no mention of Bonn or even of German sovereignty? Why, certainly this must not be called in question—it would be strange indeed if Britain, France, and, above all, the United States were not only to accept the integration of Berlin to the Federal Republic, but to draw the international consequences that follow logically from their acceptance!

Having noted in chapter 5 the principal dates that mark the recovery by both Germanies of more or less complete sovereignty, we shall now consider in more detail the machinery and stages involved.

Whereas the Grotewohl cabinet formed in the G.D.R. on October 11, 1949 already included a Minister of Foreign Affairs, there was no such post in Adenauer's government formed under the Occupation Statute on September 20 of that year. Two ministries, however, were concerned with matters beyond the confines of the Federal Republic—namely, all-German affairs and the Marshall Plan. On December 15, the Chancellor and the U.S. High Commissioner, John J. McCloy, signed the agreement on American aid that became the first state treaty concluded by the Federal Republic in accordance with the formula in the Occupation Statute on "international agreements *by* or on behalf of Germany." The occupying powers, however, also continued thereafter to sign agreements *on behalf of* Germany. This represented a considerable branch of their diplomatic activity, as may be seen from the annex to the Bonn Convention of May 26, 1952, listing international agreements concluded by them: 84 agreements with over 20 countries and half a dozen international bodies were still in force, while over 300 agreements with over 70 countries and organizations had lapsed for one reason or another.

In January, 1950, the Allied High Commission invited the Federal Government to open consulates-general at Washington, London, and Paris. A "Foreign Affairs Department" (*Dienststelle für Auswärtige Angelegenheiten*) was set up as part of the Chancellor's Office. On March 3, the Federal Republic and the Saar were invited to become associate members of the Council of Europe at Strasbourg. On May 9, the French Foreign Minister proposed the creation of the European Coal and Steel Community, which involved some forfeiture of sovereignty by all the participants except the Federal Republic. The latter's position was in fact a curious one: in order to give up of its own free will rights that it did not yet possess, it had first to be given other rights that had so far been refused to it, particularly the right to negotiate, conclude, and ratify international agreements.

Furthermore, it is not usual for states to join with their enemies to form supranational institutions. Yet, although hostilities with Germany had ceased on May 8, 1945, there had been no peace treaty and the state of war therefore still existed. Nor was this purely theoretical, at least until 1951, as we may see from the French Government's "Decree No. 51-883 of July 9, 1951 terminating the effects of the state of war with Germany as regards the position of German nationals in France":*

The President of the Council of Ministers,
On the proposal of the Minister of Foreign Affairs,
In view of the Berlin declaration of 5 June 1945 regarding the defeat of Germany and the assumption of supreme authority by the Allied governments, and the conclusions of the conference of the Foreign Ministers of France, Great Britain, and the United States of America, held at New York on 15 September 1950,
Having taken the advice of the Council of Ministers,
Decrees as follows:

*Similar measures were enacted in Britain and the United States in July and October, 1951 respectively.

Article 1. As from the date of publication of this decree, German citizens shall no longer be deemed enemy nationals.

Article 2. This decree does not affect the validity of measures that have been or may be taken in regard to German property, rights, and interests under international agreements to which France is a party, or in order to permit the implementation of such agreements.

Four months earlier, on March 6, 1951, the "First Instrument of Revision of the Occupation Statute" was signed. Article II provided that:

Paragraph 2 (c) [on reserved powers] is amended to read as follows:

(c) . . . foreign affairs, including international agreements made by or on behalf of Germany: but the powers reserved in this field will be exercised so as to permit the Federal Republic to conduct relations with foreign countries to the full extent compatible with the requirements of security, other reserved powers, and obligations of the Occupying Powers relating to Germany.

At the same time, in exercise of its reserved powers, the Allied High Commission issued the following Decision:

Article 1
The Federal Government is hereby authorized to establish a Ministry of Foreign Affairs and shall have exclusive responsibility for the choice of the personnel of its diplomatic, consular, and trade missions.

Article 3
1. the establishment of diplomatic or consular relations or trade missions shall be subject to the prior approval of the Allied High Commission.
2. The Federal Government may, however, establish without such approval diplomatic missions in those countries, other than France, the United Kingdom, and the United States of America, in which prior to the effective date of this Decision it has been authorized to establish consular offices.

Article 4
The Federal Government is hereby authorized to appoint official agents in the capitals of France, the United Kingdom, and the United States of America.

Article 6
The Federal and *Land* Governments shall keep the Allied High Commission informed of any international negotiations. The Allied High Commission may intervene in negotiations relating to the fields reserved to the Occupation Authorities.

Clearly, external sovereignty was still far from having been achieved; but in practice these provisions were never strictly applied, for many reasons including the astuteness of Dr. Adenauer, who became his own Minister of Foreign Affairs on March 15, 1951. The main reason, however, was that the Allies needed the Federal Republic's help in the military sphere. The rearmament issue gave a decisive impulse toward the restoration of West German sovereignty, though it did not arise in an acute form until the Korean war broke out in June, 1950. Previously, there had been a good deal of discussion, but it had always ended negatively. Article III of the Petersberg agreement of November 22, 1949 between the Chancellor and the High Commissioners stated that "The Federal Government . . . declares its earnest determination to maintain the demilitarization of the Federal territory and to endeavor by all means in its power to prevent the re-creation of armed forces of any kind. To this end the Federal Government will cooperate fully with . . . the work of the Military Security Board." But the international tension of mid–1950 soon caused the United States and its NATO allies, except France, to abandon once and for all the idea of Germany as a defeated enemy to be kept under control, and to regard the Federal Republic as a prospective partner on a basis of free consent.

It was some time, however, before the new situation was recognized in a formal text. The decisions of September-October, 1950 eventually resulted in the Bonn agreements of May 26, 1952, including the important Convention on Relations between the Three Western Powers and the Federal Republic of Germany, which declared that:

The United States of America, the United Kingdom of Great Britain and Northern Ireland, and the French Republic, of the one part, and the Federal Republic of Germany, of the other part: . . .

Whereas it is the common aim of the Signatory States to integrate the Federal Republic on a basis of equality within the European Community, itself included in a developing Atlantic Community;

Whereas the achievement of a fully free and unified Germany through peaceful means and of a freely negotiated peace settlement, though prevented for the present by measures beyond their control, remains a fundamental and common goal of the Signatory States:

Whereas the retention of the Occupation Statute with its powers of intervention in the domestic affairs of the Federal Republic is inconsistent with the purpose of integrating the Federal Republic within the European Community;

Whereas the United States of America, the United Kingdom of Great Britain and Northern Ireland, and the French Republic (hereinafter referred to as "the Three Powers") are therefore determined only to retain those special rights of which the retention is necessary, in the common interest of the Signatory States, having regard to the special international situation in Germany; . . .

Have entered into the following Convention setting forth the basis for their new relationship:

Article 1
1. The Federal Republic shall have full authority over its internal and external affairs, except as provided in the present Convention.

The exceptions which followed were considerable; however, they remained academic because, like the Convention as a whole, they were linked with the treaty signed at Paris on the following day for the institution of a European Defense Community, the fate of which was sealed two and a half years later when the French Assembly refused to ratify it on August 30, 1954. The Bonn Convention thus never came into force, and during negotiations in September-October, 1954 it was extensively revised and amended in the direction of West German independence. Thus the opening words of the instrument signed in Paris on October 23, 1954 indicated that it was not, like the original Convention, a treaty between the Western Allies on the one hand and Federal Germany on the other, but an agreement among four equal partners—who, moreover, had meanwhile reached agreement on West Germany's entry into NATO. The preamble to the amended Convention read simply: "The United States of

America, the United Kingdom of Great Britain and Northern Ireland, the French Republic, and the Federal Republic of Germany have entered into the following Convention setting forth the basis for their new relationship." The new Article 1, moreover, seemed perfectly straightforward:

1. On the entry into force of the present Convention the United States of America, the United Kingdom of Great Britain and Northern Ireland, and the French Republic . . . will terminate the Occupation Regime in the Federal Republic, revoke the Occupation Statute, and abolish the Allied High Commission and the Offices of the *Land* Commissioners in the Federal Republic.

2. The Federal Republic shall have accordingly the full authority of a sovereign state over its internal and external affairs.

However, this "full authority" was still limited in three areas: the legislative, the military, and the international. In internal affairs, the long and complex Convention on the Settlement of Matters Arising out of the War and the Occupation, signed at Bonn in 1952 and maintained in force by the Paris agreement, laid down the limits within which the Federal Republic might repeal or amend legislation enacted by the Control Council, the military governors, and the High Commission. The provisions of the main Convention governing the stationing of forces and their use on German territory were less discriminatory than in 1952, but under Article 5 (2), the Western powers enjoyed a right of intervention that, as we saw in chapter 5, did not lapse until 1968:

The rights of the Three Powers, heretofore held or exercised by them, which relate to the protection of the security of armed forces stationed in the Federal Republic and which are temporarily retained, shall lapse when the appropriate German authorities have obtained similar powers under German legislation enabling them to take effective action to protect the security of those forces, including the ability to deal with a serious disturbance of public security and order.

But the most important limitation was that contained in Article 2, which we quoted in the chapter on the foundations of the Federal Republic, and which is technically still valid:

In view of the international situation, which has so far prevented the reunification of Germany and the conclusion of a peace settlement, the Three Powers retain the rights and the responsibilities, heretofore exercised or held by them, relating to Berlin and to Germany as a whole, including the reunification of Germany and a peace settlement.

In other words, the Federal Republic's full authority over its external affairs extends only in a westerly direction and does not apply to the "German problem," although that is a major subject of concern to it. The purpose, of course, apart from security, was to safeguard the quadripartite principle and the doctrine that the Republic's powers were delegated to it by the Allies. However, by the time the Paris agreements entered into force in May, 1955, the restrictions appeared highly theoretical: no one doubted that in practice Adenauer possessed the right to conduct his foreign policy in all respects as he saw fit, and that he had made full use of that right for the past five years.

Nevertheless, the *alter Herr* himself felt, and rightly so, that his main effort had come to fruition and that the Paris agreements represented the consecration of his policy. When, on June 6, 1955, he formed a new government that, for the first time, included a Minister of Defense, he showed his sense that a milestone had been reached by himself relinquishing the foreign affairs portfolio.

How far was it in fact Adenauer's policy, conceived and conducted by him alone? To answer this fully would require a long dissertation on the part played by individual leaders in determining the course of politics and history.[3] In Adenauer's case, the controversy, far from dying down, has become more acute than ever in 1970, when the reappraisal of policy in regard to German unity has inevitably led to postmortems on the choices of the past twenty years. It is equally inevitable that the debate should be lacking in serenity. Even the ablest analyses (and much more so the use made of them by the press) seem designed to build up a case rather than to examine how much latitude really existed at the time.[4] From the days of the Parliamentary Council onward, and especially in and after 1949, Adenauer has been accused of having sacrificed reunification by integrating the Federal Republic into one of the two camps that divided the world, whereas it would, according to his critics, have been possible to take a different course.

The theory that events were determined by Adenauer's personal decisions and influence has found support in two very different quarters. It was upheld by his adversaries, especially the future President Heinemann,[5] insofar as they themselves subsequently embraced important features of his policy— since they were at pains to show not that he had been right all along but that he had brought about situations which left them no alternative. Second, and above all, the theory enjoys the authority of Adenauer himself, whose *Memoirs*, for all their coolness of style, go further than strict truth would allow in explaining everything that took place as due to his own lucid will power.[6] Even when he was still in office, he used his personal status as a diplomatic weapon: time and again he urged foreign negotiators to agree to his demands on the ground that the Federal Republic would be swept off course if he were to relinquish the helm—as though the international situation had not, in a sense, created an automatic pilot system.

Certainly Adenauer took important decisions without too much regard for the deliberative processes of democracy: for example, the rejection of the Soviet note of March, 1952 (of which more later), his visit to Moscow in 1955, or, first and foremost, his offer of a German military contingent in August, 1950.[7] Moreover, his personality soon became an important element of Federal German foreign policy because of his prestige and the confidence he inspired in the Western Allies. As the 1953 election slogan quite rightly declared, he "linked Germany with the free world." His funeral on April 25, 1967 was more than a solemn act of homage paid to a great man by the heads of foreign states and their governments: it was a symbol of the return to international life of a Germany that was respected and admired throughout the Western world.

Nevertheless, it did not rest simply with Adenauer to adopt whatever course he chose. He had to use deception to induce German public opinion to accept the idea of rearmament, in much the same way (irrespective of the ends in view) as Roosevelt tricked the Americans into accepting the idea of entering the war, or de Gaulle the French into accepting Algerian independence. In all three cases, it was a question of playing on sentiments that already existed, but which it was the politician's task to amplify. The Germans, in particular, had already opted for security and alignment with the West when the Chancellor set about persuading them that rearmament was a necessary consequence of that choice. It would be a grave exaggeration of his role and opportunities to depict him as the creator of an international situation to which in fact he submitted while shaping it to the best of his ability. Certainly the situation itself was not unwelcome to him. When, in October, 1945, he predicted in a press interview that Germany would remain divided and that the three western zones would be formed into a state, he was not only manifesting a gift for prophecy but also expressing his own wishes. He did not have to fight a rearguard action, but merely to conform his policy to the trend of history that, as he believed, was in the right direction. Schumacher, if he had come to power, would no doubt have had to moderate his tone and accept situations that, in opposition, he was free to declare avoidable; but his skill and energy would have been devoted, in the main, to preventing or at least delaying what he considered a harmful process.

While Adenauer held firmly to the guidelines that he himself regarded as essential, he showed flexibility in adapting to new situations, though he did not always do so at once. In 1961, when Schröder succeeded Brentano as Minister of Foreign Affairs, the Chancellor had just acknowledged, contrary to the views of his most faithful associate, that the modification of relations between the two superpowers must involve a change in German foreign policy. The new minister, however, tried to carry the change a good deal further than Adenauer thought desirable.

From the point of view of personalities, the change of Foreign Minister had in fact a double significance. Brentano went further than the Chancellor in justifying the government's policy from the ideological point of view: while moderate in his methods, he was a man of conviction and threw himself passionately into the cause of European integration and the defense of the Christian West. Schröder, on the other hand, went further than the Chancellor in his determination to secure results and not allow ideology to obscure or falsify analysis. Brentano's absolute loyalty to his chief made him seem more dominated by the latter than he really was,[8] but it is true even so that he never properly asserted his authority, and that his staff, from state secretary Walter Hallstein downward, behaved as though Adenauer were still Foreign Minister. When Schröder took over, it was not long before he succeeded in keeping the Chancellor to some extent at arm's length: by this time, indeed, Adenauer was beginning to be a spent force. When Erhard became Chancellor in 1963, Schröder had no difficulty in accentuating his own independence, and for the next three years he was seen to be the real architect of the country's foreign policy. This was so although the present-day trend in all countries is for the head of government to exercise a dominant influence in the sphere of foreign affairs, which affects nearly all departments of state and requires an over-all view of the country's interests at home and abroad.

From 1966 to 1969, Kiesinger and Brandt cooperated somewhat uneasily as Chancellor and Foreign Minister respectively. When Brandt became Chancellor in October, 1969, his ability and prestige, and the weight he carried as head of the government and chairman of one of the main parties, were such that he had some difficulty in not overshadowing the new Foreign Minister, Walter Scheel, a man of intelligence but somewhat lacking in strength of judgment and firmness in action, and too much involved in the internal conflicts of the FDP. In April, 1970, the appointment of two state secretaries for foreign affairs represented a sort of compromise: Baron Sigismund von Braun had not only been an excellent ambassador in Paris but was a member of the FDP, while Paul Frank, until then "political director" of the ministry, was a man of sound and independent judgment who had won Brandt's esteem and friendship when the latter was still Foreign Minister.

The foreign service that the state secretaries are called upon to direct is of a somewhat unusual kind. In most countries, it is true, diplomats are not quite on a par with ordinary civil servants and have some difficulty in adapting to a world in which foreign policy is no longer elaborated behind the closed doors of European chancelleries.[9] In most countries, too, ambassadors nowadays have less and less share in framing foreign policy or even providing the information on which the government makes up its mind. But in Britain, France, and even the United States, there is a tradition of the conduct of foreign affairs to which diplomats can appeal by way of justifying their existence as a profession. When the Federal Republic was set up, however, the diplomatic service had to be reconstituted at a time when the Chancellor was already in the habit of acting for himself and drawing information from other than official sources. Adenauer took little interest in administrative detail and failed to concern himself as he should have done with the staffing of the new ministry. Thanks to a subtle "old-boy" network of cooperation and behind-the-scenes influence, far too many senior posts in the Koblenzerstrasse at Bonn were filled by veterans from the Wilhelmstrasse in Berlin. We should not generalize too sweepingly or paint too dark a picture.[10] But many of these officials were prone to justify, in their own eyes at any rate, their subservience to the Nazi regime by the redoubled zeal of their anti-Communism. What is more, they endeavored, often with success, to shoulder aside people of merit who had been recruited from other walks of life to staff the new Foreign Ministry and especially the first diplomatic missions abroad.

Nevertheless, a fair number of newcomers made their way in the diplomatic arena. They were men who had known Germany's wartime sufferings and the problems of her defeat; they chose the foreign service with a sense of political vocation, and they provided it with a type of diplomat that is not overplentiful at the Quai d'Orsay—men without personal or patriotic arrogance, acting from conviction and not for amusement, less interested in cocktail parties than in studying political and social conditions in the countries where they reside. Unfortunately this type has not become the norm: as early as the middle 1950's, diplomacy was visibly reverting to its old routine, and since then the tendency has become still plainer. There is, however, a training college for diplomats at Bonn—managed by the personnel department, having previously for some years existed at Speyer on a more independent footing—where new entrants receive a more up-to-date training than their predecessors, with less emphasis on etiquette and the purely legal aspects. But their intellectual and social background seldom fits them to understand the modern world and resist the temptation to be absorbed by the trivialities of their careers. Out of the 584 attachés (male and female) recruited in the first twenty-four competitions, two-thirds had studied only law; 10 per cent came from noble families, and 27 per cent were the sons or daughters of senior officials. However, 11·6 per cent were the children of clerks who had not had a university education, and 1·9 per cent had parents who belonged to the artisan or working class—which makes the intake of the *Diplomatenschule* at any rate slightly more proletarian than that of the Paris *Ecole Nationale d'Administration*![11]

The country that the German diplomat represents abroad is unlike all others for two main reasons: the Nazi past, and the postwar division of Germany.

There was once a saying: *"Am deutschen Wesen soll die Welt genesen"* ("the world shall be the healthier for the German spirit"). No one in Germany would think of quoting this now. When General de Gaulle talked in the same way about France, people might be amused or irritated, but they were not outraged as they would have been had a German leader uttered, *mutatis mutandis*, such a phrase as: "Our activity in the outside world . . . is designed to achieve objectives which are linked together and which, because they are French, correspond to the interests of mankind."[12] The notion of Germany's special vocation or mission in the world was blown to pieces by the barbarous caricature of Nazism. As a result, German diplomacy has to operate in a minor key. Its representatives accept this and are even inclined to overdo the attitude of modesty, especially in cultural matters. The Goethe Institutes in foreign countries very often allow the most interesting features of postwar Germany to go by default: they concentrate on the literary and artistic riches of the past and fail to project aspects of Germany that might serve for instruction in the present day, given Germany's anxiety and self-questioning, its conflicts and accusations, its achievement in broadening the idea of culture and bringing it to a larger public. The Institute in Paris is a fortunate exception and perhaps an augury of what the Federal Republic may do on the lines laid down by Professor Ralf Dahrendorf before he left for Brussels on July 1, 1970 to become a member of the European Commission.[13]

Twenty-five years after Germany's surrender, her foreign policy is still hampered by the weight of the past. All three political parties are aware of this, as witness the anniversary statements made in parliament on May 8, 1970 by Chancellor Brandt for the government, Richard von Weizsäcker for the CDU/CSU, Volker Hauff for the SPD, and Frau Lieselotte Funker for the FDP. They have had opportunity enough in previous years to judge how strong feelings still were in foreign countries. When General de Gaulle withdrew from NATO in 1966, the anxiety his decision caused in Norway or the Netherlands was less due to the possible loss of efficiency to NATO than to fear lest the Federal Republic should take France's place among the "privileged" members of the alliance. In November, 1968, when the Deutsche Mark for the first time resisted the combined pressure of the U.S., British, and

French treasuries, the situation at once conjured up the German bogy even in Allied government circles. "Bonn puts 'Nein' back into its vocabulary" was the startled headline in the *International Herald Tribune*,[14] while the *Bild-Zeitung*, on November 23, came out triumphantly with "Germany Now Leads Europe" (*Jetzt sind die Deutschen Nr 1 in Europa*). This excited such general alarm as to throw an ironical light on the subtitle that followed: "Foreign countries congratulate Bonn" (*Das Ausland gratuliert Bonn*).

The foreign-exchange crisis showed, if only by the fact that the finance ministers met at Bonn, that the Federal Republic had become an economic power of the first rank. But it also spotlighted a reality of which German governments would have to take account if they ever wished to exploit that power, for instance, if Franz Josef Strauss should become Chancellor: namely, that increasing strength means, for West Germany, not so much an addition to her prestige and influence as a risk of isolation. Rightly or wrongly, Hitler's memory still outweighs millions of tons of peaceful and creative steel production.

In one important respect, the past influenced West Germany's choice of a foreign policy as early as 1949, when Adenauer resolved on a course that was honorable and advantageous, but difficult to steer. The new state, he decided, must accept responsibility for Germany's appalling heritage in order to be once again respected among nations and recognized as the true successor of the undivided Reich. Reference to the past was not, of course, the only means of achieving this end: the American alignment, for instance, enabled West Germany to obtain certificates of internal democracy and international good behavior.[15] But acceptance of civil liability for Germany's former commitments and crimes represented a more basic choice than any other.

The decisive year in this respect was 1952. On August 8, after negotiations lasting six months, Hermann J. Abs signed at London on behalf of his government an agreement on the settlement of German external debts; in it, the Federal Republic agreed, on terms varying from one case to another, to repay with interest international loans granted in the past to Germany and the *Länder* including Prussia, more especially the Dawes and Young loans of 1924 and 1930 for World War I reparations. Then, on September 10, West Germany signed a reparations agreement with Israel.

The policy of claiming and accepting continuity with the former Reich was not successful in all respects, and had one formidable consequence. The three powers had no objection to regarding the Federal Republic as the sole successor of the Reich when it came to paying off interwar debts, and they did not insist that the other Germany should bear its share; but they were less forthcoming over the general implications of the doctrine of continuity. For example, after Egypt nationalized the Suez Canal in 1956, Britain invited the Federal Republic and not the G.D.R. to take part in a conference to discuss what course to adopt, but the invitation was on the ground that Federal Germany was one of the main users of the canal, not that she was identical with the Germany that had signed the 1888 Convention. At all times, the three powers have carefully distinguished between the Federal Republic's right, which they recognize, to be regarded as sole representative of the German people in international affairs, and its right, which they deny, to speak as if its jurisdiction extended theoretically to the whole of Germany.

As to the formidable consequence, it concerns Federal Germany's public image. By undertaking to pay the score for Germany's past, the Republic made itself the continuation of that past. Even in 1970, all the residual anti-German feeling in the Western world is concentrated on the Federal Republic only: those who hate the G.D.R. do so because of its regime and not because of its past.

Chancellor Adenauer spoke for the first time of the German people's desire "to make amends for the injury done to the Jews in its name by a criminal regime" in an interview published on November 25, 1949 in the German Jewish weekly, the *Allgemeine Wochenzeitung der Juden in Deutschland*.[16] After eighteen months of difficult, indirect, and secret contacts with the Israeli leaders, and less difficult ones with the World Jewish Congress and its president Nahum Goldmann, the Federal Government made a solemn declaration to the Bundestag on September 27, 1951 expressing its readiness "to seek a solution to the problem of material reparations with representatives of the Jewish people and the state of Israel, which has welcomed so many homeless refugees." The only deputies who did not applaud were the Communists and the extreme right. The whole Bundestag then rose and observed one minute's silence. At that stage, the idea of concluding any kind of agreement with any kind of Germany still appeared sacrilegious to the people of the young state of Israel. Further long negotiations followed: they were full of setbacks and were only brought to a conclusion when Adenauer ruled in favor of Professor Franz Böhm, who was negotiating with the Israelis at Wassenaar near The Hague, and against Hermann Abs at the London debt conference, who wanted to keep Germany's obligations within stricter bounds. When the treaty was finally signed in a chilly atmosphere at Luxembourg, the attitude on both sides had changed. The Israeli Government had managed to induce a reluctant majority of the *Knesset* to approve the negotiations and the agreement itself, whereas the Bundestag made considerably more difficulty about ratifying the agreement than about giving its blessing at the outset. When the vote took place on March 18, 1953, the 238 "ayes" included 125 members of the SPD opposition and only 106 of the government coalition: the latter accounted for 15 of the 34 "noes" and 68 of the 86 abstentions. The entire CSU rejected the government proposal: five of its members voted "no" and the other 39 abstained.

The deputies' reluctance was due to three different but related considerations: the financial burden of the agreement, the implications of the acknowledgment of guilt, and the fear of losing Arab markets. The 3,000 million marks' worth of credits and supplies represented a heavy charge at the time, though less so as the Federal Republic's economy continued to expand. The treaty was faithfully executed until its expiry in March, 1966, and this required courage on the West Germans' part. In 1952, Adenauer had sent Ludger Westrick to Cairo to make sure that the Arabs would not carry out their threat of reprisals against the Federal Republic if the treaty were signed; but later developments, particularly after the appearance of the G.D.R. on the international scene, made Bonn's respect for its obligations especially praiseworthy. This was shown as late as February-March, 1965, when an extraordinary confusion of threats and counterthreats led to an official visit by Walter

Ulbricht to Cairo which did *not* result in Egypt recognizing the G.D.R., while West Germany cancelled arms deliveries to Israel but, on May 12, established diplomatic relations with it. Up till then, agreements and contacts had taken place without the two countries entering into normal relations: at first the Israelis were opposed, later the West Germans hesitated. The most favorable juncture for some time was reached when the two "grand old men," Adenauer and Ben Gurion, had a spectacular meeting in New York on March 14, 1960. Two months later came the kidnapping of Eichmann in Argentina and his trial by an Israeli court which condemned him to death: the effect was to revive many tragic memories in Israel, and some indignation in West Germany at the Israeli action. Indeed, German-Israeli relations could never be really "normalized," as the Israeli humourist Ephraim Kishon made clear in the following imaginary dialogue:[17]

"That may be," I said to my friend the unprejudiced citizen, "but I don't want any German films in Israel. They make me want to vomit."
"Just a moment. What about Austrian films?"
"Same thing."
"So you're a chauvinist."
"No, I'm not."
"Of course you know that Herzl [the father of political Zionism] spoke and wrote in German?"
"Yes, I do."
"Do you think Goethe was responsible for Germany's crimes?"
"No, I don't."
"You admit that there were Germans who saved Jews at the risk of their own lives?"
"Yes, I admit that."
"Do you know that Germany is paying us reparations, on schedule and on a large scale?"
"I do."
"Germany is one of the few countries that support us in international affairs."
"Yes, she is."
"We need Germany's help, don't we?"
"Absolutely."
"Is it possible to hate a nation for all times?"
"No, it's not."
"Very well then, tell me what you think about having German films in Israel."
"I don't want any here. They make me want to vomit."
"What kind of logic is that?"
"Logic went up in smoke at Auschwitz."

On the German side, however, pro-Israeli feeling became increasingly strong, as was most noticeable during the Six Days' War of 1967, although the Federal Republic's economic interests lay more on the side of the Arab states. Only the extreme right and the rebellious extreme left talked of Israeli crimes and American-Zionist imperialism. The reasons for pro-Israeli sentiment in West Germany are as complex as the various grounds for pro-Israeli reactions in France; they include, as in France, anti-Arab racialism and emotional anti-Communism. But, apart from a somewhat facile desire to clear one's conscience retrospectively, the dominant feeling is a deep and sincere inclination to side with the victims of Nazi barbarism and their descendants.

In 1965, the Egyptian threat to recognize the G.D.R. clashed with Bonn's threat to cut off economic aid to Egypt. Nasser's weak point was that the G.D.R. was not sufficiently wealthy to replace the Federal Republic as a source of aid. The latter's weak point was and is that its policies toward Israel and Egypt are of necessity a function of its policy in regard to the German problem.

Whether this necessity is real or only supposed, we shall consider presently. In any case it is clear that the present division of Germany weighs on the Federal Republic's foreign policy even more heavily than do the atrocities of the past. The existence of the problem has led to a sort of Germanocentrism in Bonn's attitude to world politics and its behavior on the international scene. From the outset, world problems have been considered as a function of the German question in its two major aspects: first, German unity and the status of the G.D.R., and second, the security of the Federal Republic and especially Berlin. When, on December 21, 1965, Erhard signed a joint communiqué at Washington with President Johnson proclaiming, in the context of the Vietnam war, "the determination of his government to continue to assist in this effort for the cause of freedom," he was carrying to its utmost extreme the twofold logic of Germanocentrism and the obsession with Germany's security. If the Americans ceased to hold fast at Saigon, what would they do in Berlin? And even if their Asian policy was a mistake, would they be so firmly resolved to defend Berlin if the Federal Republic did not align itself with them in all other parts of the world?

At that time, Erhard's "subservience" to Johnson was sharply criticized in the German press, not to mention the rebel students in Berlin who protested when a consignment of small replicas of the Berlin "Liberty bell" was sent to the U.S. troops in Vietnam. Times had changed since the honeymoon of June, 1963, when President Kennedy had proclaimed to the enraptured crowds of Berlin: "*Ich bin ein Berliner!*" What he had meant was that he took their cause under his protection; but his hearers and millions of other Germans assumed that, like themselves, he regarded Berlin as the hub of world affairs, and this encouraged them to maintain their Germanocentric view of diplomatic problems.

In any case, the German question continued to dominate Bonn's foreign policy well after 1965. Not only so, but the Brandt government's first year of office was marked by a re-emphasis of German unity as its main preoccupation, despite—or because of—its determination to have done with illusions and empty formulas. This time, however, the problem is clearly dissociated from that of security, which has in the meantime lost its obsessive character.

Policy in the West

To be a state like others, Germany had to overcome the burden of the past and earn the good will and trust of its allies. It is hardly a paradox to say that, in retrospect, Adenauer's policy was vindicated by the SPD, while Schumacher's true heir, as well as his exemplar, was General de Gaulle.

The world outside Germany has perhaps not paid sufficient attention to the importance of this quest for confidence. Whenever the scare of neo-Nazism is raised, the Western public should reflect that in the 1960's the three main parties took the attitude that their surest way of gaining votes was to appeal to the electorate's sense of Western solidarity, making it clear that Germany's national problems would only be broached in a spirit of friendship toward her European and Atlantic partners, and that every effort would be made not to shake their confidence which, after all, was of recent date and consequently vulnerable.

To a large extent, this attitude on West Germany's part is due to her need for security. Contrary to appearances, security is in fact the overriding priority of her foreign policy, more important in itself than German unity, let alone that of Europe. The word "security" is heard even more often in the Federal Republic than it was in France between the wars—both because of the reality of the Soviet threat and because, as we saw in chapter 4, its existence favors West German diplomacy. The tension between the two camps tends to speed up the process by which Federal Germany is integrated, on a footing of equality, into one of them, and becomes a free agent in the West instead of a mere object of international politics. The price is a deepening of the gulf between the two Germanies, but the Federal Republic gains greatly in prestige and influence.

For some time past there has been a divergence between French and German interests in this respect, which is fundamental though rarely brought out into the open. The confrontation of the two blocs has harmful effects on French internal policy (because it dramatizes the role of the Communist opposition), and on France's international status (because it reduces her to the condition of a minor ally and protégé). At a time of *détente*, on the other hand, France is one of the four powers responsible, among other things, for the fate of Germany—a Germany that East-West tension has helped to transform from an object of policy into an agent. During the acuter phases of the cold war, American strategists recalled that the German troops had given a good account of themselves against the Russians, and wondered how far one could trust a French army one-quarter of whose manpower voted Communist.

The threat to Berlin has always been real, even when there was no blockade or saber-rattling such as Khrushchev indulged in in November, 1958. The physical presence of Allied and especially American troops has never ceased to be necessary, especially since the Soviet Union became able to drop atomic bombs on American cities. Had the U.S. troops not been there, the U.S.S.R. and G.D.R. would have been strongly tempted to put an end to the vexation of a Western enclave in the middle of Communist territory. If, one day, a few thousand SED workers, having come across a supply of arms somewhere, had, in a fit of spontaneous anger, occupied the strategic points of West Berlin, they would have created an irreversible *fait accompli*. No one in such a case would take seriously an American threat to retaliate by nuclear means, for no President of the United States would risk national suicide to reconquer Berlin, so that the risk run by the U.S.S.R. for the acquisition of Berlin would be practically zero. If, on the other hand, U.S. troops are there to oppose the raid and if a single one of them were killed, no President could fail to send in at least one tank to avoid defeat and humiliation. This would lead to the arrival of two Soviet tanks and so to an escalation that neither great power could be sure of controlling or putting a stop to, short of a nuclear conflict. It follows that the risk attaching to the stake of West Berlin is sufficient to rule out forcible action.

Does not the same reasoning apply to Western Europe as a whole? The presense of American troops is an indispensable guarantee of full U.S. involvement, providing as nothing else can the certainty that the nuclear umbrella really extends over Western Europe; and the best way to make sure of that presense is the integration of forces in NATO. This basic fact is not affected by whether the West German Minister of Defense is called Franz Josef Strauss or Helmut Schmidt. When France pulled out of NATO in 1966, the General's decision caused annoyance chiefly because it savored of humbug: he well knew that the Federal Republic would not follow France's example, and the latter could therefore strike an independent attitude at no expense to herself, since geography ensured that France would continue to be protected by the presense of American troops in Germany.

In 1950, the strategic picture was different, as the balance of terror did not yet exist. The United States had agreed, at the request of Britain and France, to enter into an alliance that afforded such guarantees to the latter as might have prevented the second world war, not to speak of the first. But, as it was unlikely that atomic weapons would be used against the Soviet Union from the outset, conventional units were required in order to hold up the Red Army long enough to ensure that the bomb would be used in case of need. There was, however, no reason why these units should be solely American. At a time when the French regular army was more and more bogged down in Indochina, while the Korean war seemed to prove that the physical threat of world Communism was a real one, and the United States was obliged to put forward a big military effort in Asia, it was natural to think of using German manpower to defend Western Europe.

In July, 1949, when the French Assembly was debating the ratification of the North Atlantic Treaty, the Minister of Foreign Affairs, Robert Schuman, declared: "As regards Germany I have several times been asked: 'Can she become a member of the Atlantic Pact?' This is a question which does not arise, either at present or in the future . . . It is unthinkable, either from France's point of view or that of her allies, that Germany should be permitted to joint the Atlantic Pact for the purpose of defending herself or helping to defend other nations."[18]

By October, 1950, however, René Pleven, the French Prime Minister, was telling the Assembly that: "Germany, although not a party to the Atlantic treaty, is nevertheless a beneficiary of the security system for which it provides. It is therefore right that she should make her contribution to the defense of Western Europe." What had happened to change the position was the outbreak of the Korean war in June, 1950 and the tough negotiations in Washington in September, when the French ministers fought a lone battle against the American proposal, supported by the other Allies, to rearm the Federal Republic—a proposal based on a memorandum Adenauer had handed to McCloy on August 29, two days before the Federal cabinet was invited to approve the offer of German forces.

The Chancellor undoubtedly took the Soviet threat seriously, but he also saw German participation in the alliance as a decisive step toward equality of rights. This was a matter not of enjoying equal power with the American protector, but of moral equality with the West and the development of legal equality with the other European nations. France having proposed the creation of a European army as a substitute for Germany's admission to NATO, it seemed desirable to link as closely as possible the issues of equal rights for Germany, security, and European integration. In reasoning thus, Adenauer underrated the negative intention of the French proposal. As a German cartoonist suggested, the French Government and the bulk of the French people really wanted a German defense force that was stronger than the Red Army but weaker than the French.[19] The treaty of 1952 establishing the European Defense Community (EDC) owed its birth and death to this contradictory wish.

The French Assembly's rejection of the EDC on August 30, 1954 was a heavy blow to the Chancellor: he had believed almost to the end that it would be ratified, trusting to the optimism of his MRP friends rather than the predictions of the German embassy in Paris and of the French Premier himself. Adenauer was perhaps to be excused for being disconcerted by the want of logic in the French performance: how could he have supposed that the disciples of Descartes would propose Germany's entry into NATO rather than agree to the EDC, when they had previously devised the EDC rather than agree to Germany's entry into NATO?

On October 23, 1954, Germany became an ally of the Western powers by her accession, together with Italy, to the Brussels treaty of 1948 between Britain, France, and the Benelux countries, the enlarged alliance being known as the Western European Union (WEU). At the same time, it was agreed that Germany would become a member of NATO, which she formally did in May, 1955. The WEU, in accordance with French wishes, united Britain with the six continental powers (or "little Europe") in an alliance that, on paper at least, contained very stringent provisions.

Germany, however, was even now an ally whose status involved special problems and special restrictions. In Article 1 of Protocol III on the Control of Armaments, the members of WEU "take note of and record their agreement with the Declaration . . . in which the Federal Republic of Germany undertook not to manufacture in its territory atomic, biological, and chemical weapons." In theory, the Federal Republic might manufacture such weapons elsewhere than on its territory or acquire them without manufacturing them; but the understanding was that German rearmament would be purely "conventional," especially as none of the Six at that time possessed any nuclear forces.

Since 1955, the problem presented by the Federal Republic as a great economic power forbidden to possess nuclear equipment has assumed different forms, becoming graver at some times and less so at others, but never completely disappearing. Not that the West German leaders were at any time really anxious for the ban to be lifted, since they knew that any chance of negotiating German reunification would be lost if the Federal Republic possessed nuclear weapons. On the other hand, they wanted to be associated in NATO decisions on the same footing as the British and French, and to reduce the psychological and military disadvantages of a situation in which

Germany provided only the rank and file of the alliance, playing the part of a trip-wire or the glass in a fire alarm.

In 1963, the MLF proposal for nuclear submarines with crews of mixed nationality at first met with a doubtful reception in Germany, but was then taken up by the two main parties with such enthusiasm as seriously to damage relations with General de Gaulle, who saw it as a kind of resurrection of the EDC. When President Johnson came to power and was told about the plan, he decided that it was absurd and shelved it at the beginning of 1964, thus making his faithful German allies look rather foolish.

The Grand Coalition experienced the perplexity into which Germany as a whole was cast by the American–British–Soviet treaty of 1968 on the non-proliferation of nuclear weapons, first in its draft form and then finally signed on July 1. Should the Federal Republic adhere to the treaty, as several other states did, or follow France's example and refuse? The two main parties were in disagreement on this issue. The CDU saw no reason for Germany to tie her hands indefinitely without receiving any concession in return; the SPD argued that it made no sense to hold on to a theoretical right that no one had any intention of using in the foreseeable future, if by so doing they would be frustrating the chance of a *détente* and therefore of any progress on the German question. The CDU viewpoint was represented in a more violent form by organs of the press that, like the CSU, chose to regard the SPD's attitude as an abdication, the acceptance as it were of a new Yalta or a new Versailles.

Chancellor Brandt showed a good deal of political courage when, on November 28, 1969, he caused the Federal Republic's signature to be appended to the treaty in Moscow, London, and Washington.[20] A headline in the *Rheinische Merkur* on October 10, had spoken of "Germany's sell-out": the paper devoted little attention to considering why Federal Germany's great ally and protector had all along pressed her to sign the treaty. To do so, it would have had to analyze the course of U.S.–German relations during the 1960's and even as far back as 1957, when John Foster Dulles was still secretary of state. Yet Dulles's ideas and policy were much more in tune with the old Chancellor's than those of his predecessor Dean Acheson. Dulles knew Germany better, having had to do with the German iron and steel industry when practicing as a lawyer in the 1920's. A strict Presbyterian—a kind of moral theologian turned diplomat—he rejoiced to find that his German opposite number had no less clear-cut ideas than himself of what was good and what was evil in politics. Adenauer soon came to represent for Dulles the incarnation of German democracy. Throughout the period of uncompromising hostility to the Communist bloc, the elder statesman at Bonn was a wise, trustworthy ally whom Dulles took pleasure in consulting. Adenauer's first invitation to the United States, in April, 1953, was a sort of reward. His second visit, in October, 1954, also had a triumphal character: it came after his great electoral success of the previous year, and a few weeks after the French Assembly rejected the EDC treaty. In 1955, soon after the entry into force of the Paris agreements, he was at last able to cross the Atlantic as the head of a free and independent government. When he next came to America, in June, 1956 and May, 1957, the climate had changed: Europe was no longer in the forefront of Washington's concerns, and Bonn's advice on Afro-Asian problems was not much sought after, though lip-service was still paid to the importance of reunifying Germany.

There was, however, no actual tension in U.S.–German relations until President Kennedy came to power with a team of intellectuals who took an unemotional view of the German situation and were anxious to reach a *modus vivendi* with the Soviet Union on the European sector of the cold war so as to concentrate on the problems of Asia and Latin America. Personal relations between the young President and the old Chancellor were not of the best either. However, this did not affect the basic "Atlanticism" of West German policy, which, one may say, reached its peak in 1965, when Johnson and Erhard found that they had a similar approach to life and politics and shared a distaste for the style of General de Gaulle. On November 29, Rainer Barzel—who, as CDU/CSU spokesman, made the full-dress statement to the Bundestag that Erhard ought to have made as Chancellor—laid stress on the Atlantic community and expressed the hope that the President's "great society" would truly embrace both Europe and America. Three weeks later, the same idea was reflected in the Johnson-Erhard communiqué to which we have already referred, and which drew a parallel between the President's ideal and Erhard's concept of the "formed society" (*formierte Gesellschaft*).

Kiesinger's inaugural statement of the policy of the Grand Coalition made no mention of the Atlantic community but only of the "Atlantic alliance," a more military concept with less suggestion of integration. While not wishing to estrange the United States, Kiesinger's object was to pursue an open policy toward the Soviet Union and Eastern Europe, if possible with French support; and the notion of a closely knit Atlantic community was not congenial either to the Communist bloc or to General de Gaulle.

"As much NATO as possible—as far as possible with France." This headline in the *Frankfurter Allgemeine Zeitung* of March 19, 1966 well expressed the Bundestag's dilemma in the debate that followed the announcement of France's withdrawal from NATO. Fritz Erler, no doubt the soundest and best informed of German politicians in the field of foreign affairs, used to state the case similarly: Europe could not exist without France, nor could it be secure without the United States.

Franco-German *rapprochement* had been a basic and constant preoccupation of Chancellor Adenauer. In his endeavor to achieve it, he had sometimes to face violent personal attacks: he was charged with having been a Rhineland separatist after the first world war or a paid agent of the French secret service after the second. As the exponent of his policy in Paris, he had in the early days Wilhelm Hausenstein, a man whose merits he never fully appreciated. Aided by a staff of high quality and by the warmth of character of his wife, a Jew of Belgian origin, the ambassador succeeded in dispelling much ill-feeling and in creating an atmosphere in which it was possible to pursue a realistic policy. The Chancellor's own relations with his French opposite numbers varied from one to another. In Schuman he found a statesman whose thoughts in many matters ran parallel to his own. The Adenauer–Schuman–de Gasperi trio were in fact united not so much by their Catholicism as by the fact that they were natives of "borderland" areas—the Rhineland, Lorraine, and the Trentino respectively—who were determined to eliminate the causes of strife among Europeans. Bidault, who succeeded Schuman in 1953, was not among those MRP leaders who were in regular touch with Christian Democratic parties in other countries. As Foreign Minister, he practiced a more traditional style of diplomacy than his predecessor but did not, as had been feared in Germany, revert to the intransigence that had marked his policy from 1944 to 1948, but which was now outdated. Mendès-France (Prime Minister and Foreign Minister in 1954–55) was at first a symbol of iniquity in the Chancellor's eyes, especially after the rejection of the EDC treaty. Later on, however, the two men, who shared a taste for efficiency and realism, came to enjoy a fairly close relationship, though one would not think so from reading Adenauer's *Memoirs*.

There were many reasons for the improvement of Franco-German relations in the 1950's: the settlement of particular disputes, the slow progress of German rearmament, growing European integration, the normalization of diplomatic relations, which finally became cordial as never before, and the fading of mutual resentment as public opinion in the two countries found other subjects of concern, such as reunification or Algeria. In almost every field of public life—from local government to youth movements, from engineers' associations to political parties, from trade unions to popular culture and church groups—the leaders and active members of parallel organizations in France and Germany maintained closer and more regular contacts than they did with any other countries.

The question of the Saar is worth studying in detail as an illustration of Franco-German relations at this time. For over seven years, amid sometimes violent reactions in the parliaments and public opinion of both countries, there was a confused alternation of good will and setbacks, both sides being determined to defend their national interests but also to avoid a final breach.

When the Federal Republic was created in 1949, the Saar was in a customs union with France. At the beginning of 1950, the Chancellor broached the problem, at first with no result except to increase the powers of the Saar government headed by Johannes Hoffmann and diminish those of Gilbert Grandval, the military governor since 1945 and High Commissioner from January, 1948, with the title of ambassador from January, 1952. In March, 1950, the Chancellor protested against the "unilateral" French action in signing a general convention with the Saar. He agreed, however, against SPD opposition, to the Federal Republic becoming an associate member of the Council of Europe in July, despite the fact that the Saar was given the same status: the Schuman Plan and Germany's readmission to the concert of Europe seemed to him important enough to justify concessions over the Saar that were, as the event showed, to be temporary ones. From 1952 to 1954, there was an alternation of crisis and calm, with the Bundestag declaring that the Saar was a German territory and the Federal Government protesting in the Council of Europe against the violation of its political liberties. The parties in the Saar that favored a return to Germany were still banned at the legislative elections of November 30, 1952, when, despite an intensive campaign, supported by the Federal Ministry for All-German questions, to induce voters to spoil their ballots, the "official" parties secured two-thirds of the votes.

On January 6, 1953, René Mayer, the French Premier, declared to the Assembly that the approval of "European" status for the Saar was a precondition of the ratification of the EDC treaty. But Franco-German negotiations met with one setback after another, despite a compromise proposal by Van der Goes van Naters, the Dutch rapporteur at the Council of Europe. On October 23, 1954, after the rejection of the EDC treaty, Adenauer and Mendès-France signed an agreement giving the Saar "a European statute within the framework of the Western European Union," to be supervised by a European Commissioner. Political parties, associations, newspapers, and assemblies were to be freed from restriction; the Franco-Saar currency union was to be maintained, but economic relations between the Saar and the Federal Republic were to be made progressively similar to those between the Saar and France. The agreement provided that the statute would be approved by a referendum but did not say what would happen if the Saar population rejected it, as in fact they did. The Chancellor, who urged acceptance of the statute, was charged with having yielded to Mendès-France's pressure during their last dramatic night of negotiations, and the Saar witnessed an outburst of nationalism. On October 23, 1955, 96·6 per cent of registered voters went to the polls and 67·7 of these voted "No." On June 5, Adenauer and the new French Premier Guy Mollet reached an agreement which became the Luxembourg treaty of October 27. The Saar was to be politically united with the Federal Republic on January 1, 1957, while transitional arrangements were provided for in the economic field. The French demand for the canalization of the Moselle was agreed to, and France also obtained a large measure of satisfaction over the Warndt coal deposits, which were the main economic object of contention.

A German cartoonist depicted the story as follows: Little Miss Saarland comes to the Chancellor and asks to be taken back into the German home, but he refuses. Some friends come along and help her to get in after all, whereupon the Chancellor poses for photographers with the little girl on his knee and receives congratulations on the return of his long-lost child. Did the Saar in fact become a *Land* of the Republic thanks to Adenauer's policy or in spite of it? Illogical as it may seem, both answers are true. It is true that Adenauer was at pains to emphasize the provisional character of the European statute, so as not to prejudice the question of Germany's eastern frontiers; but, by agreeing to it, he did in effect renounce the prospect of the Saar acceding to Germany, and the unexpected result of the referendum forced his hand. But it was largely due to his policy of securing equal rights for Germany that the French attitude changed: whereas in 1949 the future of the Saarland was a matter between France and the local inhabitants and did not concern Germany, by 1955 it was a Franco-German issue on which the Saar government was taken into consultation. Moreover, the Chancellor's policy was directly responsible for the excellent climate of relations between France and Germany, thanks to which the vote of 1955 did not provoke a crisis and it was possible to arrive at the 1956 agreement in which both sides made reasonable concessions.

The Luxembourg treaty regulated the last outstanding issue between France and West Germany, and its application gave rise to few problems. The canalized section of the Moselle was opened to navigation by the heads of state of Germany, France, and Luxembourg on May 26, 1964. The integration of the Saar into the Federal Republic proceeded smoothly during a period when its coal output was becoming more of a liability than an asset, as Europe's shortage gave way to overproduction. From 1956 onward, Franco-German differences were not of a bilateral kind—apart from one or two incidents such as the kidnapping of the OAS leader Colonel Argoud at Munich in February, 1963—but were concerned with policy within a wider framework: European unity, the Atlantic alliance, relations with the Communist countries. Even when intergovernmental relations were strained by such issues, France and Germany continued to get on extremely well in other spheres: this was shown by their leaders' statements, by contacts and exchanges between individuals and groups, and also in the sphere of commerce as each country became the other's principal supplier and customer.

Nonetheless, when de Gaulle returned to power in 1958 there was anxiety at Bonn on account of his attitude toward Germany in 1944–46 and the vigor with which he had criticized his successors' policies, especially in regard to European unity. However, on September 14, the Chancellor and the General had a long meeting at Colombey-les-Deux-Eglises, and a bond of friendship sprang up between them that endured until Adenauer's death. In the political sphere, they came to a sort of tacit agreement that the Federal Republic would show understanding for France's ambition to play an independent role in various parts of the world, and especially in Atlantic affairs, while France would firmly support West Germany vis-à-vis the Communist bloc. When Erhard altered the emphasis of Bonn's policy, de Gaulle was quick to drop a hint that France might change her mind also: in his broadcast of December 31, 1963, he mentioned Pankow (East Berlin) among the capitals of the East European totalitarian states—totalitarian, but a "state" all the same.

De Gaulle's triumphal visit to Germany in September, 1962 marked the high point of relations between the two leaders, and perhaps between their countries. It inspired a plan to institutionalize Franco-German relations: a French memorandum of September 18 led to the signature not of a protocol, as at first intended, but of a regular treaty, the Koblenzerstrasse lawyers having explained to the Chancellor that a protocol would not suffice if he wanted to have the agreement solemnly ratified by the Bundestag. The treaty signed at Paris on January 22, 1963 provided for an extensive system of consultation: the heads of state or heads of government were to meet at least twice a year, the foreign ministers every three months, their senior officials once a month; the ministers of defense were to meet once a quarter, as were the French minister of education and the spokesman of the Länder in this field; the chiefs of staff and the ministers for family and youth affairs every two months. All this machinery worked well in one sense, less well in another. Its defect was that instead of consulting, Bonn and especially Paris were apt to use the meetings simply to inform each other of what they had been doing. As against this, the regularity of meetings and the resulting continuous dialogue served a valuable purpose in keeping relations on an even keel despite the stresses of 1963–66. Moreover, the system of binational ministerial councils which grew up was a complete novelty in relations between states, though their style of course varied according to the individuals concerned. At the outset, the French President's personality lent substance to the picture of affairs conjured up by the ceremony of signature, as seen in an impressive photograph: General de Gaulle in the center, with Chancellor Adenauer and M. Pompidou to his right and left, and beyond them M. Couve de Murville and Dr. Schröder; the emperor of Europe, as it were, flanked by his prime ministers and foreign ministers of Germany and France.

The treaty also provided for the setting up of an institution whose statute was laid down in a separate agreement of July 5, 1963. The *Office franco-allemand pour la jeunesse* is a new type of body presided over by the two ministers for youth affairs, with a board consisting of ten French and ten German representatives, four of each being government officials and six belonging to private associations. The office is administered on a binational basis with a secretary-general and his deputy and two directors, one at Paris and the other at Rhöndorf. During the first five years the secretary-general was French and the secretariat functioned in Germany; since 1969 there has been a German secretary-general and the secretariat is located in Paris. An initial budget of 50 million francs a year was placed at the office's disposal, and its activities expanded rapidly thanks to the multiple relations already established since 1945, as described in chapter 3. In 1968, it was able to draw up an encouraging report for its fifth anniversary; the past year or two have been marked by further achievements, but also some uncertainty in regard to funds and management.

The creation of the youth office and other consultative arrangements did not obscure the fact that the treaty represented a culmination rather than a point of departure. At the very time when it was signed, Franco-German relations were overcast owing to de Gaulle's veto on British entry into the EEC. Later came the developments of which de Gaulle spoke as follows in a press conference on October 28, 1966: "It is not our doing that the preferential links which Bonn has contracted with Washington independently of us, and which grow closer day by day, have robbed the Franco-German agreement of inspiration and substance. It may well be that our German neighbors have thereby lost some opportunities for what might have been the joint action of our two countries, since events were moving elsewhere while they were putting into effect not our bilateral treaty, but the preamble which they added to it of their own accord and which completely altered its sense." The reference is to the preamble the Bundestag added to the law ratifying the treaty on May 8, 1963; which in its main paragraph contained a far from Gaullist interpretation of Franco-German policy:

[The Bundestag] . . . Resolved to serve by the application of this treaty the great aims to which the Federal Republic of Germany, in concert with the other states allied to her, has aspired for years, and which determine her policy—to wit, the preservation and consolidation of unity of the free nations and in particular of a close partnership between Europe and the United States of America; the realization of the right of self-determination for the German people and the restoration of German unity; collective defense within the framework of the North Atlantic Alliance and the integration of the armed forces of the states bound together in that

Alliance; the unification of Europe by following the course adopted by the establishment of the European Communities, with the inclusion of Great Britain and other states wishing to accede; the further strengthening of those Communities, and the elimination of trade barriers by negotiations between the European Economic Community, Great Britain, and the United States of America, as well as other states, within the framework of the General Agreement on Tariffs and Trade.

Between 1963 and 1966, relations between the French and German governments were in fact marked by varying degrees of coolness, owing in part to the hostility felt in Paris toward Dr. Schröder even more than Chancellor Erhard. An improvement set in when the Grand Coalition came to power, the basic reason being the evolution of Bonn's East European policy. Up till then, the people who were called "Gaullists" in Germany, such as Strauss and Guttenberg, wanted to work with de Gaulle but advocated an Eastern policy very different from his, whereas "anti-Gaullists" such as Schröder were pursuing a policy very like his in opposition to him. Under the coalition, both these groups became allies of the General, with more or less common objectives vis-à-vis the Soviet Union and the other Comecon countries. Nevertheless, there were still sharp differences between France and Germany over Atlantic and European issues, which were not mitigated until President Pompidou took office in June, 1969.

The "European idea" was popular from the beginning. It was natural enough that the Federal Republic should be more "European-minded" than France, which in turn was more so than Britain. The Germans were aware of the catastrophe into which nationalism had led them; the French knew that they owed their victory to the Allies, but the war had not shattered the fabric of the French nation; the British, on the other hand, did not forget the upsurge of national pride that had been their salvation in 1940. However, pro-European sentiment in Germany has never been all of a piece: there is enthusiasm at one extreme and cynicism at the other. The former was chiefly found among young people, many of whom showed for years a genuine idealistic attachment to European unity. Their zeal was attractive, but their emotional impatience was not always proof against the inevitable disappointments. Instead of symbolically burning frontier posts, they might have done better to spend some time studying the political, economic, and social problems that had to be solved before the European dream could become a reality. Moreover, they did not always grasp that it was easier for Germany to give up rights that she had not yet regained than for her neighbors to abandon those they still possessed. As for the cynics, European unity represented to them chiefly, or rather exclusively, the quickest way for Germany to achieve equality of rights: once she had done so, Europe could fend for itself. Between the two extremes, there were large numbers of Germans of all persuasions, sentimentally attached to the European idea but seldom conscious of the difficulties and contradictions that its pursuit involved.

The first honeymoon of the European policy lasted about six weeks: from May 9, 1950, when Robert Schuman launched his proposal for the European

Coal and Steel Community, to the outbreak of the Korean war. The SPD raised objections such as the lack of British participation, continued foreign control of the Ruhr, and the conflict between European integration and German reunification, but these weighed little against the manifestly hopeful aspects of a new and creative gesture. From the autumn of 1950 onward, the problem was complicated by the argument over the EDT, since the European idea could be represented as a popular means of glossing over the unpopular rearmament policy.

The second auspicious period began with the revival of European ideas in 1955 and the conversion of the SPD, symbolized by Ollenhauer's membership of Jean Monnet's Committee for the United States of Europe. The atmosphere of the negotiations that led to the signature of the Rome treaties on March 25, 1957 showed that politicians, diplomats, and high officials were beginning to feel a true Community spirit. As for the change of regime in France in 1958, it not only did not interfere with the creation of the EEC but enabled France to play a full part in it, thanks to the December currency reform that put French finances on a sound basis. In January, 1958, the Six appointed as President of the EEC Commission the West German State Secretary for Foreign Affairs, Professor (of law) Walter Hallstein, a man of integrity and precision who had been rector of Frankfurt University from 1946 to 1948 and was chairman of the German UNESCO Commission when he first became acquainted with the Chancellor.

The Common Market was successful as a market, that is to say it stepped up commercial exchanges within the Community to a remarkable degree. The Federal Republic's foreign trade for 1969 may be broken down as follows (in milliards of DM):

Groups of countries	Exports	Imports
EEC (Common Market)	45·2	42·4
EFTA (European Free Trade Association: Britain, Scandinavia, etc.)	25·6	15·2
North America	11·9	11·5
Developing countries	14·0	17·0
Communist countries	5·1	4·0

But economic progress within the EEC has been offset by disillusionment from the political and psychological points of view. Despite the views expressed by the German press in the 1960's, de Gaulle was not solely to blame for this. Besides technical difficulties, there have been more fundamental grounds for uncertainty. The German leaders, in effect, complained to de Gaulle: "You want Europe to have a will of its own, but you refuse to give it a body"—to which the General replied: "What you want is a body with an American soul." However, de Gaulle's aversion to the whole idea of majority voting in the Community, without which it hardly deserves its name, was no less an obstacle to political progress than was his horror of "vassalization."

Do the West Germans really want the Community to be an organic unity? They are in favor of British membership, and Britain's application has not affected her distrust of political integration. Moreover, as long as Erhard was Economic Minister, the Federal Republic was opposed, in the name of the "market economy," to any Community policy that involved more than the removal of economic barriers, the organization of energy resources, and the channeling of investments. Finally, for ten years or more, from 1958 to 1969, the Federal Republic managed to avoid asking itself seriously the key question: do we really want an integrated Europe with a single foreign policy if that means that decisions about our relations with Poland or even with the "other Germany" can be taken by a majority vote?

During the national and international polemics of 1950–54, a question that came up again and again was that of the finality or otherwise of West Germany's association with the EEC: what would happen if Germany were reunified? Annexed to the Rome treaties of 1957 was a "Protocol relating to German internal trade and connected problems," which is a minor masterpiece of self-contradiction, paragraphs 2 and 3 offering in vague outline a solution to a problem whose existence is denied in paragraph 1:

1. Since exchanges between the German territories subject to the Basic Law for the Federal Republic of Germany and the German territories to which the Basic Law does not apply are part of German internal trade, the application of this treaty requires no amendment of the existing system of such trade within Germany.

2. Each member state shall inform the other member states and the Commission of any agreements affecting exchanges with the German territories in which the Basic Law for the Federal Republic of Germany does not apply, as well as of the provisions for their implementation. Each member state shall ensure that such implementation shall not conflict with the principles of the Common Market and shall, in particular, take appropriate measures to avoid any prejudice which might be caused to the economies of the other member states.

3. Each member state may take suitable measures to prevent any difficulties which might arise for it from trade between another member state and the German territories in which the Basic Law for the Federal Republic of Germany does not apply.

Thus the Europe of the Six has an indeterminate shape: it has no Eastern frontier, because the dividing line between the two Germanies is a frontier only in the eyes of the G.D.R. and its allies. As long as the Federal Republic was on bad terms with the G.D.R., this state of affairs was little more than a legal curiosity. But as far back as 1966, when Herbert Wehner put forward the idea of an economic confederation of the two Germanies, the problem of the nature of the Federal Republic became topical once more. The meetings between Willy Brandt and Willi Stoph in 1970 have spotlighted a reality hardly anyone in West Germany is prepared to face. The only way in which the Federal Republic can seek to improve its relations with the G.D.R. and at the same time pursue a policy of European unity is, on the one hand, to limit the extent of its political or even economic integration and, on the other hand, to accept the demarcation line in Germany as a true frontier. The recognition of the G.D.R. as a state in the full sense of the term is not only a precondition of any agreement with it, but is essential to the structural and psychological stabilization of the European Community; and, until the stabilization is achieved, the Federal Republic cannot itself pursue a constructive Eastern policy.

Ostpolitik

On June 5, 1947 (it will be recalled), the Minister-Presidents of the *Länder* comprising the Soviet zone "walked out" of the Munich conference immediately before it was due to open. On May 21, 1970, Willi Stoph, the G.D.R. Prime Minister, left Cassel after a second, more or less inconclusive meeting with Willy Brandt, the Chancellor of the F.R.G.

The course of events between these two setbacks was intricate yet consistent. Consistent in that it reflects a gradual but steady development toward the division of Germany into two states; intricate because of important fluctuations in international politics and changes in the Federal Republic's policy toward the Communist bloc in Europe (known as the "Eastern policy" or *Ostpolitik*).

The Federal Republic and the G.D.R. came into existence on a different basis from each other. Both were products of the cold war, but whereas the West German democracy was based on the free consent of its citizens, the Germans in the Soviet zone were forced into a regime similar to that which the Soviet Union, aided by the local Communists, had imposed on the other countries "liberated" by the Red Army. It was natural therefore that the SED leaders should be seen in the West as quislings, henchmen of the detested occupying power and oppressors of their countrymen. To have any dealings with them seemed like a betrayal of fellow Germans. In any case, was it not more important to defend the West against the Soviet threat? What proof was there that the Russians would stop at the Iron Curtain? It might be that their ambition went no further than to stabilize the demarcation line between the two hostile camps; but there was no means of knowing this, and even if it were so, how could West Germany accept a stabilization that left 17 million Germans on the wrong side of the line? A strong Federal Republic within a strong Western world—this seemed the best way of ensuring the defense of free Germany and exerting pressure on the Russians to withdraw, to let go of their prey and allow the 17 million to choose their own way of life.

Adenauer's policy was based on solid facts and motives, but its main weakness was that in practice it excluded all possibility of German reunification. From this point of view, Article 146 of the Basic Law ("This Basic Law shall become invalid on the day when a constitution adopted in a free decision by the German people comes into force") was unrealistic. It suggested that the united Germany of the future would not be a merger of the two existing states into something different from either, but would simply be an eastward extension of the Federal Republic—which must involve, apart from anything else, a major diplomatic defeat of the Soviet Union. The Russians, for their part, had every interest in preventing the consolidation of the West by holding out the hope of a merger of the two Germanies to those Germans, Frenchmen, and others who dreaded the political or military consequences of the division of Germany and of the world. Were the Soviet proposals, especially those of

1952, in regard to Germany anything more than propaganda designed to arouse false hopes of this kind? If not, there was hardly any sound alternative to the Chancellor's policy. If, however, the Russians were sincere in their offer, he would bear a heavy responsibility before the German nation.

The early 1950's witnessed a lively debate on this issue, which later died down but has revived since 1966. It focused, as it still does, on the Soviet note of March 10, 1952 proposing the conclusion of a peace treaty with a reunified Germany bounded by the Oder-Neisse frontier. The draft treaty annexed to the note comprised political, economic, and military provisions. Among these were:

Political Provisions

1. Germany is restored as a united state. The partition of Germany is thereby ended, and the united Germany obtains the possibility of developing as an independent, democratic, peace-loving state.

2. All armed forces of the occupying powers shall be withdrawn from Germany not later than one year from the day the peace treaty comes into force. Simultaneously, all foreign military bases on the territory of Germany shall be liquidated.

3. Democratic rights shall be guaranteed to the German people so that all persons under German jurisdiction, irrespective of race, sex, language, or religion, may enjoy the rights of man and fundamental freedoms, including freedom of speech, press, religion, political convictions, and assembly.

4. The free activity of democratic parties and organizations shall be made secure in Germany, granting them the right freely to decide their internal affairs, hold congresses and assemblies, and enjoy freedom of press and publication.

5. The existence on German territory of organizations hostile to democracy and to the cause of maintaining peace shall not be permitted.

6. All former servicemen of the German army, including officers and generals, and all former Nazis, except those who are serving terms of imprisonment on conviction for crimes which they committed, shall be granted civil and political rights on an equal footing with all other German citizens so that they may take part in building a peace-loving democratic Germany.

7. Germany pledges herself not to take part in any coalitions or military alliances aimed against any Power which participated with its armed forces in the war against Germany.

Military Provisions

1. Germany shall be permitted to have the national armed forces—land, air, and naval—necessary for the defense of the country.

2. Germany may produce military equipment and material, the quantity and types of which shall not exceed what is required for the Armed Forces established for Germany by the peace treaty.

One purpose of this rather surprising document was obviously to delay the signature of the EDC treaty. The Russians also had to justify "democratic" rearmament, since up to then they had denounced German rearmament in any shape or form. Had the proposed treaty ever come into force in a reunified Germany, Article 5 would have been used to confer on the Soviet Union a permanent right to interfere in Germany's internal affairs, on a par with the suppression of "anti-democratic" and "anti-peace" organizations and persons in the "People's Democracies." Although Ulbricht often spoke in after years of the new situation that acceptance of the Soviet note would have created, it is hardly possible to believe that Stalin was really prepared to surrender such a vital portion of the glacis which he had carefully built up. Adenauer, at all events, branded the document as a mere diversionary maneuver. For this he was criticized by politicians and commentators in the 1950's and 1960's, but meanwhile he had the satisfaction of signing the EDC treaty and the convention that put an end to the occupation regime in West Germany—an achievement that would have been postponed by interminable negotiations on the Soviet proposal.

There may have been times when one or another of Stalin's successors had ideas for altering the Soviet Union's German policy—indeed both Beria and Khrushchev were charged with this after they fell from power, the former in 1953 and the latter in October, 1964, a few weeks after the announcement of his visit to Bonn. But it would seem that the Russians accepted the partition of Germany, on balance, as a good thing from the early 1950's, some years before Khrushchev took to repeating to foreign visitors, especially those from France, that the situation was to everybody's advantage. It is significant that the Soviets remained silent at the only time when a Soviet proposal might have seemed to offer constructive possibilities instead of being intended merely to block progress in the opposing camp. This was at the beginning of September, 1954, when the EDC had been killed and the Paris agreements were not yet born, so that the French Government, at least, might have been expected to welcome a reasonable Soviet offer.

As it was, the Russians did everything possible to justify those who believed that they would accept the integration of the Federal Republic into NATO and the Six-power grouping when these became a *fait accompli*. Certainly they took no reprisals apart from denouncing the Franco-Soviet treaty of 1944, and the *détente* that had begun after Stalin's death became more pronounced. On July 18, 1955, two months after the Paris agreements came into force, the four powers met at head-of-government level for the first time at the Geneva conference. On September 9, Adenauer visited Moscow accompanied by Karl Arnold, representing the Bundesrat, and by Kiesinger and Carlo Schmid, the chairman and vice-chairman of the Bundestag foreign affairs committee. The visit marked an evolution on both sides. To the Soviet leaders, the "henchman of the American imperialists and war mongering trusts" had become a respectable negotiator, the spokesman of a sovereign state. Adenauer for his part assured Khrushchev and Bulganin that "no one in Germany imagines that it is possible to deal with the Soviet Union from a position of strength." The conversations resulted in the establishment of diplomatic relations between the Soviet Union and the Federal Republic, a promise to release thousands of German prisoners of war who were being held in Russia contrary to inter-Allied agreements, and negotiations for the development of trade relations.

From 1956 onward, there were thus two rival German ambassadors in Moscow. To prevent this situation recurring all over the world, with the two German states appearing on an equal footing in international life, the Chancellor declared to the Bundestag on his return from Moscow that the establishment by any other state of diplomatic relations with the "so-called German

Democratic Republic" would be considered an unfriendly act by the Federal Republic, since it would contribute to accentuating the division of Germany. This marks the origin of what came to be called the "Hallstein doctrine," though it was not really a doctrine nor was it the work of the state secretary in question. Based on a memorandum by Professor Wilhelm Grewe, the head of the political department at the Koblenzerstrasse, the policy soon lost its flexibility and took on in practice a simple, indeed an oversimple form: diplomatic relations with any state that recognized the G.D.R. in future would be broken off, and they would not be established with any states other than the Soviet Union which had already recognized it, such as the people's democracies of Eastern Europe.

On this basis, in October, 1957, the F.R.G. broke off diplomatic relations with Yugoslavia, which had just recognized the G.D.R. and had proclaimed its opinion that a peaceful reunification of Germany could only take place through a *rapprochement* between the two German states. The breach of relations was out of keeping with hints of a more flexible policy toward Poland, at a period when Gomulka was resisting pressure from the Soviet Union seconded by the G.D.R. In the autumn of 1956, one or two courageous persons—Carlo Schmid at a Franco-German conference at Bad Neuenahr, and Professor Grewe in the *Süddeutsche Zeitung* of November 17—raised their voices in favor of a frank discussion of the German-Polish frontier question; but the feelers that had gone out toward Warsaw were nullified by the breach with Belgrade. A fresh opportunity arose at the end of 1960, when Berthold Beitz, the representative of Krupp's, who had saved many Poles from the SS and enjoyed the friendship and esteem of President Cyrankiewicz, secured the Chancellor's blessing for contacts with the Warsaw leaders. However, these came to nothing owing to the stiffness and lack of tact shown by Adenauer and his officials.[21]

The 1950's were a period of intransigence, not only at Bonn but in West German public opinion. In a poll at Hamburg, 50 per cent of those questioned said that anyone who advocated the recognition of the Oder-Neisse frontier should not be allowed to lecture publicly; 57 per cent thought such a person should be kept off television, and 68 per cent would not allow him to teach in a *Gymnasium*.[22] In March, 1959, the SPD went so far as to put forward a "plan for Germany,"[23] but withdrew it next year. It was based on Polish Foreign Minister Rapacki's proposal for a neutral zone in central Europe and suggested, as a means of reunification, a conference on an equal footing between the F.R.G. and the G.D.R. (the plan actually used this latter term) and the creation of a German common market (*Gesamtdeutscher Markt*) This largely Utopian document is worth rereading in 1970 in the light of Chancellor Brandt's policy. While the hope of free elections in both parts of Germany was certainly unrealistic, the acceptance of the G.D.R. as an actual entity was less so. At the Geneva four-power conference on the German problem in May, 1959, the Western powers and their Federal German allies had, after all, agreed to an arrangement whereby delegations from the two Germanies were seated at separate tables adjacent to the round table of the conference proper.

The erection of the Berlin wall made clear to the blindest eye what should already have been clear after the East German revolt of June 17, 1953 and the crushing of the Hungarian insurrection 1956—namely, that the West was helpless to prevent the Russians doing anything they chose within their zone of Europe, even on its periphery. "Pressure" of any sort was useless; whether anything could be achieved by negotiation either was far from certain, but from then on West German foreign policy underwent a change which Schröder emphasized after Adenauer's departure. Naturally, not too much attention was paid to the long Soviet note of December 27, 1961 which, after a barrage of criticism, explained that the Federal Republic was a victim of the West and would do better to understand that its real interest lay in dealing with the friendly Soviet Union. But by degrees Bonn came to adopt a more open attitude toward Eastern Europe. Trade missions were set up at Warsaw in September, 1963, and at Bucharest, Budapest, and Sofia in May, July, and October, 1964. In January, 1963, relations with Castro's Cuba were broken off because the latter had recognized the G.D.R., but in May, 1965 Schröder declared to the Bundestag that doctrinaire principles were even more out of place in diplomacy than elsewhere and that no "abstract conceptions" stood in the way of diplomatic relations with the East European countries. From then onward, a distinction was made between those states that had recognized the G.D.R. since its inception (and that could be said to have had no choice in the matter) and those that might decide to recognize it in the future.

In the nongovernmental sphere, 1966 saw the two abortive dialogues of unequal importance between the F.R.G. and the G.D.R. The FDJ (the East German youth organization) rejected a detailed offer by the VDS (*Verband Deutscher Studentenschaften*) for permanent contacts between the two bodies and between the students and universities they represented, thus showing how apprehensive the G.D.R. still was of even a controlled interchange between any but the heads of organizations.[24] Second, after preliminary conversations and letters in April and May, the SPD and the SED agreed on an exchange of speakers: an SPD leader would make a speech at Karl-Marx-Stadt (Chemnitz) on July 14 and an SED leader at Hanover on the 21st. But a legal obstacle arose: were not the Soviet zone leaders "bureaucratic murderers" (*Schreibtischmörder*) who had signed orders whereby dozens of Germans had been shot in the vicinity of the wall or the demarcation line? That being so, were they not liable to arrest if they set foot on Federal territory? In June, the Bundestag, against the opposition of many CDU deputies, passed a law giving them "temporary immunity from German jurisdiction" (*befristete Freistellung von der deutschen Gerichtsbarkeit*). On the 29th, Albert Norden announced that the SED regarded the law as an insult and that the exchange was off.

Five months later, the SPD joined the coalition under Kiesinger, whose declaration of policy contained some new features and emphasized the desire for reconciliation with Germany's eastern neighbors. On January 31, 1967, the Rumanian Foreign Minister, Corneliu Manescu, visited Bonn and it was announced that the two countries would exchange diplomatic representatives. A year later, relations with Belgrade were restored, but the Federal Republic at the same time warned the unaligned countries outside Europe that it would not take it kindly if they recognized the G.D.R.

On April 12, 1967, the government issued a detailed statement of measures it considered acceptable and desirable in the field of inter-German relations;

these included economic and commercial arrangements and "framework agreements" (*Rahmenvereinbarungen*) for scientific, academic, technical, and cultural exchanges. On May 10, Willi Stoph addressed a letter to Kiesinger, whose reply on June 13 made a new departure by addressing Stoph as "Chairman of the Council of Ministers." The correspondence led to no immediate result, but by the spring of 1968 there was a prospect of meetings between ministers in technical departments of government. Two facts, again of unequal importance, interfered with this development and with the West German policy which, in theory, coincided with that of France—General de Gaulle vouching, as it were, to the Soviet and Polish leaders for the Federal Government's good faith. The policy in question was based on a painful choice: not only was a *détente* the only way of making progress on the German question, but West Germany was prepared to make unilateral concessions to bring it about, in the hope that one day it would be of benefit to all Germans. The object was to improve relations with the Soviet Union and the other Communist countries, not playing the Soviets off against the others but hoping for a liberalization of regimes throughout the bloc: how could Ulbricht's Germany then remain the only East European country to accuse the Federal Republic of militarism and revanchism, and to refuse to allow its citizens any contact with the West Germans?

The approach of the 1968 elections made Kiesinger more sensitive to pressure from those within his party who urged him not to alienate conservative support; this put a check on government policy and led to friction with Brandt, then Minister of Foreign Affairs. In Kiesinger's first "Report on the state of the nation in divided Germany," submitted on March 11, 1968 to the Bundestag—the latter having, in June, 1967, expressed the wish for an annual report of this kind—he expressed himself in prudent and rather vague terms. But a decisive blow, or so it seemed, was dealt to the "open" policy by the invasion of Czechoslovakia on August 20, 1968, which showed the depths of Soviet intolerance and marked Ulbricht's victory over Dubcek. Brandt, however, despite his indignation and disappointment, drew the same conclusions as the United States and France, though he had more reason than they to feel the tragedy that had befallen Dubcek's experiment in "humane socialism:" since we can do nothing to help the Czechs, we should continue with our policy as before; it is the only possible course to follow if, as de Gaulle put it, we are to advance from a *détente* to an understanding, and from that to a state of cooperation.

This line of thought is certainly acceptable to the Soviet Union, since it enables it to prove to its own citizens and to other countries that the West does not bear it a serious grudge for blighting the "Prague spring." When Brandt became Chancellor, he sent to Moscow Egon Bahr, his closest adviser, to embark on lengthy negotiations. He also caused a forthcoming reply to be returned to a letter addressed by Ulbricht, Chairman of the Council of State, to President Heinemann. Thus in due course the Erfurt and Cassel meetings took place. The Russians put pressure on the G.D.R. leaders to agree to Erfurt, but they did not forbid Stoph to dig his toes in at Cassel. Contacts yes, concessions no—or rather the concessions must all be on the Federal Government's side.

The main disadvantage of the setback at Cassel was that it exposed the Brandt government to criticism from the CDU, which quite properly hoped to return to power. But, except for Schröder—who recognized his own policy in his successor's—the CDU went a good deal too far in attacking the government's line, which it well knew to be the only one with any chance of achieving results. The policy in question, however, is one that calls for much courage, and this fact is too little realized outside Germany. Courage, that is to say, of the same order as Rathenau's in about 1920, when the necessity that lay before Germany was that of accepting in full the consequences of her defeat. Adenauer in his time was accused, both by men of the Right and by Social Democrats, of giving in and giving up too much; yet what he gave up was compensated for by a real and considerable increase in Germany's standing as compared with 1945. Brandt has an even harder task before him: that of throwing off the dead weight of a complex of moral and legal factors that no longer reflect reality. To accept reality as it is today means ignoring these factors, legitimate though they may be in themselves: it means becoming in literal truth, though in a very different spirit, what the conservatives scornfully call a *Verzichtpolitiker*—a renouncer of claims, a man who "sells Germany short." Luckily for Brandt, the climate of opinion is no longer what it used to be—partly because of the mere passage of time, partly too because he himself has changed it by the exercise of his will, by a determination stronger and more outspoken in this field than that of any of his predecessors, not by any means excluding Adenauer.

On one specific point no one in West Germany except the *Sudetendeutsche Landsmannschaft* raises any difficulty: the Munich agreement of 1938 is no longer valid, and the Sudeten territory is part of Czechoslovakia. This was firmly declared in Kiesinger's inaugural statement of policy. In 1967 and 1968, the Czechoslovak Government continued to demand an acknowledgment by the F.R.G. that the treaty was null and void from the beginning. But this claim had ceased to be a major obstacle to a *rapprochement* by the time Czechoslovakia was invaded, after which she was forced to put her signature to a very different type of agreement and her talks with West Germany for the time being came to an end.

The position with regard to Poland's frontier is less clear. The parties all treat this question like a hot potato, although public opinion has moved to some extent as the refugees have become integrated and as a result of the educative action of the EKD and some organs of the press and television.[25] The fact is not only that the former German territories have become thoroughly Polish but also that the Oder-Neisse frontier is regarded as definitive by all the Federal Republic's allies, though de Gaulle was alone in having the frankness to make his position publicly clear. One can understand the Poles' impatience with the last lingering juridical subtleties on the West German side. In the 1950's, recognition of the frontier might have been worth some Polish concession in exchange; but now that so much time has elapsed, it is a question of accepting the facts of life rather than bargaining. Nevertheless, people outside Germany, and especially in France, should realize clearly the kind of renunciation that is at stake. Algiers and Oran were never French towns in the proper sense of the term, and they were not under French rule for more than a hundred years or so. Breslau (Wroclaw) and Königsberg (which the Russians are pleased to call Kaliningrad) were thoroughly German cities and belonged to Austria or Germany for centuries. Yet France in 1961 was almost plunged into civil war on account of Algiers and Oran. There is no other place in the world where any country is called on to make a permanent sacrifice of this order as an acknowledgment of reality and for the sake of peace.

What of the demarcation line between the two Germanies? Is it a reality of the same order, and should the F.R.G. accord full recognition to the G.D.R. and expect nothing in return? The question is difficult to answer. Certainly, by the end of the 1960's it was high time to do away with some formulas and practices that bordered on the comic. It was hard for the foreign observer not to smile when the West German television blipped the strains of the G.D.R. national anthem during the European swimming championships at Budapest in September, 1966, and one is apt to feel impatient with the inverted commas that the *Frankfurter Allgemeine Zeitung* sedulously places round the term "G.D.R." in reports of Brandt's speeches. When the "Hallstein doctrine" meant that West German diplomats had to expend most of their talents on preventing recognition of the G.D.R., or when Guinea was able to extort large subsidies by a little simple blackmail, or again when the West Germans refused to open their large pavilion at the Algiers Fair because the East Germans put up a small one at the last moment—how did all this serve the true interest of the Federal Republic? An attitude more in keeping with common sense would also enable West Germany to secure due recognition for its large and growing contribution of aid to developing countries through the Ministry of Economic Cooperation. This work, begun by Scheel when the ministry was first set up in November, 1961, has been continued and expanded by his successors and in particular by Erhard Eppler, whose approach is the reverse of Germano-centric.[26]

But juridical factors cannot be dismissed from politics. As every reader of de Gaulle's *War Memoirs* will remember, when it is a question of achieving or defending legitimacy the least quibble of protocol has its own importance and its own relevance. A state whose legitimacy is rooted in the free choice of German citizens will not easily waive its claim to be, and to be treated as, the sole legitimate German state, at least until it has obtained some assurance of elementary freedom for the inhabitants of the other state, who, though no longer fellow citizens of the West Germans, are perhaps still their compatriots.

Moreover, the refusal to recognize the G.D.R. "in terms of international law" is not a matter of pure legalism. When, in 1969, the Federal Ministry for All-German Affairs was renamed the "Ministry for Internal German Relations" (*innerdeutsche Beziehungen*), this signified the fulfillment of a certain line of development and the abandonment of the idea of Germany as a single state. If the notion of *innerdeutsch*, implying a single nation, must be given up likewise, at least relations between the two Germanies should be so defined as to indicate that they are not exactly of the same kind as relations between any two states in the world. At the beginning of 1968, it looked as though a compromise might be worked out. Wilhelm Wolfgang Schütz, the clear-minded and courageous chairman of an organization with the awkward title *Kuratorium Unteilbares Deutschland* (Committee for Indivisible Germany), circulated a memorandum in which he proposed that the G.D.R. should be recognized as a state but that the concept of a single "German nation" should at the same time be upheld.[27] Although this idea met with many objections, it was clearly in accordance with the prevailing government view at that time in both parts of Germany. When the new G.D.R. constitution was adopted in April, 1968, the propaganda chief, Albert Norden, was called to order by *Neues Deutschland* for saying that relations between the two Germanies should be on a par with those between any states that were foreign to each other: on the contrary, said the SED journal (and the constitution), the G.D.R. is a "socialist state of the German nation." Two years later, however, the attitude of the G.D.R. leaders seems to have become more negative on this point also.

Nor are the G.D.R. leaders any more forthcoming as regards intellectual and human contacts between the two Germanies. One of the hopes or assumptions on which the F.R.G.'s present policy rests is that the more the G.D.R.'s position is strengthened, the safer its leaders will feel in adopting a more liberal policy. To judge from Stoph's attitude at Cassel, the result might well be the opposite, with consolidation of the regime leading to fresh intransigence. In these circumstances, is it right for the Federal Republic to take the final step of recognition without any prior guarantee of humaner conditions in the G.D.R.?

In any case, the West Germans have no choice. Having decided that the only justification for legalism on their part is that it may induce the G.D.R. to remove hindrances to individual freedom, they are committed to taking advantage of every possibility of contacts and exchanges, especially in the economic field,[28] and also to removing barriers in the West—for example, to the circulation of the G.D.R. press. Their policy must be to make use of every reality in order to bring influence to bear on the G.D.R., and this involves recognizing first and foremost the reality of the G.D.R. itself.

At the same time, however, the G.D.R. and its Soviet ally must themselves take account of realities, including the major one that West Berlin belongs to the West. Instead of admitting this, they insist that this enclave in East German territory must become a third German political entity, neither forming part of the Federal Republic nor protected by the quadripartite regime.

West Berlin is going through a slow process of demographic and economic decline. It is possible that in the long run the *status quo* will operate in the East's favor. But neither the Federal Republic nor its allies could accept a situation in which the security of West Berlin was in doubt or in which its inhabitants were once again cut off from West Germany. Is it not enough for the G.D.R. leaders that the West Berliners are deprived of all contact with their relatives on the other side of the wall, since the agreements under which a certain number of Christmas and Easter passes were issued have not been renewed since June, 1966?

The concept of the *status quo* is in fact central to the whole debate. In order to free West German policy, both domestic and foreign, from the myths and obsessions by which it has been beset, Chancellor Brandt seems prepared to pursue to its fullest extent the evolution that has been going on for the past decade and to accept facts as they are, from the Polish frontier to the division of Germany into two states. But he does not want the evolution to stop at this point, or the whole picture to be turned to stone. At Erfurt and Cassel, his

325

opposite number demanded that the existing reality should be taken as the final stage of development: accepting the *status quo* meant renouncing all hope of change. This is a fundamental divergence, and it is a faithful image of the dialogue between the Soviet Union and those in the West who, like the French Government, show the greatest good will in trying to come to terms with it. The Russians expect the West to move toward their position and hold out the hope that when it has done so, everything will stay the same forever—as though there could be a *rapprochement* with one side remaining still, and as though it was only Western society that stood in need of change!

Conclusion:
Germany in Our Time

IN 1945, Germany lay in ruins—shattered, execrated, enslaved by her conquerors. In 1970, there are two Germanies, both powerful, prosperous, and respected, both forces to be reckoned with in the economic and political life of the world community. It would be hard to imagine a greater contrast.

Let us look again. In 1945 the victors' "united front" was a mere façade. The Soviet Union took possession of its part of Germany, the three Western powers took theirs. In 1970, the Erfurt and Cassel meetings, by the very fact that they took place, have shown that the integration of each Germany into one of the opposing camps is a complete and accepted fact. Has there really been any basic change, when the situation that prevailed in 1945 has been thus stabilized and recognized after a quarter of a century?

Both sides of the picture are true. There has been a prodigious recovery, but the state of tutelage has turned out to be a permanent one. The economic power of the Federal Republic is certainly greater than that of France, and that of the G.D.R. far exceeds Rumania's; but France and Rumania are less fully integrated than either Germany in the transnational structure dominated by the respective superpowers.

The division of Germany is both a cause and a consequence of the division of the world, but basically more of a consequence than a cause; and divided Germany has remained sensitive to changes in the climate of relations between the two blocs. This has been especially true of the Federal Republic. A similar tendency was perceptible in postwar France, Britain, and Italy: first, a strong leftward trend, a general hankering after a form of Socialism combining justice and freedom; then, as the cold war intensified, a rightward swing toward restoration of the old order; and, finally, a less powerful reaction the other way, which brought Labour back to power in Britain and produced the *apertura a sinistra* in Rome. But in no other country, certainly not France, can the successive movements be traced so clearly and in so many spheres as in the Federal Republic.

The evolution of postwar France was largely determined by the repercussions on her internal affairs of the two great midcentury conflicts: the East-West antagonism and the revolt of Afro-Asia. The importance of the Communist Party has meant that the political scene in France has long been dependent in some degree on such faraway events as Stalingrad or the invasion of Czechoslovakia. But the only change of regime that France has known since the war, from the Fourth to the Fifth Republic, was brought about by the

Algerian war. In Federal Germany, on the other hand, internal developments are unaffected by the division of the world into North and South, and are entirely geared to the conflict between East and West.

The division of Germany is accepted and stabilized: the evolution in this case is complete, and the United States and the Soviet Union have tacitly agreed that the European sector of their worldwide confrontation should remain calm. West Berlin is an embarrassment to both of them because, by existing, it prevents the division between the two worlds from being completely stabilized.

But this division does not mean that there must be constant aggressiveness or that the differences must grow deeper and deeper. The way in which each of the two worlds evolves may be such as either to estrange them further or to bring them closer together. Policies adopted on either side may be such as to widen the gulf or help to bridge it. For many years, statesmen in the Federal Republic refused to understand that narrow legalism only served to defeat what was supposed to be their aim, namely the preservation of at least some degree of affinity between the two Germanies. The refusal to maintain official contacts meant the breakdown or prevention of unofficial ones, for lack of which the two states became more and more foreign to each other. If the division had been acknowledged sooner, it might have been possible to do more to preserve the feeling that both were members of one nation.

It was simpler, however, to keep on talking about reunification but to act as if it would never come about, taking virtually no steps to prevent the other Germany becoming a foreign country. The East Germans for their part showed a strong and constant wish to be different and to cut themselves off from the Federal Republic. But by their lack of interest and deliberate ignorance of conditions that shaped the minds and daily life of 17 million of their compatriots, the West Germans abetted the breach.

As time goes on, the division itself becomes less and less a fact in anyone's memory. The young people of Munich will soon feel more at home in Lyons than they would in Dresden, unless the tendency is reversed so that the West shows more desire to learn and the East ceases to prevent contacts. Meanwhile the division continues to perpetuate and multiply absurd or tragic situations of which non-Germans should take more notice than they do. In September, 1969, the runner Jürgen May was forbidden by the International Amateur Athletics Federation to take part in the European championships at Athens: the rules lay down that no one who has represented one country in the past may represent another until he has resided in it for a certain length of time, and May, the East German, had not been long enough in West Germany. We may understand the indignation of the West German team, who withdrew from the meeting in protest at the suggestion that May had changed his nationality by transferring from one part of Germany to the other!

"Was ist des Deutschen Vaterland?" ("Where is the German's fatherland?") For the past twenty years there has been no proper answer to this question, first posed in a famous nineteenth-century poem that asserted the unity of all the Germanies. In East Germany, the official answer now is that the G.D.R. is itself a *patrie*. In the West, after an unsuccessful attempt at making Europe the object of patriotic sentiment, the idea of a German nation is once more

emphasized; but a compromise is still sought between identifying the Federal Republic with Germany and preserving the emotional attachment to a greater Germany transcending its borders.

This is a matter of great importance, but is it fundamental in the last resort? When we see nationalism triumphant in Afro-Asia, does this signify that it is the wave of the future or simply that the young states are going through a phase that the industrialized countries have left behind them? In Europe itself, is Gaullism the portent of a fresh upsurge of nationalism or merely the defiant reaction to a tendency for the nation-state to be unduly depreciated as a frame of reference or an inspiration?

If the Federal Republic succeeds on the one hand in escaping the contagion of overgrown nationalism, and on the other in overcoming the state of inertia in which its highest collective ambition is to achieve comfort and respectability, then the world will have little cause to complain. Perhaps the solution of our problems is destined to be achieved through the discovery and practice of transnational solidarities by national groups. In the Eastern bloc, this may prove to be the means of achieving a Socialism free from oppression. In the West, it may produce a Europe conscious of its unity and desirous of playing its full part among the underprivileged peoples. The Germans, like the rest of us, must have their patriotism, but it must be within bounds and not *über alles*. Precisely because the Federal Republic aspires to be European and because it is not the whole of Germany, it may succeed in setting the example of an outward-looking patriotism which is both rational and creative.

Each of the two Germanies is firmly implanted in the world to which it belongs. It is a long time since the G.D.R. was merely the "Soviet occupation zone"; but, while it is less strictly subordinate to the U.S.S.R., their economic dependence on each other has increased. Moreover, as Léon Blum said in 1945 of the French Communist Party in its relation to the Soviet Union: "There is a psychological and emotional dependence which has the strength of both passion and habit. Members of the Party are not actuated by mere obedience or self-interest, but by something rooted in their being which is akin to love." This feeling may prove to be less strong in the next generation of G.D.R. rulers, but one way or another the Soviet hold is strong enough to make it certain that the internal evolution of the G.D.R. will continue to depend on that of the Soviet Union. Notwithstanding the special features of the G.D.R.'s position and development, its future depends basically on the answers to two questions: how far will the U.S.S.R. permit changes in the countries under its hegemony, and what changes may take place in the U.S.S.R. itself, since these will inevitably affect the bloc as a whole?

The situation of the Federal Republic is paradoxical. In no other West European country does the past weigh so heavily on the present state of its international relations; yet no other country is so completely divorced from its own history before 1945 and conditioned by what has happened in the past twenty-five years. Of course German attitudes and types of behavior survive from the past. Some of them are unpleasing—self-satisfaction and self-pity, the stifling narrowness of the small town with its caste-ridden society. Others are attractive: the sober, kindly delight in everyday pleasures and a job well done. But what is not there is the sense of history, above all by comparison

329

with France or Great Britain. Vercingetorix, Joan of Arc, and Napoleon are living figures to the French imagination—as Jefferson and Lincoln are in America, or Alfred the Great, Cromwell, and Disraeli in England—whereas the modern Germans, by and large, spare no thoughts for the Emperor Otto, Frederick the Great, or Bismarck. Similarly, when it comes to allusions in political debate, or to films, television, and magazine serials, the real or romanticized past is very little in evidence. There is nothing corresponding to the fall of the Bastille or the Three Musketeers, the Wild West saga, the Armada or Trafalgar. This lack is not affected by the existence of rather dreary school readers which harp on a Germany of enchanted woods and meadows: the breach with history is much more strongly felt in Germany than in the other industrial countries.

What is more, even references to the recent past are gradually becoming less common. We have seen some of the reasons in previous chapters: the integration of the refugees and expellees and the disappearance of those old enough to remember the expulsion itself; the rise of a generation in Germany and abroad for whom Nazism is a word in a history book; and the slow acceptance of the division of Germany by those who have never known it as a united state.

More and more, the Federal Republic presents the appearance of a normalized state and society, playing a sober and useful part in international life and especially in the building of Europe. It might even be described as normal to excess. In other countries, such as France or Britain, it is impossible to explain everything in terms of factors common to all nations of the same type, whereas in the Federal Republic the transnational elements are so strong that one is tempted to ignore the existence of specifically German features. It has been a difficulty throughout the writing of this book that the Federal Republic is too much a part of its own surroundings in time and place. The Social Democratic Party, the distribution of economic power, Catholicism in Germany, German students—none of these subjects can be adequately discussed without first describing and analyzing a pattern of society, behavior, and ideology that has nothing to do with Germany as such. If we have drawn comparisons with France or even Britain more frequently than with the G.D.R., it is not only because of our ignorance of the latter and our desire to make things clear to readers in the West, but above all because the analogies in Western Europe are so much closer and more numerous than those between the two Germanies.

Germany in 1970, with its mode of existence determined by international politics and its two halves each assimilated into one of the rival camps, is indeed a Germany of the present day. We in France, Britain, and the United States have a duty to understand what this means in terms of solidarity and responsibility. The West Germans, for their part, should ask themselves how soon and in what way Germany, instead of being merely absorbed into the contemporary world, can begin to make a fully creative contribution to it.

Notes

Introduction

1. Text in E. R. Huber, *Dokumente zur deutschen Verfassungsgeschichte*, 2d ed., I (Stuttgart, 1964), p. 410.
2. Karl Bachem, quoted in E. Matthias and R. Morsey, eds., *Das Ende der Parteien* (Düsseldorf, 1960), p. 443.
3. Full text in "Les entretiens franco-allemands. Mai–Octobre 1951," special number of *Bulletin de la Société des professeurs d'histoire et de géographie de l'enseignement public* (March, 1952).
4. For a fuller account of the period from April, 1932 to July, 1933, see A. Grosser's short work *Hitler: la presse et la naissance d'une dictature* (Paris, 1959).
5. Quoted in *Das Ende der Parteien*, p. 401.
6. Quoted in Walther Hofer, *Der Nationalsoziliasmus. Dokumente 1933–1945* (Frankfurt, 1957), p. 102.
7. Text of November 3, 1933, reproduced in Martin Heidegger, *Die Selbstbehauptung der deutschen Universität* (Breslau, 1934); quoted in the exhaustive summing-up by Karl-Dietrich Bracher, *Die deutsche Diktatur. Entstehung, Struktur, Folgen des Nationalsozialismus* (Cologne, 1969), p. 293. (English-language edition: *The German Dictatorship*, New York: Praeger, 1970.)
8. All these and many other texts will be found *in extenso* in the convenient and basic collection by H. A. Jacobsen and W. Jochmann, *Ausgewählte Dokumente zur Geschichte des Nationalsozialismus* (Bielefeld, 1966).
9. *Frankfurter Allgemeine Zeitung*, January 30, 1963.

1. The Take-over

1. Quoted in *Cahiers du Bolchevisme* (1940), p. 49, and reproduced in A. Rossi, *Les Cahiers du Bolchevisme pendant la Campagne de 1939–1940* (Paris, 1952).
2. Memorandum cited by Harold Macmillan at Strasbourg in 1949; quoted in Pierre Billotte, *Le Temps du choix* (Paris, 1950), p. 25.
3. Quoted in *Les Cahiers du Bolchevisme*, p. 26.
4. In general, references will not be given for published texts that are easily accessible in the many collections of documents, most of which are cited in the bibliography.
5. *Memoirs of Cordell Hull* (New York, 1948), p. 1603.
6. Lucius D. Clay, *Decision in Germany* (New York, 1950), p. 5.
7. Sumner Welles, *The Time for Decision* (New York, 1944), p. 340.

8. Quoted in the too-little known book by James Stuart Martin, *All Honorable Men* (Boston, 1950), p. 14.
9. Robert E. Sherwood, *Roosevelt and Hopkins* (New York, 1948), pp. 781 and 798.
10. *Ibid.*, p. 894.
11. Quoted in Harold Strauss, *The Division and Dismemberment of Germany* (university thesis, Geneva, 1952), p. 97.
12. Letter to Secretary of State Byrnes, dated January 5, 1946, quoted in William Hillman, *Mr. President* (New York, 1952), p. 22.
13. Charles de Gaulle, *Mémoires de guerre*, III, *Le Salut* (Paris, 1959), pp. 366 and 368 (notes of conversations drawn up by French Ambassador Roger Garreau). The English title of volume III is *Salvation*; see accompanying volume entitled *Documents* (New York: Simon and Schuster, 1960), pp. 85–6 and 88.

2. *Nuremberg and Denazification*

1. Georges Castellan, *D.D.R.—Allemagne de l'Est* (Paris, 1955), p. 28.
2. André François-Poncet, *De Versailles à Potsdam* (Paris, 1948), p. 300.
3. Basic observations by the Tribunal prefaced to the verdict on organizations; see *Das Urteil von Nürnberg 1946* (Munich, 1961), pp. 136–39.
4. *Cf.* Raymond de La Pradelle, *L'Affaire d'Ascq* (Paris, 1948).
5. A dispassionate but moving account, translated from Danish, is given in Jens Kruse, *Oradour* (Frankfurt, 1969). On the moral problems raised by the Bordeaux trial and the issues discussed in this chapter generally, the reader should refer to chapter III, "Le crime et la mémoire," of A. Grosser, *Au nom de quoi? Fondements d'une morale politique* (Paris, 1969).
6. On the origin of this directive, *cf.* Walter L. Dorn, "Die Debatte über die amerikanische Besatzungspolitik für Deutschland," in *Vierteljahreshefte für Zeitgeschichte*, January, 1958, pp. 60–77; also the supplementary documents cited by G. Moltmann, *ibid.*, July, 1967, pp. 299–322.
7. Quoted in Justus Fürstenau, *Entnazifizierung* (Neuwied, 1969), p. 25.
8. In the film based on the play, with Curt Jürgens in the leading role, the dilemma took a less acute form: the sabotaged planes were unable to take off.
9. For a chronological list from 1945 onward, see Fürstenau, *op. cit.*, pp. 233–35.
10. See graph, *ibid.*, p. 227.
11. *Cf.* p. 207 of Otto Bachof, "Die Entnazifizierung," quoted in *Deutsches Geistesleben und Nationalsozialismus* (Tübingen, 1956), pp. 195–216.
12. Lucius D. Clay, *Decision in Germany* (New York, 1950), p. 67.

3. *The Occupying Powers and the German People*

1. Title of articles by Joseph Rovan in the review *Esprit* for October, 1945 and after. Contemporary views of a similar kind are recalled in the 100th and last number, published in April, 1967, of *Allemagne: bulletin d'information du Comité français d'échanges avec l'Allemagne nouvelle*.
2. See below, chapters 9 and 11.
3. Victor Gollancz, *In Darkest Germany* (London, 1947).
4. See below, chapter 6.
5. For these debates and the incidents that gave rise to them, see especially F. Roy Willis, *The French in Germany* (Stanford, Calif., 1962), pp. 218–27.

6. R. Maier, *Ein Grundstein wird gelegt. Die Jahre 1945–1947* (Tübingen, 1964), especially pp. 350–56. The book is dedicated to the memory of Dawson, who died in 1947.
7. Raymond Ebsworth, *Restoring Democracy in Germany—The British Contribution* (London and New York, 1960), p. 121. Extracts and a brief commentary on the basic text setting out British policy are given in W. Rudzio, "Export englischer Demokratie?" in *Vierteljahreschefte für Zeitgeschichte*, April, 1969, pp. 219–36.
8. For the history of the parties as such in 1945–49 see below, chapter 7.
9. See chapters 3 and 10.
10. Présidence du Conseil, "La zone française d'occupation en Allemagne," *Cahiers français d'information*, No. 77, Paris, February 1, 1947, p. 25.
11. Epigraph and p. 12 of section II of the 1947 Report of the Secretary-General of the Inter-Allied Reparation Agency.
12. See chapters 8 and 11.

4. Cold War, Political Division and Limited Sovereignty

1. Quoted in A. Grosser, *La Quatrième République et sa politique extérieure* (Paris, 1961), p. 130, where there is a study of the main lines of French policy.
2. For details and analysis of the various kinds of reparations see Castellan, *D.D.R.—Allemagne de l'Est* (Paris, 1955), pp. 57–60.
3. See chapter 10. Tables and figures, including a comparison with the British zone, will be found in Guy Roustang, *Développement économique de l'Allemagne orientale depuis 1945* (Paris, 1963), pp. 19–34.
4. Quoted in James Stuart Martin, *All Honorable Men* (Boston, 1950), p. 202.
5. A good simplified account of the conference is given in E. Deuerlein, "Das erste gesamtdeutsche Gespräch," in the supplement "Aus Politik und Zeitgeschichte" to the weekly *Das Parlament* for June 7, 1967. The basic work, however, on the evolution of political ideas at this period is Hand-Peter Schwarz, *Vom Reich zur Bundesrepublik* (Neuwied, 1966).
6. For the full membership of all the bizonal institutions, see Tilman Punder, *Das bizonale Interregnum* (Cologne, 1966), pp. 331–48.
7. For a fuller analysis, see chapter 11; and, for the principal documents, see Hans George Ruge, *Das Zugangsrecht der Westmächte auf dem Luftweg nach Berlin* (Berlin, 1969).
8. For a convenient collection, in German, of the important documents of 1946–49 and after, see *Einigkeit und Recht und Freiheit. Westdeutsche Innenpolitik 1945–1955* (Munich, 1955).

5. The Foundations of the State

1. See chapter 11.
2. For the text of the exchange of letters see *Bulletin des Presse- und Informationsamtes der Bundesregierung* (hereinafter cited as *Bulletin*) for May 28 and 31, 1968.
3. See chapter 8.
4. See chapter 9.

5. See chapter 11.

6. Jürgen Seifert, ed., *Die Spiegel-Affäre*, I (Olten, 1966), p. 362.

7. See chapter 11.

8. *Cf.* F. K. Fromme, "Wie das Grundgesetz wirklich zustande kam. Ein Streitgespräch von Historikern und Dabeigewesenen," *Frankfurter Allgemeine Zeitung*, June 24, 1969.

9. On taking possession of the keys to the Court's new building on May 6, 1969. Full text in *Bulletin*, May 9, 1969.

10. The law on the Constitutional Court (*Bundesverfassungsgerichtsgesetz*), with appendices and a commentary (Munich and Berlin: C. H. Beck, 1965). Most of the main laws of the F.R.G. have been published by this firm. In addition to the text, Heinz Laufer's fundamental work should be studied: *Verfassungsgerichtsbarkeit und politischer Prozess*, (Tübingen, 1968).

11. See the severe comments of Ernst Friesenhahn, formerly a judge of the Court, in *Juristenzeitung*, No. 21 (1966), pp. 704–10.

6. Political Institutions

1. See chapter 11.

2. Lists for six ministries of this *Land*, as in 1964, will be found in Renate Kunze, *Kooperativer Föderalismus in der Bundesrepublik. Zur Staatspraxis der Koordinierung von Bund und Ländern* (Stuttgart, 1968), pp. 135–44.

3. The legal and political aspects are discussed, with texts, in Hans-Jürgen Toews, *Die Schulbestimmungen des niedersächsischen Konkordats* (Göttingen, 1967).

4. For the full text see *Bulletin*, April 17, 1968. (All agreements of this kind appear regularly in *Bulletin* a few days after their conclusion.)

5. For a detailed and instructive table see Franz Klein, "Die Finanzreform zwischen Bund, Länder und Gemeinden," in Supplement to *Das Parlament*, July 26, 1969, p. 30.

6. *Cf.* Heuss's memoir of Naumann, originally a lecture delivered at the Sorbonne on March 8, 1960: T. Heuss, *Friedrich Naumann und die deutsche Demokratie* (Wiesbaden, 1960).

7. Republished with an interesting commentary by Eberhard Jaeckel: T. Heuss, *Hitlers Weg. Eine Schrift aus dem Jahre 1932* (Tübingen, 1968).

8. Letter of February 1, 1955, published in Theodor-Heuss-Archiv, *Theodor Heuss. Der Mann, das Werk, die Zeit. Eine Ausstellung* Stuttgart, (1967).

9. T. Heuss, "Soldatentum in unserer Zeit" (1959), *ibid.*, pp. 15, 17, and 29; text of speech in T. Heuss, "Die grossen Reden. Der Staatsmann" (1965), *ibid.*, pp. 281–301.

10. We suggested this explanation of the Chancellor's behavior in the issue of *Express* referred to in the text. It still seems to us the most probable.

11. For the more "official" reasons, see interview with Fritz Erler, chairman of the parliamentary SPD, "Wir wissen, was wir an Lübke haben," *Der Spiegel*, June 17, 1964.

12. See chapter 9.

13. "Respekt für Heinrich Lübke?" *Der Stern*, March 12, 1968.

14. These are the final figures, slightly different from those announced at the session.

15. See chapter 9.

16. See chapter 7.

17. See chapter 7.
18. Full text, with comments by Kiesinger and F. J. Strauss, in *Frankfurter Allgemeine Zeitung*, March 12, 1969.
19. The full text is given as an Annex to Karl Dietrich Erdmann, *Adenauer in der Rheinlandpolitik nach dem ersten Weltkrieg* (Stuttgart, 1966), p. 329. This work is an able summing up of a question that is still the subject of much debate.
20. See Rudolf Morsey, "Die Rolle Konrad Adenauers im Parlamentarischen Rat," *Vierteljahreshefte für Zeitgeschichte*, I (1970), pp. 62–94.
21. Quoted from Walter Henkels, *Doktor Adenauers gesammelte Schwänke* (Düsseldorf, 1966), p. 95.
22. Cartoons by H. E. Koehler in the *Deutsche Zeitung*, reproduced in W. Freisburger, ed., *Konrad, sprach die Frau Mama . . . Adenauer in der Karikatur* (Oldenburg, 1955), pp. 95 and 117.
23. Full text in *Süddeutsche Zeitung*, November 7, 1961.
24. "Persilscheinstelle," *Der Stern*, November 13, 1966.
25. For a chart of the office in 1968, see N. Kaps and H. Kueffner, *Das Presse und Informationsamt der Bundesregierung* (Bonn, 1969), pp. 167–69.
26. Text in the excellent study by Heinz Laufer, *Der Parlamentarische Staatssekretär* (Munich, 1969).
27. For detailed figures, covering twenty years of parliamentary activity, see *Das Parlament*, August 30, 1969, and, especially, *Bulletin*, September 5, 1969.
28. A detailed sociological study down to 1965 will be found in the basic work by Gerhard Loewenberg, *Parlamentarismus im politischen System der Bundesrepublik Deutschland* (Tübingen, 1969), pp. 115–68.
29. For a lively analysis, see Peter Schindler, "Die Fragestunde des deutschen Bundestags," *Politische Vierteljahresschrift*, November, 1966, pp. 407–43.
30. *Quick*, June 21, 1964 and following numbers. On the role of the commissioner, see H. P. Secher, "Controlling the New German Military Élite. The political Role of the Parliamentary Defense Commissioner," *Proceedings of the American Philosophical Society*, April, 1965, pp. 63–84.
31. *Cf.* A. Grosser, "The Evolution of European Parliaments," in S. Graubard, ed., *A New Europe?* (Boston, 1964), pp. 219–44.

7. Elections and Party Politics

1. For the full text, including the amendment of July 22, 1969, see Irene Maier, *Recht der politischen Parteien. Parteiengesetz, Wahlkampfkostengesetze der Länder, ergänzende Vorschriften* (Opladen, 1969).
2. For additional figures, see D. Nohlen and R. O. Schultze, "Die Bundestagswahl 1969 in wahlstatistischer Perspektive," Supplement to *Das Parlament*, December 20, 1969. For a geographical analysis of the results, see also F. G. Dreyfus, "Les élections du 28 septembre 1969," *Revue d'Allemagne*, I (1970).
3. For a systematic presentation of numerous examples see Heino Kaack, *Wer kommt in den Bundestag? Abgeordnete und Kandidaten 1969* (Opladen, 1969).
4. Rudolf Wallraf, "Die finanzielle Situation der politischen Parteien," *Berichte des Deutschen Industrie-Instituts*, October 1, 1967 (multigraphed).
5. Results of polls in successive volumes published by the Institut für Demoskopie Allensbach, *Jahrbuch der öffentlichen Meinung* (Bonn and Allensbach). See especially, I, p. 139, and IV, pp. 174 and 216.

6. For dates and texts see A. Grosser, "Les Internationales de partis politiques," in La Vie internationale, XI, *Encyclopédie française* (Larousse, 1957).
7. For a factual summing up, see H. Soell, "Fraktion und Parteiorganisation. Zur Willensbildung der SPD in den 6oer Jahren," *Politische Vierteljahresschrift*, December, 1969, pp. 604–26.
8. For precise data, see the essential work by Lewis J. Edinger, *Kurt Schumacher. A Study in Personality and Political Behavior* (Stanford, Calif., 1965), pp. 319–22. Friedrich Heine's *Kurt Schumacher* (Göttingen, 1969), is at the same time hero-worshipping and impersonal.
9. See chapter 12.
10. F. Brühl, ed., *Ollenhauer in der Karikatur* (Berlin and Hanover, 1957), last page.
11. *Cf.* the admirable portrait in Günter Gaus, "Der Schwierige. Versuch über Herbert Wehner," *Der Monat*, January, 1969, pp. 51–60.
12. *Cf.* the interesting article by Conrad Ahlers, "Strauss hat sich gewandelt," in the Christian-Democratic review *Civis*, January, 1966.
13. Facsimile in Leo Schwering, *Frühgeschichte der Christlich-Demokratischen Union* (Recklinghausen, 1963), p. 209.
14. Details in Jürgen Domes, *Bundesregierung und Mehrheitsfraktion* (Cologne, 1964).
15. For the text of his report (supposedly confidential) to the executive committee, see the *Süddeutsche Zeitung*, October 8–9, 1966.
16. See the amusing satire "Da fehlt doch einer!" in *Der Stern*, March 8, 1970.
17. Full text in *Die Entscheidung*, December, 1969.
18. See the significant cartographic analysis by F. G. Dreyfus in "Les élections au Cinquième Bundestag—Etude de géographie électorale," *Revue française de Science politique*, April, 1966, pp. 286–305; "denominational" maps reproduced in A. Grosser, *Die Bundesrepublik Deutschland* (Tübingen, 1967), pp. 82–83. (English-language edition: *The Federal Republic of Germany*, New York: Praeger, 1964.)
19. For a systematic analysis of the party's changes and inconsistencies, see the excellent study by Kurt Körper, *FDP—Bilanz der Jahre 1960–1966* (Cologne, 1968), pp. 186–238.
20. The different arguments are well set out in the report of an inquiry by P. Knorr, "Was wählen Deutschlands Linke?" in the satirical monthly *Pardon*, September, 1969.
21. These are analyzed year by year in a detailed report by the Federal Ministry of the Interior, reproduced as an Annex to the weekly *Das Parlament*: "Rechtsradikalismus in der Bundesrepublik," Nos. dated March 17, 1965, March 16, 1966, June 14, 1967, April 10, 1968. See below, chapter 9.
22. Quotations from a pamphlet issued by the NPD in 1968. For a detailed comparison of the party's program with those of the NSDAP, the SRP in 1951, and the DRP, see Werner Smoydzin, *NPD. Geschichte und Umwelt einer Partei* (Pfaffenhofen, 1967), pp. 260–65. The subject is, of course, also treated in all the studies of the NPD mentioned in the bibliography to the present work.
23. *Cf.* in particular, besides the remarkable studies by Professor Erwin Scheuch, that by Klaus Liepelt (Director of the Institut für Angewandte Sozialwissenschaft [INFAS] at Bad Godesberg), "Anhänger der neuen Rechtspartei," *Politische Vierteljahresschrift*, June, 1967, pp. 237–71.

24. Texts in *Das Parlament*, January 31, 1970.
25. Very full information is available, based on the most varied techniques of analysis. Besides the reports of the major institutes (Allensbach, EMNID, INFAS) and the Federal Statistical Office, attention should be given to the important academic studies by Professors Scheuch at Cologne, Wildenmann at Mannheim, and others, as well as to the admirable computer analyses by INFAS, for example, *Wäher 1969. Woher? Wohin?*, published the day after the election.

8. Economic and Social Forces

1. The figures for 1961 and 1969 include the Saar and West Berlin. German statistics do not always make it very clear from what date the Saar is included and whether West Berlin is taken into account, as a *Land* or otherwise.
2. See especially pp. 256–59 of what is now the fundamental work on this subject: Jean François-Poncet, *La politique économique de l'Allemagne occidentale* (Paris, 1970).
3. Figures from p. 227 of the excellent study by Paul Becher, "Die Sozialpolitik der V. Legislaturperiode. Eine kritische Bilanz," in *Civitas, Jahrbuch für Sozialwissenschaften* (Mannheim, 1969).
4. Detailed proof of this is afforded by the whole second part of an original study by Reinhard Blum, *Soziale Marktwirtschaft* (Tübingen, 1969).
5. W. Röpke, *Ist die deutsche Wirtschaftspolitik richtig?* (Stuttgart, 1950).
6. Ludwig Erhard, *Une politique d'abondance*, with preface by A. Grosser (Paris, 1963), p. 335.
7. *Ibid.*, p. 87.
8. *Das Parlament*, May 1, 1963.
9. On the Bank's powers and method of operation, see especially J. von Spindler, W. Becker and O. E. Starke, *Die Deutsche Bundesbank*, 3rd rev. ed. (Stuttgart, 1969).
10. *Cf.* G. Leber, "Program zur Gesundung des deutschen Verkehrswesens," *Bulletin,,* September 26, 1967.
11. For a detailed account of agricultural policy, see J. François-Poncet, *op. cit.*, pp. 285–301. See also, "Grüner Bericht" for 1970 in *Bulletin*, March 3, 1970.
12. See the thoughtful study by Paul Ackermann, *Der deutsche Bauernverband im politischen Kräftespiel der Bundesrepublik. Die Einflussnahme des DBV auf die Entscheidung über den europäischen Getreidepreis* (Tübingen, 1970). For the French side of the picture, *cf.* Hélène Delorme and Yves Tavernier, *Les paysans français et l'Europe* (Paris, 1969).
13. Interview in *Der Spiegel*, March 30, 1970, p. 65.
14. See organizational chart annexed to an article by its director, Eberhard Günther, "Le Bundeskartellamt et la politique allemande de concurrence," in *Concurrence*, III (Paris, 1969), pp. 8–20.
15. The terms of the settlement of December 21, 1967 and the Foundation's statute of November 24 are given as an Annex to the excellent work by Bernt Engelmann, *Krupp. Legende und Wirklichkeit* (Munich, 1969), pp. 577–88. A remarkable chart of the *Konzern* was given in an article "Das war Krupp" in the monthly *Capital*, April, 1967.

337

16. See, for example, Eberhard Czichon, *Der Bankier und die Macht. Hermann Josef Abs in der deutschen Politik* (Cologne, 1970).
17. Impressive tables can be found in Kurt Pritzkoleit, *Männer, Mächte, Monopole*, new ed. (Düsseldorf, 1960), pp. 38 and 43.
18. *Cf.* Wolfgang Zapf, *Beiträge zur Analyse der deutschen Oberschicht*, 2nd (enlarged) ed. (Munich, 1965), p. 124.
19. An amusing report can be found in "Dem deutschen Adel bekommt auch die zweite Republik," *Süddeutsche Zeitung*, December 31, 1969.
20. *Cf.* Zapf, *op. cit.*, especially the chapter "Die deutschen Manager. Sozialprofil und Karriereweg," and also the series of comparative studies in *Die Zeit*, with contributions by Erwin Scheuch on the German "*Macht-Elite,*" November 24, and December 1, 1967.
21. The reader is directed to an interesting map, under the somewhat vulgar title "Wo sitzt bei uns das dickste Geld?" in *Der Stern*, August 31, 1969.
22. Among numerous press investigations in *Der Spiegel* and elsewhere, see especially S. Bluth, "Deutsche Slums—im Wahlkampf vergessen?" *Christ und Welt*, August 29, 1969.
23. An excellent table can be found in Hermann Marcus, *Wer verdient schon was er verdient?* (Dusseldorf, 1969), p. 31.
24. ECA Technical Assistance Commission, *Die Eingliederung der Flüchtlinge in die deutsche Gesellschaft* (Bonn, 1951).
25. See chapter 11.
26. For definitions in this sense see Statistisches Bundesamt, *Statistisches Jahrbuch 1969* (Stuttgart, 1969), p. xix. The figures that follow are taken from p. 39.
27. This will shortly be seen from a very thorough, useful, and up-to-date thesis by Jean-Claude Hervé: *Rapatriés et refugies allemands en Rhénanie du Nord et en Hesse du Sud.*
28. Full text in *Bulletin*, August 8, 1957.
29. *Ibid.*, May 28, 1969. The definition of the *Landsmannschaft* is from Göttinger Arbeitskreis, *Die ostdeutschen Landsmannschaften* (Göttingen, 1951), p. 5.
30. A striking facsimile is annexed to the excellent thesis, with a systematic account of the *Landsmannschaften*, by Hans W. Schönberg, *Germans from the East. A study of their migration, resettlement and subsequent group history, 1945–1961*, with preface by A. Grosser (The Hague, in press).
31. For such an account, see François-Poncet, *op. cit.*, pp. 271–83.
32. Very clear tables for different branches of industry can be found in "Betriebliche Altersversorgung," *Capital*, March, 1970.
33. A basis of comparison is afforded by the detailed study in Françoise Marnata, *Financement et délais de la construction* (Paris, 1970), *cf.* table on p. 8.
34. *Cf.* K. Bingemer *et al.*, eds., *Leben als Gastarbeiter. Geglückte und missglückte Integration* (Cologne, 1970).
35. *Cf.* for example the table of incomes, classified by occupation and sex, in D. Claessens, A. Klönne, and A. Tschöpe, *Sozialkunde der Bundesrepublik Deutschland*, rev. ed. (Düsseldorf, 1968), p. 247. An enlightening analysis of electoral motivations for specified groups is given in Klaus Liepelt, "Esquisse d'une typologie des électeurs allemands et autrichiens," *Revue française de sociologie*, IX (1968), pp. 13–32.
36. See the very clear graph in *Statistisches Jahrbuch 1969, op. cit.*, p. 75.

37. *Ibid.*, p. 117 (based on information from 1,163 polling stations).

38. For an excellent schematic analysis of the leadership, see "Die BDI-Spitze: Club der Spitzen-Manager," *Capital*, November, 1969.

39. List and composition can be found in *Statistisches Jahrbuch 1969, op.cit.*, p.138.

40. *Wenn Sozialisten regieren . . .* (Cologne, 1957).

41. *Bulletin*, October 22, 1959.

42. *Jahresbericht* of BDA for 1952, p. 196.

43. All figures (as given by the unions themselves) from *Statistisches Jahrbuch 1969, op. cit.*, p. 140. Useful statistical studies of membership and organization rates in Hartmut Schellhoss, *Apathie und Legitimität. Das Problem der neuen Gewerkschaft* (Munich, 1967).

44. A good summary of views and publications at the beginning of the election campaign was given in "Mitbestimmung," a special number of *Frankfurter Hefte*, May, 1969. The Biedenkopf report was published under the title *Mitbestimmung im Unternehmen* (Stuttgart, 1970).

45. For a good account of the problem in 1965–67, see Friedhelm Baukloh, "Der DGB und die neue Ostpolitik," *Frankfurter Hefte*, November, 1967.

9. Moral and Intellectual Trends

1. See, for example, Hermann Giesicke, "Die Krise der politischen Bildung—ein Literaturbericht," in the monthly *Deutsche Jugend*, January, 1970, pp. 35–45.

2. Institut für Demoskopie Allensbach, *Jahrbuch der öffentlichen Meinung 1965–1967* (Bonn and Allensbach), p. 146.

3. Text in *Der Spiegel*, November 21, 1966. For a fuller examination of this question, and for the whole range of problems touched on in this section, *cf.* the chapter "Le crime et la Mémoire" in A. Grosser, *Au nom de quoi? Fondements d'une morale politique* (Paris, 1969).

4. The work by Alexander and Margarete Mitscherlich, *Die Unfähigkeit zu trauern. Grundlagen kollektiven Verhaltens* (Munich, 1967) is important despite some exaggerations.

5. *Quick*, October 23, 1966.

6. *Cf.* Peter Schönbach, *Reaktionen auf die antisemitische Welle im Winter 1959–60* (Frankfurt, 1960).

7. On the first incident, *cf.* A. Grosser, "Les Zind sont parmi nous," *L'Arche, Revue du Fonds social juif unifié*, May–June, 1958. On the second, *cf.* the (Protestant) *Deutsches Pfarrerblatt* for July 15, 1959.

8. B. Engelmann, "Wer Jude ist, bestimmt der Grosse Brockhaus," *Deutsches Panorama*, June, 1966.

9. If the events discussed by Edgar Morin in *La rumeur d'Orléans* (Paris, 1969) had taken place in Germany, one can imagine the sort of conclusions that would have been drawn.

10. *Cf.* A. Grosser, "L'évêque et les otages," *Le Monde*, August 6, 1969.

11. "Das allzu offene Geheimnis," *Der Monat*, May, 1969, pp. 7–9.

12. The reports in the *Frankfurter Allgemeine Zeitung* were reprinted in Bernd Naumann, *Auschwitz. Bericht über die Strafsache gegen Mulka u.a. vor dem Schwurgericht Frankfurt* (Frankfurt, 1965; English-language edition: *Auschwitz*, New York: Praeger, 1966.)

13. From the excellent editorial "Jugendsünde?" in the Berlin student monthly *Colloquium*, December, 1964.

14. *Die Geschichte des PG 2633930 Kiesinger*, with preface by H. Böll (Darmstadt, 1969).

15. "Prognosen für Bonn. Eine Stimme aus Frankreich," in the Protestant weekly *Junge Stimme*, January 7, 1967.

16. Kurt Ziesel, *Das verlorene Gewissen*, 6th ed. (Munich, 1960).

17. *Cf.* excellent commentary by Gerhard Mauz, "Die Kommandeuse und die Kollektivschuld," *Der Spiegel*, September 11, 1967.

18. For a lively but exaggerated denunciation of the hypocrisy involved, see Armin Mohler, *Vergangenheitsbewältigung. Von der Läuterung zur Manipulation* (Stuttgart, 1968).

19. Told in the *Frankfurter Rundschau*, November 22, 1956.

20. See R. Wildenmann and H. Schatz, "Das Wahlverhältnis in Bundeswehr-Standorten," in *Sozialwissenschaftliches Jahrbuch für Politik*, I (Munich, 1969), pp. 61–154.

21. Full text in *Frankfurter Allgemeine Zeitung*, January 29, 1970. Most of General Baudissin's articles and speeches are collected in his *Soldat für den Frieden. Entwürfe für eine Zeitgenössische Bundeswehr* (Munich, 1969).

22. Many figures are given in the *Statistisches Jahrbuch, 1969*. Supplementary material on resources and activities will be found in Klaus Martens, *Wie reich ist die Kirche?* (Munich, 1969).

23. Quoted in "Taufschein und Parteibuch," *Die Gegenwart*, June 18, 1955.

24. P. Saturnin Paueser, OFM, *Die Mischehe—ein Weg ins Glück?* (Constance, 1960). Paul Bulkovac, SJ, *Atheisten, Christen. Atheismus im Westen* (Kevelaer, 1966).

25. For a critical summing-up, see John S. Conway, "Der deutsche Kirchenkampf. Tendenzen und Probleme seiner Erforschung," *Vierteljahreshefte für Zeitgeschichte*, October, 1969, pp. 423–49. For a discussion of the substantive issue, see A. Grosser's afterword to S. Friedländer, *Pie XII et le IIIe Reich* (Paris, 1964).

26. Quoted in *Süddeutesche Zeitung*, September 3, 1956.

27. *Cf.* the somewhat over-optimistic study by its president, Harry Neyer, "Zwischen Protest und Establishment—ein neuer BDKJ?" in *Deutsche Jugend*, November, 1968, pp. 453–63.

28. For an excellent thematic presentation see D. A. Seeber, ed., *Katholikentag im Widerspruch* (Freiburg, 1968).

29. Texts in Otto B. Roegele, *Versöhnung oder Hass? Der Briefwechsel der Bischöfe Polens und Deutschlands und seine Folgen* (Osnabrück, 1966), with an interpretation very different from ours. For the Bensberg document, see *Ein Memorandum deutscher Katholiken zu den polnisch-deutschen Fragen. Hgg. vom Bensberger Kreis* (Mainz, 1968).

30. Quoted in Centre d'études de politique étrangère, *Les Eglises en Allemagne* (Paris, 1949).

31. Text in *Frankfurter Rundschau*, February 27, 1962.

32. For full text, see R. Henkys, ed., *Deutschland und die östlichen Nachbarn. Beiträge zu einer evangelischen Denkschrift* (Stuttgart, 1966), pp. 176–217.

33. Charts and tables, including themes of the thirteen congresses from 1949 to

1969, in Carola Wolf, ed., *Zwanzig Jahre Kirchentag* (Stuttgart, 1969). Documents of the 1969 congress in *Deutscher Evangelischer Kirchentag 1969, ibid.*, 1970.

34. For elements of an answer see W. Harenberg, ed., *Was glauben die Deutschen? Die Emnid-Umfrage* (Munich, 1968).

35. Figures in E. G. Mahrenholz, *Die Kirchen in der Gesellschaft der Bundesrepublik* (Hanover, 1969).

36. The problem, as we see it, is set forth in chapter 4, "Information et éducation," of *Au nom de quoi?, op. cit.*

37. *Cf.* the concise presentation in the very useful book by Hermann Meyn, *Massenmedien in der Bundesrepublik Deutschland*, rev. ed. (Berlin, 1968). Laws and regulations of the different corporations in Günter Hermann, *Rundfunkgesetze. Textsammlung* (Cologne, 1966).

38. An interesting table will be found in the remarkable study by H. Meyn, "Gefahren fur die Freiheit von Rundfunk und Fernsehen?" Supplement to *Das Parlament*, November 29, 1969, pp. 17–30.

39. *Cf.* Klaus von Bismarck in a fundamental article "Wie zersetzend darf eine Sendung sein? Erfahrungen eines Intendanten," *Die Zeit*, February 4, 1966.

40. Script of the banned program in *Der Spiegel*, January 10, 1966.

41. "Politik im Fernsehen." See also, for example, K. W. Fricke, "Manipulation auf dem Bildschirm," in the review *Die politische Meinung*, No. 4 (1968), pp. 109–13.

42. For an overcritical sketch, see *Der Monat*, September, 1969. From March, 1969 onward, this monthly has published short, caustic monographs on Federal German daily and weekly papers.

43. The paper is discussed, with extracts, in H. D. Müller, *Der Springer-Konzern* (Munich, 1968), pp. 73–126 and 332–72. The Springer press is compared with other papers over a given period in A. Silbermann and A. Zahn, *Die Konzentration der Massenmedien und ihre Wirkungen* (Dusseldorf, 1970), pp. 298–336. *Cf.* also the ironical "glossary" in H. Kulas, "Ein Springer-Lexikon," in B. Jansen and A. Klönne, *Imperium Springer* (Cologne, 1968), pp. 189–204.

44. Figures and analyses can be found in the intelligently critical work by D. Just, *Der Spiegel. Arbeitsweise. Inhalt. Wirkung* (1967).

45. *Cf.* for instance Martin Faltermeier's article ironically entitled "Mit allen Kräften?" in the review *Deutsche Jugend*, which he publishes for the *Bundesjugendring*, March, 1956.

46. "Das Selbstverständnis des Deutschen Bundesjugendringes und seiner Mitgliederverbände," *ibid.*, December, 1968.

47. *Cf.* the figures quoted by Viggo Graf Blücher in "Die Unruhe in der Jugend und das Generationsverhältnis," *ibid.*, March, 1969.

48. *Cf.* for instance Friedhelm Neidhardt, *Die Junge Generation. Jugend und Gesellschaft in der Bundesrepublik* (Opladen, 1967), pp. 46–50.

49. Some particularly revolutionary documents are to be found in M. Lieber and F. Wellendorf, *Schühlerselbstbefreiung* (Frankfurt, 1969), pp. 162–200.

50. *Cf.* the poll published in *Der Spiegel*, February 12, 1968.

51. Figures given to parliament by Professor Leusink (*Bulletin*, January 23, 1970).

52. George Picht, *Die deutsche Bildungskatastrophe* (Olten and Freiburg, 1964 and Munich, 1965).

53. See Henri Menudier, "Eléments bibliographiques de la crise universitaire allemande," *Revue d'Allemagne*, No. 2 (1969), pp. 157–75.
54. Described in too sober a fashion in the VDS review launched at that time, *Input*, No. 1 (1968).
55. Text in G. Heinemann, *Plädoyer für den Rechtsstaat* (Karlsruhe, 1969), pp. 63–64.
56. *Cf.* A. Dietzel and K. Gintzel, *Demonstrations—und Versammlungsfreiheit. Kommentar zum Gesetz über Versammlungen und Aufzüge vom 24 Juli 1953* new ed. (Cologne, 1970).

10. The "Socialist State of the German Nation"

1. *Cf.* the very partisan work by Gilbert Badia and Pierre Lefranc, *Un pays méconnu: la République Démocratique Allemande* (Leipzig, 1963); also G. Badia, *Histoire de l'Allemagne contemporaine*, II, (Paris, 1962), 1933–62.
2. Marion Gräfin Dönhoff, R. W. Leonhardt, and Theo Sommer, *Reise in ein fernes Land, Bericht über Kultur, Wirtschaft und Politik in der DDR* (Hamburg, 1964). This investigation by members of the staff of *Die Zeit* created a sensation at the time.
3. Hanns Peter Schwarze, *Die DDR ist keine Zone mehr* (Cologne, 1969). A lively work, somewhat imprecise and exaggerated in parts, of which we have made much use.
4. Poll conducted in March, 1966. Institut für Demoskopie Allensbach, *Jahrbuch der öffentlichen Meinung* (Bonn and Allensbach), p. 395.
5. The results of the poll are described, with some humorous exaggeration, in Schwarze, *op. cit.*, pp. 47–51.
6. For an impressive critical analysis, see Peter Christian Ludz and K. J. Kuppe, "Literatur zum politischen und gesellschaftlichen System der DDR," *Politische Vierteljahresschrift*, September, 1969, pp. 328–87. We refer readers to this as a bibliography of the subject, since we have not the necessary knowledge to include the G.D.R. in our own bibliographical analysis.
7. Hence the sub-title of the useful study by Ernst Richert, *Das zweite Deutschland. Ein Staat, der nicht sein darf* (Gütersloh, 1964).
8. As is done in F. Fejtö's excellent *Histoire des démocraties populaires*, II, 1953–68 (Paris, 1969); English-language edition: *History of Popular Democracies*, New York: Praeger, 1971).
9. Georges Castellan, *La République démocratique allemande*, prefatory note to 1st ed., 1961. (3d rev. ed., Paris, 1968.)
10. At the end of 1968. Most of our figures are taken from *Statistisches Jahrbuch der Deutschen Demokratischen Republik 1969* (East Berlin, 1969).
11. For a good legal analysis, now somewhat out of date, see Siegfried Mampel, *Der Sowjetsektor von Berlin. Eine Analyse seines äusseren und inneren Status* (Frankfurt, 1963).
12. Badia and Lefranc, *op. cit.*, p. 308.
13. Full text in the handy collection by Ernst Deuerlein, *DDR. Geschichte und Bestandaufnahme* (Munich, 1966), pp. 124–25. Additional information in Hermann Weber, *Von der SBZ zur "DDR"*, 2 vols. (Hanover, 1966–67).
14. "Statistik der Flüchtlinge und Übersiedler," *Bulletin*, February 16, 1968, and "Notaufnahme," *Statistisches Jahrbuch für die Bundesrepublik Deutschland 1969*, p. 59.

15. Historical introduction and text of the constitution in Dietrich Müller-Römer, *Ulbrichts Grundgesetz. Die sozialistische Verfassung der DDR* (Cologne, 1968). English-language edition of the full text may be found in L. Holborn, C. Carter, and J. Herz, *German Constitutional Documents Since 1871* (New York: Praeger, 1970).

16. For his memoirs, see E. Gniffke, *Jahre mit Ulbricht*, with preface by H. Wehner (Cologne, 1966): a valuable source of first-hand information.

17. Many figures on the composition of the Chamber by parties and social or professional origin, also on the mass organizations, can be found in *Statistisches Jahrbuch der DDR 1969*, pp. 487–500.

18. Historical account and documents in R. Kulbach and H. Weber, *Parteien im Blocksystem der DDR. Aufbau und Funktion der LDPD und der NDPD* (Cologne, 1969).

19. See especially Carola Stern, *Porträt einer bolschewistischen Partei. Entwicklung, Funktion und Situation der SED* (Cologne, 1957).

20. *Cf.* the valuable study by P. C. Ludz, *Parteielite im Wandel. Funktionsaufbau, Sozialstruktur und Ideologie der SED-Führung* (Cologne, 1968).

21. *"Vom Helfer der Besatzungsmacht mit Hilfe der Besatzung zur Macht,"* in Schwarze, *op. cit.*, p. 188.

22. See especially Carola Stern, *Ulbricht. Eine politische Biographie* (Cologne, 1964); and, for additional information, Ernst Richert, *Die DDR-Elite oder Unsere Partner von morgen?* (Hamburg, 1968), with political sketches of most of the leaders.

23. Chronology in Badia and Lefranc, *op. cit.*, p. 306. Narrative and careful analysis in Arnulf Baring, *Der 17 Juni 1953* (Cologne, 1965).

24. Significant estimates, though on the dark side, will be found under *"Reparationen"* in the full and well-informed reference work issued by the Federal Ministry for All-German Affairs: *SBZ von A bis Z. Ein Taschen- und Nachschlagebuch über die Sowjetische Besatzungszone Deutschlands*, 10th ed. (Bonn, 1966). This work is used by most writers though they do not always acknowledge it. In the 11th edition (1969), the reference to the Soviet Occupation Zone (SBZ) has disappeared from the title, which now speaks only of "the other part of Germany": it runs *A bis Z: ein Taschen- und Nachschlagebuch über den anderen Teil Deutschlands.*

25. Willi Herferth and others, *Von der demokratischen Bodenreform zum sozialistischen Dorf* (East Berlin), quoted in François Reitel, *Les Allemanges. Les hommes, la terre, les régions* (Paris, 1969).

26. Wolfgang F. Stolper, *The Structure of the East German Economy* (Harvard, 1960).

27. Guy Roustang, *Développment économique de l'Allemagne orientale depuis 1945* (Paris, 1963), pp. 230 and 229.

28. Hans Apel, *Wehen und Wunder der Zonenwirtschaft* (Cologne, 1966): includes some rather doubtful forecasts; Joachim Nawrocki, *Das geplante Wunder. Leben und Wirtschaften im anderen Deutschland* (Hamburg, 1967).

29. Bibliographical list by B. Heidenhain and E. Kämpfer, "Ausgewählte Literatur zur Soziologie der DDR," in *Soziologie der DDR*, ed. by P. C. Ludz (Cologne and Opladen, 1964), pp. 465–540.

30. On this and the following, see especially the very thoughtful study by John Dornberg, *The Other Germany* (New York, 1968).

31. *Cf.* "Nr. 4532251," *Die Zeit*, September 13, 1969.

343

32. Quoted by F. W. Schlomann, "Erziehung zum Hass," *Die Entscheidung*, September, 1968.
33. Schwarze, *op. cit.*, p. 376. Quotations could, of course, be multiplied.
34. Text of the voluminous 1963 statutes in Rudolf Märker, *Jugend im anderen Teil Deutschlands* (Munich, 1969), pp. 144–68. Fuller documentation in S. Baske and M. Engelbert, *Zwei Jahrzehnte Bildungspolitik in der Sowjetzone Deutschlands*, 2 vols. (Heidelberg, 1966). On higher education, see the documented analysis by Ernst Richert, *Sozialistische Universität. Die Hochschulpolitik der DDR* (Berlin, 1967); or, more conveniently, the study by Hildegard Hamm-Brücher, later state secretary at Bonn: *Lernen und Arbeiten. Berichte über das sowjetische und mitteldeutsche Schul-und Bildungswesen* (Cologne, 1965).
35. Märker, *op. cit.*, pp. 94–122.
36. Text in Deuerlein, *op. cit.*, pp. 268–73.
37. Description of ceremonies in Schwarze, *op. cit.*, pp. 295–97.
38. *Cf.* Klemens Richter, "Anpassung in der DDR. Die Situation der katholischen Kirche im anderen Deutschland," *Publik*, October 24, 1969.
39. *Cf.* the series *Die Sprache im geteilten Deutschland*, published from 1964 onward by Hugo Moser (Düsseldorf); also Hans H. Reich, *Sprache und Politik* (Munich, 1968).
40. Gérard Sandoz, *La Gauche allemande de Karl Marx à Willy Brandt* (Paris, 1970), p. 208.
41. For the staffing of the Foreign Ministry see Walter Osten, *Die Aussenpolitik der DDR* (Opladen, 1969), pp. 100–9.
42. *Cf.* the analysis by Ernst Kohler, *Economic Integration in the Soviet Bloc, with an East German Case Study* (New York, 1965).
43. See E. and H. P. Schulz, *Braucht der Osten die DDR?* (Opladen, 1968).
44. Complete table, as of June, 1969, in Osten, *op. cit.*, pp. 115–19.
45. Review of ten years' activity in the special number of its bulletin *Rencontres franco-allemandes*, No. 51, March–May, 1968.
46. *Statistisches Jahrbuch*, p. 408. An exaggerated picture of East German sporting life and the cult of prizewinning is given in Willi Knecht, *Verschenkter Lorbeer. Deutsche Sportler zwischen Ost und West* (Cologne, 1969). The material is better presented in Karl Heinz Gieseler, *Sport als Mittel der Politik. Die Sportbeziehungen im geteilten Deutschland* (Mainz, 1966).

11. Foreign Affairs and World Policy

1. End-of-year television broadcast, December 31, 1963.
2. *Cf.* A. Grosser, "Les conditions de la renaissance d'une politique étrangère allemande depuis 1945," in Association française de Science politique, *La politique étrangère et ses fondements* (Paris, 1954), pp. 202–22.
3. For an exact and well-informed study, see the second part, "L'homme d'état," of Pierre Renouvin and Jean-Baptiste Duroselle, *Introduction à l'histoire des relations internationales* (Paris, 1964; English-language edition: *Introduction to the History of International Relations*, New York: Praeger, 1967). This problem figures centrally in A. Grosser's studies of French foreign policy under the Fourth and Fifth Republics.
4. See especially, Werner Conze, *Jakob Kaiser. Politiker zwischen Ost und West 1945–1949* (Stuttgart, 1969).

5. *Cf.* Gustav Heinemann, *Verfehlte Deutschlandpolitik. Irreführung und Selbsttäu-schung, Artikel und Reden* (Frankfurt, 1966).
6. *Erinnerungen*, 4 vols. (Stuttgart, 1965–68).
7. The rearmament question furnished the occasion for an outstanding study of the decision-taking machinery in Arnulf Baring, *Aussenpolitik in Adenauers Kanzlerdemokratie. Bonns Beitrag zur Europäischen Verteidigungsgemeinschaft* (Munich, 1969).
8. *Cf.* the very interesting account of him by Willy Brandt in a long commemorative speech: text in *Bulletin*, June 25, 1969.
9. Illuminating remarks in Hans von Herwarth, "Der diplomatische Dienst in einer sich wandelnden Welt. Zwischenbericht der Kommission für die Reform des Auswärtigen Dienstes," *Politische Studien*, September–October, 1969.
10. As is done—but on a factual basis—by the journalist Michael Mansfeld in his story *à clés: Bonn. Koblenzerstrasse. Der Bericht des Robert von Lenwitz* (Munich, 1967).
11. Figures from S. Reuter, "Bonner Diplomatenschule: Reform in Vorbereitung," *Süddeutsche Zeitung*, May 20, 1969.
12. End-of-the-year television broadcast, December 31, 1967.
13. See the noteworthy account of his policy given in the Bundestag on November 28, 1969: text in *Bulletin*, December 3, 1969.
14. November 25, 1968.
15. See, *e.g.*, James K. Pollock, ed., *German Democracy at Work* (Ann Arbor, Michigan, 1955), where the SPD is held to be undemocratic because unaligned.
16. This account is based on a valuable thesis, not yet published, by Isaac Israel, "Les relations germano-israéliennes de 1949 à 1965" (Paris, 1970). The original documentation in this work and the lucidity of its political and psychological analysis make it far superior to the earlier works cited in our bibliography.
17. *Yedioth Hayom* (Tel Aviv), January 23, 1959. Quoted by Israel, *op. cit.*, pp. 145–46.
18. For all aspects of French policy, A. Grosser, refer once more to *La Quatrième République et sa politique extérieure* and *La Politique extérieure de la Vème République*. For the evolution of Franco–German relations *cf.* A. Grosser's editorials from 1949 to 1967 in *Allemagne*; also the following: "France and Germany: the divergent outlook," *Foreign Affairs*, October, 1965; "France and Germany: Less Divergent Outlooks?" *ibid.*, January, 1970; and "Paris und Bonn: Freundschaft im Widerspruch," in *Das 198. Jahrzehnt. Eine Team-Prognose* (Hamburg, 1969), pp. 72–96.
19. Cartoon by F. Behrendt: see the collection already quoted, W. Freisburger, *Konrad, sprach die Frau Mama . . . Adenauer in der Karikatur* (Oldenburg, 1955), p. 62.
20. English and German text of the treaty, and 19-point statement of the Federal Government's position at the time of signature, in *Bulletin*, November 29, 1969. See also "Dokumente zur Unterzeichnung des Kernwaffen-Sperrvertrags durch die Bundesrepublik Deutschland," *Europa-Archiv*, January 10, 1970. This fortnightly publication is essential for the study of German foreign policy.
21. See the account by Hansjakob Stehle, former Warsaw correspondent of the *Frankfurter Allgemeine Zeitung*, in *Nachbar Polen* (Frankfurt, 1963; English-language edition was published under the title *The Independent Satellite*,

(London, 1965); see also, the enlarged German edition (1968) and his "Verpasste Gelegenheiten. Bonns Verhältnis zu Polen," *Die Zeit*, November 28, 1969.

22. W. Hartenstein and G. Schubert, *Mitlaufen oder Mitbestimmen* (Frankfurt, 1961), p. 61.

23. See *Deutschlandplan der SPD. Kommentare. Argumente. Begründungen* (Bonn, 1963).

24. Text of the very interesting exchange of letters in *Deutsche Jugend*, July, 1966.

25. *Cf.* the very detailed poll and a remarkable editorial by Henri Nannen, "Nun sag', wie hast du's mit der Illusion?," in *Der Stern*, March 5, 1968.

26. Statements and decisions in the bulletin *BMZ-Mitteilungen*, published by the *Bundesministerium für wirtschaftliche Zusammenarbeit*. *Cf.* also the Minister's interesting commentary on the report of the Pearson Commission on International Development (*Partners in Development*, New York, 1969), in *Publik*, December 12, 1969.

27. W. W. Schütz, *Deutschland-Memorandum. Eine Denkschrift und ihre Folgen* (Frankfurt, 1968).

28. See report and details of contacts and exchanges in "Materialien der Bundesregierung zum Bericht zur Lage der Nation," *Bulletin*, January 14, 1970.

Critical Bibliography

Introduction

Rather than encumber the chapters of this work with multiple references, we have confined the notes to factual indications, designed in particular to help the reader to follow up developments that have had to be too much compressed in the main text. It is our hope that the book will be read by a wide public—rather than merely consulted or criticized by specialists—and more especially by those in Britain, America, and elsewhere for whom it was written and who may not know German or be very well informed on German affairs.

At the same time, the work has been published in German under the title *Deutschlandbilanz. Geschichte Deutschlands seit 1945* (Munich: C. Hanser Verlag, 1970). It is hoped that this edition will help students and researchers who are not hampered by the language problem and whose national preconceptions are not too strong to enable them to study and understand the facts.

In view of the limited scope of the notes, we are giving a fairly comprehensive bibliography. Even so, we have omitted over three-quarters of the works discussed either in the bibliographies attached to our previous books on Germany or those published by us from 1954 to 1967 in *Allemagne*, the bulletin of Comité français d'échanges avec l'Allemagne nouvelle, and, since the beginning of 1969, in the *Revue d'Allemagne* published by the Centre d'études germaniques at Strasbourg. In particular, we have omitted books that have been overtaken by better or more up-to-date ones, and works that owe their origin to a particular occasion and are to that extent unrepresentative. Other omissions, of course, may simply be due to our ignorance of works that we ought to have known about.

The chief gap from this point of view, as we pointed out at the beginning of chapter 10, is in respect of East Germany, first as the Soviet occupation zone and then as the German Democratic Republic. It would be out of place to attempt to guide other students when we are ourselves finding our way about the subject. Instead of trying to complete the bibliographical indications contained in the notes to that chapter, we would refer the reader to the excellent survey by Peter Christian Ludz and Johannes Kuppe, "Literatur zum politischen und gesellschaftlichen System der DDR," *Politische Vierteljahresschrift*, X, No. 2–3, September, 1969, pp. 328–87. This covers sixty-six books, which themselves contain further useful bibliographies.

The present survey is an instrument of research within limits only. It does not give information on the specialities of different university centers and libraries, the localization of sources, or the various other instruments that are an aid to research.

Such information will be found in the *Guide de recherche sur l'Allemagne con-temporaine* compiled by Henri Menudier at the Centre d'études des relations inter-nationales de la Fondation nationale des Sciences politiques. We may, however, mention one of two particularly useful aids to bibliographical work.

With only a few exceptions, all books and articles in journals by French writers on Germany since 1945, along with those by German writers on France, are listed and classified in Deutsch-französisches Institut Ludwigsburg, *Deutschland-Frankreich*, IV, *Bibliographie 1945–1962* (Stuttgart, 1966); the volume covering 1963–67 is in press. The interesting work by R. Meunnig, *Deutschland und die Deutschen im englischsprachigen Schrifttum, 1948–1955. Eine Bibliographie* (Göt-tingen, 1958) has unfortunately not been continued. However, almost all works in English are listed in Helen Kehr, ed., *After Hitler. Germany, 1945–1963* (London, 1965) (the Wiener Library Catalogue Series), which contains many gaps in other respects. For German authors, see the excellent index to the monumental *Karlsruher Juristische Bibliographie. Systematischer Titelnachweis neuer Bücher u. Aufsätze in monatlicher Folge aus Recht, Staat, Gesellschaft*, 3rd ed. (Munich, 1967), with nearly 7,000 items; the 1968 supplement reaches item 8,476. Less complete but better focused lists are, e.g., those by Hans Schneider, *Bibliographie zum öffentlichen Recht in der Bundesrepublik Deutschland, ibid.*, 2nd ed. (1964), or Forschungsinstitut der deutschen Gesellschaft für auswärtige Politik, *Schrifttum über Deutschland 1918–1962* (Bonn, 1962), both of which are very useful. German journals unfortunately give very little in the way of critical bibliography. The purely factual booklists in each number of *Vierteljahreshefte für Zeitgeschichte* chiefly relate to the period 1919–45. The *Politische Vierteljahresschrift*, however, has gradually adopted the excellent habit of publishing accounts of the state of research on specific topics.

The French reader is well off as far as journals are concerned. *Documents*, once a monthly and now a bimonthly review of German problems, published by the Bureau international de liaison et de documentation, contains good articles and information on all aspects of postwar Germany. *Allemagne d'Aujourd'hui*, which was published from 1951 to 1957 by French scholars and cultural representatives in Germany, reappeared in 1966 as a quarterly edited by Félix Lusset. Since January, 1969, another quarterly, the *Revue d'Allemagne*, has published academic studies of political, economic, social, and cultural developments in the whole of Germany since 1918. Comparable journals do not exist in other countries, where academic German studies are largely confined to language and literature.

In Germany, the *Vierteljahreshefte für Zeitgeschichte*, published since 1953 by the Institut für Zeitgeschichte at Munich, does not quite live up to its title, as its usually excellent articles are mostly concerned with the period between 1919 and 1945. Only recently has more attention been devoted to the occupation; the years since 1949 are still neglected. The old *Zeitschrift für Politik*, founded in 1911 and revived in 1954, is not of much value despite a recent rejuvenation. The other political science review, the *Politische vierteljahresschrift*, has since 1960 contained studies that are few in number but nearly always sound and informative. Two reviews come closer to current events but are less scientific: *Politische Studien* (known as *Politische Bildung* from 1951 to 1954), published by the Munich Institute of Political Studies, and *Die Politische Meinung,* of Christian Democratic tendency. *Die Neue Gesellschaft,* edited by trade unionists and Social Democrats to the left of the DGB and the SPD, originally contained independent ideas and analyses but, since 1967, though still useful, it has become a somewhat uncritical champion of SPD positions. *Der Monat,* the counterpart to the London *Encounter* and the Paris *Preuves,* went through a dull phase in the 1960's but has improved and contains many articles of social and political criticism. The *Frankfurter Hefte,* founded immediately after the war, was at that time somewhat on a par with the French *Esprit.* It is less important or influential than it was, but it is improving after many years during which its quality was indifferent. Among reviews that have ceased publication, two are especially to be missed and should be consulted for any study of the years during which they appeared: the monthly *Deutsche Rundschau* (1946–64) and the fortnightly *Die Gegenwart* (1946–58).

There can be no question of listing here the specialized reviews, scholarly or otherwise, dealing with the various subjects touched on in the present work. Reference may be made to *Archiv des öffentlichen Rechts* for the study of institutions and to *Kölner Zeitschrift für Soziologie und Socialpsychologie.* Failing any review that deals with economic questions in a thorough yet convenient fashion, *Der Volkswirt* and *Wirtschaft und Statistik,* the latter published by the Statistisches Bundesamt, provide up-to-date comments and figures. The *Gewerkschaftliche Monatshefte* seldom oversteps the official line of the DGB; *Deutsche Jugend,* on the other hand, in its discussion of youth problems does not shrink from criticizing on occasion its parent organization, the Bundesjugendring. Catholic developments can be followed in the documents and articles of the *Herder-Korrespondenz* and *Stimmen der Zeit.* For foreign policy, *Aussenpolitik* is not of much use, whereas the fortnightly *Europa-Archiv,* published by the Gesellschaft für auswärtige Politik, provides a great deal more than its title suggests: apart from the quality of its articles, its chronology of international events and selection of documents make it an indispensable working tool.

For weeklies and dailies, chapter 9 may be consulted. We should however express here our debt to *Der Spiegel, Die Zeit,* the *Frankfurter Allgemeine,* and the *Süddeutsche Zeitung,* as well as to such other publications read regularly as *Die Welt* and *Pardon, Der Stern* and the *Rheinischer Merkur, Publik,* and *Christ und Welt.*

Finally, two noncommercial publications are essential for the study of German politics. These are the daily *Bulletin des Presse—und Informationsamts der Bundesregierung,* containing communiqués and speeches, official documents and statistics (the English and French versions of the *Bulletin* bear no relation to the original and are wretchedly inadequate), and the weekly *Das Parlament,* which provides a convenient way of reading parliamentary debates and a great deal of other information about political activities at Bonn and in the *Länder.*

Introduction: 1945—The Legacy of the Past

The breach with the past in 1945 does not of course mean that the study of the old Germany and the Nazi period should be neglected. For French readers, there is now a first-class general introduction, both solid and readable, in François G. Dreyfus, *Histoire des Allemagnes** (1970), with a systematic bibliography: this begins with the Holy Roman Empire and takes the story down to the 1969 elections. Golo

*All French books mentioned in this bibliography are published in Paris unless otherwise stated.

Mann, *Deutsche Geschichte des neunzehnten und zwanzigsten Jahrhunderts* (Frankfurt, 1958) has become a classic, and the conclusions of its full analyses are subject to little dispute (English-language edition: *The History of Germany Since 1789*, Praeger, New York: 1968). By contrast, the assessment of the Kaiser's Germany before and after 1914 in Fritz Fischer, *Griff nach der Weltmacht*, 2nd ed. (Düsseldorf, 1962; English-language edition: *Germany's Aims in the First World War*, New York: Norton, 1967) caused lively reactions among historians, which have not yet died away.

H. A. Jacobsen and H. Dollinger, eds., *Hundert Jahre Deutschland 1870–1970* (Munich, 1969), gives a pictorial account of men and situations, while economic and financial aspects, which are often neglected, are covered without jargon by G. Stolper, K. Häuser and K. Borchardt, *Deutsche Wirtschaftsgeschichte seit 1870* (Tübingen, 1964) and Rudolf Stucken, *Deutsche Geld-und Kreditpolitik 1914–1963* (Tübingen, 1964). On society and ideology in the past and present, the brilliant essays of able journalists such as Hans Heigert, *Deutschlands falsche Träume. Die verführte Nation*, 2nd ed. (Hamburg, 1968) and Johannes Gross, *Die Deutschen* (Frankfurt, 1967) should be read in conjunction with Henri Burgelin, *La société allemande 1871–1968* (1969), and with the fundamental work by Rolf Dahrendorf, *Gesellschaft und Demokratie in Deutschland* (Munich, 1965; English-language edition: *Society and Democracy in Germany*, New York: Doubleday, 1967).

The Weimar period is treated in a clear and thorough work (for which there is no equivalent in German): Georges Castellan, *L'Allemagne de Weimar 1918–1933* (1969), with bibliography. The same period is treated in a serious fashion, though from the Communist angle, in the first volume of Gilbert Badia, *Histoire de l'Allemagne contemporaine*, 1962 (vol. I: 1917–33), whereas his second volume, covering 1933–62, is a polemical rather than a historical work. There is an excellent introduction by Helmut Heiber, *Die Republik von Weimar* (Munich, 1966), in the DTV pocketbook series. The climate of the period is depicted in Ernst Deuerlein, *Der Aufstieg der NSDAP 1919–1933* in *Augenzeugenberichten* (Düsseldorf, 1968) and Wilhelm Treue, *Deutschland in der Weltwirtschaftskrise in Augenzeugenverichten* (Düsseldorf, 1967). The subject matter of H. and E. Hannover, *Politische Justiz 1918–1933* (Frankfurt, 1966), is of great importance for the understanding of subsequent periods.

The collapse of the Republic and the Nazi takeover can be studied in E. Matthias and R. Morsey, eds., *Das Ende der Parteien* (Düsseldorf, 1960), and especially Karl Dietrich Bracher, *Die Auflösung der Weimarer Republik*, 2d ed. (Düsseldorf, 1957) and K. D. Bracher, W. Sauer, and G. Schulz, *Die nationalsozialistische Machtergreifung* (Cologne and Opladen, 1960).

The substance of these two monumental works is fortunately comprised in K. D. Bracher's masterly summing-up *Die deutsche Diktatur. Entstehung, Struktur, Folgen des Nationalismus* (Cologne, 1969; English-language edition: *The German Dictatorship*, New York: Praeger, 1970). It may be supplemented by the following works: Martin Broszat, *Der Staat Hitlers* (Munich: DTV, 1969); Hans Adolf Jacobsen, *Nationalsozialistische Aussenpolitik 1933–1938* (Frankfurt, 1968); David Schoenbaum, *Hitler's Social Revolution. Class and Status in Nazi Germany* (New York: Doubleday, 1966); Arthur Schweitzer, *Big Business in the Third Reich* (Bloomington, Ind.: Indiana University Press, 1964), which in fact deals with medium-sized enterprises and the middle class; Hans Jochen Gamm,

Der braune Kult (Hamburg, 1962), and the same author's *Führung und Verführung. Pädagogik des Nationalsozialismus* (Munich, 1964). A vast documentation is offered by Max Domarus, *Hitler. Reden und Proklamationen. 1932 bis 1945*, 4 vols. (Munich, 1965). Gerhard Grimm's bibliography "Die deutsche Universität von 1939 bis 1945," in *Politische Studien*, March–April, 1969, pp. 222–30, covers a subject of importance in postwar years.

The literature on Nazi atrocities is abundant; there is a comprehensive view in Olga Wormser-Migot, *Le système concentrationnaire nazi* (1968). One of the first books, Eugen Kogon, *Der SS-Staat* (Frankfurt, 1946; English-language edition: *The Theory and Practice of Hell*, London, 1950), is still of the highest value. The nature and extent of the most systematic of the Nazi massacres may be studied in documents and figures in L. Poliakov and J. Wulf, *Le IIIème Reich et les Juifs* (1959), and the narratives and illustrations in Gerhard Schönberger, *Der gelbe Stern. Die Judenverfolgung in Europa* (Hamburg, 1960). On the German resistance, which is still underrated outside Germany, see Peter Hoffmann, *Widerstand—Staatsstreich—Attentat. Der Kampf der Opposition gegen Hitler* (Munich, 1969); also Günter Weisenborn, *Der lautlose Aufstand*, 2nd ed. (Hamburg, 1954), the first Western account in which justice was done to the fight put up by obscure men and women of the extreme left; Eberhard Zeller, *Geist der Freiheit*, 5th rev. ed. (Munich, 1965), the best account of the July 1944 plot, and Christian Petry, *Studenten aufs Schafott. Die Weisse Rose und ihr Scheitern* (Munich, 1968).

The Conquerors' Germany

By way of general introduction, one may read the able analysis by André Fontaine, *Histoire de la guerre froide*, 2 vols. (1965 and 1967; English-language edition: *History of the Cold War*, New York: Pantheon, 1968 and 1970): the first volume covers 1917–50, the second 1950–70. The chief landmarks as regards postwar Germany are given in Ernst Deuerlein, *Deutschland nach dem zweiten Weltkrieg* (Constance, 1963) and Gerhart Binder, *Deutschland seit 1945. Eine dokumentierte gesamtdeutsche Geschichte* (Stuttgart, 1969).

Ingo von Münch, ed., *Dokumente des geteilten Deutschland* (Stuttgart, 1968) is probably the best and most convenient collection of documents. It may be supplemented by Beate Ruhm von Oppen, ed., *Documents on Germany under Occupation, 1945–54* (London, 1955); J. Hohlfeld, ed., *Dokumente der deutschen Politik und Geschichte*, Berlin, 1952–55 (vol. VI, 1945–50; vol. VII, 1951–52; vol. VIII, 1953–54); and H. von Siegler, *Dokumentation zur Deutschlandfrage 1941–1961*, 3 vols. (Bonn, 1961). In Thilo Vogelsang, *Das geteilte Deutschland* (Munich: DTV, 1966), the documents are linked by an excellent explanatory text; a fuller work of outstanding quality is the detailed study by Gerhard Wettig, *Entmilitarisierung und Wiederbewaffnung in Deutschland 1943–1955. Internationale Auseinandersetzung über die Rolle der Deutschen in Europa* (Munich, 1967).

The origins and history of the Berlin problem may be studied in the collections of documents published by the Forschungsinstitut der deutschen Gesellschaft für auswärtige Politik, *Dokumente zur Berlin-Frage 1944–1962* (Berlin, 1962), and in Alois Riklin, *Das Berlin-Problem* (Cologne, 1964); also, Hans George Ruge, *Das Zugangsrecht der Westmächte auf dem Luftweg nach Berlin* (Berlin, 1969).

The necessary background to a study of the occupation is given in Fritz Faust, *Das Potsdamer Abkommen und seine völkerrechtliche Bedeutung*, 4th enlarged ed. (Frankfurt, 1969), and Michael Balfour in *Four-Power Control in Germany and Austria, 1945–1946* (New York: Oxford University Press, 1956). Soviet policy from 1943 to 1953 is ably treated by a specialist in Boris Meissner, *Russland, die Westmächte und Deutschland* (Hamburg, 1953); the student should also read Bodo Scheurig, *Das Nationalkomitee 'Freies Deutschland' und der Bund deutscher Offiziere in der Sowjetunion* (Munich, 1960; DTV 1965).

G. Rhode and W. Wagner, *Quellen zur Entstehung der Oder-Neisse-Linie* (Stuttgart, 1956) is a fairly objective collection of material (English-language edition: Wagner, *The Genesis of the Oder–Neisse Line*, Stuttgart, 1959). Georges (Jerzy) Zdziechowski, *Le problème-clé de la construction européenne: la Pologne sur l'Oder* (1965) states the Polish view of recent and earlier history. The sober work by Elizabeth Wiskemann, *Germany's Eastern Neighbours. Problems relating to the Oder–Neisse line and the Czech frontier regions* (New York: Oxford University Press, 1956) aroused sharp and at times unedifying controversy in Germany.

The policy and actions of the occupying powers need much fuller treatment than they have yet had if they are to be judged on any other basis than official texts and statements of intention. Raymond Ebsworth, *Restoring Democracy in Germany. The British contribution* (New York: Praeger, 1960), is a useful study by a member of the occupying forces with some degree of detachment. This is also true of Harold Zink, *The United States in Germany, 1944–1955* (Princeton, N.J.: Princeton University Press, 1957), and the former senior officials who contributed to E. H. Litchfield, ed., *Governing Postwar Germany* (Ithaca, N.Y.: Cornell University Press, 1953). John Gimbel, *The American Occupation in Germany. Politics and the Military, 1945–1949* (Stanford, Calif.: Stanford University Press, 1968) deals only with the subject of its subtitle; the same author, in *A German Community under American Occupation: Marburg, 1945–1952* (Stanford, Calif.: Stanford University Press, 1961), wrote one of the very few monographs giving some idea of grass-roots conditions. We also need more critical testimony such as that of J. S. Martin, *All Honorable Men* (Boston, 1950) on the internal conflicts of the occupation.

So far, the only general study of the occupation in any of the zones is F. Roy Willis, *The French in Germany, 1945–1949* (Stanford, Calif.: Stanford University Press, 1962). It will soon be supplemented by Richard Gilmore's valuable thesis on *France's cultural relations with Germany in the post-war era, 1945–56*; this was prepared for the Institut d'études internationales at Geneva, as was Adalbert Korff's thesis *Le revirement de la politique française à l'égard de l'Allemagne entre 1945 et 1950* (Annemasse, 1965). French researchers do not seem to be interested in the French occupation.

The cost of the occupation to Germany is depicted with a heavy brush in Institut für Besatzungsfragen, *Sechs Jahre Besatzungslasten* (Tübingen, 1951). A more precise and sober analysis is given by Nicholas Balabkins, *Germany under Direct Controls. Economic aspects of industrial disarmament, 1945–1948* (New Brunswick, N.J.: Rutgers University Press, 1964) and Wilhelm Treue, *Die Demontagepolitik der Westmächte nach dem 2. Weltkrieg. Ihre Wirkung auf die Wirtschaft in Niedersachsen* (Göttingen, 1967).

A general idea of conditions in occupied Germany is given in the large, well illustrated work edited by Hans Dollinger, *Deutschland unter den Besatzungsmächten*

(Munich, 1967). The confusion and misery is described from different angles by the courageous minister responsible for food policy in Bizonia in Hans Schlange-Schöningen, *Im Schatten des Hungers. Dokumentarisches zur Ernährungspolitik 1945–49* (Hamburg, 1953); Victor Gollancz, *In Darkest Germany* (London, 1947); Josef Müller-Marien, *Deutschland im Jahre 1. Panorama 1946–48* (Hamburg, 1960); and most strikingly of all in the law cases reported in G. H. Mostar, *Im Namen des Gesetzes. Menschen und Paragraphen* (Hamburg, 1950).

The Nuremberg trial is better described in Gerhard Gründler and A. von Manikowski, *Das Gericht der Sieger* (Oldenburg, 1967) than in J. Heydecker and J. Leeb, *Der Nürnberger Prozess. Bilanz der Tausend Jahre* (Cologne, 1968). Constantine FitzGibbon, *Denazification* (New York: Norton, 1969), does not add much to our knowledge, especially in comparison with the outstanding work by Justus Fürstenau, *Entnazifizierung* (Neuwied, 1969).

Karl Jaspers, *Die Schuldfrage* (1946; English-language edition: *The Question of German Guilt*, New York: Peter Smith, 1947) is still a fundamental work: it was reprinted in the author's *Hoffnung und Sorge. Schriften zur deutschen Politik 1945–1965* (Munich, 1965). A well-documented study by Albrecht Schröder, *La réaction du public allemand devant les œuvres littéraires de caractère politique pendant la période 1945–1950* (Geneva, 1964) discusses *inter alia* the success of *The Devil's General*. The best account of the atmosphere during the dark years is given in a German novel that deals harshly with both the occupying powers and the German people: Hans Habe, *Off Limits. Roman der Besatzung Deutschlands* (Munich, 1955; English-language edition with same title, New York: Frederick Fell, 1956). The recovery of at least some of the people from their hardships and pangs of conscience is illustrated by Curt Riess, *Sie haben es noch einmal geschafft. Schicksale im Nachkriegsdeutschland* (Berlin and Frankfurt, 1955).

Others, however, were more concerned with their country's recovery than with their own. Hermann Beer, in *Vom Chaos zum Staat. Männer, die für uns begannen. 1945–1949* (Frankfurt, 1961), depicts such men in too uniformly favorable a light; there is more solid evidence in the interviews with Heinemann, Carlo Schmid and others collected in Albert Wucher, ed., *Wie kam es zur Bundesrepublik? Politische Gespräche mit Männern der ersten Stunde* (Freiburg, 1968). Valuable first-hand material is also contained in T. Heuss, *Aufzeichnungen 1945–1947* (Tübingen, 1966); also Reinhold Maier, *Ein Grundstein wird gelegt. Die Jahre 1945–1947* (Tübingen, 1964) and his *Erinnerungen 1948–1953* (Tübingen, 1966). We need, however, more studies, even though of a rapid kind, like Thilo Vogelsang, *Hinrich Wilhelm Kopf und Niedersachsen* (Hanover, 1963), and above all such detailed and fascinating works as Werner Conze, *Jakob Kaiser. Politiker zwischen Ost und West. 1945–1949* (Stuttgart, 1969).

The main stages of political recovery can be traced in the documents and linking text of Theo Stammen, *Einigkeit und Recht und Freiheit. Westdeutsche Innenpolitik 1945–1955* (Munich: DTV, 1965). Electoral results are tabulated in Richard Schachtner, *Die deutschen Nachkriegswahlen* (Munich, 1956). The informative but dry compilation by Walter Vogel, *Westdeutschland 1945–1950. Der Aufbau von Verfassungs- und Verwaltungseinrichtungen* (vol. I, Coblenz, 1956; vol. II, Boppard, 1965) is not a substitute for works like Wolfgang Rudzio, *Die Neuordnung des Kommunalwesens in der britischen Zone* (Stuttgart, 1968); Walter Först, *Geschichte Nordrhein-Westfalens. I. 1945–1949* (Cologne, 1969); and especially Tilman Pünder,

Das bizonale Interregnum. Geschichte der Verwaltung des Vereinigten Wirtschafts-gebietes (Cologne, 1966).

Pending publication of the book on the Parliamentary Council by Eberhard Pikard, director of the Theodor-Heuss-Archiv, use may be made of the general account by Peter Merkl, *The Origin of the West German Republic* (New York: Oxford University Press, 1963), and two remarkable works that, together with that by Pünder, show that German research on the occupation period has thrown off its lethargy: Werner Sörgel, *Konsensus und Interesse. Eine Studie zur Entstehung des Grundgesetzes* (Stuttgart, 1969), with emphasis on economic interests and doctrines, and Hans-Peter Schwarz, *Vom Reich zur Bundesrepublik Deutschland. Im Widerstreit der aussenpolitischen Konzeptionen in den Jahren der Besatzungsherrschaft* (Neuwied, 1967), a particularly shrewd and informative *Habilitationsschrift*.

The Federal Republic and Its Institutions

Apart from the large but readable volume edited by Hans Dollinger, *Die Bundes-republik in der Ära Adenauer 1949–1963. Ihre Geschichte in Texten, Bildern und Dokumenten* (Munich, 1960), it is hard to find a good historical study of the Federal Republic. Klaus Bölling, *Die zweite Republik. 15 Jahre Politik in Deutschland* (Cologne, 1963) is still useful. Heinz Abosch's works *L'Allemagne sans miracle. D'Hitler à Adenauer* (1960) and *L'Allemagne en mouvement* (1968) are too relentlessly critical. Fritz René Alleman wrote an excellent summing-up in *Bonn ist nicht Weimar* (Cologne, 1956), after which he merely republished a collection of articles in *Zwischen Stabilität und Krise. Etappen der deutschen Politik 1955–1963* (Munich, 1963), as did the other eminent Swiss journalist Fred Luchsinger in *Bericht über Bonn. Deutschlandpolitik 1955–1965* (Zurich and Stuttgart, 1966). These articles are useful, but exemplify a regrettable tendency whereby professors and good journalists in Germany are led to publish only collections of brief scattered studies. The other regrettable feature of German publishing is that instead of a systematic work by a single author one gets collective volumes with a dozen or a score of ill-matched contributions from different hands. Fortunately two works exist that are enlightening, though of a somewhat anecdotal character: Rudolf Strauch, *Bonn macht's möglich. Idee und Wirklichkeit im politischen Leben der Bundesrepublik* (Düsseldorf, 1969), and especially (despite its absurd title) Eduard Neumaier, *Bonn das provisorische Herz* (Oldenburg, 1969), in which a member of the staff of *Publik* gives a lively, critical, and well-informed account of the six periods into which he divides the history of the Federal Republic.

Many political surveys are overpessimistic: some of these are brilliant, like Erich Kuby, *Das ist des Deutschen Vaterland. Siebzig Millionen in zwei Wartesälen* (Stuttgart, 1957). Others reflect convictions based on grave ignorance: these include Karl Jaspers, *Wohin treibt die Bundesrepublik?* (Munich, 1966), which is sad in view of the author's personality. Among other general or particular surveys that are worth reading are: Rüdiger Altmann, *Das Erbe Adenauers* (Stuttgart, 1960); Marion Dönhoff, *Die Bundesrepublik in der Ära Adenauers. Kritik und Perspektiven* (Hamburg, 1963); K. G. von Stackelberg, *Attentat auf Deutschlands Talisman. Ludwig Erhards Sturz* (Stuttgart, 1967); and Alois Rummel, ed., *Die Grosse Koalition 1966–1969. Eine kritische Bestandaufnahme* (Freudenstadt, 1969).

There are many good studies of features and institutions as opposed to reviews of developments. The best is certainly that of Thomas Ellwein, *Das Regierungssystem der BRD*, 2nd ed. (Cologne, 1965), which contains abundant documentation on the working of institutions. A work with a much stronger emphasis on sociology is Lewis Edinger, *Politics in Germany. Attitudes and Processes* (Boston: Little, Brown, 1968). This is less abstract than the difficult and ambitious book by Rudolf Wildenmann, *Macht und Konsens als Problem der Innen- und Aussenpolitik* (Frankfurt, 1963). *Staat und Gesellschaft in Deutschland*, by the Tübingen Professor Theodor Eschenburg (Stuttgart, 1956), was, despite its title, an excellent manual on political institutions. The author has not brought it up to date, but there is useful material on the history of institutions in his collections of articles *Institutionelle Sorgen in der Bundesrepublik. Politische Aufsätze 1957–1961* (Stuttgart, 1961) and *Die politische Praxis in der Bundesrepublik. Kritische Betrachtungen 1961–1965* (Munich, 1966). The best critical account in this field is perhaps Gert Schäfer and Carl Nedelmann, eds., *Der CDU-Staat. Analysen zur Verfassungswirklichkeit der Bundesrepublik*, 2 vols. (Frankfurt, 1969).

For a handy edition of the Basic Law see G. Dürig, ed., *Grundgesetz* (Munich: DTV, 1969), which also includes the Emergency Legislation of 1968, the 1954 Convention on Germany, the electoral law, and the laws on parties and the Constitutional Court. The same material, organized quite differently, may be found in L. Holborn, G. Caster, and J. Herz, *German Constitutional Documents Since 1871* (New York: Praeger, 1970). For a commentary, see Friedrich Karl Fromme, *Von der Weimarer Verfassung zum Bonner Grundgesetz. Die verfassungspolitischen Folgerungen des parlamentarischen Rats aus der Weimarer Republik und nationalsozialistischer Diktatur* (Tübingen, 1964), and two professorial interpretations from opposite viewpoints: Konrad Hesse, *Grundsätze des Verfassungsrechts der BRD* (Karlsruhe, 1966) and Wolfgang Abendroth, *Das Grundgesetz. Eine Einführung in seine politischen Probleme* (Pfullingen, 1966). Detailed proposals for amendment are contained in a work by a member of the Bundestag, Hans Dichgans, *Vom Grundgesetz zur Verfassung. Überlegungen zu einer Gesamtrevision* (Düsseldorf, 1970). For comments on the 1968 legislation, see Egon Schunk, *Das Notstandsrecht* (Frankfurt, 1969); Jürgen Seifert, *Der Notstandsausschuss* (Frankfurt, 1968); and Dieter Sterzel, ed., *Kritik der Notstandsgesetze* (Frankfurt, 1968). For a detailed legal study, use should be made of the periodical revisions of commentaries prepared for law faculties: the "Bonner Kommentar" (Hamburg), the Maunz/Dürig/Herzog (Munich) and the von Mangoldt/Klein (Berlin and Frankfurt).

On the Constitutional Court, the fundamental political study is Heinz Laufer, *Verfassungsgerichtbarkeit und politischer Prozess* (Tübingen, 1968), which should be supplemented by the close analyses in G. Leibholz and H. J. Rinck, *Grundgesetz für die BRD. Kommentar an Hand der Rechtssprechung des Bundesverfassungsgerichts* (Cologne, 1966). The Court's account of its own proceedings in *Das Bundesverfassungsgericht* (Karlsruhe, 1963) is still useful; one of its perennial problems, the election of judges, is studied closely in Werner Billing, *Das Problem der Richterwahl zum BVerfG.* (Berlin, 1969). The Court's decisions are collected in the series *Entscheidungen des BVerfG.*, published at Tübingen (index in vol. 10, 1960). Documents relating to important cases will be found in F. Giese and F. A. von der Heydte, eds., *Der Konkordatsprozess* (Munich, 1956); G. Pfeiffer and H. G. Stricker, eds., *KPD-Prozess*, 3 vols. (Karlsruhe, 1956–58); G. Zehner, ed., *Der Fernsehstreit vor dem BVerfG.*, 2 vols. (Karlsruhe, 1964–65). More concise notes in Wiltraut Rupp von Brunneck (a judge of the Court), *Die Grundrechte im juristischen*

Alltag (Frankfurt, 1970), and the booklets by Christian Starck, *Verfassungsrecht in Fällen*, published at Baden-Baden since 1968, e.g. No. 2: *Meinungs- und Pressefreiheit*. Until a book is published on the political role of the Federal High Court, see Otto Bachof, *Verfassungsrecht. Verwaltungsrecht. Verfahrensrecht in der Rechtsprechung des Bundesverwaltungsgerichts* (Tübingen, 1963). (For the administration of justice, see below, Moral and Intellectual Trends).

Special mention should be made of the series *Ämter und Organisationen der BRD* (Frankfurt, later Bonn): these small monographs, while not especially critical, are clear and well informed and give an account, with charts and bibliography, of the ministries and parliamentary bodies, the Chancellor's office, the Federal Press Bureau, the defense commissioner's office, etc.

Researchers have not given much attention to the Federal system. One may read Karlheinz Neunreither, *Der Bundesrat zwischen Politik und Verwaltung* (Heidelberg, 1959); Edward Pinney, *Federalism, Bureaucracy and Party Politics in Western Germany. The Role of the Bundesrat* (Chapel Hill, N.C.: North Carolina University Press, 1963); the subtitle indicates the real subject; and especially Renate Kunze, *Kooperativer Föderalismus in der Bundesrepublik. Zur Staatspraxis der Koordinierung von Bund und Ländern*. In connection with the 1970 referenda, *cf.* the documentary volume *Der Kampf um den Südweststaat* (Munich, 1952). For *Land* politics, there is now Anna Christine Storbeck, *Die Regierungen des Bundes und der Länder seit 1945* (Munich, 1970). Regional political life is also studied in Richard Lehners, ed., *Porträt eines Parlaments. Der Niedersächsische Landtag 1947–1967* (Hanover, 1967); Gabriele Strecker, *Der Hessische Landtag* (Bad Homburg, 1966); Wolfgang Leirich, *Politik in einem Bundesland. Die Landtagswahl vom 8. Juli 1962 in Nordrhein-Westfalen* (Cologne, 1968)—especially interesting; and R. J. C. Preece, *"Land" Elections in the German Federal Republic* (London, 1968), on the same elections.

Administration and local government have been even more neglected. Works of very different types are: Friedrich Fonk, *Die Behörde des Regierungspräsidenten* (Berlin, 1967); Heinz Burghart, *Ich und das Rathaus. Kommunalpolitik in den sechziger Jahren* (Munich, 1965); and Werner Freiberg, *Grundfragen der Kommunalpolitik* (Mainz, 1970).

Incomplete studies of the Presidential Office are to be found in Ulrich Scheuner, *Das Amt des Bundespräsidenten als Aufgabe verfassungsrechtlicher Gestaltung* (Tübingen, 1966), and H. J. Winkler, *Der Bundespräsident. Repräsentant oder Politiker?* (Opladen, 1967). Pending a full biography of Heuss, one may read Modris Eksteins, *Theodor Heuss und die Weimarer Republik* (Stuttgart, 1969) and K. D. Bracher, *Theodor Heuss und die Wiederbegründung der Demokratie in Deutschland* (Tübingen, 1965). Heuss's faithful companion Hans Bott uttered a spate of praise in *Theodor Heuss in seiner Zeit* (Göttingen, 1966). The picture may be completed with T. Heuss, *Die grossen Reden. Der Staatsmann* (Munich: DTV, 1967); his *Würdigungen. Reden, Aufsätze und Briefe 1949–1955* (Tübingen, 1955); and Margarete Vatter, ed., *Bürgerin zweier Welten. Elly Heuss Knapp. Ein Leben in Briefen und Aufzeichnungen* (Tübingen, 1961). For the views of the third President prior to his election, see G. Heinemann, *Verfehlte Deutschlandpolitik*, 2nd ed. (Frankfurt, 1969) and *Plädoyer für den Rechtsstaat* (Karlsruhe, 1969), with an important interview by G. Gaus.

The admirable thesis by Jean Amphoux, *Le chancelier fédéral dans le régime constitutionnel de la République fédérale d'Allemagne* (1962) has no parallel in German and would be worth bringing up to date. The problems are well set out in Wilhelm

Hennis, *Richtlinienkompetenz und Regierungstechnik* (Tübingen, 1964), while the sphere of governmental activity is more closely examined in Ernst Wolfgang Böckenförde, *Die Organisationsgewalt im Bereich der Regierung* (Berlin, 1964). An official account of the activity of each ministry is given in Presse- und Information-samt der Bundesregierung, *Regierung Adenauer 1949–1963* (Wiesbaden, 1963). See also Heinz Laufer, *Der parlamentarische Staatssekretär.. Eine Studie über ein neues Amt in der Bundesregierung* (Munich, 1969). A fundamental problem of government is studied in Adolf Schule, *Koalitionsvereinbarungen im Lichte des Verfassungsrechts* (Tübingen, 1964) and especially in H. Weber and F. H. Timmermann, *Der Koalitionsvertrag* (Bonn, 1967), with the text of the CDU/FDP agreement of 1961.

There is as yet no major biography of the first Chancellor, covering his whole career as is done for a single episode of it in Karl-Dietrich Erdmann, *Adenauer in der Rheinlandpolitik nach dem ersten Weltkrieg* (Stuttgart, 1966). The limitations of Paul Weymar, *Konrad Adenauer. Die autorisierte Biographie* (Munich, 1955; English-language edition, New York: Dutton, 1957) are well indicated by its subtitle. Charles Wighton, *Adenauer, Democratic Dictator. A Critical Biography* (New York: Coward-McCann, 1963) lacks precision as to both facts and interpretation. The four volumes of Adenauer's *Erinnerungen* (Stuttgart, 1965–68; English-language edition: *Memoirs*, Chicago: Regnery, 1966) are indispensable but should be used with caution; their frigid style makes them unattractive reading. The most trustworthy volume is the last, covering 1959–63, which the author did not live long enough to revise. See also Robert d'Harcourt, *Konrad Adenauer* (1955); E. P. Neumann and E. Nölle, *Umfragen über Adenauer. Ein Porträt in Zahlen* (Allensbach, 1961); and Anneliese Poppinga, *Meine Erinnerungen an Konrad Adenauer* (Stuttgart, 1970). There are handsome photographs in W. McBride and H. W. Finck von Finckenstein, *Adenauer. Ein Porträt* (Starn-berg, 1966). Instruction as well as amusement may be gained from the cartoon anthologies by Wilhelm Freiburger, *Konrad, sprach die Frau Mama . . .* (Oldenburg, 1955) and *Konrad, bleibst du jetzt zu Haus?* (Oldenburg, 1963); also from the anec-dotes collected in Walter Henkels, *"Gar nicht so pinkelig"* (Düsseldorf, 1965) and *Doktor Adenauers gesammelte Schwänke* (Düsseldorf, 1966).

Michael Caro's biography *Der Volkskanzler Ludwig Erhard* (Cologne, 1965) is pleasant and sensible in tone and content; for opposite reasons this cannot be said of Klaus Hoff, *Kurt Georg Kiesinger. Die Geschichte seines Lebens* (Berlin, 1969), nor particularly of Beate Klarsfeld, *Die Geschichte des PG 2633930 Kiesinger* (Darmstadt, 1969). Kiesinger's speeches are collected in *Stationen 1949–1969* (Tübingen, 1969). (For Willy Brandt, see below, Elections and Party Politics.)

There is a first-class survey of *Parliament in the German Political System* by the American professor Gerhard Loewenberg (Ithaca, N.Y.: Cornell University Press, 1966). The German version *Parlamentarismus im politischen System der BRD* (Tübingen, 1969), although not much more up to date, is preferable on account of the excellent critical biography, which goes up to June, 1968 and also covers related fields. In addition to this fundamental work, other recent studies should be con-sulted: Hans Trossmann, *Parlamentsrecht und Praxis des Deutschen Bundestages* (Bonn, 1968), by a clerk of the parliament with over twenty years' experience; Hanswerner Müller, *Handbuch der Gesetzgebungstechnik*, 2nd ed. (Cologne and Berlin, 1968)—how German laws are drafted; E. Hübner, H. Oberreuter, and H. Rausch, eds., *Der Bundestag von innen gesehen* (Munich, 1969)—fairly frank testi-mony; and especially Hans Maier, ed., *Zum Parlamentsverständnis des fünften deutschen Bundestages* (Munich, 1969), with the comments of 227 members of parliament on ways of improving its method of work.

Important aspects of parliament in its relation to political life and administration are studied in Norbert Gehrig, *Parlament—Regierung—Opposition* (Munich, 1969); Wolf-Dieter Hauenschild, *Wesen und Rechtsnatur der parlamentarischen Fraktionen* (Berlin, 1968)—unfortunately much too narrowly juridical; and especially T. Ellwein and A. Görlitz, *Parlament und Verwaltug*: vol. I, "Gesetzgebung und politische Kontrolle" (Stuttgart, 1962), vol. II, "Haushaltsplanung und Haushalts-kontrolle" (Stuttgart, 1968).

Studies of political atmosphere and personalities may be found in Walter Henkels, *Lokal-Termin in Bonn. Der 'Hofchronist' erzählt* (Düsseldorf, 1968)—by the Bonn correspondent of the *Frankfurter Allgemeine Zeitung*, and the same author's *111 Bonner Köpfe* (Düsseldorf, 1966). There is even some good to be found in Ingelore Winter, *Bonn in Frack und Schärpe. Anatomie einer Gesellschaft* (Stuttgart, 1969), a book as snobbish and pretentious as the social life it describes. However, the best work in this field is Günter Gaus, *Zur Person. Porträts in Frage und Antwort* (Munich: DTV, 1965): the value of these interviews is such as to make one regret that the author gave up television to become editor of *Der Spiegel*.

Elections and Party Politics

The basic work for the study of parties is Hans-Gerd Schumann's excellent *Die politischen Parteien in Deutschland nach 1945. Ein bibliographisch-systematischer Versuch* (Frankfurt, 1967). For party programs and statutes, legal texts, etc., see the large and valuable work by Ossip K. Flechtheim, *Dokumente zur parteipolitischen Entwicklung in Deutschland seit 1945* (Berlin, 1962–66), 5 vols. to date. A clear perspective of the postwar period may be gained from Helga Grebing's short but reliable *Geschichte der politischen Parteien* (Wiesbaden, 1962).

Pending the general study by Heino Kaak, which will be indispensable, one may read this author's *Die Parteien in der Verfassungswirklichkeit der Bundesrepublik*, 2nd ed. (Bonn, 1964) and Wolf-Dieter Narr, *CDU-SPD: Programm und Praxis seit 1945* (Stuttgart, 1966)—an intelligent, critical, and well-informed book, covering more ground than the title suggests. An introduction to a range of problems affecting all parties is afforded by Bodo Zeuner, *Innerparteiliche Demokratie* (Berlin, 1969) and Ulrich Lohmar, *Innerparteiliche Demokratie* (Stuttgart, 1963): this work by an SPD deputy is very objective and reasonably frank. However, there is a crying need of studies like Heinz Josef Varain, *Parteien und Verbände. Studie über ihren Aufbau, ihre Verflechtung und ihr Wirken in Schleswig-Holstein 1945-1958* (Cologne, 1964). Among the flood of publications on electoral reform, attention should be drawn to the elaborate calculations of Heino Kaak, *Zwischen Verhältniswahl und Mehrheit-swahl* (Opladen, 1967) and the disillusioned account by the ex-minister Paul Lücke, *Ist Bonn doch Weimar? Der Kampf um das Mehrheitswahlrecht* (Frankfurt, 1968); also the writings by various academic opponents of the majority vote, especially Ferdinand Hermens.

Opinion polls play an ever increasing role in election campaigns and even in day-to-day politics. Their methods may be studied in the work by Elisabeth Nölle, the head of the Allensbach Institute, *Umfragen in der Massengesellschaft* (Hamburg, 1963). For a record of the Allensbach polls, see *Jahrbuch der öffentlichen Meinung* (Allensbach and Bonn, 1956 and 1965), covering respectively 1947–55 and 1958–64.

The case against polls is presented intelligently in Wilhelm Hennis, *Meinungsforschung und repräsentative Demokratie* (Tübingen, 1957), and with comic exaggeration in Kurt Gayer, *Das grosse Verhör. Fug und Unfug der Demoskopie* (Gütersloh, 1969): this should be corrected by the able analysis of methods and principle in Gerhard Schmidtchen, *Die befragte Nation. Über den Einfluss der Meinungsforschung auf die Politik* (Freiburg, 1959).

The debate should in any case take more account of serious studies of electoral motivations. Klaus Liepelt, the head of INFAS at Bad Godesberg, and A. Mitscherlich have produced an analytical study, based on thorough and extensive research, in *Thesen zur Wählerfluktuation* (Frankfurt, 1968). The Federal Republic forms part of the subject of a general work by two eminent specialists in electoral sociology, Erwin Scheuch and Rudolf Wildenmann, *Zur Soziologie der Wahl* (Cologne and Opladen, 1965). But there is a lack of monographs like Hans-Dieter Klingemann, *Bestimmungsgründe der Wahlentscheidung. Eine regionale Wahlanalyse* (Meisenheim, 1969), and of approaches from a different angle such as Werner Kaltefleiter, *Wirtschaft und Politik in Deutschland. Konjunktur als Bestimmungsfaktor des Parteisystems* (Cologne and Opladen, 1966).

There are good studies of general elections: W. Hirsch-Weber and Klaus Schütz, eds., *Wähler und Gewählte. Eine Untersuchung der Bundestagswahlen 1953* (Berlin and Frankfurt, 1957), and Reinhard Vogel and Peter Haungs, *Wahlkampf und Wählertradition. Eine Studie zur Bundestagswahl 1961* (Cologne and Opladen, 1965). There is also the brilliant study by Uwe Kitzinger, *German Electoral Politics. A study of the 1957 campaign* (New York: Oxford University Press, 1960; abridged German edition *Wahlkampf in Deutschland*, Göttingen, 1960) and the monumental work by Fritz Sänge and K. Liepelt, eds., *Wahlhandbuch 1965. Sammlungen von Texten, Daten, Dokumenten zu Wahlrecht, Wahlkampf, Wahlergebnissen, Wahlkreisen* (Frankfurt), which is about 2,000 multigraphed pages that appeared before the election. Vera Gemmeke, *Parteien im Wahlkampf. Eine Analyse der Bundestagswahl 1961 im Wahlkreis Arnsberg Soest* (Meisenheim, 1967), and K. Kaufmann, H. Kohl, and P. Molt, *Die Auswahl der Bundestagskandidaten in zwei Bundesländern* (Cologne, 1961), are good monographs of a type that is too rare, in two important fields.

Kommunistische Partei Deutschlands, *Dokumente der KPD 1945–1956* (East Berlin, 1965) may be supplemented and corrected by Hermann Weber, ed., *Völker, hört die Signale. Der deutsche Kommunismus 1926–1956* (Munich: DTV, 1967); one may also read W. Abendroth and H. Ridder, eds., *KPD-Verbot. Mit den Kommunisten leben?* (Hamburg, 1968).

Gérard Sandoz, *La gauche allemande de Karl Marx à Willy Brandt* (1970) is a concise, lively and well-informed account covering the KPD, SED, and SPD. The history of the SPD may also be conveniently studied in F. Osterroth and D. Schuster, *Chronik der deutschen Sozialdemokratie* (Hanover, 1963). For the role and activity of the exiled Social Democrats, see Kurt R. Grossmann, *Emigration. Geschichte der Hitler-Flüchtlinge 1933–1945* (Frankfurt, 1970); Werner Röder, *Die deutschen sozialistischen Exilgruppen in Grossbritannien* (Hanover, 1968); and E. Matthias, ed., *Mit dem Gesicht nach Deutschland. Eine Dokumentation über die sozialdemokratische Emigration* (Düsseldorf, 1968). The problems of the returning exiles and their contacts with the Communists are described in Albrecht Kaden, *Einheit oder Freiheit. Die Wiedergründung der SPD 1945/46* (Hanover, 1964).

Every other year, before the party congress, the SPD publishes a *Jahrbuch* and subsequently a *Protokoll der Verhandlungen*: these are basic documents for a study of the postwar party. Works on it include David Childs, *From Schumacher to Brandt. The story of German Socialism, 1945–65* (London, 1966) (clear and concise); Theo Pirker, *Die SPD nach Hitler* (Munich, 1965) (an incisive left-wing criticism); Douglas A. Chalmers, *The Social-Democratic Party of Germany. From Working-class Movement to Modern Political Party* (New Haven, Conn.: Yale University Press, 1964) (able and sympathetic); and Harold K. Schellenger, *The SPD in the Bonn Republic. A socialist party modernizes* (The Hague, 1968) (with new information on the origin of the Godesberg program). Despite all these, there is still room for a thorough general study and for more works on particular aspects such as Abraham Ashkenazi, *Reformpartei und Aussenpolitik. Die Aussenpolitik der SPD* (Berlin–Bonn–Cologne–Opladen, 1968), which concentrates heavily on the Berlin Socialists. Among works by members of the party may be mentioned *Sozialdemokratie und Bundeswehr* (Hanover, 1957) (documents); H. Wehner, B. Friedrich, and A. Nau, *Parteiorganisation* (Bonn, 1969) (which gives some idea of the actual structure); Günter Gaus, *Staatserhaltende Opposition. Hat die SPD kapituliert? Gespräche mit H. Wehner* (Hamburg, 1966) (of great retrospective interest); and Horst Ehmke, ed., *Perspektiven. Sozialdemokratische Politik im Übergang zu den siebziger Jahren* (Hamburg, 1969) (text and comment on electoral attitudes).

Lewis J. Edinger, *Kurt Schumacher. A Study in Personality and Political Behavior* (Stanford, Calif.: Stanford University Press, 1965; German-language edition: 1967) is full of information but has been criticized for its emphasis on the psychological approach. It can be supplemented by Waldemar Ritter, *Kurt Schumacher. Eine Untersuchung seiner politischen Konzeption* (Hanover, 1964). The speeches and writings of the party's first three postwar leaders can be studied in K. Schumacher, *Reden und Schriften* (Berlin, 1962); E. Ollenhauer, *Reden und Aufsätze* (Hanover, 1964); and F. Erler, *Politik für Deutschland. Eine Dokumentation* (Stuttgart, 1968). Reuter's biography can be read in W. Brandt and R. Löwenthal, *Ernst Reuter, Ein Leben für die Freiheit* (Munich, 1956). Works by the present party chairman and Chancellor include *Mein Weg nach Berlin. Aufgezeichnet von Lea Lania* (Munich, 1960; English-language edition, *My Road to Berlin*, New York: Doubleday, 1960); *Draussen. Schriften während der Emigration* (Munich, 1966); and *Begegnungen mit Kennedy* (Munich, 1964). To these may be added Klaus Harpprecht, *Willy Brandt. Portrait und Selbstportrait* (Munich, 1970). (See also below for writings by the political leaders on foreign affairs.)

On the CDU/CSU, the documentary basis is furnished by *Politisches Jahrbuch der CDU und CSU 1968* (Recklinghausen, 1968 and its predecessors). Arnold J. Heidenheimer, *Adenauer and the CDU* (The Hague, 1960) is much the best general account of the early period and the problem of leadership within the party. E. Deuerlein, *CDU/CSU 1945–1957* (Cologne, 1957) is an able, uncritical narrative which can be supplemented by Leo Schwerin, *Frühgeschichte der christlich-demokratischen Union* (Recklinghausen, 1963). Rainer Barzel pays homage to his former leader in *Karl Arnold. Grundlegung christlich-demokratischer Politik in Deutschland* (Bonn, 1960), a work which contrasts somewhat with the same author's views expressed in *Gesichtspunkte eines Deutschen* (Düsseldorf, 1968). The friendly portrait of the CSU chairman by Thomas Dalberg in *Franz Josef Strauss. Porträt eines Politikers* (Gütersloh, 1968), may be set against Erich Kuby's attack in *Franz Josef Strauss. Ein Typus unserer Zeit* (Munich, 1963). But all these works do not take the place of scientific studies, and it is a pity there are not more like Renate Mayntz, *Parteigruppen in der Grossstadt. Untersuchungen in einem Berliner Kreisverband der CDU* (Cologne, 1959).

There are some substantial works on the other parliamentary parties; Herbert Bertsch, *Die FDP und der deutsche Liberalismus 1789–1963* (Berlin, 1965); Kurt Körper, *FDP. Bilanz der Jahre 1960–1966* (Cologne, 1968); Hermann Meyn, *Die Deutsche Partei* (Düsseldorf, 1965); and Franz Neumann, *Der Block der Heimatvertriebenen und Entrechteten 1950–1960* (Meisenheim, 1968).

Among the mass of publications concerning the extreme right and particularly the NPD we may mention Manfred Jenke, *Verschwörung von rechts? Ein Bericht über den Rechtsradikalismus in Deutschland nach 1945* (Berlin, 1951); Carl-Christoph Schweitzer, ed., *Eiserne Illusionen. Wehr- und Bündnisfragen in den Vorstellungen der extremen Rechten nach 1945* (Cologne, 1969); Werner Smoydzin, *NPD. Geschichte und Umwelt einer Partei* (Pfaffenhofen, 1967); R. Kühnl, R. Rilling, and C. Sager, *Die NPD. Struktur, Ideologie und Funktion einer neofaschistischen Partei* (Frankfurt, 1969); Lutz Neithammer, *Angepasster Faschismus. Politische Praxis der NPD* (Frankfurt, 1969) (with excellent bibliography); and Friedrich Bröder, '*Deutsche Nachrichten*'. *Ein Sprachrohr des Rechtsradikalismus* (Mainz, 1969). Also the hagiographic D. Rufer, *Adolf von Thadden. Wer ist dieser Mann?* (Hanover, 1969).

At the other end of the political spectrum, themes and personalities are depicted in F. Hitzer and R. Opitz, eds., *Alternativen der Opposition* (Cologne, 1969), and Hans Dollinger, ed., *Revolution gegen den Staat? Die ausserparlamentarische Opposition* (Munich, 1968). The picture may be brought into focus in the light of excellent debates organized at Nuremberg: see Hermann Glaser, ed., *Opposition in der Bundesrepublik. Ein Tagungsbericht* (Freiburg, 1968). (For the neo-Nazis and the "extraparliamentary opposition," see also below.)

Economic and Social Forces

There is no work in German comparable to the excellent survey by Jean François-Poncet, *La politique économique de l'Allemagne occidentale* (1970). Similarly, the initial period is best studied in André Piettre, *L'économie de l'Allemagne contemporaine, 1945–1952* (1952), to which may be added Henry Wallich, *Mainsprings of German Revival*, (New Haven, Conn.: Yale University Press, 1955) and Michel Beaud, *La croissance économique de l'Allemagne de l'ouest, 1949–1962* (1966). The doctrinal background and political context of the policy adopted in 1949 are analyzed in François Bilger, *La politique économique libérale dans l'Allemagne contemporaine* (1964) and Reinhard Blum, *Soziale Marktwirtschaft. Wirtschaftspolitik zwischen Neoliberalismus und Ordoliberalismus* (Tübingen, 1969). The principal speeches and writings of the chief inspirer and executant of this policy are collected in L. Erhard, *Deutsche Wirtschaftspolitik* (Düsseldorf, 1962) and Müller-Armack, *Wirtschaftsordnung und Wirtschaftspolitik* (Freiburg, 1966). The development of the policy in the light of events can be followed in the discussions of the Aktionsgemeinschaft Soziale Marktwirtschaft, published at Ludwigsburg. There is a good summing-up in Hans-Joachim Arndt, *West Germany: Politics of Non-Planning* (Syracuse, N.Y.: Syracuse University Press, 1966).

Jörg Huffschmid, *Die Politik des Kapitals. Konzentration und Wirtschaftspolitik in der BRD* (Frankfurt, 1969) gives a systematic account of the facts that may be inferred from Kurt Fritzkoleit, *Männer. Mächte. Monopole*, rev. ed. (Düsseldorf,

1960). There are enlightening monographs by Eberhard Czichon, *Der Bankier und die Macht. H. J. Abs in der deutschen Politik* (Cologne, 1970); Berndt Engelmann, *Krupp. Legende und Wirklichkeit* (Munich, 1969); and K. A. Schenzinger, H. Simon, and A. Zischka, *Heinrich Nordhoff* (Munich, 1969); also a curious self-portrait by Günter Henle: *Weggenosse des Jahrhunderts als Diplomat, Industrieller, Politiker und Freund der Musik* (Stuttgart, 1968). However, the power of such striking characters as these is threatened by the Americanization denounced in Kurt .Blauhorn, *Ausverkauf in Germany?* (Munich, 1967), and more specifically in Dieter Grosser, ed., *Konzentration ohne Kontrolle* (1969), which discusses the problems raised by concentration in various fields such as the press, codetermination, etc. Meanwhile, the tycoons are still among those criticized by Peter Brügge in *Die Reichen in Deutschland* (Frankfurt, 1966).

To understand the sufferings of those expelled from the eastern territories, rather than the large volumes of accusatory reports published in West Germany one should perhaps read Göttinger Arbeitskreis, *Dokumente der Menschlichkeit aus der Zeit der Massenaustreibungen* (Kitzingen, 1950), and especially Hans Graf von Lehndorff, *Ostpreussisches Tagebuch. Aufzeichnungen eines Arztes aus den Jahren 1945–47* (Munich, 1961). Two theses about the expellees will shortly be available: Hans Schönberg, *Germans from the East. A study of their migration, resettlement and subsequent group history* (The Hague, 1970), and Jean-Claude Hervé, *Rapatriés et réfugiés allemands en Rhénanie du Nord et en Hesse du Sud*. Meanwhile there is an imposing but unequal compilation edited by E. Lemberg and F. Edding, *Die Vertriebenen in Westdeutschland. Ihre Eingliederung und ihr Einfluss auf Gesellschaft, Wirtschaft, Politik und Geistesleben*, 3 vols. (Kiel, 1959); also Hiddo Jolles, *Zur Soziologie der Heimatvertriebenen und Flüchtlinge* (Cologne, 1965), and Linus Kather, *Die Entmachtung der Vertriebenen*, 2 vols. (Munich, 1964–65). The bitter and sometimes petty accusations in the latter work are an unwilling testimony to the success of the integration policy.

As regards sociology, the excellent bibliographical notes by Peter Haungs, "Sozialstruktur und Demokratie in der BRD," in *Civitas, Jahrbuch für Sozialwissenschaft*, VIII (Mannheim, 1969), pp. 264–89, will serve as an introduction to such works as D. Claessens, A. Klönne, and A. Tschöpe, .*Sozialkunde der BR*, new ed. (Düsseldorf, 1968); Friedrich Fürstenberg, *Die Sozialstruktur der BRD* (Cologne, 1967); K. M. Bolte, ed., *Deutsche Gesellschaft im Wandel* (Opladen, 1966); and Leo Baumanns and Heinz Grossmann, *Deformierte Gesellschaft. Soziologie der BRD* (Hamburg, 1969). Having noted Wolfgang Zapf, *Wandlung der deutschen Elite. Ein Zirkulationsmodell deutscher Führungsgruppen* (Munich, 1965), one may speculate with Klaus von Dohnanyi—*Japanische Strategien. Das deutsche Führungsdefizit* (Munich, 1969)—as to where Germany will find the ruling class that she needs as much as any other society.

The result of a searching inquiry by a government commission, *Soziale Sicherung. Sozialenquete in der BRD*, 2 vols. (Stuttgart, 1957), takes stock of the effect of legislation on social conditions. The historical background may be studied in Gerhard Erdmann, *Die Entwicklung der deutschen Socialgesetzgebung* (Göttingen, 1957). Neither of these publications covers the important special problem of foreign workers in Germany, which is dealt with from both a human and a statistical point of view in K. Bingemer and others, *Leben als Gastarbeiter. Geglückte und missglückte Integration* (Cologne, 1970).

A grave aspect of social inequality, viz. in the field of education, is ably analyzed in Hansgerdt Peisert, *Soziale Lage und Bildungschancen in Deutschland* (Munich, 1967), which may be supplemented by the gloomy work edited by B. Lutz, L. Bauer, and J. von Kornatzki, *Berufsaussichten und Berufsausbildung in der BR*, new ed. (Hamburg, 1965). The underprivileged situation of girls in particular was already depicted in G. Wutzbacher, W. Jaide, and others, *Die junge Arbeiterin* (Munich, 1958). This may be brought up to date with Helga Pross, *Über die Bildungschancen der Mädchen in der BRD* (Frankfurt, 1969), which makes instructive comparisons with the G.D.R. (For books on youth problems, see also below.) The role of women in political life is described, more particularly as regards organizations, in Mechtild Fülles, *Frauen in Partei und Parlament* (Cologne, 1969), and in a more general fashion in Gabriele Bremme, *Die politische Rolle der Frau in Deutschland. Der Einfluss der Frauen bei Wahlen und ihre Teilnahme in Partei und Parlament* (Göttingen, 1969).

Two types of study are less common than they should be: first, the investigation in depth of a particular geographical area—on the lines of T. Ellwein and G. Zimpel, *Wertheim*, vol. I: "Fragen an eine Stadt" (Munich,1969) and, second, the study of individual cases. Perhaps the best as well as the most depressing book on West German society and others of the same kind is the collection of interviews in depth by Jürgen Neven du Mont, *Zum Beispiel 42 Deutsche* (Munich, 1968).

Herbert Schneider, *Die Interessenverbände* (Munich, 1966) is a good general account of group organizations. The consumer as such is dealt with in Christa von Braunschweig, *Der Konsument und seine Vertretung* (Heidelberg, 1966), while farmers' problems that will be familiar to a French reader in the European context are described in Paul Ackermann, *Der Deutsche Bauernverband im politischen Kräftespiel der BR* (Tübingen, 1970). Pierre Waline, an eminent former member of French employers' associations, has described the German scene in a rich and unusual work, *Cinquante ans de rapports entre patrons et ouvriers en Allemagne* (vol. I, 1968: covering 1918–45; vol. II, in press: covering 1945–70). The two great organizations of employers, the BDI and the BDA, publish substantial annual reports (*Jahresberichte*). Their activities are described in G. Erdmann, *Die deutschen Arbeitgeberverbände im sozialgeschichtlichen Wandel der Zeit* (Neuwied, 1966), and especially Gérard Braunthal, *The Federation of German Industry in Politics* (Ithaca, N.Y.: Cornell University Press, 1965). The employers are not the only theme of Peter von Schubert, *Antigewerkschaftliches Denken in der BRD* (Frankfurt, 1967).

Hans Limmer, *Die deutsche Gewerkschaftsbewegung*, new ed. (Munich, 1968), gives a concise but accurate account of the history and activity of German trade unions. The traditional atmosphere and background of the unions is described in such works as Karl Anders, *Stein für Stein. Die Leute von Bau-Stein-Erden und ihre Gewerkschaften, 1869–1969* (Hanover, 1969); H. G. Schumann, *Nationalsozialismus und Gewerkschaftsbewegung* (Göttingen, 1958); and Else Klein-Viehöver, *Hans Böckler* (Cologne, 1952). There is no fully satisfactory general account of postwar developments. Albert Behrendt and others, *Die westdeutschen Gewerkschaften und das staatsmonopolistische Herrschaftssystem 1945–1966* (East Berlin, 1968) contains abundant documentation but systematically distorts the facts. Günter Triesch, *Die Macht der Funktionäre. Macht und Verantwortung der Gewerkschaften* (Düsseldorf, 1956) was much more objective and remarkably well informed, from a viewpoint close to the employers'. The excellent analytical account by Theo Pirker, *Die blinde Macht. Die Gewerkschaftsbewegung in Westdeutschland* (Munich, 1960) (vol. I, 1945–52; vol. II, 1953–60), is rather too strongly marked by the bitterness of the defeated left wing. Sources that should be consulted are the large volumes of debates and resolutions of the DGB congresses.

On codetermination, Xavier Herlin, *Les expériences allemandes de cogestion. Techniques et réalisations* (1958) gives a clear account of the laws of 1951 and 1952 and their application in the initial years. For the origin of codetermination on a parity basis, see W. Hirsch-Weber, *Gewerkschaften in der Politik* (Cologne, 1959).

Many earlier works on this subject have become out of date since the appearance of the Biedenkopf commission's report *Mitbestimmung im Unternehmen* (Stuttgart, 1970). Its publication, however, has revived the debate on the basis of the views and attitudes expressed in interviews and otherwise in Heiner Radzio, *Warum Mitbestimmung und wie?* (Düsseldorf, 1970). (For the "confessional" debate on codetermination, see below.)

The impressive picture of the DGB's material power in Kurt Hirche, *Die Wirtschaftsunternehmen der Gewerkschaften* (Düsseldorf, 1970) may be supplemented by W. Hesselbach, *Die gemeinwirtschaftlichen Unternehmen. Der Beitrag der Gewerkschaften zu einer verbandsorientierten Wirtschaftspolitik* (Frankfurt, 1966) and by Gerhard Wuthe, *Gewerkschaften und politische Bildung* (Hanover, 1962). The ideas of the union leaders as expressed, e.g., in L. Rosenberg, *Entscheidungen für morgen. Gewerkschaftspolitik heute* (Düsseldorf, 1969), or O. Brenner, *Gewerkschaftliche Dynamik in unserer Zeit* (Frankfurt, 1966), should not obscure the grass-roots reality depicted in a striking study by Hartmut Schellhoss, *Apathie und Legitimität. Das Problem der neuen Gewerkschaft* (Munich, 1967).

Moral and Intellectual Trends

The worst aspects of the Nazi past have been recalled in connection with trials. The volume edited by Reinhard Henkys, *Die nationalsozialistischen Gewaltverbrechen. Geschichte und Gericht* (Stuttgart, 1964) contains contributions of great importance. To these may be added Bernd Naumann, *Auschwitz. Bericht über die Strafsache gegen Mulka und andere* (Frankfurt, 1965; English-language edition: *Auschwitz*, New York: Praeger, 1966); Hermann Langbein, ed., *Der Auschwitz-Prozess. Eine Dokumentation*, 2 vols. (Frankfurt, 1966); and H. G. von Dam and R. Giordano, eds., *KZ-Verbrechen vor deutschen Gerichten*, 2 vols. (Frankfurt, 1962 and 1966). The record thus laid bare does not prevent nostalgia for the past in some quarters, as described with some degree of exaggeration in Kurt B. Tauber, *Beyond Eagle and Swastika. German Nationalism Since 1945*, 2 vols. (Middletown, Conn.: Wesleyan University Press, 1967). A clearer and more manageable presentation will be found in Heinz Brüdigam, *Der Schoss ist fruchtbar noch . . . Neonazistische, militaristische, nationalistische Literatur und Publizistik in der BR* (Frankfurt, 1964), to which may be added Kurt Hirsch, *Kommen die Nazis wieder?* (Munich, 1967).

Criticism from opposite angles may be compared in Armin Mohler, *Vergangenheitsbewältigung. Von der Läuterung zur Manipulation* (Stuttgart, 1969) and Jean Amery, *Jenseits von Schuld und Sühne, Bewältigungsversuche eines Überwältigten* (Munich, 1966). The facts may be read in R. Kühnl, *Das Dritte Reich in der Presse der Bundesrepublik* (Frankfurt, 1966); Karl-Ferdinand Werner, *Das NS Geschichtsbild und die deutsche Geschichtswissenschaft* (Stuttgart, 1967); and Karl Mielcke, *1917–*

1945 in den Geschichtsbüchern der BR (Hanover, 1961). The picture may be completed by examining the "presentation of the past" in the best of the books discussed by H. Giesecke in "Die Krise der politischen Bildung. Ein Literaturbericht," in *Deutsche Jugend*, January, 1970, pp. 35–45. The manner in which the past is judged is of especial concern to a particular category of survivors and their children: *cf.* Leo Katcher, *Post Mortem. The Jews in Germany Now* (New York: Dell, 1968) and Walter Oppenheimer, *Jüdische Jugend in Deutschland* (Munich, 1967). But the general attitude that required or still requires to be eradicated is the one criticized, dissected, or satirized in works like Hermann Glaser, *Kleinstadt-Ideologie. Zwischen Furchenglück und Sphärenflug* (Freiburg, 1969); W. Hartenstein and G. Schubert, *Mitlaufen oder Mitbestimmen* (Frankfurt, 1961); or Felix Rexhausen, *Mit deutscher Tinte. Briefe und Ansprachen für alle Wechselfälle des Lebens* (Frankfurt, 1965). These, of course, are not a substitute for more profound studies like A. and M. Mitscherlich, *Die Unfähigkeit zu trauern. Grundlagen kollektiven Verhaltens* (Munich, 1967), and Jürgen Habernas, *Strukturwandel der Öffentlichkeit* (Neuwied, 1962).

As regards the army, there is an excellent bibliographical survey by Wilfrid von Bredow: "Die BR und ihre Streitkräfte. Ein Literaturbericht," in *Politische Vierteljahresschrift*, September, 1969, pp. 415–47. The same author wrote *Entscheidung des Gewissens. Kriegsdienstverweigerer heute* (Cologne, 1969) and *Der Primat militärischen Denkens. Die Bundeswehr und das Problem der okkupierten Öffentlichkeit* (Cologne, 1970). Other important works are Georg Picht, ed., *Studien zur politischen und gesellschaftlichen Situation der Bundeswehr*, 3 vols. (Witten, 1965–66); Wolf von Baudissin, *Soldat für den Frieden. Entwürfe für eine zeitgemässe Bundeswehr* (Munich, 1969); and Wids Mosen, *Bundeswehr—Elite der Nation? Determinanten und Funktionen elitärer Selbsteinschätzung von Bundeswehrsoldaten* (Neuwied, 1970).

On the judicial system, Richard Schmid's *Justiz in der Bundesrepublik* (Pfullingen, 1967) and *Einwände. Kritiken an Gesetzen und Gerichten* (Stuttgart, 1965) may serve as an introduction to the documented but in part exaggerated criticism in such works as: Wolfgang Böhme, ed., *Weltanschauliche Hintergründe in der Rechtsprechung* (Karlsruhe, 1968); Rudolf Wassermann, ed., *Erziehung zum Establishment. Juristenausbildung in kritischer Sicht* (Karlsruhe, 1969); Lutz Lehmann, *Legal und opportun. Politische Justiz in der BR* (Berlin, 1966) (too systematic altogether); Xavier Berra, *Im Paragraphenturm. Eine Streitschrift zur Entideologisierung der Justiz* (Neuwied, 1966); and Frank Benseler, ed., *Im Namen des Volkes? Vier Richter über Justiz und Recht* (Neuwied, 1968). The background without which these criticisms cannot be understood is set out fully but soberly in *Die deutsche Justiz und der Nationalsozialismus*, I (Stuttgart, 1968) (together with H. Weinkauff, "Ein Überblick").

The churches are dealt with from the external standpoint in Gottfried Mahrenholz, *Die Kirchen in der Gesellschaft der BR* (Hanover, 1969); Klaus Martens, *Wie reich ist die Kirche?* (Munich, 1969); and Werner Harenberg, ed., *Was glauben die Deutschen? Die EMNID-Umfrage* (Munich, 1968). To assess internal changes, we should need a new version of Thomas Ellwein, *Klerikalismus in der deutschen Politik* (Munich, 1955) (some interesting reactions to which were collected in *Kritikspiegel*, Munich, 1956). We should also need many more studies like Erhard Blankenburg, *Kirchliche Bindung und Wahlverhalten. Die sozialen Faktoren bei der Wahlentscheidung in Nordrhein-Westfalen 1961–66* (Freiburg, 1967); Günter Kehrer, *Das religiöse Bewusstsein des Industriearbeiters* (Munich, 1967); or J. M. Lohse, *Kirche ohne Kontakte. Beziehungsformen in einem Industrieraum* (Stuttgart, 1967).

The survey by John S. Conway, "Der deutsche Kirchenkampf. Tendenzen und Probleme seiner Erforschung an Hand neuer Literatur," *Vierteljahreshefte für Zeitgeschichte*, October, 1969, pp. 423–49, makes it unnecessary to list the vast number of books on the attitude of the churches, especially the Catholic Church, toward Hitler. Postwar developments in German Catholicism are briefly dealt with in Hans Maier, ed., *Deutscher Katholizismus nach 1945* (Munich, 1964) and N. Greinacher and H. T. Risse, eds., *Bilanz des deutschen Katholizismus* (Mainz, 1966). The extent of change may be measured by comparing Pater P. E. Fichthaut, *Deutsche Katholikentage 1848–1958 und soziale Frage* (Essen, 1960), with D. A. Seeber, ed., *Katholikentag im Widerspruch. Ein Bericht über den 82. Katholikentag in Essen* (Freiburg, 1968), and Josef Örtlinger, *Wirtschaftliche Mitbestimmung. Positionen und Argumente der innerkatholischen Diskussion* (Cologne, 1967). The latter may be supplemented by the writings of the late Oswald von Nell-Breuning, a great "social theologian," *Mitbestimmung. Wer mit wem?* (Freiburg, 1969), and his basic studies *Wirtschaft und Gesellschaft heute*, 3 vols. (Freiburg, 1956–60).

Stewart Herman, *The Rebirth of the German Church* (London, 1946) is still valuable for the prewar period and the formation of the EKD. Three individual studies should be noted: D. Schmidt, *Martin Niemöller* (Hamburg, 1959); Otto Dibelius, *Ein Christ ist immer im Dienst. Erlebnisse und Erfahrungen in einer Zeitwende* (Stuttgart, 1961); and, especially, Propst Heinrich Grüber, *Erinnerungen aus sieben Jahrzehnten* (Cologne, 1968). These throw much light on the developments leading to the animated reports and debates of the *Deutscher Evangelischer Kirchentag* (Stuttgart, 1967, 1970), to which may be added the more or less annual publication (since 1966) *Protestantische Texte aus dem Jahre* . . . ; also R. Henkys, *Deutschland und die östlichen Nachbarn. Beiträge zu einer evangelischen Denkschrift* (Stuttgart, 1966) and Rat der EKD, ed., *Sozialethische Erwägungen zur Mitbestimmung in der Wirtschaft der BRD* (Hamburg, 1968).

The more "advanced" theses of, e.g., Karl-Bernard Hasselmann, *Politische Gemeinde. Ein kirchliches Handlungsmodell am Beispiel der evangelischen Kirchengemeinde an der Freien Universität Berlin* (Hamburg, 1969) go some way to explain opposed reactions such as Hans-Georg Studnitz, *Ist Gott Mitläufer? Die Politisierung der evangelischen Kirche. Analyse und Dokumentation* (Stuttgart, 1969).

The best introduction to the study of the press and television is Hermann Meyn, *Massenmedien in der BRD*, new ed. (Berlin, 1968), with good bibliographical notes. The concentration of the press is the subject of intense study in Germany: an impressive bibliography forms the main part of Jörg Aufermann *et al.*, eds., *Pressekonzentration* (Munich, 1970), pp. 35–282. Mention should also be made of Hans-Dieter Müller, *Der Springer-Konzern* (Munich, 1968) and A. Silbermann and E. Zahn, *Die Konzentration der Massenmedien und ihre Wirkungen* (Düsseldorf, 1970). H. Grossmann and O. Negt, eds., *Die Auferstehung der Gewalt. Springerblockade und politische Reaktion in der BR* (Frankfurt, 1968), is a copious but somewhat slanted collection of material. For a legal view from the opposite angle, see Ernst Forsthoff, *Der Verfassungsschutz der Zeitungspresse* (Frankfurt, 1969), Dieter Just, *Der Spiegel. Arbeitsweise, Inhalt, Wirkung* (Hanover, 1967) is a model of shrewd and honest analysis. A collection of *Spiegel* interviews has been published as . . . *wir danken Ihnen für dieses Gespräch. 24 'Spiegel'-Gespräche* (Munich: DTV, 1970), the "speakers' including Ulbricht, Dutschke, and Baudissin. The famous "*Spiegel* affair" is treated exhaustively in Jürgen Seifert, ed., *Die Spiegel-Affäre* (Freiburg): I. "Die Staatsmacht und ihre Kontrolle" and II. "Die Reaktionen der Öffentlichkeit." The power wielded by such "free-thinking" organs as *Der Spiegel* is denounced by the indefatigable K. Ziesel in *Der deutsche Selbstmord. Diktatur der Meinungsmacher*, 2nd ed. (Recklinghausen, 1965).

A good idea of German TV programs is given by Zweites Deutsches Fernsehen, *Jahrbuch* (Mainz, since 1965). The treatment of a specific event is described in Christian Longolius, ed., *Fernsehen als Aufgabe. Die Bundestagwahl 1969 als journalistische Aufgabe* (Mainz, 1970). One may also read selectively Dieter Stolte, ed., *Fernsehkritik. Im Streit der Meinungen von Produzenten, Konsumenten, Rezensenten* (Mainz, 1969), and C. Longolius, ed., *Fernsehen in Deutschland. Gesellschaftspolitische Aufgaben und Wirkungen eines Mediums* (Mainz, 1967), with interesting material on the polls carried out by E. Nölle and R. Wildenmann. The program reproduced in book form as *Hallo Nachbarn. Television schwarz auf weiss* (Hamburg, 1967) specialized in a similar type of satire to the *Kabarette*, the words of whose songs and sketches are unfortunately hardly ever published. One may get an idea of them from Kai Lorentz, *Das Kommödchen-Buch* (Düsseldorf, 1955); less well from Klaus Budzinski, *Die öffentlichen Spassmacher. Das Kabarett in der Ära Adenauer* (Munich, 1966). The reasons why we have had hardly anything to say about the German cinema are explained ferociously by Joe Hembus in *Der deutsche Film kann gar nicht besser sein* (Bremen, 1962).

The French scholar Robert Minder has written two excellent studies of the literary world in France and Germany: *Kultur und Literatur in Deutschland und in Frankreich* (Frankfurt, 1962) and *Dichter in der Gesellschaft. Erfahrungen mit deutscher und französischer Literatur* (Frankfurt, 1966). These form a good introduction to the problems ably outlined in Paul Noack, *Die Intellektuellen. Wirkung, Versagen, Verdienst* (Munich, 1961). On the subject of "committed" intellectuals one may read Reinhard Lettau, ed., *Die Gruppe 47. Bericht, Kritik, Polemik* (Neuwied, 1967) and Günter Grass, *Über das Selbstverständliche. Reden, Aufsätze, offene Briefe, Kommentare* (Neuwied, 1968). The special status of professors and teachers in the present and in regard to the past is shown in Hans-Peter Bleuel, *Deutschlands Bekenner. Professoren zwischen Kaiserreich und Diktatur* (Munich, 1958) and Gerwin Schefer, *Das Gesellschaftsbild des Gymnasiallehrers* (Frankfurt, 1969).

Sixty-seven works on university problems are discussed in Henri Menudier, "Eléments bibliographiques sur la crise universitaire allemande," *Revue d'Allemagne*, II, 1969, pp. 157–75. The spate continues. Before plunging into current problems, it is as well to read Raymond Arnold's excellent *L'Université en Allemagne de l'Ouest. Histoire, structures, caractères* (1963). Massive documentation is available in W. Albert and C. Öhler, eds., *Materialien zur Entwicklung der Hochschulen 1950 bis 1967* (Hanover-Döhren, 1969). It seems a long time since the takeover that appeared to threaten from the right-wing groups as described with approval in Bernard Oudin, *Les corporations allemandes d'étudiants* (1962) and with ferocity in Lutz Finke, *Gestatte mir Hochachtungsschluck. Bundesdeutschlands korporierte Elite* (Hamburg, 1963). Ulrich Preuss, *Das politische Mandat der Studentenschaft* (Frankfurt, 1969) discusses a basic problem, while the origins and consequences of the recent crisis are analyzed in H. Maus and F. Fürstenberg, eds., *Freie Universität und politisches Potential der Studenten. Über die Entwicklung des Berliner Modells und den Anfang der Studentenbewegung in Deutschland* (Neuwied, 1968). The breach between liberal-minded teachers and student extremists may be seen from Erwin Scheuch, ed. *Die Wiedertäufer der Wohlstandsgesellschaft*, new ed. (Cologne, 1968); Gerhard Schulz, ed., *Was wird aus der Universität? Standpunkte zur Hochschulreform* (Tübingen, 1969); and, especially, Jürgen Habermas, *Protestbewegung und Hochschulreform* (Frankfurt, 1969).

The needs of educational development in general are urged with fervor in Helmut Becker, *Quantität und Qualität. Grundfragen der Bildungspolitik* (Freiburg, 1962); G. Picht, *Die deutsche Bildungskatastrophe* (Munich: DTV, 1965); R. Dahrendorf, *Bildung ist Bürgerrecht* (Hamburg, 1965); and Hildegard Hamm-Brücher, *Auf Kosten unserer Kinder? Reise durch die pädagogischen Provinzen der BR und Berlin* (Hamburg, 1965). The financial problem is set out in Deutscher Bildungsrat, *Sozialprodukt. Öffentliche Haushalts- und Bildungsaufgaben. Eine Projektion bis 1975* (Stuttgart, 1969). The young people to whom this "projection" applies will not be the same individuals as those described in the books mentioned in Bundeszentrale für politische Bildung, *Jugend heute. Eine Auswahlbibliographie* (Bonn, 1968), or even Viggo Graf Blücher, *Die Generation der Unbefangenen. Zur Soziologie der jungen Menschen heute* (Düsseldorf, 1966), still less Helmut Schelsky's celebrated *Die skeptische Generation. Eine Soziologie der deutschen Jugend* (Düsseldorf, 1957). One may well not welcome the prospect of a permanently rebellious younger generation, such as seems to be held out in M. Lieber and F. Wellendorf, *Schülerselbstbefreiung* (Frankfurt, 1969), with startling contributions from grammar-school pupils.

Foreign Policy

An introductory bibliography will be found on pp. 334–474 of the basic study by Arnulf Baring, *Aussenpolitik in Adenauers Kanzlerdemokratie. Bonns Beitrag zur europäischen Verteidigungsgemeinschaft* (Munich, 1969). Such interesting works as R. Wildenmann, *Macht und Konsens* (Frankfurt, 1963; English-language edition, Atheneum) and Wolfram Hanrieder, *German Foreign Policy 1949–1963. International Pressure and Domestic Response* (Stanford, Calif.: Stanford University Press, 1967) still leave room for more chronological or analytical surveys such as the excellent but too short work by Karl Kaiser, *German Foreign Policy in Transition* (New York: Oxford University Press, 1968). Failing these, we have surveys from the point of view of different geographical areas such as those in Helmut Reuther, ed., *Deutschlands Aussenpolitik seit 1955* (Stuttgart, 1965), or collections of documents such as H. A. Jacobsen and O. Stenzl, eds., *Deutschland und die Welt. Zur Aussenpolitik der Bundesrepublik 1949–1963* (Munich: DTV, 1964).

Among original works or collections of speeches and articles by ministers, diplomats, and others engaged in politics may be mentioned W. Grewe, *Deutsche Aussenpolitik der Nachkriegszeit* (Stuttgart, 1960); H. von Brentano, *Deutschland, Europa und die Welt* (Bonn, 1962); K. G. Pfleiderer, *Politik für Deutschland* (Stuttgart, 1961); G. Schröder, *Wir brauchen eine heile Welt* (Düsseldorf, 1963); F. J. Strauss, *Entwurf für Europa* (Stuttgart, 1966); K. T. Guttenberg, *Wenn der Westen will* (Stuttgart, 1964); H. Schmidt, *Strategie des Gleichgewichts* (Stuttgart, 1969); and A. Brandt, *Friedenspolitik in Europa* (Frankfurt, 1968).

Texts on the recovery of sovereignty will be found in Herman Mosler and Karl Döhring, eds., *Die Beendigung des Kriegszustandes mit Deutschland nach dem zweiten Weltkrieg* (Cologne, 1963). Psychological aspects of returning confidence between Germany and the West are discussed in D. C. Watt, *Britain Looks to Germany. British Opinion and Policy Towards Germany Since 1945* (London, 1965) and Christine Totten, *Deutschland: Soll und Haben. Amerikas Deutschlandbild* (Munich, 1964). Gilbert Ziebura, the best German specialist on contemporary France, is preparing a book on Franco–German relations since the war; meanwhile one may read F. Roy Willis, *France, Germany and the New Europe* (Stanford, Calif.: Stanford University Press, 1964); Fernand Chanrion, *Une victoire européenne: la Moselle* (1964); and Jacques Freymond's extremely valuable *Le conflit sarrois 1945–1955* (Brussels, 1959).

On rearmament, Norbert Tönnis, *Ser Weg zu den Waffen. Die Geschichte der deutschen Wiederbewaffnung 1949–1961* (Rastatt, 1961) may be used as an introduction to G. Wettig, *Entmilitarisierung und Wiederbewaffnung, 1963–1965* (Munich, 1967); and the essential documentation in Institut für Staatslehre und Politik Mainz, *Der Kampf um den Wehrbeitrag*, 3 vols. (Munich, 1952–58). The valuable and penetrating study by James Richardson, *Germany and the Atlantic Alliance. The interaction of strategy and politics* (Cambridge, Mass.: Harvard University Press, 1966) may be supplemented by Horst Mendershausen, *Troop Stationing in Germany. Value and cost* (Santa Monica, Calif.: RAND, 1968) and Otto Kimminich, *Völkerrecht im Atomzeitalter. Der Atomsperrvertrag und seine Folgen* (Freiburg, 1969).

For relations with the United Nations against the background of a divided Germany, see H. Dröge, F. Münch, and E. V. Puttkammer, *Die BRD und die Vereinten Nationen* (Munich, 1966). For relations with Israel against the background of the past, see Felix Shinar, *Bericht eines Beauftragten. Die deutsch-israelischen Beziehungen 1951–1966* (Tübingen, 1967). Rolf Vogel, ed., *Deutschlands Weg nach Israel* (Stuttgart, 1967) may be read pending Isaac Israel's admirable thesis *Les relations germano-israéliennes*, as may Inge Deutschkron's remarkable *Israel und die Deutschen. Zwischen Ressentiment und Ratio* (Cologne, 1970). Both Germany's past and her divided state have been a check on relations with the Third World since the inception of the Federal Republic; these are described in Paul Gache and R. Mercier, *L'Allemagne et l'Afrique. Analyse d'une pénétration économique contemporaine* (1960), while the later activities, in a different style, of the Ministry of Economic Cooperation are the subject of Jürgen Dennert, *Entwicklungshilfe geplant oder verwaltet? Entstehung und Konzeption des BMWZ* (Bielefeld, 1968).

For *Ostpolitik* there is ample documentation in Auswärtiges Amt, *Die Bemühungen der deutschen Regierung und ihrer Verbündeten um die Einhet Deutschlands 1955–1966* (Bonn, 1966) and the massive but oddly selective work edited by Boris Meissner, *Die deutsche Ostpolitik 1961–1970* (Cologne, 1970). Georg Bluhm needed less courage to write *Die Oder-Neisse-Frage* (Hanover, 1967) than to publish, four years earlier, his thorough and lucid work *Die Oder-Neisse-Linie in der deutschen Aussenpolitik* (Freiburg, 1963). Other bold works testifying to a new understanding of the problem are Martin Broszat, *200 Jahre deutsche Polenpolitik* (Munich, 1963) and Hansjakob Stehle, *Deutschlands Osten—Polens Westen?* (Frankfurt, 1965).

Hans-Werner Richter, ed., *Die Mauer oder der 13. August* (Hamburg, 1961) describes the erection of the Berlin wall and the shocked feelings of intellectuals, even those hostile to the Federal Republic. Hans Speier, *Die Bedrohung Berlins* (Cologne, 1961; English-language edition: *Divided Berlin*, New York: Praeger, 1961) traces the course of the crisis provoked by Khrushchev in November, 1958. Almost the only serious analysis of the risk of Berlin declining from within is Kurt Pritzkoleit, *Berlin. Ein Kampf ums Leben* (Düsseldorf, 1962); the reactions of its inhabitants to pressure from without are described in Kurt Snell, ed., *Bedrohung und Bewährung. Führung und Bevölkerung in der Berliner Krise* (Cologne and Opladen, 1965). The fullest study of Berlin is Jürgen Fijalkowski and others, *Berlin. Hauptstadtanspruch und Westintegration* (Cologne and Opladen, 1967).

The sufferings of prisoners returning belatedly from the U.S.S.R., and passing through the same West German reception camps as the expellees and refugees before them, are described with some sensationalism in Josef Reding, *Friedland. Chronik der grossen Heimkehr* (Recklinghausen, 1956). Against the background of this work, one may read criticisms of Federal policy toward the U.S.S.R. in Hans Kroll, *Lebenserinnerungen eines Botschafters* (Cologne, 1967); Nikolas Ehlert, *Grosse Grusinische Nr 17. Deutsche Botschaft in Moskau* (Frankfurt, 1967); H. W. Kahn, *Die Russen kommen nicht. Fehlleistungen unserer Sicherheitspolitik* (Munich, 1969); or Klaus Erdmenger, *Das folgenschwere Missverständnis. Bonn und die sowjetische Deutschlandpolitik* (Freiburg, 1967).

On the division of Germany, Rudolf Schuster, *Deutschlands staatliche Existenz im Widerstreit politischer und rechtlicher Gesichtspunkte 1945–1963* (Munich, 1963), is a valuable summing-up of the facts, while Kurt Tudyka, ed., *Das geteilte Deutschland. Eine Dokumentation der Meinungen* (Stuttgart, 1965) provides useful reminders. There is a thorough analysis in Ferenc A. Vali, *The Quest for a United Germany* (Baltimore, Md.: Johns Hopkins, 1967), and Eleanor Lansing Dulles, *One Germany or Two* (Stanford, Calif.: Hoover Institution, 1970) is interesting in many respects. The evolution of West German ideas on the future of the "other Germany" may be traced by comparing successive editions of the huge *Tätrigkeitsberichte* of the research advisory council for reunification matters (*Forschungsbeirat für Fragen der Wiedervereinigung*) of the Ministry for All-German Affairs (3rd ed., 1961; 4th, 1965; 5th, 1969). For German books on the "German question," see the notes to chapters 10 and 11. Two should be mentioned here as they have had a special impact: Peter Bender, *Offensive Entspannung. Möglichkeit für Deutschland* (Cologne, 1964) and especially Karl Jaspers, *Freiheit und Wiedervereinigung. Aufgaben deutscher Politik* (Munich, 1960). Note also W. W. Schütz, *Antipolitik* (Cologne, 1969), with its final chapter "Deutschlandpolitik als Gesellschaftspolitik."

But reasoning should not allow us to forget the tragedy of the divided nation as it appears, in varied lights, in such works as *Hochverrat und Staatsgefährdung. Urteile des Bundesgerichtshofes*, II (Karlsruhe, 1958); Heinz Brandt, *Ein Traum, der nicht entführbar ist. Mein Weg zwischen Ost und West* (Munich, 1967); Otto John, *Zweimal kam ich heim* (Düsseldorf, 1969); and Claus Zeller, *Marx hätte geweint. Der Porst-Prozess. Geteilte Nation im Zwielicht* (Stuttgart, 1969).

Doubtless all Germans—and not only they—should read and meditate upon the excellent little Socratic volume by Richard-Matthias Müller, *Über Deutschland. 103 Dialoge* (Freiburg, 1965).

Index

371